THE AFRICAN DIASPORA

THE
AFRICAN
DIASPORA

African Origins and New World Identities

Edited by   ISIDORE OKPEWHO

CAROLE BOYCE DAVIES

ALI A. MAZRUI

INDIANA UNIVERSITY PRESS

Bloomington and Indianapolis

#40218848

This book is a publication of
Indiana University Press
601 North Morton Street
Bloomington, IN 47404-3797 USA

http://www.indiana.edu/~iupress

Telephone orders   800-842-6796
Fax orders   812-855-7931
Orders by e-mail   iuporder@indiana.edu

© 1999 by Indiana University Press

The paper used in this publication meets the minimum requirements
of American National Standard for Information Sciences—Permanence
of Paper for Printed Library Materials, ANSI Z39.48-1984.

Manufactured in the United States of America

Library of Congress Cataloging-in-Publication Data

The African diaspora : African origins and New World identities /
    edited by Isidore Okpewho, Carole Boyce Davies, Ali A. Mazrui.
        p.   cm.
    Includes index.
    ISBN 0-253-33425-X (cloth : alk. paper)
    1. Africans—America—History. 2. Africans—America—Ethnic
identity. 3. Africans—America—Intellectual life. 4. America—
Race relations. 5. African diaspora. 6. America—Civilization—
African influences. I. Okpewho, Isidore. II. Davies, Carole
Boyce. III. Mazrui, Ali Al 'Amin.
    E29.N3A49   1999
    305.896' 073—dc21   98-49472

1   2   3   4   5   04   03   02   01   00   99

CONTENTS

RECONNECTING WITH AFRICA

ACKNOWLEDGMENTS

We would like to express our deep appreciation to all those who responded to our initial call for papers and especially those who actually participated in the conference from which this book has emerged. The Rockefeller Foundation provided funds that made it possible for us to hold the conference. We are most grateful for the help. We are equally grateful to the President, Provost, Dean of Harpur College, and the various units of the State University of New York, Binghamton, that contributed generously to our conference budget. We appreciate the kindness of many of our colleagues in providing various kinds of ancillary support, such as hosting conference participants in their homes. Three of our graduate students—Chiji Akoma, Meredith Gadsby, and Miriam Gyimah—facilitated the editing of this volume at the initial stages, and we thank them for their diligence. Finally, we highly appreciate the willingness of the Africana Studies department secretary, Barbara Kumiega, to work with us beyond the normal call of duty to ensure that this project achieved its goals.

INTRODUCTION

Isidore Okpewho

This book is the product of a conference held under roughly the same title by the Africana Studies Department of the State University of New York, Binghamton on April 11–13, 1996. In recent years, there has been so much scholarly debate between those who affirm the centrality of Africa in the identity and outlook of Blacks in Western society and those who seriously question the validity of the effort, that it seemed to us necessary to explore whatever wisdom may be garnered from the controversy. In the prospectus with which we announced our intention to hold the conference, we specifically invited prospective participants to ponder a few key questions underlying the controversy: Is derivation from Africa enough to account for the African presence in the New World? How did the Africans manage to create a viable life for themselves after they got here? How were they able to negotiate the social, political, cultural, and other spaces they encountered here? How successfully have their ancestral peculiarities coexisted with those of the other peoples that history has forced them to live with over the years?

Neither these questions nor the responses to them could pretend to be exhaustive, despite the growing vogue of discourse (in conferences, symposia, and academic programs) on the subject of the African diaspora.[1] Our conference was basically intended to encourage discussion, along the major lines of approach so far recognized, of the modes of formation and continued survival of the diaspora. After the conference, we did our best to select those papers that seemed reasonably representative not only of the principal sites—Africa, the United States, Latin America, and the Caribbean—but also of these major approaches to the subject.

What premises did we set ourselves in our exploration of the subject of the African diaspora? One of these, evident enough from the preceding paragraph, was spatio-temporal. It seemed convenient to limit ourselves to Africa on the one hand and, on the other, to the area usually referred to as "the Americas," because the latter accounted for by far the largest concentration of Africans who were dispersed from the mother continent. We are aware, of course, of the significant work done by scholars like Bernard Lewis, Joseph Harris, and John Hunwick in establishing the prior settlement of Africans in Mediterranean and Asian societies.[2] But not even the Arab slave trade, to which a major proportion of this presence is traceable, accounted for anything close to the traffic in Africans that took place across the Atlantic to the Americas. We have also omitted discussion of the African diaspora in the colonial metropoles especially of Britain and France, where Africans have not been as influential in social evolution as in the Americas.

We have been just as cautious in subsuming a time-frame for the African presence in this region. Any discussion of the idea of *diaspora* is, inevitably perhaps, referable to the Jewish experience of "dispersal" as enshrined in the *Book of Deuteronomy* (28:25) and explored by various scholars, Jewish and non-Jewish; there is, therefore, a real temptation to evoke as large a time-frame as possible for the exercise. Thus, a scholar like Ivan van Sertima, in his *They Came Before Columbus*, has given evidence, plausible enough, of the presence of Africans in the Americas well before Columbus's arrival and—on the basis of the "Africoid" stone sculptures found in Mexico—even before the Christian era. The Senegalese Pathe Diagne would invoke the saga of the Mandingo king Bakari II, whose ships may have crossed the Atlantic from West Africa before 1312.[3] Finally, in his book *The Making of the African Diaspora in the Americas 1441–1900*, Vincent Bakpetu Thompson adopts the pre-Columbian scheme without providing much justification for the early date. It may safely be assumed that the contributions in this volume—to the extent, that is, that they make a historical argument—accept the sixteenth century as the era during which black Africans began to come to the Americas in any significant numbers.

This brings us to the second premise by which we sought to frame the project of the conference. Whatever time-frames we set for the African presence in the New World, it seems reasonable to subsume a few key paradigms in accounting for the various shades of that experience and indeed for the repercussions of America's history upon Africa. These paradigms may be represented by the following three eras or phases.[4] The first, the era of the *labor imperative*, was marked by the one thing the West wanted most from Africa: the labor of her sons and daughters. The slave trade was launched, and millions of Africans were exported to the Americas, or perished in the Middle Passage.

The second phase of Africa's intersection with the Americas may be seen as the era of the *territorial imperative*—the era of imperialism. It is true that, apart from helping to settle freed African Americans in Liberia, the United States did not colonize Africa directly. However, President James Monroe did issue the Monroe Doctrine (1823), asserting U.S. monopoly of power in most of the Western hemisphere. Western European powers might have attempted to recolonize parts of the former Spanish empire in Latin America but for the Monroe Doctrine. By closing the door of the Western hemisphere against any further European colonization in the area, the United States forced those imperialists to look for alternative worlds to conquer. Much of the Caribbean had of course been colonized by European powers before the Monroe Doctrine, and remained colonized. Before long, however, these powers turned their designs on Africa. To some extent, then, the Monroe Doctrine contributed to the European scramble for Africa.

The third phase may be called the era of the *extractive imperative*, when Africa's mineral wealth had become the main focus of Western interest in the continent. With regard to these minerals, Africa and the West were in some vital respects rivals rather than complementary economies: a good case in point is petroleum. But there were instances in which the United States, for instance, depended heavily on Africa for items like chrome and cobalt. At any rate, in its postcolonial intersection with a New World it has helped to build, Africa has experienced moments of tension as well as complementarity in the development of what may indeed be characterized as an Afro–worldwide web.

The intersections between Africa and America (especially the United States) are best understood in the context of the labor imperative, the source of the diaspora of enslavement which has played a crucial role in shaping American cultural and social history. Here, it is arguable that whatever is uniquely *American* in U.S. culture and lifestyles has been influenced by two very different forces: the frontier, and the Black presence. Thomas Jefferson and the "founding fathers" looked to European thinkers like John Locke and Montesquieu for inspiration; Euro-Americans liked to think of themselves as heirs to Greece and Rome. European influences were therefore a "given": but where was the *American* personality?

Frederick Jackson Turner provided one answer by arguing the significance of the frontier in American history. For him, the American character was decisively shaped by the rugged conditions on the frontier which instilled qualities like "coarseness and strength . . . acuteness and inquisitiveness, that practical, inventive turn of mind . . . restless, nervous energy . . . that buoyancy and exuberance which comes with freedom," and all other ciphers of what has been recognized as the American personality. Turner felt that what was uniquely American in U.S. institutions was not the Mayflower but boundless land, and the urge to tame the rugged frontier.[5]

What is missing in the characterization above is the role of other social elements—not just Americans of European descent who were arguably uppermost in Turner's mind—in the formation of the American personality. In this regard, what was uniquely American was also the Black presence, along with the frontier. Perhaps the most readily advertised aspect of this presence is the cultural aspect, whereby African Americans have left an enduring mark on American music, speech, literature, food culture, sports, and performing arts.

An even more intrinsic presence may be cited. This is the presence which nurtured American capitalism in its infancy, and American democracy in its maturation. In its infancy, American capitalism needed Black labor. In its maturation in the twentieth century, American democracy needed the civil rights movement and deracialization to realize its founding concept that "all men are created equal." It was the Blacks who held American democracy accountable to its own ultimate ideals. The echoes reverberated all over Africa as she struggled to free herself of centuries-old legacies of exploitation, stretching from the era of labor through the era of the territorial imperatives. Even the era of the extractive imperative has been implicated in the struggles which eventually saw the liberation of mineral-rich South Africa from the complicit bonds of race and capital.

The paradigms we have subsumed in our discussion so far have been useful in establishing the concept of *diaspora* that will help us not only to contextualize the contributions in this book but especially to understand the network of relations binding the regions of the Black world under study. For a long time the word was employed in reference only to the unidirectional movement of Black peoples from Africa outwards, a tendency that Gilroy is no doubt right in denouncing as "purist" and "absurd" (*The Black Atlantic*, 96). Given the fluid movement of persons and of ideas from both sides of the Atlantic, and in light of the shifting political and economic relations between Africa and west Atlantic society we have drawn attention to, it becomes clear that *diaspora* represents a global space, a worldwide web, that accounts as much for the mother continent as for wherever in the world her offspring may have been driven by the unkind forces of history.[6]

The fact remains, however, that African societies had attained *some* level of stabilization, in terms of lifestyles and outlooks, before their sons and daughters were forcibly seized and settled in Western societies. The burden of the conference that gave rise to the contributions in this book was to examine the ways in which these transplanted Africans and their progeny confronted the host environment and built a life for themselves, and especially the ideologies of selfhood that have guided these efforts of adjustment to the world in which they find themselves.

The alternatives represented in our subtitle should be seen less as polar distinctions than as the two major directions that discussions of the subject have taken so far. It is true, of course, that the debates between Melville Herskovits and E. Franklin Frazier a few decades ago did much to institutionalize polarities in the study of the African presence in the New World. But the continued study of the subject which their seminal views have encouraged has equally drawn attention to the ways in which the lines they once drew have steadily blurred. Although we have divided this book into sections under which the various papers may be thematically aligned, we believe the special contribution of the book is in examining the major orientations that have guided the formation of the African diaspora. For the rest of this introduction, therefore, we will be exploring the general thrusts of these orientations, with sample illustrations from the positions taken by our contributors.

"Essentialism" has emerged in recent diaspora discourse as an ugly label for any tendency to see the imprint of the homeland or ancestral culture—in this case, Africa—in any aspect of the lifestyles or outlook of African-descended peoples in the western Atlantic world. But we can hardly deny that Africa has had much to do with the ways that New World Blacks have chosen to address the realities before them from the moment they emerged from the ships. For a start, most of them were landed in those tropical and subtropical sites—South Carolina, Caribbean isles, Guyana, etc.—of plantations they had been brought to work. Deracination must have seemed a little easier to bear the moment the Africans discovered that the environment looked amazingly similar to home. In time, this familiarity encouraged them not only to resume skills (e.g., herbal arts) they had practiced in Africa but even to seek sanctuary, as maroons fleeing an inhuman regimen, in the protective cover of the surrounding woods.

Memory of Africa, a sense of roots, therefore served these exiles well, especially when conditions became simply intolerable. As John Blassingame (Slave Community) and others have shown, the slaves held on stubbornly to their ancestral mores not only as a political statement but as a psychological necessity, and found ways of masking their African customs with a superficial veneer of European icons when their owners sought to erase their African memories. Long after emancipation, and during reconstruction, the old sense of roots continued to express itself even when time had steadily taken a toll on memories of Africa. Clearly, this was what encouraged many ex-slaves and their offspring to opt to return to Africa under resettlement initiatives organized by the United States government and by private entrepreneurs like Cuffe.

Those who chose not to go to Africa had good enough reason: if you had never been to Africa, it was just as risky abandoning yourself to the uncertain myth of a glorious homeland as abiding with horrors that had become all too palpable and familiar. But even for such people, Africa remained in the subconscious as some kind of psychological surety, to be invoked against a system and a culture they revolted intensely against. In their folklore and their folklife, especially in tales they had learned from parents and other relatives, African-descended Americans found an outlet for reassuring themselves of indigenous values they found lacking in the culture of those who ruled their lives even in freedom.

More than half a century after African Americans had been savoring the freedom guaranteed them by Abraham Lincoln, they still had ambivalent feelings about the land they had chosen to call home. They had answered the call to fight in the Great War—far away in Europe—in defense of freedom, yet this freedom continued to elude them here at home. Once again, some of them looked to Africa for the surety needed to establish that they stood for something in the scheme of American life, despite all claims to the contrary. It is certainly no secret that the Black Renaissance of the 1920s and beyond, borrowing much wisdom from the contemporary ethnological scholarship, was fundamentally energized by a pride in African cultural ancestry.

True, some of the leading figures sought guarantees that the whole project was based on a credible sense of mission, which was why the poet Countee Cullen rhetorically asked, "What is Africa to me?" But others were like Langston Hughes, who had little hesitation in embracing Africa happily as the source of his creative instincts, giving concrete proof of his faith by visiting the continent and allying himself with those forces, political (Nkrumah) as well as cultural (Senghor), that provided firm moorings for his sense of African origins. In the decade that saw the passing of committed ancestralists like Hughes (1961) and Du Bois (1963, as a citizen of Ghana), America was to explode in a revolution deeply grounded in an appeal to African origins by leaders on both the political (Malcolm X, Stokely Carmichael) and the cultural (the Black Arts Movement) fronts. The movement we know today as Afrocentricity is, as its founder Molefi Asante has frequently affirmed, simply an institutionalization of a commitment that Black revolutionary leaders before him have had to make as they rallied their people around their beleaguered fate as a race.

If, therefore, a sense of African origins continues to be invoked by New World Africans at crucial points in their history, surely scholars are quite as justified in turning "essentialist" lights on those aspects of diaspora African career and conduct that mirror continental African traditions. Hence some of the papers in this volume have sought to address aspects of New World experience wherein Blacks have been constrained by certain social or political factors to identify with their African sources.

Joseph Inikori's "Slaves or Serfs?" revisits an old debate in African historiography—whether Atlantic slavery was simply an extension of an institution already in existence on the African continent. Inikori summons a large body of comparative evidence in demonstrating that what was considered slavery in Africa was really closer to the system of serfdom in feudal Europe than to the chattel slavery operated on plantations in the Americas. Besides the interesting sociological insights it yields, Inikori's paper sees in this difference the background to the frequency of slave revolts on several plantations: these forced migrants had never experienced in Africa the bondage that was imposed upon them in the Americas. We are here reminded of the distinction the West African slave Ibrahima Abduhl Rahahman drew between chattel slavery in Natchez, Mississippi and servile life in his native Timbo and appreciate why, princely backgrounds apart, he violently resisted his owners' efforts to subjugate him (Alford 44–49).

That Black people have been led to summon certain African instincts, buried in the collective psyche, against systems of oppression in which they are forced to live in the New World is also the burden of Peter Ekeh's "Kinship and State." Here Ekeh invokes the concept of "primordial consciousness" in explaining African Americans' recourse, throughout their history, to the instincts and terminology of kinship (brother, sister, etc.) against an amoral machine of state that offers few guarantees of protection for their interests. We may now understand why foster communities being established in certain parts of the U.S., in which African Americans have a significant presence, have chosen to operate on an extended family structure. In this, the race is simply reaching back to an ancestral principle, enshrined in the proverb that "it takes a village to raise a child."

In Cuba, where the African element is held equally hostage to the dominant white culture, feelings of insecurity led to an aggressive cultural nationalism. In his lucid paper, Antonio Benítez-Rojo provides an insight into how the African element has become for Cubans the most cherished point of cultural reference. Against decades of official policy which imposed restrictions on various cultural forms of African origin—religion, dress, music, dance—as being "notorious as symbols of barbarity and disturbing to the social order," many artists and intellectuals rose to the defense of what they felt to be "the richest and strongest vein of our creative sources." Today, it has become conventional wisdom that Africa accounts for the most intimate ingredients "that went towards the making of a modern nationality in Cuba."[7]

Central to any argument on African origins is the interplay of three concepts David Evans summons in his discussion of the transformation of African musical instruments in the United States: *retention, continuity, survival*. The idea is especially illuminating as we read LeGrace Benson's "Habits of Attention," which explores modernist strains in contemporary Haitian art with underlying African motifs. Here is a tradition of art where an essentialist African sensibility persistently confronts the Euro-modernist culture, in a nuanced tribute to the artist's cultural roots in Africa ("Lan Ginée"). For instance, in discussing the sculptor Nacius-Joseph, Benson carefully separates his indigenous African animist regard ("attention") for the inherent essence of his material from the conventional European utilitarian view of it. The combination of African and European elements in such art may be judged a syncretism, or perhaps the African element may be seen as experiencing a *survival* in an environment dominated by Euro-modernist styles. But, says Benson, at some point we should ponder the motivating interest, the *attention*, in the art: what, in particular, does the artist have *in view*? It is at this point that we encounter the deep-seated, persistent "African grammar" underlying much contemporary Haitian art.

Still, there are stresses here, and in Benson's discussion of the work of Wilson Bigaud the argument for an essentialist African grammar begins gradually to make concessions to what may safely be called syncretism. It seems only reasonable to expect that, after so many centuries of expatriation from Africa, the New World Black sensibility would find it increasingly difficult to keep faith with its ancestral sources (which, we must add, have scarcely remained the same), given the urgency of contingent forces. After a while it becomes hard to draw lines, with any degree of calibrative accuracy, between what is *truly* African and what is not, despite our most cherished ideological convictions.

The difficulty is evident enough in current perceptions of the most essentialist of approaches used in the discussion of the history and culture of African peoples: Afrocentricity. Molefi Asante, the most recognized champion of the ideology, defines it as a perspective for "placing African ideals at the center of any analysis that involves African culture and behavior": "To be Afrocentric is to place Africans and the interest of Africa at the center of our approach to problem solving" (*The Afrocentric Idea* 6, 198).[8] However, a brief look at recent works avowedly based on this paradigm reveals a few flaws in its record so far.

One such work is Carlton and Barbara Molette's otherwise well-argued *Black Theatre: Premise and Presentation*, which Asante has endorsed as "the first genuinely Afrocentric discussion of the black American theater" (*The Afrocentric Idea* 169). True enough, in their discussion of the ritual basis of Afro-American theater—as against Euro-American theater based on Aristotelian principles—the Molettes invoke its African sources by citing a sampling of African scholarly views on various aspects of the tradition, e.g. Mbiti on the inseparability of the religious from the secular in African daily life and outlook (77), and Nkosi on the ultratextual interactions between actors (officiants) and the audience (80–81). But their basic ideas on heroism and tragedy are rooted in social and historical realities that are *peculiarly* African American: this is especially clear from their analyses of Hansberry's *A Raisin in the Sun* and William Branch's *A Medal for Willie*. The profession of an African-centered interpretation of characters' behaviors becomes more an act of faith, because if we moved beyond the actual historical circumstances that have called these behaviors into play, we would find ourselves in the zone of basic human responses to which Africa held no special claims.

Another piece of "Afrocentric" scholarship is John Roberts's *From Trickster to Badman: The Black Folk Hero in Slavery and Emancipation*.[9] This study of the African American oral narrative tradition traces the development of its heroic types to the older tradition of African trickster tales and epics, supporting its arguments with references to actual African tales, on the one hand, and on the other to strategies of evasion and confrontation that characterized relations between Black people and the ruling White authorities from slavery to reconstruction. There is much thought here. But somehow the evidence seems carefully channeled to serve a chosen end, for, among other weaknesses, the relations between trickster tales and epics in the African tradition are hardly the same as those Roberts has argued for the African American tradition.

These two works are eminently interesting, adventurous, and groundbreaking even in the connections they try to make with African culture. But, on the whole, they are as remarkable for what they underplay as for what they stress. One certainly gets the feeling that a good deal of energy employed in arguing for African origins could be usefully channeled into highlighting and celebrating the sheer creativity with which the Blacks of the New World have triumphed over determined efforts to erase their racial memories and created a viable existence for themselves *in the light of contingent realities*, cultural and otherwise. After all, even Asante himself concedes, rather grudgingly, that "in contemporary society one has to consider also the influence of acculturation on black style" (*The Afrocentric Idea* 53).

In their pivotal work *The Birth of African-American Culture*, Sidney Mintz and Richard Price explore the dynamics involved in the creation of a new world by people effectively cut off from the sustaining structures of the past. In the maroon villages that provided much of their evidence—and this is very much the picture in west Atlantic slave societies—various ethnicities and nationalities had been collapsed into some kind of "melting pot" from which the constituent ancestries might be rescued only by a most daunting archaeology of knowledge. If we respect, as perhaps we should, the conclusion that is forced upon them—that "direct formal continuities from Africa are more the exception than the rule in any African-American culture, even in those such as Saramaka, which have been most isolated" (60)—then clearly our time is much better spent exploring conditions surrounding the paths New World Blacks have had to cut for themselves beyond the encumbering mists of history.

Quite a few of the papers in this volume have endeavored to do this. In her study of Jonkonnu folk pageants in Caribbean societies like Jamaica, Sandra Richards acknowledges the African backgrounds out of which this masking tradition was originally developed by slaves and indentured workers in the eighteenth century. But the survival and popularity of the performances have been guaranteed principally by the actors' addressing issues of contemporary social and political history as well as borrowing from European literate culture. For instance, there is one report about "a company of actors who apparently offer a pantomime concerning Tippo

Sahib, the Sultan of Mysore whom Napoleon had encouraged to take up arms against the British in India; the latter stormed his capital and killed him in 1799. . . . Seemingly in a relatively short period of time, news of this event had not only reached Jamaica but was also incorporated into a pantomime enacted by blacks." Also popular in these performance routines were "portions of Shakespeare's *Richard III*, particularly the section in which Richard pleads, 'A horse, a horse, my kingdom for a horse!'"

Here, clearly, are those stresses between what Benson calls an "African grammar"—or Richards, an "African matrix"—and the all too weighty imperatives of the present that ideology ever so hastily rushes to resolve. But Richards wisely concludes that "culture is dynamic" and sees these Jonkonnu acts as instances of cultural syncretism.

Sally Price, who worked for a long time with her husband Richard in Suriname, explores developments in the plastic arts of Saramaka women in the context not only of relations with their men but also of available materials and the cultural influences impinging on their society from the outside. Here, the past is another country. In her project, she considers it "particularly important, when we attempt to understand the nature of culture, to back up from the finished forms so that we can explore the environment in which they were made—to view them, not as static objects, but as parts of a dynamic process." Although Price is careful not to indulge in ideological battles to which studies of this kind may be easily drawn, there is little doubt where her orientation lies. "If we really want to understand how gender and creativity interact in African American communities," she concludes,

> we need once in a while to shake artistic criticism free from an obsession with finished products . . . and intercontinental continuities and devote serious attention to some of the humbler dimensions of artistic expression, such as the steps by which it's made and the social context in which it's embedded. I do not believe that the artistic continuities between Africa and Afro-America will ever be fully grasped by an anthropologist who doesn't care that African 'calabashes' belong to the pumpkin family and that the American calabash grows on a tree, or by a historian who doesn't ask about the social and economic environment that leads Maroon men to work with a knife and compass and Maroon women with broken glass, or by a critic who doesn't take artistic styles seriously until they get beyond the awkward stage of crude experimentation.

In the work of these scholars there is, at any rate, a civil concession to an African past which suggests that the quest for self-definition need not entail a total disavowal of a vestigial history. This, in fact, is the significance of scholars like Houston Baker and Henry Louis Gates—in the ideas of "vernacular theory" and "signifying," respectively—as well as artists like Toni Morrison, Edwidge Danticat, and Grace Nichols, and the trope of "re-memory" or "re-membering" underlying their work.

But the bias toward revisionism can get stronger, as here in the papers by Pierre-Damien Mvuyekure and Jean Rahier. Mvuyekure discusses the fate of African religious traditions in the novels of Ishmael Reed, especially in light of Gates's theory of "signifying." In the religious world of Reed's New Orleans, much of the African pantheon of divinities has been appropriated secondhand from Haiti. With the African cultural grammar thus seriously disjointed, the artist has had to design, almost upon a clean slate, a new identity and fresh roles for those old world figures and their new world manifestations: "what Gates calls figuration is actually a reconfiguration and transformation of African gods and . . . in some cases the arc has been broken, refashioned, and then welded."

In his study of the Afro-Esmeraldian folk poetry (*Décimas*) in Ecuador, Rahier actually draws ideological blood. His point is that this tradition has been too deeply influenced by the literate structures of Renaissance poetry, from colonial Spain, for us to be rigid in foregrounding African antecedence. Taking issue with Asante, and echoing Gilroy, he insists that his paper "does not participate in the 'Afrocentric' or 'Africentric' project. . . . By their very nature, the Afro-Esmeraldian *Décimas* contradict the 'ethnic absolutism' of Africentric writers such as Asante, for instance, who choose to understand blackness as an 'entity' frozen in time and space, which implies the adoption of a concept of self as racialized, essentialized, and fundamentally monolithic, or 'African.'"

We suggested earlier that the resistance to African origins may be traced to the work of E. Franklin Frazier, whose debates with Melville Herskovits in the 1940s provided much of the energy for African diaspora studies. Frazier's voice has assumed a new stridency in the work of anti-essentialists like Clarence Walker and Paul Gilroy. Walker's *Deromanticizing Black History* is a no-holds-barred attack not only on those who look backward to Africa, but even on those who employ the concept of "community" (as does John Blassingame) to construe Afro-America as one unified racial family. Denouncing Marcus Garvey as a "virtuoso illusionist" and as "racist and reactionary" (xxv), Walker sees him as practicing "a skillful manipulation of myth as history" (43), a "megalomaniac" engaged in "the theatrics of nationhood" (49), whose "call for black emigration to Africa was endorsed by the Ku Klux Klan and the Anglo-Saxon Clubs" (53), and whose "effort to reorder the world for black people" makes him "a forerunner of Hitler and Mussolini, who also tried to make the world a better place for their people" (55). Walker's portrait of Garvey reads particularly sad in those parts where he invokes the intraracial antipathies between "West Indians" and U.S. Blacks, especially the politics of the phenotype.

Gilroy, who is of part-British, part-Caribbean background, has not been so hard on Garvey in his work. But in his densely argued book *The Black Atlantic*, one soon comes to feel certain misgivings about the anti-essentialist project.

Incidentally, it should be pointed out that Gilroy is not quite the author of the idea of a "black Atlantic," as is generally assumed. The idea has some respectable ancestry in the thought of C. L. R. James who, in his discussions of the Atlantic slave trade, speaks of the series of political and cultural movements of communities in the Atlantic world. The phrase itself may be traced to Robert Farris Thompson—whom, strangely enough, Gilroy does not mention in his book—and the series of courses he taught at Yale University in the '70s on the subject of Black Atlantic civilizations. In the introductory chapter of his book *Flash of the Spirit*, Thompson sees "ancient African organizing principles of song and dance" as a key element in the evolution of cultural forms in New World societies, an idea that Gilroy would hesitate to acknowledge. Indeed Peter Linebaugh, whom Gilroy does cite in his book, may have done the necessary spade work in several areas of his thought: using the ship and seaman metaphors as central to the concept of the Atlantic world; speaking of the "profound and hemispheric events that originate beneath the surface of things and which are not confined to any particular nation but arise from all four corners of the Atlantic"; suggesting we go beyond the simple idea of the triangular slave trade to a more complex notion of the movement of capital across the Atlantic; and, most significantly perhaps, recognizing the importance of language in the creation of a new Atlantic culture and of writer-activists like Ottobah Cugoano in the emergence of a type of "proto-Pan-Africanism" ("All the Atlantic Mountains Shook").

Gilroy's book is, moreover, weakened by certain flaws in its internal logic. First, in adopting a paradigm that distinguishes "modernity" from the "pre-rational, spiritual mode" of especially African thought, he retools an old prejudice in Western ethnology which failed to take account of the real dynamics of traditional culture. In her paper in this volume, art historian Nkiru Nzegwu explores the political and cultural factors subtending the growth of precolonial West African art, thus exposing the absurdity in considering European artists like Picasso "modern" while judging their sources of inspiration "primitive."[10]

A second and perhaps more crucial flaw in Gilroy's position stems from his postmodernist disdain for the idea of "nation," which reveals itself in an obsessive phobia against all forms of essentialism (as in attribution of a "Black" quality to anything) or particularism (as in the invocation of African origins). This flight from "home" is a curious paradox, because nothing could be more essentialist or particularist than recognizing a geocultural site (however unstable) as peculiar to a certain set of cultural integers; an isle (even a floating one) of self-elected *deracinés* is nonetheless a "home," something Gilroy has been looking for ever since lamenting "There Ain't No Black in the Union Jack." It is precisely the same "home" Martin Delany was looking for when he went in search of a place to relocate the Blacks of the United States; that Richard Wright painfully missed when he confessed to Ellison, "Really, Ralph, after I broke with the Communist Party I had nowhere else to go" (*The Black Atlantic* 150);[11] that Quincy Jones celebrates with his album *Back on the Block*, which for him recalls "traditions of the African griot storyteller that are continued today by the rappers" (108); that ultramodernist jazz artists like Albert Ayler and Archie Shepp embrace when, having sampled a range of musical sources across the globe, they return dutifully to revitalize their roots in albums titled *Goin' Home*; and that more popular artists like Arrested Development and Erykah Badu acknowledge in openly identifying themselves as "Afrocentric."

In his analysis of a Tshimshian tale under the title "The Story of Asdiwal," Claude Lévi-Strauss made the remarkable point that whereas on the surface the story portrayed the hunting and fishing habits of the group, underneath it really explored the confrontation, in their culture, between ideas of lineage and residence. Our discussion above has indeed brought to light two seminal concepts in Afro-diasporic discourse: positionality and identity.

There is no doubt that, as we suggested earlier, relations between the various units of the Black world have grown to the point that it hardly makes sense to take a unidirectional view of the concept of *diaspora* or to privilege any sector of it above all others. One useful role played by Gilroy's work may be in challenging the centrality of Black America—with imposing icons like Delany, Du Bois, Wright—in diaspora discourse, thus giving recognition to other sites.[12] This freed space facilitates the dissolution of boundaries that geography and ideology may have erected between national entities. Some of the more challenging work in this regard has been done by Black female scholars in terms of reconfiguring the female subject beyond national borders and in the light of the complex identity subsumed by her agency: Filomina C. Steady's (ed.) *Black Woman Cross-culturally*, Susheila Nasta's (ed.) *Motherlands*, and Carole Boyce Davies's *Black Women, Writing, and Identity* are representative of this trend.

The early years of this century saw efforts made by various organizations and movements in the New World toward the spiritual and political well-being and emancipation of Africa, as in the work of religious evangelists and various leaders of the Pan-Africanist movement. Some of the contributions in this volume explore this reconnection in equally respectable ways. Alvin Tillery traces the roles of African Americans in the development of American policies toward Africa: although we see here varying degrees of racial empathy, it is nonetheless clear that many African Americans (Randall Robinson and the TransAfrica group being a good example) are determined that Africa shall no longer be shortchanged, as it was in the past. Joseph McLaren explores the problems—not least from African scholars—facing Alice Walker's concerns with Africa in her fictional and other work.[13] Laura Pires-Hester examines the continuing commitment shown by Cape Verdean–Americans to the political and economic welfare of their original African homeland: the essay is interesting because inter alia it brings to light an instance of voluntary migration of Africans to the Americas even in the era of the slave trade.[14]

In the final analysis, these gestures of positionality are, in a fundamental sense, statements of identity as well. This issue has become particularly relevant in the light of President Clinton's call for an open dialogue on "race" in the U.S. and the impending recognition of the classification "mixed race" for some categories of Americans in various official documents.

But there are other imperatives as well, here brought to our attention especially in the essays by Sharon Bryant and Patience Elabor-Idemudia. Bryant highlights the differences, in cultural and other backgrounds, between native-born African American and immigrant black women that affect their dispositions to health care programs and the successes of such programs; Elabor-Idemudia investigates the obstacles that immigrant African women, despite being well qualified, encounter in the Canadian labor market. Although they address the predicaments of black women from two different perspectives, what unites them is their interest in what Elabor-Idemudia has fittingly called the "new African diaspora" and the need to reconfigure a community, even an identity, that an overly historical view has long encouraged us to treat as homogeneous.

Here, we are in what we earlier identified as the era of the *extractive imperative*, responsible in no small degree for the postcolonial woes of many black (especially African) societies that have necessitated the flight of their citizens to the United States. The growing presence of the new migrants has (let's face it) brought some stresses into the solidarity we have generally assumed binds all black people together. On the one hand, the resultant competition for berths in America's racially determined socio-economic space has brought new dimensions to animosities that have analogues in the old slave society. On the other hand, the newcomers have left their homelands under circumstances that qualify their relations with American society and their general sense of belonging, especially since they still have social and cultural roots back in their original homelands.

These circumstances have implications for the ways in which members of the new African diaspora have been inclined to define themselves. For instance, children born in the U.S. to recent African immigrants may be so unfamiliar with their ancestry, and may have so grown up with

American speech and other behavioral habits, that they may be classified as *African Americans* almost as much as those traditionally so identified. But there are many (both parents and children) who continue to arrive in the U.S. with a strong sense of their African roots, as well as adequate knowledge of their indigenous languages. For such immigrants Mazrui has suggested the classification *American Africans* ("The African Diaspora and Globalization"), especially because many of them insist that, although America does have a claim to their present situation, they still cherish ties to the old homeland and maintain the option to return there should the conditions that forced them to leave cease to exist.

The concept of *diaspora* therefore becomes more problematic, precisely because it has been circumscribed by much recent social and political history. And yet there is a sense in which that same history has succeeded in enshrining certain sensibilities in us, especially since society has failed to live up to the promise of change and to its avowed ideals.[15] Those who believe that the proposed classification "mixed race" offers an escape from the limitations imposed by the old systems of identification, or that, as Ibrahim Sundiata has recently argued, certain New World societies have "passed out of the Black Diaspora" (16), may need to beware they do not misread the signs as woefully as has often been done with Brazil. In his contribution here, Michael Echeruo obviously has such subterfuges in mind when he says that "in matters of identity, you cannot not belong. . . . In simple terms, even were we not to claim any particular identity, we would be assigned one, by the simple logic of either appearances or essences." We might even advise, borrowing a thought from Houston Baker: "No matter how far you travel, you are still black."

While therefore we should, as scholars, recognize the ways in which time has severely qualified the easy certainties of the past, little is gained by the determined assault on ideologies that seek to protect a race's sense of itself in the annals of human cultural history. Hence, in this volume, Elliott Skinner acknowledges the efforts by which Afrocentric intellectuals try to "bring their own brick to the construction of a universal civilization" as a worthwhile endeavor, and advises, "Let us get on with the job."

NOTES

1. The following are a few of the works that have appeared in recent times on the subject: M. L. Kilson and R. I. Rotberg, eds., *The African Diaspora: Interpretive Essays* (1976); Graham W. Irwin, ed., *Africans Abroad: A Documentary History of the Black Diaspora in Asia, Latin America, and the Caribbean During the Age of Slavery* (1977); Joseph E. Harris, ed., *Global Dimensions of the African Diaspora* (1982); Vincent B. Thompson, *The Making of the African Diaspora in the Americas 1441–*

1900 (1987); John Thornton, *Africa and the Africans in the Formation of the Atlantic World, 1450–1680* (1992); Sidney W. Mintz and Richard Price, *The Birth of African-American Culture: An Anthropological Perspective* (1992); Mario Azevedo, ed., *Africana Studies: A Survey of Africa and the African Diaspora* (1993); and Michael L. Conniff and Thomas J. Davis, eds., *Africans in the Americas: A History of the Black Diaspora* (1994).

2. See especially Lewis, *Race and Color in Islam* and "The African Diaspora and the Civilization of Islam"; Harris, *The African Presence in Asia*; and Hunwick, "Black Africans in the Islamic World" and "African Slaves in the Mediterranean World." See also R. Brunschvig, "*Abd,*" and J. Comhaire, "Some Notes on Africans in Muslim History."

3. See Ajayi and Mazrui, "Trends in Philosophy and Science in Africa," 660–661.

4. See Ali A. Mazrui, "The African Diaspora and Globalization," an unpublished paper presented at the conference on the African Diaspora, SUNY Binghamton, April 13, 1996.

5. See Turner's *History, Frontier, and Section* for some of his seminal ideas in this connection.

6. See Elliott Skinner's essay "The Dialectic Between Diasporas and Homelands" for an important contribution to this line of thinking.

7. See also Kimberly Welch's "'Our Hunger Is Our Song'" (in this volume) for other shades of Afro-Cubans' marginalization by official policy.

8. In his earlier *Afrocentricity* (1980, rev. 1988) Asante says that "Afrocentricity is the belief in the centrality of Africans in post modern [*sic*] history" (6).

9. For a detailed discussion of this work and the issues it raises, see Okpewho, "The Cousins of Uncle Remus."

10. Compare Joan Dayan: "What Gilroy dubs oddly as 'pre-slave history' means little when considering how mixed and diverse were African cultures and religions *before* New World slavery" (9).

11. "*The Black Atlantic* fails," charges Ntongela Masilela, "to register that the peregrinations of Richard Wright, W. E. B. Du Bois, C. L. R. James, and others *in* Europe were a search for the historical meaning of Africa" (89).

12. Natasha Barnes is of course right in castigating Gilroy's focus on African American—and male—figures in *The Black Atlantic*. However, the sites of his interest are by no means exclusively *American*.

13. A recent volume of essays edited by Obioma Nnaemeka, *Sisterhood, Feminisms, and Power*, also exposes the stresses within black feminist ranks.

14. In his "African Diaspora: Concept and Context," George Shepperson observes that "*diaspora* has always included some element of voluntary exile," citing the two Jewish words *galut* for "forced dispersion" (as in the Atlantic slave trade) and *tephuztzot* for voluntary movement.

15. In response to Gilroy's agenda in metaphorizing the experience of slavery (ships, etc.), Joan Dayan rightly points out: "It is not yet time to look back to some fossilized theme of slavery, for slavery still exists under other names" (11).

REFERENCES

Ajayi, J. F. A. and Ali Mazrui. "Trends in Philosophy and Science in Africa." *UNESCO General History of Africa. Vol. VIII: Africa Since 1935.* Berkeley: University of California Press, 1993.

Alford, Terry. *Prince among Slaves.* New York: Oxford University Press, 1986 [1977].

Asante, Molefi Kete. *The Afrocentric Idea.* Philadelphia: Temple University Press, 1987.

———. *Afrocentricity.* Trenton: Africa World Press, 1988 [1980].

Azevedo, Mario, ed. *Africana Studies: A Survey of Africa and the African Diaspora.* Charlotte: Carolina Academic Press, 1993.

Baker, Houston A. *No Matter Where You Travel, You Still Be Black: Poems.* Detroit: Lotus Press, 1979.

Barnes, Natasha. "Black Atlantic—Black America." *Research in African Literatures,* 27.4 (1996):106–107.

Blassingame, John. *The Slave Community: Plantation Life in the Antebellum South.* New York: Oxford University Press, 1972.

Brunschvig, R. "Abd." *The Encyclopedia of Islam: Vol. 1.* Leiden: E. J. Brill. Pp. 24–28.

Comhaire, J. "Some Notes on Africans in Muslim History." *Muslim World,* 46 (1956):336–341.

Conniff, Michael L. and Thomas J. Davis, eds. *Africans in the Americas: A History of the Black Diaspora.* New York: St. Martin's Press, 1994.

Davies, Carole Boyce. *Black Women, Writing, and Identity: Migrations of the Subject.* London: Routledge, 1994.

Dayan, Joan. "Paul Gilroy's Slaves, Ships, and Routes: The Middle Passage as Metaphor." *Research in African Literatures,* 27.4 (1996):7–14.

Gilroy, Paul. *The Black Atlantic: Modernity and Double Consciousness.* Cambridge, MA: Harvard University Press, 1993.

———. *"There Ain't No Black in the Union Jack": The Cultural Politics of Race and Nation.* Chicago: University of Chicago Press, 1987.

Harris, Joseph E. *The African Presence in Asia.* Evanston: Northwestern University Press, 1971.

———, ed. *Global Dimensions of the African Diaspora.* 2nd. ed. Washington, DC: Howard University Press, 1993.

Hunwick, J. O. "African Slaves in the Mediterranean World: A Neglected Aspect of the African Diaspora." *Global Dimensions of the African Diaspora,* ed. Joseph E. Harris.

———. "Black Africans in the Islamic World: An Understudied Dimension of the Black Diaspora." *Tarikh,* 5 (1978):20–40.

Irwin, Graham W., ed. *Africans Abroad: A Documentary History of the Black Diaspora in Asia, Latin America, and the Caribbean During the Age of Slavery.* New York: Columbia University Press, 1977.

Kilson, M. L. and R. I. Rotberg, eds. *The African Diaspora: Interpretive Essays.* Cambridge, MA: Harvard University Press, 1976.

Lévi-Strauss, Claude. "The Story of Asdiwal." *Structural Anthropology: Vol. 2.* London: Allen Lane, 1977.

Lewis, Bernard. "The African Diaspora and the Civilization of Islam."
    The African Diaspora: Interpretive Essays, eds. M. L. Kilson and R. I.
    Rotberg.
————. Race and Color in Islam. New York: Oxford University Press, 1971.
Linebaugh, Peter. "All the Atlantic Mountains Shook." Labour/Le Tra-
    vailleur, 10 (1982):87–121.
Masilela, Ntongela. "The 'Black Atlantic' and African Modernity in South
    Africa." Research in African Literatures, 27.4 (1996):88–96.
Mintz, Sidney W. and Richard Price. The Birth of African-American Cul-
    ture: An Anthropological Perspective. Boston: Beacon Press, 1976.
Molette, Carlton W. and Barbara J. Molette. Black Theatre: Premise and
    Presentation. Bristol, IN: Wyndham Hall, 1986.
Nasta, Susheila, ed. Motherlands: Black Women's Writing from Africa, the
    Caribbean, and South Asia. London: The Women's Press, 1991.
Nnaemeka, Obioma, ed. Sisterhood, Feminisms, and Power. Trenton:
    Africa World Press, 1998.
Okpewho, Isidore. "The Cousins of Uncle Remus." The Black Columbiad:
    Defining Moments in African American Literature and Culture, eds.
    Werner Sollors and Maria Diedrich. Cambridge, MA: Harvard Univer-
    sity Press, 1994.
Roberts, John. From Trickster to Badman: The Black Folk Hero in Slavery
    and Emancipation. Philadelphia: University of Pennsylvania Press,
    1987.
Shepperson, George. "African Diaspora: Concept and Context." Global Di-
    mensions of the African Diaspora, ed. Joseph E. Harris.
Skinner, Elliott P. "The Dialectic Between Diasporas and Homelands."
    Global Dimensions of the African Diaspora, ed. Joseph E. Harris.
Steady, Filomina Chioma, ed. The Black Woman Cross-Culturally. Cam-
    bridge, MA: Schenckman, 1981.
Sundiata, Ibrahim K. "Africanity, Identity, and Culture." Issue: A Journal
    of Opinion, 24.2 (1996):13–17.
Thompson, Robert Farris. Flash of the Spirit. New York: Random House,
    1983.
Thompson, Vincent Bakpetu. The Making of the African Diaspora in the
    Americas 1441–1900. Harlow: Longman, 1987.
Thornton, John. Africa and Africans in the Formation of the Atlantic
    World, 1450–1680. Cambridge: Cambridge University Press, 1992.
Turner, Frederick Jackson. History, Frontier, and Section. Albuquerque:
    University of New Mexico Press, 1993.
van Sertima, Ivan. They Came Before Columbus. New York: Random
    House, 1976.
Walker, Clarence E. Deromanticizing Black History: Critical Essays and
    Reappraisals. Knoxville: University of Tennessee Press, 1991.

THE DIASPORA:
ORIENTATIONS AND DETERMINATIONS

1

AN AFRICAN DIASPORA: THE ONTOLOGICAL PROJECT

Michael J. C. Echeruo

Obviously, the shadow of the title of Paul Gilroy's book *The Black Atlantic: Modernity and Double Consciousness* hangs over any discussion of "the African diaspora." Gilroy's book is a justly bold attempt to create a basis for contemplating the idea of an African or black diaspora without resorting (as it were) to the spectacular paradigms of race or soul, which (Gilroy believes) was the crucial limitation to the visions and conclusions of both Martin Delany and W. E. B. Du Bois. Gilroy's project also avoids the easy pluralism of mainstream modernism, which refuses to acknowledge that anything significant had happened to the people of African descent in the process of their immersion in Euro-American life and thought. Gilroy writes from a particularly privileged position within the British Black Establishment and from within traditions of cultural studies which can look across the Atlantic with some sense of superiority at the sometimes bizarre turns which the desire for authenticity and identity can take. Gilroy is right to feel agitated.

Here, I want to raise some questions I consider important to any fruitful discussion and proper appreciation of Africanity, especially in its many trans-Atlantic manifestations. My basic argument is that, in a major sense, we have appropriated both the language and the theology of another historic diaspora into our discourse, without fully addressing, much less acknowledging, the consequences of that appropriation. In sum, I believe that something fundamental has been happening to European and (if I may be allowed the phrase) to white discourse of identity since the Enlightenment and the Haskala, and that that "something" has now culminated in the crisis of postmodernism. The obsession which we now witness in the discourse of the West concerning a global, multinational culture and economy, and of a gloriously undifferentiated identity, whether sexual, national, or racial, can be directly traced to those climactic events. The European Enlightenment, like the Haskala, redefined identity and the disaporadic condition by resituating the place of nationhood and nationality. Foucault put his finger on it when (in "What is 'Enlightenment'") he said:

The critical ontology of ourselves has to be considered not,
certainly, as a theory, a doctrine, nor even as a permanent body
of knowledge that is accumulating; it has to be considered as an
attitude, an ethos, a philosophical life in which the critique of
what we are is at one and the same time the historical analysis
of the limits that are imposed on us and an experiment with the
possibility of going beyond them. (Foucault, 50)

Foucault was referring to Immanuel Kant and Moses Mendelssohn.
Specifically, he was suggesting that although Kant's search for a proper definition of "Enlightenment"—and so, of modernity—was not exactly contemporaneous with Mendelssohn's, yet that Jewish philosopher had opted
to move beyond "making a place for Jewish culture within German
thought," or else, of "identifying problems common to Jewish thought and
German philosophy" (Foucault, 33). Kant and Mendelssohn had in fact
moved beyond all that: "they [were] seeking to identify the common processes from which they stem. And it is perhaps a way of announcing the
acceptance of a common destiny—we now know to what drama that was
to lead" (Foucault, 33).

Since the European "Enlightenment," then, nationality has become
essentially a legal fiction, and nationhood a political and subjective condition which one can claim without having to acknowledge it as a defining
mark of identity. "Emancipation" has become the liberation, not only of
those previously confined to the European ghettoes, but of those "nation-
als" who defined their identity in terms of a natural fatherland. In the
spirit of the new dispensation, James Joyce's Bloom can claim to be Irish:
"I was born here." Since that event, and in consequence of it, but unlike
Mendelssohn, Paul Gilroy and many others besides can propose to belong
to a category of being that is not founded on race, color, or national origin.
They can posit a category, a Black [African] Atlantic, for example, to which
they can belong, without any obligation to be identified with Blackness,
Africa, or the mythical Atlantis. Gilroy writes:

In opposition to both of these nationalist or ethnically absolute
approaches, I want to develop the suggestion that cultural historians
could take the Atlantic as one single, complex unit of analysis in
their discussions of the modern world and use it to produce an
explicitly transnational and intercultural perspective. (Gilroy, 15)

Many distinguished African American scholars have been in that business for some time, an argument that rests on a similar construction of
modernity as an ocean of intercultural enterprise: Esu Elegbara was signifying and deconstructing long before Mercury and Lacan. Modernity is
thus not the god we worship in imitation of the West, but a mark of our
prescience in having moved into the future without the crisis of an En-

lightenment. Although there is a great deal to celebrate in this realization, there is much precious cargo that, I fear, we would then have to throw overboard, like so many black bodies of the Middle Passage, in the amazing grace of this new Atlanticism. The result, I submit, would be a golden age of nothingness, a state of mind that cannot stand national or racial particularity, a situation which would, as *The Black Atlantic* phrases it, avoid "the brutal absurdity of racial classification."

But there is no running away from these absurdities. Many years ago, St. Clair Drake reminded us of the "British practice of calling the children of African and West Indian fathers and British mothers 'Black' but sneering at those who use the same designation for similar types among ancient Egyptians" (Drake, 141). Although we must avoid reading these assertions too closely as autobiographical gestures (Gilroy himself takes pains to establish his bona fides in this matter), still what he proposes in *The Black Atlantic* is no more than a re-theorizing of what he calls "creolisation, métissage, mestizaje, and hybridity" (Gilroy, 2). In effect, Gilroy is theorizing (and naturalizing) our hybridity; or more politely, the condition of "special stress" which, Gilroy says, grows "with the effort involved in trying to face (at least) two ways at once" (Gilroy, 3).

It does seem odd, to say the least, that our theoreticians would want to see our "modernity" in these terms, and, further, that they would suggest that this condition (of mulattoism) is our natural and peculiar condition in the modern world. Our theorists seem unable to wear their various identities with any kind of equanimity. Rather, in a replay of a once-upon-a-time complex, they would celebrate their condition as a special burden. I am not thinking of the gift or predicament of "Double Consciousness" as Du Bois understood and codified it. I am, instead, thinking of that other version of it, implied in *The Black Atlantic*, that we are victims, inevitable casualties, of such a condition. That, precisely, is the point of the very first sentence of *The Black Atlantic*, which asserts that "striving to be both European and black requires some specific forms of double consciousness" (Gilroy, 1). It is a curious way of thinking, and the conjunction of "European" and "black" does immediately underscore the kind of blindness of vision required to understand the predicament. For the problem apparently is the striving to be "white" *and* "black" at the same time, to be simultaneously "European" and "African." Phrased in such equal terms, the problem would become utterly insane.

But the very phrasing shows that what is at stake is not the possibility of living as an African (or a black) in the modern European (or white) world, but in supposing that both identities are equivalent in ontological terms. For it would not occur to any European advocate of modernity to phrase the the European condition in similarly quixotic terms. It certainly would be difficult, if not impossible, for a European to strive to be African and white at the same time in the sense that Gilroy means it. And the explanation would be that the African is the unique species of the human as likely as ever to feel his ontological self suffocated by the environment of his modern situation. It is always the African self that is so creolised. And this is so because we do not think we are anything in particular. Says Gilroy:

> The contemporary black English, like the Anglo-Africans of earlier generations and perhaps, like all blacks in the West, stand between (at least) two great cultural assemblages, both of which have mutated through the course of the modern world that formed them and assumed new configurations. At present they remain locked symbiotically in an antagonistic relationship marked out by the symbolism of colors which adds to the conspicuous cultural power of their central Manichean dynamic—black and white. (Gilroy, 1–2)

The question arises: why should this particular plague be visited on black people? Why is it that creolisation is always an event attachable only to one of the two sources of hybridity? Or, phrased less polemically, why are Africans the ones to be "inserted" in modernity? Why are we not the makers of modernity? Why is it that Europe, for all the changes and transformations it has undergone over the centuries, has remained a recognizable entity, whereas Africa—the multifarious anomaly of *In My Father's House*—is always the sufferer, and its children the natural victims of this unique mental disorder of double consciousness?

The answer is as old as the history of our theorizing of ourselves. It is emblematized in that exasperated predicament Phyllis Wheatley worked herself into centuries ago. When she asks:

> The happier *Terrence* all the choir inspir'd
> His soul replenish'd and his bosom fir'd
> But say, ye *Muses*, why this partial grace,
> To one alone of *Afric's* sable race;
> From age to age transmitting thus his name
> With the finest glory in the rolls of fame?

she is not initiating an argument or proposition. Her argument is an *appositional* gesture which stands between a discursive world of her own and the world of the Others to whose assumptions and conclusions hers is addressed in spite of itself. If her question is essentially rhetorical, this is because the speech event itself is also essentially rhetorical, not political. We cannot even begin to determine the implications and reverberations of her phrase "*Afric's* sable race" without considering the political particulars of a *counter*-discourse that she was not, at that point, interested in addressing at length. Even so, it is clear not only that Phyllis Wheatley did want to make Terrence an African poet, and herself a continuation of his heritage, but that she also wanted to make herself a poet, like all other poets within and outside the "Western" tradition, through Terrence, her re-generated middleman, the literal and metaphorical link between two discourse-worlds.

Phyllis Wheatley herself did not create Terrence's "grace." That reputation (the condition for the meaning/significance of "Terrence") was already granted by the Other. Her argument thus assumes the first liability of counter-discourse, namely that it must begin with a premise from the primary discourse. Phyllis Wheatley had to begin from the West and re-posit, even if not accept, what Western discourse had claimed and/or acknowledged. In doing so, she also rhetorically uses (which, in political terms, means subscribing to or accepting) the judgment of the "Other" which had conferred that grace. What might her discourse have been without "Terrence"? Whatever her choice of model or starting point, her goal was not so much to re-place or re-position other poets, still less to separate Terrence and herself from the poets of the West, but (after naming Terrence and herself as African) to then make a new pantheon for *all* poets. Phyllis Wheatley was making herself the subject of a discourse in which she was, until then, only object, subject-matter. We have yet to develop adequate theoretical tools by which to read our own writing.

If I here give credit to Wheatley, it is because she does not quite succumb to asserting what is at best only thinkable as a question, a mode of anxiety. Gilroy (and several others) do not see a question or an anxiety, but an exciting predicament. A similar predicament led Claude McKay to lose his bearing entirely, not only in his native West Indian world and later in his Harlem refuge, but also in his Afro-Britisher world. Of course Africa itself never counted for anything. Still, it was McKay's realization of the need for "group identity" that was his saving grace; it was his conviction that such identity did not exist in Harlem and could not exist in England that fed his desperation, because it left him with two communities on both sides of the Atlantic that he never really believed in: the community in exile in the West Indies, and the community of the fatherland in Africa. While McKay worried about details, he failed to make the first necessary leap of faith: identification with kin, without the associated angst about shades of blackness; dialect, language, and toilet manners.

If Gilroy, unlike McKay, does not believe in kinship, why, then, does he speak of a *black* Atlantic? The answer, I believe, is that Gilroy, in spite of himself, is thinking of an African *diaspora*, that is, of those people who have blood links with blackness and who are to be found everywhere on the wrong side of the Atlantic. He is thinking of us all. But Gilroy gives a particular turn to the idea of a diaspora in his adoption of James Clifford's trope of the "travelling culture" (Gilroy, 17). In place of the traumatic event that precipitates exile in classical diasporas, Gilroy pictures a different scenario: diasporas as travellers, if not outright wanderers. The consequence is that the experience of the Middle Passage begins to seem not so different after all from Phyllis Wheatley's visit to Europe or Ida B. Wells's travels in England. Both journeys become analogous to Frederick Douglass's journey of the mind into the kingdom of English and Scottish radicals, or of Du Bois's spiritual and actual journeys into the mind of Germany and of Bismarck. Given such re-situation of the Black experience in exile, the task, appropriately enough, becomes that of determining "the impact that this outer-national, trans-cultural re-conceptualization might have on the political and cultural history of Black Americans and that of blacks in Europe" (Gilroy, 17).

The diasporadic condition is, of course, not new; nor is it simply a condition precipitated by a epochal event in remote history. It is a phenomenon which recurs, and can be theorized and reimagined. There is, for example, an active Irish diaspora. In an address to both houses of the Oireachtas on 2 February 1995, Irish president Mary Robinson spoke of the "seventy million people worldwide who can claim Irish descent" and of the "inextinguishable nature of our love and remembrance" in Ireland of those "who leave it behind."

> In places as far apart as Calcutta and Toronto, on a number of visits to Britain and the United States, in cities in Tanzania and Hungary and Australia, I have met young men and women throughout the island of Ireland who felt they had no choice but to emigrate. I have also met men and women who may never have seen Ireland but whose identity with it is part of their self-definition. . . .
>
> The more I know of these stories the more it seems to me an added richness of our heritage that Irishness is not simply territorial. In fact Irishness as a concept seems to me at its strongest when it reaches out to everyone on this island and shows itself capable of honouring and listening to those whose sense of identity, and whose cultural values, may be more British than Irish. . . . In fact, I have become more convinced each year that this great narrative of dispossession and belonging, which so often had its origins in sorrow and leave-taking, has become—with a certain amount of historic irony—one of the treasures of our society." (Robinson, 1–2)

I have quoted President Robinson at some length to draw attention to the indecent haste with which our own spokespersons seek to create new identities to accommodate those of the diaspora who (for whatever reason) do not belong, speaking analogically, to the mainland. The Irish see in the "narrative of dispossession" a parallel "story of belonging." For a diaspora is a "nation in exile," a "race in exile," and a "people in exile," however vaguely we define "exile" and irrespective of how long it lasts or can last. If it does not mean any of these things, it means nothing at all. The problem with those who try to understand the diaspora through the Enlightenment is that they can have no name for the entity to which the dispersed members belong. The issue, in short, is that of identity. It is not a matter of classification, but of being. It is an ontological question.

The Jewish diaspora, to take another example, is evidence that the issue is not one of taxonomy but of ontology. The Jews of the diaspora manifest characteristics and can attest to experiences so various that it is a miracle that they still can be said to constitute a people. Indeed, the State of Israel has been justly described by a student of the Jewish diaspora as "a palimpsest of the Diaspora" in which "the Jewish citizenry of the Zionist republic comprises a vast melding of races, ethnic types, even colors, as well as of linguistic groupings and subgroupings. The people of Israel in fact are the peoples of Israel. In their variety and diversity, they are living testament to the integrative power of an extraordinarily tenacious creed" (Sachar, 470). I have already referred to the Haskala and its consequences for the Jewish diaspora in modern times. But even in antiquity, the very fact that members of a diaspora had to operate (live their lives and earn a livelihood) in an alien and often hostile land did not always result in the kind of disorientation of the self which we celebrate so regularly in our own case.

Of course, as Joseph M. Modrzejewski and others have pointed out, there were Jews in Hellenistic Egypt who were torn between being "Hellenes" and being "Jews"; but they did not doubt that they were Jews. The task was how to relate their ontological being (their Jewishness) to their other forms of being, whether they were voluntary immigrants, indentured servants, or naturalized Hellenes. There is a further lesson in the example. Modrzejewski also points out that Jews in Hellenistic Egypt were both Greeks ("Hellenes") and Jews ("Joudaios") apparently without much anguish. "The inclusion of the Jewish diaspora within the Greek group of colonists did not inevitably lead to the compromising or destruction of Jewish identity either by assimilation or through hostile action of the surrounding society" (Modrzejewski, 83). Dual allegiance was thus technically possible. That is, using modern terms, it was possible to be an African American or a black Englishman. But, as the article points out, with the supersession of Roman law over the Greek, the super-subtle duality of that identity came to a certain ruin. "Given favorable circumstances," he argues, "dual allegiance falls within the realm of possibility; but they give us due warning that, in the long term, it can prove disastrous. They also remind us that the success of any acculturation is closely linked to social and political status. It could be of vital importance for those who occupy positions of responsibility in our modern democracies to meditate upon the lesson that Alexandrian Jewry teaches us" (Modrzejewski, 91).

I state, therefore, that in matters of identity, you cannot not belong. Hegel, to whom Gilroy is much indebted, does remind us that "Identity, as self-consciousness, is what distinguishes man from nature, particularly from the brutes which never reach the point of comprehending themselves as 'I', that is, pure self-contained units" (Hegel, 137). In that sense, as Foucault would phrase it, "the modern man"—à la Baudelaire—is one who "tries to invent himself" (Foucault, 42). But this way of looking at identity has been mistaken by the Black Atlanticists as meaning that our identity awaits our decision to belong; that it is entirely contingent on our moments of subjectivity. This is patently absurd. As Hegel himself would have explained, our identity is not only constructed out of what, in today's lingo, we call "the real" us, but of everything that we are not. That extraneous condition of Being makes all the difference. That is to say, even in advance of our choosing what to be, we are excluded from being all the things we are not, and our subsequent elections are relevant only to the extent that they are conformable to that preselection. A black man whose subjective identity is that of a white woman is clearly in for some challenging times. Certain options are, by the realities of our being, not open to us. For me, for example, being "white" is not a valid option. I cannot actually face two ways at once.

This does not, in any way, mean that subjective identities do not have their kind of validity; I cannot, while claiming identity with the African diaspora, act and think differently. It simply means that since such identities (and similar delusions, generally) are self-assumed and remain unmediated, only the cold reality of external constraints define what we eventually can be. In simple terms, even were we not to claim any particular identity, we would be assigned one, by the simple logic of either appearances or essences. If we talk the talk and walk the walk, we might be tagged one way; if we only talk the talk, but cannot walk the walk, we might be classified differently. And the classification may be wrong, either because of a material error (in judging our color or understanding our dress code), or from a misjudgment of our essences (as when we think a fellow is being nice who is actually out to do us in). But we cannot be left alone in nonentity. There is, ontologically speaking, no such thing as an identity-less being. And to say this is not to propose a "monolithic and static conception" of identity, as Denis-Constant Martin would call it (Martin, 5–20). This view of identity supposes that choices can be made. Indeed, in the view of this school of thinkers, the individual is seen, not as a person—an individual—but as the occupant of a "social area"

> where a great number of groups overlap, and in the course of his life he encounters innumerable possibilities of identifying with certain groups and adhering to certain organizations. Although many identifications are compatible, or made compatible by a rationalization process which deals with the past and the present, to identify with one or several groups always amounts to selecting certain refer-

ence groups and rejecting others. It means an acceptance to participate in certain symbolical systems of which the person becomes
actively or passively a carrier. (Martin, 13)

Recall Langston Hughes's poem "Theme for English B" and the lines:

It's not easy to know what is true for you or me
at twenty-two, my age. But I guess I'm what
I feel and see and hear, Harlem, I hear you!

Yet, as both the poet and his teacher already knew, he is "the only colored
student" in his class; and besides, "Being me, it [what I write] will not be
white."

Therein we have slipped into what Hegel might have thought an understandable error, making the "Abstraction" stand for the "Thing." "Abstraction," he says, "is the imposition of this Identity of form, the transformation of something inherently concrete into this form of elementary
simplicity." Whence all things "A" are all "A's." We correct this fallacy
by admitting difference into the equation, by making "A" include the spe-
cification "non-A," so that, in our particular case, "colored" in Langston
Hughes's text excludes all "non-colored." In any event, Hughes cannot be
simultaneously "colored" and "non-colored"; worse still, he does not have
the option of being neither. That he chose consistently to identify himself as "colored" does not prove that he was colored. It only confirms that
choices have to be made, and are often made based on the conditions that
exist extraneous to our being, "the us, inside." As I have argued elsewhere
(Echeruo, passim), the predicament for those who have a problem choosing
where to belong is that they cannot quite get themselves to realize that
their options in the matter are very limited indeed. Put bluntly, they have
none. Paul Gilroy does not have a choice of identities. It is a spurious ser-
mon therefore to speak (as Gilroy does) in this context of the "instability and mutability of identities which are always unfinished, always being made" (Gilroy, xi). What the history of the black diaspora teaches us
is that black identity must always be predicated on black experience, and
to whatever additional extent possible, on the experience of those others
touched enough by black blood to identify themselves with it. Nothing in
that act of commitment restricts the growth of the inside.

In "Culture and Reasonableness," a review of Kwame Appiah's In
My Father's House, Simon Gikandi makes the important point that criticisms of modernist Atlanticists based on ad hominem charges of mixed-
race politics serve little to explain the importance of the issues which
these theorists raise (Gikandi, 778). It is an important point to bear in
mind, not least because, as other diasporas long ago realized, identity
markers are not always self-evident. Actually, we make more of this than

we ought. Recall the title Shaye J. D. Cohen chose for the inaugurating lecture of the Program in Judaic Studies at Brown University in 1991: " 'Those Who Say They Are Jews and Are Not': How Do You Know a Jew in Antiquity When You See One?" Professor Cohen's was pointing to the "ambiguities inherent in Jewish identity and 'Jewishness' especially in the diaspora."

> . . . in the diaspora Jewishness was a conscious choice, easily avoided or hidden, and at best tolerated by society at large. . . . How was Jewishness expressed? What did a Jew do (or not do) in order to demonstrate that s/he was not a gentile? If someone claimed to be a Jew, how could you ascertain whether the claim was true? In sum, how did you know a Jew in antiquity when you saw one? . . . Not a single ancient author says that Jews are distinctive because of their looks, clothing, speech, names, or occupation. (Cohen, 3)

Cohen is not entirely persuasive, but the point he makes is relevant to any discussion of the black diaspora; for in that context, the question surely would not be whether a black would be recognized as such in Europe and America, although there would be some people claiming not to be black who might on closer inspection be found to be merely "passing." The equivalent test to that often threatened in ancient times by the elders (that is, confirming circumcision) would be quite problematic in our case, and one would have to be content to do as the Romans did: reject those they would not want to claim, just as Europe does to the black.

That in spite of this invisibility, as it were, the Jewish diaspora retained a certain plausible coherence through the centuries argues again that identity is not entirely a subjective event, although a subjective essence may run counter to otherwise important (even crucial) elements of the identity claimed. And it is not the case, either, that the nonsubjective identity is purely public and peripheral. For (as in the case Cohen is making) claiming that identity meant defining one's essential self; that is, not our present, but our forever self, the self that we may manipulate within history. A diaspora is possible only when there is an acceptance of such an ontological entity.

This line of thought can easily become a distraction, and the caution which Gilroy advises in the consideration of issues of identity between black and Jewish history has to be heeded. "I want to resist the idea," he writes, "that the Holocaust is another instance of genocide. I accept arguments for its uniqueness. However, I do not want the recognition of that uniqueness to be an obstacle to better understanding of the complicity of rationality and ethnocidal horror to which this book is dedicated" (Gilroy, 213). Yet, as Gilroy soon realizes in his rather critical comments of Zygmunt Baumann's *Modernity and the Holocaust,* among other texts, there is a sense in which his Black Atlantic is modelled on a notion of identity so unique in its constitution that it can never have a replicate. Nearly thirty years ago, the *New Cambridge Modern History* had high praise for Buchez's definition of nation as "not only the nation, but also the something in virtue of which a nation continues to exist even when it has lost its autonomy" ("Nationalities . . . ," 213). Recent history, especially the history of ethnic self-determination, points to the power of the "something" imagined by Buchez. Gilroy can think of no such "something," except perhaps the experience of ships and sailorship, from the desperate image of horror and salvation recovered in Turner's famous painting, to the experiences of Richard Wright and Langston Hughes.

Still the point made by Baumann that the Jews constitute the "only 'non-national' nation" (which Gilroy decries as ignorant and chauvinistic) is nevertheless the basis, properly speaking, of their condition both as a diaspora and as veritable citizens of the modern world. I raise the matter here to draw attention to the blindness which often leads our intellectuals into forever overstating their inclinations to fairness. For in the same breath that he criticizes Baumann, Gilroy reviews Edward Blyden's attitudes to Zionism and the Jewish Question, but cannot see that Blyden's response was not simply the result of a childhood spent in a predominantly Jewish community, nor the result of a simpleminded fascination with the Old Testament. Blyden had a veritable admiration for the Jews as a people, precisely the same way that he was proud of himself and of black people generally. Those who speak of Blyden as a "race man" have no clue whatsoever to what makes people a people. Gilroy's question is therefore answered by his own quotations from James Baldwin in connection with Warsaw and Watts. That he did not follow through on it in his earlier discussion of Delany, Du Bois, and Crummell must remain a matter of great disappointment, and it is to these three men that I now turn for another view of our ontological quest.

Here, let me raise another matter of some theoretical interest: the burden of Return. I consider this element the primary condition for the possibility of a diaspora. For although, as is obvious from the Irish and Jewish examples already cited (and Gilroy does return to it now and again) the idea of communal suffering experienced by its members is at the heart of the condition of the diaspora, yet it is the idea of an eventual Return that is its most fundamental source of sustenance. The members of a diaspora must have once had a home of their own, a nation, if you like, but nevertheless a covenanted forever home, a site from which they may be (for a while) excluded, but which is theirs, inalienably. This home, this land is not important only as a physical place; it is even more important as the source, root, final location for a determinable lineage. No person can claim to be part of a diaspora who cannot, however improbably, claim also to be traceable by descent to a lineage and (hence) to a place. The point of *Roots* is not, in my view, that a particular location on a map has been identified, but that a claim can be made to such a location.

Neither is returning a romantic journey to a dreamland of our fathers. The power of the idea lies in the principle of it: that a return is possible forever, whenever, if ever. It is this possibility—this inalienable right to wish a return, to reclaim connections to a lineage, however fractured, that makes one individual a part of a diffuse and disparate collection of persons we call the diaspora. Moreover, that retrospective capacity makes brothers and sisters of all who are *authorized*, or who claim the right to claim connection to the lineage. Such a capacity, above all else, permits us to be African. A situation in which a member of this "Black Atlantic" could not seriously entertain the capacity, the authority to claim to be African, does not leave him much room to maneuver in any kind of diaspora.

The commitment to return is not an obligation. It is only a prophetic expectation to be realized in Never-time. It is this condition, as well, that makes the difference between the exile, properly speaking, and the mere wanderer, the beast of no nation. But in adopting the challenge and opportunity of this Return, the diaspora inevitably distinguishes itself from all others who must choose a different homeland, a different prophetic expectation, a different identity. Only through this condition can a person be presumed to belong (or not belong) to a specific diaspora, in this instance, the Black Atlantic.

Martin Delany was the first of our major writers to properly understand the true measure of this condition as it applied to us. He first understood that we, of the Black Atlantic, were Africans before we were anything else; he first made the ontological assertion of our identity, and then proceeded to relate that being to our historical condition. He it was who made a distinction which Gilroy has no way of understanding, between the history and being, between the self and the un-doing of the self. Delany understood history, and (by implication) the many jokes that history plays on identity. The early settlers of St. Domingo, for example, thought of themselves as belonging to two broad groups: those who were free, called "people of colour," and those who were not, called "blacks." When the Bureau of the Census dropped "Mulatto" from its racial categories earlier this century, it became impossible for so-called mixed-race persons to claim other than black identity, since whiteness was not an available option. In short, Delany understood that history does not create our identities, it restructures that identity. In that sense, our modern (or postmodern) condition is not our identity, and does not negate our identity. It is our history, including the many ways our intellectual history has permitted us to reflect on our selfhood, that has modified the circumstances under which we express our identity.

Du Bois began where Delany left off. Gilroy is quite sympathetic to Du Bois's views, but grudgingly so. Without a doubt, Du Bois was one peculiar and complicated product of the historical conditions we have been examining. But he, like Delany, had an uncomplicated response to his historical situation. Du Bois was what his age called a mulatto; unlike many others, however, he was troubled by it. I suspect he was troubled by the suggestion implicit in the concepts of race taught him at Harvard, Tufts, and in Germany, that the African part of him was a disastrous admixture, the source, ultimately, of the inferiority attaching to his being. It was a particularly galling experience, since neither of the two possible theories on the matter—first that mulattoes (like the children to be born of black professionals and English prostitutes in the bizarre experiment proposed in the nineteenth century for the Gold Coast) would be a better breed of persons, liable therefore to lead to what was called the amelioration of the race; and second, that mulattoes were the rank product of an ill-fated union of two related but different species, whose character would be bound up in tragedy and shame—served to create self-esteem. Du Bois chose to identify, not with particular black people, but generically with the black people of Africa. Robert H. Brisbane's account of Du Bois's relationship with Marcus Garvey is well taken. Du Bois called Garvey "a little, flat black man, ugly, but with intelligent eyes and a big head" (quoted in Brisbane, 85); but then James Baldwin, in *Notes of a Native Son*, had called his own father worse. The point surely is that Du Bois regarded his identity in ontological terms, not by assembling all black people to determine whether he was in a kind of primitive unanimity with them on all issues of faith and conduct, but by accepting his Africanness as a given to be deployed and explained in the full glare of history. What he gave us in the process (the gestures to Bismarck and Herder, as well as to Hegel, notwithstanding) is the foundation for that doctrine of Being intended to link motherland Africans with their kin in the diaspora. I am, of course, referring to Negritude.

A third captive, a very much maligned one, too, is Alexander Crummell. He is a problem child of the American experience in this regard because, as post–race men would suggest, he was still caught up in the miserably outdated notion of an African identity. Gilroy has rescued him from the pits into which *In My Father's House* would consign him. Still, it is not often realized how important it was that he clung to Christianity for the vindication and salvation of the Black race. It was not naiveté that led him to that. Gilroy, who rails a great deal against the complicity of rationality and science in the ascendancy of racism, nevertheless ignores a fact of the late nineteenth century, that the Bible was the only "European" document to which the African intellectual could turn for *any* reassurance that he or she belonged with the rest of the human race. We sometimes forget how fundamental it was for the blacks of the diaspora to rely on the Adamic origin of all races, in the face of much scholarship and even more sermonizing on the alternative reading of Genesis which allowed for polygenesis. Crummell's texts are an answer to those charges. When Henry Louis Gates, Jr. criticizes Crummell, I believe he underrates this circumstance.

What Crummell does say about the responsibility of the black person of the diaspora in relation to the mother country is worth quoting in full here:

> For when God gives a man, or a number of men,—a nation, place, circumstance, opportunity, advantage, and appliance, with
>
> 'Ample room and verge enough,'
>
> thereunto added, for a great and noble work; such as the deliverance of a people, or the freedom of a race, or the laying the foundations of a new state, or the building up of a great commonwealth, or the development of civilization in a new sphere, or introducing the kingdom of Christ into the very domain of Satan; and they have neither sight to see, nor judgment to gauge, nor brains to understand, nor hardihood of soul to endure and to achieve, nor manly honor to meet their duty and to fulfil their work and mission; then the avenging angel of God stands in the way of such a people, and Jehovah's glittering sword cuts the cumberers down to the ground. (Crummell, 100)

It seems to me that the issue of the regaining of "Africanity" is currently being beclouded by two currents in Euro-American intellectual life. The first, as I have been trying to suggest, is the very habit of our transatlanticists to leave their identity up in a nebulous air of postmodern doubt; to theorize blackness while excluding themselves in all but the most peripheral sense from its true embrace; to believe, in other words, that because we read Foucault and Derrida, visit the Prada, drink Coca Cola, and watch Mapplethorpe and David Letterman with Richard Rorty, we are no longer African: Africans in America, Africans in Britain, and Africans everywhere. We imagine that the historical conditions which have shaped our experiences in these various locations negate this identity; that, because we are so various, we are not, therefore, also, identical and African. We call any notion that we might have remained African through these experiences a form of "essentialism" and are only too glad to choose to be nothing.

The other (and second) current is not, as Gilroy would imagine, those so-called essentialists (or, in his way of thinking, Afrocentrists) who are thought not to have grown up to the realization (as the phrase goes) that, "Hey! This is America. Welcome to the twenty-first century." These Afrocentrists have a limited and perfectly innocuous role to play. The dangerous second current is the tradition which celebrates the dissolution of identity in pluralism or multiculturalism. I recall a scene from Langston

Hughes's short story "A Good Job Gone," where the young black narrator hears a woman laughing in his employer's living room.

> I knew it was a colored laugh—one of ours. So deep and pretty, it couldn't have been nothing else. . . . She was colored, all right. One of those golden browns, like an Alabama moon. Swell looking kid. . . . Jesus! She was like gin and vermouth mixed. You know." (*The Ways of White Folks*, 61)

Passages like this smell of essentialisms, of permanently knowable, identifiable black women; or permanently, forever nameable Alabama moons; and of something fixed and eternal in the mixture of gin and vermouth. There is also the essentialism of female allure, the potency of a black sexuality (or sensuality) which needs only be named to be realized. As Hughes in fact says, "She had the old man standing on his ears. . . . She kept him laughing till daylight, hugging and kissing. . . . a sugar-brown had crowded the white babies out." She belonged naturally to the class which Hughes's narrator calls "my people." I know no American writer as cosmopolitan as Langston Hughes; and I know of none who belonged as perfectly in his new nation, America, as well as in the world of the African peoples generally. He would call himself black or colored or negro, or whatever the current term was, and not mind if all it did was link him up with people he believed (in the context of history) were his kin. His "The Negro Speaks of Rivers" is modelled on Du Bois, but Hughes's river runs deeper; and no writer, I suspect, has a greater sense of what hierarchies there are in the order of our various identities, gender not excluded. There are those, however, who do not believe in a hierarchy of identities, who do not see that a "tall black man" is not a "black tall man," even if you translated the phrase into Latin. Those constitute the second and dangerous tradition working against the affirmation of our Africanity.

For us all, though, there is a practical and cautionary lesson to be learned from the work of Nadine Gordimer. She is, as some may know, Jewish; she is also, as some would have guessed, white; she is decidedly a woman. But Gordimer has not gone so far, herself, to claim more than that. Her being African is a historical and contingent reality, the experience of its historicity being the context of many parables of fluctuating identities. Hillela, the heroine of her *A Sport of Nature*, who is ostensibly Jewish and white, is also ostensibly a reject, as it were, from the old fold. She is, as Gordimer's epigraph admits, "a spontaneous mutation, a new variety produced in this way." She "exhibits abnormal variation or a departure from the parent stock or type." She is a reject, cast from the fold, unclaimable by any diaspora. In Gordimer's novel, as we know, she gets married to an African general by whom she has a daughter named after Winnie Mandela. When that general is assassinated she marries another freedom fighter who becomes President of a newly liberated African country. Gordimer's joke of nature, this "lusus naturae" as Darwin would call her, is granted a new birth. She is adopted into a new identity and given a new name: Hillela becomes Chiemeka, "God has done very well." Welcome to the Diaspora!

REFERENCES

Baumann, Zygmunt. *Modernity and the Holocaust*. Cambridge: Polity Press, 1989.

Brisbane, Robert H. *The Black Vanguard*. Valley Forge, PA: Judson Press, 1970.

Cohen, Shaye J. D. " 'Those Who Say They Are Jews and Are Not': How Do You Know a Jew in Antiquity When You See One?" in *Diasporas in Antiquity*, ed. Shaye J. D. Cohen and Ernest S. Frerichs. Atlanta, GA: Scholars Press, 1993, pp. 1–45.

Crummell, Alexander. *The Future of Africa* (1862). Detroit, MI: Negro Universities Press, 1969.

Drake, St. Clair. *Black Folk Here and There: Essays in History and Anthropology*. Vol. 1. Los Angeles: UCLA, Center for Afro-American Studies, 1987.

Echeruo, Michael J. C. "Edward W. Blyden, W. E. B. Du Bois, and the 'Color Complex'." *Journal of Modern African Studies* 30:4 (1992), 669–84.

Foucault, Michel. "What Is Enlightement," in *The Foucault Reader*, ed. Paul Rabinow. New York: Pantheon Books, 1984, 32–50.

Gikandi, Simon. "Culture and Reasonableness," in *Contemporary Literature* 34:4 (1993), 777–82.

Gilroy, Paul. *The Black Atlantic: Modernity and Double Consciousness*. Cambridge, MA: Harvard University Press, 1993.

Gordimer, Nadine. *A Sport of Nature*. New York: Penguin Books, 1987.

Hegel, G. W. F. *Phenomenology of Mind* (1967), tr. with notes by J. M. Bailie. New York: Harper and Row, 1967.

Hughes, Langston. "A Good Job Gone," in *The Ways of White Folks*. New York: Vintage Books, 1990, pp. 57–68.

——. "Theme for English B," in *Selected Poems*. New York: Vintage Books, 1990, pp. 247–48.

Martin, Denis-Constant. "The Choices of Identity," *Social Identities* 1:1 (1995), 5–20.

Modrzejewski, Joseph M. "How to Be a Jew in Hellenistic Egypt?" in *Diasporas in Antiquity*, ed. Shaye J.D. Cohen and Ernest S. Frerichs. Atlanta, GA: Scholars Press, 1993, pp.65–91.

"Nationalities and Nationalism," in *New Cambridge Modern History*. Vol. X: The Zenith of European Power, 1830–1870, ed. J.P.T. Bury. Cambridge: Cambridge University Press, 1967.

Robinson, Mary. "President Robinson's Address to the Oireachtas," 2 February 1995. http://celtic.stanford.edu/pmurphy/uachtaran.html, pp. 1–7.

Sachar, Howard M. *Diaspora: An Inquiry into the Contemporary Jewish World*. New York: Harper and Row, 1985.

2

CULTURAL RECONFIGURATIONS
IN THE AFRICAN CARIBBEAN

Maureen Warner-Lewis

Unlike the Jewish, European, Indian, or Chinese disaporas, the scattered communities of the African diaspora are united around no venerable scripted text or texts, nor do they share codified and institutionalized religions. But the awareness of the disapora nexus is centuries old, and, not surprisingly, has been more ardently articulated by spokespersons from the West Atlantic than by persons from Africa, the diasporic matrix itself. This is because those in exile and moreover in vulnerable socioeconomic conditions tend to be preoccupied by imaginaries of a homeland and by the implications of demographic and cultural dispersal rather than those Africans whose occupation of a homeland is centuries, even millenia, long. The latter not only occupy that homeland from which the ancestors of the dispersed peoples came, but further their occupation is consolidated by political hegemony in certain defined continental spaces and by intermarriage between later migrant ethnic groups and aboriginal inhabitants of these geographical locations: some of the more identifiable of these aborigines are the Khoi-Khoi and the San of the Kalahari, and the Twa of the Central African forests.

Speaking from a Caribbean perspective, the most notable advocates in African diasporic discourse have been publicists, historicans, and anthropologists, among them Edward Blyden from the Danish West Indies (now the Virgin Islands); the Jamaicans T. E. S. Scholes, J. A. Rogers, Robert Love, Marcus Garvey, and Leonard Barrett; Arthur Schomburg of Puerto Rico; Jean Price-Mars of Haiti; John Jacob Thomas, George Padmore, and C. L. R. James of Trinidad; and George James, Norman Cameron, Ivan Van Sertima, and Walter Rodney from Guyana. Among the creative writers have been Aimé Césaire and René Maran of Martinique; George Lamming and Kamau Brathwaite of Barbados; Maryse Condé, Joseph Zobel, and Simone Schwarz-Bart of Guadeloupe; Nicolás Guillén from Cuba, and the Jamaicans Erna Brodber, Lorna Goodison, and Mutabaruka. The call of Africa and reminders of African affiliation have been prominent messages in the popular musics of the Caribbean, among them the calypso[1] and reggae. Bob

Marley, Burning Spear, Peter Tosh, and Bunny Wailer of Jamaica, and Black Stalin and Chalkdust of Trinidad come readily to mind. The diasporic worldview also informs the genesis of the Rastafari movement, just as it inspires work in the visual and plastic arts of Haiti, Suriname, and Jamaica. As such, it is not a concern exclusively for the intelligentsia, since the popular arts as well testify to an ongoing embeddedness of diasporic awareness among the Caribbean masses.

Having spent some thirty years in the recovery of language, orature, and family histories in the Caribbean which validate the lived strength and expressions of the African diaspora,[2] I wish to testify to that embeddedness of the people's sense of filiation to a larger though fractured ethnic community. It is a filiation which coexists with a general Eurocentricity of moral, cultural, and aesthetic values and institutions in the Caribbean, often by the very bearers of African culture forms themselves, values and institutions which have resisted reciprocity and symbiosis with the African historical and cultural connections of a major part of the Caribbean population. Such resistance to African culture has been evident in the history of the calypso, carnival, and steelband of Trinidad, the rumba and *comparsa* carnivals of Cuba, and the reggae of Jamaica.[3] This resistance has created the ambivalences of opinion and attitude which characterize the peoples created by the ethnic and cultural hybridities peculiar to the region.

Remnants of African languages have been recovered from individual speakers in the second half of this century, one century after their original speakers had arrived in the Caribbean from Africa; such African language texts have been recuperated in Martinique, Trinidad, Jamaica, and Cuba, while African-derived words occur there as well as elsewhere.[4] The continuity of African language use even during the slave era is substantiated by evidence that shared language was the basis on which freed ex-slaves and post-emancipation African migrant laborers cooperated to constitute homesteads in the new civil society which came into being when the category of slave was abolished and that of free citizen was created.[5] In any case, there is abundant evidence of the existence under hispanophone slavery of confraternities called *cabildos* which united persons of similar ethnicity, and in the anglophone countries of ethnic-based secret and mutual aid societies.[6] The significance of the recovery of African language texts in this century emphasizes the dialectics of change and evolution, in that African languages have coalesced with European languages to create new languages indigenous to the Caribbean—the Dutch, French, English, and Spanish Creoles,[7] yet African languages, in out-surviving that fusion have themselves been reshaped in phonology and syntax by European language forms.[8]

Some of the oral texts themselves serve as refractions of the knowledge brought by those who had crossed the Middle Passage, meanings in large part lost to subsequent generations who preserve the phrases of song, legend, or prayer.[9] But an analysis of Yoruba songs recorded in Trinidad indicates an affective and informational range of themes which restore personality to their original singers, reflecting their traumas and religious beliefs. The songs speak to pride in family status, a sense of ethnic group consciousness, experiences of war and dislocation, alienation and exile, joy at personal freedom, the desire for personal advancement and material acquisition; songs expressive of religious belief and ritual state confidence in immortality, respect for ancestors, for deities, and natural forces.[10]

Thus within the ethnic communities which the enslaved established across plantation boundaries,[11] and within their later ethnic and multiethnic homesteads founded in freedom, they passed on to their children and wards varieties of African knowledge: in cooking styles and food combinations,[12] herbal skills, games,[13] concepts of musical and vocal instrumentation and form,[14] and cosmological frameworks.[15] Such knowledge was not necessarily disseminated in formal, conscious modes, though sometimes it was, as in the case of santería and Abakuá notebooks in Cuba;[16] all the same, intergenerational reticence typified explication regarding aspects of religious ritual. This was in line with traditional resistance to the transfer of particular areas of mystical information, while awareness that certain forms of religious conduct transgressed European law invited the evasive strategy of secrecy. But mimesis and memory, as well as the fear of ancestral sanction, served as bases for the continuation of certain beliefs, strategies, and lifestyles.

The coexistence in the Caribbean of transplanted Africa and Europe led to the layering and multiplicity of identities. African personal names retained their self-referential valency and were used within the in-group, even as Africans took and/or received European pet and official names; indeed, African names were given by some parents to their children and grandchildren.[17] In corresponding fashion, African ethnic groups which continued to celebrate and petition their deities identified congruent Christian iconographies and nomenclatures for them, especially in West Atlantic environments where the Catholic pantheon of saints facilitated such a conflation or layering of supernatural identities.[18] Such recognition of similar divine personalities and iconographies has also taken place cross-culturally among, and even within, African-derived religious communities: metallic associations link the Koongo power Zarabanda and Yoruba Ogun in Cuban Palo Monte; the serpent iconography intertwines the Koongo deity Bumba and the Dahomean Damballa in Haitian vodun; in Trinidadian orisha religion Yoruba and Dahomean deities are correlated, and within Trinidad orisha worship Oshun and Yemanja, both Yoruba female water deities, are often twinned.

Thus compromise and syncretism have been inevitable strategies for personal and group survival. Such transformation and readjustment necessarily involved the fracturing of customs and ritual from their African institutional hierarchies of authority and governance, from African systems of work allocation and gender socialization, and African calendrical and spatial locations for particular events. This has produced variations of practice, interpretation, and emphasis within the West Atlantic diaspora, all in the context of changes over time. For instance, there has been secularization of sacred ritual, occasion, and liturgy, exemplified in the Eastern Caribbean by the connection between the ancestral rite *saraka* and the dance occasion called *bèlè*; but the opposite has also occurred, whereby the secular has been appropriated into the sacred as the African cultural core has narrowed. This is evident in the incorporation of secular songs into Yoruba-derived Cuban and Trinidadian religion. In tandem with this phenomenon, there has been the retention of symbol but a reallocation of function and context: for example, this occurred when individuals were designated king or chief in Caribbean plantations and villages—such persons served as spokesmen for the group in its representations to the wider society, as headmen of work groups, and head arbitrators of disputes. Retention of symbol but reassignment of function surfaces in the association in Cuban santería of the Yoruba tempest deity Oya with death, whereas in Yorubaland her fame rests on her physical power and her unflinching fidelity to her husband Shango. There also exist multiple labels for the same item or phenomenon, such as the several Koongo names for marijuana in Jamaica (*dyamba* or *chianga, makoni, kaya*)[19] and the multiple names for Koongo-based religion in Cuba (Palo Monte, Kinfuiti, Mayombe, Kimbisa, Briyumba). This bifurcation is partially a reflection of the influence of particular African ethnicities and sub-ethnicities in differing locales in the Caribbean. A related phenomenon has been the application of African methodologies to usage of raw materials more accessible in new environments. The replacement in Cuban Yoruba-derived Ifa divination of dry coconut segments for kolanut valves is an example; so too is the replacement of palm oil by coconut oil and coconut milk in Caribbean cuisine.

These various forms of restructuring, together with the assimilation of non-African cosmologies in the West Atlantic, have served, in large measure, to blur the ethnic distinctions brought from Africa. The assimilationist pressures of plantation and colonial societies subjected various African ethnicities to the same marginalization and stigmatization, so that over time Koongo or Igbo or Yoruba became Africans, their children became African Creoles, Creoles became Negroes, Negroes became Coloreds, Coloreds became Blacks, and now Africa is reclaimed in labels such as Afro-Caribbean or African. This necessary loss of primordial ethnic specificity, as I have indicated, has been accompanied by complex, contradictory processes of accommodation and realignments in power relations and cultural influence among African ethnicities themselves, such that

Fon or Yoruba or Akan or Koongo ethnic influence may predominate and subsume other African ethnicities in particular localities or in particular activities or customs. For example, Hausa Arabic-derived *saraka* in the Eastern Caribbean has informed the ancestral remembrance rites of Yoruba and Koongo descendants, not only Hausa; Fon and Koongo influences vie for prominence in Haitian vodun rites; Akan day-names, such as Kojo, Kofi, Kwashi, Mimba, Kwasheba, and Juba, appear to have been applied in Jamaica and throughout the Caribbean plantation system to Akan- and non-Akan-descended children alike.

At the same time, as these processes have been in train among the African ethnic groups, there have been concurrent processes of assimilation, accommodation, masking, and resistance by Africans and their descendants to European legal, political, social, and religious institutions and worldviews. These are the informal processes of deconstruction and recombination which are ongoing. These processes have not necessarily received attention in the macrocosmic visions of the publicists and historians mentioned above, but these processes are daily enacted in the expressive arts, in the use of the indigenous languages of the Caribbean, in their idioms, sound symbolisms, and proverbs—even in the still existent personal memories of interaction with grandparents who crossed the Atlantic. The past continues in the present.

Yet I end with the reminder of the heterogeneous, structurally fragile nature of the African diaspora, even in the face of its ethnic, cultural, and migrant interconnectedness. The formation of new nations in the Caribbean and of new national loyalties fostered since the latter part of the nineteenth century challenge, cut across, even undercut diasporic loyalties. The rallying cry issued by Eric Williams, radical historian and former Prime Minister of Trinidad and Tobago, encapsulates the anglophone Caribbean's post–World War II nationalist repositioning of loyalties and identity: it was in its cosmovision essentially "creole" in the sense of "divorced from/renouncing ancestral heritage":

> There can be no Mother India for those whose ancestors come from India . . . there can be no Mother Africa for those of African origin . . . there can be no Mother England and no dual loyalties. . . . there can be no Mother China even if one could agree as to which China is the mother; and there can be no Mother Syria and no Mother Lebanon. A nation, like an individual, can have only one mother. The only mother we recognize is Mother Trinidad and Tobago, and Mother cannot discriminate between her children.[20]

Meanwhile, the homeland African faces the challenge of consolidating transethnic nation-states, but for better or worse, s/he confronts this complexity, incorporating within his/her identity the traditions and history of the clans and subgroups of larger ethnic groups. The West Atlantic Africans similarly operate in multiethnic contexts. But unlike the continental African, the Africans of the West Atlantic embody intimate or distant relationships with miscegenated fragments of earlier African ethnic cultures. These various ethnic cultures have converged in the West, and some ethnic cultures have even been hegemonized by others. Fragmentation implies that elements of a putative whole may have been erased and lost, but the surviving fragments have been reconstituted into modalities which are peculiar to each diasporic location, modalities which themselves continue to renegotiate their relationship to each other. But the reconstituted elements of African cultures in the West Atlantic are also renegotiating their relationships to non-African ethnic discourses and matrices of power given their complex multiethnic environments, and over time they continue to respond to the pressures and innovations produced by immigration, outmigration, and modernization.

NOTES

1. See Boyce-Davies 1985.
2. See Warner-Lewis 1991a, 1995, 1996.
3. See Pearse 1956; Hill 1972:16–22; Clarke 1980:57–97; Hill 1993:34–43; Moore 1997.
4. See Fernando Ortiz, *Revista Bimestre Cubana* 30:117, 5–35 and 30:118, 126–164, 1922; Lydia Cabrera, *Anagó, Vocabulario Lucumí*, Miami: Colección Chicherekú, 1970; David Dalby, Ashanti Survivals in the Language and Traditions of the Windward Maroons of Jamaica, *African Language Studies* 12, 1971, 31–51; Gema Valdés Acosta, Descripción de Remanentes de Lenguas Bantúes en Santa Isabel de las Lajas, *Islas* 48, 1974, 69–85; Manuel Álvarez Nazario, *El elemento afronegroide en el español de Puerto Rico*, San Juan, Instituto de Cultura Puertorriqueña, 1974; Robert Damoiseau, Kikongo en Martinique, *Etudes Créoles: Culture, Langue, Société* 3:2, 1980, 100–106; Carlos Esteban Deive, La Herencia Africana en la Cultura Dominicana Actual, *Ensayos sobre cultura dominicana*, Santo Domingo, Museo del Hombre Dominicano, 1981, 105–141; Kenneth Bilby and Bunseki Fu-Kiau, *Kumina: A Kongo-based Tradition in the New World*, Brussels, Centre d'Étude et de Documentation Africaines, 1983; Ama Mazama, The Nature of Language Contacts in Guadeloupe during Slavery: Sociological and Linguistic Evidence, Paper presented to the 1992 Conference of the Society for Caribbean Linguistics; Warner-Lewis 1996; Hazel Carter, Annotated Kumina Lexicon, *African-Caribbean Institute of Jamaica Review* 3, 1996, 66–129; Abiodun Adetugbo, The Yoruba in Jamaica, *African-Caribbean Institute of Jamaica Review* 3, 1996, 41–65.
5. After the emancipation of slaves in the anglophone Caribbean in 1834 in Antigua, and 1838 elsewhere; in the French Antilles, after 1848, in Cuba, after 1886, and the Dutch Antilles, after 1863.

6. See Rodway 1891:297–298; Acosta Saignes 1955; Bolland 1987; Friedemann 1988, Ortiz 1992.

7. See Chaudenson 1979; Alleyne 1980; Robertson 1993; Lipski and Schwegler 1993; Granda 1994; Kouwenberg 1997.

8. See Warner-Lewis 1996:118–136, 182–183.

9. See Warner-Lewis 1996; Schwegler 1996.

10. See Warner-Lewis 1995.

11. See Hall 1989 for the movement of slaves from one plantation to another for social functions such as death wakes and birth celebrations; evidence from Nelson 1966 regarding Monteath's encounters with slaves from other estates.

12. Note the continued use in the Caribbean of steamed starchy flours, or baked starchy flour paps, and combinations of green banana and root crops boiled in thick sauces, called "oil down" and "run down" in various Caribbean locations.

13. Among the games should be noted *warri*, a draughts-like activity, and *kalinda*, a sport of combat with sticks. For *warri*, see Zaslavsky 1973:116–136.

14. See Warner-Lewis 1991a; Whylie and Warner-Lewis 1994.

15. See, among others, Barrett 1977; Cabrera 1979; Cabrera 1986; Jorge 1991; Warner-Lewis 1991b.

16. See Leon 1971.

17. See Warner-Lewis 1996:78.

18. See Simpson 1965; Bascom 1972.

19. Bilby 1985:85–87.

20. Williams 1964:278.

REFERENCES

Acosta Saignes, Miguel. 1955. Las Cofradías Coloniales y el Folklore. *Cultura Universitaria* 47, 79–99.

Alleyne, Mervyn. 1980. *Comparative Afro-American: An Historical-Comparative Study of English-based Afro-American Dialects of the New World.* Ann Arbor: Karoma.

Barrett, Leonard. 1977. African Religion in the Americas: The Islands in Between. *African Religions: A Symposium.* Ed. Newell Booth, 183–215. New York: NOK Publishers.

Bascom, William. 1972. *Shango in the New World.* Austin: The University of Texas Press.

Bilby, Kenneth. 1985. The Holy Herb: Notes on the Background of Cannabis in Jamaica. *Caribbean Quarterly*, monograph, 82–95.

Bolland, Nigel. 1987. African Continuities and Creole Culture in Belize Town in the Nineteenth Century. *Afro-Caribbean Villages in Historical Perspective. African-Caribbean Institute of Jamaica Research Review* 2, ed. Charles Carnegie, 63–82.

Cabrera, Lydia. 1986a. [1979] *Reglas de Congo: Palo Monte, Mayombe.* Miami: Ediciones Universal.

———. 1986b. *El Monte: Igbo-Finda, Ewe Orisha, Vititi Nfinda*. Miami: Colección Chicherekú.

Chaudenson, Robert. 1979. *Les Créoles Français*. Paris: Fernand Nathan.

Davies, Carole Boyce. 1985. The Africa Theme in Trinidad Calypso. *Caribbean Quarterly* 31:2, 67–86.

Friedemann, Nina de. 1988. Cabildos Negros: Refugios de Africanía en Colombia. *Montalban* 20, 121–134.

Granda, Germán de. 1994. *Español de América, español de África y hablas criollas hispánicas: Cambios, contactos y contextos*. Madrid: Editorial Gredos.

Hall, Douglas. 1989. *In Miserable Slavery: Thomas Thistlewood in Jamaica, 1750–86*. London and Basingstoke: Macmillan.

Hill, Donald. 1993. *Calypso Calaloo: Early Carnival Music in Trinidad*. Gainesville: The University Press of Florida.

Hill, Errol. 1972. *The Trinidad Carnival: Mandate for a National Theater*. Austin and London: University of Texas Press.

Jorge, Angela. 1991. Cuban Santería: A New World African Religion. *African Creative Expressions of the Divine*. Ed. Kortright Davis and Elias Farajaje-Jones, 105–120. Washington D.C.: Howard University School of Divinity.

Kouwenberg, Silvia. 1997. Creole and Substrate: The Identification of Kalabari Properties in Berbice Dutch Creole. Paper presented to Conference on "West Africa and the Americas: Repercussions of the Slave Trade," University of the West Indies, Jamaica.

León, Argeliers. 1971. Un caso de tradición oral escrita. *Islas* 39–40: 139–151.

Lipski, John and Armin Schwegler. 1993. Creole Spanish and Afro-Hispanic. *Bilingualism and Linguistic Conflict in Romance*. Eds. John Green and Rebecca Posner, 407–432. Berlin: Mouton de Gruyter.

Moore, Robin. 1997. *Comparsas* and Carnival in the New Republic: Four Decades of Cultural Controversy. *Nationalizing Blackness*. Pittsburgh: University of Pittsburgh Press.

Nelson, Vernon, ed. 1966. Archibald John Monteith: Native Helper and Assistant in the Jamaica Mission at New Carmel. *Transactions of the Moravian Historical Society* 21:1, 29–52.

Ortiz, Fernando. 1992 [1921]. *Los cabildos y la fiesta del Día de Reyes*. Habana: Editorial de Ciencias Sociales.

Pearse, Andrew. 1956. Carnival in Nineteenth Century Trinidad. *Caribbean Quarterly* 4:3 and 4, 175–193.

Rodway, James. 1891. *History of British Guiana*. Vol. II. Georgetown: J. Thomson.

Schwegler, Armin. 1996. *"Chi ma nkongo": Lengua y rito ancestrales en El Palenque de San Basilio (Colombia)*. Vols. I and II. Frankfurt: Vervuert Verlag.

Simpson, George. 1965. *The Shango Cult in Trinidad*. Rio Piedras: Institute of Caribbean Studies.

Warner-Lewis, Maureen. 1991a. The Influence of Yoruba Music on the

Minor-Key Calypso. *Guinea's Other Suns: The African Dynamic in Trinidad Culture.* Dover, MA: The Majority Press. 141–158.

——. 1991b. The Ancestral Factor in Jamaica's African Religions. *African Creative Expressions of the Divine.* Ed. Kortright Davis and Elias Farajaje-Jones, 63–80. Washington D.C.: Howard University School of Divinity.

——. 1995. *Yoruba Songs of Trinidad.* London: Karnak House.

——. 1996. *Trinidad Yoruba: From Mother Tongue to Memory.* Tuscaloosa and London: The University of Alabama Press.

Whylie, Marjorie and Maureen Warner-Lewis. 1994. Characteristics of Maroon Music from Jamaica and Suriname. *Maroon Heritage: Archaeological, Ethnographic and Historical Perspectives.* Ed. Kofi Agorsah, 139–148. Kingston: Canoe Press.

Williams, Eric. 1964. *History of the People of Trinidad and Tobago.* London: Andre Deutsch.

Zaslavsky, Claudia. 1973. *Africa Counts: Number and Pattern in African Culture.* Westport: Lawrence Hill.

3

THE RESTORATION OF AFRICAN IDENTITY FOR A NEW MILLENNIUM

Elliott P. Skinner

The determination of African peoples to end the feeling of self-alienation and to restore our civilizations is an imperative for the twenty-first century. For over four centuries, those of us whose ancestors were torn away from Africa's shores by the slave trade have been victims of what has been termed an "exilic" agony. We can empathize with Cullen, who asked in his poem "Heritage,"

> What is Africa to me
> Copper sun or scarlet sea
> Jungle star or jungle tract
> Strong black men or regal black
> Women from whose loins I sprang
> When the birds of Eden sang?
> One three centuries removed
> From the scenes his father told
> Spring grove, cinnamon tree
> What is Africa to me?[1]

It is more troubling, but quite revealing, when one notices the same kind of alienation and the questioning of Africa from Africans whose ancestors never left the continent. Senegalese-born David Diop lamented:

> Africa, I have never known you
> But my gaze is full of your blood . . .
> Africa tell me Africa
> Is this you this back that is bent
> This back that breaks under the weight of humiliation
> This back trembling with red scars
> And saying yes to the whip under the midday sun
> But a grave voice answers me
> Impetuous son, that tree young and strong
> That tree there

In splendid loneliness amidst white and faded flowers
That is Africa your Africa
That grows again patiently obstinately
And its fruit gradually acquires
The bitter taste of liberty

(Extract from "Africa")

The self-doubt that arose among African peoples led them to lose that simple human pride that normally prevented people from readily accepting the notion that they and their cultures were inferior to others. Generations of African peoples experienced the onus of seeing themselves through the eyes of others. As "bastards" of the West, they always sensed that in many subtle and obvious ways they were illegitimate. It was out of this recognition that the drives for equal rights, national independence, and cultural autonomy arose. With the presidency of Nelson Mandela, the ancestral continent has finally thrown off the yoke of alien rule, and African peoples in the diaspora are anxious to achieve full equality. Today the twin desires of a cultural renaissance and economic development are necessary if African peoples should attain equality with human beings everywhere.

The nature of the earliest encounters between African peoples and outsiders took place "before history" and will never be known to us. But if contemporary paleontological evidence is accepted, the first humans appeared in Africa and literally gave rise to other human beings who subsequently left the ancestral continent. The earliest records we have about Africans, those in ancient Egypt (Ethiopia), reveal people quite sure of themselves and their traditions and freely acknowledging that they had all the virtues and vices that flesh is heir to. They gave as much as they got, and they were often as much the conquerors as the conquered.

The contact between Africans and the West was so traumatic that we began to question our very humanity. We forgot that our ancestors could not believe their eyes when they encountered the first Western Europeans. Mungo Park could not contain his surprise when the Africans, especially the women, teased him about the whiteness of his skin and the prominence of his nose and "insisted that both were artificial" (Park, 1813:45). We forgot the report of William Bosman, who in 1705 declared that the "Inhabitants of *Great Benin* are generally good-natur'd and very civil, from whom it is easy to obtain whatever we desire by soft means. If we make them liberal Presents, they will endeavor to recompense them doubly." But they insist that they "expect that their Courtesy should be repaid with Civility, and not with Arrogance or Rudeness; for to think of forcing anything from them, is to dispute with the Moon" (1967:433).

The image of Africa that emerged after the period of this initial contact was one of a "Dark Continent" whose peoples were subhuman, heathen, and barbarous. The developing biblical Hamitic myth, said to be of

Babylonian Talmudic origin, assigned Africans the role of servants to other peoples because of Canaan's misdeeds. Linnaeus's *Systema Naturae* (1735) not only classified all living things with human beings at the top, but stimulated the notion that the black race was quite low among humans in the "Great Chain of Being" (Curtin, 1964:36–37). Almost all the major philosophers of that period believed this to be true. Kant, Rousseau, and Voltaire all suggested that Africans were naturally inferior to Europeans in mental ability. David Hume, the British philosopher, argues that

> There never was a civilized nation of any other complexion than white, nor even any individual eminent either in action or speculation. No ingenious manufacturers amongst them, no arts, no science. . . . Such a uniform and constant difference could not happen, in so many countries and ages, if nature had not made an original distinction between breeds of men. (Curtin, 1964:42)[2]

Hume dismissed as nonsense the report that an African slave in Jamaica had exhibited remarkable intellectual ability (Williams, 1970:208).

In a manner reminiscent of Hume, Wilhelm Friedrich Hegel added:

> It [Africa] is no historical part of the world; it has no movement, or development to exhibit. Historical movements in it—that is in its northern part—belong to the Asiatic or European world. Egypt does not belong to the African Spirit. What we properly understand by Africa, is the Unhistorical, Undeveloped Spirit, still on the threshold of World History.[3]

This was the intellectual and moral climate with which Africans had to deal when they became conscious of their position vis à vis Western Christendom. Imperial Europe wished to remake the world in its image, or in its shadows, and estranged Africans from themselves. It was therefore not surprising that those who were either sent away to Europe for education or were taken as slaves to the New World started to devalue themselves and their traditions.

Philip Quaque from Cape Coast (Ghana), who was sent to England in 1754 to be trained as an Anglican priest and returned home with an English wife to serve as official chaplin at Cape Coast Castle, wrote back to England that he had discovered that the customs of his people were "detestable," "barbarous and inhuman," and generally unbelievable (Curtin, 1967:129). Quaque had been psycho-culturally estranged by the hegemonic paradigm of his day and denigrated himself and his culture.

Phillis Wheatley, who was transported as a slave to English North America, would write in 1773, in a poem entitled "On Being Brought from Africa to America,"

Twas mercy brought me from my Pagan land,
Taught my benighted soul to understand
That there's a God, and there's a Saviour too:
Once I redemption neither sought nor knew.
Some view our sable race with scornful eye,
"Their colour is a diabolic die."
Remember, Christians, Negroes, black as Cain,
May be refin'd, and join th' angelic train.

It might have helped these early Africans if their European mentors had permitted them to join the Christian or human community. But as W. E. B. Du Bois noted in 1897, the white world yielded the African "no self-consciousness, but only [let] him see himself through the revelation of the other world . . . that looks on in amused contempt and pity" (1897).

Many black people succumbed to these notions about themselves and accepted the existential superiority of the West, portrayed through various texts and discourses. But it is important to note that many of the early enslaved were the very ones who started the process of vindicating their humanity and African cultures in the face of European detractors. Their problem was that, while adopting what we would call today a counter-textual stance in reacting to European discourse, continental and diasporic African intellectuals faced a dilemma: how to free themselves from this hegemonic, paradigmatic control?

In order to accomplish this, African peoples faced the intellectually daunting problem of having to use the same lenses and analytical tools as their detractors. After all, the dominant Europeans had the power to control the available discourse, and woe to the black captives in the New World who could not speak "bucra." Coming readily to mind is the poem by Countee Cullen that laments "[making] a poet black and bid him sing." There is also the anguish of a Leopold Sedar Senghor having to express the feelings of the soul in a strange tongue. Mazrui reported that Kenyatta, frustrated by the English language which prevented him from communicating with his people, literally threw it aside and broke into Swahili to the applause of his auditors. Almost all these persons were quite familiar with the lament of the Hebrews in exile who resisted the invitation to "sing the Lord's song in a strange land." What this meant then, as it does now, is that people of African descent had to be prepared to pay a high price if they would attempt to reconstruct themselves and Africa. Perhaps an important but troublesome step toward our emancipation is to realize the nature of the problem.

Equiano of Benin, who had been transported as a captive to Barbados in 1756, and who finally ended up in London (where he bought his freedom and wrote his memoirs in 1788), faced this dilemma when he attempted to vindicate Africans and their cultures. A convert to Christianity,

Equiano viewed the Bible as the canon of Christendom and relished comparing African behavior and cultures with those of the Hebrews. Citing the culture of "Abraham and the other patriarchs," Equiano wrote: "We had also our circumcision (a rule I believe peculiar to that people); we had also our sacrifices and burnt-offerings, our washings and purifications, on the same occasions as they had" (Curtin, 1967:82). Equiano's argument was that if King David danced before the Lord, what right had Western European converts to Christianity to criticize the behavior of Africans when this was comparable to that of the ancient and venerated Israelites whose religion the Europeans treasured? Yet Equiano could not break out of the Hebraic-Christian paradigm that demanded his conversion and the abandonment of his culture.

When in 1792 Benjamin Banneker, a free man and possibly a "free thinker" (meaning that he was not a practicing Christian), sought to defend the race against the opinions of Secretary of State Jefferson (also something of a free thinker), he was caught in the same dilemma. Tackling the issues of culture and race, Banneker believed that as a man of "the African race, and in that color which is natural to them of the deepest dye," he was capable of astronomical and mathematical accomplishments.[4] Banneker knew that Jefferson disdained Phillis Wheatley's poetry, but hoped that a man who considered himself an equal of positivist French philosophers would examine another bit of evidence attesting to the intellectual capacity of African Americans.[5] Banneker remarked that African Americans had "long been considered rather as brutish than human, and scarcely capable of mental endowments."[6] But he urged Jefferson to take fully into consideration the "state of degradation, to which the unjustifiable cruelty and barbarism of men" had reduced the African Americans.[7] Jefferson was not convinced of Banneker's brilliance, believing instead that George Ellicott had helped him.

Those eighteenth- and nineteenth-century intellectual companions and heirs of Banneker who refrained from going so far as becoming "free thinkers" were nevertheless disgusted with the bigotry of their brethren in Christ. They left the white denominations and organized "African" branches. Besides now being free to "fellowship" with each other, they invented spirituals that not only made joyful noises "unto the God of Jacob," but invoked a longing for the lands over "Jordan" whence would come their help. In beseeching the Lord to let his people go, they transformed themselves into Hebrews and the Egyptian Pharaoh into the slave master. The paradox here was that they also wished to use the "glory" that was Egypt and the power of its princes to bring about their salvation.

In time, the contradiction that was inherent in the biblical paradigm induced many blacks to move even further away from Christianity. In the persons of "Father Divine" and "Daddy Grace," they venerated their own messiahs and created their own heavens. Those who remained faithful to

Jesus Christ would later experience their own Gethsemane in Birmingham jails, when they could not rouse the sleeping sentiment of fellow pastors.

Reacting to the cultural paradigm of African inferiority, many African American intellectuals of the mid-nineteenth century invented the paradigm known as "black nationality," an interesting conflation of culture and religion. Its major trope was "Egyptian princes and Ethiopia's hands."[8] These persons challenged their detractors to explain how they could expect African Americans to be moral superpeople while held in bondage and subjected to hostility and discrimination. Their one consolation was that God worked in mysterious ways His wonders to perform, and that African Americans may be instruments of His scheme "until the princes shall come forth from Egypt and Ethiopia stretch out her hand unto God."[9]

When these persons employed the biblical "exodus" as a metaphor for fleeing slavery and sought an Eden that became identified with Africa, it was but a small step for them to insist (even before Darwin) that the first human beings appeared in Africa and that it was the source of all civilization. Out of this "black nationality" would come the first signs of "Afrocentricity."

The Reverend Henry Highland Garnet, undeterred by his Christian vocation, complained that, among other things, his world appeared determined to pilfer Africa of her glory. It was not enough, he said, "that her children have been scattered over the globe, clothed in the garments of shame—humiliated and oppressed—but her merciless foes weary themselves in plundering the tombs of our renowned sires, and in obliterating their worthy deeds, which were inscribed by fame upon the pages of ancient history."[10] He asserted that during a period when the representatives "of our race were filling the world with amazement, the ancestors of the now proud and boasting Anglo-Saxons were among the most degraded of the human family."[11]

Garnet's spirited defense of African peoples and African civilization also encouraged a subtext of African primacy, namely, "black superiority" (Aptheker, 1971:165–179). His lead was followed by Edward Wilmot Blyden, who invoked "the sphinx of African history" and "the glory that was Egypt" to foster Afrocentricity as a counter-Eurocentric paradigm. Blyden loved comparing African institutions with the African-derived ones of the Hellenic Greeks and the Romans. For him, in solving the riddle of the Sphinx lay the way to understanding the rise of all civilizations. He had no doubt about what the Sphinx was.

Her [sic] features are decidedly that of the African or Negro type, with "expanded nostrils." If, then, the Sphinx was placed here—looking out in majestic and mysterious silence over the empty plain where once stood the great city of Memphis in all its pride and glory, as an "emblematic representation of the king"—is not the inference clear as to the peculiar type of race to which the king belonged? (Quoted in Du Bois, 1915:34)

But Blyden was not content to assert that human civilization began in Africa, that Africa civilized Greece, and that Greece civilized Europe; he also attacked the other paradigm used by blacks, namely, Christianity. For Blyden, Islam was more in harmony with the "Negro race" than was Christianity, a religion that he associated with Western imperialism. His attitude toward Islam started a paradigmatic process that affected later generations of African Americans and has echoes today.

W. E. B. Du Bois was too much of a "free thinker" to buy into the Hebraic paradigm of "Ethiopia's hand." He admired Blyden's cultural approach and often employed the trope of the Sphinx of history in the light of unsolved problems. Committed to the struggle of blacks for equality, Du Bois challenged the social Darwinists of his day, bolstered by the work of Franz Boas of Columbia.[12] In hoping for a culturally pluralistic United States of America, Du Bois felt that blacks had to "break the mental shackles of a white-imposed inferiority . . . in an overwhelming white-and-hostile America" and come to grips with themselves and Africa (Drimmer, 1968:2).

Du Bois challenged the Hegelian notion that Africans had made no contributions to world civilization, and asserted that specifically in the case of Egyptian civilization, it was clear that the "Negro did make some contributions to world history."[13] Du Bois remained intrigued with Africa. He published a small book entitled *The Negro* in 1915 which was regarded as "one of the first serious American works on African cultures" (Du Bois, 1969:xiv). In it, he described Africa in lyrical and visionary terms:

This is not a country, it is a world—a universe of itself and for itself, a thing Different, Immense, Menacing, Alluring. . . . Africa is the Spiritual Frontier of human kind—oh the wild and beautiful adventures of its taming! But oh! the cost thereof and ever, ever young the day when there will spring [up] in Africa a civilization without coal, without noise, where machinery will sing and never rush and roar, and where men will sleep and think and dance and lie prone before the rising sun, and women will be happy. . . . (Du Bois, 1915)

This statement reveals that Du Bois had "a visceral faith in the historic significance of Africa" (Lewis, 1993:352), but behind the romantic was the pragmatist who while extolling African culture insisted that African Americans had to come to grips with life in America. He did not believe blacks should attempt to Africanize America, "for America has too much to teach the world and Africa." Nor, said Du Bois, should they "bleach" their "Negro soul in a flood of white Americanism," for "Negro blood has a message for the world." Du Bois simply wished to make it possible for a man to be both a Negro and an American, without being cursed and spat upon by his fellows and without having the doors of Opportunity closed roughly in his face (1961:17).

The continental contemporaries of Du Bois who knew his work and had closely followed the debate in the diaspora about "African culture," "black nationality," and "Pan-Africanism" joined the battle over African culture. They had long resented the notion that African societies were judged "primitive" and that Africans possessed "primitive mentalities." They, too, started to insist that while the "African personality" was different from that of the Europeans, it warranted respect. Chief among these African intellectuals was Joseph Ephraim Casely Hayford, who in a pair of books, *Ethiopia Unbound* and *Gold Coast Native Institutions*, systematically compared African institutions with those of the Europeans.

A lawyer by training, Casely Hayford was less prepared than the later Afrocentrics to claim a primacy for African institutions. He simply wanted to defend them from unwarranted attacks. Casely Hayford was especially perturbed by reports that a former British governor of the Gold Coast had "declared that the Gold Coast was neither 'fit' for a white man, nor a black man, nor a Chinaman, nor yet for a dog. . . ." He rebutted that the governor was in error and that as far as the local people were concerned, "The Gold Coast is, and will always be, 'fit' for the Gold Coast man. So has God ordained it" (Hayford, 1903:238). The Gold Coaster conceded that in many respects, European institutions had advanced beyond those possessed by Africans. Nevertheless, he urged the British "to apply a little common sense and practical statesmanship" in dealing with Africans. Arguing like Equiano before him, Casely Hayford declared:

Take the case of your own national evolution. It is a matter of history that, at the beginning of the Christian era, you were worse off than we are to-day; greater darkness brooded over your intellectual horizon. By the absorption of Grecian and Roman culture and the science of the Eastern world, you gradually emerged from darkness into light, and were able to develop what was natural and innate in you, and to, in time, contribute your quota to the world's work. In a word, given the conditions of development, you developed on your own lines, until you became the great nation you are today. (1903:239–240)

Casely Hayford felt that the problem that the Gold Coast people faced "in its naked form" was pressure to emulate or imitate the West. He warned that for a century, the Gold Coast people had observed the attempts of the British "to mould their institutions, and that you have signally failed. They see in the civilization you offer much that is fair, but cannot fail to perceive the weak spots and blemishes in the same. They say to you, 'We are anxious to take part in the race of nations towards the attainment of higher ideals, if you will give us a chance to work out our own salvation.'" He did not believe that it was either right or fair for the British to regard the Gold Coasters as innocents forced to act like "pigmies" and march with the Colossus whether it was expedient or not (1903:7).

Curiously, two important actors in the African diaspora, while equally concerned about advancing the causes of African peoples, were not overly interested in African culture. Although more of a "race-man" than is commonly realized, Booker T. Washington felt that accommodating white political and economic power, rather than emulating their culture, would improve the lot of blacks. He frequently ridiculed the trouser-less African who attempted to read Cicero, indicating that this was not the road to salvation. Yet the same Booker T. Washington wrote:

> There is . . . a tie which few white men can understand, which binds the American Negro to the African Negro; which unites the black man of Brazil and black man of Liberia; which is constantly drawing into closer relations all the scattered African peoples whether they are in the old world or the new. There is not only the view of race, which is strong in any case, but there is colour, which is especially important in the case of the black man. It is this common badge of colour, for instance, which is responsible for the fact that whatever contributes, in any degree, to the progress of the American Negro, in South America and the West Indies. When the African Negro succeeds, it helps the American Negro. When the African Negro fails, it hurts the reputation and the standing of the Negro in every part of the world.[14]

If Booker T. Washington was often too economic in his approach to the African problem, Garvey could be said to have been too political. Stimulated by the same desire to "improve the race," Marcus Garvey left Jamaica and came to a Harlem that had emerged as a mecca for African peoples (in the same way the rest of New York City was viewed by European migrants) with his Universal Negro Improvement Association (UNIA) to politicize the question of Africa. He described his epiphany:

> I had read "Up From Slavery," by Booker T. Washington, and then my doom—if I may call it—of being race leader dawned upon me in London after I had traveled through almost half of Europe. I asked, "Where is the black man's Government?" "Where is his

King and his kingdom?" "Where is his President, his country, and his ambassador, his army, his navy, his men of big affairs?" I could not find them, and then I declared, "I will help to make them."[15]

From Harlem's Liberty Hall he boldly proclaimed that "Africa belonged to Africans at home and overseas," and planted UNIA cells wherever blacks lived. Attempting to build institutions to support his trope, Garvey appointed nobility with symbolic fiefs named after African countries and rivers (Garvey, 1983; Skinner, 1992).[16]

Meanwhile, Garvey's Harlem was the arena of a veritable cultural revival or renaissance. This led to negritude, a paradigmatic revolt of diasporic Africans who felt culturally stifled. The early musicians who discarded the funeral marches as mourners left the cemeteries of New Orleans invented Jazz. These musicians followed the Mississippi northward to Chicago, and would later send their descendants east to Harlem and to Paris, where "Le Jazz Hot" attracted expatriate Americans, the French, and African students studying there.

In tandem with this, the Harlemites celebrated their "blackness" in dialect poetry based on the singing sermons of black preachers. Langston Hughes conflated the rivers of the old world with those in the new, equally celebrating those who built ziggurats along the Euphrates and pyramids on the banks of the Nile, and loaded cotton on the Mississippi. Cullen raised and answered his relationship to Africa in his poem "Heritage." Their companions from the Caribbean rhapsodized about "hibiscus in the snow." Zora Neale Hurston came down from Columbia's Morningside Heights and researched the folklore of rural African Americans and that of Jamaicans and Haitians as sources of the African tradition. Diasporic blacks understood the reasons why Professor Price-Mars asserted that the Haitian Creole language was a proper vehicle of discourse and that Vodun was a religion worthy of respect (1928).

It was partly these developments in the New World African diaspora that gave birth to negritude, and to the debate as to whether African cultural specificity could be a debilitating or liberating paradigm. Brilliant students such as Aimé Césaire and Franz Fanon from Martinique, Leopold Sedar Senghor of Senegal, and Leon Damas of French Guiana championed negritude and spent innumerable long evenings in the cafés of Paris's Latin Quarter, debating the nature of African culture (Mouralis in Mudimbe, 1992). Senghor felt that

Negritude is the whole complex of civilized values—cultural, economic, social, and political—which characterize the black peoples, or, more precisely the Negro African world. . . . the sense of communion, the gift of myth-making, the gift of rhythm, such are the essential elements of Negritude, which you will find indelibly stamped on all the works and activities of the black man. (Senghor 1961:1211)

Franz Fanon was sympathetic to the need of many young people in Paris for a cultural renaissance to support political action and to establish an African orientation ("presence africaine") in all aspects of human life and culture, from art to zoology. Yet, swayed by marxist notions, Fanon remained skeptical and quite suspicious of the possibility that negritude could be a balm to the psychosocial and cultural dependency of his colleagues. For him, this attempted "return to the source" and embrace of African culture was comparable to the "the desperation of a drowning man." Fanon observed:

> This culture, abandoned, sloughed off, rejected, despised, becomes for the inferiorized an object of passionate attachment. . . . The customs, traditions, beliefs, formerly denied and passed over in silence are violently valorized and affirmed. . . . Tradition is no longer scoffed at by the group. The group no longer runs away from itself. The sense of the past is rediscovered, the worship of ancestors resumed. . . . The past, becoming henceforth a constellation of values, becomes identified with the Truth.[17]

Fanon warned that the archaic cult of negritude had no relationship to technical development. Moreover, he felt that the institutions that the Africans were attempting to valorize no longer corresponded to the elaborate methods or actions that were needed.[18] Instead of "mystification," Fanon wanted a thorough understanding of the relationship between technologies, social structures, and culture.[19] He did attract followers, but others felt that this particular God had feet of clay and would fail because it defined as "false consciousness" a "racial" reality that crippled their lives.

Defined by Jean-Paul Sartre as an "anti-racist-racism," negritude was very much in the Afrocentric paradigmatic tradition. Then, as now, it was the center of debate among persons of African descent, involving as it did ontological, epistemological, and methodological disagreements about the nature of African culture, and especially the issue of Eurocentricity versus Afrocentricity, a battle over hegemony. This battle was grounded in the existential reality of authority and power, and in the words of one of its contemporary practitioners, was and is "a radical critique of the Eurocentric ideology" (Asante, 1987:3). The notion was that as long as there was or is contestation about the place of African peoples and their cultures within the world system, the paradigmatic debate was/is judged necessary.[20]

For others, Afrocentricity was viewed as reinforcing the belief in the inferiority of African peoples and their cultures and was therefore unacceptable. They pointed out that one serious drawback with Afrocentricity as "a legitimate defense" of Africans against Euro-American paradigmatic superiority was and is that it often led to a greater preoccupation with European culture, or "the stolen legacy," than with the experiences of Africans and their descendants in the various diasporas.[21] The issue here is how and why paradigms are invented. Except when purposely framed to mobilize their people for action, human beings usually create paradigms to vaunt their characteristics or values.

I submit that the task of dealing with contemporary hegemonic paradigms should be less an exercise in *Afrocentricity* that an attempt to develop the capacity of *Africanity*. Paradigms, whether developed by African peoples or by others, provide a way of looking at the world in which people live, and a manner of providing succeeding generations ways in which to shape and to understand their lives. Given our reality and our existential needs, it is necessary that we delve into the African past and our own existence for ideas and processes for paradigms to effect our renaissance.

The approach of Africanity is not as simple as it seems, however, because it challenges its practitioners to shift the focus away from Europe, even from "Black Athena," and come to grips with the experience of African peoples. This experience is quite complex because over the past five centuries there has been "self-fashioning" as African peoples reacted to severe sociocultural, geno-phenotypical, historical, and linguistic pressures. But we must realize that paradigms have always been created, invented, and reaffirmed as conditions dictated.

It is clear that given the requirements of the modern world and the imperatives of the new millennium, African peoples cannot rely exclusively upon our own paradigms and traditions as guides for action. It must not be assumed, however, that our paradigmatic achievements must be undervalued as we assert ourselves in the contemporary world. Instead of talking about syncretism of African cultures with those of others, we must emphasize redefinition and, more importantly, the "retrieval" and enhancement of African culture traits. For example, many persons were uncomfortable when an African praise-singer appeared on the podium when Nelson Mandela took the oath of office as the first black president of South Africa. They did not feel that this tradition was in keeping with modern political culture. (The Afrikaners in the stands were visibly upset, especially Mrs. F. W. De Klerk).

Unnoticed or unknown is that rural Africans confronted by modern institutions have always initially viewed those developments through their own cultural lenses. It is only later that they accept alien models. For example, in working on a book on sources of the African tradition, I attempted to find examples of traditional African polities that had elements of "democracy." I could not find a coherent account of any traditional African constitution from such African scholars as Casely Hayford, Africanus Horton, or J. B. Danquah. They spent their time comparing aspects of African polities with the politics of Aristotle. To my chagrin, I had to resort to the work of Captain R. S. Rattray, a British anthropologist, to find a fairly straightforward account of an Akan state.

I was also disappointed with written versions of African oral traditions until I realized that although rural Africans referred in their discourses and poems to "askaris," "district officers," "automobiles," and "airplanes," these accounts retained traditional forms even when serving changing functions. How far these developments can proceed without severe paradigmatic shifts is unknown, but these shifts, when they take place, should emphasize the persistence of African traditions.

In an article "Yoruban Astrophysics," which appeared in *The Washington Post* of April 9, 1995, Wole Soyinka sought to explain "How My Nigerian Past Prepared Me for the Mysterious Future." Wole explained that "The Yoruba respond to new, alien experiences by integrating them into the domain of the deities. Today, for instance, with the penetration of computer technology in everyday life, the only problem might be to decide whether the computer belongs to Obong, the god of electricity, or to Sango, the god of metals. I suspect it will be Ogun of the Cyber-Superhyways!"

Perhaps in response to Franz Fanon, Soyinka continued: "Technology is not considered alien in Nigeria. From childhood, I knew roadside mechanics adept at fixing almost every kind of mechanical contrivance, and I have no doubt that we shall soon produce our own computer experts." What intrigued him, however, was that so far Western scientific theories did not have the answers to cosmic issues. He said that "Until a spacewalker brings back irrefutable evidence, the Big Bang theory, black holes, time warps and allied notions of space, eons of light years away, convulsing in labor pains or collapsing inwards—they occupy the same realm of mystification as the most outlandish myths. A truly rational explanation seems, for now, beyond the most sophisticated instruments or inspired projection of the mind. I remain optimistic however. One of these days, the darkest secret of space will be laid bare." Then, the Yoruba cosmic view of interlocking worlds, ancestors, the living, and the unborn "will find a triumphant correlation in the universe of astrophysics."

Closer to home, here is an intriguing example from the contemporary United States about how we can create traditions to suit our needs. With tongue in cheek, and with its Oxbridge nose in the air, *The Economist* of December 17, 1994, did a story examining the year's-end holidays in the United States that stretched from "Thanksgiving through Hanukkah and Christmas, all the way to Kwanza." It explained to its British readers that Kwanza was a "festival of African American heritage, celebrated for seven days starting the day after Christmas," and that it now received "equal holiday-season treatment in many schools and museums. Not bad for an upstart." After all, *The Economist* said, Hanukkah was 2,159 years old, and Christmas 1,194 (or thereabouts), whereas Kwanza was "a mere babe of 28." What intrigued *The Economist* was that Mr. Karenga had "concocted his festival by borrowing from a number of cultural sources. . . . His idea was to create a ritual for America's blacks to express pride in their African roots." The magazine noted, inter alia, that Kwanza cannot be found anywhere in Africa. It is entirely African-American. Being not a religious festival, Kwanza could "happily co-exist with Christmas" and it took on local colorations in different places in the United States.

The article noted that many blacks and whites objected to what they termed "myth-making" that harked back to an "idealized African past" and that Kwanza ignored part of the black American tradition. Nevertheless, the festival was now celebrated by about five million African Americans, and had spawned holiday expositions at which big American companies such as Pepsi Cola, AT&T, Revlon, and Hallmark exhibited their wares. The magazine quipped that those persons who did not believe that the tradition would last some 2,000 years were accused of having little faith or "imani." Unfortunately, the article was published too early to report that President Clinton understood the meaning of this festival and wished African Americans "Happy Kwanza" when he offered year-end greetings to all Americans.

What the events surrounding Kwanza demonstrate is that it was not only possible for African Americans to invent a festival that was meaningful to them, but that they were able to have it accepted by all Americans. This was probably what Du Bois had in mind when he declared at the turn of the century:

> If the Negro is ever to be a factor in the world's history—if among the gaily colored banners that deck the broad ramparts of civilization is to hand one uncompromisingly black, then it must be placed there by black hands, fashioned by black heads and hallowed by the travail of 200,000,000 black hearts beating in one glad song of jubilee.[22]

These were certainly the sentiments of Leopold Sedar Senghor, poet president of Senegal, when he echoed Du Bois by asserting that African peoples intend to bring their own brick to the construction of a universal civilization. Let us get on with the job.

NOTES

1. Countee Cullen, *On These I Stand: An Anthology of Selected Poems.*

2. It is also instructive to bear in mind that writing from their power-

ful political position in the world, the Europeans were not necessarily "Eurocentric." They naturally saw and interpreted the world from a cultural, intellectual, and psychological perspective that was congruent with their growing economic-military-political power. Edward Said (1978), in his *Orientalism*, protested against the European creation of the Orient. Unfortunately, he tells us more about how the Europeans invented the Orient than how people from that part of the world viewed themselves and their countries. Moreover, Said is not known for any important work on the culture of the "Orientals."

3. This notion dies hard. It was held by many European colonials in Africa, from Rhodes to Ian Smith. Richard Nixon is said to have shared this notion.

4. "Copy of a letter from Benjamin Banneker to the Secretary of State" (Philadelphia, 1792), Aptheker, *Documentary History*, 24.

5. Ibid., 23. In a letter accompanying his work, Banneker regretted that so distinguished a man as Jefferson had in *Notes on the State of Virginia* contributed to "the almost general prejudice and prepossession, which is so prevalent in the world against those of my complexion."

6. Ibid., 23. Banneker conceded that "we are a race of beings, who have long labored under the abuse and censure of the world; that we have long been looked upon with an eye of contempt. . . ."

7. Ibid., pp. 24–25.

8. "Two Negro Leaders Reply to Slanders—And Denounce Slaveholding," 1794, cited in Aptheker, *Documentary History*, 32–38.

9. Ibid. When faced with the same suggestion, many African Americans resisted the notion that "the superior white man must bear the burden of civilizing colonial peoples of the world, if necessary against the will of those peoples" (Drake and Cayton, 1962:47, 756). The issue then had two contradictory implications: On the one hand whites firmly believed that "it would be a matter of a thousand years before Africans could develop high forms of civilization or become dangerous to the white race." On the other hand, whites insisted that "The very existence of social order [in America] is believed to depend upon 'keeping the Negro in his place.'"

10. Henry Highland Garnet, *The Past and Present Condition and the Destiny of the Colored Race: A Discourse at the 50th Anniversary of the Female Benevolent Society of Troy, New York*, 6–12.

11. Ibid.

12. Franz Boas "supplied intellectual reinforcement at a critical point." Invited by Dr. W. E. B. Du Bois to give a Commencement Address at Atlanta University on May 31, 1906, Boas, who was interested in the physical differences between Negroids and Caucasoids, miscegenation, racism, and ethnic chauvinism in the United States, took as his subject "The Outlook for the American Negro." He sought to convince the young graduates that the lowly status of blacks in America was not immutable. Reporting upon the accomplishments of Africans, Boas complained that "we have no place in this country where the beauty and daintiness of African work can be shown; but a walk through the African museums of Paris, London, and Berlin is a revelation" (Stocking:313).

13. W. E. B. Du Bois, *The Conservation of Races.*

14. Booker T. Washington, *The Story of the Negro: The Rise of the Race from Slavery,* 1, 33–34.

15. Marcus Garvey, "The Negro's Greatest Enemy," *Current History,* 18, No. 6 (September 1923), 951–57. Garvey, who had been attracted by the pioneering work of Booker T. Washington, was disappointed that the principal of Tuskegee had died, and wished to replace him. He declared that now that Washington had raised the "dignity and manhood of his race to midway," it was the duty of those who shared his ideals and felt his influence "to lead the race on to the highest height in the adopted civilization of the age." Marcus Garvey, 1983: 1, 166.

16. Marcus Garvey, 1983: 1, 166.

17. Fanon, *Toward the African Revolution,* pp. 40ff; Fanon, *The Wretched of the Earth,* pp. 212ff.

18. Fanon, *Toward the African Revolution,* p. 84ff.

19. The events surrounding the publication of Amos Tutuola's *Palm Wine Drinkard* (1953) is a case in point. See Chinweizu, O. Jemie and I. Madubuike, *Toward the Decolonization of African Literature.*

20. Later paradigms such as diffusionism, structural-functionalism, marxism, structuralism, structural-marxism, hermeneutics, and the like that were largely created by European scholars to analyze and understand African cultural data have also been used when judged useful or rejected when deemed detrimental.

21. The iconoclastic and Afrocentric Cheikh Anta Diop was quite prepared to challenge existing paradigms that hesitated to take Africa and Africans seriously. Basil Davidson recognized the source of the problem when he admitted that "with one or two exceptions," source books for the study of Africa still conceived that "subject as no more than an extension to the study of Europe or the New World" (1991:4). These books were "strictly European in standpoint, and their value lies less in any light they may throw on African life than in the movement they reveal of European penetration and conquest" (Ibid). For his part, Davidson did attempt to deal with Africa in terms of itself and not with respect to other regions (cf. Bernal, 1987). Cf. Diop, *Civilization and Barbarism.*

22. Du Bois, *Conservation of Races.*

REFERENCES

Aptheker, Herbert. 1951. *A Documentary History of the Negro People in the United States.* New York: Citadel Press.

Asante, Molefi. 1987. *The Afrocentric Idea.* Philadelphia: Temple University Press.

Bernal, Martin. 1987 and 1991. *Black Athena: The Afro-Asiatic Roots of Classical Civilization.* Vols. I and II. New Brunswick: Rutgers University Press.

Bosman, William. 1967 [1705]. *A New and Accurate Description of the Coast of Guinea.* New York: Barnes and Noble.

Chinweizu, O. Jemie, and I. Madubuike. 1980. *Toward the Decolonization of African Literature.* Enugu: Fourth Dimension.

Cullen, Countee. 1947. *On These I Stand: An Anthology of Selected Poems.* New York: Harper and Brothers.

Curtin, Philip D. 1964. *The Image of Africa: British Ideas and Action, 1780–1850.* Madison: University of Wisconsin Press.

———. 1967. *Africa Remembered: Narratives by West Africans from the Era of the Slave Trade.* Madison: University of Wisconsin Press.

Davidson, Basil. 1991. *African Civilization Revisited: From Antiquity to Modern Times.* Trenton, NJ: African World Press.

Diop, Cheikh Anta. 1991. *Civilization and Barbarism.* New York: Lawrence Hill.

Diop, David. "Africa." 1966. *Modern Poetry from Africa.* Gerald Moore and Ulli Beier, eds. Baltimore: Penguin.

Drake, St. Clair, and Horace Cayton. 1962. *Black Metropolis: A Study of Negro Life in a Northern City.* New York: Harper and Row.

Drimmer, Melvin. 1968. *Black History: A Reappraisal.* Garden City, NY: Doubleday.

Du Bois, W. E. B. 1897. *The Conservation of Races.* Washington, DC: American Negro Academy, Occasional Papers, II.

———. 1961 [1903]. *The Souls of Black Folk: Essays and Sketches.* Greenwich, Conn.: Fawcett.

———. 1969 [1915]. *The Negro.* New York: H. Holt.

Fanon, Frantz. 1963. *The Wretched of the Earth.* Trans. Constance Farrington. New York: Grove Press.

———. 1967. *Toward the African Revolution: Political Essays.* Trans. Haakon Chevalier. New York: Monthly Review Press.

Garnet, Henry Highland. 1848. *The Past and Present Condition and the Destiny of the Colored Race: A Discourse at the 50th Anniversary of the Female Benevolent Society of Troy, New York.* Troy, NY: J. C. Kneeland.

Garvey, Marcus. 1923. "The Negro's Greatest Enemy." *Current History* 18, Number 6:951–57.

———. 1983. "UNIA Memorial Meeting for Booker T. Washington." In Robert A. Hill, ed. *The Marcus Garvey and the Universal Negro Improvement Association Papers.* Berkeley: University of California Press.

Hayford, J. E. Casely. 1903. *Gold Coast Native Institutions.* London: Sweet and Maxwell.

———. 1911. *Ethiopia Unbound.* London: C. M. Phillips.

Lewis, Bernard. 1993. *Islam and the West.* New York: Oxford University Press.

Mouralis, Bernard. 1992. "*Presence Africaice*: Geography of an Ideology." *The Surreptitious Speech*, ed. V. Y. Mudimbe. Chicago: University of Chicago Press. 3–13.

Park, Mungo. 1813. *Travels in the Interior Districts of Africa.* New York: Evert Duyckinck.

Price-Mars, Jean. 1928. *Ainsi parle l'oncle: essais d'ethnographie*. Port-au-Prince: Compiegne.

Said, Edward. 1978. *Orientalism*. New York: Pantheon Books.

Senghor, Leopold Sedar. 1961. "Negritude." *West Africa*, November 4.

Skinner, Elliott P. 1992. *African Americans and U.S. Policy toward Africa*. Washington, DC: Howard University Press.

Soyinka, Wole. 1995. "Yoruba Astrophysics." *The Washington Post*, April 9.

Stocking, George W. 1974. *The Shaping of American Anthropology: A Franz Boas Reader*. New York: Basic Books.

Tutuola, Amos. 1953. *The Palm Wine Drinkard*. New York: Grove Press.

Washington, Booker T. 1969 [1900]. *The Story of the Negro: The Rise of the Race from Slavery*. New York: Negro Universities Press.

Williams, Eric. 1970. *From Columbus to Castro: The History of the Caribbean*. London: Andre Deutsch.

ADDRESSING THE CONSTRAINTS

4

SLAVES OR SERFS? A COMPARATIVE STUDY OF SLAVERY AND SERFDOM IN EUROPE AND AFRICA

Joseph E. Inikori

After decades of neglect, slavery in Africa took the center stage in African historiography in the 1970s and 1980s. Suddenly there was a lot of excitement about the subject among European and North American historians and anthropologists, although, somewhat curiously, the then vibrant schools of history on the African continent, in particular the Ibadan school in Nigeria, showed little interest. The excitement sustained for about two decades an impressive amount of empirical research into African socioeconomic institutions which the researchers labelled "slavery." Historians studying slavery in other continents—especially in the New World where the slave population comprised people of African descent— were surprised to be told that "there were certainly more slaves in Africa in the nineteenth century than there were in the Americas at any time," and that

> The scholarship of the last twenty years [1970s and 1980s] has demonstrated that the variety and intensity of servile relationships and methods of oppression that can be equated with slavery were probably more developed in Africa than anywhere else in the world at any period in history.[1]

Some part of the research also reports that in 1897 the slave population of northern Nigeria alone was "certainly in excess of 1 million and perhaps more than 2.5 million people," and that "Northern Nigeria's slave system [was] one of the largest slave societies in modern history."[2]

But can we be certain that the institution studied by the Africanists approximates that studied by historians of classical history, European history, Asian history, and New World history? As Claude Meillassoux has stressed, "Slavery, rigorously defined, may have universal characteristics, but its definition . . . must be generally accepted if a real discussion is to take place."[3] Certainly, the use of terms such as slave and slavery invites

49

comparison. And students of slavery in Africa have not been insensitive to the need to compare. They have, in general, compared the slaves they discovered in Africa with those of the Americas. While conceding that there were some differences, it is argued that enough similarities existed for the people they identify as slaves in Africa to approximate the universal social category of slave and slavery.[4] It is even argued that there were extensive slave plantations in many African regions approximately comparable to New World slave plantations.[5]

A few scholars have mildly expressed their discomfort with this analytical thrust, which certainly characterizes the mainstream literature on the subject. Some have argued that the late-nineteenth-century servile institutions in Africa were not equivalent to slavery, but, not finding what they consider an appropriate alternative term, they have reluctantly used both terms, with quotation marks.[6] Others have employed terms such as "captives" or "serfs" without offering a convincing explanation for their use. This occasioned Frederick Cooper's criticism that these scholars are shying away from the ugly implications which the word "slave" usually carries. As he put it, "the word 'slave' carries with it a bundle of connotations—all of them nasty. This has led some Africanists to use terms like 'adopted dependents,' 'captives,' or 'serfs' for a person whom others would call a slave." In a footnote to this statement, Cooper adds:

> The first euphemizes a process that was based on violence and coercion; the second distracts from the various possible fates that befell people and their descendants once the act of capture was completed; and the third misrepresents the nature of dependence and the slave's relationship to the land.[7]

This intervention by Cooper seems to have silenced the few dissenters. Apart from one or two lonely voices, it has been business as usual in the study of slavery in Africa since the 1980s. Meillassoux has stated that the inclusion of non-slaves is responsible for the claim that slavery in Africa was mild or benign,[8] but apart from his very helpful effort to provide a universal definition, he has not shown which social categories to include or eliminate. Similarly, elsewhere I have complained of terminological looseness in the study of slavery in Africa,[9] but failed to show systematically how to bring precision and discipline to the enterprise. The outline for that exercise is attempted here. For that purpose, I propose to conduct a comparative examination of servile social categories in medieval Europe and precolonial Africa. I argue that slavery and serfdom under the socioeconomic conditions of medieval Europe provide better comparative insights for a precise and disciplined study of servile institutions in precolonial Africa than the New World comparisons that have hitherto been conducted. This is so because the societies of medieval Europe were closer in all respects to those of precolonial Africa than were the New World slave societies that were specifically organized for the large-scale production of commodities for an evolving capitalist world market. What is more, at some point slavery coexisted with other dependent social categories in precapitalist Europe. This coexistence of slavery and non-slave servile categories has been carefully studied by students of European history. I propose to show how students of European history distinguish between slave and non-slave dependent social categories in precapitalist Europe. Their method of separation and classification is then applied to the descriptive evidence on precolonial African servile categories in order to determine which of them approximated slavery or serfdom or some other category. To make the exercise manageable, I have chosen two extreme geographical points in Europe: England, to the west, and Russia, to the east.

I

Slavery was first brought to England by the Romans. But the departure of the Romans and their legions in AD 407 did not end slavery in England. The chaos which followed the collapse of the Roman empire provoked slave raids and encouraged slave use in England and other parts of Europe. Continental Europeans from the Danish peninsula and the coastlands of northern Germany and Holland, called Anglo-Saxons, raided England for slaves and eventually took over the country.[10] Many of the indigenous people, the Celts, were enslaved. After their settlement, the Anglo-Saxon kingdoms continued to fight among themselves and take captives. In consequence, slaves made up a large proportion of the population of Anglo-Saxon England.[11]

Slave raids and slave trading by various groups in the British Isles continued into the eleventh century, with Bristol as the main exporting port and Ireland a major export market. The Anglo-Saxon bishop of Worcester, who fought hard against the slave trade from England, lamented: "You might well groan to see the long rows of young men and maidens whose beauty and youth might move the pity of the savage, bound together with cords, and brought to market to be sold."[12] In the end, the conquest of the warring groups in Britain and Ireland by the Normans stopped the slave raids and the trade in captives. The Westminster Council of 1102 proclaimed "That no one is henceforth to presume to carry on that shameful trading whereby heretofore men used in England to be sold like brute beasts."[13]

But the Normans did not enact a law abolishing slavery in England. They had met an England in which slaves were a statistically important part of the population. Based on the Domesday enumeration of 1086, it has

been estimated that all categories of free peasants taken together constituted only 14 percent of the total population of rural England in 1086.
Various categories of unfree peasants made up the remaining 86 percent,
of whom slaves were 10.5 percent of the whole rural population and different groups of serfs accounted for 75.5 percent.[14] Thus, over a period of
time whose actual length is uncertain, slavery coexisted with other servile
institutions in England. The disappearance of the slaves was a long drawn-
out process, in which the slaves were gradually converted to other dependent social categories.

   This long process of conversion has been examined in some detail by
Postan.[15] It started in the Dark Ages when Anglo-Saxon slaveholders, like
their counterparts in the Frankish kingdoms, began to move their slaves,
whether manumitted or not, into separate landholdings of their own. The
new arrangement allowed them much freedom to cater to themselves and
maintain households of their own, while continuing to render labor services to the lords in the cultivation of their estates. These new landholding
dependent cultivators were distinguishable from their pre-existing counterparts mainly in terms of the greater labor services which they owed to
the lords. At the same time, however, the lords continued to hold other
slaves directly in their estates. These were housed, fed, and clothed by the
lords, and they spent most of their time working the latter's estates. As a
recognition of the significant difference between these groups of dependent cultivators, contemporary practice and modern medievalists limited
the application of the term "slave" to those directly resident on the lords'
estates and largely maintained by them. The slaves enumerated in the
Domesday Inquest of 1086 belonged to this category.[16]

   The process of converting slaves to landholding dependent cultivators
in England was completed in the twelfth century. But, by this time, the
most recently converted groups were still somewhere between slaves and
fully settled landholding dependent peasants. Their holdings were small,
and these had been carved out recently from the lords' estates and, therefore, were located close to them.[17] They still spent the greater part of their
time cultivating the lords' estates, from which they earned much of their
livelihood in food and money. And, like the fully settled dependent peasants, by law they were not free to move.[18] Postan calls them serf smallholders settled on servants' holdings. The medieval sources refer to them
as *bovarii* or *famuli*. What happened in England in the twelfth century,
according to Postan, was a wholesale conversion of the remnants of the
slave class to *bovarii*. As he put it,

> a *bovarius* was a serf who possessed few rights or franchises de-
> nied to the late-Roman or German slaves, and whose greater inde-
> pendence resulted not so much from his superior status as from his
> separate holding and his life away from the lord's *curia* [estate]. It

is in this physical separation that the key to the change must be sought. The smallholder was able to set up a family and have some inducement to exploit to the full the land of his holding.[19]

Postan insists that the smallholders settled on servants' holdings, the *bovarii*, were not slaves:

> Twelfth-century *bovarii* were not slaves; and neither were the bulk of their Domesday namesakes. Twelfth-century *bovarii* were serfs, and the difference of status between slave and serf may have been very slight. Yet it is impossible wholly to identify medieval serfs with slaves without repudiating the accepted view of medieval serfdom as a condition intermediate (though of course far from equidistant) between those of slavery and freedom. Now and again the Domesday scribes, more especially those responsible for recording the Herefordshire entries, go out of their way to underline the difference between the *bovarius* and the slave.[20]

Thus, by contemporary practice and by the method of separation and classification adopted by medieval historians, there were several categories of serfs in England in the twelfth century. The common denominator for all of them was the possession of some land which they cultivated for themselves. Linking them also was the labor service they owed to their lords and their lack of freedom to move under the law. They were, on the other hand, separated by the amount of labor dues they had to render to the lords, and the amount of land they held and the amount of time available to them to cultivate it. Serfs without slave origin, by local custom and tradition, had larger holdings and more time to cultivate them. For serfs of slave origin, the labor dues, the size of holdings, and the amount of time available to work them all tended to depend on the distance in time from the slave ancestors. On these differences, we quote Postan again at length:

> The services of a smallholder regularly employed as a *famulus* were, relative to his holding and rent, incomparably greater than the labour dues of an ordinary villein. . . . The latter, unlike the true manorial servant, was left enough time to work his own holding, and had enough substance to employ a servant himself if he needed one. There was no question of maintaining him and his family by the lord's plough-team, food and money. In economic fact he was still a customary tenant, discharging his labour obligations, while the full-time *famulus* . . . was a labourer working another man's land and deriving his livelihood wholly or in the main from his employer's wages.[21]

In order to place Postan's examination of England's case in the general context of medieval Europe, it is enough to refer to the summary statement by R.H. Hilton. According to Hilton, the words "serf" and "slave" generally employed by modern historians of medieval Europe come from two words, both of which meant "slave" at different times. *Serf* comes from the Latin *servus*, which in classical times meant "slave," while in the early Middle Ages *slave* was derived from the ethnic term *Slav*. By the latter time the descendants of the slaves of the classical period, and most of the slaves of the late Dark Ages, had been settled on separate holdings of their own and were now *servi casati*. Many of the slaves still resident on their lords' estates were Slavonic captives acquired by the Germans in their eastward expansion and sold in the slave markets of Western Europe. Medieval historians, therefore, use both words to distinguish between the conditions of the two broad categories of dependent cultivators. As Hilton puts it,

> Although some slaves in antiquity were by no means completely without property the distinction between slaves and serfs is based on the fact that, on the whole, slaves were the chattels of their master, employed as instruments of production in agriculture or industry, receiving food, clothing and shelter from the master and possessing nothing. . . . Some peasants were descended from the *coloni* of the late Empire, who . . . sank into serfdom under the heavy weight of the obligations imposed on them by the estate owners and the state. . . . Other peasants were descendants of full slaves, some of their ancestors having been slaves under the Roman Empire, others having been enslaved during the wars of the Dark Ages. What distinguished these serfs from their slave ancestors was, of course, the fact that they were now *servi casati*, provided with their own holdings from the landowner's estate. Other medieval peasant serfs were descended from free men who had entered into various forms of dependence under lords.[22]

Like England and the rest of Western Europe, slavery antedated serfdom in Russia. But while in England slavery died naturally in the twelfth century and serfdom in the fifteenth, in Russia slavery remained alive up to the early eighteenth century and serfdom began its development only in the mid-fifteenth, to be abolished by state law not until the second half of the nineteenth century. The enserfment of the Russian peasants was associated with the construction and expansion of the Russian state. Muscovy had been one of several Russian principalities until the fifteenth century. But in about a hundred years from 1462, a Russian empire ruled by the Muscovite state was established. The creation of the Russian empire was accompanied by the rise of a powerful nobility. The size of this aristocracy and its capacity to dominate the peasantry grew *pari passu* with the geographical expansion of the empire and the power of the Russian tsar. As all this happened, the previously free Russian peasants increas-

ingly lost their freedom. The development followed an observable historical sequence. In the first instance the peasants' general freedom was gradually curtailed in the second half of the fifteenth and the greater part of
the sixteenth century. This was followed by a total prohibition of their
right to move in the late sixteenth and early seventeenth centuries. And
between the seventeenth century and the first half of the eighteenth, the
changes were formally codified. Thereafter the conditions of the Russian serfs moved closer and closer to those of chattel slaves as the powerful
nobles acted in total disregard of the law and tradition.[23]

Meanwhile the Russian slaves (*kholopy* in Russian) were being transformed into serfs. From the mid-fifteenth to the early eighteenth century the enserfed peasants coexisted with their older servile "cousins," the
slaves. In the course of the seventeenth century, however, slaves and serfs
gradually merged. The remnants of the slave class were moved into the
rank of serfs by the tsar Peter I in 1723.[24] Now, how do students of Russian
history distinguish the slaves from the serfs in the period during which
they coexisted? On this, a recent writer states that

> The main distinction between kholopy [slaves] and serfs was that
> whereas the latter were usually self-supporting, growing their own
> food on allotted plots of land, the former were usually maintained
> by their owners; instead of living in a village with the peasants,
> they lived in or near their owners' residences.[25]

However, as was mentioned earlier, the conditions of the Russian
serfs deteriorated considerably over time. The practice of selling and buying serfs by noblemen, which began in the second half of the seventeenth
century, became generalized by the eighteenth. It has been said that in the
course of the eighteenth century, serfs were "bought and sold, traded, won
and lost at cards."[26] But legally they remained serfs, and the Russian government made it clear that what was abolished by state law in the 1860s
was serfdom, not slavery. In 1858, on the eve of emancipation, there were
a total of 11.3 million male serfs (11,338,042). In 1795, the figure had been
9.8 million (9,787,802).[27] Assuming an equal proportion of female serfs,
the totals come to 19.6 million in 1795 and 22.7 million in 1858. The
literature has regularly referred to all of them as serfs.[28]

II

The foregoing evidence on England and Russia (and generally on
Europe) makes it clear that the formula employed by students of European
history to distinguish serfs and other dependent social categories from
slaves incorporates unambiguous elements: First and foremost, the serfs
or non-slave dependent people must possess the means of production of

their own (mainly land) large enough to provide a potential income that could support a household with unproductive children and old members; second, they must have enough free time to produce for themselves in order to realize the potential income from the employment of their means of production; third, they must be allowed to retain for their own use as they please the income realized; and fourth, their residences must be physically separated from those of their lords. On the other hand, for a dependent people to be slaves, they must spend virtually their entire working day on their lords' estates—they may be allotted some plots, but both the size and the time available to work them would be so limited that they would have to be fed, clothed, and housed by their lords; and their owners must be free, under the law and by tradition, to sell them to any buyer. I now proceed to apply to the evidence on the dependent social categories of precolonial Africa the formula applied to those of precapitalist Europe by modern historians.

Incidentally, the pioneers of modern African historiography conducted a somewhat similar exercise more than three decades ago when they debated the issue of whether the concept of feudalism could be applied to any of the political systems in precolonial Africa. Some aspects of that debate are relevant for the present purpose. It is, therefore, appropriate to start with that debate.

Following efforts being made in the 1940s and 1950s to constitute a typology of political organizations in precolonial Africa, Jacques Maquet suggested in 1962 that "The feudal system deserves to be considered as an important type of political organization in traditional Africa."[29] The defining features of feudal regimes that should be considered in applying the feudal concept to Africa were outlined. It was made clear that the concept was originally employed by historians of Europe to describe the main features of the dominant political regimes which existed in Europe between the ninth and thirteenth centuries. The defining features were, therefore, stated in accordance with the conceptions of feudalism employed by two broad groups of students of medieval European history—Marxists and non-Marxists. For non-Marxists, the essential element of feudal regimes is vassalage bond; for Marxists, the distinguishing element is the relation of surplus extraction defined by a particular form of land ownership.[30]

Jack Goody criticized these attempts to apply the concept of feudalism to precolonial African regimes. He began with the problem of transferring to African history a term for which there are conflicting conceptions. A case in point was an Anglo-Soviet discussion on feudalism, in which the English speaker dwelled on military fiefs, while the Russian participant concentrated on class relations of surplus extraction between lords and peasants. Goody concluded that "In general, however, the core institution of feudal society is seen as vassalage associated with the granting of a landed benefit (fief), usually in return for the performance of military duties."[31] Specific cases of the application of the concept to African societies were then examined. Goody's summary of Potekhin's description of Asante is of particular interest and deserves to be reproduced:

> Potekhin writes that "Feudal land ownership constitutes the foundation of feudal relations." Land belongs to a restricted circle of big landowners, while the peasant pays rent or performs services for the right to cultivate his land. In Ashanti, he finds "the exclusive concentration of land in the hands of the ruling upper strata," together with the conditional land tenure and hierarchies of dependence "typical of feudal society."[32]

Goody did not question the factual accuracy of the description, but thought that defining feudalism in terms of the ownership of land was not appropriate.

Of all the cases cited and summarized by Goody, only that of Basil Davidson specifically touched upon the question of slavery in Africa. Davidson's main point was that African feudalism shared many common features with feudalism in medieval Europe. Thus he pointed out that during the formative period of feudalism in the European Dark Ages slaves were gradually transformed into serfs, while in Africa strong states and empires destroyed tribal equality and produced a mass of dependent people who were serfs and not slaves. Comparing Asante with England at the time of the Norman conquest, Davidson showed further similarities:

> Thus the titles and the rights of great lords, the obligations of the common people, the customs of trade and tribute, the swearing of fealty, the manners of war—all these and a hundred other manifestations have seemed to speak the same identical language of feudalism.[33]

Davidson seems to imply that slavery is incompatible with feudalism. For our present purpose, however, that issue is not important. Suffice it to say that we do not have to prove the existence of feudalism in order to establish the existence of serfs. Feudalism is a form of sociopolitical organization with several elements. At a given moment and place some elements may be present without others. Had Davidson been primarily concerned with the issue of slavery or serfdom in Africa, the right question to ask would have been whether the conditions of the people being considered more closely approximated those of serfs or those of slaves in medieval Europe.

However, these were not the issues queried by Goody, whose main discomfort was with Davidson's tailoring of African history too tightly to European history. At that stage of African historiography, Goody thought that African institutions should be studied in depth in their own right, without European labels. While encouraging comparative studies, he admonished African historians to stay clear of terms such as "tribalism," "feudalism," and "capitalism," which invite crude comparison.[34]

Beattie concurred. In his study of Bunyoro in modern Uganda, he found that the political regime there contained three of the five features listed by Marc Bloch as defining feudalism in Europe. The missing elements were a special military class and evidence of the disintegration of a preexisting strong state. On the basis of this, Beattie concluded:

> Like Goody, I consider it to be more useful and illuminating to retain the term "feudalism" and its associated vocabulary for the complex European polities to which they were first applied (and perhaps to such other systems, like the Japanese one, which can be shown to resemble it in all or most of its essential features), and to describe the political Institutions of traditional Bunyoro and of other African kingdoms as far as possible in their own terms.[35]

It is a pity that the debate did not proceed further to examine in depth the issue of slavery and serfdom raised by Basil Davidson. Apparently it was concluded that these are terms to be avoided in the writing of African history. But that may not be altogether correct. As will be shown shortly, slaves and serfs, properly defined, can be encountered in African societies at some point in time and in specific regions. The problem is how to distinguish them from each other, and from other dependent social categories, and trace their historical development.

Let us now attempt to resolve this conundrum by applying the formula employed by historians of precapitalist Europe, as outlined above. The main difficulty is the scantiness of descriptive evidence on the dependent social categories in question. However, the research of more than three decades has produced enough evidence to make the exercise feasible. Particularly important, this research has been most intensive in the geographical areas where dependent populations in precolonial Africa were mostly concentrated: the Western Sudan; the Sokoto Caliphate in the Central Sudan; and the East African Coast. These constitute the main focus of the exercise. Scattered evidence from other areas will be examined to provide the basis for a continental generalization.

The dependent populations of the nineteenth-century Sokoto Caliphate of modern northern Nigeria were among the first groups of such populations in tropical Africa to be scientifically studied by modern scholars. As early as the late 1940s, Michael Smith and his wife, Mary Smith, conducted elaborate data collection on the socioeconomic conditions of the servile populations among the Hausa-Fulani in the northern parts of the Zaria emirate in the Sokoto Caliphate.[36]

Smith's descriptive evidence shows a hierarchical sociopolitical organization of the Zaria emirate. The population was distributed into two spatial locations—walled towns, which included the capital city of Zaria, and agricultural villages where the peasants lived, groups of which were located near each walled town. Administratively, the ruler of the emirate was the Emir of Zaria, referred to as "king" by Smith. Being part of the Sokoto Caliphate, he was answerable to the overall ruler of the Caliphate, whose seat was in Sokoto city. Assisting the emir in the administration of the emirate were fief-holding officials, all of whom resided in the capital city of Zaria. The walled towns and agricultural villages were held as personal fiefs by the fief-holding officials. Each fief-holder administered his fiefs through his own appointed subordinate staff (*jekadu*). At the lowest level of authority, the agricultural communities were run by village chiefs. Several of these agricultural villages were made up of servile cultivators. Such villages were known locally as *rinji* (pl. *rumada*). Smith described them as slave-villages. They belonged mostly to the emir and his fief-holding officials residing in the capital city, although some also belonged to merchants and other non–office holders. These, like the other villages, had their own village chiefs.

The servile cultivators in the *rumada* lived in separate households, and possessed lands of their own allotted to them by their lords. These lands were separate from the lords' fields and the harvests were retained by the servile peasants for the support of their households. The dependent cultivators worked with their families on their own farms from the early hours of the morning to 9:30 A.M., at which time they went to their lords' fields. There they worked until midday, when food was sent to them on the fields by their lords. By 2:30 P.M. work on the lords' fields was over and they were free to return to their own farms. Apart from the meal provided on the field, the servile cultivators were responsible for the maintenance of their households.

According to Smith, the dependent populations of Zaria were of two categories, the native-born (*dimajo*, pl. *dimajai*) and those brought from outside by capture or by purchase. Those brought from outside could be sold, but the native-born could not be alienated. The latter provided the core of the emirate's military personnel: they "formed the main body of the military force, of the police, and of the administrative staff at a subordinate level."[37]

Polly Hill's study of Kano emirate, one of the largest emirates in the Sokoto Caliphate (covering an area of over 16,000 sq. miles), adds further descriptive evidence. Of particular interest is the servile village belonging to the Emir of Kano. A member of the village and of servile descent, who was born in about 1885, narrated in 1972 how the village functioned in the precolonial days. Polly Hill's summary of the account is here reproduced:

He said that in the early days there had been "about fifty" men and
women slaves working on the land; that many were strangers who
spoke poor Hausa; that they lived in separate houses they had built
themselves, since there was no house corresponding to a *rinji*; that
each slave was given a farm plot (*gayauna*) for his own use, a plot
that could be inherited by a son (though not by a daughter) or lent
to someone else (*aro*) but could not be sold. He said that the usual
crops (grains, cassava, groundnuts, etc.) were grown on the main
estate (*gandu*); that some slaves became rich enough to ransom
themselves; that the slave households cooked or bought most of
their own food, though during the farming season cooked meals
were provided in the evening as well as on the farmland at midday;
that the slaves were paid for any work (such as thatching) done for
the Emir in the dry season; that some free men worked alongside
the slaves. . .[38]

In general, Hill's description of the conditions of the servile populations in Hausaland complements Smith's evidence, although she is critical
of some of the points. For example, she points out that the restriction on
the sale of bonded people was not based on generational differences; rather,
Hausa tradition and public opinion imposed severe limitations on the
rights of masters to sell servile individuals living in a household. She states
further that most bonded people in Hausaland lived in households "with
their spouses and children, richer male slaves being polygynous."[39]

Another elaborate study of bonded populations in the Sokoto Caliphate is the one on the Bida emirate by Michael Mason. Mason narrates how
the Bida state, a unit of the Sokoto Caliphate, was established by a Fulani
aristocratic family and expanded from 1857 to 1901. The expansion led to
the subjugation of the indigenous populations that were forcefully incorporated into the expanding state. These indigenous populations were Nupe
who had lived all along in the geographical area that became the Bida emirate, with Bida City as the capital. Bida's military incursions into neighboring territories also brought captives from other ethnic groups, such as the
Yoruba, Afenmai, Igbirra, and even the Hausa and Fulani. Both the subjugated Nupe populations and the captives brought from outside were settled
in agricultural villages around Bida, the capital of the emirate. These captive villages or settlements were known locally as *tungazi* (sing. *tunga*).
By 1859 there were 55 of them; between 1859 and 1873, 694 new captive
settlements were created; and by 1901, there were a total of 1,601 captive
villages in the Bida emirate. The bulk of these, about two-thirds, were settlements composed of subjugated indigenous Nupe populations.[40] Mason
believes that the total population of these villages must have been around
100,000 by 1901.[41]

The dwellers in these captive villages did not work collectively on
their lords' fields; they did not render any labor services to their lords.

Rather, they produced entirely for themselves and paid tributes to their lords in cash (cowries) and in kind (farm products).[42] Mason calls them slaves, and the settlements, slave plantations. However, he says,

> In Nupe, although slaves did not live together with the lineages of their owners, we do not see that the social relations between slaves and their masters were fundamentally different from the relations between the lords or *egbazi* (sing. *egba*) and the peasants who paid them tribute. Slaves and peasants both paid tribute. Otherwise, the slaves kept their own products.

Mason adds that there was only one social relation of production in nineteenth-century Nupe, "and that is the one which we have called 'tributary.' This mode colored all relations between masters and slaves and between lords and peasants."[43]

Now, based on the descriptive evidence presented, how do we categorize the servile populations of the Sokoto Caliphate in the nineteenth century, using the formula employed by students of European history? We need to stress at this point that the studies presented do not cover all the emirates of the Caliphate. The extent to which the emirates studied are representative of the whole Caliphate is not easy to say. However, it can be said that the emirates included adequately represent the ethnic composition of the Caliphate: Kano Emirate (predominantly Hausa); northern Zaria (servile settlements studied were held mostly by the Fulani); and Bida Emirate (predominantly non–Hausa-Fulani). Whether the geographical location and the ethnic composition of the emirates affected the conditions of the servile populations is unclear. What is clear is that they were all involved primarily in agricultural production. It should also be pointed out that in all the emirates of the Caliphate, members of the Fulani aristocracy were large holders of servile populations.

Having said this, I think it is possible to agree that in parts of the Caliphate some captives newly acquired by purchase or through capture, and some of those who lived within the residences of their masters lived and worked under conditions that approximated to those of slavery. These would be the ones Jan Hogendorn refers to as "unmarried slaves," who were fed by their masters throughout the year.[44] Certainly, unmarried members of servile households worked and ate with their parents. Based on the evidence presented, it is clear that this category of dependent cultivators did not constitute a large proportion of the total servile population in the Sokoto Caliphate in the late nineteenth century. The vast majority were householders settled on holdings of their own and were, therefore, *servi casati*. They possessed enough land, and had enough time and motivation, to produce for themselves and maintain a household.[45] Both in status and in economic independence, most of them were superior to the *bovarii* of twelfth-century England. Many were in the category of the villein of medieval Europe. Certainly, as the evidence of Mason shows, the dwellers of the captive villages in Bida had greater economic independence than even the villeins of medieval Europe. What is more, the dwellers of the servile villages in the Sokoto Caliphate were superior in economic independence and social status to the nineteenth-century Russian serfs. Applying to the evidence from the Sokoto Caliphate the formula employed by European historians to distinguish between slaves and serfs in precapitalist Europe leads, therefore, to the conclusion that the bulk of the servile populations in the Caliphate hitherto referred to as slaves by scholars were in fact *servi casati*, that is, serfs. To call the servile villages in Bida and other parts of the Caliphate slave plantations, we have to accept that the medieval manor in England and the serf villages in nineteenth-century Russia were all slave plantations.

In fact, several of the authorities cited earlier are uncomfortable with the use of "slave" or "slavery" to describe the servile populations they studied. Thus, Michael Mason explains:

> I have used the term "slave" only because of its familiarity and its currency in discussions of unfree labour in African societies. As I have suggested in the title, "captive" is a more appropriate term, as it is principally the mode of recruitment which the West African "slave" had in common with his brother in Cuba or Brazil.[46]

Polly Hill also says:

> Unlike genuine chattel slaves in ancient Greece and Rome, in the United States, and in Brazil and Haiti, who were always totally devoid of rights, farm-slaves in rural Hausaland normally enjoyed so many rights (including those of self-ransom) that it is reasonable to ask whether the term slave is, in fact, an appropriate translation of the Hausa *bawa*. However, quite apart from the impossibility of finding any alternative English word, it is clear that present-day definitions ... are sufficiently commodious to include the Hausa variant.

When a definition is too "commodious" it ceases to define anything, for Hill later complains: "So it seems that, after all, the use of the term 'slavery' does confuse certain essential issues in rural Hausaland and that a substitute ought to be coined."[47] Michael Watts has also argued that the extent to which the upper classes in the Sokoto Caliphate depended on the surplus produced by slaves has been "implausibly inflated":

> In some of the northern and peripheral emirates, perhaps less than 10 percent of the populace was servile, and while Kano and Sokoto

may have been high-density systems, we are after all referring to a society constituted by perhaps 8 to 10 million 'free' peasants. . . . The rights of ownership and production that farm slaves possessed converged with the slaveholders' ideology of the Islamic patriarch, assimilation, and the possibility of manumission. In short, the political, economic, and ideological tendencies in the Caliphate were toward the *production of peasants* who, if not entirely free, could at least be taxed or retained in a quasi-client status.[48]

So, while some members of the servile population in the Sokoto Caliphate were approximately slaves, a more precise use of terms, in the manner of modern historians of precapitalist Europe, would compel scholars to describe the vast majority of them as serfs. In other words, what the British colonial administration ended in Northern Nigeria in the early twentieth century was more serfdom than slavery.

The evidence for the Western Sudan is similar in many ways to that for the Sokoto Caliphate. Martin Klein, who has written extensively on the servile populations of the region, describes how their labor was rationally exploited in the nineteenth century: "[S]laves were settled in separate villages or separate quarters and there was increasing control over labour, feeding and dues."[49] He points to two possible ways of grouping the populations—the native-born versus those acquired by purchase or by capture, and those who resided within their lords' compounds versus those settled in separate villages. The native-born could not be sold, while many of those residing within their masters' compounds were those newly acquired and some trusted retainers and concubines. The latter group were fed and clothed by their masters, and those settled in villages worked under chiefs of servile descent. As Martin Klein reports, "the larger numbers and the relative autonomy" of those living in separate villages "made possible the development of leadership."[50]

The microstudies by Marion Johnson and by William Derman provide descriptive detail for the region. Johnson studied the state of Masina, which was established by a Muslim teacher and his followers in the region generally referred to as the Niger Bend (including Timbuktu and areas to the west). The state was created in the early nineteenth century and lasted up to the 1860s, when its capital was destroyed by Al-Hajj Umar. The process of establishing the state and expanding its geographical area created subjugated populations, referred to individually as *rimaibe* (sing. *dimadio*); some were held by the state and others by private Fulani pastoralists. Many of them were settled in villages. They were given lands with which to produce for themselves and maintain their own families, one-sixth of the harvest being paid as rent for the land. In addition, a quantity of grains was paid in dues called *diamgal*. Those held by the state paid only the dues in grains; they did not pay the land rent. Marion Johnson dismissed the suggestion that the settlement of the servile populations in separate villages of their own was brought about by the founder of the Masina state, who transformed preexisting chattel slaves into serfs with defined rights: "[T]he Masina system," she explained, "is so similar to the arrangements in adjacent territories which never came under control of the Masina theocracy, that it seems more probable that Sheku Ahmadu [the founder of the Masina state] formalized and regulated a pre-existing system."[51]

The study by William Derman was conducted in the Fouta-Djallon area of the modern Republic of Guinea. Here, in a Fulani-led *jihad* from about 1727, the indigenous Diallonke, Susu, and Poullis were conquered and reduced to servile status. The subjugated indigenous population and captives brought from outside were settled in villages where they produced for themselves on lands rented from the Fulani overlords: "they were economically self-sufficient. They lived in their own villages, they cultivated their own fields and women's gardens (although they did not own the land), owned property and had their own kin groups."[52] The rent for the land was 10 percent of the harvest. Quite often the servile cultivators rented lands from their masters, but sometimes the land was rented from other Fulani landowners. Apart from the rent, they owed their masters labor dues: "Men, women, and children worked five days a week for their masters from early morning until early afternoon." Although Derman thinks that they were reduced to poverty by the amount of labor demanded by their masters, the labor dues would seem to be of about the same magnitude as those of Kano and Zaria in the Sokoto Caliphate. The fact that the servile population of the Fouta-Djallon grew naturally after French conquest ended the wars and stopped the supply of new captives is an indication that the servile cultivators produced enough from their lands to support households with unproductive children and old members.[53]

The servile villages also had a good amount of autonomy to look after their own affairs at some level. For example, disputes in a village were settled by the elders, while political leadership was provided by a member whose master was a chief. This political leader was also the link between the servile village and the Fulani overlords.

Taking all the evidence together, we can agree with Martin Klein that many of the newly acquired captives and some others in the nineteenth-century Western Sudan lived and worked under conditions which approximated to those of slaves. But the majority of the servile population did not belong to this category. The evidence shows clearly that those in the servile villages were *servi casati* living in households and supporting themselves. These constituted the majority of the people in servitude in the region on the eve of French conquest.

We now come to servitude on the East Coast of Africa. Here, Frederick

Cooper has studied servitude in four important locations: two islands, Zanzibar and Pemba, where Omani Arabs produced cloves on a large scale in plantations, and two towns on the mainland, Malindi and Mombasa (both in modern Kenya), where Arabs, Swahili, and migrant Africans employed servile labor to produce grains for local and export markets. The evidence shows considerable differences in the socioeconomic conditions of the servile populations in these places. In the clove plantations of Pemba and Zanzibar, they lived in huts "scattered around the plantations, dispersed among the clove trees." The main tasks of the servile workers were harvesting, planting, and tending the young clove trees. There were two harvests each year, a large one in November or December and a smaller one in July to September. Planting, watering the young plants, and weeding around them was a year-round task. During the harvest season, these servile cultivators worked eight or nine hours a day, seven days a week; at other times they worked five or six days a week. They were allotted some plots where they produced some of their own food, mostly cassava.[54]

In Malindi, the servile cultivators worked in the grain fields of their masters in groups of five to twenty under a headman of servile status. The work week was between 40 and 50 hours. They were allotted small plots of between 200 by 10 yards and 200 by 50 yards where they produced some of their own food. During the dry season, Thursdays and Fridays were set aside for them to work their own plots, while in the wet season (the main agricultural season) they had only Fridays off. According to Cooper, "Most informants claimed that masters provided slaves with a daily ration of food and that the produce of the slaves' own plots was a supplement to this. Masters were also expected to provide their slaves with clothes."[55]

In Mombasa, on the other hand, servile cultivators held by several masters lived in villages of their own, each village containing from 50 to 300 people. Some of them worked on their own and paid their masters a monthly or annual sum called *ijara*. Others cultivated the nearby fields of their masters on their own without supervision; a quantity of grain (rent in kind) was paid to their town-dwelling masters, who went to the villages periodically to collect it. The dwellers of these servile villages around Mombasa were left with much autonomy to run their own affairs. On this, Cooper's descriptive evidence is instructive:

> In the Mombasa area, slaves often lived in villages containing slaves owned by various masters. They were governed by a slave headman elected by their own elders. He was expected to arrest any suspected criminals and send them to Mombasa for trial.[56]

Taking the evidence together, we agree entirely with Cooper that the servile cultivators of the clove plantations and those in mainland Malindi were slaves. Even though they had some small plots allotted to them, they certainly did not have enough time to produce for themselves and maintain a reasonable level of socioeconomic independence. The small size of the plots, less in area than a soccer field, is itself indicative. Although the demographic evidence is scanty, it clearly indicates that the servile populations in the clove plantations did not reproduce themselves socially, in spite of the rather favorable sex balance. The observation of contemporary visitors that the rate of reproduction was low and the death rate high is consistent with the hard data showing that mainland-born people were two-thirds of the servile population in 1900–1901. Since large-scale slave imports from the mainland were concentrated in the first four decades of the nineteenth century, as the growth of clove exports suggests, a reasonable reproduction rate should have given rise to a much greater proportion of island-born people in the population by this time. This demographic piece of evidence[57] points further to the low level of socioeconomic autonomy among the servile populations of the clove plantations. The case of those in the mainland area of Mombasa is a different matter. Here we are dealing with people whose socioeconomic autonomy was greater than that of even the villeins in medieval Europe, not to talk of the *bovarii* of twelfth-century England and the serfs of nineteenth-century Russia. It is an inexcusable terminological looseness to lump together the dependent cultivators of the Mombasa area and the servile populations of Malindi, Zanzibar, and Pemba under the same dependent social category. The former certainly were more similar to serfs than to slaves.

After examining the regions with high densities of servile populations in precolonial Africa, it is tempting to generalize that nothing very different existed in the other regions. That may very well be the case in places like Asante, Dahomey, and the Benin kingdom of southwestern Nigeria. In places such as these, a significant population of dependent people, whose socioeconomic conditions approximated those of slaves, existed side by side with others, in greater numbers, whose conditions were closer to those of serfs. But there are regions in which the people described as slaves by scholars had so much freedom that it will not even be appropriate to call them serfs. Such was the case of the Puna and Kuni societies of modern Congo. Here, the so-called slaves labored the same way as their free counterparts: they could hold any office in the society; and they were usually married to free spouses from the lineages of their masters.[58] Then we have the interesting case of the servile warriors of Mozambique in the period from 1825 to 1920, who look more like the knights of medieval Europe. They lived in their own villages, which were scattered all over the land; they had their own leaders, appointed from among them by their masters; and they constituted the instruments with which the lordly class dominated the peasants: they were employed in collecting tribute from the peasants and in imposing discipline on the peasant communities. The most important service they rendered to their masters, however, was in military duties.[59]

III

To conclude, it must be said that we owe a significant intellectual debt to the historians and anthropologists who have studied slavery in Africa for the past two decades or so. Their research has helped to call attention to social and economic issues in the study of African history after the initial emphasis on political questions. However, the sociology of knowledge which directed the research, it would seem, encouraged lack of attention to terminological precision. As we know too well, slavery in Africa was a major theme constructed by the European slave traders to defend their business against the abolitionist onslaught in the eighteenth century. The same theme also became very fashionable for the agents of European colonialism in the late nineteenth and early twentieth centuries, as the abolition of slavery was presented to the moral conscience of Europeans as a part of the European "civilizing mission" to Africa. The propaganda by the slave traders and by the agents of colonialism was so effective that it was given intellectual respectability in history textbooks. One part of the propaganda—that the preexistence of widespread slavery in Africa gave rise to and helped to sustain the Atlantic slave trade—was strongly challenged in the mid-1960s by the late Walter Rodney.[60] It is fair to say that the subsequent encounter between Rodney and Fage set the stage for the research of the 1970s and 1980s on servile institutions in precolonial Africa. Rodney himself, while questioning the existence of slavery in the coastal societies of Western Africa before the Atlantic slave trade, accepted uncritically the colonial propaganda that slavery was everywhere in late-nineteenth-century Africa.

Given the sociology of knowledge which informed the study of slavery in Africa, it is understandable why very little attention has been paid to terminological precision that characterizes the study of dependent social categories in the history of precapitalist Europe. I have attempted to redress this weakness in the literature by applying to the African evidence the formula employed by modern historians to separate slaves from serfs in precapitalist Europe. The result shows unequivocally that, while there were slaves in late-nineteenth-century Africa, the bulk of the people hitherto so described were approximately serfs. The phenomenon of what scholars refer to as intergenerational mobility among the slave populations in Africa[61]—the tendency for the children of slaves to become free persons or nearly so—meant that the slave class in Africa could not reproduce itself, not only because its rate of reproduction was low in the context of Meillassoux's theory, but largely because the children of slaves normally did not remain in slavery. They either became free or became serfs. Apart from the clove plantations of East Africa, most of what scholars have called slave plantations in Africa were, in fact, serf villages. To accept them as slave plantations, we must also accept the medieval manors in Europe and the serf villages of nineteenth-century Russia as slave plantations. In that case, Russia would have had the largest concentration of slaves in the nineteenth century, with over 22 million.

It is thus clear that the chattel slavery experienced by Africans in the Americas was something new for them for two fundamental reasons. First, the vast majority of the forced migrants from Africa were entirely legally free people captured in wars or raids, or kidnapped like Olaudah Equiano. These people had no previous experience of bondage, not even in serfdom. The claim that the preexistence of chattel slavery in the coastal societies of Western Africa facilitated the growth and development of the trans-Atlantic slave trade is not borne out by the evidence. Second, for the few who were already in bondage before capture and forced transportation to the Americas, their socioeconomic conditions in Africa were much closer (in many cases even superior) to those of serfs in medieval Europe than to those of chattel slaves. All of this may help explain the phenomenon observed by students of slave societies in the Americas that the greater the proportion of African-born people in the population, the greater the incidence of resistance or revolt.[62]

NOTES

1. Paul E. Lovejoy, "Foreword," in Claude Meillassoux, *The Anthropology of Slavery: The Womb of Iron and Gold*, translated by Alide Dasnois (Chicago: University of Chicago Press, 1991), p. 7. This view, expressed in the foreword by Paul Lovejoy, is totally contrary to Meillassoux's argument in the book. Meillassoux states unambiguously that tropical Africa was the last region in the world to develop a trade in slaves and the institution of slavery, many centuries after similar developments in Euro-Asia and around the Mediterranean (pp. 20–21).

2. Paul E. Lovejoy and Jan S. Hogendorn, *Slow Death For Slavery: The Course of Abolition in Northern Nigeria, 1897–1936* (Cambridge: Cambridge University Press, 1993), pp. xiii and 1.

3. Meillassoux, *The Anthropology of Slavery*, p. 22.

4. Martin A. Klein, "The Study of Slavery in Africa," *Journal of African History*, XIX, 4 (1978), pp. 599–609; Frederick Cooper, "The Problem of Slavery in African Studies," *Journal of African History*, XX, 1 (1979), pp. 103–125; Paul E. Lovejoy, "The Characteristics of Plantations in the Nineteenth-Century Sokoto Caliphate (Islamic West Africa)," *American Historical Review*, 84, 5 (1979), pp. 1267–1292.

5. Paul E. Lovejoy, "Plantations in the Economy of the Sokoto Caliphate," *Journal of African History*, XIX, 3 (1978), pp. 341–368; Lovejoy, "The Characteristics of Plantations."

6. Igor Kopytoff and Suzanne Miers, "African 'Slavery' as an Institution of Marginality," in Suzanne Miers and Igor Kopytoff (eds.), *Slavery in Africa: Historical and Anthropological Perspectives* (Madison: University of Wisconsin Press, 1977).

7. Cooper, "The Problem of Slavery," p. 105 and fn. 11, p. 105.

8. Meillassoux states that "One approach to African slavery, which stresses its benevolent character by comparison to American or West Indian slavery, tends to play down the differences between slaves and other dependent or dominated social categories, such as pawns, serfs, or even married women." Claude Meillassoux, "Female Slavery," in Claire C. Robertson and Martin A. Klein (eds.), *Women and Slavery in Africa* (Madison: University of Wisconsin Press, 1983), p. 50.

9. Joseph E. Inikori, *The Chaining of a Continent: Export Demand for Captives and the History of Africa South of the Sahara, 1450–1870* (Mona, Jamaica: Institute of Social and Economic Research, 1992), p. 37.

10. David Pelteret, "Slave raiding and slave trading in Early England," in Peter Clemoes (ed.), *Anglo-Saxon England*, 9 (Cambridge: Cambridge University Press, 1981), pp. 99–114. Pelteret explains that the Anglo-Saxons did not use slaves themselves before they moved into England: "In contrast to the Roman world, slavery seems not to have been an integral element in the social structure of the Germanic peoples living outside the Empire at the time when Tacitus was writing about them" (p. 100). But the Anglo-Saxons were involved in taking captives and exporting them to places in the Roman empire before they moved into England. That practice of taking and selling captives continued for centuries after they settled in England.

11. Pelteret, "Slave raiding," pp. 99, 102.

12. *Life of St. Wulstan, Bishop of Worcester*, translated by J. H. F. Peile (Oxford, 1934), pp. 64–65, cited by Pelteret, "Slave raiding," fn. 107, p. 113.

13. *Eadmer's History of Recent Events in England*, translated by G. Bosanquet (London, 1964), p. 152, cited by Pelteret, "Slave raiding," fn. 111, p. 113.

14. H. E. Hallam, "England before the Norman Conquest," in H. E. Hallam (ed.), *The Agrarian History of England and Wales: Volume II, 1042–1350* (Cambridge: Cambridge University Press, 1988), pp. 10–12. M. M. Postan has suggested that the percentage of slaves in the total population may actually have been less than the Domesday figures imply: "Corrected by the coefficients which historians employ to translate the Domesday figures of households into numbers of heads, the proportions of slaves to the total Domesday population would probably turn out to be smaller than the gross figures in the Domesday might suggest. For we must assume that whereas a large proportion of the slaves were not in a position to establish families, all the other social groups were counted in family units." M. M. Postan, *The Famulus: The Estate Labourer in the XIIth and XIIIth Centuries* (The Economic History Review Supplements 2, London: Cambridge University Press, 1954), pp. 5–6.

15. Postan, *The Famulus*. Much of the account of the English case which follows is based on this work.

16. Postan holds that by 1086 the conversion process had not gone far enough to engulf "that portion of the slave class whom lords were still employing in their *curia*." Postan, *The Famulus*, p. 11.

17. Postan, *The Famulus*, pp. 12–13.

18. Ibid., p. 23.

19. Ibid., p. 36. Earlier in the same work, Postan states: "How fundamental the change-over from slave to *bovarius* was, is not a question to which a simple answer is possible. It may have signified nothing more than a modification of their status, and may not have been of very great economic importance. On the other hand it may have been one of habitation—the resident slave may have been transformed into a landholding servant—in which case it was of great economic significance" (p. 11).

20. Ibid., p. 9.

21. Ibid., p. 25. This way of looking at slavery and serfdom would seem to be consistent with Meillassoux's theoretical construct, which distinguishes slavery from serfdom on the basis of the dependent producer's capacity to retain a proportion of his surplus large enough to raise a family and maintain a household. Under Meillassoux's framework, if the dependent producer possessed enough land and had enough time to work it and keep a surplus large enough to raise children and maintain old members of the household, then he was a serf. On the other hand, if the lord's demand for surplus labor was so great that the dependent producer was unable to maintain a household, then he was a slave. Hence, the observation that in all slave systems the slave class is unable to reproduce itself socially, being born of the "womb of iron and gold"—capture by force of arms and purchase with money on the market. See Meillassoux, *The Anthropology of Slavery*.

22. R. H. Hilton, *The Decline of Serfdom in Medieval England* (London: Macmillan, 1969), pp. 9–11.

23. Peter Kolchin, *Unfree Labor: American Slavery and Russian Serfdom* (Cambridge, Mass.: The Belknap Press of Harvard University Press, 1987), pp. 2–4, 41. The discussion of the Russian serfs is based largely on the evidence from this work.

24. Ibid., pp. 2–3.

25. Ibid., pp. 37–38.

26. Ibid., p. 43. By the mid-eighteenth century there were two broad groups of peasants, state peasants and serfs. The latter, owned almost exclusively by noblemen, constituted over 50 percent of the peasant population. The state peasants were made up of those who escaped enserfment and those recently freed (Ibid., p. 39).

27. Ibid., Table 3, p. 52. It is not clear whether "male serfs" refers to heads of household or to all males, including children. If reference is to heads of household, then the total serf population was much greater than what is stated here.

28. It should be noted that historians have debated the issue of whether the nineteenth-century Russian serfs were actually slaves or if they were serfs in the main, although their conditions came close to those of chattel slaves. Based on the evidence, this is an important distinction to make,

contrary to the view of Peter Kolchin, who thinks that the dispute is mere hairsplitting. The sale of the serfs certainly moved them very close to chattel slaves. But, as Kolchin himself acknowledges, most serfs continued to receive allotments of land of their own from their owners, with which they supported themselves (Ibid., pp. 43–45). For this reason they were *servi casati*. And the demographic evidence indicates that they were able to maintain a household and reproduce themselves socially. Even their sale was, at least, regulated by state laws. Peter I decreed in 1721 that family members must not be separated by sale, and in the nineteenth century, Nicholas I twice outlawed the selling of unmarried children away from their parents (Ibid., p. 117). It is fair to say that in the main these were serfs, but over time their conditions came close to those of chattel slaves.

29. Jacques J. Maquet, "A Research Definition of African Feudality," *Journal of African History*, III, 2 (1962), p. 307.

30. Maquet thought that the Marxist conception would be difficult to apply to precolonial Africa, where the notion of land ownership embodied in Roman law was nonexistent. We shall comment on this later. See Maquet, "African Feudality," p. 309.

31. Jack Goody, "Feudalism in Africa?" *Journal of African History*, IV, 1 (1963), p. 3.

32. Goody, "Feudalism in Africa?" p. 10. Reference here is to I. I. Potekhin, "On the Feudalism of the Ashanti," Paper read to the Twenty-fifth International Congress of Orientalists, Moscow, 1960.

33. Basil Davidson, *Black Mother: The Years of the African Slave Trade* (Boston: Atlantic Monthly Press, 1961), pp. 11 and 12.

34. Goody, "Feudalism in Africa?" pp. 10–13. Goody may as well have included words like "slavery" and "plantations."

35. J. H. M. Beattie, "Bunyoro: An African Feudality?" *Journal of African History*, V, 1 (1964), pp. 26 and 35.

36. Of the many publications arising from this research, the following have been consulted: *Baba of Karo: A Woman of the Muslim Hausa*, edited by Mary F. Smith, with introduction and notes by Michael G. Smith (London: Faber and Faber, 1954); M. G. Smith, "A Study of Hausa Domestic Economy in Northern Zaria," *Africa*, XXII, No. 4 (1952), pp. 333–347; M. G. Smith, "Slavery and Emancipation in Two Societies," *Social and Economic Studies*, Vol. 3, Nos. 3 and 4 (December, 1954), pp. 239–290; M. G. Smith, *Government in Zazzau, 1800–1950* (London: Oxford University Press, 1960).

37. Smith, "Slavery and Emancipation," pp. 244, 253, 264–267; Smith, *Government in Zazzau*, pp. 86, 89–90; Smith, "Introduction," in Mary Smith (ed.), *Baba of Karo*, p. 22.

38. Polly Hill, "From Slavery to Freedom: The Case of Farm-Slavery in Nigerian Hausaland," *Comparative Studies in Society and History*, Vol. 18, No. 3 (1976), p. 418.

39. Ibid., pp. 402–404.

40. Michael Mason, "Captive and Client Labour and the Economy of the Bida Emirate, 1857–1901," *Journal of African History*, XIV, 3 (1973), Tables 1 and 2, pp. 459 and 460.

41. Mason, "Captive and Client Labour," pp. 467–468.

42. Mason, "Captive and Client Labour," pp. 465–466.

43. Michael Mason, "Production, Penetration, and Political Formation: The Bida State, 1857–1901," in Donald Crummey and C. C. Stewart (eds.), *Modes of Production in Africa: The Precolonial Era* (Beverly Hills: Sage Publications, 1981), pp. 214–215.

44. Jan Hogendorn, "The Economics of Slave Use on Two 'Plantations' in the Zaria Emirate of the Sokoto Caliphate," *International Journal of African Historical Studies*, 10 (1977), p. 378.

45. According to the more detailed work schedule presented by Hogendorn, the dependent cultivators in Zaria rose by 4:00 A.M. for the morning prayer, after which they went with their families to their own farms. By 9:00 A.M. they moved to their lords' fields and worked to midday, when they rested and had their meals brought to them on the fields by their lords. By 2:00 P.M. work on the lords' fields was over and they were free to return to their own farms. This is the schedule during the farm season, which lasted (including the harvesting period) probably no more than six or seven months. For the whole of the dry season, about November to April, they worked mostly for themselves and were paid when they worked for their lords. See Hogendorn, "The Economics of Slave Use," pp. 375–376; Hill, "From Slavery to Freedom," p. 418. Assuming that the morning prayers lasted an hour, the servile cultivators must have had at least six hours daily to devote to their own farms during the farming season (allowing for movement to and from the lords' fields), while spending at the very most about four hours on their lords' fields. And then, of course, there was a lot of time during the dry season to engage in non-agricultural activities for themselves—hunting, handicraft production, etc.

46. Mason, "Captive and Client Labour," fn. 2, p. 453.

47. Hill, "From Slavery to Freedom," pp. 397, 413.

48. Michael Watts, *Silent Violence: Food, Famine and Peasantry in Northern Nigeria* (Berkeley: University of California Press, 1983), pp. 77–78. This telling criticism notwithstanding, Michael Watts still talks of "several million slaves" in the Sokoto Caliphate in the late nineteenth century (p. 191).

49. Klein, "The Study of Slavery," p. 607.

50. Martin A. Klein, "Slave Resistance and Slave Emancipation in Coastal Guinea," in Suzanne Miers and Richard Roberts (eds.), *The End of Slavery in Africa* (Madison: University of Wisconsin Press, 1988), pp. 208–209.

51. Marion Johnson, "The Economic Foundation of an Islamic Theocracy—The Case of Masina," *Journal of African History*, XVII, 4 (1976), pp. 488–489.

52. William Derman, *Serfs, Peasants, and Socialists: A Former Serf Village in the Republic of Guinea* (Berkeley, California: University of California Press, 1973), p. 30.

53. Derman, *Serfs, Peasants, and Socialists*, p. 34.

54. Frederick Cooper, *Plantation Slavery on the East Coast of Africa* (New Haven: Yale University Press, 1977), pp. xi, 156–170.

55. Cooper, *Plantation Slavery*, p. 173.

56. Cooper, *Plantation Slavery*, p. 173-176, 228.

57. Cooper, *Plantation Slavery*, pp. 51, 52, 61, 131, 221-225.

58. Klein, "The Study of Slavery," p. 605.

59. Allen Isaacman and Anton Rosenthal, "Slaves, Soldiers, and Police: Power and Dependency among the Chikunda of Mozambique, ca. 1825-1920," in Miers and Roberts (eds.), *The End of Slavery*, pp. 220-253.

60. Walter Rodney, "African Slavery and Other Forms of Social Oppression on the Upper Guinea Coast in the Context of the Atlantic Slave Trade," *Journal of African History*, VII, 3 (1966), pp. 431-443; John D. Fage, "Slaves and Society in Western Africa, c. 1445-1700," *Journal of African History*, 21 (1980), pp. 289-310; Claude Meillassoux, "The Role of Slavery in the Economic and Social History of Sahelo-Sudanic Africa," in Joseph E. Inikori (ed.), *Forced Migration: The Impact of the Export Slave Trade on African Societies* (London and New York: Hutchinson and Africana, 1982), pp. 74-99; J. Devisse and S. Labib, "Africa in inter-continental relations," in D.T. Niane (ed.), *UNESCO General History of Africa: IV, Africa from the Twelfth to the Sixteenth Century* (Berkeley: Heinemann, University of California Press, UNESCO, 1984), p. 672.

61. Klein, "The Study of Slavery," p. 605.

62. David Barry Gaspar, "Slave Importation, Runaways, and Compensation in Antigua, 1720-1729," in Joseph E. Inikori and Stanley L. Engerman (eds.), *The Atlantic Slave Trade: Effects on Economies, Societies, and Peoples in Africa, the Americas, and Europe* (Durham and London: Duke University Press, 1992), pp. 311-317.

REFERENCES

Beattie, J. H. M. "Bunyoro: An African Feudality?" *Journal of African History* 5, No. 1 (1964): 25-35.

Cooper, Frederick. "The Problem of Slavery in African Studies." *Journal of African History* 20, No. 1 (1979): 103-25.

———. *Plantation Slavery on the East Coast of Africa*. New Haven: Yale University Press, 1977.

Davidson, Basil. *Black Mother: The Years of the African Slave Trade*. Boston: Atlantic Monthly, 1961.

Derman, William. *Serfs, Peasants, and Socialists: A Former Serf Village in the Republic of Guinea*. Berkeley: University of California Press, 1973.

Devisse, J., and S. Labib. "Africa in Inter-Continental Relations." *UNESCO General History of Africa: IV. Africa from the Twelfth to the Sixteenth Century*, ed. D. T. Niane. Berkeley: Heinemann, University of California Press, UNESCO, 1984, 635-672.

Eadmer's History of Recent Events in England. Trans. G. Bosanquet. London, 1964.

Fage, John D. "Slaves and Society in Western Africa, c. 1445-1700." *Journal of African History* 21 (1980): 289-310.

Gaspar, David Barry. "Slave Importation, Runaways, and Compensation in Antigua, 1720–1729." *The Atlantic Slave Trade: Effects on Economies, Societies, and Peoples in Africa, the Americas, and Europe.* Joseph E. Inikori and Stanley L. Engerman, eds. Durham and London: Duke University Press, 1992, 311–317.

Goody, Jack. "Feudalism in Africa?" *Journal of African History* 4, No. 1 (1963): 1–17.

Hallam, H. E. "England Before the Norman Conquest." *The Agrarian History of England and Wales: Volume II, 1042–1350.* Hallam, ed. Cambridge: Cambridge University Press, 1988, 1–44.

Hill, Polly. "From Slavery to Freedom: The Case of Farm-Slavery in Nigerian Hausaland." *Comparative Studies in Society and History* 18, No. 3 (1976): 395–426.

Hilton, R. H. *The Decline of Serfdom in Medieval England.* London: Macmillan, 1969.

Hogendorn, Jan. "The Economics of Slave Use on Two 'Plantations' in the Zaria Emirate of the Sokoto Caliphate." *International Journal of African Historical Studies* 10 (1977): 369–383.

Inikori, Joseph E. *The Chaining of a Continent: Export Demand for Captives and the History of Africa South of the Sahara, 1450–1870.* Mona, Jamaica: Institute of Social and Economic Research, 1992.

Isaacman, Allen, and Anton Rosenthal. "Slaves, Soldiers, and Police: Dependency among the Chikunda of Mozambique, ca 1825–1920." In Miers and Roberts, 220–253.

Johnson, Marion. "The Economic Foundation of an Islamic Theocracy—The Case of Masina." *Journal of African History* 17, No. 4 (1976): 481–495.

Klein, Martin A. "The Study of Slavery in Africa." *Journal of African History* 19, No. 4 (1978): 599–609.

———. "Slave Resistance and Slave Emancipation in Coastal Guinea." In Miers and Roberts, 203–219.

Kolchin, Peter. *Unfree Labor: American Slavery and Russian Serfdom.* Cambridge: The Belknap Press-Harvard University Press, 1987.

Kopytoff, Igor, and Suzanne Miers. "African 'Slavery' as an Institution of Marginality." In *Slavery in Africa: Historical and Anthropological Perspectives,* Kopytoff and Miers, eds. Madison: University of Wisconsin Press, 1977.

Life of St Wulstan, Bishop of Worcester. Trans. J. H. F. Peile. Oxford, 1934.

Lovejoy, Paul E. Foreword. In *The Anthropology of Slavery: The Womb of Iron and Gold,* by Claude Meillassoux; trans. Alide Dasnois. Chicago: University of Chicago Press, 1991, 7–8.

———. "Plantations in the Economy of the Sokoto Caliphate." *Journal of African History* 19, No. 3 (1978): 341–68.

———. "The Characteristics of Plantations in the Nineteenth-Century Sokoto Caliphate (Islamic West Africa)." *American Historical Review* 84, No. 5 (1979): 1267–92.

Lovejoy, Paul E., and Jan S. Hogendon. *Slow Death for Slavery: The Course* of *Abolition in Northern Nigeria, 1897–1936.* Cambridge: Cambridge University Press, 1993.

Maquet, Jacques J. "A Research Definition of African Feudality." *Journal of African History* 3, No. 2 (1962): 307–310.

Mason, Michael. "Captive and Client Labor and the Economy of the Bida Emirate, 1857–1901." *Journal of African History* 14, No. 3 (1973): 453–471.

———. "Production, Penetration, and Political Formation: The Bida State, 1857–1901." In *Modes of Production in Africa: The Precolonial Era,* Donald Crummey and C. C. Stewart, eds. Beverly Hills: Sage Publications, 1981, 205–226.

Meillassoux, Claude. "The Role of Slavery in the Economic and Social History of Sahelo-Sudanic Africa." In *Forced Migration: The Impact of the Export Slave Trade on African Societies,* ed. Joseph E. Inikori. London and New York: Hutchinson and Africana, 1982, 74–99.

———. "Female Slavery." In *Women and Slavery in Africa,* Claire C. Robertson and Martin A. Klein, eds. Madison: University of Wisconsin Press, 1983, 49–65.

———. *The Anthropology of Slavery: The Womb of Iron and Gold.* Trans. Alide Dasnois. Chicago: University of Chicago Press, 1991.

Miers, Suzanne, and Richard Roberts, eds. *The End of Slavery in Africa.* Madison: University of Wisconsin Press, 1988.

Pelteret, David. "Slave Raiding and Slave Trading in Early England." In *Anglo-Saxon England* 9, Peter Clemoes, ed. Cambridge: Cambridge University Press, 1981, 99–114.

Postan, M. M. *The Famulus: The Estate Labourer in the XIIth and XIIIth Centuries.* The Economic History Review Supplements 2. Cambridge: Cambridge University Press, 1954.

Potekhin, I. I. "On the Feudalism of the Ashanti." Twenty-fifth International Congress of Orientalists, Moscow, 1960.

Rodney, Walter. "African Slavery and Other Forms of Social Oppression on the Upper Guinea Coast in the Context of the Atlantic Slave Trade." *Journal of African History* 7, No. 3 (1966): 431–443.

Smith, Mary F., ed. *Baba of Karo: A Woman of the Muslim Hausa,* with Introduction and Notes by Michael G. Smith. London: Faber and Faber, 1954.

Smith, M. G. *Government in Zazzau, 1800–1950.* London: Oxford University Press, 1960.

———. "Slavery and Emancipation in Two Societies." *Social and Economic Studies* 3, Nos. 3 and 4 (1954): 239–290.

———. "A Study of Hausa Domestic Economy in Northern Zaria." *Africa* 22, No. 4 (1952): 333–347.

Watts, Michael. *Silent Violence: Food, Famine, and Peasantry in Northern Nigeria.* Berkeley: University of California Press, 1983.

5 MODERNITY, MEMORY, MARTINIQUE

Richard Price

In his great poem "The Schooner Flight," Derek Walcott writes:

> I met History once, but he ain't recognize me,
> a parchment Creole, with warts
> like an old sea bottle, crawling like a crab
> through the holes of shadow cast by the net
> of a grille balcony; cream linen, cream hat.
> I confront him and shout, "Sir, is Shabine!
> They say I'se your grandson. You remember Grandma,
> your black cook, at all?" The bitch hawk and spat.
> A spit like that worth any number of words.
> But that's all them bastards have left us: words.

During the past three decades, the populations of the French Caribbean—
Martinique, Guadeloupe, and Guyane—have been subjected to an intense
program of *francisation*, a development scheme designed to integrate, assimilate, and restructure these former colonies as full *départements* of
France (and now, so-called Ultra-Peripheral Regions of Europe). Here, I
want to talk about one aspect of this modernization process—the ways
it has affected people's views of their past, in particular the ways that
the colonial past has been refashioned to better fit people's current aspirations and activities. If George Lamming is right that "the word 'development' . . . is, perhaps, the most dangerously toxic word in our vocabulary"
(1995:30), one reason surely is that it corrodes a people's sense of its past,
their collective identity. It is this ugly, silent, corrosive process I want
to invoke here—a postcolonial process in which people are participating,
complicitously, in the destruction of their own identity and selfhood. I'll
use Martinique, where I live, as the prime example. And despite the brev-
ity of this piece, I'll try not to caricature.

Colonial nostalgia, 1990s Martinique-style, provides one quick entrée
into this tangle of interlinked phenomena. Consider the following (as reported by the main local newspaper, *France-Antilles*). Just off the north-
south road that skirts the Atlantic coast, "a mini-village made up of rural

cabins from the 1950s . . . permits the new generation to discover the scenes their ancestors knew, the way of life of their parents and grand-parents. . . . Four years in the making, this open-air museum is a gem of tradition. On Sunday afternoons . . . members of the folkloric troupe Madinina install themselves there to recreate a living portrait of that by-gone era" (Staszewski 1993). A few kilometers to the south, in the cove of Anse Figuier, another privately run museum, the island's first *écomusée*, also targets the 1950s—"the traditional society we have forgotten in our rush to modernity . . . *la Martinique profonde*" (E.H-H. 1992).

Alongside these idealized recreations of the good old days of not so long ago, generally depicted as a timeless and ahistorical moment, there is another mode of institutionalized nostalgia—restorations of elegant eight-eenth-century plantation houses, filled with period furniture. It may be worth noting that there is very little information provided, in either the "1950s" museums or the eighteenth-century exhibits, about the social relations of production—the fact that most work in both periods was agricultural gang labor (whether by slaves or waged men and women). Nor is colonialism more than a silent backdrop in either context. The 1950s exhibits, ostensibly depicting the domestic economy, focus on such activi-ties as household food processing and artisanal production. And the eight-eenth-century restorations portray leisured life in the great house. Both these pastorals exude contentment.

More generally, nostalgia for the "ancestral" way of life, for "the way we used to live," is omnipresent in 1990s Martinique. Celebration of the cultural patrimony permeates the press, radio, and TV, animated by art-ists, musicians, dancers, tale-tellers, writers, theater groups, and cultural associations. Commercialized folklore is available at every village fête and large hotel, and it floods the airwaves.

The unusually rapid modernization that has taken place in Martinique, largely imposed from the metropole, is profoundly assimilationist in spirit. And it demands the concomitant rejection of much of Martiniquan culture as it had developed during the previous three centuries—at least as a viable way of life for today's forward-looking generation. Television ads ridicule the country bumpkin, visiting his bourgeois cousins, who grates fruit to make juice rather than buying it readymade in a carton at the su-permarket, and such promotional campaigns have successfully created a whole range of "needs," such as electronic front gates, home security sys-tems, travel agents, and canned dog food, that were virtually unknown just two decades ago. In terms of values and self-perception, Martiniquans have been encouraged to situate themselves as thoroughly modern, bourgeois members of the First World (and Europe), and to look with benevolent con-descension upon, say, Haitians, Saint Lucians, or Brazilians as their dis-advantaged, sometimes picturesque, but backward Third World neighbors. All of this has produced tremendous tension for Martiniquans—by struggling to become more and more French, Martiniquans have developed an acute double consciousness. As Fred Constant has recently written, "Les dominés devinrent alors leurs propres dominants [the dominated thus became their own dominators, the oppressed became their own oppressors]."[1]

Some years ago, Edouard Glissant argued that cultural symbols of Martiniquan identity—music and dance, the Creole language, local cuisine, carnival—take on remarkable power in this modernizing context by fostering in people the illusion that they are representing themselves, that they are choosing the terms of their "difference," while at the same time obscuring the rapidity and completeness of the assimilationist project. This focus on *the Cultural* and *the Folkloric*, he wrote, serves both the assimilators and the assimilating, by lulling the latter into complacency and helping mask the crushing force of the French "Civilizing Mission" (Glissant 1981:213). Richard Burton, writing in Glissant's wake, argues that the agricultural base on which traditional creole culture was founded "has been eroded beyond all possibility of restoration, leaving that culture—where it survives at all—increasingly bereft of any anchorage in the actual lived experience of contemporary French West Indians and, as such, subject to a fatal combination of folklorization, exoticization, and commodification" (Burton 1993:7–8). The modern Martiniquan, he claims, is "as much a spectator of his or her 'own' culture as the average tourist: 'culture,' like everything else in Martinique today, is something to be consumed rather than actively produced in a living human context" (Ibid.).

In terms of the colonial past, such processes encourage a denial of conflict, an overall laundering of struggle and oppression. Take this example from Guyane (see R. and S. Price 1996 for details): In the projected Regional Museum, one of the expository labels stresses that "the earliest colonists, often poor, lived under conditions that were scarcely better than those of their slaves." And the brutality of slavery is relegated wholesale to the neighboring colony of Suriname. The physical objects highlighted in the plantation section of the museum are pottery and a Creole stringed instrument allegedly made by an eighteenth-century slave. There is no mention of chains, iron collars, or other instruments of discipline and control. And that museum does the same for the famous French Guiana penal colony (Devil's Island)—nothing on its raison d'etre or the conditions of life within the institution. Rather, a display of pretty crafts items made by prisoners. All this is reminiscent of the advertisements reported from 1995 Barbados for hotel floor shows, where visitors are invited to "see the cultures of the Caribbean as influenced by the Spanish, French and African *settlers*" (Potter 1996:3).

Similarly, in Martinique, the leading younger generation of writers, the Créolistes, are busy recasting the Caribbean past (see R. and S. Price 1997 for details). And among their reformulations is the idea that it was not the heroic Maroon, the freedom-fighter who fueled the imagination of an earlier generation of Caribbean intellectuals, who stands as their identitarian model but rather the slave *conteur*, the plantation man-of-words they describe as an Uncle Tom whom the master didn't fear and who therefore could subtly and more effectively serve as spiritual leader. While Aimée Césaire's generation proudly identified themselves as modern Maroons, that of Raphaël Confiant and Patrick Chamoiseau identify themselves instead as modern *conteurs*. And doesn't it make sense? The violent resistance of the Maroon *worked* as an anticolonial model, but for those who are at one and the same time basking in French literary prizes and trying to preserve folkloric aspects of Martiniquan identity, the more muted and partial resistance of the man-of-words seems far more appropriate to the current situation. Or take another recent reformulation of Martinique's past, the idea that Martinique is, and always has been, an unusually diverse society—ethnically, racially, and linguistically (what the créolistes call *diversalité*). Françoise Vergès has argued, quite appropriately I think, that this kind of *métissage* is now being packaged as a consumable cultural product (along the lines of the United Colors of Benetton), and that it can serve as "an 'artifact' in the Great French Museum of Human Diversity as long as the historical conditions that gave birth to this diversity—colonial wars, slavery, the construction of the French nation—are denied or swept under the rug" (1995:81).

I would argue that the Créolistes' novels—which have been winning all of France's biggest literary prizes during the past few years—tend to celebrate a museumified Martinique, a diorama-ed Martinique, a picturesque and "pastified" Martinique that promotes a "feel-good" nostalgia for people who are otherwise busy adjusting to the complexities of a rapidly modernizing lifestyle. And constant state-sponsored events—Culture Week, the Day of Local Cuisine, the Festival of Tradition—take people's daily lives and turn them into official folklore, or official History. In short, I'm trying to call attention to one of the traps of modernization, the process of museumification or patrimonialization of which Derek Walcott wrote: "Stamped on that image is the old colonial grimace of the laughing nigger, steelbandsman, carnival masker, calypsonian and limbo dancer . . . trapped in the State's concept of the folk form . . . the symbol of a carefree, accommodating culture, an adjunct to tourism" (Walcott 1970:7).

In this brief essay I am unable to demonstrate any of these claims—I hope that my book *The Convict and the Colonel* does the trick in that regard. But here I will at least introduce the case that forms the centerpiece of that book.

In 1980 I first saw this wooden statue in a rumshop near where we live in Martinique (Fig. 1). For the past sixteen years I've been following its story. The first part of the book narrates a massacre in 1925, by French colonial forces, of local people trying to cast their vote for mayor. During

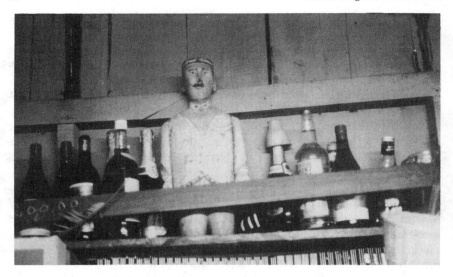

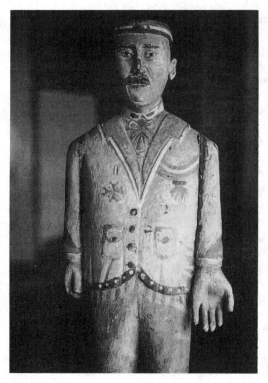

FIGURE I.
The Colonel, by Médard
Aribot, ca. 1924 (2 views).
All images in this chapter
are from Richard Price,
*The Convict and the
Colonel* (Boston: Beacon,
1998) and appear courtesy
of Beacon Press.

the demonstration that preceded the massacre, the crowd paraded this statue around the town square, shouting insults. It depicts a retired colonel, the white owner of the local sugar mill, who was running for mayor against the people's candidate, a black socialist. It was the colonel who is said to have ordered the colonial troops to open fire on the crowd, killing ten and wounding twelve. The statue was the work of a man at the opposite end of the social scale from the colonel—a marginal who lived in a cave by the sea and who survived by petty theft and by selling artworks: ships (Fig. 2), images of people (Fig. 3), and other objects (all of which, I argue in the book, play subtly with the theme of colonial domination).

The second part of the book recounts how Médard Aribot—for that was his name—spent some fifteen years in the French Guiana penal colony at hard labor, returning to Martinique around 1950, after the penal colony was finally closed. Working with archival materials in both French Guiana and metropolitan France, and combining this information with oral materials gathered over many years in Martinique, I am able to reconstruct a rather detailed picture of Médard's life before, during, and after his stay in Guyane. Before Médard died in 1973, he built a miniature house, a little masterpiece of bricolage, looking out toward Diamond Rock (Fig. 4).

We can take that house as a symbol of the broader processes I am trying to evoke today. This picture shows the house, abandoned and beaten by the winds, as it stood ten years after Médard's death. At that time, fishermen and peasants from throughout the region used the house as a mnemonic device, as a way of recalling a story that mattered a great deal to them. What they said was this: the house belonged to Médard, who was sentenced to hard labor in the penal colony because he had made that image of the colonel, an image that was "too true" and therefore insolent and insulting. For people all along the south coast of Martinique, Médard's house recalled Médard's life, which stood for all the horrors of colonial oppression. "Médard," they would say, "was sweet as a lamb. He never stole. He never killed. And yet, the colonial powers sentenced him to life at hard labor simply for making a statue of the colonel. . . . "

Now, this is what people said only fifteen years ago. Today, now that Martinique drinks more champagne per capita than anywhere in the world (except Guadeloupe) and some local women sport French poodles on leashes, consciousness of the past has, perhaps inevitably, changed radically. Indeed, the third and final part [of my book] is devoted to the ways that this once-central part of rural Martiniquans' historical consciousness, this story they liked to tell themselves about their own past, has become folklorized or laundered, how Médard and his house have become distanced, sanitized, and appropriated by the tourist industry.

The house was taking its more or less natural course in the late 1980s (Fig. 5—some Rastas had squatted there for a while), when a local cultural

FIGURE 2.
Ship, by Médard Aribot,
ca. 1970.

FIGURE 3.
An African King, by
Médard Aribot, ca. 1960.

FIGURE 4.
Médard's House, 1983.

FIGURE 5.
Médard's House, 1986.

FIGURE 6.
Postcard.

group, supported by the municipality, decided to rehabilitate it because of its potential picturesqueness. Soon, the house was appearing on postcards sold at every tourist hotel, with the label "Diamond Rock and the House of the Fisherman, or of the Convict" (Fig. 6).

The rest of the story is a bit convoluted, but by the early 1990s, Médard had become pretty fully folklorized. Local people below the age of fifty rarely knew anything about him or even about the existence of the massacre of 1925. And official sources now denied that anything like that could ever have happened. In 1993 the weekend supplement to *France-Antilles* devoted an article to Médard under their weekly "History" rubric.

MÉDARD ARIBOT, ARTIST OR CONVICT? HIS LIFE SEEMS CLOSEST TO A MARVELOUS FOLKTALE, HOWEVER SAD. WAS HE A CONVICT? THERE'S NOTHING THAT PROVES IT. BUT THAT HE WAS AN ARTIST COULDN'T BE CLEARER!

Is there a single tourist who has passed through Anse Cafard in Diamant and not conscientiously photographed that delicious little multicolored structure, said to be "the house of the convict"? Facing the illustrious Rock, it is a miniature masterpiece, the work of an original.

It is said that he was condemned to fifteen years banishment in French Guiana, though no one seems to know the name of the judge or the tribunal that sentenced him. There is no record of the matter in the contemporary press. Even the leftist papers, so ready in those agitated times to make accusations at the drop of a hat, contain not a whisper. "Médard came back from Cayenne fifteen years later, after 1940" say his faithful defenders today, even specifying that he was "crippled and twisted because they'd kept him in a tiny underground cell." But such claims owe more to dreams and imagination than to reality.

The Archives of the Bagne at Aix-en-Provence have not found a single trace of this alleged convict. If Médard Aribot went to French Guiana, it would have been for a wholly different reason and at some wholly different time. And the idea that he might have been registered under some other name is equally ridiculous.

Thus, the martyrdom of Médard Aribot can be considered simply a legend growing from the fertile popular imagination (Rabussier 1993a, 1993b).

David Dabydeen, in his muscular poem "Turner," echoes Walcott about the legacy of slavery, when he writes of the European colonizer:

> His tongue spurting strange potions upon ours
> Which left us dazed, which made us forget
> The very sound of our speech.

I wonder whether a parallel process isn't taking place in postcolonial Martinique. After three hundred years in which slaves and their descendants, who at first were indeed "dazed," managed to build a new, vibrant Afro-American culture of their own, the French-engineered process of rapid modernization has again left people dazed—and made them forget the sound of their speech. For the final apotheosis of Médard's story—which was, remember, only fifteen years ago a heroic part of local historical consciousness, something that *mattered* to local people—the final chapter (to date) is that local younger people now know *nothing* of Médard or the massacre of 1925, and that *this* is the cover of the new Guide Gallimard to Martinique, the largest-selling tourist guide to the island, which is published in Paris (Fig. 7).

NOTES

This essay, written for the conference "The African Diaspora: African Origins and New World Self-Fashioning," SUNY Binghamton, April

FIGURE 7.
Cover of Guide Gallimard.

11–13, 1996, draws on several works then in progress and in press: R. and S. Price 1996, R. and S. Price 1997, and, especially, R. Price 1998.

    1. I neglected to save the clipping—or reference—for this quote, which appeared in an article Constant wrote for *France-Antilles* in early 1996.

REFERENCES

Burton, Richard
    1993   "*Ki Moun Nou Ye?* The Idea of Difference in Contemporary French West Indian Thought." *New West Indian Guide* 67:5–32.
Dabydeen, David
    1994   "Turner." In *Turner: New and Selected Poems*. London: Jonathan Cape, pp. 1–40.
E.H-H.
    1992   "Le premier éco musée de Martinique." *France-Antilles Magazine* 28 November–4 December, pp. 44–45.
Glissant, Édouard
    1981   *Le discours antillais*. Paris: Seuil.
Lamming, George
    1995   *Coming, Coming Home: Conversations II*. St. Martin: House of Nehesi Publishers.
Potter, Robert B.
    1996   "The 'New Tourism,' Postmodernity and the Culture and History of the Caribbean." *Caribbean Studies Newsletter* 23(1):3–4.
Price, Richard
    1998   *The Convict and the Colonel*. Boston: Beacon.
Price, Richard and Sally Price
    1996   "Museums, ethnicity, and nation-building: reflections from the French Caribbean," in *Ethnicity in the Caribbean: Essays in Honor of Harry Hoetink*, edited by Gert Oostindie, London, Macmillan, pp. 81–105.
    1997   "Shadowboxing in the Mangrove." *Cultural Anthropology* 12:3–36.
Rabussier, Dominique
    1993a   "Médard Aribot, artiste ou bagnard? (1)." *France-Antilles Magazine*, 14–20 August, pp. 48–49.
    1993b   "Médard Aribot, artiste ou bagnard? (2)." *France-Antilles Magazine*, 21–27 August, pp. 48–49.
Staszewski, Gérard
    1993   "Images et couleurs d'un village d'antan." *France-Antilles Magazine* 6–12 March, pp. 48–50.
Vergès, Françoise
    1995   "Métissage, discours masculin et déni de la mère," in *Penser la créolité*, edited by Maryse Condé & Madeleine Cottenet-Hage, Paris, Karthala, pp. 69–83.
Walcott, Derek
    1970   "What the Twilight Says: An Overture," in *Dream on Mon-*

key Mountain and Other Plays, New York, Farrar, Straus and Giroux, pp. 3–40.

1979   "The Schooner Flight." From *The Star-Apple Kingdom*, in *Derek Walcott, Collected Poems 1948–1984*, New York, Farrar, Straus and Giroux, pp. 345–361.

6

KINSHIP AND STATE IN AFRICAN AND AFRICAN AMERICAN HISTORIES

Peter P. Ekeh

Africans and their relatives-in-diaspora in the United States share similar historic experiences in the sphere of their interactions with state organizations. In their tumultuous encounters with state institutions, they have also reacted in ways that are alike. Because states and their functionaries have persecuted ordinary Africans and African Americans for much of the past three to four centuries, both groups of blacks, during various portions of their histories, have resorted to building up kinship corporations as a counterweight to the state, often relaxing their kinship ties whenever state institutions become helpful or benign.

From such experiences both Africans and African Americans have constructed kinship bonds that have resulted in strong primordial consciousness, but with widely differing consequences. On the African continent, Africans have carefully fabricated myriad ethnic forms of consciousness, each of which nurtures loyalties for the benefit of an exclusive membership of a well-defined kinsfolk, excluding the vast majority of other Africans and often antagonizing some other ethnic groups. On the American continent, an unmatched common historic experience, under slavery and other kinds of subordination, has enabled African Americans to construct a unique type of primordial consciousness that is different from expressions of kinship in Africa. In Black America, there is an absence of ethnic consciousness; instead, there is an exaggerated form of race consciousness that includes other African Americans and indeed blacks everywhere in shared sentiments. That is to say, whereas Africans on the African continent lack any conception of race in their behaviors, African Americans' folkways are suffused in race consciousness. Interactions between Africans and African Americans have sometimes been brittle because of these differing patterns of primordial consciousness.

This essay seeks to trace the routes that Africans and their trans-Atlantic relatives have followed in acquiring these contrasting forms of consciousness from a shared emphasis on kinship bonds. In order to ensure its theoretical underpinnings, I will begin this exercise indirectly by examining disputed relationships between state and kinship in African history and social science. Contrary to our viewpoint on the primacy of kinship in African history and societies, two leading perspectives in studies of African social development offer bold propositions suggesting that state institutions would outlive and outlast kinship domains in Africa.

I argue that in the long historical run the proper relationship between state and kinship hinges on how much each of these societal institutions services individuals' basic security needs. Kinship disappears from societal structures whenever alternative institutions, principally states, provide for individuals' basic security needs. If states fail to do so, kinship becomes a source of security for the individual, acquiring the status of surrogate statehood in some instances. Indeed, if the state becomes the source of individuals' insecurities, if the state persecutes individuals, they will construct a kinship system that will enable them to survive the state's transgressions. Africans on the African continent and African Americans have both experienced conditions that predispose them to be subject to this thesis.

TWO PERSPECTIVES ON AFRICAN SOCIAL DEVELOPMENT: MODERNIZATION THEORY AND THE SOCIAL HISTORY OF THE SLAVE TRADE

Modernization theory, a staple of the social sciences in the early decades of the postcolonial era, was as dominant in African studies in the 1950s–1970s as cultural studies have proved to be in the 1990s. Although it was festooned with tedious phraseology from fashionable Parsonian sociology,[1] modernization theory had a well-organized central thesis: Postcolonial African nations—like other "developing" countries of the Third World in Asia and Latin America—would emerge from backward and traditional circumstances into full-fledged modernity as soon as the *nation state* became relevant and central to the lives of its citizens, displacing benighted *kinship* systems which had hitherto ruled Africans' lives. Richard Fox (1971: 129) made this point forcefully: "Kinship withers away as society passes from primitive to the complex. Familial etiquette gives way to class relationship." Morton Fried, another influential modernization theorist, saw the relationship between state and kinship as incompatible, with kinship receding as state institutions become entrenched: "A state is better viewed as the complex of institutions by means of which the power of the society is organized on a basis superior to kinship" (Fried 1967: 229). Thus, modernization theory posited an inverse relationship between kinship and state in the evolution of a political society. According to this view, the expansion of one necessarily doomed the existence of the other, even in Africa. The march from tradition to modernity would follow along the pathways carved out by such modernization measures as mass education of young people in Western schools and ways, the introduction of mass communications, and the economic improvement of these nations—leading to enhanced per capita income for their citizens (thus see Lerner 1958).

Unlike the current regnant regime of cultural studies in African studies of the 1990s, modernization theory was much more than a passive perspective coined by intellectuals. On the contrary, it was generously sponsored by several Western governmental agencies and foundations in the heat of the competition of the Cold War between Western capitalist nations and Soviet communism. The independence decade of the 1960s was bolstered by the intellectual stimulation of the Cold War that urged on the West an expansion of its commitments to the newly independent countries of Africa and Asia. Its mission was to save these new nation-states from the "appeals of communism" (see Almond 1965) by endowing them with economic progress and the whole package that is associated with the totality of development (thus, Almond and Coleman 1960; Rostow 1961). These aids were given on the grounds of the intellectual suasion that as standards of living of Africans rose with the economic development of their new nation-states, as their educational capabilities were elevated with improved educational facilities, as communications between communities multiplied with expanded print and electronic media, so would the prospects of democracy increase in the new nations of Africa, allowing individuals to free themselves from kinship domains and to associate with one another across kinship fault lines in new emergent civil communities of the nation-state.

Modernization theory in the social sciences had its counterpart in historical scholarship. J.D. Fage's influential historical interpretation of the slave trade was based on the idea that the international slave trade was good for African political development because it helped to modernize Africa by upgrading its capabilities to construct state institutions while it destroyed Africa's rampant kinship systems. He writes:

> On the whole it is probably true to say that the operation of the slave trade may have tended to integrate, strengthen and develop unitary, territorial political authority, [and] to weaken or destroy more segmentary [i.e., kinship] societies. Whether this was good or evil may be a nice point; historically it may be seen as purposive and perhaps as more or less inevitable. (Fage 1969: 402)

From the point of view of this argument, there was the presumption that the abundant kinship that colonial social anthropologists chronicled for most communities on the continent in the late nineteenth and early twentieth centuries was natural to Africa and that it predated the slave trade. Fage views the destruction of kinship as slave trade's major achievement. Thus, he chided Walter Rodney (1966, 1972) for having "regarded as wholly bad what happened in Africa as a consequence . . . of the trade with Europeans and the trade in slaves in particular" (Fage 1989: 109–110). In Fage's view, Rodney had

> underestimated what Africans themselves were achieving in West Africa through their imposition on small-scale kinship societies of the ever larger and more determinate economic, political, military and bureaucratic structures that we call kingdoms and empires. As I see it, much of this was more or less inevitable as horizons were opened up. It seems not unreasonable to think that what was happening in West Africa by the seventeenth and eighteenth centuries (if not in the nineteenth) was not at all different from what had happened rather earlier in western Europe. (Fage 1989: 110)

Because modernization theory was clear in its intentions and indeed had a predictive character, its validity could be assessed directly. In this respect, modernization theory proved to be invalid and incorrect in most of its claims. For instance, the expected decay of kinship that would accompany the invigoration of African states never occurred. On the contrary, kinship expanded enormously even as the state grew under the aegis of modernization theory's programs of development, virtually following a course that Clifford Geertz (1963) anticipated in an influential paper that, in effect, challenged the linear projection of modernization theory and the view that modernization of traditional societies would only involve rational civil ties (also see Ekeh 1975). As one observer of these modernization programs put it,

> Within the process of modernization in the West, the features of intensive urbanization, extensive migration, geographical and social mobility have been associated with a concomitant decline in the importance of wide kinship ties. . . . By contrast, in Africa strong and extensive kinship ties . . . have altered little. Ethnic associations have not only persisted, in many cases they have increased in importance in the new towns and cities. (Plotnicov 1970: 1970: 66–7)

Nor has the retrospective application of modernization theoretical perspectives in the interpretation of the slave trade fared well. Fage's claims of benefits of the slave trade for the enhancement of state traditions and the concomitant weakening of kinship have been challenged—with one counterclaim that the slave trade weakened state traditions in Africa (Wrigley 1971), and another that it emboldened kinship (Ekeh 1990: 673–683), during slave trade's centuries of dominance.

How would one account for the failures of modernization theory and its counterpart in African history in predicting the demise of kinship in African social life? The truth of the matter is that modernization theory's daring proposition that kinship would wither away from African history, while the state advanced, and Fage's interpretation of the slave trade as being inimical to kinship and beneficial to state formation were adaptations from one particular version of European history. These strands of African studies have lifted such propositions from classical experiences in the relationships between state and kinship in those areas of European history that experienced feudalism and then applied them to Africa. In order to fully explain the weaknesses of these faulty applications and to see why kinship has continued to grow while state traditions have been imperiled in Africa, we must visit with the history of European kinship and its relationship to the European state.

STATE AND KINSHIP IN EUROPEAN HISTORY AS MODELS FOR AFRICAN HISTORY

The protestation of Afrocentricism[2] notwithstanding, the dominant interpretations and analyses of African history and social science have largely been borrowed from models of Western European historic experiences. Modernization theory was one glaring example of a theory of African societies that was crafted on the European historic experience. It made the path of European history of development a universal one and then projected Africa's future along it. In the course of European history, kinship gave way to state institutions and withered away. Borrowing from such experiences, modernization theory assumed that the strategy of strengthening the postcolonial state would yield the same results for Africa, leading to robust states while kinship would grow jejune and eventually die out of African history.

What was critically amiss in modernization theory is a clear recognition of the intervening role of individuals' security needs in the interplay between kinship and state in the evolution of political society. The relationship between state and kinship in the European history of progress that modernization theory mimicked was not a direct one. Rather, it was mediated by the imperatives of ordinary individuals' basic security needs. When kinship corporations supplied these, it mattered in the lives of ordinary individuals and kinship corporations flourished in ancient European communities. When it failed to do so, they looked elsewhere to meet their basic security needs, including protection from violence, allowing feudal state institutions to replace kinship.

Historians applying such reasoning as grounds for the emergence of state institutions in their work in Africa have been more detailed and more skillful than modernization theorists. They have followed the process by which kinship died out of European history. Two notable instances will make my point. Fage assumed that the history of the African slave trade followed European history of development in which individuals coped with violence by seeking the protection of powerful princes. The slave trade, argued Fage, introduced a level of violence that compelled individuals to seek protection from feudal chieftains, building up new bonds between state functionaries and the "subjects" of these chieftains. He writes: "Not to belong to a king or one of his feudatories was to be dangerously exposed" during the violence of the slave trade (Fage 1974: 14). Therefore, Fage reasoned, kinship was weakened while state institutions were strengthened by the slave trade. This appears to be an undisguised extrapolation from the record of the ways in which individuals reacted to the European history of violence in medieval times. Another student of African history directly applied the model of European history to the career of violence in Borno among the Kanuri of northeastern Nigeria. Ronald Cohen (1966: 92–95) believed that Borno was on the verge of developing feudal institutions from its history of violence, in the same way Europe developed one. Cohen cited Marc Bloch's theory of the rise of feudalism in Europe as the right authority for his interpretation.

Marc Bloch (1940) theorized that feudalism arose in Western Europe in response to external violence—from the Vikings in the north, Hungarians in the east, and Arabs in the south—that besieged Western European communities in medieval times. Kinship, which had previously protected individuals from small-scale violence, was no longer able to do so in the face of such a volume of violence. Individuals were then compelled to seek new sources of security from feudal lords. Bloch (1940: 443) says, "feudal ties were developed when those of kinship proved inadequate." Accordingly, feudal ties, and subsequently state institutions, grew at the expense of kinship (also see Maine 1888: 155–6; Hintze 1929: 27). It is this version of European history that has been applied to African history and social science.

There is another version of the European history of progress which Africanist applications of models of European history have ignored. Kinship did not perish from all of European history by yielding to feudal forces. As Bloch (1940: 142) himself noted, "the only regions in which powerful agnatic groups survived—German lands on the shores of the North Sea, Celtic districts of the British Isles—knew nothing of vassalage, the fief and the manor." In this respect Irish history provides another compelling model in European history of kinship. Although the Irish shared with the rest of the inhabitants of the British Isles the torments of Vikings' invasions, it is the subjugation of the Irish by the English that had a greater impact on their social institutions. While corporate kinship had collapsed from English, German, and French societies quite early in the medieval era, yielding to feudalism (see Phillpotts 1913, Murray 1983, and Miranda 1974), kinship flourished in Irish history well up to late Medieval times.

Irish kinship survived and indeed expanded alongside English rule and its colonial state in Ireland. Arguing against an evolutionary interpretation that minimized kinship in Irish history in the interest of a false assumption "that a reduction in the scale of kinship organization is a sign of advancing modernity," Nerys Patterson (1991: 27) cogently maintains that "Ireland swarmed with kinship corporations of all sizes until the Tudor conquest." "In this respect, Ireland in the late Middle Ages was far more of a kinship-based society than England [which had ceased to be so] for centuries" (1991: 11). Nor did the English conquest and rule of Ireland extinguish its kinship. In fact, English rule had to combat Ireland's "lax" kinship customs and laws which favored kinsmen with light communal punishment and reserved "capital punishment, mutilation, flogging and incarceration as fates for those who were not native members of the local [kindred], such as slaves" (Patterson 1991: 317). Kinlessless was a major calamity for affected individuals in kin-conscious medieval Ireland and frequently resulted in enslavement[3]—just as statelessness imposed hardship on, say, Jews in many state-conscious European countries in ancient and medieval times.

What can one gain from these models of the European history of kinship for studying African history and societies? And which of these two models is more appropriate for Africa's historical circumstances? We may now properly turn to these questions.

KINSHIP AND STATE IN AFRICAN HISTORY

Despite the sharp contrasts between the history of England (and feudalized Europe) and Celtic Irish history, these societies faced a common generic problem which, however, they solved differently. In feudal England, the state and its functionaries attempted to provide security for ordinary individuals against violence from outside the realm. In Ireland, the Irish state had been co-opted by Tudor conquerors who were perceived as enemies by the Irish. In Irish history, individuals could not entrust their security to state functionaries. In Irish circumstances, individuals had to construct alternative security systems against the insecurities inflicted by the state. Kinship was available for this function and did provide some security.

Because African and English encounters with state and kinship are dramatically distant from each other, it is an error for historians and social scientists to model African history on English experiences. And in seeking patterns of ancient and medieval European history that have parallels in African history, it is a blunder to ignore Irish experiences with state and kinship. This is so because Irish experience along these lines under Tudor conquest and imperialism bear remarkable similarities with fragments of African history during the eras of the slave trade and colonialism.

The generalized misfortunes that have befallen ordinary persons in African history began with the collapse of Songhai in 1591. Songhai, and the two pristine regimes of Ghana (550–1250) and Mali (1250–1350) that it succeeded in the West African region (otherwise called the Western Sudan by historians), had established state traditions of peace and justice. In the fourteenth century, an Arab traveler could testify to the responsibility of these kingdoms: "Among the virtues of the Sudanese, Ibn Battuta [an itinerant Arab scholar] counted the care they took in protecting the trade routes. On his way from Walata to the capital of Mali, he traveled with only one guide, because it was not necessary to go in caravan. In these conditions trade flourished and foreigners settled and conducted business in the Sudan" (Levtzion 1973: 163). Justice and peace were the undeniable emblems of the states of this region until the end of the sixteenth century.

Songhai's defeat and humiliation in 1591 by Arab Moroccan forces began an irreversible trend of the loss of autonomy for most African states. Morocco attacked Songhai in large part because it showed much independence and protected its citizens from exploitation by Muslim Arabs. Among the many consequences of Songhai's fall was a radical change in traditions of African state behaviors. Henceforth, successful African states relied on alliances with foreign potentates, rather than the imperatives of internal legitimacy, in their activities. These changes eventually sanctioned the slave trade and colonialism, in which African states became agents of either Arab or Western European nations and corporate interests in the exploitation and violation of ordinary Africans.[4]

The Slave Trade and the Strengthening of Kinship in Africa

In the sweep of world history, the slave trade from Africa by Arabs (c. 950–1850 CE) and Western Europeans (1460–1850) must be seen as embodying international organizations that implicated Arab and European states and nations, on the one hand, and local African states and their functionaries on the other. Among historians of the African slave trade, Rodney has been most perceptive in noting the reduction of African states to dependencies of European nations and factors that compelled African states to participate in the evil trade:

> Once trade in slaves had been started in any given part of Africa,
> it soon became clear that it was beyond the capacity of any single
> African state to change the situation. . . . [An] example of African
> resistance during the course of the slave trade comes from the Baga
> people in what is now the Republic of Guinea. The Baga lived in

small states, and in about 1720 one of their leaders (Tomba by name) aimed at securing an alliance to stop the slave traffic. He was defeated by local European resident-traders, mulattoes, and other slave trading Africans. . . .

Of course, it is only as a last resort that the capitalist metropoles need to use armed force to insure the pursuit of favorable policies in the dependent areas. Normally, economic weapons are sufficient. In the 1720s, Dahomey [through Agaja Trudo, Dahomey's greatest king] opposed European slave traders, and was deprived of European imports—some of which had become necessary by that time. . . . [The Europeans] failed to unseat him or to crush the Dahomean state, but in turn Agaja failed to persuade them to develop new lines of economic activity . . . being anxious to acquire firearms and cowries through the Europeans, he had to agree to the resumption of slave trading in 1730. (Rodney 1972: 80–81)

The dependency on, and addiction of many African states to, the traffic in captives can be amply illustrated from the plaintive request from the king of Asante to the King of England to agree to reopen the slave trade. Adu Boahen, the well-known Ghanaian historian, has brandished the following fragment of an entry in the diary of a British diplomat as a "very interesting and illuminating discussion that took place in 1820 between Joseph Dupuis, the British Counsel sent to Kumasi, the capital of the Asante Empire, and the Asantehene, [King] Osei Bonsu":

"Now," said the king, "A long time ago the great king [of England] liked plenty of trade, more than now; then many ships came, and they bought ivory, gold and slaves; but now he will not let the ships come as before, and the people [who do come] buy gold and ivory only. . . . Why does the king do so? . . .

"The white men who go to council with your master . . . do not understand my country, or they would not say that the slave trade was bad. But if they think it bad now, why did they not think it bad before? . . . If the great king would like to restore this trade it would be good for the white men and for me too. . . ." (Cited in Boahen 1987: 2–3)

For every such an instance of the corruption of African state traditions that can be traced to the European slave trade from Africa, many more can be attributed to the Arab slave trade, which spanned over eight centuries.

Who were the victims of such state corruption? They were mostly ordinary individuals,[5] particularly from stateless societies bordering or near slave trading states. These people were stateless and probably hated state organizations that threatened their perilous existence. They could neither trust nor rely on state functionaries and institutions for meeting their basic security needs. For them kinship formed the first and last lines of defense.

How then did kinship fare in Africa during the centuries of the slave trade? Unfortunately, there cannot be a direct answer to this question because colonial social anthropology, whose self-proclaimed business was the study of kinship, made the crippling intellectual assumption that kinship was eternal to Africa and was not variable in historical scholarship.[6] This has largely discouraged historical studies of kinship in Africa. In fact, however, there is great probability that kinship became entrenched during the centuries of the slave trade. Although we may no longer garner historical evidence on the increase or decrease in kinship networks in any given ethnic groupings during the slave trade, we have enough comparative data for coming to some important conclusions on the relationships between the slave trade and kinship in Africa. On the whole, it may be stated that kinship has tended to be strong in areas of Africa where the slave trade was prominent, particularly among its victims, whereas it has tended to be weak in regions where the slave trade was minimal or nonexistent.

Evidence for weak kinship comes from an area where the state was strong enough to resist pressures to participate fully in the slave trade. Of the major ancient African states that were dominant before the onset of the slave trade, Benin City (in modern southwestern Nigeria) stands out as one that concluded that it was not in its interest to become a slave trading power.[7] Such a policy apparently resulted from the painful history of the loss of many of its citizens through emigration in previous centuries. The modern ethnic neighbors of the Bini, principally the Urhobo to their east and the Ishan to their north, fled Benin City (commonly called *Ore-Edo*), between the thirteenth and sixteenth centuries (see Bradbury 1957). Remarkably, the Bini constructed a formidable moat around the city before the fifteenth century, not to fend off attacks from outside but to prevent large emigration.[8] The lack of Benin enthusiasm for the slave trade was therefore consistent with its history. The state and its citizens, of course, were spared the wholesale wars and ravages emanating from the slave trade that were visited on such other competing powers as Oyo in Yoruba country.

It is therefore remarkable that Benin's lack of elaborate participation in the slave trade is matched by a weak kinship system. Its kinship system was much weaker than those in other comparable African states that were riddled with the slave trade. The British anthropologist, R. E. Bradbury, was well impressed by the fact that Benin's kinship system was weaker than that in the neighboring Yoruba country (1973: 10–16). Bradbury went so far as to make this an Africa-wide comparison:

As compared with most [indigenous precolonial] African states (even nineteenth century Buganda or Dahomey) corporate descent

groups played a negligible role in Benin political organization. . . .
Neither at the village nor at the state level were political roles conceived in terms of the representation of descent groups. (Bradbury
1973: 78)

Surely, it is fair to assume that Benin's weak kinship system—as measured against comparable kingdoms which, however, participated in the
slave trade—had something to do with an absence of a history of heavy
involvement in the slave trade, in which participating states were predisposed to ignore the security needs of the common person.[9]

The evidence for the abundance of kinship in areas that suffered
greatly from the slave trade is even more compelling. All the classic cases
of stateless societies celebrated by colonial social anthropologists as segmentary lineage societies (see Middleton and Tait 1970), in which individuals developed profound agnatic ties, were communities that suffered
from the slave trade. The Tiv in northern Nigeria, the Tallensi in northen
Ghana, and the Nuer and Dimka in the Sudan were not only stateless societies, but also victims of state organizations. Kinship was their constant
companion because it offered some protection against the depredations
of the slave trade engineered by some neighboring slave-trading states and
powers and a consortium of international slave trading nations.

In these African societies kinship had the surrogate status of states.
Existence outside kinship networks was unacceptable and dangerous. That
this is so may be gleaned from the harsh treatment of kinlessness by the
Ibos of southeastern Nigeria. Nineteenth-century Iboland was ravaged by
the slave trade organized by the eastern Niger states of the Efik and the
Ijo, which were founded as primary slave-trading states with the help of
slave-trading Europeans (see Forde 1956, Jones 1963). To be kinless was a
moral transgression in an Ibo society suffused in kinship. Kinless persons
were exposed to dangers which they avoided by offering themselves and
their descendants as *osu*, community slaves who then were ritually protected as public wards by the priests of village gods (see Basden 1938, Isichei 1976)—obviously comparable to the phenomenon of fuidhirs among
the Irish in medieval times.

Colonialism and the Construction of Meta-Kinship in Africa

Among its many other virtues, Eric Williams's (1944) *Capitalism and
Slavery* eternally serves the scholarship of African history for having highlighted the key point that European colonialism in Africa was an extension of the economic logic of the slave trade. Both the slave trade and colonialism were compelled by the economic imperatives of the English
Industrial Revolution and its resulting social formation of capitalism.
While the slave trade helped the growth of mercantile capitalism in

England, colonialism supplied the tropical raw materials demanded by the second phase of capitalism, namely, industrial capitalism.

On the ground in Africa, colonialism made use of the same institutions as the slave trade. Whereas the European slave traders and their national European sponsors befriended Africa's indigenous states as their chief mechanism for gaining control of the captives from raids compelled by the slave trade, European imperialists subjugated Africa's indigenous states during the last two decades of the nineteenth century and the first two of the twentieth, turning them to new uses in the governance of their colonies. The resulting colonial state in Africa was an imported bald model of the Western state. It was supplemented in its operations by subjugated indigenous African states.

Colonialism also used the resources of kinship, which had become exceedingly entrenched in the centuries of the slave trade. The major European colonial powers funded social anthropological researches whose main purpose was to discover the principles of kinship organization in Africa (see Lackner 1973, Ekeh 1990: 665–669). The European imperialists' chief goal in these efforts was to discover African folkways that would allow their new subjects to develop in their customary paths of kinship.[10] Colonialism thus deliberately encouraged kinship, whose institutions would enable Africans to ply their wonted existence, causing little disruption in the colonies. Colonialism entailed administration on the cheap, encouraging any low-cost method of governance, which kinship and its ideologies readily supplied.

Colonialism's fraternization with kinship helped its expansion during the colonial era by allowing it to spawn meta-kinship corporations. Under the regime of the slave trade, kinship was compact, usually bonding immediate kinsfolk in village settings. Under colonialism, its range and ideology expanded into ethnic groups, many of which used the new technologies of literacy to knit related fragments of kinship groupings and languages into composite ethnic groups (see Ekeh 1983, 1994; Abernathy 1969: 110). Ironically, the difficult years of European colonialism saw the crystallization of large ethnic groups that expanded the meaning of kinship from little bodies of kinsfolk, villagers, or small communities of agnates to vast numbers that the ethnic groups now claimed and served.[11]

The Postcolonial State and Expansion of Meta-Kinship in Africa

The irony in the career of kinship in Africa is that the postcolonial era saw its continued growth rather than its demise. There are two principal reasons for the consolidation of kinship in postcolonial Africa. First, the state and its functionaries continued the colonial practice of keeping a distance from meeting the basic needs of its citizens. In effect, the postcolonial African state has accepted the norms of colonial statehood in its relations to citizens by assuming that the basic needs of citizens should be met by kinship groupings rather than the state. These basic needs include the rules for the socialization and education of young people (for which few African states assume any responsibility); the burial and funeral needs of individuals; and the welfare of families of deceased persons, including the management of the deceased's estate. In all these respects, there is widespread assumption that the state has little or no role to play in periods when an individual is helpless to make decisions affecting his life and the welfare of his family. In all these circumstances, kinship groups have become dominant, while the state's role has been exiguous.

A second reason for the consolidation of kinship in the postcolonial era is the increasing campaign of terror by state agencies against the masses. Widespread dictatorship has ruined democratic prospects in many African nations, turning the police and other state agencies on their own citizens with impunity (see Lawyers Committee for Human Rights 1992). In countries like the Democratic Republic of the Congo, where the state has become a liability for the individual, kinship has flourished with a brilliance that was unimaginable a few decades ago. The failure of rulership and the rise of military and personal dictatorships have caused considerable alienation of Africans from state institutions, pushing them into the entrails of kinship (see Ekeh 1995).

KINSHIP AND STATE IN THE AFRICAN AMERICAN EXPERIENCE

Although Africans and their kinsfolk across the Atlantic have been separated for centuries now, they share common experiences with respect to relationships with the state. In some sense, having been subjected to double-barreled persecution by state institutions in Africa and America, African Americans' collective memories probably provide the most outstanding examples of the state's capacity to commit acts of oppression. Their ancestors were victims of the international slave trade organized by state forces in Europe and Africa. In America, their ancestors and they themselves have been subjected to unprecedented abuse and discrimination in the hands of a well-organized state system which for most of its history of more than two hundred years allowed race to be a basis of state policy. It is fair to say that until the mid-1960s, and in spite of regional and temporal exceptions to a widespread pattern, blacks were alienated from the American state in a manner that was ingrained and pandemic.

Did African Americans respond to their abuse at the hands of state institutions and functionaries, as Africans did, by building up formidable kinship corporations? There are of course remarkable differences in the circumstances of Africans and their migrant kinsfolk in America. First, kinship as an ideology and as a form of social organization has always been privileged in African social history. Its existence as a social institution has not been attacked and challenged. In contrast, in Black America, there were deliberate attempts to disrupt the ideas of kinship and marriage among African Americans as imagined by their ancestors from Africa.[12] Second, whereas most social institutions, such as religion, that help persecuted individuals to survive have been appropriated by kinship in Africa, they grew independently of kinship among African Americans. Thus the Black Church has grown as a source of succor for blacks persecuted by the state in America (thus see Lincoln and Mamiya 1990, Paris 1985). Third, of the various fractions of the African diaspora in the Americas, blacks in the United States have been a distinct minority in ways that, for instance, African Caribbeans have not experienced.[13]

Given these circumstances and differences between African Americans and their African and Caribbean relatives, it would be logical to expect that kinship would be less outstanding among African Americans than it is with blacks on the African continent or in the Caribbean. It is therefore remarkable that, during slavery and after, African Americans constructed an elaborate kinship tradition. In his masterful book on Black American kinship, Herbert Gutman shows convincingly how "Afro-Americans . . . adapted to enslavement by developing distinctive domestic arrangements and kin networks that nurtured a new Afro-American culture, and how these, in turn, formed the social basis of developing Afro-American communities" (Gutman 1976: 3). The origins of African Americans' penchant for enacting kinship behaviors probably dates back to an era when "to the negro the plantation is his country and the 'family' his state" (Gannet 1865: cited in Gutman 1976: 185).

African American kinship is distinctive. It may have profited from memories of African kinship practices that were passed from generation to generation. But it had (and still has) features which are either absent or minimal in African kinship. First, kinship in Africa has been built around two attributes which African American history lacks. African kinship is closely tied to ownership of an ethnic territory and to an ethnic language.[14] Lacking these attributes, kinship in Black America has been far more intellectual and less localized. African kinsmen clothe themselves in the idioms of shared territory and language. The New World of America removed these restrictive attributes from enslaved Africans. They had to reconstruct their kinship norms in nonterritorial and nonlinguistic ideologies. Robert Staples (1974: 4) makes this point well:

> In their state of involuntary servitude, the slaves began to form a new sense of family. Whereas, in African society, the family was based on the system of kinship within the tribe, under slavery it was the community of slaves in which the individual found his identity. *Tribal affiliation was reorganized to encompass those individu-*

als bound together by the commonality of their blackness and their enslavement. It was in this context that many of the traditional functions of the family were carried out and the former philosophical principle of survival of the tribe held fast. (Emphasis added.)

Second, the use of names to construct kinship is uniquely African American, not necessarily borrowed from African kinship practices. Although naming practices are very much part of African kinship, they largely serve symbolically to cement existing blood relationships. In Black America, naming routines were used in an instrumental way to construct kinship: "slave naming practices . . . indicate how kin obligation was transformed into enlarged slave social obligation" (Gutman 1976: 182) in the face of an intrusive state and slave-owning functionaries who sought to curtail the freedom of everyone in the slave community and disrupt its social organization. Thus, despite the fact that the state recognized only "uterine" descent for the offspring of slaves, "children were named for fathers [possibly] because fathers were more likely to be separated from their children than mothers" (Gutman 1976: 190). Similarly, naming children for grandparents and extended blood relatives consolidated kinship networks in a dramatic way.

Third, the creative use of fictive kinship—including the employment of such terms as "auntie," "uncle," and "brother" or "sister"—to enlarge African American kin bonds and communities was especially an invention of African American kinship: "Fictive, or quasi, kin played yet other roles in developing slave communities, *binding unrelated adults to one another* and thereby infusing enlarged slave communities with conceptions of obligations that had flowed initially from kin obligations rooted in blood and marriage" (Gutman 1976: 220, italics in original; also compare Mintz and Price 1992).[15]

Why did African Americans resort to constructions of such elaborate kinship systems? Answers vary considerably—from habitude with kinship, from their African past (thus see Foster 1983, Nobles 1974), to mundane necessities of fellowship among persecuted persons. While such suggestions may well have some merit, an intellectually credible response to this question should take into account the larger history of the harsh circumstances of state control that African Americans have survived on the American continent for several centuries. A great deal of that history is related to their basic security needs and the American state's role in denying them access to mechanisms for wholesome survival. Kinship grew brilliantly under slavery and after, when blacks were persecuted—many times through the actions and laws of the state. In those circumstances, kinship played the role of state surrogate. The expansion of kinship compassion and norms of behavior to those blacks in peril—but who could not rely on the state for their basic security needs—indicates the extraordinary role of kinship among African Americans. Gutman (1976: 226) notes: "Obligations toward nonslave kin were most powerfully expressed during and just after the Civil War in the attention ex-slaves gave to black children orphaned by the sale and death of their parents, by parental desertion, and by wartime dislocation. . . . Some were absorbed into extended kin-groups, and others found places with non-kin." In effect, this form of extended kinship was playing the role of the state in meeting the security needs of an expanded community of kinsfolk which was now imagined as being coextensive with all blacks.

The unique construction of extended kinship by African Americans, who operated outside the benefits of the state's security and legal systems, contrasted sharply with those of contemporary whites. In this regard, we must note, with respect, Herbert Gutman's wise speculation about kinship among whites in America before the Civil War:

> It will be surprising if . . . Lewis Sterling and his family as well as the family of John Foster Dulles's forebears knew anything like the complex kin networks . . . as the enslaved men, women, and children they owned. . . . [Any study of this subject] will probably show that enlarged kin networks and the social obligations flowing from them were comparatively much more important to Afro-Americans than to lower-class native white and immigrant Americans. (Gutman 1976: 212–213)

That the construction and strength of African American kinship are tied to the state's activities with respect to black Americans' basic security needs may be imagined from the weakening of kinship bonds since African Americans gained access to the American state in the 1960s (see Jewell 1988). Older African Americans bemoan the careless disregard for kinship among younger blacks who were born into an America whose governments now include blacks in legal and social security concerns. Even so, unease in the relationships between the American state and African Americans lingers on. So also is the greater prominence of African Americans' regard for kinship than that of whites, as witness the clan-like assemblies of black "family reunions" during America's famous week-end public holidays.[16]

KINSHIP AND THE CONSTRUCTION OF PRIMORDIAL CONSCIOUSNESS

One outstanding consequence of kinship is its constitutive social formation of primordial consciousness. Wherever kinship has a powerful sway, its adherents are moved at the visceral level to demonstrate a community of feelings among the putative kindred when the basic security needs of its members are threatened. Primordial consciousness embodies a degree of empathy for putative kinsmen that one will not exercise for those who are outside the perimeters of the assumed kindred. On the positive side, primordial consciousness can generate mutual compassion for those in the primordial fold, allowing individuals to sacrifice heavily for members whose welfare and security needs are in danger. On the negative side, primordial consciousness can generate hostility to groups that appear to threaten the survival of adherents' kinship identity.

Kinship's hold over the putative kindred is therefore a great deal stronger than would be indicated by rational calculations of measurable economic benefits that its members gain from their interrelationships. Kinship is, in a manner of speaking, an underground spring of sentiments which sometimes will remain dormant in periods of normalcy but which will erupt into mighty passions in periods of crises that threaten the corporate existence of the kindred. It exercises a moral bond among those who share in its sentiments. Primordial consciousness will of course vary from one form of kinship to another, and the primordial consciousness associated with African kinship is remarkably different from that which has developed from African American kinship.

Ethnic Consciousness in Black Africa

The primordial consciousness that has been cultivated as an aspect of kinship in Africa is closely associated with ethnic groups. Largely defined by its two central attributes of land and language, the dominant form of kinship in Africa has produced a specialized form of primordial consciousness that has sought to include all members who share these characteristics. They have a region and a specified land area that they point to as theirs, and they speak a common language. Often, they will sacrifice their lives defending the domains of their ethnicity. But they will also help to protect weak ones within their kinship's domains. At many other times, members will sacrifice much to defend the sanctity of their kinship heritage against outsiders. Interethnic conflicts will often involve issues that puzzle nonpartisan observers as to their economic and rational value. But ethnic primordial consciousness is not always about rationality. It can be ferociously irrational. Ethnic consciousness in Africa often precludes the wide domain of race consciousness. Indeed, most Africans have no conception of race.[17] Among Africans, the power of race is displaced by ethnic consciousness.

Race Consciousness in Black America

Most white Americans identify with two forms of primordial consciousness. They identify first with an ethnic grouping and secondly with the white race. Thus, Polish Americans will identify with their ethnic Polish origins while also asserting their membership in a dominant white race in America. The same can be said of Italians, Irish, and other fractions of European Americans. This pattern of primordial identity is also common with Asian Americans, who will express Japanese, Chinese, or Korean identities while claiming a common Asian identity. These forms of primordial consciousness are different from Africa's, largely because freedom of movement and the dominance of a common English language have endowed American ethnicity with an expansiveness and mobility that are lacking in Africa.

Remarkably, by exercising a single form of primordial consciousness, African Americans are different from Asian and white Americans. African Americans lack any sense of ethnic consciousness. Their common history under slavery and after has predisposed them to forgo an ethnic identity. Instead, they evince a bold form of race consciousness in which they have invested a great deal of sentiment. While an Italian or Irish American will share sentiments between ethnic consciousness and racial consciousness, African Americans' sentiments are concentrated on the single identity of race. This singularity of primordial identity, as well as the absence of land and language as defining parameters of identity, has foisted on African Americans an intellectual representation of their primordial consciousness in ways that are unique—at any rate in ways far removed from the localization of African kinship's primordial identities. Race among African Americans is an intellectual construction in much the same way as Jewish history has intellectualized Jewish identities. Such intellectualization has enabled African Americans to incorporate many black groups into their form of primordial consciousness, although they have been unable to understand the strength of ethnic primordialism in Africa.

Primordial Consciousness and Interactions between Africans and African Americans

Interactions between African Americans and their African relatives have a long history with various shades of comfort and discomfort. In modern times, African Americans have expressed concern about the chronic inability of Africa's ethnic groups to get along with one another. "Why should the Zulu fight the Xhosa? Are they not all black?" is a common query. The answer, of course, is that Africans are governed by a form of primordial consciousness that is different from that of their American relatives-in-diaspora, not allowing them to exercise the type of unity of action that African Americans are used to.[18]

What is remarkable is that the predominance of race consciousness among African Americans allows them to see Africa differently from blacks on the African continent. Black Americans see and consider Black

Africa and its problems as a single piece. On the other hand, Africans' own perspectives on Africa and its problems are sieved through their fragmented primordial ethnic consciousness. Ironically, then, African Americans have more wholesome viewpoints on African problems than do native Africans. Two examples of African Americans' superiority in this respect will serve to establish my point.

Pan-Africanism. Pan-Africanism was a movement of the early twentieth century that attempted to bring the benefits of the modern world to Africa and allow its nations to gain freedom from foreign rule. Its origins were in Black America and its steady influence and guardian was the African American intellectual W. E. B. Du Bois (see Geiss 1974, Padmore 1963). Pan-Africanism's origins fully reflect the character and dimensions of African Americans' primordial consciousness. Although it is doubtful that Pan-Africanism could have been constructed inside Africa, the movement eventually had its African following. Two of Du Bois's intellectual followers, Nnamdi Azikiwe of Nigeria and Kwame Nkrumah of Ghana, did a great deal to popularize the principles of Pan-Africanism inside Africa. But the opposition to both of these protagonists of Pan-Africanism, largely based on the narrow grounds of primordial ethnic sentiments, ruined their efforts.

Kente Cloth. A more recent indication of the power of African Americans' primordial sentiments in shaping social usages inside Africa is the spread of the Asante cloth called *kente*. Kente is a traditionally embroidered cloth donned on ceremonial occasions among the Asante. It was hardly a Ghanaian national ceremonial dress, given its identification with the strongly ethnic Asante. But some time in the mid 1980s, Black America decided to adopt this clothing item in ceremonies. It began to appear at academic graduations and other ritual occasions among African Americans. Now, in the short order of less than ten years, kente is appearing as Africa's international dress—in Southern, East, and even West Africa! Again, the use of kente as a pan-African customary wear could only be successfully originated in Black America. It is doubtful that West Africa's other strong ethnic groups—in Nigeria and elsewhere—would have considered kente as a pan-African wear, without its introduction by African Americans.

NOTES

1. Talcott Parsons, a major exponent of the so-called school of structural functionalism in sociology, supplied the main concepts and tools, in a series of publications (thus see especially Parsons 1951, 1960), that modernization theorists applied in their analysis of projected social change in the developing countries of Asia and Africa.

2. Afrocentricism seeks to study African history and societies in their own terms, without gratuitous borrowing from the methodologies of Western history and social science. It adopts its authority from Cheika Anta Diop's (e.g. 1955, 1981) studies of Egypt and other pre-Arab civilizations of the Nile Valley as the sole foundations of authentic African history. Consider the following from Diop (1955: xiv): "Ancient Egypt was a Negro civilization. The history of Black Africa will remain suspended in air and cannot be written correctly until African historians dare to connect it with the history of Egypt. . . . The African historian who evades the problem of Egypt is neither modest nor objective, nor unruffled; he is ignorant, cowardly and neurotic."

3. See Maine's (1888: 172–75) analysis of the dangers of kinlessness in medieval Irish society: "The territory of every Irish tribe appears to have had settled on it . . . certain classes of persons whose condition was much nearer to slavery than that of [impoverished] free tribesmen. . . . It consisted of the *Fuidhirs*, the strangers or fugitives from other territories, men, in fact, who had broken from the original tribal bond which gave them a place in the community, and who had to obtain another as best they might in a new tribe or a new place. . . . Now, the Fuidhir tenant was exclusively a dependent of the Chief, and was through him alone connected with the Tribe. The responsibility for crime, which in the natural state of Irish society attached to the Family or Tribe, attached in the case of the Fuidhirs, to the Chief, who in fact became to this class of tenants that which their original tribesmen or kindred had been. Moreover, the land which they cultivated in their place of refuge was not theirs but his."

4. Walter Rodney's scepticism about African scholars' celebration of these states avoids their remarkable distinction—reckoned in terms of their autonomy and integrity—from the states that succeeded them. Rodney (1972: 56) writes: "The Western Sudanic empires of Ghana, Mali, and Songhai have become by-words in the struggle to illustrate the achievements of the African past. That is the area to which African nationalists and progressive whites point when they want to prove that Africans too were capable of political, administrative, and military greatness in the epoch before the white men." The problem with Rodney's caution is that it fails to indicate that after Songhai's fall, state traditions became subservient to Arab and European imperatives. Rodney also fails to note that Arab incursions into Africa did at least as much harm to African state traditions as European subjugation of Africans in the slave trade and colonialism.

5. It should be added, though, that the corruption of state institutions during the era of the slave trade did not spare even the aristocratic and military classes. Thus, in Abubakar Balewa's *Shaihu Umar*, which provides a realistic ethnohistory of the slave trade and its slave raids in the Fulani empire of the Sokoto Caliphate, palace intrigues led to the banishment and enslavement of members of chiefly families (see Balewa 1967). The Oyo state of Yoruba country fought a ferocious civil war in the nineteenth century, from which military captives were sold into the slave trade (see Mabogunje and Omer-Cooper 1971).

6. Thus, in his extensive analysis of kinship in Africa, Radcliffe-Brown

(1950: 2), doyen of British colonial social anthropology, vowed, "We cannot have a history of African institutions."

7. See Ryder's (1969: 198) conclusion on this point: "There is no evidence that Benin ever organized a great slave raiding network similar to that which supplied the ports of the eastern [Niger] delta, or that it ever undertook systematic slave raiding. . . . Benin either could not or would not become a slave-trading state on a grand scale."

8. This is how Jacob Egharevba, the native Benin historian, narrated this aspect of his city's history: "In the midst of the [turmoil in the fourteenth century] many more of the citizens migrated in several groups and became founders and settlers of [neighboring territories]. . . . The people therefore cried out . . . [to the King]: 'King Ewuare, let the City of Benin be increased.' The *Oba* [King] then hysterically dug the ditch or moat which is in the heart of the City to prevent his few remaining subjects from further desertion" (Egharevba 1973: 11).

9. Another piece of evidence for Benin's weak kinship system may be gleaned from its protofeudal tradition of primogeniture. Royal succession is regulated by the fixture of primogeniture, whereas in the neighboring Yoruba country, royal succession is based on a system of rotation among kin groups (see Egharevba 1934: 43–44; Bradbury 1973: 16, 97; Ekeh 1976: 70, 1990: 678).

10. Frederick Lugard, a main architect of British colonial policies in Africa, designed the famous colonial doctrine of indirect rule, which required the administration of Africans on their own separate terms, different from European modes of governance. Such a policy would engender "the true conception of the inter-relation of colour: complete uniformity in ideals . . . [but] in matters social and racial a separate path, each pursuing his own inherited traditions, preserving his own race-purity and race-pride" (Lugard 1922: 87).

11. The following passage, highlighted by Terrence Ranger (1983) in his survey of invented tradition in colonial Africa, is typical of this form of social formation under colonialism: "The British wrongly believed that the Tangayikans belonged to tribes; Tangayikans created tribes to function within the colonial framework. . . . [The] new political geography . . . would have been transient had it not coincided with similar trends among Africans. They too had to live amidst bewildering social complexity, which they ordered in kinship terms and buttressed with invented history" (Iliffe 1979: 324).

12. Thus among the characteristics and disadvantages of freed blacks listed by Keating (1903: 180) is the following: "*Suspicion of his own race.* He was taught to watch other Negroes and tell all that they did. This was slavery's native detective force to discover incipient insurrection." For views on the disruption of African marriages during slavery and efforts to regain lost freedom to raise a family through legal marriage, see Blasingame (1972: 87) and Absuz (1971).

13. Thus see Fogel and Engerman (1974: 22): "The absence of a sugar industry in the U.S. colonies also affected the size of the units on which [African slaves] lived. . . . Blacks in Jamaica and the other Caribbean is-

lands had little contact with the European culture of the white slaveowner both because of the small percentage of whites who lived on these islands and because of the enormous size of the typical sugar plantation. But blacks in the U.S. colonies were typically a minority of the population and lived on small units which brought them into continuous contact with their white masters."

14. There are two noteworthy exceptions to these rules of kinship in Africa. The Fulani in Nigeria have no territorial demarcations that they claim as their ethnic land, although they regard all Hausaland as theirs by right of conquest. They have also adopted the language of the Hausa, among whom they have lived for centuries and whom they conquered some two centuries ago. Another immigrant ethnic group with a similar history (conquest of an indigenous people whose land and language it has appropriated) is the Tutsi in Rwanda and Burundi in central Africa.

15. Also see Drew and Sims (1977: 62): "During the days of chattel slavery and for a considerable number of years afterwards, many Black families tended to be of the extended variety. This was so because the sale of slaves separated children from mothers, and husbands from wives. It was common for a slave mother to care for her own as well as the children from other unions. These siblings, in many cases, were destined never to know their real parents; too, the offspring of the slave master and an African woman could be found among them."

16. Thus, consider Littlejohn-Blake and Darling (1993: 460): "African Americans and Euro-American families have historically met the instrumental and expressive needs of their families differently. Most Euro-American families are a unit in which all or most of the functions and activities of family life are carried out in isolation from other kin. However, the African American family unit exists within the extended family and such functions and activities are shared by both. Whereas Euro-American families are more compatible with individualism and materialism, African American families show an interdependence or communal cooperation born out of necessity of providing a living."

17. This point was powerfully brought home to me when I read material in an autobiographical essay that my son, Anthony Ekeh, had written for a university course at Buffalo. Here is the relevant fragment: "I attended an International School at Ibadan where I learned to live beyond my means, discriminate against those who didn't try to be European in manners. . . . Interestingly enough, it was only when I got to America that I realized that I was black. And it is that kind of realization that one has to be thankful for. . . . A lot of everyday Africans back home hardly consider themselves to be anything other than who they are, everyday Africans. . . . Well, being a 'Black African' in the United States has broadened my perspectives and given me a view which Africans back home don't get. I can see a bigger picture concerning not just Africans in America (that is, African Americans), Africans in the Caribbean, or Africans on the African continent, but of all black people the world over."

18. When Rodney King was ferociously beaten by members of the Los

Angeles Police Department, there was an outpouring of outrage from all types of African Americans—old and young, wealthy and poor, and educated and uneducated—from all regions of America. I was impressed by this community of feelings and did inquire from a Nigerian compatriot what he thought would happen if such a beating occurred in Lagos, Nigeria. His answer was: "the Yoruba [ethnic group] would mourn him if the victim of such police brutality was Yoruba and the Ibo would complain if he was Ibo."

REFERENCES

Abernathy, David B. 1969. *The Political Dilemma of Popular Education. An African Case.* Stanford: Stanford University Press.

Absuz, Robert H. 1971. "The Black Family During Reconstruction." Pp. 26–39 in Nathan Huggins et al., eds., *Key Issues in the Afro-American Experience.* New York: Harcourt, Brace and Jovanovich.

Almond, Gabriel A. 1965. *The Appeals of Communism.* Princeton: Princeton University Press.

Almond, Gabriel A., and James S. Coleman. 1969. *The Politics of Developing Areas.* Princeton: Princeton University Press.

Balewa, Abubakar Tafawa. 1967. *Shaihu Umar.* English translation by M. Hiskett. London: Longmans.

Basden, G. T. 1938 [1966]. *Niger Ibos.* London: Frank Cass.

Blasingame, John. 1972. *The Slave Community.* New York: Oxford University Press.

Bloch, Marc. 1940 [1961]. *Feudal Society.* Chicago: The University of Chicago Press.

Boahen, A. Adu. 1987. *African Perspectives on Colonialism.* Baltimore: The Johns Hopkins University Press.

Bradbury, R.E. 1957. *The Benin Kingdom and the Edo-Speaking Peoples of South-Western Nigeria.* London: International African Institute.

Cohen, Ronald. 1966. "The Dynamics of Feudalism in Borno" in *African History,* vol. 2 of *Boston Papers on Africa,* Jeffrey Butler, ed., 85–105. Boston: Boston University Press.

Diop, Cheik Anta. 1955 [1974]. *The African Origin of Civilization, Myth or Reality.* Edited and translated by Mercer Cook. Chicago: Lawrence Hill Books.

———. 1981 [1991]. *Civilization or Barbarism: An Authentic Anthropology.* Chicago: Lawrence Hill Books.

Drew, James, and Ed Sims. 1977. "The African-American Clan." *The Pennsylvania Heritage,* 4(1, December).

Egharevba, Jacob. 1934 [1968]. *A Short History of Benin.* Ibadan: Ibadan University Press.

Egharevba, Jacob U. 1949–1952 [1971]. *The City of Benin . . . Benin Law and Custom . . . Some Stories of Ancient Benin . . . Some Tribal Gods of Southern Nigeria.* Nendeln, Kraus Reprint.

Ekeh, Peter P. 1975. "Colonialism and the Two Publics in Africa: A Theoretical Statement." *Comparative Studies in Society and History*, 17(1, January): 91–112.

———. 1976. "Benin and Thebes: Elementary Forms of Civilization." Pp. 65–93 in Werner Muensterberger, Aaron H. Esman, and L. Bryce Boyer, eds., *The Psychoanalytic Study of Society, Volume 7*. New Haven and London: Yale University Press.

———. 1983. *Colonialism and Social Structure. An Inaugural Lecture Delivered at the University of Ibadan*. Ibadan: Ibadan University Press.

———. 1990. "Social Anthropology and Two Contrasting Uses of Tribalism in Africa." *Comparative Studies in Society and History*, 32: 660–700.

———. 1994. "The Public Realm and Public Finance in Africa." Pp. 234–258 in Ulf Himmelstrand, Kabiru Kinyanjui and Edward Mburugu, eds., *African Perspectives on Development: Controversies, Dilemmas & Openings*. London: James Curry.

———. (1995). "African (Democratic) Theory." Pp. 1231–1238 in Seymour Martin Lipset, ed., *The Encyclopedia of Democracy, Volume IV*. Washington, DC: Congressional Quarterly Books.

Fage, J.D. 1969. "Slavery and the Slave Trade in the Context of West African History." *Journal of African History*, vol. 10, 393–404.

———. 1974. *States and Subjects in Sub-Saharan African History*. Johannesburg: Witwatersrand University Press.

———. 1989. "African Societies and the Atlantic Slave Trade." *Past & Present*, No. 125 (Nov.), 97–115.

Fogel, Robert William, and Stanley L. Engerman. 1974. *Time on the Cross*. Boston: Little, Brown.

Forde, Daryll, ed. 1956. *Efik Traders of Old Calabar. Containing the Diary of Antera Duke, an Efik Slave-Trading Chief of the Eighteenth Century*. London: International African Institute.

Foster, H. J. 1983. "African Patterns in the Afro-American Family." *Journal of Black Studies*, 14(2): 201–232.

Fox, R. G. 1971. *Kin, Clan, Raja and Rule: State-Hinterland Relations in Preindustrial India*. Berkeley: University of California Press.

Fried, Morton H. 1967. *The Evolution of Political Society*. New York: Random House.

Gannett, William G. 1865. "The Freedmen at Port Royal." *North American Review*, 208 (July), 1–28.

Geertz, Clifford. 1963. "The Integrative Revolution." In Clifford Geertz, ed., *Old Societies and New States: The Quest for Modernity in Asia and Africa*. Glencoe, Ill.: Free Press.

Geiss, Imanuel. 1974. *The Pan-African Movement: A History of Pan-Africanism in America, Europe, and Africa*. Translated by Ann Keep. New York: Africana Pub. Co.

Gutman, Herbert G. 1976. *The Black Family in Slavery and Freedom, 1750–1925*. New York: Pantheon Books.

Hintze, Otto. 1929 [1968]. "The Nature of Feudalism." Pp. 22–31 in Frederick L. Cheyette, ed., *Lordship and Community in Medieval Europe. Selected Readings*. New York: Holt, Rhinehart, and Winston, Inc.

Iliffe, John. 1979. *A Modern History of Tanganyika*. Cambridge [England]: Cambridge University Press.

Isichei, Elizabeth. 1976. *A History of the Igbo People*. New York: St. Martins Press.

Jewell, K. Sue. 1988. *Survival of the Black Family: The Institutional Impact of U.S. Social Policy*. New York: Praeger.

Jones, G. I. 1963. *The Trading States of the Oil Rivers: A Study of Political Development in Eastern Nigeria. Rivers. A Study of Political Development in Eastern Nigeria*. London: Oxford University Press.

Keating, H. T. 1903. "The Characteristics of the Negro People." Pp. 161–185 in Booker T. Washington, et al., *The Negro problem; a series of articles by representative American Negroes of To-day*. Miami, Fla.: Mnemosyne Pub. Inc., 1969.

Lackner, Helen. 1973. "Colonial Administration and Social Anthropology" in *Anthropology and the Colonial Encounter*, Talal Asad, ed., pp. 123–151. London: Ithaca Press.

Lawyers Committee for Human Rights. 1992. *The Nigerian Police Force: A Culture of Impunity*. Washington, DC: Lawyers Committee for Human Rights.

Lerner, Daniel. 1958. *The Passing of Traditional Society: Modernizing the Middle East*. With the collaboration of Lucille W. Pevsner, and an introduction by David Riesman. Glencoe, Ill.: Free Press.

Levtzion, Nehemia. 1973. *Ancient Ghana and Mali*. London: Methuen and Co.

Lincoln, C. Eric, and Lawrence H. Mamiya. 1990. *The Black Church in the African American Experience*. Durham, NC: Duke University Press.

Littlejohn-Blake, Sheila M., and Carol Anderson Darling. 1993. "Understanding the Strengths of African American Families." *Journal of Black Studies*, 23 (4, June): 460–471.

Lord Lugard. 1922 [1964]. *The Dual Mandate in British Tropical Africa*. London: Frank Cass & Co.

Mabogunje, A. L., and J. D. Omer-Cooper. 1971. *Owu in Yoruba History*. Ibadan: Ibadan University Press.

Maine, Sumner Henry. 1888. *Lectures on the Early History of Institutions*. New York: Henry Holt and Company.

Middleton, John, and David Tait, eds. 1970. *Tribes Without Rulers: Studies in African Segmentary Systems*. London: Routledge and Kegan Paul.

Mintz, Sidney Wilfred, and Richard Price. 1992. *The Birth of African-American Culture: An Anthropological Perspective*. Boston: Beacon Press.

Miranda, Pierre. 1974. *French Kinship: Structure and History*. The Hague: Mouton.

Murray, Alexander C. 1983. *Germanic Kinship Structure: Studies in Law and Society in Antiquity and the Early Middle Ages*. Toronto: Pontifical Institute of Medieval Studies.

Nobles, Wade. 1974. "African Root and American Fruit: The Black Family." *Journal of Behavioral and Social Science*, 20(Spring).

Padmore, George, ed. *History of the Pan-African Congress*. London: Hammersmith Bookshop, 1963.

Paris, Peter J. 1985. *The Social Teaching of the Black Churches*. Philadelphia: Fortress Press.

Parsons, Talcott. 1951. *The Social System*. Glencoe, Ill.: Free Press.

——. 1960. *Structure and Process in Modern Societies*. Glencoe, Ill.: Free Press.

Patterson, Nerys Thomas. 1991. *Cattle-Lords and Clansmen. Kinship and Rank in Early Ireland*. New York and London: Garland Publishing.

Phillpotts, Bertha Surtees. 1913 [1974]. *Kindred and Clan in Middle Ages and After: A Study in the Sociology of the Teutonic Races*. New York: Octagon Books.

Plotnicov, Leonard. 1970. "Rural-Urban Communications in Contemporary Nigeria: The Persistence of Traditional Institutions" in *The Passing of Tribal Man in Africa*, Peter C. Gutkind, ed., pp. 66–82. Leiden: E.J. Brill.

Radcliffe-Brown, A. R. 1950. "Introduction" in *African Systems of Kinship and Marriage*, A.R. Radcliffe-Brown and Daryll Forde, eds., pp. 1–85. London: Oxford University Press.

Ranger, T. O. 1983. "The Invention of Tradition in Colonial Africa" in *The Invention of Tradition*, Eric Hobsbawm and Terence Ranger, eds., pp. 211–262. New York: Cambridge University Press.

Rodney, Walter. 1966. "African Slavery and Other Forms of Social Oppression in the Context of the Atlantic Slave Trade." *Journal of African History*, 7(3): 431–443.

——. 1972. *How Europe Underdeveloped Africa*. Washington, DC: Howard University Press.

Rostow, Walt W. 1961. *The Stages of Economic Growth: A Non-Communist Manifesto*. Cambridge [England]: Cambridge University Press.

Ryder, A. F. C. 1969. *Benin and the Europeans, 1485–1897*. New York: Humanities Press.

Staples, Robert. 1974. "The Black Family in Evolutionary Perspectives." *The Black Scholar*, 5(9, June): 2–9.

Wrigley, C. C. 1971. "Historicism in Africa: Slavery and State Formation." *African Affairs: Journal of the Royal African Society*, vol. 170(no. 279, April), 113–124.

7

WAGES OF MIGRATION: JOBS AND HOMEOWNERSHIP AMONG BLACK AND WHITE WORKERS IN MUNCIE, INDIANA, 1920

Jack S. Blocker, Jr.

The migrations of African Americans during and after the Civil War represent a distinct phase of the African Diaspora. During this phase, African Americans initiated three historic self-transformations: ecological displacements from the southern to the northern United States and from rural to urban settings, and a socioeconomic metamorphosis from farmers and agricultural laborers into industrial workers. These changes flowed from decisions made by African Americans, and the greater scope for choice afforded by emancipation most clearly distinguishes this from the preceding stage of their diaspora. The contrast should not be overdrawn, as a generation of slavery scholarship has demonstrated that rarely were American slaves totally without options. Nevertheless, it seems clear that emancipation brought a much wider range of choices, and of these perhaps the most obvious and far-reaching was the decision to stay or to move.

During the years between the Civil War and the Great Depression, southern blacks' decisions about mobility were conditioned by the vicissitudes of the southern economy and the convolutions of political struggle to protect their constitutional rights. As southern white élites increasingly gained the upper hand through terrorism and legal manipulation, they directed their energies toward binding their black work force ever more tightly within the confines of southern society. Despite their best efforts, however, the South could not be walled off from the rest of the United States, and consequently the decision to migrate remained a choice open to blacks.[1] This essay explores the nature and the outcomes of the choices made by the migrants who settled in one northern city, Muncie, Indiana, before 1920.

The migrants who came to Muncie had chosen to leave the South or to move on from other places in the North. In addition, they chose Muncie in preference to other possible northern destinations: either the large cities which after 1890 received the lion's share of black migrants, or other small cities or towns. Their choices were typically informed by foreknowledge of their destination provided by friends or family members already in Muncie, and even migrants who had no personal contacts in Muncie often possessed some information about conditions there.[2] Given this degree of foreknowledge, what was there in Muncie that could have motivated them to choose this over other possible destinations?

Those who chose to move to Muncie could have justified their decision on a variety of grounds, including personal, familial, and communal as well as economic, social, and political. Of these, I investigate in this paper only the economic. By restricting my focus to economic conditions, I do not mean to imply that aspirations for material improvement are or were more "basic" than other possible motivations, or that a decision made on economic grounds precluded other reasons for migration. Indeed, I hope to illuminate the spectrum of possible motivations by defining as precisely as possible the scope of the economic.

Muncie in 1920 was a diversified industrial city. Its best-known works, the Ball Brothers Glass Manufacturing Company, had been for two decades the nation's leading maker of glass fruit jars, but the town also held other significant glass factories, such as the Hemingray Company, which made insulators for the rapidly expanding electrical industry. In addition, foundries, other metalworks, and a recently built Chevrolet assembly plant figured large on the local industrial scene. Industrialization had come to Muncie hard on the heels of major discoveries of natural gas in east central Indiana during the late 1880s, and many industries remained after the gas boom ended about fifteen years later.[3]

Muncie's industrialization fuelled rapid population growth, from about 5,000 in 1880 to more than 36,000 in 1920. Most of those who came to the Magic City during the third of a century before 1920 were whites, but Muncie's black population grew even faster, rising from only 3.6 percent of the total in 1880 to 5.6 percent in 1920. The proportion of blacks rose consistently during this period, with the sole exception of the decade of the 1890s, when a 77 percent increase in black population was surpassed by even faster growth in the white population (85 percent) (Table 1). In 1920, the proportion of African Americans in Muncie's population exceeded that in New York, Chicago, Cleveland, or Detroit.[4]

The acceleration of black population growth stimulated by the gas boom and Muncie's subsequent industrialization allowed the city to escape the fate of most other places in the middle of the midwestern urban hierarchy, whose black populations began deserting them after 1890 in favor of the region's biggest cities. This urban shift represented a new direction in African-American migration in the lower Midwest, as much of the movement of blacks into and within the region during the quarter-century after the Civil War had been directed toward smaller places.[5] In Indiana,

Table 1: Black Population of Muncie, 1860–1930

Year	Total Population	Black Population	Black Percentage
1860	1,782	16	0.9
1870	2,992	48	1.6
1880	5,219	187	3.6
1890	11,345	418	3.7
1900	20,942	739	3.5
1910	24,005	1,005	4.2
1920	36,524	2,054	5.6
1930	46,548	2,646	5.7

Sources: Joseph C. G. Kennedy, *Population of the United States in 1860* (Washington: Government Printing Office, 1864), 116; *Statistics of the Population of the United States at the Tenth Census, 1880* (Washington: GPO, 1883), 418; *Eleventh Census, 1890, Part I* (Washington: GPO, 1895), 457; *Fourteenth Census, 1920, Vol. II: Population* (Washington: GPO, 1922), 63; U.S. Bureau of the Census, *Negroes in the United States, 1920–32* (Washington: GPO, 1935), 58.

for example, just 20 percent of the state's black population in 1890 lived in Indianapolis, the only city of over 100,000. More than a third of Indiana's 1890 black population was rural, and nearly one-half lived in small towns and cities. During blacks' emigration from small cities, towns, and rural areas after 1890, only industrial communities in the gas belt and in the state's northwestern corner near Chicago were spared.[6] Muncie, then, in 1920 was not only a city which had consistently attracted black migration over the past 40 years, but also one which had drawn blacks who were increasingly reluctant to settle in most other small and mid-size towns and cities in its region.

To explore the outcomes of the choices made by Muncie's black migrants in 1920, I drew a sample from the federal manuscript census returns.[7] The sampling procedure was designed to select adult African Americans in such a manner as to reflect the distribution of black population across Muncie's nine wards and 21 enumeration districts; it produced a file of 384 cases (203 males and 181 females), which represents 18.7 percent of Muncie's black population.[8] For comparison, a sample of adult whites was drawn in similar fashion. The white sample consists of 358 cases (176 males and 182 females), 1.0 percent of Muncie's white population.[9] In order to provide further information on geographic mobility than could be obtained from a single census, both samples were linked to the 1910 manuscript census.[10]

As might be expected for such a rapidly growing city, most of the adult inhabitants of Muncie in 1920 had migrated there. The census schedules afford no precise measure to distinguish migrants from nonmigrants, but information on place of birth and presence in the community at the previous federal census demonstrate the migratory status of the population clearly enough. Only 30.1 percent of the combined sample were present in the Muncie area ten years before; of those who were, only a handful, 27 blacks and 73 whites, were natives of Indiana. And some of the native Hoosiers among both groups had no doubt moved to Muncie from some other place within the state. The maximum percentage of the sample who could have been native Munsonians (that is, who were both born in Indiana and present in 1910) is only 7.0 percent of the blacks and 20.4 percent of the whites, and the actual percentage who were Muncie-born is certainly lower. At least thirteen out of fourteen adult blacks and four out of five adult whites were migrants.

Consistent with the normal pattern of migration, most black migrants to Muncie in 1920 came from nearby origins. The two largest groups were Indianans and Kentuckians, each of whom represented nearly one-third of the sample. In view of the overall urban direction of black migration within Indiana, it is likely that those black Hoosiers who travelled to Muncie had come from smaller places—rural areas or small towns—within the state. Ohioans and Tennesseans were the next largest groups, at about ten percent each. In comparison to the pattern of origins of all United States–born Indiana blacks in 1920, Muncie was similar in its attraction to Indianans, Kentuckians, and Tennesseans, more attractive to Ohioans, North Carolinians, and Virginians than the statewide norm, and less appealing to migrants from Alabama and Georgia.[11]

In order to measure the outcomes of migrants' choices to come to Muncie, this study focuses on two aspects of their lives in 1920, jobs and real wealth accumulation in the form of homeownership. Although there is a substantial social-historical literature in which occupation is taken as a gauge of achievement, in this study jobs are considered as a means, not an end. Most jobs available in Muncie in 1920 were industrial jobs in mechanized factories, which means that they consisted of highly routinized, repetitive operations carried out under close supervision in uncomfortable and often dangerous conditions. Tenure was insecure, and an individual worker's chances for advancement were small. Under these conditions, workers' wives interviewed by Robert and Helen Lynd during the mid-1920s tended to regard the wages provided by their husbands' work as the principal reward for their labor.[12]

Whether families achieved homeownership will be taken as a measure of the rewards their members received for their labor. As historians John Bodnar, Roger Simon, and Michael Weber point out, "In the early twentieth century the purchase of a home was the most common form of wealth accumulation achieved by persisting unskilled workers and newcomers to the city." This was because "homeowning had several distinct advantages over renting. In addition to providing a sense of status, it gave the owners greater control over their environment, provided a form of enforced savings with a resultant equity, and had the potential of providing a source of income."[13] "Workers," adds historical geographer Richard Harris, "viewed their homes as a source of security in times of unemployment, sickness, and old age. Among a group of people who had little say in how their work was done, the home could be a place of real, if limited autonomy."[14]

Despite its advantages, homeownership was not necessarily the goal of every black family's efforts. Although they attribute lower rates of African-American homeownership in part to discrimination in jobs and housing, Bodnar, Simon, and Weber note evidence of higher career aspirations among black migrants to Pittsburgh than among European immigrants, as well as greater faith in the value of formal education. Such aspirations and such faith might have encouraged family strategies that de-emphasized homeownership in favor of pursuing better jobs for both the current and coming generations.[15] Some of the force of this contrast is lost in Muncie, which in 1920 held only a tiny immigrant population.[16] Nevertheless, because of the possibility that the aspirations of blacks and whites varied with regard to homeownership, comparisons between the two groups must be handled with care.

Interviewed in 1980, a black migrant to Muncie who had worked in one of the city's foundries recalled, "You could always get a job in Muncie when you couldn't get a job any place else. Used to be plenty of work here in the factories and the foundaries [sic]. . . . "[17] Comparison of the occupational distribution of blacks and whites reveals that for black men the available jobs were usually unskilled positions in factories (Table 2).[18] Only a handful of black men held white-collar positions, including two physicians and two ministers. Shop owners were few: two barbers, a cobbler, a grocer, and the owner of a shoe-shine parlor. Although a quarter of a century earlier a black clerk had been hired in the Muncie post office, the 1920 sample contained no black clerks or salesmen.[19] While unskilled wage laborers made up less than 20 percent of the white sample, nearly three out of five black workers fell into this category. The largest single group worked in foundries and metalworks, with another substantial group in glass factories. Black workers were significantly underrepresented among skilled and semi-skilled wage laborers, a grouping that included less than one in five blacks compared to nearly half of white workers; the most drastic difference was in Muncie's newest industry, autos and auto parts. Nevertheless, the glass and metals industries do seem to have offered some opportunity for black occupational advancement. In both industries, such opportunities were in apparently segregated jobs. Among white skilled and semi-skilled workers in glass factories were a foreman, a time keeper, a glass blower, and a pipefitter; none of these job titles was held by blacks, who were instead gas makers, white liners, a temperer, a takeoff man, and a fireman, titles which were not applied to white glassworkers. The only job title held by both a black and a white glassworker was "machinist." Among metalworkers, although the only job title shared by a

Table 2: Occupational Category by Color, Male Workers, Muncie, 1920 (in percentages)

	Whites	Blacks
Professional	1.8	2.5
High white collar	1.2	0.3
White collar	12.7	0.0
Nonretail proprietors	6.1	4.0
Retailers	1.8	0.5
Craftsmen	1.8	1.0
Skilled and semi-skilled wage labor	46.1	18.1
Glass	4.8	9.5
Metals	7.9	5.0
Autos and auto parts	15.8	1.5
Wood	0.6	0.5
Skilled and semi-skilled service workers	6.7	3.5
Unskilled wage labor	19.4	59.3
Glass	3.6	11.1
Metals	2.4	28.1
Autos and auto parts	4.8	3.5
Wood	3.0	2.5
Unskilled service workers	2.4	10.6
Total	100.0	100.0
N	165	199

Source: Study data.

white and a black worker was "drawer" in a wire mill, blacks clearly held skilled positions in both wire- and boiler-works: electrical engineer, crane operator, electrician, and boilermaker.

As Muncie's ability to attract black migrants after 1890 placed it in a class with larger industrial centers, so too did the occupational distribution of its male black work force. Although the use of varying classification schemes makes comparison difficult, Muncie's large majority of industrial workers ranks it alongside Chicago, Cleveland, Detroit, Milwaukee, and Norfolk, whose industrial workers seem to have numbered between one-third and three-quarters of the black male work force.[20] Muncie's concentration of industrial workers in fact places it toward the higher end of the distribution.

Besides the availability of industrial jobs, one probable reason for the relatively large concentration of black men in Muncie's industries was the small size of its black population, which afforded few opportunities for businesses dependent on the African-American community. Dependence of black-owned businesses upon black trade was a function of white reluctance to patronize them. As other historians have concluded, "By 1920 the black businessman was a rarity in the urban northeast."[21]

Another reason for the industrial concentration was the small number

*Table 3: Occupational Category by Color, Female Workers,
Muncie, 1920 (in percentages)*

	Whites	Blacks
White collar	40.0	1.4
Nonretail proprietors	14.3	11.1
Retailers	0.0	1.4
Craftswomen	5.7	2.8
Skilled and semi-skilled wage labor	14.3	4.2
Glass	2.9	4.2
Metals	5.7	0.0
Skilled and semi-skilled service workers	11.4	13.9
Unskilled wage labor	2.9	5.6
Glass	0.0	5.6
Unskilled service workers	11.4	59.7
Total	100.0	100.0
N	35	72

Source: Study data.

of black male Munsonians in domestic and personal service work. In larger urban centers this had historically been a major source of employment for black men, and the opening of industrial jobs in some of these cities during the decade 1910–20 generally represented new, and no doubt welcome, opportunities for higher-wage work.[22] But in Muncie, blacks had found a foothold in factory work from an early stage of the city's industrialization. Of the African-American men listed in the city directory in 1889, during the first flush of the gas boom, at least one-quarter worked in industrial occupations, and few were to be found in domestic or personal service jobs.[23] The principal shifts in the black male occupational structure over the ensuing thirty years were an increase in industrial occupations and a shift from wood industries to metals, a transition that paralleled the alteration of the city's industrial structure.

For African-American women, too, Muncie offered a limited array of jobs similar to those available in larger industrial cities (Table 3). In Chicago and Cleveland in 1920, domestic service provided work for about three-fifths of the female black work force, while factories employed another 10–15 percent. Their situation contrasted drastically with that of white women, who were flooding into newly created clerical and secretarial positions rarely open to blacks.[24] In Muncie, three-fifths of employed black women were unskilled service workers, while nearly ten percent worked in the glass factories. The "nonretail proprietors" (11.1 percent) were generally keepers of boarding or rooming houses. Among white women workers, in contrast, two-fifths held white-collar positions. The principal dissimilarity between black and white women in Muncie was not, however, in the structure of the work force but in its size: while only

35 of the 182 white women in the sample held gainful occupations (19.2 percent), 72 of the 181 black women did (39.8 percent).

Insofar as Muncie's appeal to black migrants rested on the availability of jobs, it must have been its factories that burned brightest on the migrants' horizon, like the spires of flaming natural gas which had heralded the town's entry into the machine age a third of a century before. For black men, industrial jobs in Muncie were overwhelmingly unskilled, although limited opportunity for advancement to semi-skilled or even skilled positions beckoned in the glass and, more often, the metals industry. For women, the same menial domestic labor available to women in cities across the country could be found in Muncie; but, alongside domestic work, some avenues existed into industrial jobs in Muncie's glass factories. Given the nature of industrial work for men or women, however, it is unlikely that migrants travelled to Muncie for factory jobs because they enjoyed the work. Rather, like other workers, they sought it out because of the wages that industrial work offered, as well as its autonomy and impersonality, all of which contrasted favorably with the conditions of agricultural work in the South.[25]

Too rarely, however, were African Americans able to find in large industrial cities that industrial work led to wealth accumulation in the form of homeownership, because of the forces that combined to create black urban ghettoes, in particular white hostility to potential black neighbors expressed through a multitude of forms, from restrictive covenants to violence. In large northern cities, black residents, even if they held relatively well-paying industrial jobs, typically lived in rented accommodations in overcrowded, under-maintained buildings located in unsanitary and vice-ridden neighborhoods.[26] Black homeownership in three largely black districts in Pittsburgh in 1930 ranged from 0.5 percent to 13.2 percent.[27] Detroit in 1920 reported rates of black homeownership among household heads ranging from 2.6 percent to 4.8 percent.[28] A 1928 survey in Milwaukee revealed that, although 42 percent of all dwellings in the city were owned by their occupants, only one percent of blacks—only ten families in a population of about 7,000—owned the dwelling they occupied.[29] Yet in 1920, the census reported rates of black homeownership in southern states ranging from 14.5 percent in Georgia to 41.2 percent in Virginia, and averaging around 20 percent.[30] This contrast goes far to suggest why migration to northern cities became for many migrants, as Langston Hughes put it, "a dream deferred."

In Muncie the situation was different. Although fewer blacks (31.7 percent) than whites (42.9 percent) in the 1920 sample lived in a home owned by a member of their family, the rate of black homeownership was much higher than in any other northeastern city for which data are available for a comparable point in time.[31] This high rate suggests that black migrants were able to translate rewards from the jobs they found in Muncie into a basic form of wealth. Yet aggregate ownership rates by themselves cannot prove this, since house purchases could conceivably have been made using resources brought to Muncie. Before concluding that migrants were able to accumulate wealth through their labor in Muncie, it is necessary to analyze homeownership further.

The question to be asked is whether a "structure of opportunity" was present in the Magic City before 1920. The concept of a "structure of opportunity" refers to the possibilities of material improvement in a community according to the time spent there. If a structure of opportunity existed, then it should be reflected in greater accumulated assets among those who have had the longest exposure to the community. The fundamental comparison in such an analysis, then, is between newcomers and persisters. The analysis can and should be sharpened by taking account of age, since life-cycle differences can affect wealth comparisons in several distinct ways.[32] Controlling for age can also address the possibility that migrants may have arrived in the community with varying resources, since older migrants would be more likely than younger ones to come with accumulated earnings or the proceeds from sale of assets. Furthermore, the analysis should recognize that a national structure of opportunity characterized by regional differences forms the context for local endeavors. In particular, because of the retardation of economic development in the South compared to the North in the early twentieth century, southern-born migrants may have been handicapped relative to their northern-born counterparts. Because of the distinct male and female occupational structures in Muncie, if for no other reason, separate analyses must be conducted for men and women. An examination of homeownership incorporating time spent in the community, age, and origin as independent variables should reveal, insofar as available data can, whether migrants to Muncie found some portion of the rewards they presumably sought through mobility.

Simple correlation analysis shows that persistence in the community did produce an increased likelihood of homeownership, as residence in Muncie for at least ten years raised the chance of occupying a home owned by a member of one's family by about 10–14 percent for whites and about 40 percent for blacks (Tables 4 and 5).[33] Age, too, increased one's chances of occupying a family-owned home, but the effect of neither age nor persistence can be definitely established, since the two variables were intercorrelated among women and among black men (Tables 4B and 5B). Birth in a northern state conferred a small advantage on white men and a large one on white women. Northern birth, however, bestowed no advantage on blacks, as southern-born black men were nearly as likely as northern-born to live in family-owned homes, while southern-born women were considerably more likely than northern-born to live in a family-owned dwelling. Again, however, the effect of age makes any conclusion premature, since

Table 4: Possible Determinants of Homeownership,
Adult Males, Muncie, 1920

A. Occupancy of Family-Owned Homes by Color (in percentages)

	Whites		*Blacks*	
	Group Size	Percent Occupying Owned Homes	Group Size	Percent Occupying Owned Homes
Persistence				
Newcomer since 1910	110	34.5	138	18.8
Present in 1910	64	48.4	57	56.1
Age				
21–39 years	86	30.2	124	17.7
40 years and over	87	48.3	70	51.4
Origin				
Southern-born	14	35.7	115	29.6
Northern-born	151	41.1	78	30.8
Foreign-born	8	25.0	1	0.0
All	174	39.7	195	29.7

B. Correlation Matrices

Whites (N=164)			
	Persistence	Age	Origin**
Family-owned home	+.15*	+.19*	+.03
Persistence		+.08	+.05
Age			+.07

Blacks (N=192)			
	Persistence	Age	Origin**
Family-owned home	+.38*	+.31*	−.01
Persistence		+.13*	+.05
Age			−.18*

* Significant at the .05 level.
** Excluding foreign-born.

Source: Study data.

southern-born blacks tended to be older than northern-born (a median age
of 38 years for southern-born men and 39 for southern-born women compared to 33 for northern-born men and women), so that their chances of
occupying a family-owned home could have been affected by their age,
rather than their southern origin. For whites, northern birth operated independently to increase the likelihood of living in a family-owned home,
since age was not correlated with region of birth. It is noteworthy that,
despite blacks' lower overall likelihood of occupying a family-owned

Table 5: Possible Determinants of Homeownership,
Adult Females, Muncie, 1920

A. Occupancy of Family-Owned Homes by Color (in percentages)

	Whites		*Blacks*	
	Group Size	Percent Occupying Owned Homes	Group Size	Percent Occupying Owned Homes
Persistence				
Newcomer since 1910	121	43.0	133	24.1
Present in 1910	57	52.6	41	65.9
Age				
21–39 years	87	44.8	106	26.4
40 years and over	91	47.3	68	45.6
Origin				
Southern-born	20	15.0	85	41.2
Northern-born	154	50.0	89	27.0
Foreign-born	8	25.0	0	n.a.
All	178	46.1	174	33.9

B. Correlation Matrices

Whites (N=174)			
	Persistence	Age	Origin**
Family-owned home	+.09	−.01	+.22*
Persistence		+.18*	+.02
Age			−.06

Blacks (N=174)			
	Persistence	Age	Origin**
Family-owned home	+.37*	+.20*	−.15*
Persistence		+.37*	−.13*
Age			−.16*

* Significant at the .05 level.
** Excluding foreign-born.

Source: Study data.

home, in four groups—male and female persisters, men aged 40 years or over, and southern-born women—African Americans' chances of living in a family-owned home were as great or greater than those of their white counterparts.

The question of whether a structure of opportunity existed in Muncie can be addressed more directly by examining the incidence of family ownership using more precise categories (Tables 6 and 7). For whites, there is some evidence to indicate a local structure of opportunity, as persistence

Table 6: An Opportunity Structure for Men in Muncie?

A. Occupancy of Family-Owned Homes by Color (in percentages)

| | Whites | | Blacks | |
	Group Size	Percent Occupying Owned Homes	Group Size	Percent Occupying Owned Homes
Older northern-born persisters	31	58.1	7	85.7
Younger northern-born persisters	25	36.0	18	44.4
Older southern-born persisters	2	100.0	20	65.0
Younger southern-born persisters	2	50.0	11	45.5
Older northern-born newcomers	43	44.2	13	46.2
Younger northern-born newcomers	51	29.4	40	10.0
Older southern-born newcomers	3	33.3	30	36.7
Younger southern-born newcomers	7	14.3	53	9.4
All	164	40.2	192	30.2

B. Multiple Regression Analysis of Homeownership

Variable	Coefficient	*t* value	p
	Whites		
Intercept	.10		
Age	.18	2.3	.02
Origin	.01	0.1	.91
Persistence	.14	1.8	.08
R^2 = .054			
	Blacks		
Intercept	−.18		
Age	.27	4.1	.00
Origin	.04	−0.6	.51
Persistence	.34	5.2	.00
R^2 = .213			

Source: Study data.

in the community paid off for all groups except southern-born women. The differences in homeownership between white persisters and newcomers, however, were not great. The structure of opportunity in Muncie operated within the context of a national structure which rewarded northern birth as well as persistence in Muncie. All groups of white women benefitted from northern birth; among men, northern newcomers both old and young did better than southern newcomers. Persistence in the community allowed the few southern-born men to equal or exceed the homeownership rates of their northern-born counterparts. Multiple regression analysis, however, reveals that among white men opportunity was structured primarily by age: when age was controlled, origin and persistence became statistically nonsignificant. Increasing age bolstered men's chances of oc-

Table 7: An Opportunity Structure for Women in Muncie?

A. Occupancy of Family-Owned Homes by Color (in percentages)

	Whites		*Blacks*	
	Group Size	Percent Occupying Owned Homes	Group Size	Percent Occupying Owned Homes
Older northern-born persisters	30	56.7	13	69.2
Younger northern-born persisters	21	57.1	3	66.7
Older southern-born persisters	5	20.0	16	56.3
Younger southern-born persisters	1	0.0	9	77.8
Older northern-born newcomers	49	46.9	15	20.0
Younger northern-born newcomers	54	46.3	58	17.2
Older southern-born newcomers	5	20.0	24	41.7
Younger southern-born newcomers	9	11.1	36	25.0
All	174	46.0	174	33.9

B. Multiple Regression Analysis of Homeownership

Variable	Coefficient	*t* value	p
	Whites		
Intercept	.13		
Age	−.01	−1.1	.91
Origin	.22	3.0	.00
Persistence	.09	1.2	.24
R^2 = .058			
	Blacks		
Intercept	.22		
Age	.05	0.7	.48
Origin	−.10	−1.3	.18
Persistence	.34	4.5	.00
R^2 = .153			

Source: Study data.

cupying a family-owned dwelling, whether persister or newcomer, southern- or northern-born. Among white women, age did not bring the same opportunities: only northern birth conferred advantage.

For whites, then, the factors affecting access to homeownership seem to have been largely independent of the local context in Muncie. For blacks, the opposite was true. Even when age and persistence are controlled, it is clear that blacks were not usually favored by northern birth. Among both men and women, older northern-born persisters had a greater likelihood of living in family-owned accommodations than older southern-born persisters, but both northern- and southern-born older persisters were much more likely to enjoy such accommodations than were blacks as a whole. Among women—in contrast to white women—the southern-born consistently exceeded the homeownership rates of the northern-born. Among black men, origin exerted no consistent effect.[34] Persistence in Muncie invariably paid off for blacks among groups of the same sex, age, and origin. Among men, age, too, was rewarded by advancement toward family home ownership, though its effect was not consistent for women. The importance for blacks of the local structure of opportunity is confirmed by the multiple regression analysis, which shows persistence and age as the only significant independent correlates of family ownership among men, while persistence remained powerful among women when age and origin were controlled. The greater importance of this local structure of opportunity for blacks compared to whites is shown by the coefficients of variation for the two equations: for whites the three variables—age, origin, and persistence—together explain less than six percent of the variance in levels of family ownership among both men and women, while for blacks the same variables explain 15 percent among women and 21 percent among men.

The foregoing analysis implies that color played little part in determining a person's chances of living in family-owned accommodations in Muncie, and therefore the apparent difference in levels of family ownership between blacks and whites was actually produced by differences in age (blacks' mean age was about two-and-one-half years less than whites'), origin (86 percent of blacks were southern-born while 64 percent of whites were northern-born), and persistence (26 percent of blacks had been living in Muncie ten years earlier compared to 34 percent of whites). Multiple regression analysis using a step-wise procedure to select the most powerful determinants of family ownership confirms that this was in fact the case. Among all men, persistence was the best predictor, followed by age; with account taken of age and persistence, region of birth and color added nothing to the explanatory power of the model.[35] For women, only persistence was a statistically significant predictor of family ownership.[36] The differing meaning of region of birth for black and white women cancelled out the potential effect of this variable, and neither age nor color was statistically significant once persistence was entered into the equation. This analysis confirms the existence in Muncie before 1920 of a structure of opportunity organized according to time spent in the community and age, although the local structure exerted far less effect on whites' homeownership patterns than on blacks'.

Thus far it seems clear that black and white families had roughly equal opportunities to become homeowners in Muncie, but the evidence examined does not, of course, bear on the question of the quality of housing available to members of the two groups (except that the high level of black homeownership meant that decisions about maintenance were more likely in Muncie than elsewhere in the urban North to be made by a dwelling's occupants rather than by a landlord). African-American housing may

have been overcrowded and segregated. Or black owners may have disproportionately occupied mortgaged properties, while whites were predominantly freeholders. Census evidence, however, supports none of these possibilities. White sample members actually lived in larger households, with
a median size of four members, compared to three for blacks. To measure
residential segregation, I tabulated the "color or race" recorded by the enu-
merator for neighbors preceding and following each sampled household
on the census schedule. Only 5.4 percent of white sample members had
one or more black neighbors, but this is not unexpected, since blacks comprised 5.6 percent of Muncie's population. Blacks, for their part, were by
no means evenly distributed throughout the city. Only one of Muncie's
nine wards contained no black sample members, but 82 percent of the
black sample lived in three wards (4, 6, and 7).[37] Yet whites also lived in
those wards, and blacks often lived next door to them. Three-fifths of
black sample members resided in households with at least one white
neighbor; one-quarter lived in households both of whose neighbors were
white.[38] Black homeownership was more geographically concentrated than
the black population, as 56 percent of blacks living in family-owned quarters resided in Ward 4, which contained only one-third of Muncie's black
population. But black homeowners were scattered across five other wards,
and even in Ward 4 more than half of all African Americans lived in homes
with at least one white neighbor. Finally, there was no difference at all
between blacks and whites, among those listed in the census as "family
heads," in whether their homes were owned freehold or mortgaged.[39] None
of this evidence proves that blacks did not live in smaller or cheaper
homes, or in the poorer neighborhoods of Muncie. Some of black families'
homes on the outskirts of Muncie may have been built by their occupants.
Self-building, however, did not necessarily distinguish black from white
workers, both of whom found "sweat equity" a means (perhaps the only
means) to locate outside a crowded central city.[40] The important fact still
remains that black workers' chances for ownership of some housing were
not hindered by the color of their skin, and they were therefore able to
convert the earnings from their industrial jobs into the most basic form of
wealth accumulation.

For African-American families in Muncie, homeownership could possibly confer an additional benefit beyond autonomy and security. This is
evident when women's patterns of family ownership are compared with
structures of gainful employment as indicated by the census.[41] Access to
gainful occupations was not correlated with family ownership for white
women, but black women without gainful occupations were significantly
overrepresented among those living in family-owned accommodations.[42]
This pattern is consistent with the possibility that women in black families who owned their homes were relieved of the obligation to seek work
in the menial jobs that were the principal source of black female employ-

ment in Muncie, as in other urban places. For white women in homeowning families, in contrast, work outside the home more often meant white-collar employment in expanding clerical and sales occupations. The security implied by homeownership therefore may have allowed the women of black families the opportunity to stay at home.

Clearly, Muncie could not offer migrants the excitement of Chicago's South Side or the vibrancy of Harlem on the verge of its Renaissance. Nor did its slightly over 2,000 black population form a large enough community to support many black businesses or an extensive network of community institutions.[43] Nevertheless, Muncie, and possibly other small industrial cities as well, could provide not only the manufacturing jobs available in large cities, but also something the big cities could not: fulfillment of aspirations for home ownership and what that could bring in safety, security, and support for family life.

Beyond Muncie, what we now know about African Americans' opportunities to find industrial jobs and attain homeownership in similar places suggests hypotheses which may illuminate unexplored dimensions of the migration experience in the early-twentieth-century United States. In particular, the opportunities for black migrants in Muncie, limited as they were, stand out in contrast to the even more restricted openings in the wall of prejudice and discrimination facing blacks elsewhere in the North. Most striking about the pattern of black achievement in Muncie are the differences in the structures of opportunity for blacks and whites. For whites, the legacy of free forebears and a relatively open society was a pattern of advancement that differed for some from South to North, but within the North seems not to have been very place-specific.[44] White migrants, it appears, did not need to obtain precise information about the opportunities available at a particular destination in the North, or at least information as exact as that required by prospective black migrants. For would-be black migrants, the differences between the opportunities—and dangers—present in North and South were perhaps not so crucial as those between different kinds of places in the North. Before 1919, for example, public violence against blacks occurred in the Midwest only in nonmetropolitan areas.[45] Then, in 1919, the pattern was reversed, as white mobs attacked blacks in many northern big cities. Jobs other than the menial domestic and personal-service variety were available not just in places of a certain size, but also only in certain places within a size category. Furthermore, even where relatively remunerative jobs were open to blacks, chances for homeownership were not always good. And possible destinations that offered tangible rewards for hard labor might not provide the thriving community life or chances for cultural expression which some migrants sought. Different people made different choices, and some still wound up in places they would rather not have been. For African Americans, migrating to the Midwest in the age of the first Great Migration meant choosing among a wide range of options of which few would pay off. If those who chose to settle in Muncie before 1920 hoped to establish a relatively firm basis for family life, moving to Muncie was one choice that did.

NOTES

Research for this study was supported by Huron College and the Indiana Historical Society. The author wishes to thank Stacey Demay and Laura Wackman for their careful and conscientious assistance in linking the 1920 sample to the 1910 census schedules, the members of the U.S. historians' seminar at the University of Western Ontario for useful criticism of an earlier version of the essay, and participants at the Binghamton University African Diaspora conference for their helpful comments on another version.

1. William Cohen, *At Freedom's Edge: Black Mobility and the Southern White Quest for Racial Control, 1861–1915* (Baton Rouge: Louisiana State University Press, 1991).

2. I have explored the reasons given for migration to Muncie by migrant respondents to oral-history interviews in "Black Migration to Muncie, 1860–1930," *Indiana Magazine of History* 92 (December 1996): 297–320.

3. Discussions of Muncie's economy may be found in Robert S. Lynd and Helen Merrell Lynd, *Middletown: A Study in Modern American Culture* (New York: Harcourt, Brace and World, 1929), chs. II–VI; Scott Ray, "The Depressed Industrial Society: Occupational Movement, Out-Migration and Residential Mobility in the Industrial-Urbanization of Middletown, 1880–1925" (Ph.D. dissertation, Ball State University, 1981), 125–31; Clifton J. Phillips, *Indiana in Transition: The Emergence of an Industrial Commonwealth, 1880–1920* (Indianapolis: Indiana Historical Bureau and Indiana Historical Society, 1968), 192–202, 276.

4. U.S. Bureau of the Census, *Negroes in the United States, 1920–1932* (Washington: Government Printing Office, 1935), 55.

5. By the lower Midwest I mean Ohio, Indiana, and Illinois.

6. During the 20 years after 1890, while the black population of Indiana increased more rapidly than the white, the growth of white population was more rapid in places of 2,500–9,999, 10,000–24,999, and 25,000–99,999; black population grew more rapidly only in places of over 100,000 (Indianapolis). Blocker, "Black Migration to Muncie," Table 2.

7. Manuscript U.S. Census, Delaware County, Indiana, 1920.

8. Within the range of possible page numbers in Muncie's enumeration districts, numbers were selected using a table of random numbers (the page numbers drawn were 3, 4, 7, 11, 17, 19, 27, and 31). On each selected page all of those 21 years and over who were identified as "black" or "mulatto" were taken. In enumeration district 30, Ward 6, two of the selected pages were illegible, so pages 1 and 2 were used instead.

For estimating the proportion of the population living in family-owned homes, a sample of this size will be accurate within five percentage points either way at the .95 level of confidence.

9. On the pages selected as described above, four numbers within the range 1–100 were taken from a random number table for selection of "white" individuals (the numbers were 23, 38, 67, and 98; each double page of the census schedule contains 100 lines). If a person 21 years of age or over was not listed on the selected line, I moved alternately up and down the page until I found one who fit the age and "color" criteria. If the person found on the selected line was designated as "black" or "mulatto," that person was taken for the sample, and no "white" person was selected.

For estimating the proportion of the population living in family-owned homes, a sample of this size will be accurate within six percentage points either way at the .95 level of confidence.

10. The linkage was done manually using the following information from the 1920 census schedules: name, sex, "color," age, and place of birth. Only definite matches were considered to reflect presence in the Muncie area in 1910. The search for possible links in 1910 covered not only the 18 enumeration districts in Muncie, but also districts 19 (Normal city), 20 (Riverside city), 21 (Whitely, a heavily black neighborhood), 22, and 23, at least some of which were annexed to Muncie before 1920.

11. Blocker, "Black Migration to Muncie," 306.

12. Working conditions are described in Lynd and Lynd, *Middletown*, chs. VI–VII.

13. John Bodnar, Roger Simon, and Michael P. Weber, *Lives of Their Own: Blacks, Italians, and Poles in Pittsburgh, 1900–1960* (Urbana and Chicago: University of Illinois Press, 1982), 153–54. For a different view, see Daniel D. Luria, "Wealth, Capital, and Power: The Social Meaning of Home Ownership," *Journal of Interdisciplinary History* 7 (Autumn 1976): 261–82. In arguing that homeownership did not confer social power or lead to occupational advancement, Luria does not deny that workers sought home ownership.

14. Richard Harris, "Working-Class Home Ownership in the American Metropolis," *Journal of Urban History* 17 (November 1990): 47.

15. Bodnar, Simon, and Weber, *Lives of Their Own*, 31–37, 158.

16. The foreign-born represented only about two percent of Muncie's population in 1920. Lynd and Lynd, *Middletown*, 9.

17. Interview, James D., June 6, 1980, Black Middletown Project, Special Collections, Bracken Library, Ball State University.

18. The occupational categorization used is a slightly modified form of that adopted by Olivier Zunz in *The Changing Face of Inequality: Urbanization, Industrial Development, and Immigrants in Detroit, 1880–1920* (Chicago: University of Chicago Press, 1982), described in Appendix 3. In addition to specifying the type of industry in which wage laborers were employed, I reassigned cooks, drivers, and chauffeurs from the category of unskilled service workers to the category of skilled and semi-skilled service workers and shifted washerwomen and laundresses working on "own

account" from the category of nonretail proprietors to the category of unskilled service workers.

19. Hurley Goodall and J. Paul Mitchell, *A History of Blacks in Muncie* (Muncie: Ball State University, 1976), 7.

20. Alan H. Spear, *Black Chicago: The Making of a Negro Ghetto, 1890–1920* (Chicago: University of Chicago Press, 1967), 153–54; Kenneth L. Kusmer, *A Ghetto Takes Shape: Black Cleveland, 1870–1930* (Urbana: University of Illinois Press, 1976), 200; Zunz, *Changing Face of Inequality*, 340–41; Peter Gottlieb, *Making Their Own Way: Southern Blacks' Migration to Pittsburgh, 1916–30* (Urbana and Chicago: University of Illinois Press, 1987), 91; Joe William Trotter, Jr., *Black Milwaukee: The Making of an Industrial Proletariat, 1915–45* (Urbana and Chicago: University of Illinois Press, 1985), 48; Earl Lewis, *In Their Own Interests: Race, Class, and Power in Twentieth-Century Norfolk, Virginia* (Berkeley: University of California Press, 1991), 34.

21. Bodnar, Simon, and Weber, *Lives of Their Own*, 134. Kusmer, *A Ghetto Takes Shape*, 191–95, is somewhat more positive about the "moderate gains" in black business after 1915.

22. Spear, *Black Chicago*, 151; Kusmer, *A Ghetto Takes Shape*, 199–202; Richard W. Thomas, *Life for Us Is What We Make It: Building Black Community in Detroit, 1915–1945* (Bloomington and Indianapolis: Indiana University Press, 1992), 30; Trotter, *Black Milwaukee*, 47. In Pittsburgh, the decline in the percentage of black men in domestic and personal service occupations was accompanied by a contraction in skilled industrial jobs for blacks. Gottlieb, *Making Their Own Way*, 89–103.

23. The number working in factories was 29 out of a total of 119 males listed with occupations: seven in glass factories, 20 in factories working in wood, and two in iron manufactories. *Emerson's Muncie Directory, 1889* (Indianapolis: Chas. Emerson and Co., 1889). The situation in Muncie contrasts with opportunities for black workers in Milwaukee in 1880 and in 1900. In 1880, five occupations (porters, waiters, servants, cooks, and common laborers) made up 69.7 percent of black jobs in Milwaukee; in Muncie, these five occupations represented only 30.3 percent (37 of 122) of jobs held by blacks listed in the city directory. In Milwaukee in 1900, an African-American population twice the size of Muncie's in 1889 included the same number of skilled workers (7), and "few Afro-Americans entered the industrial work force." Trotter, *Black Milwaukee*, 10–13. The quotation is on p. 13. In Chicago, only 8.3 percent of the black male work force in 1900 held jobs in manufacturing. Spear, *Black Chicago*, 32.

24. Spear, *Black Chicago*, 154–55; Kusmer, *A Ghetto Takes Shape*, 200, 203. Milwaukee had a larger proportion of its female black work force (39.1 percent) in semi-skilled positions, and a correspondingly smaller percentage (39.4 percent) in domestic service. Trotter, *Black Milwaukee*, 49. Norfolk had about the same proportion of black women workers in manufacturing as Chicago and Cleveland, but a much larger proportion (81.9 percent) in domestic service. Lewis, *In Their Own Interests*, 37.

25. James R. Grossman, *Land of Hope: Chicago, Black Southerners, and*

the Great Migration (Chicago and London: University of Chicago Press, 1989), 260–61.

26. Florette Henri, *Black Migration: Movement North, 1900–1920* (Garden City, N.Y.: Anchor Press, 1975), ch. 3; Gilbert Osofsky, *Harlem: The Making of a Ghetto, 1890–1930* (New York: Harper and Row, 1963); Spear, *Black Chicago*; Kusmer, *A Ghetto Takes Shape*; Trotter, *Black Milwaukee*; Zunz, *Changing Face of Inequality*; Bodnar, Simon, and Weber, *Lives of Their Own*; Emma Lou Thornbrough, "Segregation in Indiana during the Klan Era of the 1920's," *Mississippi Valley Historical Review* 47 (March 1961): 596. In Cincinnati, blacks are reported to have found neither industrial jobs nor opportunities for homeownership. Nancy Bertaux, "Structural Economic Change and Occupational Decline among Black Workers in Nineteenth-Century Cincinnati," in Henry Louis Taylor, Jr., ed., *Race and the City: Work, Community, and Protest in Cincinnati, 1820–1970* (Urbana: University of Illinois Press, 1993), 126–55; Henry Louis Taylor, Jr., "City Building, Public Policy, the Rise of the Industrial City, and Black Ghetto-Slum Formation in Cincinnati, 1850–1940," in ibid., 156–92.

27. Bodnar, Simon, and Weber, *Lives of Their Own*, 211.

28. Zunz, *Changing Face of Inequality*, 287.

29. Trotter, *Black Milwaukee*, 70.

30. U.S. Bureau of the Census, *Fourteenth Census, 1920: Vol. II: Population* (Washington: Government Printing Office, 1922), 1282. The census reported what proportion of homes were owned or rented, not what percentage of families owned their homes. Since more than one family could occupy a dwelling, the percentage of families owning their home would probably be lower than the percentage of homes owned by their occupants. Nevertheless, the contrasts drawn in the text should be sufficiently great to make the point that most migrants moved from a setting in which homeownership was more possible to one in which it was less so.

31. The closest rate of homeownership to Muncie's is for 20 years later in Evansville, Indiana, where Darrel Bigham reports that "less than a fifth of black household heads owned their homes." *We Ask Only a Fair Trial: A History of the Black Community of Evansville, Indiana* (Bloomington and Indianapolis: Indiana University Press, 1987), 223. A survey in 1918 of parents of children aged 2–7 years in Gary revealed that 11.3 percent of blacks owned or were buying their homes, compared to 35.1 percent of native-born whites and 51.2 percent of foreign-born. Elizabeth Balanoff, "A History of the Black Community of Gary, Indiana, 1906–1940" (Ph.D. diss., University of Chicago, 1974), 25. In Los Angeles in 1910, 36.1 percent of dwellings occupied by blacks were owned by their occupants. Quintard Taylor, *The Forging of a Black Community: Seattle's Central District from 1870 through the Civil Rights Era* (Seattle and London: University of Washington Press, 1994), 85.

32. J. R. Kearl and Clayne L. Pope, "The Life Cycle in Economic History," *Journal of Economic History* 43 (March 1983): 149–58.

33. This analysis uses the entire sample. As an alternative, only the 316 sample members designated in the census as "family heads" could have been used, so as to distinguish those most likely to have been owners from

those less likely. To do so, however, would have had three damaging consequences: (1) accepting the hierarchical notion of "family head"; (2) excluding many younger people and women from the analysis, thereby neglecting their historical experience; and (3) reducing the size of the population under study considerably. A parallel analysis has been carried out for "family heads" only without differentiating by sex, and it shows generally similar patterns to those found in analysis of the full sample without differentiation by sex. The principal difference is that among both black and white "family heads" the variation between northern-born and southern-born is reduced.

For the correlation and regression analyses, the dichotomous nominal variable measuring whether a person rented or occupied a family-owned home is recoded as an indicator variable (0 = rented home, 1 = family-owned home). So are the variables measuring region of birth (0 = Southern-born, 1 = Northern-born) and persistence (0 = newcomer since 1910, 1 = present in 1910). Age is left as originally entered from the census.

34. Bodnar, Simon, and Weber found a slightly higher rate of homeownership among northern-born than southern-born black families in Pittsburgh in 1900, but without controlling for age or persistence. By 1910, however, among persisting black families the southern-born had attained slightly higher rates of homeownership, a lead they maintained in 1915, 1920, and 1930. *Lives of Their Own*, 156–60. Studies of black advancement in northern cities using occupation as a measure show conflicting results. Olivier Zunz, using a small sample of black household heads, shows northern-born doing better than southern-born. Darrel Bigham, after analyzing a sample from the 1910 census, concludes that Indiana origins conferred no advantage among Evansville blacks over southern birth. Zunz, *Changing Face of Inequality*, 338–39; Bigham, *We Ask Only a Fair Trial*, 171. Neither study controls for age or persistence in the community.

35. Persistence explained seven percent of variance in ownership, and age added an additional five percent.

36. Persistence explained five percent of variance in ownership.

37. The Pearson chi-square for crosstabulation of ward with color equals 257.8 which, with 8 degrees of freedom, is significant at the .00001 level.

38. Oral-history evidence confirms that residential neighborhoods in Muncie were not segregated, nor were schools, buses, or streetcars. Restaurants, theaters, parks, and swimming pools were. Blocker, "Black Migration to Muncie," 314–15.

Muncie's 38.2 percent of blacks having two black neighbors placed the Indiana city between the proportions Spencer Crew reports for Camden (58.2 percent) and Elizabeth (35.4 percent), New Jersey, in 1915. "A black ghetto characterized by a high concentration of black residents living largely in one area of the city," Crew concludes, "had not yet developed in either Camden or Elizabeth by 1920." *Black Life in Secondary Cities: A Comparative Analysis of the Black Communities of Camden and Elizabeth, N.J., 1860–1920* (New York and London: Garland Publishing, 1993), 48, 65 (quotation).

39. Forty-two percent of blacks were freehold owners, compared to 41

percent of whites. For oral-history testimony to blacks' ability to obtain mortgages, see Mrs. M., Interview, July 1, 8, 1980, Black Middletown Project, Special Collections, Bracken Library, Ball State University.

40. Richard Harris, "Self-Building in the Urban Housing Market," *Economic Geography* 67 (January 1991): 1–21. For oral-history accounts of black migrants who built their own homes, see Tolbert Bragg and Preston Tate (both of Portland, Indiana) and Charles Green and Dulcinda Baker Martin (Springfield, Ohio), Interviews, *The American Slave: A Composite Autobiography*, ed. George P. Rawick, 41 vols. (Westport, Connecticut: Greenwood Press, 1972–79), Supplement, Series 1, vol. 5, 20–21, 220–21, 351, 416, and Julia Williams, Interview, June 10, 1937, ibid., Series 2, vol. 16, 107.

41. The qualifier "as indicated by the census" is necessary, since the census systematically underreported women's gainful work. Marjorie Abel and Nancy Folbre, "A Methodology for Revising Estimates: Female Market Participation in the U.S. Before 1940," *Historical Methods* 23 (1990): 167–76.

42. The incidence of family ownership was as follows: nonemployed white women, 47.9 percent; employed white women, 38.2 percent; nonemployed black women, 41.5 percent; employed black women, 22.1 percent. For white women, correlation of employment status and family ownership yields a chi-square statistic of 1.0, which, with one degree of freedom, is not significant at the .30 level. For black women, the same correlation produces a chi-square statistic of 7.0, which, with one degree of freedom, is significant at the .01 level.

43. Muncie's black population in 1921 supported five churches, or one for every 411 persons. There were 34 churches serving the white population, one for every 1,014 persons. *Emerson's Muncie Directory, 1921–1922* (Cincinnati: The Williams Directory Company, 1921).

44. A study of white Appalachian migration to Muncie—which began during the 1920s and continued through the 1960s—concludes that "the 'push' of Fentress County [Tennessee] superseded the 'pull' of Muncie." Margaret Ripley Wolfe, "Appalachians in Muncie: A Case Study of an American Exodus," *Locus* 4 (Spring 1992): 172.

45. See the listings for Ohio, Indiana, and Illinois in the NAACP's *Thirty Years of Lynching in the United States, 1889–1918*, reprint edn. (New York: Arno Press, 1969 [1919]).

REFERENCES

Bertaux, Nancy. "Structural Economic Change and Occupational Decline among Black Workers in Nineteenth-century Cincinnati." In Henry Louis Taylor, ed.

Bigham, Darrel E. *We Ask Only a Fair Trial: A History of the Black Community of Evansville, Indiana*. Bloomington: Indiana University Press, 1987.

Blocker, Jack S., Jr. "Black Migration to Muncie, 1860–1930." *Indiana Magazine of History* 92 (December 1996):297–320.

Bodnar, John, Roger Simon, and Michael Weber. *Lives of Their Own: Blacks, Italians, and Poles in Pittsburgh, 1900–1960.* Urbana: University of Illinois Press, 1982.

Cohen, William. *At Freedom's Edge: Black Mobility and the Southern White Quest for Racial Control, 1861–1915.* Baton Rouge: Louisiana State University Press, 1991.

Crew, Spencer. *Black Life in Secondary Cities: Camden and Elizabethtown, New Jersey, 1860–1920.* New York: Garland, 1993.

Goodall, Hurley, and J. Paul Mitchell. *A History of Negroes in Muncie.* Muncie: Ball State University, 1976.

Gottlieb, Peter. *Making Their Own Way: Southern Blacks' Migration to Pittsburgh, 1916–30.* Urbana: University of Illinois Press, 1987.

Grossman, James R. *Land of Hope: Chicago, Black Southerners, and the Great Migration.* Chicago: University of Chicago Press, 1989.

Harris, Richard. "Self-building in the Urban Housing Market." *Economic Geography* 67 (January 1991):1–21.

———. "Working-class Home Ownership in the American Metropolis." *Journal of Urban History* 17 (November 1990):46–69.

Henri, Florette. *Black Migration: Movement North, 1900–1920.* Garden City, NY: Doubleday, 1975.

Kearl, J. R., and Clayne L. Pope. "The Life Cycle in Economic History." *Journal of Economic History* 43.1 (1983):149–58.

Kennedy, Joseph C. G. *Population of the United States in 1860.* Washington, DC: Government Printing Office, 1864.

Kusmer, Kenneth L. *A Ghetto Takes Shape: Black Cleveland, 1870–1930.* Urbana: University of Illinois Press, 1976.

Lewis, Earl. *In Their Own Interests: Race, Class, and Power in Twentieth-Century Norfolk, Virginia.* Berkeley: University of California Press, 1991.

Luria, Daniel D. "Wealth, Capital, and Power: The Social Meaning of Home Ownership." *Journal of Interdisciplinary History* 7 (Autumn 1976):261–82.

Lynd, Robert S., and Helen Merrell Lynd. *Middletown: A Study in Modern American Culture.* New York: Harcourt, Brace, & World, 1929.

National Association for the Advancement of Colored People. *Thirty Years of Lynching in the United States, 1889–1918.* New York: Arno, 1969 [1919].

Osofsky, Gilbert. *Harlem: The Making of a Ghetto.* New York: Harper and Row, 1966.

Phillips, Clifton J. *Indiana in Transition: The Emergence of an Industrial Commonwealth, 1880–1920.* Indianapolis: Indiana Historical Bureau and Indiana Historical Society, 1968.

Rawick, George P., ed. *The American Slave: A Composite Autobiography.* 41 volumes. Westport, Conn.: Greenwood Press, 1972–79.

Ray, Scott. *The Depressed Industrial Society: Occupational Movement,*

Out-migration and Residential Mobility in the Industrial-urbaniza-tion of Middletown, 1880–1925. Ph.D. Dissertation, Ball State University, Muncie, Indiana, 1981.

Spear, Allan. *Black Chicago: The Making of a Negro Ghetto, 1890–1920.* Chicago: University of Chicago Press, 1967.

Taylor, Henry Louis, Jr. "City Building, Public Policy, the Rise of the Industrial City, and Black Ghetto-slum Formation in Cincinnati, 1850–1940." In Henry Louis Taylor, Jr., ed., 156–92.

——, ed. *Race and the City: Work, Community, and Protest in Cincin-nati, 1820–1970.* Urbana: University of Illinois Press, 1993.

Taylor, Quintard. *The Forging of a Black Community: Seattle's Central District from 1870 through the Civil Rights Era.* Seattle: University of Washington Press, 1994.

Thomas, Richard W. *Life for Us Is What We Make It: Building Black Com-munity in Detroit, 1914–1945.* Bloomington: Indiana University Press, 1992.

Thornbrough, Emma Lou. "Segregation in Indiana during the Klan Era of the 1920's." *Mississippi Valley Historical Review* 47 (March 1961):594–618.

Trotter, Joe William, Jr. *Black Milwaukee: The Making of an Industrial Proletariat.* Urbana: University of Illinois Press, 1985.

U.S. Bureau of the Census. *Eleventh Census, 1890, Part I.* Washington, DC: Government Printing Office, 1895.

——. *Fourteenth Census, 1920. Volume II: Population.* Washington, DC: Government Printing Office, 1922.

——. *Manuscript Census Schedules, Delaware County, Indiana, 1920.*

——. *Negroes in the United States, 1920–1932.* Washington, DC: Gov-ernment Printing Office, 1935.

——. *Statistics of the Population of the United States at the Tenth Cen-sus, 1880.* Washington, DC: Government Printing Office, 1883.

Wolfe, Margaret Ripley. "Appalachians in Muncie: A Case Study of an American Exodus." *Locus* 4 (Spring 1992):169–89.

Zunz, Olivier. *The Changing Face of Inequality: Urbanization, Industrial Development, and Immigrants in Detroit, 1880–1920.* Chicago: University of Chicago Press, 1982.

8

THE SIGNIFICANCE OF COGNITIVE-LINGUISTIC ORIENTATION FOR ACADEMIC WELL-BEING IN AFRICAN AMERICAN CHILDREN

Ira Kincade Blake

This essay represents an attempt to situate my own research on African American preschoolers within the growing yet fragmented body of sociocultural research and theory about the language behavior of African American children of various ages. Much of this work has focused on the role of language in the performance difficulties of African American children in mainstream schools. Historically, the core has shifted from a primary interest in grammar and vocabulary to include pragmatic issues about conversational style, narrative style, and the oral-literate dichotomy in discourse. Methodologically, researchers have moved from the singular use of a Black/White comparative design to examining the data on African American children in its own right. This movement has produced explanations grounded in the experience of African American children, unlike Eurocentric perspectives that explain Black/White differences as the result of African American children lacking mainstream Anglo-American experiences. It is my intention to amplify this effort by constructing a broad language picture in three ways: (1) how cultural factors influence what African American children learn and know about the world, thereby creating a distinctive cognitive-linguistic orientation; (2) how their use of both oral and written language reinforces that learning and knowledge, thereby maintaining the cultural assumptions undergirding the orientation; and (3) how this cognitive-linguistic orientation is manifested across their formal education experience. In addition, I propose that this interplay between culture and language represents an extension of a West African heritage, albeit one adapted to the demands of new sociohistorical circumstances.

THE CULTURAL BASIS OF HUMAN BEHAVIOR

Theory and research indicate that culture plays an important role in human lives by providing an objective and subjective context for human interaction, serving as an organizing filter of valued information from the environment, and providing approved scripts for the manner of personal and interpersonal activities (see Brislin, 1990; McAdoo, 1990; Segall, Dasen, Berry, and Poortinga, 1990; and Willis, 1992 for discussion). Kitayama (1996) characterizes the relationship between what the individual thinks and does, and the cultural practices and meanings of his/her group as a "mutual constitution." Specifically, aspects of the cultural collective facilitate the acquisition of particular psychological processes and mechanisms in the individual; with these ways of thinking and acting the individual then participates in the culture; and accordingly, the manner of the individual's participation works to maintain the practices and meanings of the cultural collective. Culture, then, represented in customs and historical wisdom, helps persons make sense of what is important within their cultural context, enabling them to be effective and comfortable in the world their group experiences (see Blake, 1993; Schieffelin and Ochs, 1986; Shade, 1992; Willis, 1992).

As children develop, they acquire primarily the understanding of the world offered by the adults (and older children) around them. This offering supplies information not only about *what* is to be learned but also *how* to determine the worth of various kinds of information available in the world. Bloom (1993) speaks of this process as a "tuning in" to certain features of the environment. This valuation for the purpose of collective meaning-making generally influences the content of children's personal ideas, beliefs, feelings, and attitudes as well as their ways of expressing that content behaviorally. Thus, children learn to express their own ideas, feelings, attitudes, and behavior in ways that are interpretable to and shaped by those around them in their everyday experiences. Reciprocally, children learn to interpret the expressions of others in those culturally sanctioned ways. Consequently, what children are in the process of learning, thinking, and doing in their physical and social environment reflects and is part of what Kitayama designates as "mutual constitution."

What happens when children engage in an activity where the cultural practices and meanings of their group may not be coincident with those underlying the activity? A well-documented example is apparent when one examines the structure and content of teacher-requested oral and written narratives by African American children (Gee, 1985). These children often demonstrate a narrative structure called "topic-associating" (Michaels, 1981a; 1981b), which includes topical content that seems only marginally related to a perceived "topic-centered" structure that highlights the main

theme for a story. In another study, John-Steiner and Panofsky (1992) analyzed the re-told stories of school-age children from several culturally distinct backgrounds. The children's accounts included culturally familiar
features even though there were fewer components in the stories. When
taken together, such findings suggest that children utilize their cultural
strengths in various settings, participating through their group's conventional strategies for learning the content as well as negotiating situational
demands.

Thus, children's strategies for dealing with information are culturally
grounded in at least two fundamental ways: determining (1) what is
worthy of knowing and (2) the manner in which it is to be understood
and used most effectively. Here the emphasis is not only on identifiable
cultural products—e.g., the structural forms of Black English (or the topic-
associating narrative structure mentioned above)—but also on subjective
cultural products, such as an emphasis on personal expressiveness that
shapes the manner in which Black English is used (or the use of stress,
rhythm, and repetition in narration). In other words, the way children
come to know and learn is culturally conditioned to support their effective
participation in reality as adults view it. Moreover, the way they learn and
use language reveals cultural conditioning.

EVIDENCE OF CULTURE'S INFLUENCE: A LOOK ACROSS STUDIES OF LANGUAGE BEHAVIOR IN AFRICAN AMERICAN CHILDREN AND YOUTH

Turning to the literature on the language of African American children, a review of most studies reported since the 1960s reveals two general
facts: (1) the language behavior of African American children is different from the expected mainstream norms across grade levels (Blake, 1984;
Deutsch, 1967; Feagans and Farran, 1982; John-Steiner and Panofsky, 1992;
Labov, 1972; Smitherman, 1986/1977); and (2) the differences are attributed a pivotal role in the children's school difficulties (Ball, 1995; Smitherman, 1981; Stockman and Vaughn-Cooke, 1981; 1982). What is generally
important about these facts is that they have been typically reported with
little reflection on why—or an investigation of how—differences persist
across grades. For example, when compared with mainstream norms, African American preschoolers use less complex speech (see Hale-Benson,
1986/1982); early schoolers produce dissimilar frequencies of various sentence types (see Tough, 1977; 1982), and tell personal narratives that are
diffuse in focus (Michaels, 1981b) as well as evaluative in quality (Potts,
1989); middle schoolers use a participatory style for storytelling and personal writing (Nichols, 1989); high schoolers respond distinctively to elements of literary texts by personally aligning themselves with the reported
actions of main characters (Spears-Bunton, 1993); undergraduates high-

light personal opinion in course papers (Blake, 1994). In addition, research reports that culturally based language features influence the style and content of academically successful African American students (Ball, 1995). These studies represent only a portion of the growing literature that describes what these children actually do with language. This literature connects the patterns of language behavior to the discourse communities of African American children (Ball, 1995). Moreover, such knowledge permits us insight into the constructive factors of their behavior.

Thus, the aforementioned body of research reveals that they use language, in oral and written form, to express information that is distinctive from that expected within formal learning settings across grade levels. The differences are continuous with African American children's cultural experiences but discontinuous with Euro-American cultural expectations that traditionally frame the schooling experience of all students (Ball, 1995; Cazden, 1988). Thus, for African American children, the kind of information emphasized and the manner of its expression not only contribute to the reported persistent differences but undoubtedly influence their sense of competency as learners in school contexts at one time or another. The need to question oneself as a learner in school becomes necessary when the children realize that their knowledge is not supported in assessment or by teacher comments (see Ball, 1995; Kohl, 1991; Michaels, 1981b). A case in point is seven-year-old African American Mica,[1] who realized, without her teacher explicitly saying so, that the speech of two other black girls—her friends—was unacceptable for expressing ideas by the teacher's continual refusal to let the girls respond to her questions and repeated inquiry about whether they would like to go to the language lab. The teacher was reacting strictly to the form of the girls' language, providing no opportunity for them to demonstrate their knowledge and learning, even though the girls were highly motivated. Moreover, the girls did not interpret the teacher's entreaty to go to the language lab as just that, but rather as a genuine choice they could make. Unlike the insightful and subsequently self-concerned classmate, these girls did not understand the teacher's intended meaning. The girls continued to raise their hands without realizing that they would be given no chance to respond. However, Mica's distress centered on the teacher's belief that the girls did not speak well enough to answer questions. As a result, the ongoing personal issue for her was to make sure her own speech was less similar to that of her friends so that she would be given opportunities to demonstrate her knowledge. Clearly, Mica's academic ability was seriously challenged, at least in her mind, thereby affecting her sense of well-being.

As in the example, rarely is the performance of African American children seen as the expression and interpretation of what they know about culturally effective ways of responding in the world. Rather, the worth of their behavior is consistently undermined by the proverbial comparative mainstream lens through which most studies and evaluations of nonmainstream children take place (Greenfield and Cocking, 1994). Language comparisons typically focus on the distinctive phonological features, grammatical constructions, and vocabulary found in the variety of English spoken by African Americans. The variety, generally known as Black English and African American English, has been viewed historically as a key factor in the educational achievement and occupational accomplishments of African Americans (see Atkins, 1993; Stockman and Vaughn-Cooke, 1981, 1982). Although its status as a valid language system has been documented by prominent sociolinguists such as J. L. Dillard, William Labov, and Geneva Smitherman, African American English remains linguistically and socially suspect for many. Moreover, much research indicates that bias against nonstandard varieties of English, particularly the speech of African Americans, influences not only perceptions of nonstandard speakers' ability to perform but the quality of interaction with them as well (Atkins, 1993; Burg, 1975; Markham, 1984; Newmeyer, 1973; Washington and Miller-Jones, 1989).

Recently, the legitmacy of African American English as a tool of expression resurfaced with the announcement by the Oakland, California School District that Ebonics (another term for African American English) would be used to teach Standard English to African American students (Oakland Unified School District, 1997). In an attempt to develop a comprehensive program for language development, the policy included the training of the district's teaching and administrative staff not only in Ebonics but also African American history and culture. The emotional responses from many fronts indicate that the speech of African Americans remains a sensitive issue, both within and outside of the Black community, particularly when mainstream settings are being considered. Yet, to understand the performance of African Americans, children and adults alike, we must begin to view their behavior as reports of culturally valued information. Behavior in general, and language in particular, should be viewed as acts of expression and interpretation (Bloom, 1993) that are grounded not only in personal intentions but shared cultural experience. Returning to classroom settings, when students behave and speak they intend to communicate what is in their minds, and this intent is shaped by what they know about culturally valued content and ways of expressing it. Conversely, when students see the behavior and hear the speech of others they decipher them in light of the "ways of knowing" (see Brice-Heath, 1982) they already possess.

A CLOSER LOOK AT CULTURAL INFLUENCE: MOTHER-CHILD COMMUNICATION

The research I will summarize is part of a larger ongoing study of the language behavior of African American children and their parents. The research focuses on what young children learn about using language in relation to the manner of adult speech they experience in parent-child interactions. The issues of distinctiveness and maintenance of African American cultural values will be discussed in terms of patterns of regularities in the naturalistic speech of young African American children and their mothers.

Method

The participants in the study were five 2–3 year olds and their mothers[2] who were videotaped for one hour in a low-structure playroom. Each pair visited with the two African American research assistants[3] once prior to the actual taping session. The setting included a child-sized table with two chairs, a large slide, a set of core toys, and a snack of juice and cookies. During the taping session, additional sets of toys were brought into the room approximately every ten minutes.

The research design and method provided the participants with numerous opportunities to engage in a variety of actions and activities. For example, there were doll figures for role play, blocks for construction, a ball for participative activity, a slide for large motor play, and a puzzle for literacy-related activity. It was assumed that the number and diversity of interactive opportunities would give the pair enough communicative latitude so that a picture of how each pair used language naturally could be constructed. The presence of a similar pattern of use for language learners and mature language models would be seen as representative of language socialization and cultural language practices. Moreover, the occurrence of an identifiable communicative pattern during play in the mothers' speech would be indicative of what the mothers value and therefore convey to their children through talk.

Analyses and Results

Written transcriptions of the children's and mothers' speech and behavior served as the raw data for analyses. The main purpose of each intelligible utterance was examined and assigned to one of eight language-function categories derived from the speech of African American children in an earlier study (Blake, 1993; 1994). Briefly, an utterance served to negotiate and establish relations with others (Interpersonal Expressive), to obtain services and material goods (Effective), to report personal feelings and opinions to others (Self-Expressive Social), to describe the features and actions of objects and other persons (Objective), to report speaker's actions (Directive), to label and practice personal feelings and attitudes for the benefit of self alone (Self-Expressive Nonsocial), to seek joint physical activity with another (Participative), and to request that another person look at an action, object, or person (Attentive) (see Blake, 1994 for more complete definitions with examples).

The absolute frequencies for the language functions were tallied and proportional frequencies were calculated for each participant. In order to determine whether the distributions of language functions were similar and hence representative of a group pattern of language use for the dyads as a group, proportional frequencies were examined in three ways: (1) between children, (2) between mothers, and (3) between children and mothers as groups.

Children's Language Functions. All five children used language to accomplish the range of purposes represented by the eight function categories. Although the relative proportions for the language functions varied for individual children, there were similarities in the most frequent (and least frequent) functions. The children used the Objective function to describe aspects of the setting (*He crash*); the Directive function to report their own actions (*I pour my own juice*); the Interpersonal Expressive function to influence their mothers' talk (*shut up*) and activity (*be careful*); the Effective function to obtain assistance and objects (*I need my cookie*); and the Self-Expressive Social function to express their internal state (*like that TV*). Because of the similarities, the proportional frequencies for each category were combined and averaged for the group. The categories accounting for more than 10% of the total functions were Interpersonal Expressive (25%), Objective (22%), Effective (15%), Directive (12%), and Self-Expressive Social (11%). Each remaining function accounted for less than 10% of the total functions for the group.

The overall distribution of functions indicated that while the children used language to express knowledge about toys and related actions in the playroom, a substantial amount of their speech was used to mediate the social space of interpersonal relations with their mothers. This pattern of language use has been identified as a social-emotional orientation in communication (Blake, 1994).

Mothers' Language Functions. Even though the language function categories were derived from the speech of young children, they adequately captured the purposes served by the mothers' speech.[4] Similar to the children, the relative proportions of each mother's function distribution varied, indicating that each mother used language to achieve personal goals as a function of context, activity, and knowledge of her child. Again, however, there was a common pattern in the overall distribution of the language functions for the mothers. Thus, the proportional frequencies for each function were combined and averaged for the mothers. The most frequent function for the mothers was Interpersonal Expressive function (45%). This function served to shape behavior (*How do you ask me nicely?*); to inquire about personal state (*You don't want your toys?*); and to establish roles (*Mine/yours* contentions). The second most frequent function for the mothers was Objective (26%), which served to inquire and provide knowledge about the physical world (*Do you know the color? Do you know what you use chalk for?*). The third most frequent was Self-Expressive Social (14%), where speech was used to express a mother's feelings to her child (*Ooh, that looks like fun*). All remaining functions accounted for less than 10% of the total functions for the group. It was concluded that the mothers used a substantial amount of their speech to negotiate relations with their children (i.e., the Interpersonal Expressive and Self-Expressive Social functions).

The overall distribution of language functions reflected a communicative orientation that emphasizes interpersonal relations. Similar to that of the children, the mothers' orientation was characterized as social-emotional. At issue, then, is whether the overall patterns of language use for the children and mothers stressed similar functions.

A Comparison of Language-Use Patterns for Children and Mothers. When proportional frequencies were compared for the children and mothers, more than half of each group's speech served functions that negotiate interpersonal activity through the active, ongoing management of relationships and expressed personal needs and feelings (represented by the Interpersonal Expressive, Effective, and Self-Expressive Social functions). Speech serving these social-emotional functions averaged 51% for the children and 68% for their mothers. Hence, children and mothers used language similarly, expressing a communicative style that emphasizes an expressively negotiatory use of language. Moreover, it was concluded that the presence of this conforming pattern of use for language learners and mature language models is indicative of language socialization and cultural language practices. Thus, mothers are demonstrating, intentionally and unintentionally, what they value, and by extension, what is valued by their cultural group.

DISCUSSION

Although the occurrence of similar language use patterns for mothers and their young children is striking, it is not surprising. Compellingly, sociolinguists have argued some time for recognizing the cultural and social bases of language acquisition (Gumperz and Cook-Gumperz, 1981; Harkness, 1990; Hymes, 1972; Labov, 1972; Smitherman, 1981; Tomasello, 1992). It is revealing to examine early language use and the manner in which it is acquired in light of the persistent language differences African American children exhibit that influence teacher perceptions of their academic competence as the children navigate the schooling experience. Ball (1995) illustrates through case studies how a variety of traditional oral language devices of African Americans find their way into the students' written language expression (e.g., rhetorical devices, folk idioms, talk-aloud protocols, and repetition). She posits that these mechanisms are culturally related and maintain a valued African American tradition of "participative sensemaking such as dialogue, tropes, hyperbole and call and response . . . (that serve) to establish an atmosphere of direct interactive communication with an assumed familiar audience" (p. 274). Moreover, Ball provides examples of how teachers' obliviousness to and perceptions of the use of orally based devices in students' writing affect the teachers' assessment of academic competence.

In the present study, maternal speech—hence early socialization—reflected a similar focus, using language to mark relations with others in a range of ways. A great deal of language was used to negotiate and to inform the other about personal feelings, wants, attitudes, and opinions. In other words, language was used to actively maintain *inter*personal engagement. Mothers used much of their language in this way, and accordingly, their young children were learning to use language in similar ways. Further, by learning to use language in a culturally relevant manner, the children were also learning to make sense of the world and value aspects of it in culturally appropriate ways as well. Consequently, learning how to use language within cultural parameters provides access to that culture's view of the world.

A consideration of the values associated with an African American world view and cultural experience (see Burlew, Banks, McAdoo, and Azibo, 1992 for overview) suggests that the cultural worth assigned to the individual's unique abilities (personal expression) and feelings (affect) at the same time the group is esteemed (interdependence) requires the ongoing monitoring of the status of self relative to group (verve). In other words, each African American group member must have a means for negotiating personal meaning within social space, while simultaneously understanding that culturally all space is first and foremost interpersonal (social time perspective).

The instrumentality of a social-emotional orientation for such a world view is apparent. The Self-Expressive Social function (personal expression and affect) enables the speaker to provide the listener with an affective status report while the Interpersonal Expressive (verve and interdependence) and Effective (interdependence) functions allow the mediation of personal goals within social space. Moreover, the maintenance mechanism for the orientation becomes evident as well. This particular communicative orientation supports and is supported by the larger cultural world view of African American people. It embodies the fundamental cultural belief of the dynamic of the personal (me) and the interpersonal (us) superimposed on all settings, thereby highlighting the primacy of social space.

In summary, the communicative orientation used by the mothers and being learned by their children reflects and supports traditional emphases in African American culture. These emphases or beliefs, which include but are not limited to the aforementioned interdependence, affect, verve, personal expression, and social time (see Abrahams, 1974; Boyd-Franklin, 1989; Boykin and Toms, 1989; Harrison, Wilson, Pine, Chan, and Buriel, 1990; Smitherman, 1986/1977), provide the framework for organizing daily activities, i.e., the culture's world view. And it is this world view that influences the way group members "do things and how they perceive the reality around them" (Rifkin, 1980, p. 5). In other words, a world view is an internalized handbook for living which prescribes behavioral, affective, and cognitive guidelines for group inclusion and conventional scripts for how an individual meets his/her desires and needs. For African Americans, then, the handbook contains a number of traditional values that are continuous with their ancestral heritage (i.e., West African roots) yet sometimes modulated in distinctive behavioral ways in line with New World experiences (see Gilman, 1993; Shade, 1992; Williams, 1993; and Willis, 1992 for discussion). Furthermore, the persistent psychological, sociological, and linguistic boundaries between mainstream and African American living experiences have contributed to the maintenance of a distinctive way of thinking, behaving, and speaking for African Americans.

CONCLUSIONS AND IMPLICATIONS

What does maintanence of an African American cultural world view and communicative style—a cognitive-linguistic orientation—signify for African American children as learners in school settings? At the very least, the children's perceptual processes would be directed to interpersonal content, whereby the quality of a person's actions and relevant contextual information for inferring quality of personal states could be determined. This interpretation is a crucial one because the most effective orientation for mainstream schooling at present would be one that directs attention to objective relationships between aspects in the world, i.e., verifiable facts rather than opinions and judgments (Brice-Heath, 1982; Cazden and Dickinson, 1981). Thus, the orientation that children use in the school context influences what children perceive as important information for learning and thereby shapes what they talk about and the way they talk within that context. This, in turn, affects the teacher's assessment of what children know and—just as crucially—what teachers think children can learn. Importantly, if the teacher and learner are approaching a learning activity repeatedly with divergent frames for interpretation and expression, at the very least frustration will result, and the child may begin to question his/her abilities as an academic learner.

Taken together, these findings argue that our knowledge of the cultural foundation of expression and interpretation for African American children must be extended. In addition, we must investigate the ways in which school contexts affect their cognitive-linguistic orientation and motivation to learn in school across their school years. Such knowledge can serve as the basis for creating more supportive pedagogical strategies for formal learning, as Ball (1995) suggests. Importantly, by drawing on the culturally based language skills with which African American children enter and participate in school, we would be better able to nurture their academic well-being.

NOTES

1. A pseudonym.

2. One child's adult sister (20 years old) is a primary caregiver and participated in study as the mother figure.

3. All research teams were comprised of two African Americans, except one team which included an African American and a Latina.

4. The one exception was Self-Expressive Nonsocial, which no mother used. However, this was not surprising, because the function refers to language used to express feelings, attitudes, and opinions with no designated listener. Generally, the children used it infrequently (5% for the group) for the purpose of labeling an internal state (e.g., *I mad*, said lowly while continuing to look at and play with a toy).

REFERENCES

Abrahams, R. D. (1974). Black talking in the streets. In R. Bauman and J. Sherzer (eds.), *Exploration in the ethnography of speaking*. Cambridge: Cambridge University Press.

Atkins, C. P. (1993). Do employment recruiters discriminate on the basis of nonstandard dialect? *Journal of Employment and Counseling*, 30(37), 108–118.

Ball, A. F. (1995). Text design patterns in the writing of urban African American students: Teaching to the cultural strengths of students in multicultural settings. *Urban Education*, 30(3), 253–289.

Blake, I. K. (1984). *Language development in working-class black children: An examination of form, content, and use*. Unpublished doctoral dissertation, Columbia University, New York City.

———. (1993). The social-emotional orientation of mother-child communication in African American families. *International Journal of Behavioral Development*, 16(3).

———. (1994). Language development and socialization in young African American children. In P. Greenfield and R. Cocking (eds.), *Cross-cultural Roots of Minority Child Development* (pp. 167–195). Hillsdale, NJ: Erlbaum.

Bloom, L. (1993). *The transition from infancy to language: Acquiring the power of expression*. Cambridge: Cambridge University Press.

Boyd-Franklin, N. (1989). *Black families in therapy: A multisystems approach*.

Boykin, A. W., and Toms, F. D. (1989). Black child socialization: A conceptual framework. In H. P. McAdoo and J. L. McAdoo (eds.), *Black children: Social, educational, and parental environments*. Newbury Park, CA: Sage Publications.

Brice-Heath, S. (1982). What no bedtime story means: Narrative skill at home and school. *Language and Society*, 11, 49–76.

Brislin, R. W. (ed.). (1990). *Applied cross-cultural psychology*. Newbury Park, CA: Sage Publications.

Burg, L. A. (1975). Affective teaching: Neglected practice in inner city schools. *Reading Teacher*, 28(4), 360–363.

Burlew, A. K. H., Banks, W. C., McAdoo, H. P., and Azibo, D. A. (eds.). (1992). African American psychology: Theory, research, and practice. Newbury Park, CA: Sage Publications.

Cazden, C. (1988). *Classroom discourse: The language of teaching and learning*. Portsmouth, NH: Heinemann.

Cazden, C. B., and Dickinson, D. K. (1981). Language in education: Standardization versus cultural pluralism. In C. A. Ferguson and S. B. Heath (eds.), *Language in the USA* (pp. 446–468). Cambridge: Cambridge University Press.

Deutsch, M. (1967). *The disadvantaged child: Studies of the social environment and the learning process*. New York: Basic Books.

Feagans, L., and Farran, D. C. (eds.). (1982). *The language of children reared in poverty: Implications for evaluation and intervention*. New York: Academic Press.

Gee, J. P. (1985). The narrativization of experience in the oral style. *Journal of Education*, 167(1), 9–35.

Gilman, C. (1993). Black identity, homeostasis, and survival: African and metropolitan speech varieties in the New World. In S. S. Mufwene (ed.), *Africanisms in Afro-American language varieties* (pp. 388–402). Athens: University of Georgia Press.

Greenfield, P. M., and Cocking, R. (1994). *Cross-cultural roots of minority child development*. Hillsdale, NJ: Erlbaum.

Gumperz, J. J., and Cook-Gumperz, J. (1981). Ethnic differences in communicative style. In C. A. Ferguson and S. B. Heath (eds.), *Language in the USA* (pp. 430–445). Cambridge: Cambridge University Press.

Hale-Benson, J. (1986/1982). *Black children: Their roots, culture and learning styles*. (Revised ed.). Baltimore: The Johns Hopkins University Press.

Harkness, S. (1990). A cultural model for the acquisition of language: Implications for the innateness debate. Special Issue: The idea of innateness: Effects on language and communication research. *Developmental Psychobiology*, 23(7), 727–739.

Harrison, A. O., Wilson, M. N., Pine, C. J., Chan, S. Q., and Buriel, R. (1990). Family ecologies of ethnic minority children. *Child Development*, 61, 347–362.

Hymes, D. H. (1972). Models of the interaction of language and social life. In J. J. Gumperz and D. Hymes (eds.), *Directions in sociolinguistics*. New York: Holt, Rinehart and Winston.

John-Steiner, V., and Panofsky, C. (1992). Narrative competence: Cross-cultural comparisons. *Journal of Narrative and Life History*, 2(3), 219–233.

Jones, R. L. (1991). *Black psychology*. Berkeley, CA: Cobb and Henry.

Kitayama, S. (1996). Culture, Self and the Collectivist View: Presentation at Center for Advanced Study in the Behavioral Sciences. Stanford University, Stanford, CA.

Kohl, H. (1991). *I won't learn from you! The role of assent in education*. Minneapolis: Milkweed Editions.

Labov, W. (1972). *Language in the inner city: Studies in the Black English vernacular*. Philadelphia: University of Pennsylvania Press.

McAdoo, H. P. (ed.). (1990). *Family ethnicity: Strength in diversity*. Newbury Park, CA: Sage Publications.

Markham, L. R. (1984, May). "De dog and de cat": Assisting speakers of Black English as they begin to write. *Young Children*, 39(4), 15–24.

Michaels, S. (1981a). Sharing time: An oral preparation for literacy. *Language in Society*, 10, 423–442.

——. (1981b). "Sharing time:" Children's narrative styles and differential access to literacy. *Language in Society*, 10, 423–442.

Newmeyer, F. J. (1973). Linguistic theory, language teaching, sociolinguistics: Can they be interrelated? *Modern Language Journal*, 57(8), 405, 410.

Nichols, P. C. (1989). Storytelling in Carolina: Continuities and contrasts. *Anthropology & Education Quarterly*, 20, 232–245.

Oakland Unified School District. (1997, January 24). Synopsis of the adopted policy on Standard American English language development. *Http://ousd.k12.ca.us/oakland.standard.html#standard*.

Potts, R. (1989). *West side stories: Children's conversational narratives in a Black low-income community*. Paper presented at the Biennial Meeting of the Society for Research in Child Development, Kansas City, MO.

Schieffelin, B. B., and Ochs, E. (1986). Language socialization. *Annual Review of Anthropology*, 15, 163–191.

Segall, M. H., Dasen, P. R., Berry, J. W., and Poortinga, Y. H. (1990). *Human behavior in global perspective: An introduction to cross-cultural psychology*. New York: Allyn and Bacon.

Shade, B. J. (1992). Is there an Afro-American cognitive style? An exploratory study. In A. K. H. Burlew, W. C. Banks, H. P. McAdoo, and D. A. Azibo (eds.), *African American psychology: Theory, research, and practice* (pp. 256–259). Newbury Park, CA: Sage Publications.

Smitherman, G. (1981). "What go round come round": King in perspective. *Harvard Educational Review*, 51(1), 40–56.

——. (1986/1977). *Talkin and testifyin*. Detroit: Wayne State University Press.

Spears-Bunton, L. A. (1993). *Cultural consciousness and response to literary texts among African American and European American high school juniors*. Unpublished dissertation, University of Kentucky, Lexington.

Stockman, I. J., and Vaughn-Cooke, F. B. (1981). *Child language acquisition in Africa and the Diaspora: A neglected linguistic issue.* Paper presented at the First World Congress on Black Communications, Nairobi, Kenya.

———. (1982). A reexamination of research on the language of black children: The need for a new framework. *Journal of Education, 164,* 157–172.

Taylor, J. B. (1983). Influence of speech variety on teachers' evaluation of reading comprehension. *Journal of Educational Psychology, 75*(5), 662–667.

Tomasello, M. (1992). The social bases of language acquisition. *Social Development, 1*(1), 67–87.

Tough, J. (1977). *The development of meaning: A study of children's use of language.* New York: Wiley.

———. (1982). Language, poverty, and disadvantage in school. In L. Feagans and D. C. Farran (eds.), *The language of children reared in poverty* (pp. 3–18). New York: Academic Press.

Washington, V. M., and Miller-Jones, D. (1989). Teacher interactions with nonstandard English speakers during reading instructions. *Contemporary Educational Psychology, 14*(3), 280–312.

Williams, S. W. (1993). Substantive Africanisms at the end of the African linguistic diaspora. In S. S. Mufwene (ed.), *Africanisms in Afro-American language varieties* (pp. 407–422). Athens: University of Georgia Press.

Willis, M. G. (1992). Learning styles of African American children: A review of the literature and interventions. In A. K. H. Burlew, W. C. Banks, H. P. McAdoo, and D. A. Azido (eds.), *African American psychology: Theory, research, and practice* (pp. 260–278). Newbury Park, CA: Sage Publications.

9

THE RELATIONSHIP BETWEEN PLACE
OF BIRTH AND HEALTH STATUS

Sharon Aneta Bryant

Culture is an amorphous concept that influences all aspects of health. It provides the context in which health behaviors are practiced and it shapes beliefs about health and illness. The Western medical paradigm views health as the absence of diseases and harmful bacteria in the body; an individual becomes ill when the body malfunctions (LaFargue, 1985). People of African descent often characterize health as the harmony between mind, body, and spirit; illness occurs when there is disharmony (Spector, 1985; Perrone, Stockel, and Krueger, 1989). Rural Southern Blacks often associate religion with health: God can protect a person's health and lack of faith in God can cause illness (Robenson, 1985). Thus health care providers accustomed to Western medicine and its practices are often surprised that other health belief systems affect the practice of medicine. Many assume that once foreign-born people immigrate to the U.S., they will abandon their cultural views about health and quickly accept and adopt Western health beliefs. Moreover, the medical care delivery system has not integrated the cultural values and traditions of non-Westerners, even though research studies conclude that African Americans are more likely to follow health care treatments when their health care providers can design treatments influenced by African Americans' cultural values (Scupholme, Robertson, and Kamons, 1991).

An individual's culture can shape how she or he recognizes and expresses symptoms of illness. As part of the socialization process, a person learns which symptoms elicit sympathy and which symptoms do not. In the United States, for example, headaches elicit more sympathy than memory problems, while in Mexico the opposite is true (Brislin, 1993).

Culture has also influenced patterns of health care use (Russell and Jewell, 1992). Consistently, studies have shown that Whites have higher rates of medical care utilization than Blacks possibly because the medical care system may support Whites' values about health and illness more than it does Blacks'. Moreover, foreign-born Blacks access health care services even less than U.S.-born Blacks. Frutcher and others (1990) report that Haitian women residing in the United States visit the doctor less frequently than U.S.-born women. Although differences in health insurance coverage, high cost of medical services, and mistrust of health providers who practice medicine differently may account for the above difference, culture plays an important role. As Americans, we tend to place our faith in the medical care system, whereas immigrants may prefer folk remedies, an indigenous healer, or a health care provider who understands their culture, especially when there is a language barrier.

The impact of culture on Black womens' health status has been ignored because we have operationalized "Black" or "African American" in a way that obscures cultural differences among women of African descent living in the U.S. Researchers who study health status indicators have demonstrated the importance of distinguishing among cultural subgroups of populations that are often considered undifferentiated (Williams, 1994). For example, low-income Haitian Americans have a different health profile than U.S.-born Blacks (Frutcher et al., 1990). While we know that people of African descent in the United States are composed of many different ethnic backgrounds (e.g., persons from the Caribbean and African countries), we have not systematically examined these differences using national data.

The purpose of this essay is to examine whether place of birth may influence subjective health information such as self-reported health status. Data from the 1990 National Health Interview Survey of Disease Prevention and Health Promotion (DPHP) was used to examine health status differences between U.S.-born and foreign-born Black women. This study addressed the following questions in particular:

1. What is the relationship between place of birth and health status?
2. What is the relationship between place of birth and the use of preventive health behavior?
3. What is the relationship between self-reported health status and preventive health behavior?

METHODS

Sample

The 1990 DPHP National Health Interview Survey was a national survey of adults aged eighteen and older, sponsored by the National Center for Health Statistics. It is a cross-sectional survey of the United States civilian noninstitutionalized population and has been conducted annually since 1957. Census Bureau personnel interviewed members of 40,000 to 50,000 households across the country to obtain health and demographic information (Kovar and Poe, 1985). Besides collecting basic health information every year, they included supplemental surveys on special health topics. In 1990, DPHP included a set of questions on health-related practices to serve as a basis for tracking progress toward the *Healthy People 2000* goals. The overall response rate for the 1990 DPHP was 86%.

Characteristics of the Sample

For this investigation, the sample was restricted to women of African descent. Table 1 provides some characteristics of the sample. There were more U.S.-born Black women between the ages of 18 to 24 (13%) than foreign-born Black women (8%). U.S.-born Black women were more likely to be aged 65 and older than foreign-born Black women. Forty percent of foreign-born Black women were married, compared to 28 percent of U.S.-born Black women. U.S.-born Black women were more likely to report their marital status as widowed, divorced, or separated (42%) than were foreign-born Black women (29%). Foreign-born Black women acquired more advanced education than U.S.-born Black women; 23% of foreign-born Black women attended college as compared with 18% of U.S.-born Black women. Eighty-four percent of foreign-born Black women had family incomes above the poverty level, compared to 64% of U.S.-born Black women. Seventy-two percent of foreign-born Black women were employed, in contrast to 52% of U.S.-born Black women. More U.S.-born Black women lived in the south (53%), and more foreign-born Black women lived in the northeast (63%). (Several shortcomings limited this study. The number of foreign-born Black women included in the study was very small compared to U.S.-born Black women, and their countries of birth were unknown. Also, the foreign-born Black women were a heterogeneous group that included women who lived in the United States from less than one year to more than fifteen years.)

FINDINGS

Cross-tabulations were used to examine the relationship between place of birth and health status. At the bivariate level Pearson's chi-square statistics were used to analyze the relationship between place of birth and health status, place of birth being used to measure culture.

Health Status

Table 2 shows the relationship between place of birth and measures of health status. U.S.-born Black women (23%) reported poorer health status than foreign-born Black women (12%). Fifty-five percent of foreign-born Black women reported their health status as excellent, in contrast to 45% of U.S.-born Black women. Twenty-four percent of U.S.-born Black women

*Table 1: Demographic Characteristics of U.S.-Born
and Foreign-Born Black Women*

Personal Characteristics	Percents U.S. Born (N=3,431)	Percents Foreign Born (N=183)
*Age***		
18–24	13	10
25–34	24	36
35–44	21	24
45–54	14	16
55–64	12	6
65–74	9	5
75 and over	7	4
*Marital Status***		
Married	28	42
Widowed/div/sep	42	30
Never Married	30	28
*Education Attainment***		
Some schooling	33	31
High school graduate	39	30
Some college	18	23
College graduate	6	10
Graduate school	4	6
*Poverty Status***		
Above poverty	64	84
Below poverty	36	16
*Employment status***		
Employed	52	72
Not employed	48	28
*Region***		
Northwest	14	62
Midwest	23	4
South	53	25
West	10	9
*Telephone status***		
Yes	87	96
No	13	4

*p<.05
**p<.01
***p<.001

reported some activity limitation, compared with 14% of foreign-born
Black women. Twenty-five percent of U.S.-born Black women stated that
in the past two weeks they frequently experienced stress, as compared with
18% of foreign-born Black women. Physicians told more U.S.-born Black
women that they had hypertension (37%) than foreign-born Black women
(19%). Eight percent of U.S.-born Black women were diagnosed with dia-

Table 2: Measures of Health Status by Place of Birth

Health Status Characteristics	Percents U.S. Born (N=3,431)	Percents Foreign Born (N=183)
Health Status***		
Excellent	45	57
Good	32	31
Poor	23	12
Activity Limitation***		
Limitation	24	14
No limitation	76	86
Amount of stress experienced in the past two weeks***		
A lot	25	18
Moderate	27	20
Relatively little/almost none	48	62
Ever told by MD you had hypertension***		
Yes	37	19
No	63	81
Now have diabetes***		
Yes	8	5
No	92	95
Have heart condition***		
Yes	10	5
No	90	95
Ever had a stroke		
Yes	3	2
No	97	98
Ever been told by MD you had high blood cholesterol***		
Yes	33	25
No	67	75

*p<.05
**p<.01
***p<.001

betes, in contrast to 5% of foreign-born Black women. Ten percent of U.S.-born Black women had heart conditions, compared with 5% of foreign-born Black women. Physicians told more U.S.-born Black women that their blood cholesterol levels were high (33%) than foreign-born Black women (25%).

Preventive Health Behavior

Table 3 presents the relationship between place of birth and preventive health behavior. Overall, U.S.-born Black women participated in more preventive health practices than foreign-born Black women. More foreign-born Black women have never had a physician perform a clinical breast

Table 3: Preventive Health Behavior by Place of Birth

Health Behaviors	Percents U.S. Born (N=3,431)	Percents Foreign Born (N=183)
Ever had mammogram		
Yes	51	52
No	49	48
Pap smear***		
Less than or equal to 1 year	52	54
Many years	43	33
Never	5	13
MD perform breast exam***		
Less than or equal to 1 year	54	53
Many years	39	33
Never	7	14
Perform breast self-exam***		
Yes	85	76
No	15	24
Smoke cigarettes now***		
Yes	65	52
No	35	48
Drinking status***		
Non-drinker	56	67
Drinker	44	33
Exercise or play sports regularly***		
Yes	27	21
No	73	79
Exercise (walking)***		
Yes	48	37
No	52	63
Average number of hours of sleep per day***		
Less than or equal to 7 hours	49	59
8 hours	36	30
More than 9 hours	15	11
Wear seatbelts**		
Yes	58	60
No	42	40
Eat Breakfast*		
Everyday	47	56
Sometime	30	26
Rarely	23	18
Regular physician***		
Yes	86	74
No	14	26
Doctor visits in past 12 months***		
Yes	84	78
No	16	22

Table 3 (continued)

Health Behaviors	Percents U.S. Born (N=3,431)	Percents Foreign Born (N=183)
Interval since last MD visit***		
Less than 1 year	85	79
1 year to less than 2	6	12
Greater than 2 years	9	9

*p<.05
**p<.01
***p<.001

examination (14%) than U.S.-born Black women (7%). Twenty-four percent of foreign-born Black women stated that they had never performed breast self-examination, compared to 15% of U.S.-born Black women. No significant differences were found between the two groups for having ever had a mammogram or for having regular mammograms. Although slightly more foreign-born Black women had had a pap smear (54%) in the past year than U.S.-born Black women (52%); 13% of foreign-born Black women reported having never had a pap smear performed, as compared with 5% of U.S.-born Black women.

More foreign-born Black women were nonsmokers (48%) than their U.S.-born counterparts (35%). Sixty-seven percent of foreign-born Black women abstained from drinking alcoholic beverages, as compared with 56% of U.S.-born Black women. U.S.-born Black women exercised (27%) more frequently than foreign-born Black women (21%). Forty-eight percent of U.S.-born Black women walked for exercise, as compared with 37% of foreign-born Black women. Slightly more U.S.-born Black women (36%) slept an average of eight hours per night than foreign-born Black women (30%). U.S.-born Black women were slightly less likely to wear seat belts (58%) than foreign-born Black women (60%). Fifty-six percent of foreign-born Black women ate breakfast every day, as compared with 47% of U.S.-born Black women. U.S.-born Black women were more likely to have a regular physician (86%) than were foreign-born Black women (74%). Eighty-four percent of U.S.-born Black women have visited the doctor at least once in the past 12 months, as compared to 78% of foreign-born Black women.

DISCUSSION

What do these findings suggest about health differences among women of African descent residing in the United States? Not only did U.S.-born

Black women report poorer health status than did foreign-born Black women, they also experienced higher rates of self-reported chronic diseases, most diagnosed by a physician. Though it appeared as if foreign-born Black women were healthier than U.S.-born Black women, foreign-born Black women engaged in fewer preventive health practices than did U.S.-born Black women, practices that could prolong their apparent good health. U.S.-born Black women have heeded the health messages concerning preventive health practices and have incorporated many of those practices into their lifestyle. One reason for such findings may be U.S.-born Black women's higher rate of using the medical care system. Once they were in the system, their health care providers were more likely to order tests to detect these chronic diseases. When women were diagnosed, they may have been more likely to change some behaviors and incorporate preventive practices into their lifestyles. Furthermore, U.S.-born Black women may have been more receptive to Western messages about preventive health practices and were thus more willing to modify their behaviors (Scupholme, Robertson, and Kamons, 1991; Russell and Jewell, 1992).

Although U.S.-born Black women were more likely to participate in preventive health practices, both groups lagged behind national goals for participating in preventive health behaviors. For example, *Healthy People 2000* includes health care goals that Americans should reach by the year 2000. Black women's health promotion activities must improve considerably to meet the targeted goals for their groups. Two health goals that illustrate the need for culturally relevant health education are as follows:

16.6d: Reduce cigarette smoking to prevalence of no more than 18 percent among Blacks aged 20 and over.

Both groups of women were found to have higher rates of smoking, 65% for U.S.-born and 52% for foreign-born.

21.3b: Increase to at least 95 percent the proportion of Blacks who have a specific source of ongoing primary care for coordination of their preventive and episodic health care.

Both groups of women were found to have lower rates of regular medical care, 86% for U.S.-born Black women and 74% for foreign-born Black women.

These two examples illustrate the need to design and develop health education messages and programs that are culturally relevant to the targeted groups. In the past, general health messages were translated into different languages; apparently, these generalized messages did not work effectively. Health messages need to reflect the beliefs, values, and traditions of diverse cultures and be language-appropriate. Many HIV/AIDS preventive messages targeting diverse Black cultures use, for example, African proverbs, religious symbols, images of Black people, and artwork. The same strategies need to be applied to other health concerns, such as diabetes and hypertension. For example, diet plays a big role in treating both diabetes and hypertension, and studies have shown that when health care providers develop diet plans that take into account traditional food and preparation styles, Blacks are more likely to adhere to these treatment modalities (Russell and Jewell, 1991).

Health education messages cannot be limited to health care settings but must be extended to culturally appropriate settings outside the health care system, since foreign-born Black women are less likely to use medical care services. Community representatives need to participate in designing programs to meet the needs of their communities (Russell and Jewell, 1991). Many of these representatives have worked with national agencies such as the American Heart Association, American Cancer Society, and national HIV/AIDS organizations. These organizations have been successful at getting topics such as breast cancer, heart disease, and HIV/AIDS discussed in community settings. Community representatives and organizational staff members have taught Black women the importance of health promotion activities in beauty parlors, sorority and club meetings, and at church events (Braithwaite and Lythcott, 1989). For example, training beauticians to educate their clients increases the probability the Black women will listen to the health promotion message. Furthermore, these messages need to take place in more secular community organizations.

These findings suggested that U.S.-born and foreign-born Black women may be applying different standards in evaluating their health status. More research is needed to conduct extensive interviews with foreign-born Black women to learn who serves as the referent group when a woman evaluates her health status. Also, what are some indigenous health practices that foreign-born Black women turn to before seeking formal medical care services? We also need to better understand foreign-born Black women's cultural values and traditions associated with health in order to develop appropriate health programs and messages to target this group.

This study suggested that subjective assessments of health were not unmediated reflections of something that we might consider "true health" but were influenced by an individual's culture. If groups with different social characteristics (e.g., foreign born and U.S. born) responded to questions concerning health differently than did other groups, then researchers who used this information to compare health levels could easily attribute substantive differences in health to what was actually difference in the way individuals from these different groups respond (Angel and Guaranaccia, 1989; Kleinman and Kleinman, 1985). This problem was particularly serious in the study of health, since many studies that deal with health differences between Blacks and Whites were based on subjective reports by survey respondents, and most of this information cannot be verified against objective external information. Therefore, researchers must ask themselves whether the measurement tools tap the same underlying phenomenon in different groups or whether the measurement was significantly affected by the characteristics of the groups studied. It is also necessary to understand how subjective information is influenced by cultural factors in order to begin to be confident of the accuracy of group comparisons based on self-report data.

REFERENCES

Angel, R., and P. Guarnaccia. 1989. "Mind, Body and Culture." *Social Science and Medicine* 28: 1229–1238.

Braithwaite, R., and N. Lythcott. 1989. "Community Empowerment as a Strategy for Health Promotion for Black and Other Minority Populations." *Journal of the American Medical Association* 261: 282.

Fruchter, R., et al. 1990. "Cervix and Breast Cancer Incidence in Immigrant Caribbean Women." *American Journal of Public Health* 76(7): 794–796.

Fruchter, R., et al. 1990. "Cervical Cancer in Immigrant Caribbean Women." *American Journal of Public Health* 76(7): 797–799.

Kleinman, A., and J. Kleinman. 1985. "Somatization: The Interconnections of Chinese Society Among Culture, Depressive Experiences and the Meanings of Pain." In A. Kleinman and B. Good (eds)., *Culture and Depression*. Berkeley: University of California Press.

Kovar, M., and G. Poe. 1985. *The National Health Interview Design*. Hyattsville, MD: National Center for Health Statistics.

LaFargue, J. 1985. "Mediating Between Two Views of Illness." *Topics in Clinical Nursing* 7(3): 70–77.

Mechanic, D. 1980. "The Experience and Reporting of Common Physical Complaints." *Journal of Health and Social Behavior* 21: 146–155.

National Center for Health Statistics. 19. *Healthy People 2000*. Washington, DC: U.S. Government Printing Office.

Perez-Stable, E., et al. 1986. "Tuberculin Reactivity in United States and Foreign born Latinos." *American Journal of Public Health* 76(6): 643–645.

Robenson, M. 1985. "The Influence of Religious Beliefs on Health Choices of Afro Americans." *Topics in Clinical Nursing* 7:57–63.

Rosenwaike, I., and K. Hempstead. 1990. "Differential Mortality." *Social Biology* 37(1–2): 11–25.

Russell, K., and N. Jewell. 1992. "Cultural Impact of Health Care Access." *Journal of Community Health Nursing* 9(3): 161–169.

Scupholme, A., E. Robertson, and A. Kamons. 1991. "Barriers to Prenatal Care in a Multiethnic Urban Sample." *Journal of Nurse-Midwifery* 36: 111–116.

Spector, R. 1985. *Cultural Diversity in Health and Illness*. Norwalk, CT: Appleton-Century-Croft.

Zola, I. 1964. "Illness Behavior of the Working Class: Implications and Recommendations." in A. Shostak and W. Gomberg (eds)., *Blue Collar World*. Englewood Cliffs, NJ: Prentice-Hall.

——. 1966. "Culture and Symptoms." *American Sociological Review* 31: 615–630.

RACE, GENDER, AND IMAGE

10 IMAGES OF AFRICA AND THE HAITI REVOLUTION IN AMERICAN AND BRAZILIAN ABOLITIONISM

Celia M. Azevedo

One of the main tasks of abolitionists, wherever they lived, was to forge a general sentiment of empathy with the slave. Empathy with the slave required, above all, a picture of the slave as a human being in chains, with no will of his or her own, a bound worker under the sole power of the slaveholder: in a word, the slave as a victim. However, there were very distinct ways of forging this sympathetic sentiment.

In this essay, I intend to show how American and Brazilian abolitionists revealed different sensibilities toward the slave through the images of Africa and the Haiti Revolution presented in their writings and speeches.[1]

I shall proceed by the following steps. First, I will present American abolitionists' images of Africa and the Haiti Revolution. Second, I will dwell on Brazilian abolitionists' images of Africa and slave rebellion in general, given the fact that one hardly finds any references to Haiti in Brazilian abolitionism. Third, I will conclude by making some remarks on the striking differences of images engendered by abolitionists in the United States and Brazil as well as on the historical reasons for such contrasting ways of searching for empathy with the slave.

AMERICAN ABOLITIONISTS: THE GLORY OF AFRICA AND HAITI

The search for empathy with the slave, and the Negro in general, begins with the search for the past glory of Africa. Black and white abolitionists agreed that Africa in the present had nothing to offer as a contribution to progress and civilization. To the African American David Walker, "ignorance" was the word to define the present state of Africa.[2] But if Africa was considered the land of ignorance and heathenism, he made clear that this distressing present situation was not to be understood from a racist perspective. To Walker, the "wheel of events" was part of the history of rising and falling, from which no country in the world could escape.[3]

In discovering the decaying African land, all that Christian and "enlightened" individuals in Europe, and some in Asia, had done was to plunge the African ancestors "into wretchedness ten thousand times more intolerable, than if they had left them entirely to the Lord." But, adding to their miseries, Christians told them "that they are an *inferior* and *distinct race* of beings. . . ."[4]

To contradict this rationale of race, Walker dismissed the presupposition that Africa, as a land of darkness, had no past, and took the first steps toward writing the history of Africa from the point of view of the oppressed Africans. In the past Africa had been a land of light, for learning (that is, the arts and sciences) originated among "the sons of Africa or of Ham" and "was carried thence into Greece, where it was improved upon and refined" as well as, later, to the Romans. What made Walker so sure that the arts and sciences had been initiated by Africans was that Africans were the inhabitants of Egypt, which historians usually claimed as the cradle of world civilization.[5]

During the 1840s the theme of Africa as a land of light in the past received a more detailed treatment from another abolitionist of African descent. In an address to the Female Benevolent Society, the Reverend Henry Highland Garnet invited his audience to forget for a moment the desolation in which black people were immersed, and look upward toward "the bright scenery of the future." In considering the present as "the midway between the Past and the Future," Garnet suggested that the best way to visualize the bright future of "the colored people" was to depict the glorious past of Africa. The biblical narrative offered essential evidence that Africa had been once a land of light. For Ham, one of the three sons of Noah, was the first African, and Egypt was settled by an immediate descendant of Ham called Mesraim.[6]

In pointing to the glorious past of Africa, Garnet did not forget to suggest the degraded past of "Anglo Saxons." As he suggested, at the time the enlightened black Egyptians were filling the world with amazement, the ancestors of "the now proud and boasting Anglo Saxons" were among the most degraded of the human family. Anglo Saxons lived in caves, either naked or covered with the skins of wild beasts; and they offered human sacrifice in bloody altars.[7]

Two purposes seem to be at the root of Garnet's speech. First, by calling attention to the reverse histories of Africans and "Anglo Saxons" in the past—Africa as a land of light, Europe as a land of darkness—Garnet implied that the future might bring the same historical reversal. If the present was "the midway between the Past and the Future," the future could recapitulate the past as the closing of a life circle. Secondly, to prove that the Negro was a human being with rights equal to those of any other

human being required that Negroes be attributed a history of their own—
the history of Africa—just as white people could dwell on the history of
Europe. Otherwise, Africa would appear as a land eternally destined to
degradation because of God's punishment, or, as scientists were increasingly assuming, because of the inferiority of the "African race."

White abolitionists partook of the same purposes by incorporating the
theme of the glorious past of Africa side by side with the theme of Africa
as a land of darkness in the present. In *The Oasis*, published in 1834, Lydia
Maria Child included a special poem on the subject:

> The poor despised negro might look up,
> And smile, to hear that Greece, that classic Greece,
> Refused not to partake the enticing cup,
> Which swarthy Egypt tendered with the arts of peace:
>
> That the proud white man sought in ages back,
> The intellectual fire that lights his brow,
> And found it too, among a race as black
> As the poor slave he makes his victim now!
>
> The heir of Africa may not always be
> The "lowest link" in this our being's chain;
> There is a magic power in liberty,
> To make the smother'd flame break out and blaze again.[8]

Lydia M. Child introduces here another of the favorite themes of
American abolitionism: the sublime slave struggle for liberty. In commenting on the danger of slave insurrections, one writer for *The Liberator*
made clear that when slaves fought for their liberty, they were only listening to God's will:

> Resistance to tyrants is obedience to God, was our revolutionary
> motto. We acted upon that motto—what more did Nat Turner? . . .
> In claiming this right for themselves, the American people
> necessarily concede it to all mankind.[9]

But what made the call for liberty irresistible for the slaves was the
memory of a successful slave insurrection, the Haiti Revolution. For the
first time in the history of slavery, slaves rebelled, expelled their tyrants,
and assumed the political power of a former European colony. Moreover,
this had been a Revolution of *black* slaves, a living expression that there
was hope for the future of the American slaves. In the concluding remarks
to his book on "the tyranny and cruelty of American Republican Slave-
Masters," David L. Child expressed his admiration for Haiti by defining it
as the present "depository of the greatest trust of God to man."[10]

Haiti as the American slaves' great hope of deliverance from the present sorrows was one of the common readings of this revolutionary event by American abolitionists. Another reading was that Haiti offered living proof that people of African descent were not inferior to white people. Therefore Haiti stood also as the black people's great hope of deliverance from the sorrows of racism.

In sum, the themes of Africa as a land of light in the past, the perennial slaves' struggle for liberty, and the glorious Haiti Revolution were all part of a well-coordinated effort by black and white abolitionists to create empathy with the slave, as well as with African Americans in general.

Let's now turn our attention to Brazil, and see how Brazilian abolitionists approached Africa and the issue of slave rebellion.

BRAZILIAN ABOLITIONISTS: THE VICIOUS AFRICA AND THE DANGEROUS SLAVE

The search for empathy with the slave did not translate into empathy with people of African descent in Brazilian abolitionism. Themes which, as time went by, shaped a kind of abolitionist common sense in the United States were absent. The idea of Africa's brillant past was unknown to Brazilian abolitionists. By the same token, mention of the Haiti Revolution was absent from the abolitionist press, but for a few alarming references in early antislavery literature.

If Africa itself ever came to mind, it evoked misery, ignorance, and ugliness. Africa was the land of darkness. The problem to which Brazilian abolitionists constantly referred was that Africa had exported its vices to Brazil, along with thousands of slaves. As one of the main abolitionist leaders, Joaquim Nabuco, explained,

> When the first Africans were imported to Brazil, their [Brazil's] main inhabitants did not think . . . that they were preparing for the future a people compounded in its majority of slaves' descendants. . . . The main effect of slavery over our population was thus its africanization, saturating it with black blood. . . .
> Called by slavery, the Negro race by the mere fact of living and reproducing, increasingly became the most considerable element of the population. . . . That was the initial revenge of the victims. Each slave womb gave to the master three or four children which he reduced to money; they went on multiplying, and thus the vices of the African blood ended up by making their way into the general circulation of the country.[11]

The "africanization" of Brazil was then an inheritance from the "mother country," that is, Portugal, which had impressed a "spot" on every possible aspect of Brazilian society, including language, social manners, education.[12] Africanization was thus the ensemble of African vices circulating, along with the slaves, in Brazil. But what did Nabuco and other Brazilian abolitionists mean by "African vices"? The first arose from African superstitions, which had corrupted religion in Brazil. Nabuco believed that Africans were incapable of religion, because they could not understand the metaphysical principles that constituted the superior level of religion. Immersed in their fetishism, Africans saw in their images not the symbol, but the very substance, of the superior being. They did not learn anything from Catholicism but the exteriority of the rites.[13] Thus, the lack of a truly religious sentiment prevented slaves from acquiring the basic notions of morality that cemented marriage, family, and social contacts in general. Another African vice was laziness. The abolitionist Domingos Jaguaribe Filho implicitly suggested that Africans worked only under compulsion, for work as the source of goods, improvement, and progress was almost absent from African history:

> But when we think that the huge black population that inhabits the African continent, for more than three thousand years, has not taken one step ahead, that man there is a thing with no importance . . . that the contact between the peoples has been unable to civilize it [the African population], neither change nor take it from the apathy and misery which seems to be its greatest pride: when one reflects that [the African population] scattered throughout the world does not exhibit as other peoples the love for the homeland, nor the stimulus which guides every man in search of wealth and education, then it seems that one has the right to say nothing more, nor to predict the future of such an unfortunate race.[14]

Brazilian abolitionists were increasingly incorporating the growing scientific rationale of race to their views about the slave by the 1870s and 1880s. Social Darwinism made its entrance simultaneously in American and Brazilian society, but the thought of Herbert Spencer, which systematized the implications of Charles Darwin's evolutionism in fields other than biology itself, became influential in Brazilian society before the abolition of slavery, and not after, as happened in the United States. In Spencer, Brazilian abolitionists found the "evolutionary optimism" which underlay their presupposition that the emancipated slaves would have the chance to mentally develop toward the needs of civilized life.[15] As Nabuco argued, many of the unfavorable influences of slavery over the country "could be attributed to the Negro race, to its backward mental development, to its barbarous instincts, and also to its rough superstitions"; but for slavery, contact between white and black people would have brought about the mental elevation of the "Negro race" to the superior level of the "more advanced race," that is, the race of "caucasian blood."[16]

Social Darwinism intermingled with Positivism, another influential theory making its way in Brazilian society during the 1860s. In assimilating the thought of August Comte, abolitionists also found reasons for being optimistic about future relations between "the white race" (that is, "the intelligent race") and "the black race" (that is, "the loving or affective race"). As the "Perpetual President" of the Rio de Janeiro Positivist Society, the abolitionist Miguel Lemos explained,

> The African is a venerator by nature, and therefore he submits; it is neither fear, nor interest which holds him in slavery, but the love for the masters whom they regard as their superiors. The submission of the African is similar to the submission of the soldier to the general; we repeat, it is the product of veneration, and not interest.[17]

Given the presence in Brazilian abolitionism of themes such as Africa as a land of vices, the vicious bestial slave, as well as the rationale of race attributing intelligence to white people and stupidity to black people, it is hardly surprising that abolitionists were not prone to praise the Haiti Revolution as well as the slaves' struggle for liberty in Brazil. Despite some admiring references to African courage in poems by Fagundes Varela, abolitionists could not attribute any honorable meaning to the rebellion of irrational human beings, as they considered the slaves.[18] If there was any meaning, it was that of a mere bloody revenge by the slave, like the one the leading romantic poet Castro Alves describes in "The Negro Bandit."[19]

CONCLUSION

I would like to summarize now the contrasting views of the slave by American and Brazilian abolitionists. To American abolitionists, the search for empathy with the slave meant also an effort to nurture a sympathetic feeling toward the African and their descendents in the United States as well as toward a Revolution made by black people. In contrast, to Brazilian abolitionists, the search for empathy with the slave did not expand either toward the Africans, or toward the slaves' struggle for liberty.

How can we explain such ideological difference of views between American and Brazilian abolitionists? First, one must have in mind the differences in the informing influences on the language of abolitionism in each country. As we have seen, American abolitionists were religion-oriented and depicted the struggle for abolition as a fight between the forces of God and evil. In contrast, Brazilian abolitionists lived in an increasingly secularized intellectual environment and were inclined to find inspiration in science—as well as scientific racial theories—in order to demonstrate the wrongness of slavery. Second, one must be aware that American abolitionism was a voice speaking from outside slavery, while

Brazilian abolitionism was a voice speaking from the very heart of the slave hierarchy. When Brazilian abolitionists addressed the problem of slavery they were addressing people formed by that very evolving slave spirit, as they were themselves. American abolitionists from the 1840s onward warned of slave power rising from an almost alien society—the South— and trying to expand throughout the country and destroy the free institutions of the North. But while American abolitionists wrote about the slave power, Brazilian abolitionists wrote under the slave power, having themselves been formed by its cultural environment. Brazilian abolitionists as well as slaveholders would agree with Nabuco that if abolitionist propaganda reached the slaves' ears, the most influential and powerful class would be exposed to "the barbarous and savage revenge of a population which has been maintained up to now at the level of the animals, and whose passions, once having broken the brakes of fear, would not acknowledge any limits in the way of obtaining satisfaction."[20]

There is a third crucial difference. The relationship between abolitionism and the black community in each country may also explain the reasons why American abolitionists were inclined to fight for a double goal—abolition of slavery and abolition of racism—whereas Brazilian abolitionists showed a less radical commitment in approaching the problem of slavery as well as the racial issue.

Historians of American abolitionism have pointed to cooperation as well as conflict underlying the relationship between white and black abolitionists, beginning with formation of the first abolitionist societies in the years that followed the American Revolution.[21] Although some put more stress on cooperation and others on conflict, all agree that when white abolitionists met black abolitionists, they were meeting people with feet firmly planted in the African American community, a small but expanding northern community with its own institutions.

The fact that African Americans were already living in a segregated community in the North by the time abolitionism arose as a movement committed to immediate goals does not imply a lack of communication between black and white abolitionists. On the contrary, "the two abolitionisms"—as they were christened by Jane H. Pease and William H. Pease in stressing the conflicts—were intimately intermingled by historic and religious heritage.[22] African Americans took the Declaration of Independence at its word when it affirmed the freedom and equality of all men.[23] After emancipation in the northern states, African Americans continued to fight for abolition throughout the country, as well as against the increasing racism that weighed heavily on the northern black community.

By 1794 the emergence of the Negro independent church had improved the African Americans' ability to solidify their cultural inheritance, to draw their own interpretations from the Bible, and to criticize the inconsistency of the white children of the American Revolution toward their black brethren.[24] My point here is that the northern African American commmunity—small as it was, and increasingly attacked and segregated by the 1820s—was nevertheless able to make itself heard and understood by a small number of religion-oriented European-Americans who were equally distressed by the emerging feeling that the American Revolution had failed in its highest humanitarian promises.

In examining the relationship between abolitionists and people of African descent in Brazil, one would hardly find any kind of intellectual bridges making communication between them possible. There were no religious or political texts cementing a common ground between them and shaping their views of the slave. Abolitionists on the one side, and the mass of people of African descent on the other—although interacting daily in a thoroughly slave country—lived in two worlds apart in terms of social position and cultural differences. As for the few Brazilian abolitionists of African descent who were able to rise to the social world of the white elite, they looked upon the surrounding African Brazilian world with eyes as foreign as those of their white comrades.

Brazilian abolitionists of African descent lived in the white world of the urban elites, were imbued with European culture, and, like their white peers, could hardly feel any cultural empathy with the surrounding African Brazilian world. The "peculiar sensation," the "double-consciousness" that W. E. B. Du Bois attributed to himself as an American citizen and a black man, "of always looking at one's self through the eyes of others," would not have been unfamiliar to abolitionists of African descent living in Brazil during the 1870s and 1880s.[25] Yet, since they had effectively passed into the white world and, in contrast to American abolitionists of African descent, did not live within a black community, they seem to have believed that their antislavery struggle should not go beyond the narrow goal of abolition of slavery. Their "twoness" was not to become a public issue.[26]

NOTES

1. This essay relies partially on chapter 3 of my book *Abolitionism in the United States and Brazil: A Comparative Perspective* (New York and London: Garland Publishing Inc., 1995).

2. *Walker's Appeal, in Four Articles; together with a preamble, to the Coloured Citizens of the World, but in particular, and very expressly, to those of the United States of America, written in Boston, State of Massachusetts, September 28, 1829* (Third and Last Edition, with additional notes, corrections, &c.; Boston: Revised and Published by David Walker, 1830), p. 22.

3. Ibid., p. 22.

4. Ibid., p. 22.

5. Ibid., pp. 10, 22.

6. Henry Highland Garnet, *The Past and Present Condition, and the Destiny, of the Colored Race: A Discourse delivered at the fifteenth anniversary of the Female Benevolent Society of Troy, N.Y., Feb. 14, 1848* (Miami, Florida: Mnemosyne Publishing Inc., 1969), pp. 5–8.

7. Ibid., p. 12. For the thesis that the Africans were the first Egyptians, see also Frederick Douglass, "The Claims of the Negro Ethnologically Considered: An Address delivered in Hudson, Ohio, on 12 July 1854," in John W. Blassingame (ed.), *The Frederick Douglass Papers* (series one: Speeches, Debates, and Interviews), 3 volumes (New Haven: Yale University Press, 1979), vol. 2, pp. 497–525.

8. L. M. Child, "Ruins of Egyptian Thebes," in *The Oasis* (Boston: Allen and Tichnor, 1834), pp. 212–213.

9. "Danger of Insurrection," *The Liberator*, vol. 8, n. 28 (July 13, 1838).

10. David L. Child, *The Despotism of Freedom; or the Tyranny and Cruelty of American Republican Slave-Masters, shown to be the worst in the world; in a Speech, delivered at the First Anniversary of the New England Anti-Slavery Society, 1833* (Boston: The Boston Young Men's Anti-Slavery Association, for the Diffusion of Truth, 1833), p. 68.

11. Joaquim Nabuco, *O Abolicionismo* (London: Abraham Kindon and Co., 1883), pp. 136–137; 140. All translations from Portuguese to English are my own.

12. Ibid., pp. 140, 144–145.

13. Joaquim Nabuco, *A Escravidão* (Recife: Massangana, 1988), pp. 35–36.

14. Domingos José Nogueira Jaguaribe Filho, *Reflexões sobre a Colonisaçao no Brasil (approvado com distinçao pela Academia de Medicina da Corte)* [approved with distinction by the Academy of Medicine of the Court] (São Paulo and Paris: A. L. Garraux e Cia., Livreiros—Editores, 1878), pp. 293–294.

15. On Spencer's "evolutionary optimism," see Richard Hofstadter, *Social Darwinism in American Thought*, revised edition (Boston: Beacon Press, 1955), pp. 39–40.

16. Nabuco, *O Abolicionismo*, pp. 144–145, 252–253.

17. Miguel Lemos, *O Pozitivismo e a Escravidão Moderna Trechos estraidos das obras de Augusto Comte, seguidos de documentos pozitivistas relativos a questao da escravatura no Brazil e precedidos de uma introdução por Miguel Lemos Prezidente Perpetuo da Sociedade Pozitivista do Rio de Janeiro* (Rio de Janeiro: Sede da Sociedade Pozitivista, 1884), pp. 21, 60.

18. J. N. Fagundes Varela, "O Escravo," in *Poesias Completas*, 2nd vol. (São Paulo: Companhia Editora Nacional, 1957), pp. 118.

19. Castro Alves, "Bandido Negro," in *Os Escravos* (São Paulo: Livraria Martins Ed., no date), pp. 83–91.

20. Nabuco, *O Abolicionismo*, p. 25.

21. See among others: Leon F. Litwack, "Abolitionism: White and Black," in *North of Slavery—The Negro in the Free States 1790–1860*

(Chicago: The University of Chicago Press, 1961), chapter 7; James Brewer Stewart, *Holy Warriors—The Abolitionists and American Slavery* (New York: Hill and Wang, 1976); Jane H. Pease and William H. Pease, *They who would be free—Blacks' Search for Freedom, 1830–1861* (Urbana: University of Illinois Press, 1990); R. J. M. Blackett, *Building an Antislavery Wall—Black Americans in the Atlantic Abolitionist Movement 1830–1860* (Baton Rouge: Louisiana State University Press, 1983).

22. Pease and Pease, *They who would be free*, pp. 3–16.

23. Litwack, *North of Slavery*, pp. 10–12. Black and white Americans were "heirs of the same promise" of liberty and equality, according to Benjamin Quarles. See his *The Negro in the American Revolution* (New York: Norton and Company, 1973), pp. 182–200, chapter 10. On "the impact of the American Revolution on the Black Population" see Willie Lee Rose, *Slavery and Freedom* (New York: Oxford University Press, 1982), chapter 1, pp. 3–17.

24. Litwack, *North of Slavery*, pp. 191–196. See also Pease and Pease, *They who would be free*, pp. 17–28. On "the humanized, liberating Christology" of black priests see Carol V. R. George, "Widening the Circle—The Black Church and the Abolitionist Crusade, 1830–1860," in Lewis Perry and Michael Fellman, editors, *Antislavery Reconsidered—New Perspectives on the Abolitionists* (Baton Rouge: Louisiana State University Press, 1979), pp. 88–91.

25. W. E. B. Du Bois, *The Souls of Black Folk* (New York: New American Library, 1982), p. 45.

26. The expression "twoness" is from Du Bois, *The Souls of Black Folk*, p. 45.

REFERENCES

Alves, Castro, *Os Escravos* (São Paulo: Livraria Martins Ed., no date).
Azevedo, Celia M., *Onda Negra, Medo Branco—O Negro no Imaginário das Elites* (Rio de Janeiro: Paz e Terra, 1987).
——, *Abolitionism in the United States and Brazil—A Comparative Perspective* (New York and London: Garland Publishing Inc., 1995).
Blackett, R. J. M., *Building an Antislavery Wall—Black Americans in the Atlantic Abolitionist Movement 1830–1860* (Baton Rouge: Louisiana State University Press, 1983).
Blassingame, John, ed., *The Frederick Douglass Papers*, series one: Speeches, Debates, and Interviews, 3 volumes (New Haven: Yale University Press, 1979).
Child, David L., *The Despotism of Freedom; or the Tyranny and Cruelty of American Republican Slave-Masters, shown to be the worst in the world; in a Speech delivered at the First Anniversary of the New England Anti-Slavery Society, 1833* (Boston: The Boston Young Men's Anti-Slavery Association, for the Diffusion of Truth, 1833).
Child, Lydia M., ed., *The Oasis* (Boston: Allen and Tichnor, 1834).
Garnet, Henry Highland, *The Past and Present Condition, and the Des-*

tiny, of the Colored Race: A Discourse delivered at the fifteenth anniversary of the Female Benevolent Society of Troy, N.Y., Feb. 14, 1848 (Miami, Florida: Mnemosyne Publishing Inc., 1969).

Hofstadter, Richard, *Social Darwinism in American Thought*, revised edition (Boston: Beacon Press, 1955).

Jaguaribe Filho, Domingos José Nogueira, *Reflexões sobre a Colonisaçao no Brasil* (São Paulo and Paris: A. L. Garraux e Cia., Livreiros—Editores, 1878).

Lemos, Miguel, *O Pozitivismo e a Escravidão Moderna Trechos estraidos das obras de Augusto Comte, seguidos de documentos pozitivistas relativos a questao da escravatura no Brazil e precedidos de uma introduçao por Miguel Lemos Prezidente Perpetuo da Sociedade Pozitivista do Rio de Janeiro* (Rio de Janeiro: Sede da Sociedade Pozitivista, 1884).

Litwack, Leon F., *North of Slavery—The Negro in the Free States 1790–1860* (Chicago: The University of Chicago Press, 1961).

Nabuco, Joaquim, *O Abolicionismo* (London: Abraham Kindon and Co., 1883).

———, *A Escravidão* (Recife: Massangana, 1988).

Pease, Jane H., and William H. Pease, *They Who Would Be Free—Blacks' Search for Freedom, 1830–1861* (Urbana: University of Illinois Press, 1990).

Perry, Lewis, and Michael Fellman, eds., *Antislavery Reconsidered—New Perspectives on the Abolitionists* (Baton Rouge: Louisiana State University Press, 1979).

Rose, Willie Lee, *Slavery and Freedom* (New York: Oxford University Press, 1982).

Stewart, James Brewer, *Holy Warriors—The Abolitionists and American Slavery* (New York: Hill and Wang, 1976).

Varela, J. N. Fagundes, *Poesias Completas*, 2 volumes (São Paulo: Companhia Editora Nacional, 1957).

Walker, David, *Walker's Appeal, in Four Articles; together with a preamble to the Coloured Citizens of the World, but in particular, and very expressly, to those of the United States of America, written in Boston, State of Massachusetts, September 28, 1829*, third and last edition, with additional notes, corrections, &c. (Boston: Revised and Published by David Walker, 1830).

11 OUR HUNGER IS OUR SONG: THE POLITICS OF RACE IN CUBA, 1900–1920

Kimberly Welch

This essay examines the social, political, and economic factors that influenced the historical development of racial polarization and cultural nationalism during the early decades of the Cuban Republic. Specifically, it analyzes the collective struggles of Afro-Cubans to fight for their socioeconomic and political rights as citizens during a period of intense racial violence and discrimination. Moreover, the essay studies the response by Afro-Cuban nationalists and their allies to the imposition of North American cultural hegemony by white American politicians, entrepreneurs, and military officials upon the multicultural structure of Cuban society.

The violent struggle for independence against Spanish colonialism during the 1890s united Cubans across racial lines to fight for the creation of the Cuban Republic. Many Afro-Cubans responded enthusiastically to the great independence leader José Martí's impassioned plea for racial unity and cooperation because they regarded themselves as an integral part of the new Cuban nation. Black Cuban leader Juan Gualberto Gómez stated in 1890 that blacks wanted only to be treated as citizens with the same legal and political guarantees as white Cubans. "The Negro demands no special privileges," Gualberto Gómez asserted; "His sole desire is to make the principles of social and political prevail here and not be an outcast from society. Victim as he is of benumbing cares, he wants them to disappear."[1] Nevertheless, the young republic, controlled by elite Creole and white North American economic interests, failed to redress the social and economic inequalities faced by people of color. Instead, it exacerbated old problems while creating new ones, thus merely granting Afro-Cubans token legal equality and limited financial opportunities on the island.[2]

The penetration of North American capital into the Cuban sugar industry symbolized the predominance of foreign economic control. From

1902 to 1924, American investment went from 50 million to 600 million dollars.[3] By 1905, Americans owned 29 centrales, which represented 21 percent of the total sugar production. Deprived of any significant role within their economy except as managers and technicians, the Cuban middle class came to resent the supremacy of foreign ownership of the island's commerce, industry, and finance. José Sixto de Sola, editor of the magazine *Cuba Contemporánea*, stated in 1913 that during the early years of the republic some Cubans regarded North Americans as their "superiors."[4]

For black Cubans, daily survival was more important than the encroachment of foreign capital in the economy. The growth of Afro-Cuban peasant families in Oriente placed a strain on agricultural resources. Ridden with debt, and unable to purchase land because of higher prices, many small black landowners and tenant farmers experienced financial ruin. In addition, many Afro-Cubans lost their parcels due to costly litigation with large foreign corporations over land titles in courts sympathetic to the latter.

In the southeastern region, where a large proportion of blacks lived, sugar mills expanded their operations. In the Guantánamo Valley, for example, ten ingenios dominated the area; the "Soledad," "Isabel," and "Los Caños" centrales were owned by the Guantánamo Sugar Company from New Jersey, which possessed a total of 55,000 acres. The "Santa Cecilia" mill, property of the Santa Cecilia Sugar Company from Maine, held more than 12,000 acres. Black landownership declined from 40 percent to 35 percent between 1899 and 1907, compelling many to become rural wage earners.[5] Throughout the early years of the Republic, Afro-Cubans in Oriente steadily joined the ranks of the landless as ingenios replaced the once prosperous coffee, fruit, and cacao fincas, or farms.

In the aftermath of World War I, the euphoria over sugar prices in 1920 produced a short-lived period known as the "Dance of the Millions," when money flowed freely into the coffers of North American and Cuban investors.[6] The price of sugar reached its highest level at 22 cents per pound. The "Dance of the Millions," however, had a short duration due to an international surplus of sugar caused by the recovery of the European beet sugar industry and the expansion of sugar production in the United States and Hawaii. Cuban sugar prices collapsed during late 1920 and continued their slide the following year; during the latter part of 1920, the price of sugar fell 80 percent.[7] By 1921, sugar prices were at an all-time low of 3.10 cents per pound. As the crisis prompted a run on North American and Cuban banks, many prominent Cuban sugar merchants and bankers went bankrupt, while the savings of the Cuban middle class disappeared.[8]

The economic predicament of 1921 intensified Cuban resentment against the island's dependency on sugar. Cuban writer Luis Marino Pérez argued in 1922, for instance, that the United States, which benefited from the Cuban economy, should treat Cuba as an equal trading partner. "Our situation is not that of a petitioner asking favors. . . . Unless Cuba receives just treatment and consideration from the United States, we shall suffer."[9]

While some Cuban intellectuals demanded that the United States respect Cuba's economic sovereignty, Afro-Cubans appealed to their own government to address socioeconomic problems that they had endured. The independence movement raised the expectations of Afro-Cubans for social justice, political freedom, and equality in the new Republic. They had rallied enthusiastically to the separatist cause, lending their support to the Partido Revolucionario Cubano and the Liberation Army.[10] Indeed, the war offered mobility for those in the military, since nearly 40 percent of the commissioned ranks consisted of black officers.[11]

Furthermore, black Cubans organized their own political activities through the Directorio de las Sociedades de la Raza de Color, formed in 1892 by prominent Afro-Cuban politician Juan Gualberto Gómez.[12] In the Irijoa Theater in Havana in July 23, 1892, Gualberto Gómez united more than 100 provincial black organizations under the leadership of the Directorate. Its motto was "Inform, inform, inform" (instruirse). The organization drafted a program that emphasized social protest through the legal process and presented petitions to the Spanish government demanding the end of racial discrimination in public facilities. Gualberto Gómez urged its members to engage in civil disobedience for the integration of public facilities. During the 1890s, he led campaigns to integrate the theaters in Havana, which had traditionally relegated Afro-Cubans to the uppermost galleries. He and others successfully challenged theater owners by purchasing orchestra and box seats in mass quantities for blacks. Once these actions were brought before the colonial judiciary, Gualberto Gómez was able to win a favorable verdict from Spanish authorities.[13] The Directorate channelled Afro-Cuban resistance against the colonial regime. Believing strongly in the interracial vision of José Martí, blacks felt that their participation in the struggle would result in the creation of an equalitarian society devoid of the racial prejudice that characterized the colonial era.[14]

Despite the valiant role blacks played in overthrowing the Spanish regime, they received few benefits from the young republic. After the untimely death of progressive leaders such as José Martí and Antonio Maceo, the Cuban political leadership was dominated by white upper-class conservatives who regarded Afro-Cubans with contempt and aversion.[15] Furthermore, the demobilization of the Liberation Army destroyed one of the few institutions which allowed blacks significant representation. As racial discrimination continued, the optimism Afro-Cubans felt for the Republic disappeared.[16]

The first independent government of Tomás Estrada Palma (1901–1906), comprised principally of former exiled white Cubans, decided that no specific antidiscriminatory legislation was necessary for the new republic. The new constitution vaguely proclaimed that all Cubans were equal under the law and granted citizenship to the African-born. Estrada Palma and the Creole conservatives hoped that these pronouncements would satisfy white and Afro-Cuban liberals and moderate nationalists. Although the 1901 Cuban Constitution supported universal male suffrage, many black Cubans found it difficult to use the ballot box to promote their own political interests. The political agenda of the Liberal and Moderate parties ignored the race issue and endeavored to attract Afro-Cuban voters through patronage networks established by black Cuban politicians such as Liberal leaders Gualberto Gómez and Martín Morúa Delgado and Moderate supporters such as Lino D'Ou and Rafael Serra. In 1904, out of sixty-three congressmen only four were mulatto or Afro-Cuban. Among the twelve senators, Morúa Delgado was the single Afro-Cuban member. The few black Cuban congressmen remained party loyalists who spent their political careers advancing personal and partisan matters, thus avoiding the difficult problem of racial unity.[17]

Whereas Gualberto Gómez, Morúa Delgado, and Generoso Campos Marquetti enjoyed prominence within the Liberal Party, Afro-Cuban membership in the Liberal and Moderate parties remained low during the early years of the republic. White Cuban politicians, particularly those out of office, assiduously courted the black Cuban vote while withholding firm support for Afro-Cuban candidates.[18] Gualberto Gómez, however, continued to emphasize patience and cooperation with whites as the only viable solution to the race problem. His ideas provided little consolation to the Afro-Cuban middle class, which found white Cubans reluctant to accept them as political partners.[19]

The United States provisional government also weakened the political influence of Afro-Cubans with the imposition of a new electoral law intended to restrict male suffrage in favor of promoting what it considered a "better class" of Cuban voters. Voters were required to read and write, maintain property valued at $250, or serve honorably in the Liberation Army. This decree was intended to disenfranchise black Cuban voters in a manner similar to the imposition of poll taxes and literacy tests upon the African American electorate in the southern United States after 1865. Consequently, only half of eligible male voters cast ballots in the municipal elections of 1900. It was estimated that only 3,000 black Cubans voted, representing 19 percent of the Cuban electorate despite the fact that they comprised 37 percent of Cuban male citizens. The majority of Afro-Cuban voters qualified on the basis of their participation in the Liberation Army.[20]

Notwithstanding the formal equality guaranteed by the 1901 Constitution, Afro-Cubans were subjected to discrimination based on class and race. The absence of Afro-Cubans in the bureaucracy underscored Cuba's racial inequity. Blacks eagerly sought government employment, one of the few remaining avenues of mobility left for Cubans without capital and land. Afro-Cubans quickly discovered that they were denied entry to middle- and upper-level public administration positions through a policy of informal racial discrimination.[21] Few were employed as clerks and typists. Many blacks were consigned to the lowest-paying jobs within the government, such as porters, watchmen, and a few post office appointments.[22]

Some black leaders, such as Generoso Campos Marquetti, confronted conservative president Estrada Palma on the issue of racial discrimination in the civil service. On one occasion, Campos Marquetti met with the president to voice strong complaints regarding the absence of blacks in the Havana police force. He received no commitment from Don Tomás.[23] White officials justified the scarcity of Afro-Cubans in the government by pointing out their poor educational background. This rationale obscured the fact that even qualified black candidates were often rejected for jobs in which they possessed the required scholastic background. The diplomatic corps and the judiciary were devoid of people of color. The few Afro-Cubans who had university degrees faced great obstacles in obtaining even middle-level positions within public administration, such as clerks or teachers.[24]

The exclusion of Afro-Cubans from the government weakened their attempts to end racial discrimination. Few acquired favorable positions, such as ministerial appointments, that would insure the development of a black Cuban presence within public service.[25] Furthermore, these positions were doled out as part of the extensive patronage system sustained by Cuba's political parties. Creoles who wielded financial and political clout were the first in line to receive the best jobs and they, in turn, secured minor posts for their colleagues. Successive administrations concluded that they had little to gain economically or politically if they placed Afro-Cubans in key bureaucratic assignments.[26]

Afro-Cubans were conspicuously absent not only from the higher ranks within the civil service but from those within the private sector as well. In the cities, most blacks worked as servants, laundry workers, dock workers, newspaper sellers, and street cleaners. In the 1907 census, 23,904 people of color were listed as servants, as opposed to 6,118 native-born white Cubans.[27] Employment opportunities as store clerks, restaurant workers, and streetcar conductors were relatively rare for nonwhites. Department store owners, in particular, avoided hiring people of color because their wealthy Creole and white North American clients were offended by the sight of black salespeople.[28]

Blacks worked in industrial jobs characterized by the worst pay and, not infrequently, the hardest labor. Within the sugar industry, Afro-Cubans formed the bulk of the cane cutters while the managerial jobs generally went to Creoles, Europeans, or white Americans. An anonymous American traveler in 1903 described the racial division of labor on a sugar plantation where blacks worked as manual workers while the administrators and technicians were white:

> The blacks spent the whole day in the work gangs under a
> contra-mayoral or assistant overseer. They worked all day in the
> field—every black man, woman and child armed with a machete.
> . . . At the same time, the engineers were always white, generally
> an American who is, next to the administrator—also always white,
> the most important employee on the ingenio.[29]

Furthermore, many blacks were painfully acquainted with the old axiom, "Last hired, first fired." When unemployment hit the sugar and tobacco industries after 1921, hundreds of Afro-Cubans became the first ones affected by layoffs.[30]

Afro-Cuban women suffered from a form of triple exploitation. They were oppressed because of their poverty, gender, and color. They worked mostly as seamstresses, laundry workers, and servants.[31] Out of a total number of 9,464 female seamstresses listed in the 1907 census, 6,082 were black, while native-born white women numbered 3,121. During that same year, Afro-Cuban women comprised 19,887 out of 24,016 laundresses. In addition, 15,765 of the 23,378 female servants were black.[32] By 1919, 22,136 black women still worked in domestic service, as opposed to 10,519 Creole women.[33] Given the limited employment opportunities and racial prejudice, Afro-Cuban women were forced to toil in the drudgery of low-paid, unskilled labor.

Despite their dismal economic situation, there were a few areas of improvement for black Cuban women during the early republic, such as agricultural labor (where the proportion of Afro-Cuban women declined in 1907 as compared to numbers revealed in the 1899 census, due to the influx of young Spanish female immigrants). In addition, there remained a steady rise in the number of black Cuban women in the teaching professions, although they constituted only 325 out of 3,832 teachers. Overall, Afro-Cuban women still had limited employment opportunities.[34]

Moreover, the plight of black veterans was also dismal. Most of them emerged from the 1895 war indigent and embittered by treatment they received from the government. Many hoped the Estrada Palma regime would offer them employment in the bureaucracy as a reward for military service. Their dreams of advancement through the public administration, however, were shattered immediately. Afro-Cuban General Pedro Ivonnet complained to Liberal president José Miguel Gómez in 1908 that in Santiago de Cuba former black captains in the Liberation Army were street sweepers, while counterrevolutionaries were employed as their supervisors. He concluded that the great black general Antonio Maceo (then deceased), would have never tolerated such an adverse racial environment.[35] Former slave Esteban Montejo noted that the majority of Afro-Cuban veterans became destitute due to discriminatory hiring practices in the civil service: "Men brave as lions found themselves out in the streets."[36] Even black veterans who received government recognition for their military service were treated shabbily. One example was the distinguished general Quintín Banderas who, since 1868, had fought with distinction for the independence of Cuba. However, President Tomás Estrada Palma rewarded this dedicated fighter by giving him the position of postman and a gift of five pesos. Banderas refused this petty tribute.[37] A bust made in his honor was never restored to its original place after it collapsed.

The government's indifference toward notable Afro-Cubans was not confined to renowned veterans. The small number of black legislators felt the social ostracism of the Creole elite. In 1903, the wife of Martín Morúa Delgado, the famous mulatto writer and Liberal senator, did not receive an invitation to a presidential reception along with other wives. President Estrada Palma later apologized for the incident; however, it was repeated again in 1905. Black elected representatives Antonio Póveda Ferrer and Generoso Campos Marquetti encountered a similar problem when their families were excluded from a social function at the Presidential Palace.[38]

The prejudice endured by black Cubans led many to believe that they had become social pariahs in their own land. Indirect forms of racial segregation occurred in certain parks, private clubs, and schools. Complaints by Afro-Cuban newspapers such as *Previsión* and *El Nuevo Crillo* (The New Creole) regarding this unjust situation went unheeded by the Cuban government, which contended that such activities were too isolated to warrant any reform.[39] Still, blacks understood that since many Creole legislators were opposed to interracial social contact, they sanctioned this climate of racial animosity.

As in the case of employment, the exclusion of blacks from private and public facilities developed along class as well as racial divisions. Economics played a powerful role in barring Afro-Cubans from social mobility. Most could not afford to join affluent private social clubs, such as the elitist Havana Yacht Club, where important business relationships and transactions were pursued. These organizations, in turn, owned the beaches, where black Cubans could not gain entry unless they were members. The high cost of a university education prevented many Afro-Cubans from joining the professional ranks, accounting for their absence from medical and legal associations. Few black parents had the resources to send their children to private secular and parochial schools, which provided a better education than the public system.[40]

There were circumstances, moreover, where blacks were forced to contend with rigid segregation based entirely on race. On certain paseos, or promenades and parks in small towns and provincial capitals, whites prevented people of color from entering.[41] In 1915, a group of Afro-Cubans in Camagüey were attacked by whites after they entered Agramonte Park.[42] In most cases, the Creoles did not post "Whites Only" signs but instead enforced racial separation through unwritten local rules. Blacks who lived in these towns understood that there were public areas where they could not venture. In Cienfuegos, for example, in 1916 a group of white Cubans beat up a black man who sat in a section of the public park used by whites.[43]

Further, demonstrations of romantic affection between white and black Cubans were condemned by whites who despised interracial unions. Montejo commented that before the Cuban Revolution, some Creoles could not tolerate the sight of white men with black women and black men with white women in public.[44] These couples usually avoided walking through certain paseos and parks for fear they might be verbally or physically assaulted by indignant white Cubans. Still, interracial couples did exist despite social disapproval of racially mixed marriages.

Not all white Cubans condoned racial prejudice and discrimination on the island. There were a growing number of progressive Creoles in the labor movement who shared the same vision of racial equality as Martí. The gradual incorporation of Afro-Cuban workers during the nineteenth century laid the groundwork for future interracial labor unity after independence. The manifesto of the Congreso Obrero (Workers' Congress) in 1892, for example, vowed to fight racial inequality in public facilities and the workplace.[45] For working-class blacks, labor unions were the only institutions committed to ameliorating the economic condition of all Cubans, regardless of race. During labor unrest on the ingenios in the towns of Lajas and Cruces in Las Villas province in 1902, Evaristo Landa, a mulatto labor leader in the Union of Lajas Workers, declared that the labor movement instilled racial solidarity among all Cuban laborers.[46]

The inclusion of blacks within trade unions did present problems for some Spanish and white workers who, despite their fervent socialist convictions, did not accept the principles of racial equality. In certain unions affiliated with the Partido Obrero Socialista (Socialist Workers Party, POS), racism was also evident. In 1904, Carlos Baliño, a Spanish socialist and founder of POS, expressed amazement that Spanish and white Cuban workers insisted upon monopolizing skilled occupations at the expense of Afro-Cubans. Baliño underestimated the racial animosity between Cuban workers of color and whites. During the 1920s, leadership within communist labor organizations such as the Confederación Nacional Obrera de Cuba (National Workers' Confederation of Cuba), took a more active role in attacking racism among trade unionists.[47]

However, during the first years of the Republic, some blacks still believed that participation in the political system would instigate reform. The small Afro-Cuban petite bourgeoisie, consisting of landowners, tenant farmers, and a few professionals, identified with the Liberal Party, which espoused the interests of the middle class. By contrast, most blacks viewed the Moderate Party of Tomás Estrada Palma as elitist.[48] During the first presidential campaign in 1901, black legislator Juan Gualberto Gómez urged Afro-Cubans to vote for Liberal candidate General Bartolome Masó.[49] This attempt to form a black voting bloc presented a difficult challenge given the indifference shown by numerous black voters. Concerned with their immediate economic survival, many poor Afro-Cubans did not believe voting would substantially alter their situation. For them, neither party showed any genuine concern for their material condition. However, for the tiny but influential black middle class, collaboration in the electoral process offered the likelihood of government sinecures. Established Afro-Cuban legislators such as Morúa Delgado, a staunch integrationist, believed that only involvement within mainstream politics would open doors for blacks.[50]

The first Afro-Cubans to act collectively on the issue of racial equality were those pro-Masó veterans of the Liberation Army. On May 2, 1902, at the invitation of Generoso Campos Marquetti, two hundred veterans, presidents of sociedades de color, and individuals met at the Havana sociedad Divina Caridad to discuss the adverse economic and social treatment of black Cubans and mulattos. They elected a Comité de Acción de los Veteranos y Asociaciones de Color, presided over by Campos Marquetti and including Julian V. Sierra and Evaristo Estenoz, former officers in the Liberation Army. In early June, they presented their grievances, and their proposals for racial and social equality for Afro-Cubans, to President Estrada Palma and the Congress. Moreover, the Comité lobbied General Emilio Nuñez, governor of the Havana province and mayor of Havana, to provide more public employment to black Cubans.[51]

In the presence of a large Afro-Cuban audience, the House of Representatives on June 30, 1902 debated a memorandum presented by the Comité which proposed equal rights for black and white Cubans and the termination of all U.S. military orders that discriminated against Afro-Cubans, especially in the police forces. The debate, however, produced only a few symbolic government appointments for Afro-Cubans and no constructive legislative changes.[52]

By 1907, many Afro-Cubans had abandoned hope of receiving redress through government channels. Repeated grievances regarding their exclusion from public and private occupations were disregarded by the government. With their social and economic advancement restricted, some Afro-Cubans began to organize outside the established party system. In 1907, they formed the Agrupación Independiente de Color or Independent Group of Color which later became the Partido Independiente de Color (Independent Party of Color, PIC) in 1908.[53] A large segment of the PIC consisted of destitute black veterans and a growing number of coffee, fruit and tobacco small landholders, and tenant farmers who were in a precarious position due to the expansion of sugar production in Oriente, a traditional stronghold of Afro-Cuban peasantry.[54]

The leadership of the PIC was dominated by two Afro-Cuban generals from the Liberation Army, Evaristo Estonez and Pedro Ivonnet, who shaped the activities and ideology of the PIC. These men represented a small, nationalistic black middle class which saw the resolution of its predicament in terms of race, not through class conflict or cooperation with the status quo.[55] The independientes focused their efforts primarily on the institutional racism that obstructed their participation in the political life of the republic they helped create.[56] The principal strategy of the PIC was to focus national attention upon the economic and social inequities that Afro-Cubans suffered because of racial discrimination.[57]

The PIC argued that any resolution to Cuba's racial situation by the government should benefit the entire Cuban population, particularly the poor. In their party charter, the independientes advocated the eight-hour work day, distribution of the land to small farmers, establishment of a tribunal to mediate disputes between workers and employers, compulsory public education, and preference for the native-born over foreigners in industrial, commercial, and agricultural employment.[58] The nature of the PIC demands reflected its determination to control foreign influence in agriculture and industry and to create a more equitable Cuban society.

The independientes asserted that blacks faced an implicit yet odious form of racism. For example, the PIC contended that Afro-Cuban children felt the sting of racism when they first entered public school, despite the absence of legalized racial segregation. Their teachers deliberately separated them from whites in the classrooms. It was commonplace for Creole teachers to mortify Afro-Cubans by referring to them solely by their skin color instead of by name.[59] This learning environment was not conducive to the educational needs of young blacks. Moreover, the treatment received by these children at the hands of racist instructors instilled a feeling of low self-esteem among them.

The PIC criticized the government's colonization schemes and immigration programs, aptly pointing out that the government offered land grants to white North Americans and Europeans while many black families were being evicted from their farms. The independientes noted that certain colonization plans were merely a guise by which foreign corporations expanded their operations, recalling an incident where 3,000 caballerías of land in Baracoa were allotted to 50,000 Norwegian colonists—who never came. The land was then sold to an American sugar company. The PIC stressed that employers preferred to hire poor Spanish emigrants to the detriment of blacks who desperately needed jobs. The government's encouragement of North American and European emigration served to revive the old colonial mission to "whiten" the Cuban population.[60]

The reforms proposed by the PIC would have democratized Cuban society and the economy. However, the island's white political leaders were openly antagonistic to the PIC, which had attacked their wealth and privileges; the Liberal Party, under President José Miguel Gómez, disliked the PIC because it threatened to dislodge its grip on black voters. The organization was anathema to conservative Afro-Cuban politicians like Juan Gualberto Gómez and Martin Morúa Delgado because it challenged their influence among people of color. Distrustful of the PIC's radicalism, Morúa Delgado and Gualberto Gómez were thrown into a strange coalition with Creole reactionaries against the PIC.[61]

The independientes encountered constant harassment from the government during the brief existence of the PIC. The police broke up its rallies, confiscated pamphlets, and arrested the leaders on spurious charges. In 1909, the police in Güines raided a PIC meeting, then arrested several men who were later sentenced to thirty days' imprisonment.[62] The Liberal Party, which saw the PIC as a dangerous threat to their grip on the Afro-Cuban electorate, disrupted the first PIC meeting, held in a public park in Havana, on September 20, 1908, which resulted in police intervention. Evaristo Estonez responded to public criticism that he was leading an exclusive racial movement, stating that the PIC did not want to establish a "black republic," a fear voiced by Cuban negrophobes. Instead, the independientes hoped to create a progressive political party that would try to exert its influence upon traditional Cuban politics. In the 1908 elections, the PIC presented its first slate of candidates, which lost in every district. Ivonnet wanted the PIC to win congressional seats in the November 1908 elections, but it only managed to offer candidates for the provinces of Havana and Santa Clara, each of whom lost.[63] The PIC, only three months old at the time, lacked enough recognition among voters to win seats in the Chamber of Deputies or Senate.

Despite its initial setbacks, the PIC continued to attract Afro-Cubans to its ranks.[64] It represented a future threat to both the established party system and Afro-Cuban politicians. Morúa Delgado, believing that the radicalism of the PIC polarized Cuban politics and threatened his chances for advancement within the Liberal Party, sponsored a bill in 1910 which banned the creation of political parties based on color. It became known as the Morúa Amendment although in reality it was composed by a white senator, Gonzalo Pérez, an apologist for racial inequality.[65] In that same year, the principal leaders of the independientes were accused of being members of an illicit organization and detained, although later released from police custody.

Estranged from participation in Cuban politics and denounced by the established Afro-Cuban political leadership, the independientes felt their only recourse was armed protest. In May 1912, Estonez and Ivonnet organized separate but coordinated uprisings in Pinar del Río, Matanzas, Las

Villas, and Oriente. The ill-fated rebellion, however, suffered from a lack of direction and leadership from the beginning.[66] It was quelled immediately in the western provinces, where the Afro-Cuban population was politically weak and numerically small. In Oriente, however, the movement attracted support from its large black constituency, including some Haitian immigrants.[67] Rebels destroyed property and public buildings and sugar production briefly came to a halt as independientes attacked ingenios. The American-owned sugar mills at Santa Cecilia and Santa Lucia were demolished and their machinery dismantled by the insurgents.[68] In Guantánamo and San Luis, blacks set Spanish-owned stores on fire, derailed railroad tracks, and burned land registry records. It was estimated that 10,000 Afro-Cubans were involved in the revolt.[69]

The United States used the 1912 "Guerra de Razas" or race war to invoke the Platt Amendment, dispatching Marines to Oriente to "protect" American property while Cuban armed forces were released from their garrisons to suppress the uprising.[70] Newspapers in the United States printed lurid accounts of Afro-Cubans massacring whites while, in reality, the rebels wrecked havoc to property, not to the white population. However, the revolt raised the specter of a racial armageddon that Creoles felt had to be suppressed at all costs.[71]

The independientes and their supporters failed to escape the brutal repression that thousands of troops and volunteers launched against them. By June 27, Estonez was shot at point-blank range, together with fifty men, near Alto Songo. The government displayed his badly decomposed body in Santiago de Cuba before it was consigned to a mass grave. Moreover, many newspapers exhibited photographs of his dead body with euphoric headlines. When Ivonnet was captured near El Caney on July 18, he was "shot while trying to escape." According to an autopsy report, he had not eaten in three days. As with Estonez, the government placed his body on public exhibition, then buried him in a common grave despite the funeral arrangements that his family made to provide a memorial for his remains.[72] Nearly 4,000 to 8,000 Afro-Cubans, many of whom had no contact with the PIC, perished during the month of May.[73]

Many Creoles regarded the Guerra de Razas of 1912 as an ignominious chapter in their nation's history. Two white Cuban reporters, Rafael Conte and José M. Campany, published a journalistic account of the event in which they characterized the rebels as being motivated by racial hatred against whites.[74] Despite its many detractors, the revolt still evinced sympathy from those who saw the PIC as a reformist organization. In 1922 Bernardo Súarez, an Afro-Cuban doctor, commented that the rebels were compelled not by plunder and racial animosity but by the idea of social justice. "The campaign of Estonez was not a campaign of incitement against the life and property of whites," stated Súarez. "It was merely an effort by a group of people to obtain, through the peaceful activities of a political organization, a fuller participation in the public life of their country and a greater measure of respect and consideration from those they had shared sacrifices [with] for the cause of independence."[75]

Notwithstanding the bitterness and extreme frustration that many Afro-Cubans felt in the aftermath of the failed 1912 PIC revolt, the growing influence of white North Americans within Cuban society only intensified the racial bigotry that black Cubans suffered during first decades of the Cuban Republic. The absence of legal racial segregation on the island was anathema to many white Americans accustomed to living in a racially segregated world. A 1902 editorial in the newspaper *La Lucha* quoted a statement made by General Bragg, American consul general in Havana, that the Cuban population was characterized by a "'race' of blacks, Chinese, descendants of aborigines and assorted mongrels." He also asserted that, "you might as well try to make a whistle out of a pig's tail as to try to make anything of the Latin race."[76]

American journalist Dorothy Stanhope expressed bewilderment when she observed that black Cubans did not exhibit any sense of inferiority when they encounter a white person. "Cuban negroes consider themselves superior to anyone of fairer skin."[77] Esteban Montejo recalled that white soldiers during the military occupation used derogatory names when addressing blacks. "The Americans," stated Montejo, "Used to shout 'Nigger, nigger' and burst out laughing." Montejo remembered how he avoided white Americans whenever he could since he detested their penchant for expressing racial slurs toward Afro-Cubans. "I couldn't stomach them [white Americans] and that's the fact," he said. "I never joked with them, I gave them the slip whenever I could. After the war ended, the arguments began [between white Americans and Negroes] whether Negroes had fought or not."[78]

There were occasions when certain white Americans instigated violent racial incidents. In 1910, two Afro-Cuban senators were refused service at the bar of the American-owned Plaza Hotel. A riot ensued when the senators returned with several hundred supporters who engaged in a fight with white Americans from the hotel. In the end, two North Americans were arrested.[79] A *New York Times* editorial on the incident noted that Afro-Cubans "bitterly resented any attempt to establish in Cuba the same kind of racial distinctions known in this country."[80]

Moreover, Afro-Cubans detested the derogatory remarks made by white Americans about them. While on a baseball exhibition tour in 1911, John McGraw, a manager for the New York National Baseball Club, and an umpire from the National League were fined twenty dollars each for making racist statements about Cubans. During dinner at a café, the men had loudly remarked that all Cubans were black and inferior. When a black policeman was summoned, the two tried to resist arrest; two white Cuban policemen had to detain the Americans.[81]

An attempt by white Americans to bar Afro-Cubans from a joint United States–Cuban official ceremony for the Spanish-Cuban-American war was denounced by many Cubans as racist. In 1913, a battalion of Cuban soldiers was supposed to take part in memorial exercises for the war. North American officials insisted that Afro-Cubans were not allowed in the contingent. The Cuban Congress refused to fund such a ceremony unless Afro-Cubans could participate. President García Menocal, however, capitulated to the Americans' demands by subsidizing the trip from his own resources. García Menocal claimed that Cuba was "too greatly indebted to the United States to allow a memorial exercise to proceed without Cuban representation." The Cuban Congress refused to reimburse the president for his expenses.[82]

Many Cubans viewed with alarm attempts by white Americans to impose their racial ideas on the island and considered incidents sparked by white Americans a dangerous precedent which might lead to major acts of racial violence, such as lynchings.[83] The Creole elite, particularly after 1912, wanted to avoid any large-scale violent confrontation between whites and blacks that would trigger civil unrest.

The Cuban elite, like their counterparts in other Latin American nations with significant black populations, promoted the view that Cuba was a racial paradise despite its acrimonious racial divisions. In Brazil, authorities declared their country a "racial democracy" despite the harsh economic and social inequities faced by people of African descent there.[84] The Venezuelan elite, on the other hand, expected that the "whitening process," in which successful middle-class, educated blacks and mulattos would become "assimilated" into the white population through interracial marriage and social contact, would eventually eliminate racial problems.[85] The continued presence of indirect racial discrimination, sporadic and organized violence against blacks, and the growing impoverishment of the Afro-Cuban population only served to marginalize blacks from the mainstream of Cuban society. The impact of the Negritude movement throughout the Caribbean and the rise in Cuban nationalism during the Twenties and Thirties challenged the racial bigotry, political antagonism, and economic limitations that Afro-Cubans endured during the first decades of the Cuban Republic.

NOTES

1. Rafael López Valdés, "Discrimination in Cuba," *Cuba Resource Newsletter* 2, January 1973: 7.
2. Marianne Masaferrer and Carmelo Mesa-Lago, "The Gradual Integration of the Black in Cuba Under the Colony, the Republic and the Revolution," in *Slavery and Race Relations in the Americas*, edited by Robert Brent Toplin. Westport, CT: Greenwood Press, 1974, 371.

3. Jules Benjamin, *The United States and Cuba: Hegemony and Dependent Development, 1880–1934.* Pittsburgh: University of Pittsburgh Press, 1974, 14.

4. José Sixto de Sola, "Los extranjeros en Cuba," *Cuba Contemporánea* 8, June 1913: 106–107.

5. Juan Jerez Villarreal. *Oriente: Biografía de una provincia*, Habana: El Siglo XX, 1960: 519–522.

6. Arnaldo Silva Leon, *Cuba y el mercado internacional azucarero*, Habana: Editorial de Ciencias Sociales, 1975, 19.

7. Benjamin, *The United States and Cuba*, 15–16.

8. Ibid., 16.

9. Luis Marino Pérez, "Cuba and the United States," *Living Age* 314, September 23, 1922: 767.

10. Louis Pérez, *Cuba: Between Reform and Revolution*, New York: Oxford University Press, 1988, 211.

11. Louis Pérez, "Politics, Peasants and the People of Color: The 1912 'Race War' in Cuba Reconsidered," *Hispanic American Historical Review* 66, August 1986: 510.

12. Martha Verónica Alvarez Mola and Pedro Martinez Pirez, "Algo acera del problema negro en Cuba hasta 1912," *Universitaria de la Habana*, Mayo/Junio 1966: 80–81.

13. Jorge and Isabel Castellanos, *Cultura Afrocubana* (El Negro en Cuba, 1845–1959), vol. 2, Miami: Ediciones Universal, 1990, 260.

14. Donna Wolfe, "The Cuban Gente de Color and the Independence Movement, 1879–1895," *Revista/Review Interamericana* V, Fall 1975: 420.

15. Ministerio de Relaciones Exteriores, *Cuba: Country Free of Segregation*, Habana: Dirección de Información, 1963, 2.

16. Pérez, *Cuba*, 211.

17. Aline Helg, "Afro Cuban Protest: The Partido Independiente de Color, 1908–1912," *Cuban Studies* 21 (1991): 104.

18. Ruiz, *Cuba: The Making of a Revolution*, New York: W. W. Norton, 1968, 151.

19. Pedro Serviat, *El problema negro en Cuba y su solución definitiva*, Habana: Empresa Poligráfica del CC de PCC, 1986, 74.

20. Aline Helg, *Our Rightful Share: The Afro Cuban Struggle for Equality, 1896–1912*, Chapel Hill: University of North Carolina Press, 1995, 94.

21. Arrendondo, *El Negro en Cuba*, 58.

22. Serviat, *El problema negro*, 70.

23. Thomas Orum, *The Politics of Color: The Racial Dimension of Cuban Politics During the Early Republican Years, 1900–1912*, Diss. New York University, 1975, 96.

24. Ibid., 72.

25. Erwin Epstein, "Social Structure, Race Relations and Political Stability in Cuba under U.S. Administration," *Revista/Review Interamericana* VII, Summer 1978: 194.

26. Pérez, *Cuba*, 215.

27. *Cuba: Population and Resources, 1907*, Washington: U.S. Bureau of the Census, 1909, 220.

28. Ibid., 70–72.

29. "On a Cuban ingenio," *The Living Age* 21, 26 December 1903: 810–811.

30. Ruiz, *Cuba*, 151.

31. *Historia del movimiento obrero cubano, 1865–1958*, tomo I, Habana: Editora Política, 1985, 123.

32. *Cuba: 1907 Census*, 256.

33. *Cuba: Census of the Republic of Cuba, 1919*, Habana: Maso, Arroyo y Caso, 1920, 667.

34. Helg, *Our Rightful Share*, 102.

35. Alvarez Mola and Martinez Pirez, "El Problema Negro," 83.

36. Esteban Montejo, *Autobiography of a Runaway Slave*, New York: Vintage Books, 1968, 216.

37. Sergio Aguirre, *El Cincentenario de un gran crimen*, Habana: Empresa Consolidada de Artes Graficas, 1961, 12.

38. Antonio Olliz-Boyd, "Race Relations in Cuba: A Literary Perspective," *Revista/Review Interamericana* VIII, Summer 1973: 227.

39. Pedro Serviat, "La discriminación racial en Cuba, su origen, desarrollo y terminación definitiva," *Islas* 66, Mayo/Agosto 1980: 10.

40. Lourdes Casal, "Race Relations in Contemporary Cuba," in *The Cuba Reader*, ed. Philip Brenner, et al. New York: Grove Press, 1989, 477.

41. Johnnetta Cole, *Race Toward Equality*, Habana: José Martí Publishers, 1982, 21.

42. Leon Primelles. *Cronicas Cubanas*, Habana: Editorial Lex, 1955, 112.

43. Ibid., 220.

44. Montejo, *Autobiography*, 217.

45. Serviat, *El problema negro*, 66.

46. *Historia del movimiento obrero cubano*, 143.

47. Ibid., 149–150.

48. Ruiz, *Cuba*, 151.

49. Epstein, "Social Structure," 202.

50. Serviat, *El problema negro*, 74–75.

51. Helg, *Our Rightful Share*, 125.

52. Ibid., 126.

53. Pérez, *Cuba*, 221.

54. Alvarez Mola and Martinez Pirez, "El Problema Negro," 82.

55. Serviat, *El problema negro*, 75.

56. Pérez, "Race War," 529.

57. Alvarez Mola and Martinez Pirez, "El Problema Negro," 83.

58. Ibid., 85.

59. Serafín Portuondo Linares, *Los Independientes de Color*, Habana: Editorial Libería Selecta, 1950, 151–156.

60. Ibid., 75–76.

61. Alvarez Mola and Martinez Pirez, "El Problema Negro," 83.

62. "Raid Cuban Negro Meeting," *New York Times*, 5 December 1909: 3.

63. Helg, "Partido Independiente de Color," 108–109.

64. Alvarez Mola and Martinez Pirez, "El Problema Negro," 84.

65. Ibid., 87.

66. Pérez, "Race War," 530–531.

67. Sergio Aguirre, Un gran crimen, 23.

68. "The Cuban Insurrectionary Movement Now Growing Alarming Most Rapidly," The Miami Herald, 25 May 1912: 1

69. Pérez, "Race War," 536.

70. "Cuban Government Insists the Rebels at Present Are Not Numerous," The Miami Herald, 26 May 1912: 1

71. Orum, Politics of Color, 259.

72. Helg, Our Rightful Share, 224.

73. Ibid., 537–538.

74. Rafael Conte and José M. Campany, Guerra de Razas, Habana: Imprenta Militar de Antonio Pérez, 1912, 20.

75. Bernardo Súarez, The Color Question in the Two Americas, New York: Hunt Publishing Company, 1922, 38–39.

76. "General Bragg's Indiscretion," La Lucha, 22 July 1902: 1.

77. Dorothy Stanhope, "The Negro Race in Cuba," New York Times, 16 September 1900: 5.

78. Montejo, Autobiography, 216

79. "Americans Injured in Cuba: Riot Follows Refusal to Serve Negro Congressmen in Hotel Bar," New York Times, 3 January 1910: 4.

80. "American Ideas Resented," New York Times, 5 January 1910: 10.

81. "McGraw and Riegler Fined," New York Times, 4 December 1911: 1.

82. "Cuban Soldiers to New York," Havana Post, 6 May 1913: 1.

83. Julio Villoldo, "El lynchamiento social y juridicamente considerado," Cuba Contemporanéa, 21 September 1919: 5.

84. Thomas Skidmore, "Race and Class in Brazil: Historical Perspectives," in Race, Class and Power in Brazil, edited by Pierre-Michel Fontaine. Los Angeles: UCLA Center for African American Studies, 1985, 12–13.

85. Winthrop Wright, Café Con Leche: Race, Class and National Image in Venezuela. Austin: University of Texas Press, 1990, 74–76.

REFERENCES

Aguirre, Sergio. El Cincentario de un gran crimen. Habana: Empresa Consolidada de Artes Graficas, 1961.

Alvarez Mola, Martha Verónica and Pedro Martinez Pirez. "Algo acera del problema negro en Cuba hasta 1912." Universitaria de la Habana Mayo/Junio 1966: 79–93.

"American Ideas Resented." New York Times 5 January 1910: 10.

"Americans Injured in Cuba: Riot Follows Refusal to Serve Negro Congressmen in Hotel Bar," New York Times 3 January 1910: 4.

Arrendondo, Alberto. El Negro en Cuba. Habana: Editorial "Alfa" O'Reilly, 1939.

Benjamin, Jules. The United States and Cuba: Hegemony and Dependent

Development, 1880–1934. Pittsburgh: University of Pittsburgh Press, 1974.

Casal, Lourdes. "Race Relations in Contemporary Cuba" in *The Cuba Reader*, ed. Philip Brenner et al. New York: Grove Press, 1989. 471–486.

Castellanos, Jorge, and Isabel Castellanos. *Cultura Afrocubana (El Negro en Cuba, 1845–1959)* vol. 2. Miami: Ediciones Universal, 1990.

Cole, Johnnetta. *Race Toward Equality*. Habana: José Martí Publishers, 1982.

Conte, Rafael, and José M. Campany. *Guerra de Razas*. Habana: Imprenta Militar de Antonio Pérez, 1912.

Cuba: Census of the Republic of Cuba, 1919. Habana: Maso, Arroyo y Caso, 1920.

Cuba: Population and Resources, 1907. Washington: U.S. Bureau of the Census, 1909.

"Cuban Government Insists the Rebels at Present Are Not Numerous." *The Miami Herald* 26 May 1912: 1.

"Cuban Insurrectionary Movement Now Growing Alarming Most Rapidly." *The Miami Herald* 25 May 1912: 1.

"Cuban Soldiers to New York." *Havana Post* 6 May 1913: 1.

Epstein, Erwin. "Social Structure, Race Relations and Political Stability in Cuba Under U.S. Administration." *Revista/Review Interamericana* VII, Summer 1978: 192–203.

"General Bragg's Indiscretion." *La Lucha* 22 July 1902: 1.

Helg, Aline. "Afro Cuban Protest: The Partido Independiente de Color, 1908–1912." *Cuban Studies* 21 (1991): 101–121.

———. *Our Rightful Share: The Afro Cuban Struggle for Equality, 1896–1912*. Chapel Hill: University of North Carolina Press, 1995.

Historia del movimiento obrero cubano, 1865–1958, tomo I. Habana: Editora Política, 1985.

Jerez Villarreal, Juan. *Oriente: Biografía de una provinca*. Habana: El Siglo XX, 1960.

López Valdés, Rafael. "Discrimination in Cuba." *Cuba Resource Newsletter* 2 January 1973: 6–14.

"McGraw and Riegler Fined." *New York Times* 4 December 1911: 1.

Marino Pérez, Luis. "Cuba and the United States." *Living Age* 314, September 1922: 765–77.

Masaferrer, Marianne, and Carmelo Mesa-Lago. "The Gradual Integration of the Black in Cuba Under the Colony, the Republic and the Revolution." In *Slavery and Race Relations in the Americas*, ed. Robert Brent Toplin. Westport, CT: Greenwood Press, 1974. 348–384.

Ministerio de Relaciones Exteriores. *Cuba: Country Free of Segregation*. Habana: Dirección de Información, 1963.

Montejo, Esteban. *Autobiography of a Runaway Slave*. New York: Vintage Books, 1968.

Olliz-Boyd, Antonio. "Race Relations in Cuba: A Literary Perspective." *Revista/Review Interamericana* VIII, Summer 1973: 226–231.

"On a Cuban Ingenio." *The Living Age* 21, 26 December 1903: 809–816.

Orum, Thomas. *The Politics of Color: The Racial Dimension of Cuban Politics During the Early Republican Years, 1900–1912.* Diss. New York University, 1975.

Pérez, Louis. *Cuba: Between Reform and Revolution.* New York: Oxford University Press, 1988.

———. "Politics, Peasants and the People of Color: The 1912 'Race War' in Cuba Reconsidered." *Hispanic American Historical Review* 66, August 1986: 509–539.

Portuondo Linares, Serafín. *Los Independientes de Color.* Habana: Editorial Librería Selecta, 1950.

Primelles, Leon. *Crónicas Cubanas.* Habana: Editorial Lex, 1955.

"Raid Cuban Negro Meeting." *New York Times* 5 December 1909: 3.

Ruiz, Ramón. *Cuba: The Making of a Revolution.* New York: W. W. Norton, 1968.

Serviat, Pedro. "La discriminación racial en Cuba, su origen, desarrollo y terminación definitiva." *Islas* 66, Mayo–Agosto 1980: 4–22

———. *El problema negro en Cuba y su solución definitiva.* Habana: Empresa Poligráfica del CC del PCC, 1986.

Silva León, Arnaldo. *Cuba y el mercado internacional azucrero.* Habana: Editorial de Ciencias Sociales, 1975.

Sixto de Sola, José. "Los extranjeros en Cuba." *Cuba Contemporánea* 8 Junio 1913: 273–303.

Skidmore, Thomas. "Race and Class in Brazil: Historical Perspectives." In *Race, Class and Power in Brazil,* ed. Pierre-Michel Fontaine. Los Angeles: UCLA Center for African American Studies, 1985 11–24.

Stanhope, Dorothy. "The Negro Race in Cuba." *New York Times* 16 September 1900: 5.

Súarez, Bernardo. *The Color Question in the Two Americas.* New York: Hunt Publishing Company, 1922.

Villoldo, Julio. "El lynchamiento social y jurdicamente considerado." *Cuba Contemporanéa* 21 September 1919: 5–19.

Wolfe, Donna. "The Cuban Gente de Color and the Independence Movement, 1879–1895." *Revista/Review Interamericana* V, Fall 1975: 403–421.

Wright, Winthrop. *Café con Leche: Race, Class and National Image in Venezuela.* Austin: University of Texas Press, 1990.

12 THE ROLE OF MUSIC IN THE EMERGENCE OF AFRO-CUBAN CULTURE

Antonio Benítez-Rojo
Translated by James Maraniss

If someone ever were to publish the selected works of Fernando Ortiz, they would have to include the speech entitled "La solidaridad patriótica" (1911). In said speech, given to close the awards presentation of Havana's public schools, Ortiz defended the idea of "a fusion of all races" while warning at the same time that racial separation, brought on by slavery, "is a cause of deep disintegration of the social forces that ought to keep our homeland and our nationality together" (Ortiz 1913, 120). In the second part of his talk, Ortiz encouraged the teaching of popular music in primary school. Why? Because this would provide a social space which, because it is shared by everyone, would work to dissolve racial tensions and therefore offer a way toward a higher level of national integration.

It is impossible to know whether any of the music students present at this convocation took Ortiz's words to heart. What is certain is that ten years later Cuba would experience a musical revolution which, beginning with the popularization of the *son*, would continue with that of the *rumba, conga, mambo, cha-cha-cha*, and other rhythms. This era of musical hyper-creativity, which saw a proliferation of orchestras and combos, interpreters and recordings, would forever denote Cubanness. From then on, the cultural expression that best defines what is Cuban to a foreigner is Cuban popular music. It is no accident that the films of the 1930s and 1940s abounded in Hollywood versions of congas, nor that Marlon Brando should dance a mambo à la Pérez Prado in *Guys and Dolls*, nor that Nat King Cole would dare to sing *El bodeguero* in Spanish, nor that jazz performers should like to include the first eleven notes of *El manicero* (The Peanut Vendor) in their improvisations. To the average American, and in fact to the whole world, that which is Cuban is above all music, dance, drum, rhythm.

It should be made clear that not all Cuban music has enjoyed the same degree of world, or even national, popularity. There is an entire peasant folklore brought from Spain which is scarcely known outside the island. Why didn't this folklore—called *guajiro* in Cuba—capture the sustained interest of the world? I can find no better answer than that given by Alejo Carpentier:

> The *guajiro* attaches his poetic invention to a traditional melodic pattern, which is rooted in the Spanish ballad, or *romance*, brought to the island by the first colonizers. . . . A real poet, the Cuban *guajiro* is not a musician. He does not create melodies. All over the island, he sings his *décimas* upon ten or twelve fixed patterns, quite similar to one another, whose primary sources may be found in any traditional ballad collection from Extremadura. (Carpentier 1972, 303)

Carpentier concludes:

> In mulatto and black music, on the other hand, if the interest in the words is usually scant, the musical material is of an incredible richness. For that reason one always goes back to one of its forms or rhythms when making any attempt at a work of national expression. (Carpentier 1972, 304)

In short, the music that went toward the making of a modern nationality in Cuba was the black and the mulatto—that is, music that is African to a greater or lesser degree. It ought to be clear that modern Cuba was not born on May 20, 1902, when the interventionist flag of the United States was lowered; the twentieth century in Cuba began two decades later, when the Africanized music of the *sones* played by the *Trío Matamoros* and the *Sexteto Habanero* took Havana by storm, linking Cuba together with the horns of the Victrolas and the first radio receivers. Furthermore, the Victrola and the radio made it possible for the compositions, songs, and rhythms of black people to be listened to and danced to in white peoples' homes. Because of these new developments, black people found an unexpected place of coexistence with whites within popular music, a space where instead of being marginalized they were recognized and acclaimed; furthermore, they were sought after for playing at private parties, theaters, dance halls, and night clubs.

In noting the *son*'s sudden impact, Ortiz writes: "The first *sones* in Havana signaled a nationalist and democratic awakening, both in the music and the instruments used. It was a triumph, a vindication of popular art" (Ortiz 1954, 443).

This conquest, if indeed effective and irreversible, had been the product of years of social and cultural strife. The prejudices against everything that might sound like colored music had always been enormous. For example, in 1900, under the U.S. military government, the city hall in Havana prohibited the use of drums of African origin in meetings of all kinds; in 1903 the Abakuá secret society was banned, and in 1922 it was resolved by the Executive Power to:

> Prohibit in the entire territory of the Republic, as prejudicial to public safety, and contrary to morality and good custom, all Afrocuban ceremonial dances, especially the one known by the name of "Bembé," and whatever other ceremonies which, in conflict with the culture and the civilization of a people, are notorious as symbols of barbarity and disturbing to the social order. (Díaz Ayala 1993, 85)

The *son* itself had been the object of discrimination, being set against the *danzón* and the fox-trot, which were seen as music more appropriate for whites. But if indeed the upper class rejected the *son* at first, this class ended up by surrendering to its lively rhythm. Its popularization caused a transformation of the other genres (*danzón, bolero, guajira, guaracha*); it was the predecessor of the mambo, the cha-cha-cha, the salsa. Furthermore, in contributing to a narrowing of the distance between blacks and whites, it opened the way for a multitude of cultural components that were strongly African—the secret orbits of Afro-Cuban beliefs—to advance slowly but surely toward the first ranks of the national culture.

Right away, the young intellectuals who defined themselves as white began to regard black people in a different light. Ortiz, who had already published the compassionate pages of *Los negros esclavos* (1916), started the decade of the 1920s with the first serious investigations of the history and folklore of Cuban black people—*Los cabildos afrocubanos* (1921), *Glosario de afronegrismos* (1924), *La fiesta afro-cubana del "Día de Reyes"* (1925). Thus, after four centuries of slavery and racial violence, black men and women—almost a third of the total population—were revealed as a repository of an unexplored zone of *Cubanness*. It was that interest, sociological and artistic at once, that impelled composers such as Amadeo Roldán and Alejandro García Caturla to take the rhythms of black and mulatto music to symphony orchestras. Among the works of Roldán, those that deserve especial mention are his *Obertura sobre temas cubanos* (1925), which included batá drums and other Afro-Cuban instruments; *A Changó* (1928); and above all *La rebambaramba* (1928), a ballet presenting yoruba, congo, and Abakuá dances.

Roldán's interest in black music was followed immediately by that of García Caturla. Among his first compositions for orchestra there appeared a *Son en do menor* and an excellent *Rumba*, all from 1927. In 1929, while Roldán was premiering the Afro-Cuban ballet *El milagro de Anaquillé* in Havana, in Paris García Caturla premiered his *Bembé*, for woods, brasses, piano, and percussion, as well as his *Dos poemas afrocubanos*. In 1927, Cuban musical theater began with *La niña Rita*, a musical by Ernesto Lecuona and Eliseo Grenet, in which Rita Montaner caused a sensation by singing *Mamá Inés*, a tango congo. A year later, when the singer left to record in New York, a composer named Moises Simmons handed her the music of a *son* with an insistent rhythm, *El manicero*, which (recorded that same year by Rita Montaner) went on to be one of the greatest international successes of Cuban music.

Toward the end of the 1920s something of extraordinary significance happened: the Afro-Cuban current overflowed the limits of music and invaded the realms of literature and art. The first black poems written by Cubans appeared in 1928: "La rumba," by José Zacarías Tallet, and "Bailadora de rumba," by Ramón Guirao. The influential *Revista de Avance* published "Elegía a María Belén Chacón," by Emilio Ballagas, and "Liturgia," by Alejo Carpentier. Illustrations of the black theme often accompanied the new poetry, including drawings by Jaime Valls and Antonio Gattorno, among others. But the *negrista* poetry—as it was called—did not acquire real force until 1930, the year in which Nicolás Guillén published the eight poems of his *Motivos de son*. At their appearance, Guillén's poems differed from those written by Tallet, Guirao, Ballagas, and Carpentier—all of whom were white. It was with Guillén that the black people, both men and women, entered into Cuban national literature speaking about themselves, their dreams, their sexuality, their marginality; further, it was with Guillén that the Havana black person's manner of speech—with no hint of criticism—entered Cuban poetry. The connection between the *son* and Guillén's poetry is unquestionable: "The most marked influence in the *Motivos* (at least for me)"—acknowledged Guillén in an interview—"is that of the *Sexteto Habanero* and the *Trío Matamoros*" (Morejón 1974, 41).

The stanzas of Guillén's poems were to be taken into both popular and serious music within a few years. In a letter he wrote to Guillén, García Canturla said: "You don't need me but I do need you, since in our country there are so few poets given to *afrocubanismo*: for in music as well as our art in general, I consider it the richest and strongest vein of our creative sources" (Morejón 1974, 322).

The same point of view seems to have sustained the composers who were working for the new musical theater. If indeed their musicals were inspired by the various genres of popular music, the works that achieved the greatest success were the ones which showed a dominant emphasis not only on black and mulatto rhythms but also on the events and characters who had some bearing on the nation's race problem. From 1928 to 1932, Lecuona staged *El cafetal*, *María la O*, and *Rosa la China*; in 1932 Gonzalo Roig staged his famous *Cecilia Valdés* and Rodrigo Prats his *María Belén Chacón*. All of these titles correspond to black women characters.

In the sphere of art, the nationalist current that Víctor Manuel began at the end of the twenties also included the images of black people, for example *La negrita, Frutas tropicales,* and even to a certain extent his famous *Gitana tropical,* from 1929, which depicts a mixed-race madonna whom he would paint again many times in his work. Much later, in 1940, he would complete *Carnaval,* his painting most imbued with Afro-Cuban culture, in which a group of black dancers watch the contortions of an Abakuá mask. But in the twenties, the painter who approached negrismo most obsessively was Eduardo Abela, who between 1926 and 1928 painted *La comparsa, La casa de María la O, Los funerales de Papá Montero,* and, above all, *El triunfo de la rumba* and *El gallo místico,* probably his best works on Afro-Cuban themes. In this last painting, Abela introduced the theme of the ceremonial sacrifice. In addition, the sculptor Teodoro Ramos Blanco became known worldwide at the Seville World's Fair (1929), at which he earned a gold medal. His statues and busts, which always refer to members of his race, are characterized by the accentuated negroid features of the models, which speaks of his black pride.

In 1931 Guillén published his second book, *Sóngoro cosongo,* and three years later there appeared *West Indies, Ltd,* with whose central poem Guillén left the insular orbit and dealt with the socioeconomic picture of the entire Caribbean. If *Sóngoro cosongo* indeed was Guillén's last book to be dominated by negrista poems, the movement itself lasted in Cuba until the end of the thirties. In 1934, when Ballagas published his excellent *Cuaderno de poesía negra,* three new black poets had come to negrismo. Finally, in 1938, Guirao published his anthology *Orbita de la poesía afro-cubana,* closing the heyday of this poetic movement in Cuba. Nevertheless, what it produced has not been forgotten. Dramatic speakers such as Eusebia Cosme and Luis Carbonell and singers like Bola de Nieve helped to keep it alive through constant recitals and recordings. One can safely affirm that of all the kinds of poetry that have been cultivated in Cuba, negrista has achieved the greatest popularity and drawn the most critical attention. But above all, the happy coming together of the *son* and the rumba, the music of Roldán and García Caturla, the musicals of Lecuona and Roig, the drawings of Gattorno and Valls, the works of Abela and Ramos Blanco, and the poetry of Guillén and Ballagas, ensured that the rhythm, the image, the culture, and the language of black people would begin to be accepted as integral parts of Cuban identity. In 1934, on introducing Eusebia Cosme at a recital sponsored by Havana's most exclusive women's association, Ortiz said:

> Up until today, an act such as this one would have been impossible: a *mulatica sandunguera* before a learned and female society, artfully reciting mulatto verses. . . . Until a very few years ago, the people of mixed race had no verses of their own, in spite of the genius that had already appeared in white poetry; nor did the

whites think that there could be any interpretive literary forms
here other than those forms created and consecrated by themselves.
. . . This attitude has changed now, at least in the most liberal
reaches of the creole mentality. (Castellanos 1994, 187)

But literary negrismo was not limited to poetry; there were the stories of Lino Novás Calvo and Rómulo Lachatañeré, among others; also the
novel ¡Ecue-Yamba-O! (1933), in which Carpentier tried to document an-
thropologically the tragic life of Menegildo Cué, an Abakuá character. In
1936 Lydia Cabrera began her prolific career as a writer and folklorist with
her Cuentos negros de Cuba, published in France. The Spanish-language
edition of this extraordinary book appeared in 1940, an auspicious time
for Cuba: that year a new constitution was inaugurated. Among the social
and political improvements that this democratic constitution established
were the prohibition of discrimination and a guarantee of religious freedom. There can be no doubt that the demands of black people, who had
participated in the constitutional process, contributed to these guarantees.
But the popularization of the son and the rumba, and of Afro-Cuban culture in general, also made its contribution.

The decade of the forties can be seen in Cuba as a period of national
consolidation. It is true that, in spite of the new constitution, black people
continued to be subject to racial segregation, but not in the open and generalized manner that had existed before. Times had changed, and now
many appreciated the role that black people had played in the forming of
the nation.

The first years of the decade belonged to painting. A second generation
of artists, in union with the earlier one, gave form and color to what could
now be called the golden age of Cuban painting. Wilfredo Lam, fleeing the
German occupation of France, returned to Cuba in 1941. There he established a close friendship with Lydia Cabrera and Alejo Carpentier and re-
discovered his old cultural roots, giving his art a decisive Afro-Cuban spin.
His paintings from 1942 and 1943, shown in New York in 1944, include
his famous The Jungle, which hangs in New York's Museum of Modern
Art. From this period there came Cortadores de caña and Danza afrocu-
bana by Mario Carreño; Músicos and a whole series of Cuartos fambá by
Luis Martínez Pedro; La caoba en el jardín by Carlos Enríquez, and René
Portocarrero's series of Brujos, as well as the Afro-Cuban works of Roberto
Diago.

At this time two crucial works were published: Fernando Ortiz's Cuban Counterpoint: Tobacco and Sugar (recently reprinted by Duke University Press) and Alejo Carpentier's La música en Cuba. In the former,
Ortiz introduced his new concept of "transculturation," with which he explained the formation of Cuban culture as the shared achievement of up-
rooted peoples, principally European and African. In the latter, Carpentier

offered a fascinating history of Cuban music which documented the relevance of African influences.

Toward the decade's end, popular music entered a period of renewal. The López brothers, Orestes and Cachao, musicians and composers for Antonio Arcaño's band, transformed the *danzón*, adding to it a new syncopated segment that they called a mambo. Shortly thereafter, Dámaso Pérez Prado used the same term to denote a series of syncopated rhythms based on the ones played by Arcaño's band. Pérez Prado conceived them with the idea of their being played by a full jazz band with an additional section of Cuban drums—and the mambo as we know it today was ready to sweep the world. By that time other Afro-cuban rhythms had entered the United States. Several Cuban musicians, among them Machito, established bands in New York and Los Angeles. Stan Kenton's band recorded *El manicero* in 1947, with Machito playing the maracas, and in that same year the collaboration of the composer and conga player Chano Pozo with Dizzy Gillespie began, from which came the legendary recordings of *Manteca* and *Cubana Bip Cubana Bop*. Afterward, Machito played with Charlie Parker, Dexter Gordon, Stan Getz, Howard McGhee, and other jazz figures, contributing decisively to what we now call Latin Jazz.

Meanwhile, in Cuba, the regulations that prohibited the observance of Afro-Cuban rituals were going unenforced. In Havana alone, an average of two thousand permits used to be issued for the celebration, on September 7, of the bembé of Our Lady of El Cobre, Ochún in santería; at present, santería, which is basically yoruba religion, is perhaps the most common religion in Cuba.

REFERENCES

Carpentier, Alejo. 1972. *La música en Cuba*. Mexico City: Fondo de Cultura Económica.

Castellanos, Jorge, and Isabel Castellanos. 1994. *Cultura afrocubana*. Miami: Ediciones Universal.

Díaz Ayala, Cristóbal. 1993. *Música cubana: Del Areíto a la Nueva Trova*. Miami: Ediciones Universal.

Morejón, Nancy, ed. 1974. *Recopilación de textos sobre Nicolás Guillén*. Havana: Ediciones Casa de las Américas.

Ortiz, Fernando. 1987. *Entre cubanos*. Havana: Editorial de Ciencias Sociales.

———. *Los instrumentos de la música afrocubana* IV. Havana: Ministerio de Educación.

13 THE CENTRALITY OF MARGINS: ART, GENDER, AND AFRICAN AMERICAN CREATIVITY

Sally Price

"You know us, Sister-in-Law," Norma said with a gently reprimanding smile. "You know you can't just go off for ten years and come back to find us sitting around doing the same old thing!" I had expressed surprise at the patchwork cape she was sewing, which was in a style I'd never seen before. The last time I'd been up the Suriname River, a decade earlier, Saramaka women had been devoting all their sewing efforts to the elaborate cross-stitch art that had been the uncontested rage since the late 1960s. Norma's half-finished cape was completely different in its raw materials, the technique used to make it, and the final product.

We were sitting in an open-sided shed next to the road that linked the nearby town of St. Laurent to Cayenne, a hard three-hour drive away. Norma Amania and her husband, together with a handful of others, had permission to squat on the land in return for keeping an eye on things and supplying occasional garden produce for the owner. They had built houses, Saramaka-style, planted fruit trees and a vegetable garden, and set up a stand from which the men sold their woodcarvings to the tourists who all too rarely drove by. The men went hunting whenever they could, but their trips on foot or bicycle into St. Laurent to buy supplies such as gasoline for their chain saw were kept to a minimum, since they had no papers authorizing their presence in French Guiana and would be deported if the gendarmes picked them up. Back in Suriname, their village on the upper Suriname River had been ravaged by the civil war of the late 1980s. They were not happy to be illegals in a foreign country that didn't want them, but had decided to try to stay until, as they put it, "Suriname turned good again."

Norma was right: I shouldn't have been surprised that cross-stitch embroidery had passed from the height of fashion to a kind of second-best leftover during my absence. Nothing I had learned about Saramaka art and attitudes toward change suggested that a given fashion, no matter how popular, would settle in for the long term. Saramaka art tended to lean more in the direction of what Amiri Baraka, writing about black music in the United States, called "the changing same." The overall aesthetic of Norma's composition seemed comfortably in line with Saramaka preferences concerning color, form, and balance that I was familiar with, but the cloth on her lap was a completely new one in the specifics of its materials, layout, and technique of execution. "We call it *abena kóosu*," she told me.

In a society where people enjoy and admire artistic innovation as much as Saramakas do, it seems particularly important, when we attempt to understand the nature of culture, to back up from the finished forms so that we can explore the environment in which they were made—to view them, not as static objects, but as parts of a dynamic process. Toward that end, this essay will examine three dimensions of Saramaka art-making—its social environment, its physical production, and its stylistic transformations over time. More specifically I will suggest that, partly because of Saramaka ideas and practices concerning gender, artistic experimentation in women's media—which means mainly textile art and calabash carving—tends to be concentrated in the marginal areas of established forms, and that as these experiments catch on they migrate into the compositional centers, pushing out the styles that preceded them and taking over the (temporary) status of mainstream art. In other words, I will argue that the dynamic of Saramaka art and fashion involves, for women, a repeated process in which artistic creativity moves, in the most literal sense, from margins to centers.

ART AND GENDER IN MAROON SOCIETY

Western visitors to the interior of Suriname, from eighteenth-century explorers and colonial officers to twentieth-century anthropologists and missionaries, have rarely failed to include descriptions of Maroon men's woodcarving in their accounts, but women's artistic efforts are often passed over with barely a mention. And while the living room of nearly every tourist to Suriname boasts some piece of carved wood fashioned by a Maroon (most commonly a comb, a coffee table, or a folding stool), women's textiles and calabashes are not generally considered marketable items. In the context of the culture they're made for, however, women's arts play crucial aesthetic and social roles. During the 1960s and 1970s, Saramaka women and men helped me piece together the history of these less well known arts, and later I was able to complement the information and insights they provided by working in museums, libraries, and archives elsewhere—principally in Suriname and Holland, but also in France, Germany, and the United States. I must begin, then, by expressing gratitude to all the Saramakas, Norma included, who shared their artistic knowledge with me.

Saramaka daily life is strongly shaped by cultural ideas about men and women. Almost every social or religious role, almost every subsistence activity, almost every ritual involvement is more strongly associated with (in many cases assigned to) one than the other. It seems more "natural," from a Saramaka perspective, for men to be the ones to fell trees, make combs and canoes, drive outboard motors, live in their natal village, work on the coast, learn foreign languages, earn money, interrogate oracles, maintain historical knowledge, run council meetings, dig graves, and play drums. Similarly, it seems more "natural" for the gathering of firewood, the sewing of clothes, the planting and harvesting of rice, the cooking of meals, and the maintenance of dual residences (in natal and conjugal villages) to be the stuff of a woman's life. In the realm of artistic expression, Saramakas generally consider it more "natural" for men to produce geometric designs with well-executed symmetry and for women to produce free-form designs with imperfectly realized symmetry, for men to work with manufactured tools and for women to work with recycled bottles and umbrella spokes.

In the literature on Maroon culture, the word *têmbe* has often been translated as "woodcarving," effectively limiting most discussions of art to the male domain. But *têmbe* also functions as an adjective, modifying any kind of artistic production or even a person's overall giftedness as an artist. The kinds of objects that are complimented by this term are most frequently intended for use in the ongoing courtships that figure so prominently in Saramaka life, both between spouses and between lovers. I therefore start my exploration of the dynamics of Saramaka creativity by sketching in the main lines of the gendered division of labor and cultural notions about the material interdependence of men and women. Although women assume primary responsibility for supplying and processing food from gardens (rice, tubers, bananas, peanuts, okra, etc.) and the forest (most importantly, the palm nuts used to make cooking oil), it is the men who do the hunting and fishing, purchase imported goods (including pots and pans, cloth and soap, sugar and salt, guns and machetes, radios and tape recorders) with their earnings from wage labor, and fashion wooden objects such as houses, canoes, paddles, stools, combs, and cooking utensils. With marriage serving as the main institution through which these foods and goods pass from male to female hands, a woman without a husband is at a significant disadvantage in terms of material comfort. For various demographic reasons, including earlier first marriages for women and, since the 1870s, heavy outmigration by men, there are many more women of marriageable age than men. Both because of and in spite of the fact that most men have more than one wife, there is vigorous competition among women for the available pool of husbands. These (and a number of other) demographic and economic factors come together to produce a cultural environment in which women spend a great deal of energy trying to please men. In this setting, their artistic production plays an important role. (Further detail on these aspects of Saramaka life is provided in S. Price 1984.)

In terms of textile arts, the great bulk of patchwork and decorative sewing appears on the vibrantly designed shoulder capes that represent the most prominent item of men's formal dress; second in importance are men's breechcloths. Even when women decorate their own skirts and capes, there is a general understanding that it would be inappropriate to devote as much aesthetic attention to this kind of sewing as to that on a man's garment.[1] In the 1970s, for example, when narrow-strip patchwork capes were declining in popularity but women still had large accumulations of strips (edge pieces trimmed from the cloths they had hemmed to make their own wrap-skirts), they sometimes used the strips to make patchwork skirts for themselves. They were quick to explain, however, that they simply threw together, with an explicit avoidance of pre-planning, whatever strips they had on hand.

Similarly, while the handsomely carved calabash bowls that women produce belong to them and not to the men, the most important use of these bowls is at men's meals, a highly charged site for competition among each man's several wives. The calabash forms destined for men's meals (water-drinking and hand-washing bowls) are embellished with more elaborate and carefully executed designs than those destined for use by women (spoons, spatulas, ladles, and rice-rinsing bowls), where the carvings are sparse and simple. (Calabashes intended for use in rituals are completely undecorated.)

A CENTURY OF ART AND FASHION

The earliest mentions of Suriname Maroon clothing and textiles are frustratingly sparse in their descriptive detail. Missionaries who lived for many years among the Saramaka during the second half of the eighteenth century, for example, wrote that their hosts had "no clothing except a small covering over the abdomen," and the drawings made by one of them corroborate this description (Staehelin 1913–19, 3.2:141; R. Price 1990:161 et passim). John Gabriel Stedman described the clothing and accessories of two Maroons he encountered in eastern Suriname in the 1770s, but he neither mentioned nor illustrated any kind of patchwork or decorative sewing (1790/1988:390–392, 405, Frontispiece, Plate 53). Although other historical accounts go into some detail about costume, including both ritual accessories and coastal imports such as shirts and trousers (see S. Price 1984:125–129), the only suggestion that Maroon patchwork or decorative sewing may have existed in any form before the late nineteenth century comes not from Suriname but from Cayenne, French Guiana; there, a recaptured fifteen-year-old runaway slave declared under interrogation in 1748 that in the enclave where he had been living over an eighteen-month period, three of the men "make cloths from cotton, which provide *tanga* for the women and loincloths for the men, and that this cotton material is woven piece by piece which they assemble and which is marked with Siamese cotton" (R. Price 1973:317).[2]

We have no picture of Maroon decorative sewing that predates the very late nineteenth century. Indeed, despite clear evidence that earlier Maroons had women's wrap-skirts, two styles of men's loincloths (wider and narrower), an impressive range of jewelry and accessories (much of it intended for ritual protection), and Western-style clothing purchased in coastal Suriname (see S. and R. Price 1999: chapter 4), we do not even have reason to believe that Maroon dress included shoulder capes before the end of the century. Schumann's eighteenth-century Saramaka dictionary gives no word for cape; Coster reports in 1866 that among the Maroons of eastern Suriname both men and women wear multiple cloths over the shoulders, but his detailed frontispiece—which shows eight men in loincloths, chest sashes, neckerchiefs, hats, legbands, jewelry, and more—does not depict capes; Crevaux's description and numerous illustrations of Aluku Maroons ten years later confirms this picture; and Bonaparte's book on the Djukas and Saramakas brought to Amsterdam for the Colonial Exposition of 1883, who were systematically photographed in native garb (Fig. 1), shows all of them bare-chested (Schumann 1778; Coster 1866; Crevaux 1879; Bonaparte 1884).[3]

It seems likely that men's capes and decorative sewing made their first appearance in Maroon costume at roughly the same time, in the very late nineteenth century. That is, in any case, the point at which both of them first appear in museum collections and written documentation. And current Maroon ideas about dress might well reflect their simultaneous introduction since, as we will see below, men's shoulder capes are by far the most consistently and most elaborately decorated of any type of garment. This essay, which considers clothing styles through the 1970s, therefore covers roughly a hundred years of Maroon textile history.[4]

The oldest type of textile art that present-day Maroons remember, and that photographs and museum collections document, consists of embroidered figures on a monochrome or subtly striped cotton backing. Figure 2 (left) shows a representative example from 1908. The shapes tend to be curvilinear, their placement is roughly symmetrical around a vertical axis, and they are executed as linear outlines, often filled in with dense stitching in a contrastive color (see Fig. 3).

The absence of vibrantly colorful patchwork textiles during this early period does not mean, however, that Maroons would not already have developed both the aesthetic principles and the cutting-and-piecing technique that were to go into its creation. Not only is color contrast already present in the nineteenth-century embroidery designs, but many other domains of daily life attest to its importance as a central feature of Maroon

FIGURE I.
Djukas and Saramakas brought to Amsterdam for the Colonial
Exposition of 1883. (From Bonaparte 1884: title page)

aesthetics. Gardens are laid out in patchwork-like alternations of "red" and
"white" rice varieties, even though the different kinds look and taste the
same once they get to the cooking pot. Dress reflects an explicit preference
for wearing colors that contrast rather than blend with each other (for example, a red waistkerchief on top of a yellow and green wrap-skirt). Ideals
of physical beauty include admiration for bright white teeth against jet
black skin and dark ("green") cicatrizations on an albino woman. And the
inlays of men's woodcarving introduce tonal contrast into an otherwise
monochrome art.

In terms of the technical dimension, there exist Maroon garments
that are made by cutting cloth into pieces, repositioning them, and seaming them back together without incorporating any of the vibrant color contrasts that later came to dominate the art of patchwork. In a cape construction popular in the 1920s, for example, a length of striped cloth was cut
into five pieces which were then repositioned and sewn back together in
three vertical panels (see S. and R. Price 1999:85 and, for a similarly pieced

FIGURE 2.
A Dutch explorer with
his Saramaka guides,
1908. (From Eilerts de
Haan 1910: Fig. 24)

FIGURE 3.
Detail of cloth collected
in the 1890s.
Tropenmuseum
Amsterdam. (Photo by
Antonia Graeber)

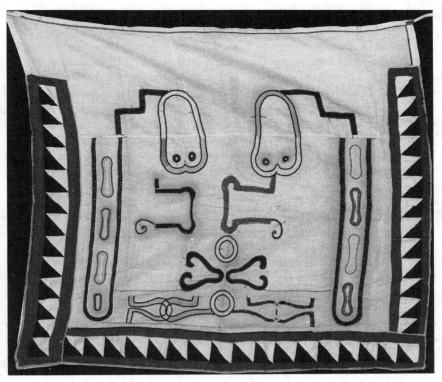

FIGURE 4.
Saramaka cape sewn 1900–1910. For more on this cape's life history,
see R. and S. Price 1991:iv. (Photo by Richard Price)

breechcloth construction, S. Price 1984: Fig 46). Here, no pattern of contrastive colors or cross-cutting stripes results; both the initial cloth and
its pieced-together follow-up are characterized by uniform stripes running
in a single direction. But while a cape made from the uncut cloth would
have either displayed horizontal stripes (which Saramakas say they don't
like on capes) or been too long and narrow, the cut-and-pieced version
forms a cape of the preferred orientation and appropriate proportions.
Similarly, the cape in Figure 4 has been discreetly pieced together, simply
because the seamstress did not have a single piece of cloth that was large
enough.[5]

Lingering a bit longer with this same cape, we can discern other aspects of Maroon textile arts as well. First, the design spread over its center

is an excellent illustration of a very common color scheme in which the basic threesome of red, white, and navy or black predominates but is complemented by yellow, blue, and orange. Second, it displays the imperfectly realized bilateral symmetry that characterizes the bulk of women's art—calabashes as much as textiles. Saramakas explicitly esteem symmetry more than off-balance visual effects, but are quite unanimous in the belief that women are less skilled at producing it than are men. A layout of motifs such as the one on this cape seems almost designed to prove their point, since it is clearly conceptualized in terms of a vertical axis but has been executed with its elements a bit off-center. Third—and here we come to the heart of my argument—the composition is framed on the sides and bottom with patchwork strips in red, white, and black, appliquéd onto the edges of the white cape.

The steps of production lend us help as we try to read the implications of such a textile's aesthetic features. Having had the opportunity of watching Saramaka women plan out many dozens of textile compositions, I have been struck that each time they begin at the center and then work out to the edges. This order governs every other kind of decorative sewing as well. Furthermore, when adjustments are made on a cape that has already been worn, they are introduced at the edges, which means that a cape's borders sometimes postdate its center by many years; it is not unusual, for example, for a cape to be enlarged in response to changing fashion by extra strips sewn onto the sides and bottom (see S. and R. Price 1999: Fig. 84). So, whether or not the patchwork strips in the embroidered cape in Figure 4 were present the first time the cape was worn, they would not in any case have been sewn on until after the embroidery design was completed. This means that the masterful realization of an established embroidery art filling the center of the cape was complemented by a three-sided frame in which the seamstress was experimenting with something new. Over the years, as both the makers and the wearers of capes began to get tired of the same old thing, the once fashionable embroidery style faded out and the newer technique and aesthetic represented in its edge strips moved center-stage.

Although the new style, which made its debut in the early years of this century, showed up on the same garments with the earlier curvilinear embroidery, it was constructed by a completely different process, used different raw materials, and produced a different aesthetic effect. Small strips, squares, and triangles were cut with a knife from monochrome red, white, and black/navy cloth, and sewn together to produce a patchwork strip, which was then appliquéd onto the backing cloth. This technique/style eventually became known variably as bè-ku-baáka ("red-and-black"), pèndê koósu ("striped/patterned cloth"), or píspísi ("pieced-together" or "bits and pieces") sewing.

Over time, the new bits-and-pieces strips began to upstage the older curvilinear embroidery as women became more proficient at designing and producing them and as men acquired a taste for clothes that featured them. With embroidery falling in the popularity charts of Maroon fashion, bits-and-pieces patchwork literally took the center. On breechcloths (see S. and R. Price 1999: 88–89), this meant a patchwork composition covering the broad rear flap—the most noticeable portion, since the front flap is small in comparison and the rest of the garment simply passes between the wearer's legs. This rear panel receives special attention because of the swinging motion it makes when its wearer walks. As Saramakas explained to me, the design itself is colorfully spread out—*wangaa!*—on the breech-cloth, and it swings jauntily—*lioliolio* . . . —as the man moves—hence their term for a breechcloth sewn in this style: *awangalió*. For shoulder capes (which, unlike breechcloths, have no nonvisible parts), the construc-tion in which a solid piece of cloth served as a backing for decorative patchwork dropped out, and the entire garment came to be formed exclu-sively of "bits and pieces," the seams of which were tucked under with a needle and meticulously hemmed to hide the raw cut edges. At the same time, the standard red, white, navy color scheme of earlier textiles was embellished with accents of yellow.

Figure 5 illustrates this development. Here, the production process be-gins with the construction of patchwork strips. One of these (often of a unique pattern—in this cape, for example, the central patchwork strip is black-and-white while all the others are black, white, and red) is chosen for the garment's "spine" (Sar. *báka míndi*), thus defining its vertical cen-ter. The "spine" is then flanked by a pair of matching strips, one to the right and one to the left, followed by another and another until the cen-ter of the composition achieves the proper size. The strips are laid out on the ground without being sewn so that changes can be made at any point. In this cape, once the patchwork strips were in place, the seamstress con-tinued the process with strips of the multicolored cotton that was being sold in coastal stores, beginning with one she had in duplicate (a red-and-yellow striped cloth), attempting to continue the symmetry (with white and then black cloth), and then finishing with a more random sequence of three strips in which only the middle one produces a left-right match. The next steps would be to select one or two warp strips (strips running in the same direction as the cloth's selvage) for the lower edge, and to attach a final warp strip, to be tied at the man's shoulder, on the top. A single stitch or two would fix the chosen order of strips, and the time-consuming proc-ess of seaming and hemming could begin.

Readers who are following the argument should already be turning their attention to the edges again, and be in a position to predict what the next rage was in men's fashion. Capes composed exclusively of narrow strips cut from multicolored striped cotton had completely driven out the "bits-and-pieces" style well before I first arrived in Saramaka in the

FIGURE 5.
"Bits-and-pieces" cape sewn 1920–40 by Peepina,
village of Totikampu. (Photo by Antonia Braeber)

mid-1960s. Despite their visual resemblance, if viewed by non-Maroon
eyes, to West African traditions of edge-sewn textiles, this style of narrow-
strip composition emerged directly from experimentation by Maroon
seamstresses, who were tiring of the older form of sewing, discovering the
properties of raw materials recently made available in coastal stores, and
elaborating in novel ways an aesthetic preference of contrasts and inter-
ruptive patterning that already ran through many dimensions of their
daily lives.[6]

We now follow these multicolor strips as they migrate from the edges
to the center of fashion (see Fig. 6). It is worth noting that in this new
textile art the raw materials themselves are "marginal" in the most literal
sense, since the strips are the left-over trimmings from women's wrap
skirts, which are made by cutting the ends and sides off two-ell lengths
of trade cotton, and even the sewing thread was sometimes salvaged from
such scraps when store-bought thread was in short supply. The earlier bits-

FIGURE 6.
Saramaka cape, probably sewn in the 1960s or early 1970s.

and-pieces construction has by this time dropped out completely, and the entire composition consists of multichrome narrow strips, though the procedure of establishing a vertical "spine" and flanking it, from the center out, with matching strips remains constant. (For examples of narrow-strip capes, see S. and R. Price 1999: chapter 4; S. Price 1984: Figs. 48, 55.)

Meanwhile, around the same time that the narrow-strip capes were dominating men's fashion in the villages of the Suriname interior, young Maroon women in the villages closest to the city, where Moravian missionaries had set up churches, medical clinics, and schools, were learning the refined art of cross-stitch embroidery, conscientiously following diagrams in the women's magazines provided by the missionaries. Saramaka men from upstream villages, who traveled the river frequently on wage-labor trips and developed romantic ties with downstream women, were

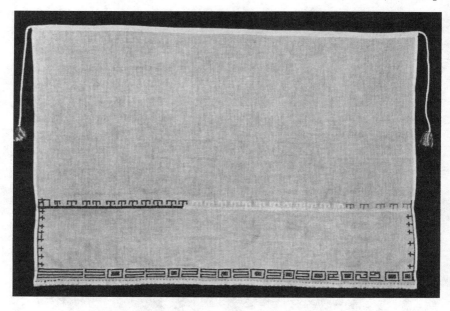

FIGURE 7.
Cape with cross-stitch embroidery, sewn 1960–65.
(Photo by David Porter)

often presented with gifts of capes and breechcloths decorated in this cross-stitch embroidery—and they wore them with pride at community events in their home villages upriver, where their wives were not insensitive to the admiration they inspired. And although the upriver women, who had never had an opportunity to go to school, were at first profoundly intimidated by this competition from their more formally educated rivals, they realized they would have to learn to embroider cross-stitch if that's what their men wanted.

So they did. For the first several years women worked on thin trade cotton like that their mothers and grandmothers had used for embroidery, first setting up a grid of horizontal and vertical guidelines for the crosses by pulling threads out of the cloth with a pin. The designs on these early "pull-the-thread" capes were linear motifs, and they were executed at the very edges of the cape (Fig. 7). Both because the thread pulling was labor intensive and because the women didn't yet feel confident in the medium, these early cross-stitch designs were rather minimal. Later on, women discovered that a heavier weave of commercial cotton, which they called *lapu*, allowed them to skip the time-consuming preparation, since its knobbier texture supplied a ready-made grid. And with time, they mastered the new embroidery technique at least as well as the downstream women had. By the mid-1970s, when men had packed almost all of their narrow-strip capes away in trunks or started using them for rags, the cross-stitch art had broken out of the edges and taken over the centers of capes, and sometimes breechcloths (see Fig. 8).

That, in a very small nutshell, is the art history of Saramaka Maroon textiles, and a summary demonstration of the idea that particular styles—defined in terms of materials, techniques, and design principles—take root in the margins, migrate to the centers as they evolve into mature arts, and eventually cede their privileged place when the next style begins moving along the exact same route.[7]

BOTTLES, BOWLS, AND BACKSIDES

We are now in a position to ask whether this progression characterizes the road from experimentation to established styles in other media as well. The second major medium exploited by Maroon women is calabash carving, an art form which has neither warp nor weft, neither selvages nor raw edges. Where, then, are the "marginal areas" and what do we see happening in them?

The earliest Maroon calabashes—as represented in historical documents, museum collections, and the memories of late-twentieth-century Maroons—were decorated in a technique and style that followed the general model of carvings done by their ancestors in many parts of Africa. In spite of the fact that the fruits utilized by the Maroons came from the American calabash tree and the fruits known as "calabashes" in Africa were picked from vines in the botanical family of pumpkins and squashes, the bowls made out of the two fruits looked a lot alike.[8] That is, the raw materials were totally unrelated, but the objects made from them, and the artistic style of their decoration, were at first strikingly similar. Early Maroon calabash carvings were, like many of their African precedents, composed entirely of intricate designs carved on the exterior surfaces of bowls and covered containers. In early Maroon communities, it was the men who made these carvings, using manufactured metal tools imported from the coast.

The history of women's calabash carving begins with a discreet takeover of this traditionally male artistic domain. While the innovative styles that young women developed in textile arts eventually replaced those of their mothers and grandmothers, the artistic territory that their calabash experimentation invaded was that of their fathers and grandfathers. If, in examining early examples of Maroon calabash carving in museum collections, we look beyond the published photographs, if we pick the bowls up

FIGURE 8.
Cape and breechcloth with
cross-stitch embroidery,
sewn in the 1970s. (Photos
by Richard Price)

off the shelf and turn them over, we notice markings in their "left-over" spaces. We see crude incisions that were clearly not made by a knife or chisel or gouge, that were clearly not designed with rigorous attention to symmetry or geometry, that were clearly not products of a coherent artistic style, that were clearly not executed with full manual control, and that were clearly not carved by the same artist who worked the bowl's exterior (see Fig. 9 and, for seven nineteenth-century examples, S. Price 1984: Figs. 15–18). The authorship of these irregular, off-center, bas-relief markings is not identified in publications or museum records, but by following them through time, we can see them evolving into a highly refined carving style. As the women gradually redefined their artistic terrain, abandoning bowls that had already been carved by men and taking over control of the entire object, their designs spread over the bowl's whole interior surface and their art became a pervasive presence in the material culture of the Maroons. In short, both the carvings themselves and the role of the art in daily life moved out of the wings and into center stage—just like each style and technique in the series of textile arts that we saw earlier (Fig. 10).

It may be worth noting that the tools for the calabash carvings also emerged from the "margins" of Maroon material culture in much the same sense as the edge trimmings that women used to make narrow-strip textiles. Maroon men had long been working on calabashes with manufactured instruments they bought in the city. But women (who had no personal access to money or city stores) discovered that by setting a bottle on the ground and breaking it with a rock, they could produce small, very sharply pointed pieces of glass, some of which, with a little experimentation and a lot of practice, served as effective tools for the carving of their bowls. This tendency to exploit the margins of material culture with artistic innovativeness can be seen in other domains as well. The colorful calfbands that men, women, and children wear as an accessory are crocheted by women using the sharpened spokes of old umbrellas. And the smoothly gradated stacks of shiny aluminum anklets that women literally build onto their lower legs are made from the insides of cables appropriated by Saramakas from the Alcoa subsidiary in coastal Suriname.

AND THE BROADER PICTURE?

Given the particular configuration of gender roles in Saramaka, it does not seem incongruous for women to construct their vibrant textile compositions from scraps, to carve their handsome calabashes with bits of broken glass, to craft their jewelry from the detritus of an aluminum smelter, or to crochet their tasseled calfbands with the spokes of discarded umbrellas. This is, after all, a society in which women eat their meals out of cooking pots with the children while men are served smoothly molded rice in a handsome bowl carefully covered with an attractive embroidered cloth.

FIGURE 9.
Top of two-piece calabash container, carved on the outside (*left*) with woodcarving tools and on the inside (*right*) with a piece of broken glass. Collected in Aluku at an unknown date. Acquired by the Musée de l'Homme in 1935. (Photo by the Musée de l'Homme, Paris)

FIGURE 10.
Saramaka calabash bowl carved with a piece of broken glass in the 1960s. (Photo by Antonia Graeber)

Where a man can tell his wife to heat water for his evening bath though she must never drop a hint that she would like him to go hunting. Where women, like men, serve as mediums for individual spirits but men are the priests of the major oracles. Where women are the seamstresses but men own the sewing machines. In this context, there's a certain logic to the idea that women do not allow themselves to be diminished by working at the edges, that they create works of stunning beauty in the margins.

My interpretation is based on a long-term dialogue with Saramakas, begun in 1966, about their lives, their artistic techniques, their ideas about men and women, their attitudes toward innovation and tradition, and much more. It would never have emerged from visual inspection of the finished forms. I am therefore not prepared to speculate in an equivalent fashion about art and gender elsewhere in the African Diaspora. But I do see arenas of artistic activity that might lend themselves to future exploration along similar lines, and I therefore conclude this essay by pointing to just a few Diaspora artists whose work suggests that attention to edges, borders, and margins—and a consideration of specific gender ideologies as an influence on how and where creativity comes alive—could provide useful insights for a fuller appreciation of the artistic wholes.

Faith Ringgold, certainly one of the most versatile and productive African American women on the art scene in the United States, has described some of her compositions as "appearing to be unframed because the glued-on borders are included as part of each painting" (1995:79), and in many of her famous story-quilts, two signature elements are squeezed into the peripheral edges of the compositions—the strips of text that tell the stories and the patchwork quilting that explicitly evokes her African American cultural heritage. When, in her autobiography, she identifies the medium of each work, the pieced-fabric border receives as much prominence on the credit line as the acrylic center does. And in some of her compositions, such as the "Harlem Renaissance Party" of 1988, the text-and-patchwork borders take up a larger amount of space than the image that they frame.

This is also true in the vibrantly creative work of Joyce Scott, as can be seen, for example, in the story quilt that celebrates with affection her mother, her nuclear family, and the ancestors she never knew (Grudin 1990:70). And countless African American patchwork quilts consist fully as much of compositions along the borders as in the center (see, for example, Grudin 1990:27 or Leon 1992:11).

How does this artistic attention to borders and margins compare with the artistic production of African American men? This question, which exceeds the margins of my own scholarly competence, is best answered by others, but it may be worth simply pointing out that Romare Bearden's compositions, for all their strongly patched quality (see, for example, "The Street" [1975] or "The Grey Cat" [1979]) and even the explicit evocation of patchwork quilts (e.g., "The Patchwork Quilt" [1970] or "Quilting Time" [1985]), do not include elaborate border designs. Nor do those of naive artists like Canute Caliste from Carriacou (see Caliste 1989), despite their inclusion of marginal texts not unlike those in Faith Ringgold's story quilts. On the other hand, the colorful borders of male-made Haitian vodou flags (see, for example, Houlberg 1996:31) might well be worth exploring in terms of both production process and stylistic change over time.

If we really want to understand how gender and creativity interact in African American cultures, we need once in a while to shake artistic criticism free from an obsession with finished products, masterpieces, star-status artists, and intercontinental continuities and devote serious attention to some of the humbler dimensions of artistic expression, such as the steps by which a work is made and the social context in which it's embedded. I do not believe that the artistic continuities between Africa and Afro-America will ever be fully grasped by an anthropologist who doesn't care that African "calabashes" belong to the pumpkin family and that the American calabash grows on a tree, or by a historian who doesn't ask about the social and economic environment that leads Maroon men to work with a knife and compass and Maroon women with broken glass, or by a critic who doesn't take artistic styles seriously until they get beyond the awkward stage of crude experimentation. For a genuine appreciation of the artistic spirit, the scratches in the margins and the scraps along the borders have, as African American seamstresses have understood for centuries, very central stories to tell.

NOTES

1. This observation applies specifically to Upper River Saramakas. Eastern Maroons and Saramakas living in the villages closest to Paramaribo have sometimes decorated skirts.

2. I have reworded the translation of this passage very slightly, rendering the verb *marquer*, for example, as "mark" rather than "decorate."

3. Robert Farris Thompson has made a valiant effort to unearth historical evidence showing that Suriname Maroons had developed decorative patchwork art before the late nineteenth century. "There must have been," he argues, after citing the 1748 testimony from Cayenne, "similar memories of West African multi-strip cloth among black runaways of neighboring Suriname, for in 1823 Ferdinand Denis describes and illustrates an article of dress, given as Carib" (1983: 215). Thompson reproduces Denis's illustration and goes on to reason that the garment, by virtue of its "two patterned narrow strips . . . separated by a single band of continuously unpatterned cloth," embodies an aesthetic that "points back to early Asante cloths of the nineteenth century, when weavers were working under Mande influences radiating from Kong and from Bonduku, northwest

of the Akan and north of Cap Lahou, whence sailed to Suriname 50 percent of a sample of Dutch slaving ships" (1983:215).

Although the object in the sketch is captioned as an Indian loincloth ("*Camiza Indien*"), Thompson dismisses this attribution on the grounds that Suriname Indians "in general make and prefer solid red loincloths" (no reference given), and that therefore the garment must have been made by Djuka Maroons, who must then have sold it to the Indians from whom it was collected. In any case, he asserts (no reference given), "the word *camiza* is not Amerindian" (1983:296). In fact, however, this word *is* (and was even in the eighteenth century) Amerindian, and the garment it referred to was not necessarily red, as any number of sources make clear. Stedman, writing of the 1770s, notes: "The only dress Wore by these Indians consists in a Strip of black, or blew Cotton, worn by the Men to cover their Nakedness, and cal'd *Camisa* [while the equivalent for women is] a Girdle made of human Hair around their Waste, through which before, and behind, they fasten a Square broad Piece of black Cotton" (1790/1988:306); P. J. Benoit describes Suriname Indian loincloths in the 1830s as being "red or blue" (1839:42); and the venerable *Encyclopædie van Nederlandsch West-Indië* reports that "the Caribs of both sexes wear a loincloth, or *kamiesa* (Sp. camisa) of dark blue cotton" (Benjamins and Snelleman 1914–17:102).

Compounding the errors in Thompson's Amerindian ethnography, there are troubling slips in his representation of Djuka history and in his use of demographic figures on the slave trade to Suriname. The sequence of events he proposes is: transfer of influence from Mande to Asante weavers of the early nineteenth century; the capture, transatlantic voyage, and selling into slavery of some of these Asantes; their escape into the interior of Suriname; their acceptance by the Djuka Maroons; the production by them (or under their influence) of the loincloth in question; its sale to Carib Indians; and its collection from those Indians by a French explorer, who then sailed back to Europe, wrote up his travel account, and published it in Paris in 1823. He caps this scenario off with a claim that the African area which influenced the hypothetical Asante weavers was one "whence sailed to Suriname 50 percent of a sample of Dutch slaving ships," giving as his source R. Price 1976:14–15.

Note, however, that (1) the Djuka Maroons had been virtually closed off to new runaways since their treaty with the Dutch Crown in 1760, and (2) the statistical sample he alludes to does not refer simply to "a sample of Dutch slaving ships," but rather to a (56-ship) sample of *those Dutch slaving ships that transported Africans from the Windward Coast*—an area which, as the cited pages make clear, supplied only 0–4 percent of Suriname slaves before 1736 and under 50 percent later in the eighteenth century.

4. A word of explanation about the 1980 end date. In 1986 Richard Price and I went to Suriname after a six-year absence. The evening before our trip upriver, we were placed under house arrest in our Paramaribo hotel and then, at midnight, brusquely put in the back seat of a Volkswagen

and "escorted to the border" by two military policemen. Although we did not know it at the time, the Maroon-led Jungle Commando had just had its first skirmishes with the Suriname military, and a civil war, which eventually lasted six years, was in the making. In the wake of that experience, compounded by encounters that Richard Price had after testifying on behalf of the Saramaka people in a 1992 Human Rights trial against the government of Suriname (see R. Price 1995), our Maroon fieldwork has been conducted in neighboring French Guiana.

5. In like manner, if the 1823 mention of "assembling" pieces of cloth in French Guiana (see above) was referring to patchwork, it could easily have been made without producing color contrasts, given that nothing is said in that testimony about dyes.

6. This view of discontinuous textile arts emerging from continuous aesthetic principles and sewing techniques, which reflects a perspective first elaborated in terms of Afro-Caribbean culture in general (Mintz and Price 1976/1992), explicitly contests the more narrowly medium-specific continuity proposed by Robert Farris Thompson (1983:214–219). His preferred scenario would link Saramaka narrow-strip cloths "of the twentieth century," Djuka equivalents "of the late nineteenth century," and coastal black patchwork "of even earlier facture" in order to explain Afro-American continuities without recourse to "a mysterious black consciousness." The "earlier facture" of coastal patchwork rests on a single verbal statement by a man Thompson met in Paramaribo, and is unsupported by illustrations, examples, or written documentation of any kind. The basis for the Djuka dating is not indicated. And Plate 141, Thompson's illustration of the "culmination [of this progression] in Djuka and Saamaka multistrip expressions of the early twentieth century," is a patchwork hammock sheet that was made by Apúmba, wife of Saramaka Tribal Chief Agbagó, as a gift to her sister-in-law Naai, who gave it to Richard Price and me in 1968 when we left Saramaka after having been her close neighbors for two years. Photographed hanging from a rod in our living room, it is presented by Thompson without acknowledgment or attribution of any kind, perhaps because our published documentation of the textile in a 1980 book made clear that it may have been sewn as late as the 1950s.

7. Like any nutshell history, this one has left out numerous details. I cite just three. Even after the early curvilinear embroidery style gave way to bits-and-pieces patchwork, a more linear, less textured version of it continued as a secondary kind of decoration for many kinds of clothing (see, for example, S. and R. Price 1999: 96, S. Price 1984: Figs. 49–50). During a transitional period between bits-and-pieces and narrow-strip patchwork, some textiles displayed bits-and-pieces composition executed with the multicolored cloth more typical of the narrow-strip art (see, for example, S. and R. Price 1999: 121–122). And in the 1980s, women were already focusing their efforts on the new *abena koósu* art, sewing patchwork that displayed striking visual similarities to that of the early twentieth century, but employed a distinctive range of colors and made significantly heavier use of appliqué.

8. For further discussion of the these two botanical species (*Crescentia*

cujete L. and *Lagenaria siceraria* [Mol.] Standl.) and the implications of differences between them for Maroon art history, see S. Price 1982.

REFERENCES

Benjamins, H. D., and Joh. F. Snelleman (eds.). 1914–17. *Encyclopædie van Nederlandsch West-Indië*. The Hague: Martinus Nijhoff.

Benoit, P. J. 1839. *Voyage à Surinam: description des possessions néerlandaises dans la Guyane*. Bruxelles: Société des Beaux-Arts.

Bonaparte, Prince Roland. 1884. *Les habitants de Suriname, notes recueillies à l'exposition coloniale d'Amsterdam en 1883*. Paris: A. Quantin.

Caliste, Canute. 1989. *The Mermaid Wakes: Paintings of a Caribbean Isle*. London: Macmillan.

Coster, A. M. 1866. "De Boschnegers in de kolonie Suriname, hun leven, zeden, en gewoonten." *Bijdragen tot de Taal-, Land- en Volkenkunde* 13:1–36.

Crevaux, Jules. 1879. "Voyage d'exploration dans l'intérieur des Guyanes, 1876–77." *Le Tour du Monde* 20:337–416.

Eilerts de Haan, J. G. W. J. 1910. "Verslag van de expeditie naar de Suriname-Rivier." *Tijdschrift van het Koninklijk Nederlandsch Aardrijkskundig Genootschap* (2e serie) 27:403–68, 641–701.

Grudin, Eva Ungar. 1990. *Stitching Memories: African-American Story Quilts*. Williamstown, MA: Williams College Museum of Art.

Houlberg, Marilyn. 1996. "Sirens and Snakes: Water Spirits in the Arts of Haitian Vodou." *African Arts* 29(2):30–35, 101.

Leon, Eli. 1992. *Models in the Mind: African Prototypes in American Patchwork*. Winston-Salem: The Diggs Gallery and Winston-Salem State University.

Mintz, Sidney W., and Richard Price. 1976/1992. *The Birth of African American Culture*. Boston: Beacon.

Price, Richard. 1973. *Maroon Societies: Rebel Slave Communities in the Americas* (Richard Price, ed.). Garden City, NY: Doubleday/Anchor.

——. 1976. *The Guiana Maroons: A Historical and Bibliographical Introduction*. Baltimore: Johns Hopkins University Press.

——. 1990. *Alabi's World*. Baltimore: Johns Hopkins University Press.

——. 1995. "Executing Ethnicity: The Killings in Suriname." *Cultural Anthropology* 10:437–471.

Price, Richard, and Sally Price. 1991. *Two Evenings in Saramaka*. Chicago: University of Chicago Press.

Price, Sally. 1984. *Co-Wives and Calabashes*. Ann Arbor: University of Michigan Press.

——. 1982. "When Is a Calabash Not a Calabash?" *New West Indian Guide* 56:69–82.

Price, Sally, and Richard Price. 1999. *Maroon Arts: Cultural Vitality in the African Diaspora*. Boston: Beacon.

Ringgold, Faith. 1995. *We Flew Over the Bridge: The Memoirs of Faith Ringgold*. Boston: Bulfinch Press.

Schumann, C. L. 1778. "Saramaccanisch Deutsches Wörter-Buch." In
   Hugo Schuchardt, *Die Sprache der Saramakkaneger in Surinam* (Am-
   sterdam: Johannes Müller, 1914), pp. 46–116.
Staehelin, F. 1913–19. *Die Mission der Brüdergemeine in Suriname und
   Berbice im achtzehnten Jahrhundert.* Herrnhut: Vereins für Brüder-
   geschichte in Kommission der Unitätsbuchhandlung in Gnadau.
Stedman, John Gabriel. 1790/1988. *Narrative of a Five Years Expedition
   Against the Revolted Negroes of Surinam* (newly transcribed from the
   1790 manuscript: edited and with an introduction and notes by Rich-
   ard Price and Sally Price). Baltimore: Johns Hopkins University Press.
Thompson, Robert Farris. 1983. *Flash of the Spirit: African and Afro-
   American Art and Philosophy.* New York: Random House.

14

GABRIELA CRAVO E CANELA: JORGE AMADO AND THE MYTH OF THE SEXUAL MULATA IN BRAZILIAN CULTURE

Eliana Guerreiro Ramos Bennett

Brazil is a country of great contrasts. For example, it has the world's fourteenth-largest economy in terms of its gross national product, but this wealth does not reach the majority of Brazilian people, most of whom can be counted among the world's poorest. Another "contraste brasileiro"—Brazilian contrast—is the fact that the richest 20 percent of the population makes 32 times as much as the poorest 20 percent.[1] A third example is the subject of this essay: the great chasm between the Brazil which Brazilian officials have traditionally portrayed, not only in Brazil, but especially outside of Brazil, and the *real* Brazil.

In the postcard picture of Brazil, the country is portrayed as a "racial paradise" where the various national ethnic groups and cultures intermingle and intermarry peacefully, to form the great happy Brazilian plantation, where everyone dances the samba with Disney's Joe Carioca. The picture of Brazil as a "racial paradise" is a Jungian exercise in collective fantasy in the sense that Brazil presents itself as it would like to be seen, even perhaps as it would like to be, but this fantasy is far from the shadowy reality of ethnic relations in Brazil. The truth—or the shadow, to use Jung's term to describe our inner reality—of Brazilian interethnic relations is that Brazil is more similar to the old South Africa than to any racial paradise.

Brazil is a country with a majority black and brown population ruled by a white minority. There is racial segregation at every level of society: not the kind of segregation found in the old South Africa or in the old American South, with public signs and laws governing interethnic human relations, but more a matter of custom. Brazilian racism, as is the case with other Latin American phenomena, has a surreal quality to it. That is, it is governed by rules largely unspoken and not clearly observable and quantifiable. It is a system in which blacks and whites each have a "proper place" in society, in a kind of "God-given" order. Although there is an emerging consciousness, mainly represented by the "Movimento Negro," the social and economic segregation of blacks is generally not questioned by most Brazilians of any ethnicity.

North American anthropologist Angela Gilliam, in an article published in a Brazilian newspaper, compares the American system of racism with the one in Brazil where, she says, "invisibility shrouds the black person and his or her daily problems."[2] The key word here is "invisibility," which indeed is a hallmark of the life of Brazilian blacks, who are truly considered nonpersons by both the political and the cultural structures. My own experience in both countries confirms Gilliam's concept of "invisibility." As one example, the work of my late father, Alberto Guerreiro Ramos, one of Brazil's foremost social scientists, was cited by President Fernando Henrique Cardoso in his inaugural address and is, in fact, studied in both Brazilian and American universities. Yet in his Rio de Janeiro police file he is a potential "subversive," a "mulato, dado a estudos sociologicos" (mulato, prone to conducting sociological studies). I remember with great sadness the year 1966, when my father learned of this file. He had by then published twelve books and was well known in Brazil. This description by the Brazilian military, who were in the process of killing or imprisoning thousands of thoughtful Brazilians, became one of the factors in our family's eventual migration to Los Angeles, California where my father was a professor at the University of Southern California from 1966 until his death, still in exile, in 1982.

The real personality of black and brown women—the specific subject of the present discussion—is mostly invisible. We are, instead, described and even experienced by (and in) Brazilian society within the context of the "myth of the sexual mulata." We do not exist as real persons but rather are seen as the middle component of the Brazilian three-part puzzle expressed in the popular saying "branca para casar, preta para cozinhar, e mulata para fazer amor"—"White woman to marry, black woman to cook, and mulata to make love." In her book *Brazilian Women Speak*, Daphne Patai refers to this very structure of social relations: "The intertwining of race, class, and gender in Brazil is further demonstrated by the patterns of interracial marriages. When their level of education (and with it access to higher incomes) permits it, many Black men marry 'up'—which means White. And they are more likely to do so as their educational attainments increase. Among higher-educated White men, however, the tendency to marry Black women decreases. It would seem that the old (androcentric as well as racist) Brazilian saying still holds: 'White woman for marriage, mulata for sex, Black woman for work'."[3]

Ours is the ultimate example of a Jungian existence: nobody knows us. We are falsely experienced. In 1982, I presented what I thought was an interesting paper on an alternative theory of development at the Fundaçao Getulio Vargas, in Rio de Janeiro. After my presentation, instead of comments I received several invitations to "lunch."

No one has contributed more to our "invisibility" as real and complete human beings than our great writer Jorge Amado, and of his novels, none has fueled the myth of the sexual mulata more than *Gabriela Cravo e Canela* (Gabriela, Clove and Cinnamon), published thirty-seven years ago. Amado's novels all deal with Afro-Brazilian culture as an outsider looking at "the other." He is what Alberto Guerreiro Ramos was thinking of when he wrote that "in order to inferiorize the Black, white social scientists transform him into a subject matter."[4] To Amado, Black Brazilian culture is exotic, mysterious, interesting. Widely read in Brazil, he has influenced at least one generation's thoughts about Afro-Brazilianism; in 1961 he was elected to the Brazilian Academy of Letters.

This novel takes place in 1925, and before the reader gets a first glimpse of Gabriela herself, we are told about life in this Brazilian city, colonial in its architecture and history as well as in social customs and rituals governed by the appearance of propriety. The *appearance* of proper social behavior is imperative, if not the behavior itself:

> The sons of the landowners attended the most expensive schools in the big cities, new houses for the families, built in the newly built streets, luxurious furniture sent from Rio, grand pianos appointed the living rooms, different stores, a growing commerce, liquor flowing in the cabares, women arriving in ocean liners, progress, after all, the much anticipated civilization.[5]

And describing an annual religious procession through the city:

> . . . in this participated the most notable citizens, the largest landowners, which is not a small feat because the colonels were not known for their religiosity, they did not attend church, rebelling against the mass and confession, leaving these weaknesses to the females of the family.[6]

As I mentioned at the outset, Jorge Amado is in fact one of our great writers. To dismiss him because of his racial prejudice would be akin to dismissing Ernest Hemingway because of his perceptions of race and gender. In my view, neither Amado nor Hemingway can be dismissed, as they, in spite of their prejudices, present interesting, often beautiful, pictures of the world. In fact, perhaps the most serious aspect of *Gabriela Cravo e Canela* and its impact on Brazilian culture is that it is a beautifully written novel, one which also contains an interesting portrait of early 1900s Brazilian society. Still, I think that it is important to strike a balance between appreciating Amado's work as a writer and being aware of his attitudes toward race. To return to the novel itself, in the thirty-seven years since its publication, *Gabriela Cravo e Canela* has contributed significantly to the manner in which brown women—mulatas—are seen and treated in Brazilian culture.

Gabriela is the story of a mulata, Gabriela, essentially incapable of leading a respectable life as a wife. She can be happy only as a mistress, fulfilling the sexual needs and fantasies of both employer and husband. Gabriela is a *retirante*, the term used in Brazil to describe the millions of people who, over the decades, have been forced to leave the Nordeste (the Northeast of Brazil) due to devastating years-long droughts during which many people die. The retirantes travel, by bus, truck, or foot, to the southern parts of the country looking for work and survival. Gabriela arrives, on foot, in the city of Ilheus, in the state of Bahia, just as Nacib, an Arab bar owner, loses his cook and is looking for a new one. Nacib hires Gabriela to be his cook on a subsistence salary.

When Nacib hires her, Gabriela is covered with dirt and dust from her months-long trip from the Nordeste. The first time that he sees her after she has bathed and cleaned herself, Nacib is stunned to find that she is, of course, a beautiful mulata:

> He came in softly and saw her sleeping on a chair, her long hair spread over her shoulders. After being washed and combed her hair had been transformed into something beautiful, black, full of curls. She was dressed in rags, but clean. A tear on her skirt showed a piece of thigh the color of cinnamon, her breasts moved up and down slightly to rhythm of her sleep, her face smiling.
> —My God!—Nacib stood in disbelief.
> To look at her in limitless surprise, how was so much beauty hidden under the dust from the road? Her round arms, her brown face smiling in her sleep, there asleep on the chair she looked like a picture. How old she must be? The body of a young woman, features of a girl.
> —My God, what a sight!—whispered the Arab almost devoutly.
> To the sound of his voice, she woke up frightened but quickly smiled and the room seemed to smile with her. She stood up, her hands fixing the rags she was wearing.
> —Why didn't you lie down and go to sleep?—was all Nacib was able to say.
> —Mister didn't say anything. . . .[7]

Nacib then ponders the possibilities, thinking about Gabriela, "Some brown woman, his maid. Such eyes, my God. . . . And of that burnt color that he liked."[8] A sexual relationship soon develops. Gabriela works all day, performing miracles as cook and housekeeper and still managing to wait each evening beautiful and "fresh" for Nacib. Here Jorge Amado describes for us the mulata as the ideal woman:

> How did she find the time to wash clothes, clean the house,—it had never been so clean!—fix the trays for the bar, lunch and dinner for Nacib? Not to mention at night she was always fresh and rested, wet with desire, not only giving herself but taking him as well, never satisfied. She seemed to guess Nacib's thoughts. . . .[9]

Nacib, of course, falls in love with Gabriela.

After a few months, Dona Arminda, another cook and Gabriela's friend, advises that Gabriela can get anything she wants from Nacib, even marriage:

> —Marry me? Why? This is not necessary . . . why would he get married? Mister Nacib should get married to a nice girl, from a good family. Why would he marry me?
>   Not necessary. . . . And you don't have any desire to be a lady, have servants, walk hand in hand with your husband, dress in nice clothes, be somebody in society?
>   —I would probably have to wear shoes every day . . . I would not like that. I might even like to marry Mr. Nacib. I would spend all my life cooking for him, helping him. . . . But, Mister Nacib has better things to do than to marry a nobody like me, that he found already lost. . . . I don't want to think about this Dona Arminda. Not even if he were mad.[10]

Nacib and Gabriela marry, and she is unable to adjust to her new status as a respectable wife. She hates wearing shoes, she falls asleep at a poetry reading, she sneaks away to see a traveling circus, and, finally, she is caught in bed with another man. Nacib is devastated; he has the marriage annulled, but keeps her as a cook. They soon resume their sexual relationship, prompted by Gabriela, who cannot control her physical desire for Nacib, missing his smell much as an animal relates to another's scent. "A Senhora Saad goes back to being Gabriela (Mrs. Saad goes back to being Gabriela)," Amado says. He adds that Gabriela was "nascida para aquilo (born for that)"—for sex.

Over the last thirty-seven years *Gabriela Cravo e Canela* has become part of Brazilian consciousness, or perhaps it would be more accurate to say unconsciousness, in the way we think of, perceive, and relate to black and brown women in Brazil.

"Mulata, Produto de Exportacao"—"Mulata, Export Product": these are Jorge Amado's words during a television interview (PBS, 1975) in which he explains that the mulata is a "product" which can show the world how Brazil has addressed the problem of racism by, he says, intermarriage between blacks and whites. Out of this union, Amado continues, has come this "beautiful product." During the interview, aired on PBS in the United States, Amado actually had a "mulata" sitting next to him to whom he proudly pointed to show what he meant. As he said, "THIS is what I mean."

Native American writer Michael Dorris said in a recent interview that "Social life, after all, is simply a collective illusion, a shared set of boundaries and possibilities. If we all believe something to be true, in an odd way it is true."[11] This is the case with the way black and brown women are perceived in Brazil, where the collective illusion is that mulatas, to use the term for a moment, are better suited for sex than for anything else. Black and brown women are readily employed in the tourist industry (for example, as samba dancers, showgirls, etc.) but those who attempt to pursue professional careers to any extent are not taken seriously.

The historical origins of the Brazilian collective illusion regarding women of color are not entirely different from what happened in the United States. The Brazilian and the North American systems of slavery share some similarities. So-called "house slaves," in general, were light-skinned. This cadre of slaves, both in Brazil and in North America, were the ones who lived in intimate proximity to the slave-owning class, performing duties associated with personal matters which ranged from cooking, to caring for children, to having sex with the master.

Both in Brazil and in the United States light-skinned slaves were, of course, the children of slave-owners and slaves, and in both countries there developed the custom of sexually exploiting black and brown women. In North America this practice was swept under the Puritan rug, whereby any sex is a sin, let alone illicit sex with Africans. In Brazil there developed the "ideology of the mulata," by which women of color are mythologized as being both less than human and overly sexual. The myth also stipulates that it is always the mulatas who tempt the otherwise perfectly pure men.

In reality, even during slavery, women of color attempted to escape the role assigned to them by the dominant society. In the words of Helena Theodore Lopes, "in spite of being shown only as the 'erotic mulata' or domestic worker, submissive, it is important to point out that the participation of black women in the fight for freedom from slavery was constant."[12] The myth of the sexual mulata is, in some ways, similar to the myth of the dumb blonde. Both are ways of dehumanizing and objectifying women. Both myths serve to impede women from participating in society as full human beings.

NOTES

1. Brown, 121.
2. Gilliam, January 15, 1995.
3. Patai, 80.
4. Ramos, 217.
5. Amado, 15.
6. Amado, 15.
7. Amado, 129.
8. Amado, 130.
9. Amado, 165.
10. Amado, 181.
11. Aronson, 35.
12. Nascimento, 102.

REFERENCES

Amado, Jorge. *Gabriela Cravo e Canela.* 71st edition. Rio de Janeiro, Brazil: Editora Record, 1995.
Aronson, David. *Teaching Tolerance.* Montgomery, AL: Southern Poverty Law Center, 1995.
Brown, Lester. *State of the World.* W. W. Norton and Company. New York and London, 1997.
Gilliam, Angela. Article published in *Folha de São Paulo,* January 15, 1995. São Paulo, Brazil.
Nascimento, Elisa Larkin, editor. *Sankofa—Resgate Da Cultura Afro-Brasileria,* 2d ed. Rio de Janeiro: Seafro, 1994.
Patai, Daphne. *Brazilian Women Speak.* New Brunswick, NJ: Rutgers University Press, 1993.
Ramos, Alberto G. *Introducao Critica a Sociologia.* Rio de Janeiro: Universidade Federal, 1995.

15

GENDER AND THE NEW AFRICAN DIASPORA: AFRICAN IMMIGRANT WOMEN IN THE CANADIAN LABOR FORCE

Patience Elabor-Idemudia

The realities that confront Africans in their struggles to create a viable life for themselves have often been presented from a Eurocentric perspective. In many circles, Euro-American education continues to distort, misappropriate, and misinterpret African people's lives and experiences by using their blackness as a political metaphor for identifying them with the disadvantaged and the dispossessed. What is often missing in the Euro-American discourse is an analysis of how a people rich in resourcefulness, self-reliance, and community bonding came to be marginalized, pauperized, and dominated. Their struggles, which started with forcible relocation through slavery to the New World, continue today in the postslavery and postcolonial era. While the nature of their relocation may have changed, today the challenges they confront continue to be mediated by their ethnicity, race, gender, and class.

In the New African Diaspora, the question has been raised as to whether there are certain peculiarly African qualities in New World black culture that do not quite sort well with the contingent culture. This essay attempts to answer that question by examining the experiences of African women in their quest for work in Canada. It applies an African-centered or Afrocentric discourse in its analysis of the histories and experiences of diasporan Africans, especially immigrant women as they struggle for everyday survival. The discourse attempts to validate and interpret the women's experiences as subjects rather than objects on the fringes of European experience (Dei, 1993). Afrocentricity, within this context, is about inclusion, particularly in an era in which the marginalization of African people's experiences and subjugation of their identities have become more problematic than ever before (Dei, 1993).

Specifically, I will examine and analyze the challenges confronted by African immigrant women in the Canadian labor force. The ideological constructs which form the basis for the devaluation of their "foreign" educational qualifications and experiences, and their limited access to training opportunities in official language programs, are racist, sexist, discriminatory, and therefore in dire need of analysis. The adoption and use of priority criteria like "bread-winner" and "being an independent immigrant" as yardsticks for determining eligibility serve to systemmatically marginalize immigrant women. In the specific case of African immigrant women in Canada, their race and gender, coupled with the stereotypic ideology and stigma endemic to their social construction as "immigrants" and/or "women of color," means that many in the dominant culture assume they have a limited knowledge of English; they speak English with an accent and come from "visibly" different cultures from "our" own (Bannerji, 1987). Moreover, their indigenous cultures are seen as inherently conservative and pathological, not oriented to developing a high level of self-esteem and self-identity, thereby rendering them incapable of successful participation in Canadian social life.

It will be argued here as elsewhere (Ng, 1988; Leah, 1991; Boyd, 1987) that immigrant women and, in this case, African immigrant women are perceived as a "special commodity," that is, a group of people lacking "Canadian experience" who are not qualified and skilled enough to engage in paid work or assume any position that would allow them to assimilate adequately into the Canadian society. It is common for African women from the continent to confront racism in the way that they are viewed as exotic specimens or victims of all sorts of patriarchal oppression, including polygamy and/or "clitoridectomy." These ideological constructs, as parameters for determining the women's suitability for life in Canada, are particularly challenging when applied to African immigrant women because of their strength and distinctiveness. The notions of self-reliance and community bond are more relevant to African women, who tend to use their local creativity and resourcefulness to address contemporary problems of daily survival and to forge ahead (Dei, 1993).

As economic survival through labor is a predominant reason for immigrant families' migration to Canada, these women, in spite of their high educational background, are forced to engage in low-paying jobs under difficult working conditions. Others engage in nonformal work in cottage industries where they are subjected to exploitation, with incomes barely large enough to subsist on. The implications of these trends will be analyzed using the findings of a study of African immigrant women in Toronto conducted during the summer of 1994. Antiracist and nonsexist alternative ways of addressing the challenges confronted by the African immigrant women will also be explored.

BLACK IMMIGRANT WOMEN:
A HISTORY OF THEIR LABOR STATUS

In Canadian society, black women's experiences are historically and institutionally structured in ways that are different from the experiences of those who are not black and female[1] (Carty, 1991). As a group, black women tend to experience their social world differently than do men and other women. For example, in their relations with men, in the roles that are available to them in the family, in the labor market, in the paid and unpaid work that they perform, in their interactions with other women, and in their knowledge of themselves, they experience oppression, subordination, and discrimination mainly because of their race and gender. Contrary to popular belief, slavery did exist in Canada, specifically in what has become Quebec, Nova Scotia, Ontario, and New Brunswick between 1629 and 1834 (Brand, 1988; Bolaria and Li, 1988). Blacks also came as Loyalists after the American Revolution and as fugitives from slavery after 1800 via the Underground Railroad. Although there is an absence in Canada of specific historical documentation on black communities, in particular on black women, one can speculate that their experiences resembled those in the United States and the Caribbean.

Historical patterns of systemic discrimination against immigrants in Canada have been well documented (Estable, 1986; Ng, 1986, 1988, 1992; Ng and Estable, 1987; Warren, 1986; Calliste, 1991; Leah, 1991; and Das Gupta, 1994) and have led to the development of a labor force that is segregated by gender, race, and ethnicity. To understand the relations between black and white communities in Canada, one has to look to the history of slavery in the Americas. It was in that context that racialized gender relations of working-class black women and white middle-class men and women crystallized (Brand, 1988). The ideology of racism was constructed to justify slavery, colonialism, and imperialism. For example, within slavery, black women were used not only for the reproduction of black children but for the reproduction of children of white slave masters, including those born of brutal rapes. As this ideology was itself reproduced, it perpetuated the belief that different racial and ethnic groups had inherent attributes which suited them to particular jobs (Calliste, 1991). Race and gender ideologies were used to justify the domination, exclusion, and restriction of blacks and other people of color, particularly women. Racially constructed gender ideologies and images portrayed black women as "naturally" suited for jobs in the lowest stratum of a labor market segmented along gender lines. Immigrants and women of color, in addition to suffering from the inequality faced by all women (such as low wages, part-time employment, lack of job security, occupational and industrial segregation in women's job ghettos, sexist discrimination, sexual harassment, and high unemployment),[2] were confronted by racism, class exploitation, and structural discrimination. They faced discrimination in employment as well as in education, housing, and immigration. Blacks, specifically, were stigmatized as unassimilable and undesirable for permanent settlement in Canada.

Black women, forced immigrants from Africa and the West Indies, worked largely on farms, in domestic service, and at home at the turn of the century. Until the 1940s, 80 percent of black women worked as domestics, mother's helpers, housekeepers, general helpers, and laundresses. It was not until World War II that labor shortages forced employers to hire black women to work in areas formerly held by white females. When white females moved into essential war-industry jobs, black women took up their spaces in hospitals, restaurants, hotels, laundries, dry-cleaning, and nonessential companies making candy, tobacco, and soft drinks (Brand, 1991:15). This segregated and racialized labor force resulted in low pay, few benefits, and little job security. Today, women employed in private domestic services—many of them recent immigrants or visa workers from Jamaica and the Philippines—generally earn below the minimum wage.

Experiences of racism and sexism have shaped, and still shape, the lives of immigrant women of color in their communities and their workplace. The exploitation of their labor has been shaped by capitalist demands for cheap labor combined with racist and sexist immigration and state policies. Immigrant women, especially nonwhite and non-English speaking, are concentrated in the lowest, most insecure, and least organized sector of traditional female occupation. Black women are generally segregated into the lowest-status service jobs while native women are largely excluded from the paid labor force. Discriminatory government policies and workplace practices serve to maintain this extreme form of exploitation. Women of color, especially blacks, face many obstacles to unionization, and within the union movement itself they face continuing discrimination. It is these lived experiences of racism, sexism, and exploitation that have shaped the demands being raised by immigrant women as they organize and demand necessary action by the government (Leah, 1991).

Related to the marginal labor status and low earning power of women of color is the high proportion of part-time employment or the casual nature of their jobs. The "First Equal Employment Opportunity Report," issued by Metro Toronto in June 1985, pointed to a 492 percent growth in temporary and part-time employment between 1977 and 1985; 79 percent of these part-time workers were women and/or members of visible minority groups, most of whom preferred full-time jobs but could not get them (Leah, 1991).

In the last two decades, the migration of large numbers of the working class from southern Europe and the Third World (non-English and non-white) has been encouraged by labor demands for unskilled workers, and immigration policy was directed toward this end (Leah, 1991). For example, black women from the Caribbean emigrated to Canada under the Jamaica-Canada domestic agreement, a policy later replaced by the recruitment of domestic workers on temporary visas. Most immigrant women and women of color are employed in labor-intensive, low-wage sectors, used as a reserve labor force, subject to intense exploitation, and often denied the most basic labor rights (Estelle and Ng, 1985; Calliste, 1991). Most black women in Canada work at low-status jobs in homes and institutions, doing "black women's work": cleaning white people's houses, bathrooms, and hotel rooms; serving white people breakfast, lunch, and dinner in private homes, in office cafeterias, and in hospitals; lifting, feeding, minding, and washing white people's children and elders; and sweeping, packaging, scouring, washing, and cooking (Brand, 1987).

As more women of color are allowed to migrate to Canada today, they are doing so as wives and dependents under the family class status (Estable and Meyer, 1989). Women who come in under the family class are assumed to have guaranteed financial support and therefore are not allowed to work outside their homes. Their primary responsibility is seen to be with childcare and housework. This in effect reproduces traditional gender ideology with regard to sexual division of labor. In addition, the sponsorship agreement of up to ten years puts the black immigrant woman into a dependency relationship with the male principal applicant. The dependent status of these women is maintained by various institutional processes upon their arrival and results in their inability to (i) access certain federal social services; (ii) voice their experiences in family abuse situations; (iii) access services and programs, depending on how provincial and municipal regulations are interpreted in relation to the sponsorship agreement (Lee, 1990). Therefore, government-subsidized programs, such as English/French as a Second Language (ESL/FSL) courses offered by the Employment and Immigration Centre (EIC), are not accessible to them since "they are not destined for the labour force." It is obvious that sponsored immigrant women are vulnerable to the good will of the male principal applicant's confirmation that the sponsorship agreement is intact. According to Estelle and Meyer (1989), this policy affects women adversely, since about 43 percent of women immigrants in 1986 did not know either official language. Community organizations representing immigrant women agree that the Employment Centre practices place women in a double bind. They are denied access to language training and language upgrading, without which they cannot find wage work. Coupled with this are the inadequacies of the childcare system and inadequate awareness of the legal rights of workers and obligations of the employers which compound the limitations under which the sponsored black immigrant woman may work.

EMPLOYMENT DISCRIMINATION: RACE AND GENDER ISSUES

In advanced capitalist societies like Canada, racism and sexism are used to maximize profit in several ways: through the devaluation of educational qualification of foreign workers; through a segregated labor market where racial minorities and women, particularly black women, are concentrated in low-status and low-paying jobs; and through a split labor market where women are paid less than white workers and men for doing the same work (Phizacklea, 1983; Calliste, 1991). For example, since the mid-1970s, immigration policies and practices have allowed a large number of professional and skilled workers to emigrate from Africa to Canada. But within this practice is the "cultural hegemony" of Western educational systems embodying a long history of Euro-American dominance of what constitutes valid knowledge and how such knowledge should be produced and disseminated internally and internationally (Amin, 1990; Said, 1979). Once in Canada, these African immigrants with professional skills often encounter many institutional barriers, and this tends to undermine the true market worth of their expertise. Many immigrants who are qualified as physicians, nurses, or teachers in their home countries may not be granted a license to practice their professions in Canada. Many with extensive qualifications and experience are underemployed in jobs that utilize their expertise but underpay their market worth relative to that of Canadian graduates. In so doing, Canada economizes on the reproduction of high-cost labor as well as reaps the fruit of the labor of foreign-trained workers without having to pay for full cost of labor.

A 1984 report of the Special Committee on Visible Minorities in Canada noted that the evaluation of foreign degrees and credentials is such that minority immigrants do not receive due recognition of their credentials, and face undue delay in becoming licensed. Their educational training is "devalued." For example, a Jamaican immigrant with a B.A. honors degree from Harvard University and a Ph.D. from Stanford University received a letter from the evaluation officer of the Ontario Ministry of Education and the Ministry of Colleges and Universities advising him that his "educational attainment in the United States may be considered comparable to the completion of at least Grade Thirteen in the current Ontario school system"[3] (as cited in Bolaria and Li, *Racial Oppression in Canada*, 1988:218). An immigrant who obtained a bachelor's degree from India with first-class standing was evaluated as only qualified for admission to the first year of one Canadian university's undergraduate degree program.[4]

These findings led the committee to recommend that the practice of evaluating non-Canadian degrees and credentials and licensing professionals be investigated.

It is obvious that although employment is a key factor in the social integration of newcomers in most societies, in Canada, most African immigrants and refugees, especially women, face severe systemic discrimination in the labor force, due mainly to their race and gender (Moussa, 1992, 1993) and their "lack of Canadian experience." A 1984 report of the Abella Commission set up to examine employment practices of eleven crown corporations revealed that racial minorities experience lower participation rates, higher unemployment and underemployment rates, occupational segregation, and low income levels. A study conducted by Henry and Ginzberg (1982) during the same period demonstrated that when education, work experience, and skills were controlled, white applicants experienced preferential treatment and black applicants experienced discrimination at the point of entry into the employment process. White job applicants had three job chances to every one for blacks.

In a study of barriers to recognition of immigrant credentials, it was revealed that racist views toward racial minorities about their ability to meet performance criteria (compared to whites) prevailed. These views varied according to occupation, country of origin, and province of settlement (Ministry of Citizenship, 1989). Again, these findings, as well as those of a Parliamentary Task Force and other research, forced the government in late 1980s to establish a mandatory Employment Equity Program (Employment Equity Act, 1986) to help achieve equity in employment for women, Aboriginal people, visible minorities, and persons with disabilities. The act stated that federally regulated employers must begin to institute measures to ensure equitable representation of designated groups throughout the workplace and to remedy and prevent the effects of both intentional and systemic discrimination (Collins and Henry, 1994). In spite of the government's actions, devaluation of non-Canadian degrees persists. The nonrecognition of prior, non-Canadian professional experience and qualifications poses difficult questions for the employment status for immigrants of color, especially black women, who are then streamlined into dead-end, entry-level jobs. These practices have implications for the social construction of knowledge, raising questions about whose interest such construction serves. Feminists and postmodernists have called for the introduction, validation, and interrogation of "other voices and ways of knowing in order to provide a more complete account of the history of ideas and events that have shaped human growth and development" (Buck, 1991; Gunew, 1991).

An analysis of sexist and racist barriers and trends in labor practices shows them to fall within the dual segmentation theory of labor. The dual segmentation theory, proposed by Edwards (1979), attempts to explain the persistence of low-wage work by examining the operation of labor markets. According to this theory, labor markets are segmented into two workforces: skilled male workers who are usually unionized and predominate in the primary labor market, which is characterized by relatively high wages, secure employment, reasonable working conditions, opportunities for advancement, and management practices circumscribed by rules and customs; and women, youth, and racial and ethnic minorities found in the secondary labor market, characterized by weak unions, poor wages, insecure employment, poor working conditions, minimal advancement, and arbitrary management practices (Phillip and Phillip, 1983). The primary labor market is usually linked to core industries, while the secondary labor market feeds into so-called peripheral industries (Gannage, 1986). Both black men and women generally find themselves in the secondary labor force.

Radical economists have linked the dual segmentation of the labor force to the motivation of capitalists to divide and rule the workforce (Gordon et al., 1987). To this, feminists have added that not only capital but also male skilled workers have played a major role in structuring the labor force along gender lines (Hartmann, 1981; Whorton and Burris, 1982). Moreover, women are both reliant upon and oppressed by their positions within the family. This is especially the case with immigrant women, whose limited networks leave them with few of the support services needed to work outside the home. Coupled with the dual segmentation theory are the interventions of race/ethnicity and gender.

Phizacklea's (1983a) anthology examines the situation of immigrant women in Britain with regard to the relationships among gender, class, and ethnicity. She found that universal concepts of labor based on gender define women as mothers and domestic laborers first, and as wage-earners second. In Britain, immigrant women are confined to certain low-paid, low-skilled work because of their gender but racial discrimination further ensures their subordination. She concludes that migrant women represent a "sexually and racially categorized class function." In other words, immigrant women and especially black women constitute a "special commodity" in the labor force. The women, therefore, compete with each other as they move from one form of "low pay manual jobs to another or the lowest rank of non-manual work" (Phizacklea, 1983b). In contrast, their male counterparts move up the skill ladder, as do Canadian-born white women.

A CASE STUDY OF
AFRICAN IMMIGRANT WOMEN

This study, conducted in Toronto in 1994, consisted of 300 African women from continental Africa who have lived in Toronto for between three and five years. Subjects included women who came to Canada as students, housewives, economic and political refugees, and migrant workers. They represented at least twelve countries in Africa and identified their countries of origin as Uganda, Kenya, Tanzania, Nigeria, Zaire, Zimbabwe, South Africa, Sudan, Ethiopia, Somalia, and Zambia. Their ages ranged from 27 to 65, and 268 of them identified their marital status as married. They all spoke some English; 180 of them could read and write English; all have a primary, and some have a secondary, level of education, with 100 having some post-secondary education. Ninety of the 300 women had lived in another, European country before proceeding to Canada.

As African migration to Canada is recent, little research has been done on this group's integration into the Canadian society (Kazosi, 1986, 1992; Neuwirth, 1989; Moussa, 1992, 1993). Although studies relating to labor market integration of other women of color and immigrants exist, no study focusing exclusively on African immigrant women's relationship with the Canadian labor force had been carried out before this study. However, related existing studies generate useful information, as already highlighted (Estable and Ng, 1985; Iacovetta, 1986; Ng, 1988; Leah, 1991; Brand, 1991). Such research findings on immigrant women show a bimodal pattern of employment, with over-representation of immigrant women in the professional sector and in the manufacturing and service sectors, in comparison to Canadian-born women (Boyd, 1986). On the other hand, findings from a general survey assessing "employment, education and training barriers" to immigrant women in Toronto indicate "the largest area of employment was in service occupations followed by industrial jobs" (Costi, 1991).

Objectives of the Study

In order to test the bimodal pattern of immigrant women's employment, the specific case of African women's relationship with the Canada labor force was examined. The objectives of the study were

- to document the current employment patterns of African women and to compare their patterns with Canadian-born women;
- to analyze African women's educational and socioeconomic background in relation to their employment patterns;
- to identify and describe the employment needs and concerns of African immigrant women in Toronto;
- to analyze current resource allocation models used for allocating employment program resources and to evaluate agencies' cost-effectiveness in meeting African women's employment needs.

The following questions guided the in-depth interviews of the research:

1. What are the barriers that have confronted African women in their efforts to become gainfully employed?
2. What perceptions about and attitudes toward the barriers African women encounter due to race, class, and gender discrimination do agency personnel and employers have?
3. What assumptions do agency personnel/employers and the women themselves make about the relative merits of gender roles and the sexual division of labor within African families in comparison to Canadian families when they counsel/employ African women?
4. What strategies do agency personnel and/or employers favor with respect to overcoming systemic discrimination?
5. What employment services do agency personnel/employers view as most suited to meeting African women's needs, and why?

Methodology

In accordance with the study's theoretical objectives, both quantitative and qualitative research methods of data collection were used. The research necessitated cooperation with individuals at three different social constituencies—immigrant women, immigration personnel and their agents, post-secondary education personnel, and employers. The duration of the field research was four months. The project followed five stages: information gathering involving a review of current literature and organizations working with African immigrant women; focus group meeting of African women, which served as a brainstorming session for the development of questionnaires; the design of the questionnaires; administration of the questionnaires to a snowball-selected 300 African women (i.e., using one person as a link to the next); and personal interviews with thirty African women, ten of them in depth. These steps were followed by collation and analysis of the data. Contacts were made with personnel of the Immigration and Employment office in Toronto in order to collect information and learn more about the process of immigration. Documents produced by the office were collected and examined in order to obtain information on the services available to immigrants. Contacts were also made with nongovernmental agencies that provide services to immigrants in Toronto.

The quantitative research method involved the administration of field survey questionnaires to collect quantitative data about immigrant women. The questionnaires were designed with sixty items on the respondents' social characteristics (marital status, educational background, income), actual employment and employment needs, aspirations, stress management behavior, and survival strategies used to cope with stress. The questionnaires were administered to 300 women who were selected using a snowball technique. Lists of names for initial contact were obtained from the telephone book, agencies working with immigrants (Canadian

African Centre for Training [CANACT] and African Research, Training, and Employment Centre [ARTEC]), and from government-funded immigrant aid community organizations. The sample consisted of a representative group reflecting age, marital status, region/country/ethnic group of origin, entry status, and education (professionals, degree holders, technicians). Telephone, face-to-face, and mail interviews were conducted. A three-tier envelope method was used to ensure confidentiality.

The qualitative aspect of the research involved holding in-depth interviews with ten immigrant women. Open-ended questions were administered and the process required the hiring of translators from the immigrant community to translate the questionnaires into ethnic languages. The use of tape recorders was eliminated because the women did not want their voices taped. Also, personnel of agencies catering to the needs of immigrant women and immigration officials were interviewed.

Participant observation method was used to gather information on how government and nongovernment agency personnel adapt to factors in the wider environment which are largely beyond their control—such as policy guidelines and funding constraints—in their efforts to deliver effective client services.

Research Findings and Analysis

The reported work-status of the 300 respondents in the study consisted of 174 women who were gainfully employed, 96 who were actively seeking jobs, and 43 who were not working or seeking jobs. One hundred and twelve of the 174 working women said that they put in twenty hours or more of work per week. One hundred and five of the 174 working women reported their hourly pay to be $6.50 per hour, as opposed to the $7.25 per hour minimum wage in Ontario. Sixty gainfully employed women reported hourly wages equal to the minimum wage, while thirty reported incomes higher than the minimum wage. The reported wages may give the impression that the immigrant women are relatively well paid; however, when annual income levels are examined, the data suggest the opposite. The nature of their jobs included cleaning, childcare, home-making, caring for the elderly, dishwashing, restaurant work, making beds in hotels, hairdressing, and sewing in garment industries. These are traditional female jobs in the service sector, but are also marginalized and with poor wages.

On the question of working conditions, 120 of the 174 working women reported that their working conditions were either adequate or very adequate. Adequate conditions were said to include a good working relationship with the supervisor, a good workplace atmosphere, or access to the allotted time for breaks. Fifty-four women said that their working conditions were inadequate. Inadequate working conditions included long hours, job insecurity, understaffing, and overwork. On the whole, there appeared to be more dissatisfaction with working conditions than the quantitative data would suggest.

Most of these African immigrant women could only find jobs in the marginal labor market, where they are subject to exploitation because of their nonunionized position. They are concentrated in the low-paying, low-status, labor-intensive jobs in the manufacturing and service industries as in the past history of immigrants. They often find it difficult to get out of these job ghettos because of their "lack" of Canadian experience and limited proficiency in English. Added to this is the nonrecognition by employers of their previous education, training, and experiences acquired before coming to Canada.

For the 96 women not gainfully employed, the stated barriers to gainful employment and the challenges they confronted in their efforts to assimilate into the Canadian society are summarized as follows:

- Difficulty in gaining recognition for education already obtained in country of origin
- Difficulty in gaining access to institutions of higher learning to upgrade their education
- Lack of access to daycare facilities for their children
- Accent and language seen by potential employers as problems
- Lacking "Canadian experience" seen as a major setback
- Seen as being overqualified for English-as-a-Second-Language classes
- Personal circumstances, social pressure to stay at home, cultural barriers, limited access to childcare, and the lack of support
- Lack of support from employment agencies
- Not knowing where to go (lack of knowledge on existing resources) and inadequate knowledge of interview procedures
- Ideological and stereotypical beliefs of potential employers were acted out in interviews and resulted in the women's poor performance

The survey also showed that no mainstream agency was currently delivering effective employment services that met the needs of the women. The African-based agencies that serviced this client group were found to be working under tremendous internal and external pressures which affected their ability to deliver services. Existing resource allocation models do not meet employment needs of the client group and therefore need to be reformed.

Based on the questionnaire responses and interviews, the challenges/barriers to getting jobs for which immigrant women were qualified were found to intertwine with institutional, systemic, and sociocultural discrimination. The findings of this study support those of previous studies which highlight the "double-day" syndrome of paid and domestic labor (Armstrong and Armstrong, 1990). The burden of the double day is intensified when immigrants experience utter isolation in the workplace. A lot of the women thus turn to their homes or ethnic community as the refuge from an alien environment. Many women were accustomed to participating in a paid labor force in their country of origin, sharing in the income, companionship, and independence such participation represented. For these women—who now find themselves unemployed in Canada, except as domestic labor—the emotional effects of immigration are staggering. For both groups of women, the situation is worsened by watching their children and husbands being integrated into the Canadian society because of their efficiency in English, which they do not have. This exclusion from integration serves as a further source of isolation.

The work life of most of the African immigrant women in the sample was found to have changed after their arrival in Canada. Some women who reported housework as their sole occupation in their country of origin became employed in the paid labor forces in Canada, in such occupations as janitors, nurse's aides, home-makers (cleaning the homes of middle-class white Canadian families or the elderly). Sixty percent of women who had worked in the paid labor force activity in both the country of origin and Canada experienced a downward mobility trend in their occupational status when they entered the Canadian work force. Twenty percent of the women who worked in the labor force in their country of origin and in Canada seem to have continued working in similar occupations. The transitions reported were from nurse's aide to janitor, and from cleaner in a hospital to cleaner in a hotel. Only 5 percent of the respondents could be said to have reported an upward mobility in the change of work situation in the Canadian labor force, including two women who worked as hairstylists in their country of origin and now own their own beauty salon. Two other women reported owning their own restaurants after working as waitresses in their countries of origin. A woman who was a dressmaker in her country of origin now works as a social worker. Fifteen percent of the women said that they could not find jobs even with average education and work experiences from their home countries: they lack the Canadian experience that is a yardstick used by employers to measure immigrant women's suitability for the labor force.

Case Histories

In order to confirm some of the findings of the survey, summaries of the in-depth interviews held with three of the ten selected cases are described below. They capture the experiences, needs, and concerns of three professionals who participated in the project.

Case 1 A husband and wife, both medical doctors specializing in gynecology and obstetrics, moved from Ghana to Toronto as landed immigrants in 1989. They sat for the Canadian evaluation and qualifying exams in 1990 and 1991 and passed, but could not attain opportunity for residency/training either in Toronto or in other provinces. They were told that if they could find a sponsor, for example a pharmaceutical company to pay for their residency, then places might be made available. "The problem is money," they were told. They looked unsuccessfully for research positions. Nor could they find any opportunity to volunteer as technicians in research so as to acquire some Canadian experience. The couple was forced to live on social assistance for over three years and began exploring opportunities in the United States after passing the American qualifying exams.

A number of issues arise from this case, including frustration, disappointment, and emotional distress at both individual and family levels. The cost to the Canadian society in terms of lost skill and contribution, the money spent on social assistance, and the loss of human capital to Canada are immeasurable. In addition, the devaluation of the knowledge of the couple because of the foreign nature of such knowledge is racist and problematic.

Case 2 This case deals with another professional woman, who qualified as a veterinary doctor at Makerere University in Uganda. She described her experience here in Canada since her arrival five years ago as a "run around." She had three years working experience before emigrating to Canada for safety reasons. She knew about the veterinary professional qualifying process, which includes writing an exam, and tried gaining admission to a university in Ontario so as to upgrade her skills. She was invited for an interview but was unsuccessful in gaining admission. Upon inquiring about why she had not been accepted, she was told that the competition was too stiff and that there were a limited number of spaces. She was advised to take three courses by correspondence in order to be better qualified for admission the next year. She endeavored to do as advised and tried again the following year, but to no avail. This time around, she was not even invited for an interview and was in fact told that the courses she had been advised to take by correspondence were not necessary for admission. "They only served as a way of assessing your capacity to function at a certain educational level," she was told. Her admission was turned down a second and even a third time, at which point she decided she was tired of trying. She is still to gain admission but is currently working with the Ontario humane society as a secretary—in an environment she loves, but not in the capacity for which she is qualified.

Case 3 The woman in this situation is from Nigeria and holds a degree in education. She accompanied her husband, a graduate student, and she is legally qualified to work in Canada, but all efforts to secure a job in the field for which she is qualified have been unsuccessful. She had sought accreditation for her degree from Nigeria but was told that it would not be recognized without additional courses. She is willing to take the make-up courses but cannot gain admission to any university because of her dependent status as the wife of a foreign student. In the past three years, she has worked as a home-care giver and has at times worked as a babysitter. While her husband is completing his studies, she is not even given the chance to upgrade her skills. She feels very frustrated and has, at times, suffered from depression because of the loss of her privileged middle-class position in Nigeria and a lack of extended family support here, especially in view of the fact that she is a mother of two.

These three interview cases, and the findings of this study, show that African immigrant women are confronted with barriers similar to those that have been established for other immigrant women of color. The endless succession of unsuccessful attempts to enter their profession or trade has inevitable and deleterious effects on their self-esteem. The interaction of cultural norms; the experience of being transplanted into a new community; the percieved lack of English language skills; pressures of raising a young family; limited resources; and lack of family connections, familiarity, and support networks have undoubtedly made assimilation into Canadian society difficult and has limited their growth and development.

Role of Change Agencies/Social Networks

From the research, it was found that African women's labor force participation conformed to the pattern for all immigrant women of color but differed from those of white immigrant women. They were confronted by discrimination based on gender and race but also on the "foreignness" of their qualifications. In order to deal with this discrimination, several agencies have been put in place to help alleviate the women's suffering. The women themselves have resorted to using social networks to get information on employment and basic survival. An assessment of the effectiveness of the social networks which African women activate to get employment found that such networks were very effective. Some of the women who were able to secure jobs as home-makers and childcare givers did so through information provided by their friends and network members. They were also introduced and recommended by other members of their social networks who were doing similar work. The social characteristics of individuals who the women identified as gatekeepers included race/ethnicity, class, language, gender, age, and length of stay in Canada. They were mostly young, middle class, Anglo-Saxon males who were either born in Canada or migrated with their parents to Canada at a very young age. They were university educated and exercised a lot of control over the process of applying for jobs. Some of the women found the gatekeepers to be unfriendly and very patronizing. On the other hand, most of the social workers working with these gatekeepers were women with limited clout in the agencies.

Agencies' effectiveness in meeting African women clients' employment needs, when measured in terms of former clients' rate of participation in the labor force after various periods of time (up to ten years), was found inadequate. Of the 300 women surveyed, only 45 found the agencies useful in meeting their employment needs. Resource allocation models used to meet the employment needs of African women were not structured, but instead developed on an ad hoc basis. They did not, in fact, meet the women's employment needs, tending to focus on training in English as a second language, even though most of the African women participating in the study already spoke and understood English. The "Canadian experience" the women lacked was not provided by the agencies and their allocation models.

CONCLUSION

The findings of this research show that African immigrant women face many of the same problems that most women face in Canadian society, and more, in view of their race and distinctiveness within Canada. Discrimination, ghettoization in the paid labor force (that is, the restrictions that limit women to low-paying and low-status jobs), and the "double day" duty of both paid labor force activities and the domestic labor of caring for home and family, are common experiences for women in Canada. In addition to these problems, immigrant women are required to adapt to the new society, to learn a new language, and to overcome the isolation and discrimination imposed by their new society. The dependence of immigrant women is dramatically perpetuated by their isolation, especially when they are in abusive familial relationships. Although not an object of the case study, it was revealed that immigrant women face a "choice": break sponsorship and risk deportation, or stay silently within the abusive marriage.

The implications of these findings for African immigrant women is that systemic practices create and perpetuate a dependency on male family members and on an inadequate welfare system. This condition is alien to women raised to be self-dependent in their countries of origin, who regard themselves as subjects in their own right. It takes a lot of adjustment and readjustment to suddenly find themselves marginalized. It not only destroys self-image, but creates a sense of worthlessness. This process has major negative implications on gender relations both within and outside black family households in the diaspora. Marriages have been known to break down from economic instability and difficulties in communication which arise as family members spend most of their time finding individual solutions to problems instead of using the communal approach to problem-solving, which is often devalued in the new capitalist world.

The alleviation of some of the challenges confronted by African immigrant women will rely on the acknowledgment of the unequal power which women of color, particularly blacks, hold within the Canadian diaspora: "groups unequal in power are correspondingly unequal in their access to the resources necessary to implement their perspectives outside their particular group" (Collins and Henry, 1994: 94). Hope for righting this imbalance lies in the fact that ethno-cultural and racially specific community-based agencies are growing to fill the gap in service delivery created by failure of mainstream institutions to serve the needs of a multiracial, multicultural immigration population. The agencies spend their time identifying the challenges and barriers to women's quality of life and are demanding, through advocacy and lobbying, amelioration of the situation. These agencies are themselves isolated from the mainstream delivery system through lack of institutional support, but they have undertaken responsibility for providing effective, responsive, and equitable services to immigrant communities. It is through these organizations that African immigrant women must fight for their rights and their children's rights to food, shelter, clothing, health care—all of which are very dependent on training and gainful employment. Using racist and sexist justifications for denying them access to their basic needs is an abuse of their human rights in a country that they have come to call home.

NOTES

1. These differences have been structured by race, class, and gender. See Paula Giddings's *When and Where I Enter: The Impact of Black Women on Race and Sex in America.* New York: William Morrow, 1984.

2. Pat Armstrong and Hugh Armstrong, *The Double Ghettos.* Toronto: McClelland and Stewart, 1991.

3. *Report on the Special Committee on Visible Minorities in Canada,* 1984:40.

4. Ibid., p. 41.

REFERENCES

Adelman, Howard et al. (1994). *Immigration and Refugee Policy: Australia and Canada Compared.* (Volumes 1 and 2). Toronto: University of Toronto Press.

Agard, R. 1987. "Access to the Social Assistance Delivery System by Various Ethnocultural Groups." In *Social Assistance Review Committee Report.* Ontario Ministry of Community and Social Services.

Amin, Samir. 1990. *Maldevelopment: Anatomy of a Global Failure.* London: Zed Books.

Armstrong, Pat and Hugh Armstrong. 1994. *The Double Ghetto: Canadian Women and Their Segregated Work*. Toronto: McClelland and Stewart.

——. 1990. *Theorizing Women's Work*. Toronto: Garamond.

——. 1978. *Canadian Women and Their Segregated Work*. Toronto: McClelland and Stewart.

Bannerji, Himani. 1987. Introducing Racism: Notes Towards an Antiracist Feminism. *Resource for Feminist Research*, 16(1):10–12.

Bolaria, B. Singh and Peter S. Li. 1985. *Racial Oppression in Canada*. 2d edition. Toronto: Garamond.

Boyd, Monica. 1986. Immigrant Women in Canada. In *International Migration: The Female Experience*, ed. R. J. Simon and C. Brettell. New Jersey: Rowman and Allanheld Publishers.

——. 1984. "At a Disadvantage: The Occupational Attainment of Foreign-born Women in Canada." Pp. 549–573 in *Immigration and Refugee Policy: Australia and Canada Compared*, vol. 2, ed. Howard Adelman et al. 1994. Toronto: University of Toronto Press.

Brand, Dionne. 1993. A Working Paper on Black Women in Toronto: Gender Race and Class. In *Returning the Gaze: Essays on Racism, Feminism and Politics*, ed. Himani Bannerji. Toronto: Sister Vision Press.

——. 1987. "Black Women and Work: The Impact of Racially Constructed Gender Roles on the Sexual Division of Labour." *Fireweed*, (25):35.

Buck, Pem D. 1991. "The View from Under the Sink: Can You Teach Anthropology Up When You Aren't Down?" *Transforming Anthropology*, 2(1):22–24.

Buijs, Gina, ed. 1993. *Migrant Women: Crossing Boundaries and Changing Identities*. Oxford: Berg.

Calliste, Agnes (1991). "Canada's Immigration Policy and Domestics from the Caribbean: The Second Domestic Scheme." In Vorst et al. (eds.), *Race, Class, Gender: Bonds and Barriers*. Toronto: Garamond Press, pp. 136–168.

Canada. Secretary of State (1988). Programme for the promotion of Immigrant Women.

Carty, Linda. 1991. "Black Women in Academia: A Statement from the Periphery." In *Returning the Gaze: Essays on Racism, Feminism and Politics*, ed. Himani Bannerji. Toronto: Sister Vision Press.

Collins, Jock and Frances Henry. 1994. "Racism, Ethnicity and Immigration." Pp. 515–548 in *Immigration and Refugee Policy: Australia and Canada Compared*, vol. 2, ed. Howard Adelman et al. Toronto: University of Toronto Press.

Costi. 1991. Report on Immigrant Women: Education, Training and Employment. Toronto: Costi.

Das Gupta, Tania. 1986. *Learning from Our History: Community Development of Immigrant Women in Ontario (1958–1986)*. Toronto: Cross-Cultural Communication Centre.

——. 1994. "Multiculturalism Policy: A Terrain of Struggle for Immigrant Women." *Canadian Woman Studies*, 14 (2):72–75.

Dei, George. 1993. "The Challenges of Anti-Racist Education in Canada." *Canadian Ethnic Studies Review*, 25 (2):72–75.

Edwards, Richard. 1979. *Contested Terrain: The Transformation of the Workplace in the Twentieth Century.* New York: Basic Books.

Estable, Alma. 1986. "Immigrant Women in Canada: Current Issues." *Canadian Advisory Council on the Status of Women.* Ottawa.

Fleras, Augie and Jean Leonard Elliott. 1993. *The Challenge of Diversity: Multiculturalism in Canada.* Scarborough: Nelson Canada.

———. *Unequal Relations: An Introduction to Race and Ethnic Dynamics in Canada.* Scarborough: Prentice-Hall Canada.

Gannage, Charlene. 1986. *Double Day, Double Bind: Women Garment Workers.* Toronto: The Women's Press.

Giddings, Paula. 1984. *When and Where I Enter: The Impact of Black Women on Race and Sex in America.* New York: William Morrow.

Gordon, David M., Richard Edwards, and Michael Reich. 1987. *Segmented Work, Divided Workers: The Historical Transformation of Labour in the United States.* Cambridge: Cambridge University Press.

Gunew, S. 1991. *A Reader in Feminist Knowledge.* London: Routledge.

Hartmann, Heidi. 1976. "Capitalism, Patriarchy and Job Segregation by Sex." In M. Blaxall and B. Reagan (eds.), *Women and the Workplace: The Implications of Occupational Segregation.* Chicago and London: University of Chicago Press.

Henry, F. and E. Ginzberg. 1984. *Who Gets the Work? A Test of Racial Discrimination in Employment.* Toronto: Urban Alliance on Race Relations and the Social Planning Council of Toronto.

Horna, Jarmila L. A. 1990. "Acculturation, Dual Cultural Identity, or Somewhere Between: A Sociological Summary." Paper presented at the 42d Congress of the Czechoslovak Association of Canada, Edmonton, Alberta.

Iacovetta, F. 1986. "Primitive Villagers and Uneducated Girls: Canada Recruits Domestics from Italy, 1951–1952." *Canadian Woman Studies*, 7 (4):14–18.

Immigrant Women of Saskatchewan (IWS). 1985. *Doubly Disadvantaged: The Women Who Immigrate to Canada.* Saskatoon: Immigrant Women of Saskatchewan (monograph).

Leah, Ronnie. 1993. "Black Women Speak Out: Racism and Unions." Pp. 157–171 in *Women Challenging Unions: Feminism, Democracy, and Militancy,* ed. Linda Briskin and Patricia McDermott. Toronto: University of Toronto Press.

———. 1991. "Linking the Struggles: Racism, Sexism and the Union Movement." In Vorst et al. (eds.), *Race, Class, Gender: Bonds and Barriers.* Toronto: Between the Lines.

Lee, Betty. 1991. *Women and Immigration.* In *Symposium Report on Immigrant Settlement and Integration.* Ottawa: Canada Employment and Immigration Advisory Council, p. 19.

Lee, I. 1990. *Multiculturalism: The Dilemmas of Implementation.* In *Cross-Cultural Communication and Professional Education,* ed.

C. Hedrick and R. Holton. Adelaide: Centre for Multicultural Studies, Flindas University.

McLean, Stuart. 1992. *Welcome Home: Travels in Small Town Canada*. Toronto: Viking.

Moodley, Kogila. 1983. Canadian Multiculturalism as Ideology. *Ethnic and Racial Studies*, 6(3):320–321.

Moussa, Helene. 1993. *Storm and Sanctuary: The Journey of Ethiopian and Women Refugees*. Dundas, Ont.: Artemis Publishers.

Musisi, Nakanyiki. 1994. Meeting the Employment Needs of African Immigrant and Refugee Women in Toronto (working paper).

Neuwirth, Gertrude. 1989. *The Settlement of Ethiopian Refugees in Toronto: An Exploratory Study*. Ottawa: CEIC (November).

Ng, Roxana. 1992. Managing Female Immigration: A Case of Institutionalized Sexism and Racism. *Canadian Woman Studies*, 12(3):20–23.

———. 1988. *Politics of Community Services: Immigrant Women, Class and the State*. Toronto: Garamond Press.

———. 1986. "The Social Construction of 'Immigrant Women' in Canada." In R. Hamilton and M. Barrett (eds.), *The Politics of Diversity: Feminism, Marxism and Nationalism*. Montreal: Book Centre Inc.

Ng, Roxana and Alma Estable. 1987. Immigrant Women in the Labour Force: An Overview of Present Knowledge and Research Gap. *Resource for Feminist Research*, 16 (1):29–33.

Ng, Roxana and Judith Remirez. 1981. *Immigrant Housewives in Canada*. Toronto: Immigrant Women's Centre.

Ottawa Ministry of Employment and Immigration. 1991. Immigration Statistics. Ottawa: Ministry of Immigration and Citizenship.

Phillips, Paul and Erin Phillips. 1983. *Women and Work: Inequality in the Labour Market*. Toronto: James Lorimer and Co., Ltd.

Phizacklea, A., ed. 1983. *One Way Ticket: Migration and Female Labour*. London: Routledge and Keagan Paul.

Report of the Special Committee on Visible Minorities in Canada. 1984. Ottawa, Ontario.

Said, Edward. 1979. *Orientalism*. New York: Vintage Books.

Silvera, Makeda. 1993. *Silenced*. 2d ed. Toronto: Sister Vision Press.

Statistics Canada. 1991. Census of Canada.

Thomas, B. 1987. *Multiculturalism at Work*. Toronto: YWCA.

Walker, James W. St. G. 1980. *A History of Blacks in Canada*. Ottawa: Ministry of Supply and Services.

Winks, Robin W. 1988. Slavery. *The Canadian Encyclopedia*, 2d ed. Edmonton: Hurtig Publishers, vol. 3: 2010–2011.

16
HORNED ANCESTRAL MASKS, SHAKESPEAREAN ACTOR BOYS, AND SCOTCH-INSPIRED SET GIRLS: SOCIAL RELATIONS IN NINETEENTH-CENTURY JAMAICAN JONKONNU

Sandra L. Richards

Jonkonnu is a masking tradition, much like that of Carnival or Mardi Gras. It is celebrated in Jamaica, Belize, the Bahamas, and the Bermudas during the Christmas season.[1] Practiced by blacks, Jonkonnu dates from at least the late seventeenth century, when slaves were given a few days of rest before the arduous task of harvesting sugar cane began. After the masquerade was banned in Kingston in 1841 because of the "commotion" it allegedly caused in "decent" people's heads, this masking tradition withdrew into the rural areas of Jamaica, where it remained almost clandestinely practiced until the 1950s, when the *Gleaner* newspaper revitalized widespread public interest through its sponsorship of festival competitions. In this essay I seek to bring together two literatures—one on Caribbean slavery and the other on nineteenth-century Jamaican theatrical practice—that in many instances seemingly do not speak to each other, though they scrutinize the same historical periods. I wish to reopen the question of what social relations were being enacted in Jamaica at a given historical moment (1800–1841), particularly if we accord serious attention to the fact that these historical agents were gendered and class stratified. More specifically, given the ways in which white and black women were oppositionally defined in Jamaica, I wish to challenge received understandings concerning white patronage of Jonkonnu troupes.

CONTEXTS

Discovered first by the Spanish, Jamaica came under British control in 1655; by 1730 sugar, produced by African slave labor, was generating the colony's chief economic activity. Unlike in the United States, a significant proportion of Jamaican plantation owners resided in England, employing a class of attorneys, bookkeepers, clerks, and artisans to supervise the actual running of the plantations; like their employers, these English, Scotch, and Irish supervisory staff also dreamed of making their fortunes in Jamaica and returning home. As the Assembly of elected property owners described the island in 1797,

> The inhabitants of this colony consist of 4 classes: whites, free people of colour having special privileges granted by private acts, free people of colour not possessing such privileges, and slaves. . . . all these classes, when employed in public service, have, as far as it has been practicable, been kept separate. (Brathwaite 105)

Though a reconstruction of population demographics is problematic, historian Edward Brathwaite calculates that in 1820, some 30,000 whites lived in Jamaica; of those, only 1,189 were men of property, and their white families resident on the island numbered another 4,800 approximately. (The fact of a relative absence of white women in Jamaica had signficant implications for social relations, as historians like Barbara Bush have demonstrated.)[2] Another 5,000 whites would have been servants to this propertied class, and as many as 3,000 soldiers were garrisoned on the island. The remaining 16,000 whites would have been attorneys, doctors, merchants, tavern keepers, and plantation artisans (Brathwaite 134). Synthesizing various contemporaneous records and subsequent scholarship, historian Gad Heuman offers the following additional demographics: the free colored population numbered between 28,000 and 31,000; free blacks were some 11,000 in number, while approximately 300,000 people were enslaved (Heuman 7). By 1810 some 53 percent of those slaves were involved in sugar production, and of that group, those who labored in the fields were predominantly women (Bush); other blacks worked as domestics, mechanics, artisans, porters, or jobbers—both men and women—who hired out their services to whomever would employ them and returned a portion of their earnings to their owners. Still other slaves who exercised some modicum of control over their labor included food vendors, fishermen, boatmen, firemen, and rat catchers. Of the slave population, it is estimated that some ten years after the abolition of the slave trade in 1807, approximately 35 percent were African, that is, born on the African continent and transported to the Americas.

The system of racial classification was more complex in Jamaica than in the United States. At the apex of the social hierarchy were whites: those who had been born in England and then those who were creoles or born in the Americas. Jews, who had settled in Jamaica when it was a Spanish colony, were considered white in the sense of legal privileges but were marginalized socially because of their religion. Negroes or Africans were at the bottom of the socioeconomic-political totem pole. The category "colored" applied to people whom we today might term "mixed race" and was elaborated through such subcategories as mulatto (the child of a white man and a negro), sambo (the child of a mulatto and a negro) through to octoroon.

> Legally, all coloured people were "mulatto" and this "corruption of blood" was visited upon "not the sins of the father but the misfortunes of the mothers" unto third and fourth generation of intermixture from the Negro ancestor exclusive. An octoroon was therefore legally white and so automatically free in Jamaica and the British West Indies. (Brathwaite 167–168)[3]

Not only did the law determine when one's genealogy made one white, but it also could, through the mechanism of special petitions, convert a "black" person into a "white" one. Generally, these rather infrequent instances of transformation were reserved for biracial or black men who had managed to acquire sufficient education, wealth, and the protection of influential white men; comments about their character and deportment, attestations about their ability to perform whiteness, were included in these special, legislative petitions. Of a different category were free people of color, those whose fathers or sexual intimates had manumitted them; while they were not owned by anyone, they did not have the full civil rights conferred by whiteness.[4]

I would like to add to these demographics a brief review of some of the history that serves as an intertext to Jonkonnu celebrations in the decade of 1830 to 1840. The last decade of the eighteenth century was a period of considerable turmoil in the Caribbean. In 1791 a slave uprising in Saint Domingue resulted in an influx of French slaveholders to Jamaica. This was a cause for concern both because France and England were adversaries during some of the period, and because immigrant slaves brought with them and disseminated among Jamaican slaves news of rebellion. Some thirteen years later Haiti would become the first independent black republic in the Americas. From 1795 to 1796, the Jamaican colonial government engaged in a protracted struggle against Maroons, or Africans who had fled Spanish enslavement, established their own independent communities in the hills, and welcomed runaways. In 1803 and again in 1805 the colonial authorities were forced to call out the militia to put down slave unrest; 1807 brought not only the official end to the slave trade but also the beginning, in the English parliament, of legislation designed to ameliorate some of the worst conditions of slavery, as well as agitation for its abolition. From approximately the 1820s on, free people of color and black freedmen waged separate campaigns to gain civil rights, often allying themselves with liberal elements in England and Nonconformists or Baptist and Wesleyan missionaries in Jamaica against Jamaican Assembly members, who also varied in the extent to which they were willing to concede rights to these freedmen. The year 1834 was designated as the beginning of a transition toward emancipation; after a four-year period of apprenticeship allegedly designed to ready the bondspeople for freedom, slavery was finally abolished in 1838.

Interestingly, because so many women refused to continue laboring in the fields (Wilmot, "Females"), workers had to be imported. Beginning in the 1840s Indians, Chinese, and free Africans from Yorubaland and what is presently Sierra Leone and the southwest Ivory Coast were brought to work in the cane fields. For the practice of Jonkonnu, the influx of Africans over two centuries meant that, to a certain extent, this performance tradition never lost contact with its African roots. But culture is dynamic: specific black ethnic practices would syncretize within an "African" matrix and reflect contact with people from England, Scotland, Ireland, and India.

THE HORNED ANCESTRAL MASK

Descriptions of Jonkonnu date from as early as the 1687 report of slave men "with rattles tied to their legs and waists and 'Cow Tails to their Rumps'" (Bettelheim 47; Hill 230). A 1750 European account observes that

> In the towns, during Christmas holidays, they have several tall . . . fellows, dressed up in grotesque habits, a pair of ox-horns on their heads, sprouting from the top of a horrid sort of visor, or mask, which about the mouth is rendered very terrific with large boar-tusks. (Hill 230; Bettelheim 47)

During this early period, the Jonkonnu or horned mask performed solo, exhibiting superior dance skills. Within the Kru, Akan, Ewe-Fon, Yoruba, Igbo, Bantu, and Mandingo cultures, from which the slaves came, this skill would have been understood as a sign of superior moral abilities (Ryman 17 and Thompson).[5] A female Connu, represented by a male dancer completely covered in an enormous, gaudy, and fearsome mask, also danced solo; both were accompanied by musicians and men and women who shouted "John Connu/Canoe" as the procession moved from plantation to plantation or from door to door in towns, hoping for hospitality in return for their performances.

Several explanations have been offered for the etymology of the word *Jonkonnu*. Anthropologist Cheryl Ryman argues that based upon their numerical representation in the slave population up until 1897, it is most plausible to argue that the word comes from the Ewe *dzono kunu* (and related *dzonku nu*), which means "deadly magician/sorcerer."[6] But the explanation repeated in most scholarly accounts centers on John Konny, who resided in the Axim area of present-day Ghana. A powerful trading partner of the Prussian Brandenburg African company, he was a slave trader who fended off British and Dutch take-over attempts for some fifteen years before being defeated and sold into slavery along with members of his ethnic group (Wynter, "Behind *Maskarade*" 16). Whether derived from an Ewe concept or from a specific, historical personage, the term signifies veneration of a powerful ancestor capable of bestowing upon or withholding blessings from his community. Though, as we shall see momentarily, the term *Jonkonnu* shifts from a horned mask to a human configuration, the horned mask does not disappear entirely. Writing in the 1920s, folklorist Martha Beckwith asserts that the oxhead mask was banned because of the fear it inspired (150), but photographs from the 1950s when Jonkonnu was brought back into the public eye clearly document the manifestation of this ancestor.[7]

HOUSEBOATS, ACTOR BOYS, AND SET GIRLS

Writing in his journal on January 1, 1816, when he had barely arrived on the western end of the island at Black River in St. Elizabeth parish, the English Matthew Gregory (Monk) Lewis recounts hearing the sounds of a "drum and banjee" procession featuring John Canoe, whom he describes as a "Merry-Andrew dressed in a striped doublet, and bearing upon his head a kind of pasteboard house-boat, filled with puppets, representing, [sic] some sailors, others soldiers, others again slaves at work on a plantation, etc." (51). Some fifteen years earlier Lady Maria Nugent, wife to the Governor of Jamaica, had encountered a similar scene. Though it is lengthy, I would like to quote the entirety of her Christmas entry for 1801 because it is rich with details; it anticipates comments other Europeans would make about seemingly ceaseless drumming which gave them headaches; and it indicates that another category of performers had already joined the procession. Living in Government House in Spanish Town (located in the eastern interior), Lady Nugent writes,

> Christmas Day! All night heard the music of tom-toms, etc. Rise early, and the whole town and house bore the appearance of a masquerade. After Church, amuse myself very much with the strange processions, and figures called Johnny Canoes. All dance, leap and play a thousand antics. Then there are groups of dancing men and women. They had a sort of leader or superior at their head, who sang a sort of recitative, and seemed to regulate all their proceedings; the rest joining at intervals in the air and the chorus. The instrument to accompany the song was a rude sort of drum, made of bark leaves, on this they beat time with two sticks, while the singers do the same with their feet. Then there was a party of actors.—
> Then a little child was introduced, supposed to be a king, who

stabbed all the rest. They told me that some of the children who appeared were to represent Tippoo Saib's children and the man was Henry the 4th of France. What a *mélange*! All were dressed very finely, and many of the blacks had really [*sic*] gold and silver fringe on their robes. After the tragedy, they all began dancing with the greatest glee. We dined in the Council Chamber, but went to bed early, but not to rest, for the noise of singing and dancing was incessant during the night.—

26th. the same wild scenes acting over and over again. (48)

Note that Lady Nugent mentions a company of actors who apparently offer a pantomime concerning Tippo Saib, the Sultan of Mysore whom Napoleon had encouraged to take up arms against the British in India; the latter stormed his capital and killed him in 1799 (Nugent footnote, 48). Seemingly in a relatively short period of time, news of this event had not only reached Jamaica but was also incorporated into a pantomime enacted by blacks. Though Errol Hill, the foremost historian of the Caribbean stage, expresses puzzlement at "[h]ow this story [of Saib's young heir] relates to a French king who ruled two centuries earlier, and how the blacks got hold of the story so soon after the event," (237) I think it entirely plausible to suspect that a bit of resistant pleasure is operative here. That is, blacks, who listen to conversations of their British masters while working, enact opposition to the colonial authority and then disguise that confrontation with the death—historically displaced—of Britain's enemy.

That these Actor Boy troupes, as they came to be known, mounted topical materials is also supported by Lewis's comments on watching perfectly executed excerpts from plays like the *Fair Penitent* or *Douglas*. These plays had recently been staged in Jamaica, and presumably some of the Actor Boy troupe members had seen the plays while sitting in the upper theater balconies and waiting to drive their masters and mistresses home. Equally popular, according to other chroniclers, were combat-death-and-rejuvenation pantomimes and portions of Shakespeare's *Richard III*, particularly the section in which Richard pleads, "A horse, a horse, my kingdom for a horse!" Presumably, literate sponsors helped performers learn the lines.

In addition to the House John Canoe (Fig. 1) and Koo-Koo Actor Boy (Fig. 2), a third masquerade had joined the Jonkonnu procession by 1837, when Isaac Belisario created a series of sketches that would come to represent Jonkonnu as its most lavish point.[8] Contingents of identically dressed young women, known as Set Girls (Fig. 3), organized themselves in Kingston into red and blue groups that paraded the streets and rivaled each other in the splendor of their costuming. The exact origin of this masquerade is not known: Monk Lewis explained that given divided allegiances, the red color stood for the British, and the blue for the Scotch.

FIGURE 1.
I. M. Belisario sketch of
"House John Canoe,"
Jamaica, 1836. Courtesy
of the National Library
of Jamaica.

FIGURE 2.
I. M. Belisario sketch of
"Koo-Koo Actor Boy,"
Jamaica, 1836. Courtesy
of the National Library
of Jamaica.

FIGURE 3.
I. M. Belisario sketch of "Set Girls," Jamaica, 1836.
Courtesy of National Library of Jamaica.

Historians surmise that a more likely explanation relates to the red coats
of the British army soldiers and the blue of the sailors, celebrated in 1782
after Admiral Rodney defeated the French fleet (Hill 239).[9] After the official presentation of arms, these military men would have retired to their
respective favorite taverns maintained by colored women who employed
other colored and black women as servants or slaves to attend to the needs
of their male customers.

SOCIAL RELATIONS

At first glance these lithographs of the Houseboat, Actor Boy, and Set
Girls argue significant cultural change. By 1840 John Konny seems to have
migrated far from his beginnings as a powerful African ancestor invoking
fearful awe in festival practitioners. But further probing of the costumes
in performance reveals not only continuities with the past but also new
political dynamics and conflicting social aspirations as various segments of the Jamaican populace participated in Jonkonnu. Veneration of

the ancestors continued, for as Monk Lewis noted, the representation of the master's Great House included figures of slaves working on the plantation. As such, the elaborate houseboat mask referred to an actual site of power and may be considered to constitute a memorial to the history and lives of those who had suffered at that site. Martha Beckwith's anthropological research lends further support to this interpretation. Conducting field research between 1919 and 1924, she learned that the construction of the houseboat was related to the African-derived religious practice of myalism, and that prior to its emergence during the Christmas festivities, it was taken to the cemetery where dances and songs were rehearsed in order to catch the spirit of the dead who would effect good medicine and remain in the house until the mask was ceremonially destroyed (151).

House John Canoe's jacket repeats aspects of the British military uniform, while his striped pants, fringed sash, and multicolored bows carnivalize that uniform; similarly, Koo Koo Actor Boys' and the Set Girls' costumes repeat European fashion. As Homi Bhabha alerts us, imitation in the colonial context is never simple mimicry but an appropriation that signals resistance and a turning of the gaze back upon power (86–89). So too here, for these people of African descent quite clearly demonstrate their ability to perform an upper-class English- or Frenchness, even though according to the discourses of slavery, they are economic units or (phrased more benevolently) unthinking, irresponsible children—Lady Nugent's term is "blackies." The suggestion of shrewdly calculated performances is contained in Monk Lewis's diary entries. In questioning the slaves on his Cornwall plantation, Lewis learns that the houseboat John Canoe has been crafted and financed by his artisans, slaves of color who have discovered that a well-crafted mask and finely executed performance will net them money to be shared amongst their fellow slaves. Though Lewis suspects at times that his slaves' joy at being in his presence and their greetings are a little too profuse, that skepticism seemingly never stops him from playing and enjoying the role of beneficent patriarch handing out coins. Presumably, it was a role that other white men also enjoyed enacting.

In the towns (free) men of color, who had acquired some financial resources either through hard work as skilled craftsmen or paternal links to rich white men, financed and shared the profits of troupes composed of men of their own class standing or those of a social class beneath them. Obviously for the performers, conviviality and involvement in a network that valued one's creative abilities would have been other important reasons for participating in a Jonkonnu troupe. In that the political arena up until the 1830s was closed to the participation of free colored and black men, Jonkonnu also functioned as one site where they could congregate and push for civil rights. To be sure, some enslaved people also saw this festival not simply as an occasion for making merry, for the history of Jamaican slavery is filled with accounts of insurrections that occur close to Christmas, when Africans and black creoles would have had physical mobility. As much of the prevailing literature on carnivals argues, Jon-konnu may have functioned as a safety valve; this certainly was a position that some proslavery whites supported as part of their argument concerning benign treatment accorded the slaves. But Jonkonnu as rehearsal for, as cover for rebellion, was perhaps another of its functions.[10]

The case of patronage of the Set Girls is interesting in its complexity and illuminates other aspects of Jamaican social relations. The Scotch planter writing under the pseudonym of George Marly reported local gossip that a trio of white women competed against each other through the outfitting of their slave women (Hill 242), and other historical accounts make similar assertions concerning financial support (Fenn). But given social constructions governing white and black women's behaviors, it seems reasonable to ask whether the patronage of white women was an exception rather than the rule. First of all, because the tropical environment posed particular health risks to whites, and the colony was regarded as a site for acquiring riches quickly, relatively few white women resided in Jamaica. In fact, the white managerial class of bookkeepers, overseers, and attorneys who managed absentee plantations were contractually forbidden to bring wives with them or to acquire them in Jamaica, because families constituted a drag on the extraction and repatriation of wealth. Not surprisingly, white men turned to black women and as Lady Nugent and another diarist, Mrs. Carmichael, noted, had multiple black and brown mistresses on the various plantations for which they were responsible;[11] their habits even became the subject of derisive songs composed by male John Canoe bands.[12] These colored "favourites" (Bush) and "brown ladies" (Lewis, Bush, Scott, *Tom Cringle*), as they were known, utilized interracial, sexual liaisons or "dense transfer points for relations of power" (Foucault) for a variety of purposes, including avoiding the backbreaking, dangerous work of the fields and of possibly securing manumission for themselves and any children they might have. Securing funds for the Set Girls—who though they started as a town masquerade were also adopted on plantations—was a way of extracting, and redistributing, some of the master's wealth while projecting the esteem with which these favorites were regarded. Similarly, patronage afforded white men an opportunity to display their own largesse and compete with other men who also had mistresses.

But cast as the chaste "embodiment of modesty and respectability" and encouraged in their social pretentiousness (Bush, "White 'Ladies'" 249), white women, whether born into wealth or ascending into it after their hard work as indentured servants, paid for their economic security and leisure by being held to a rigid double sexual standard. Furthermore, a colonial orientation toward the values of the landed English gentry (even though that gentry was being economically outstripped by a bourgeois class) placed creole women at a disadvantage. By virtue of their birth in the rough world of the Americas and sustained domestic contact with coloreds and blacks, creole white women were thought to be unsophisticated and particularly susceptible to the "taint" or contagion of the latter's customs. Lady Nugent describes a "perfect Creole" woman as "[she] says little, and drawls out that little, and has not an idea beyond her own Penn" (52); furthermore, many of these uneducated ladies speak a "broken English, with an indolent drawling out of their words, that is very tiresome if not disgusting" (98). In another instance they prove themselves "so completely stupid" (55), with their giggles and simpering, that searching for some productive activity, Lady Nugent finally sets them to stringing beads. In contrast, black and brown women had active, economic (as well as sexual) roles to play in colonial society. Why then would white ladies outfit colored favorites and black wenches as an expression of their own (white) status?[13]

In fact, historian Gad Heuman would argue that with the approach of emancipation that forced more absentee planters—including their white wives and daughters—to live in Jamaica, color distinctions intensified: "As in nineteenth century India, European women tended to introduce minute distinctions that could be carried to great lengths. . . . the[ir] increased presence . . . worked against the acceptance of browns in white society" (76).

I would posit, however, that even in earlier periods, there exist strong arguments for colored patronage and black, self-generated support for the Set Girls. As in the case of the men, participation in a network that supported sociality and individual expressivity must have functioned as powerful incentives to set up these contingents. But the dynamics fueling the impulse to make community so that "the family tree is not cut" (Bush, chap. 6) differed according to gender and class. As not only as mistresses to white men but also often as chief domestic managers of the plantations and doctors to the slaves, brown ladies negotiated a liminal space of greater privilege, greater surveillance, and greater suspicion between the master and the slaves displaced onto their persons. Membership as a Set Girl conceivably offered a safe, psychic haven in which not only were some of the plantation resources redistributed to the slaves, but affective ties linking the house and field were reaffirmed. For nondomestic, laboring black women who may have financed their own participation, the Set Girls presumably provided a slightly different kind of psychic space. It offered an opportunity to display the limited economic autonomy they had managed to wrest from the system. That is, plantation law required owners to set aside provision grounds, wherein the slaves could cultivate food for their own consumption; these grounds were by custom at some distance from the plantations, thus affording slaves the regular opportunity to leave the plantation. This law had both economic and symbolic consequences. As in West Africa, women were responsible for much of this cultivation of foodstuffs meant for internal consumption. What they and their families did not consume, they were free to sell and retain the profits therefrom.[14] In the cities many of the vendors or "higglers" were women; thus, women would have been critical to the flow of goods and information between the towns and more rural areas.

The spatial organization of the John Canoe bands and Set Girls especially reflects a social hierarchy of class and color. Chroniclers such as Belisario, Michael Scott, and the fictional Marly remark upon a pattern whereby the Set Girls masquerade consisted of four Grand Masters charged with protecting the contingent from the occasionally rowdy competition with other sets; Drummers, Singers, and other Musicians; two Adjutants carrying flags; the Queen; the Ma'am; the Commodore; more Adjutants and Musicians; a gaggle of women all dressed alike; and finally, an ancestral, vegetal figure (Hill 243–244, Dirks 184). Even though all the women—even down to very young girls—were identically dressed, the Queen was distinguishable by the greater amount of jewelry she had managed to assemble. Given that public processions were also common practice in many West African king-states, it is not inconceivable that the Set Queen and Ma'am achieved their positions in a similar manner, i.e., not only through an accumulation of material possessions but also through a communally recognized demonstration of moral stature throughout the year. Just as color was an indication of social status in nonfestival time, so too in the organization of the Set Girls, for they were rigidly segregated according to color, with the brown sets with their "clear olive complexions, and fine faces, elegant carriages, splendid figures—full, plump, and magnificent" representing the most beautiful of all, according to the nineteenth century fictional observer Tom Cringle (245).

But even while clearly influenced by the ideology of the plantocracy, another system of law, understood as a "repository of social performances" (Roach 55) regulating behavior and producing identity, was also operative in Jonkonnu. In the belief systems of many of the ethnic African groups resident in Jamaica at this time, the ground was also the symbolic site where the ancestors resided. Though transplanted into radically different social circumstances, the ancestors' force could, nonetheless, be mobilized in attempts to (self-) regulate behavior amongst the slaves, insuring in particular that black drivers or overseers were also accountable to the common good (Wynter). Removed from the purview of their masters, black women and men could dance on the provision grounds, honor their deities, and reassemble a narrative of ancestry that over time shifted from ethnic specificity to a racial identity as Ewes, Yorubas, and Bantu peoples became African or black, bound together by a history of enslavement and degradation. When they emerged in their sets of blue and red, or yellow on Christmas morning, these revelers were both performing European culture and enacting a neo-African one. In virtually each Belisario print, there in the frame is an unmistakable African referent, such as the drums which gave Europeans headaches but released black and brown bodies to the ancestors' power. Appearing with the Set Girls is a manifestation of an ancestor figure or what Europeans, from their own frame of reference, would describe as a jack-of-the-green. Furthermore, the costumes' vegetal and snaking designs, intricate inlay of pattern upon pattern (full body masking in the case of John Canoe and Actor Boy), and visual opulence that threatens (or promises) the possibility of excess recall West African masking traditions.

As the sugar economy worsened during the decade of the 1820s, and the colony moved toward greater civil liberties for men of color and emancipation for the slaves, Jonkonnu became one of the arenas in which political battles were waged. Contestants included the white landowning and merchant classes and conservative coloreds, on the one hand, against an emerging coalition of wealthy, but socially marginalized Jewish retailers and unenfranchised black and colored labor, on the other (Wilmot, "Politics").[15] Though they could not vote, lower-class women voiced their objections to legislative attempts to curtail their street vending activities, which were said to adversely affect shopkeepers; they also demonstrated against inadequate medical care in concert with their men, who in some instances sought direct political redress (Wilmot, "Females"). Kingston Mayor Hector Mitchel sought to ban Jonkonnu entirely in 1840 as part of an attempt to counteract the maneuvering of one Daniel Hart, a Jewish merchant and property owner who had effectively mobilized the unenfranchised masses to alternately intimidate conservative voters and bolster his own liberal supporters. Mitchel was initially more successful in 1841, for his rival had been convicted and jailed for inciting a riot, but "respectable blacks" as well as the unenfranchised were so determined to celebrate Jonkonnu that Mayor Mitchel eventually had to flee to ships in the bay for safety from rampaging protestors. Two men were killed and many injured before the army was finally able to restore order. "Clearly, for the Kingston ex-slaves, John Canoe was part of their folk culture and their celebration of it was not to be tampered with at the whim of Mayor Mitchel and the conservative faction in Kingston politics" (Wilmot, "Politics" 73). But the festival was also coming under assault from Nonconformist Baptists and Wesleyans who, though they had fought for the abolition of slavery, preached to their black and brown converts that the allegedly lascivious, lavish nature of the festival was unbefitting a free and civilized people (Hill 247). Jonkonnu eventually retreated to the hills. Costuming became understandably less extravagant, given rural poverty; new masquerades were introduced, but the horned ancestral mask remained. Even though the upwardly mobile colored class tended to regard the festivities as "bush" or backward, they also could not deny the uncanny power of the mask. With the approach of independence from the British crown in the 1950s and '6os, Jamaican intellectuals were prepared to rein-vestigate and reevaluate their African heritage; entrepreneurs, taking their cues from activities on other Caribbean islands like the Bahamas (Bettel-heim), saw in Jonkonnu a distinctive selling point in the competition for tourist dollars.

CONCLUSION

In summary, a festival practice like nineteenth-century Jamaican Jonkonnu consolidated onto the bodies of performers a complex network of social, economic, political, aesthetic, and philosophical histories. As this review has demonstrated, the John Canoe or horned ancestral mask metamorphosed over time, acquiring new and often conflicting meanings, losing other designations, and adding to its retinue additional masquer-ades; at no point was its construction stable. Some Europeans considered the festivities a noisy, troublesome release from the pressures of produc-ing sugar; others saw in the swirling splendor bizarre echoes of European folk traditions. Some Africans participated as a way of maintaining con-tact with ancestors—albeit adapted to a different social ecology—and of making a little profit in the process, while others used the proceedings as a way of performing and advancing their sociopolitical status. Though people of African descent enacted in Jonkonnu a community in opposition to a hegemonic plantocracy, as we have seen most clearly demonstrated in the organization of the Set Girls, that community was by no means mono-lithic. Similarly, though the European community may have been united in its overall commitment to slavery, they too exhibited contradictory mo-tivations, shaped in part by gender and class, for supporting (or declining to actively patronize) Jonkonnu troupes. Reading the histories of slavery and performance practices intertextually, through the lens of gender, re-vises earlier scholarship about white–black female relationships and un-covers hidden transcripts (Scott, *Domination . . .*) that structured the agencies of participants and observers, variously positioned within Jamai-can society on the eve of emancipation. Finally, with its polyvocality and contingency of meanings, Jonkonnu challenges social and performance historians alike to adopt more multilayered, intertextual, gendered reading strategies if we wish to understand the complexity of lived experience.

NOTES

An earlier version of this essay was presented as part of the "Perform-ance and Law" plenary session organized by Professor Joseph Roach of Tu-lane University for the 1996 Performance Studies Conference, Northwest-ern University.

1. During the U.S. American colonial period, Jonkonnu was also prac-

ticed in North Carolina; see Geneviève Fabre, "Festive Moments in Antebellum African American Culture."

2. For an overview of the extent to which scholars have devoted attention to women in Caribbean slave history, see Hilary Beckles, "Sex and Gender in the Historiography of Caribbean Slavery."

3.   Sambo = child of mulatto and negro
     Mulatto = child of white man and negro
     Quadroon = child of mulatto woman and white man
     Mustee = child of quadroon or pure Amerindian by white man
     Mustiphini = child of mustee and white man
     Quintroon = child of mustiphini and white man
     Octoroon = child of quintroon and white man (Brathwaite 167)

4. Some 80 percent of freedmen were colored; the rest were black (Heuman 4).

5. Cheryl Ryman quotes Robert Farris Thompson saying, "In Africa, horned figures have been linked to the strength and power invested in important personages by virtue of their superior physical, political, and supernatural attributes" (Thompson 1974).

6. Furthermore, she observes that the Bambara word *kono* and the Quojas *canoo* also denote concepts of power and vengeance associated with a vestigial figure (16–17).

7. Indeed, Guadalupe Garcia-Vasquez's presentation, "Mexican Crossings of the Black Atlantic," at the 1996 Performance Studies Conference, Northwestern University, 22 March 1996 helps document the extent to which this horned mask appears throughout the Afro-Americas.

8. Judith Bettelheim reports that Isaac Mendes Belisario was born in Jamaica c. 1791–1800. Quite possibly the grandson of a rabbi of the same name, he was educated in England and exhibited landscapes at the Royal Academy from 1815 to 1818 and in 1831. He returned to Jamaica in 1831 and was said to have drawn these color sketches "from life" on Christmas 1836; they were lithographed in 1837 by Duperly. See Bettelheim, fn. 12. Scholars such as Bettelheim and Hill have argued that by the time Belisario made these sketches, Jonkonnu had already begun to lose some of its splendor, but because he had had his work vetted before the lithographs were produced, one can safely assume that they did indeed accurately convey the lavishness of early-nineteenth-century Jonkonnu.

9. Red and blue were by no means the only colors available to Set Girls. Some chroniclers mention Yellow Girls, Royalists sponsored by the French-speaking community in Jamaica, and African Mabiales (Hill; Dirks).

10. James C. Scott reviews the prevailing literature that views carnival as a rather harmless "reversal of status" rite before arguing that this semi-public transcript of resistance to hegemonic domination often historically bursts into full-scale rebellion. See also Robert Dirks, who argues the rather novel view that Jonkonnu was a ritualized expression of planter–slave conflict generated by the enforced famine-feast cycle of the Caribbean sugar economy.

11. In fact, Lady Nugent attributes the immorality of blacks to the li-

centiousness of white men, who in living with slave women fail to set a proper example of moral probity (87). A defender of the plantocracy in St. Vincent and Trinidad, Mrs. Carmichael associates "demoralization" with class status, explaining that given the high cost of living in the West Indies and consequent absence of white women, white men of the managerial-bookkeeper class are forced to take up with black women until they gradually forget their "early instructions, and become as the expression is, almost a *white negro*" (59).

12. Scotch merchant Michael Scott records in *Tom Cringle's Log* (243) the following verses sung by a butchers' John Canoe band, presumably in the period 1810–1817, when Scott was employed by a Kinsgton mercantile house:

> But Massa Buccra have white love,
> Soft and silken like one dove.
> To brown girl—him barely shivel—
> To black girl—oh, Lord, de Devil!

But as the white man becomes more acclimated, his views change:

> But when him once two tree year here,
> Him tink white lady wery great boder;
> De coloured peoples, never fear,
> Ah, him lob him de morest nor any oder.

Alleging that it is black people who nurse this white buccra when he becomes ill with fever, the singers conclude,

> So always come—in two tree year,
> And so wid you massa—never fear;
> Brown girl for cook—for wife—for nurse,
> Buccra lady—poo—no wort a curse.

13. Fenn specifically argues this point of white women's patronage, pointing to the example of one Miss Edwards cited in Lewis's journal for her intense loyalty to the "blue girls of Waterloo," but Fenn may be reading contemporary norms into an historical account. That is, Monk Lewis begins his discussion of set girls by reporting that the Admirals of the Blue and Red both gave *brown* girls fancy-dress balls, with the result that all Kingston divided into parties. "Brown girls" is, of course, the term applied to mulatto women who in this instance would have enjoyed the attentions of white men. Furthermore, Lewis identifies Miss Edwards as the mistress of a hotel from which he and his friends watch the parade. Mulatto women were often innkeepers, and the term "Miss" was applied to them by other slaves; Lewis may be following suit here. Think, for example, of Maria Nugent, who though she uses the term "blackies," refers to the colored women she (privately) meets on her official tour of Jamaica as "mulatto ladies" and "coloured friends."

14. But as Dirks makes patently clear (chapter 4), we should not entertain the idea that slaves were able to raise substantial amounts of food-

stuffs for sale; in fact, for most of the year, they subsisted at near-starvation levels.

15. According to Gad Heuman, by 1830 people of color had become a significant political force because outnumbering whites, they could influence local elections as a result of low property franchise; predictably, white men responded by raising the economic barriers (51).

REFERENCES

Beckles, Hilary. "Sex and Gender in the Historiography of Caribbean Slavery." Shepherd, Brereton, and Bailey 125–140.

Beckwith, Martha Warren. *Black Roadways: A Study of Jamaican Folk Life*. Chapel Hill: University of North Carolina Press, 1929.

Bettelheim, Judith. "Jonkonnu and Other Christmas Masquerades." *Caribbean Festival Arts: Each and Every Bit of Difference*. Ed. John W. Nunley and Judith Bettelheim. Seattle: University of Washington Press, 1988. 39–83.

Bhabha, Homi K. "Of Mimicry and Man: The Ambivalence of Colonial Discourse." *The Location of Culture*. London: Routledge, 1994.

Brathwaite, Edward. *The Development of Creole Society in Jamaica 1770–1820*. Oxford: Clarendon Press, 1971.

Brereton, Bridget. "Text, Testimony and Gender: An Examination of Some Texts by Women in the English-speaking Caribbean from the 1770s to the 1920s." *Engendering History: Caribbean Women in Historical Perspective*. 63–93. Ed. Verene Shepherd, Bridget Brereton, and Barbara Bailey. New York: St. Martin's, 1995.

Bush, Barbara. *Slave Women in Caribbean Society 1650–1838*. Kingston: Heinemann Publishers, Caribbean, 1990.

——. "White 'Ladies', Coloured 'Favorites' and Black 'Wenches': Some Considerations on Sex, Race and Class Factors in Social Relations in White Creole Society in the British Caribbean." *Slavery and Abolition* 2.3 (1981): 245–262.

Mrs. Carmichael. *Domestic Manners and Social Conditions of the White, Coloured, and Negro Population of the West Indies*, v. 1. London, 1833; rpt. New York: Negro UP, 1969.

Clark, VèVè. "Developing Diaspora Literacy and *Marasa* Consciousness." *Comparative American Identities: Race, Sex, and Nationality in the Modern Text*. Ed. Hortense Spillers. New York: Routledge, 1991.

Dirks, Robert. *The Black Saturnalia: Conflict and Ritual Expression on British West Indian Slave Plantations*. Gainesville: UP of Florida, 1987.

Fabre, Geneviève. "Festive Moments in Antebellum African American Culture." *The Black Columbiad: Defining Moments in African American Literature and Culture*. Ed. Werner Sollors and Maria Diedrich. Cambridge: Harvard UP, 1994.

Fenn, Elizabeth A. "'A Perfect Equality Seemed to Reign': Slave Society and Jonkonnu." *North Carolina Historical Review* 65.2 (1988): 127–153.

Foucault, Michel. *Discipline and Punish: The Birth of the Prison.* Trans. Alan Sheridan. London, 1977.

Heuman, Gad J. *Between Black and White: Race, Politics, and the Free Coloreds in Jamaica, 1792–1865.* Westport: Greenwood, 1981.

Hill, Errol. *The Jamaican Stage 1655–1900: Profile of a Colonial Theatre.* Amherst: University of Massachusetts Press, 1992.

Lewis, Matthew Gregory. *Journal of a West India Proprietor, Kept During a Residence in the Island of Jamaica.* London, 1834; rpt. New York: Negro UP, 1969.

Roach, Joseph. *Cities of the Dead: Circum-Atlantic Performance.* New York: Columbia UP, 1996.

Ryman, Cheryl. "Jonkonnu: A Neo-African Form." *Jamaica Journal* 17.1 (1984): 13–23 and 17.2 (1984): 50–61.

Scott, James C. *Domination and the Arts of Resistance: Hidden Transcripts.* New Haven: Yale UP, 1990.

Scott, Michael. *Tom Cringle's Log.* 1829; rpt. Edinburgh: William Blackwood and Sons, 1900.

Shepherd, Verene, Bridget Brereton, and Barbara Bailey, eds. *Engendering History: Caribbean Women in Historical Perspective.* New York: St. Martin's, 1995.

Thompson, Robert Farris. *Flash of the Spirit: African and Afro-American Art and Philosophy.* New York: Random House, 1983.

Wilmot, Swithin. " 'Females of Abandoned Character'? Women and Protest in Jamaica, 1838–1865." Shepherd, Brereton, and Bailey 279–295.

———. "The Politics of Protest in Free Jamaica—The Kingston John Canoe Christmas Riots, 1840 and 1841." *Caribbean Quarterly* 36.3–4 (1990): 65–75.

Wright, Philip, ed. *Lady Nugent's Journal of her residence in Jamaica from 1801 to 1805.* 1907; rpt. Institute of Jamaica, 1966.

Wright, Richardson. *Revels in Jamaica 1682–1838.* New York: Dodd, Mead, 1937.

Wynter, Sylvia. "Behind 'Maskarade': Jonkonnu, the Queen-Mother, and the Festival Complex." Manuscript (n.d.).

———. "Jonkonnu in Jamaica: Toward the Interpretation of Folk Dance as a Cultural Process." *Jamaica Journal* 4.2 (1970): 34–48.

———. "Rethinking 'Aesthetics': Notes Towards a Deciphering Practice," *Ex-Iles: Essays on Caribbean Cinema* 237–279. Ed. Mbye Cham. Trenton: Africa World Press, 1992.

CREATIVITY, SPIRITUALITY, AND IDENTITY

17 FROM FOLKLORE TO LITERATURE: THE ROUTE FROM ROOTS IN THE AFRICAN WORLD

Oyekan Owomoyela

"FOLKLORE" AND "LITERATURE" AS TROPES

I am using the terms "folklore" and "literature" as descriptive tropes to characterize two different types of society, the first representing tradition and all those things we associate with it, and the second standing for modernization (essentially commensurate with westernization) and all those qualities and habits it entails. Suggested in the title is an opposition based on ideas African philosophers, for example, have advanced, according to which folklore (or folklorism) marks backwardness and arrested development, while literature (or literacy) symbolizes progressiveness and development. Folklore, in this usage, thus calls to mind such concepts as ethnophilosophy and what some have described as "mytho-poeic imagination" (Irele 217), while literature would suggest an analytic and deductive mindset. Embedded in my title is the suggestion of a progression—from the folklore state to the literature state—a progression that much of current scholarly thinking in African studies has endowed with some incumbency. The habit of thought to which I refer is the same one that gave the world the concept of *pre*literacy as an early stage in the supposedly necessary evolution of societies to literacy. By its logic, then, non-Western (or African) societies and cultures would be *pre*-Western, on their way, with some luck, to necessary westernization. I am, of course, subsuming traditional African societies under "folklore," and Western societies under "literature."

PARADIGMATIC OPPOSITIONS

The paradigmatic oppositions between the two kinds of society may be elaborated as follows: folklore societies (or cultures) are presumed to be exempt from the dynamic processes of history, and to be committed to the stability of their institutions and practices; they are thought to be afraid of change, and, consequently, to be reluctant to acknowledge the existence of a future, or to plan for it. In this view they exist, in short, in a state of *being*, or, as V. S. Naipaul is wont to say, they are "complete, achieved" societies (92). Literature cultures, on the other hand, are supposedly dynamic by preference. They are deemed to be comfortable with the knowledge that everything changes, that they are in a constant state of *becoming*, and, therefore, that they must always actively seek to understand the current state of things, and be prepared to face new challenges in the future.

In addition to the foregoing, folklore societies measure wealth in terms of people, their members treasuring the security of belonging to caring and reciprocative communities, whereas literature societies de-emphasize the human connection and value the security of material goods instead. One way to illustrate this difference is to resort to texts characteristic of the respective types of society: "*Èèyàn lasoò mi*" (People are my wealth of clothing), a Yoruba proverbial song declares; by contrast Macon Dead (in Toni Morrison's *Song of Solomon*) tells his son Milkman, "Let me tell you right now the one important thing you'll ever need to know: Own things. And let the things you own own other things. Then you'll own yourself and other people too" (55).

Ali Mazrui has suggested another area of difference between the two types of cultures under discussion. "Western-style time-worship marginalizes ancestors," he writes. "Past, Present and Future are re-organized in scale of importance. Present, Future and Past becomes the order of priorities. Indeed, fanatical time-worship finally becomes obsessed with the present—at the expense of both the future and the past" (1994: 172). Traditional African societies are well known for the importance they attach to the past, as indicated by their veneration of their ancestors, and by the privileged place they accord to their official storytellers, the *griot*, the *imbongi*, the *akéwì*, and other such "remembrancers." Chinua Achebe stresses this quality in *Anthills of the Savannah*, where the old man from Abazon declares that, the story being paramount among contenders for glory, the storyteller takes the eagle feather, beating out even the warrior, because "it is only the story that outlives the sound of war-drums and the exploits of brave fighters" (114). We may, I believe, legitimately substitute "history" for "story" in this context, for what the old man says of the story—"It is the story . . . that saves our progeny from blundering like blind beggars into the spikes of the cactus fence"—recalls the claim usually made for history, i.e., that those who are without its guidance are doomed to repeat the mistakes of the past.

The foregoing leads to the most important opposition (for my present purposes): folklore societies' attachment to roots, or at least to racial identity, versus literature societies' preference for raceless, rootless cosmopolitanism. In the discussion that follows I will elaborate on the desire in the African world to "progress" from a folklore complex to a literature one, and the professed, or otherwise obvious, reasons for it. It is, in any case, always a response to the conviction that while the former might have served adequately in the dark past, the latter state is better—more enlightened, more fulfilling, and more in keeping with the modern mood.

HISTORY DENIED

The appeal of westernization (literature) derives from its association with the state of technological development the world has achieved, development made possible by science. The most serious criticism of African folklore cultures recently has come from African philosophers, who regard the folkloric mind as essentially incapable of philosophy, and, therefore, incompatible with the scientific spirit which alone guarantees progress. Such is the enthusiastic embrace of the literature state that it sometimes renders the appreciation of some salutary qualities of its folklore counterpart difficult or impossible. For example, as I have indicated (above), the reverence for the past, for ancestors, is consistent with the valorization of the story, and, therefore, of history. But the powerful urge to prove folklore societies always inferior to literature societies denies this habit to folklore societies. Thus, Paulin Hountondji remarks that "the first precondition for a history of philosophy, the first precondition for *philosophy as history*, is the existence of a scientific practice, the existence of science as an organized material practice reflected in discourse. But one must go back even further: the chief requirement of science itself is writing" (99; my italics). Here history is equated with philosophy, and its existence (or possibility) is predicated on writing. Since writing (as a popular practice) came to Africa through the agency of the Europeans, the statement aligns Hountondji (and those who share his opinion) with the likes of Hugh Trevor-Roper, who believed that the Europeans introduced history to Africa.

ALMIGHTY WRITING

Henry Louis Gates has proposed a theory to explain the great importance African Americans attached to creative writing during the eighteenth-century debate over slavery. According to him,

> After Descartes, *reason* was privileged, or valorized, among other human characteristics. Writing, especially after the printing press became so widespread, was taken to be the *visible* sign of reason. Blacks were "reasonable," and hence "men," if—and only if—they demonstrated mastery of the "arts and sciences," the eighteenth century's formula for writing. (54; his italics)

The slave narratives, he adds, were attempts by blacks to *"write them-selves into being"* (57). The evidence of Hountondji's assessment of writing and its indispensability for the all-important state of "development" would suggest that writing is in fact no less a lifeline to twentieth-century African intellectuals. It is precisely that mistaken perception of writing as a necessary feature of cultural legitimacy that motivates the preference for "non-literacy" over "illiteracy" as the qualifier for traditional African cultures.

It is also the stigma with which what might be described as scripto-philic prejudices have invested non-literacy, and, by extension, African-ness, that explains the trend I have chosen to describe as the journey from roots to routes. I am using the term "routes" with deference and thanks to Paul Gilroy, whose *The Black Atlantic* argues eloquently for the claims of routes over roots. According to him, the trans-Atlantic connection is an inescapable element, in fact, the magisterial one, in fashioning the Black Atlantic, and the one that, as I understand him, he believes matters most in terms of filiation and identity. Furthermore, of primary concern to Gilroy is the inconvenient emergence in Britain of "circumstances where blackness and Englishness appeared suddenly to be mutually exclusive at-tributes" (10), along with the consequent difficulties those circumstances place in the path of "attempts to construct a more pluralistic, postcolonial sense of British culture and national identity" (11). To a significant extent, he is concerned with the frustrations that white insiderism inflicts on Blacks who hanker for unqualified and uncontested Englishness.

When the wind of change was blowing independence across Africa, though, the intellectual response to the conclusions the colonialists had drawn about Africa and Africans on the basis of the paradigmatic opposi-tions cited above was to ridicule them, and, in fact, to reverse them in favor of Africanity. That was what the negritude project amounted to. Even in Anglophone Africa, where negritude was not the fashion, our intellectuals rejected the claims of the colonialists, as when Achebe declared in his fa-mous manifesto that Africa was not enveloped in a darkness that the Euro-peans dispelled with their providential arrival (1976: 59). Many went be-yond mere rhetoric to practically embrace their roots, in the way they dressed, in the music they listened to and danced to, in the food they ate and their manner of eating it, and so forth. Francophone African writers compared themselves to *griots*, and their anglophone counterparts saw themselves as bards, both designations that hark back to oral (that is, non-literate) traditions. Gaturia, the linguistically alienated student in Ngũgĩ wa Thiong'o's *Devil on the Cross*, indicates his reorientation toward roots when he comments, "The kind of education bequeathed us by the whites has clipped the wings of our abilities, leaving us limping like wounded birds" (63). Africans in the diaspora followed suit by reestablishing and reaffirming their African connection (a process already evident in the

1920s *nigritie* movement in Haiti, the 1930s Harlem Renaissance, and the 1940s negritude movement in Paris). In the United States, also, and especially starting in the late 1950s, Blacks increasingly dropped their "slave names" in favor of African ones—famous examples that come to mind are Niara Sudarkasa and Molefi Kete Asante.

NOSTALGIA

The deeper we have advanced into independence, however, the more we seem inclined to nostalgia for our prior condition, nostalgia expressed in the form of adoption of the colonialist premise that to *be* is to be Western, and in the form of distancing ourselves from Africanity (from folklorism or "mytho-poeic imagination"). The nostalgia, one must say, is characteristically an intellectual condition: the mindset prevalent among intellectuals in Africa and the diaspora favors doing away with vestiges of folklorism. If Africa was outside of history before the arrival of the Europeans, their thinking goes, if, in other words, before the Europeans came among us our state of existence amounted to non-being, then, logically, any program that might return us to that state must be resisted. We can understand why they would regard attachment to that prior state, and ideas like Cabral's "return to the source," as repulsive and even perverse. A return to the source would be no more and no less than a reversal of the route that brought us out of the void and into history. That reasoning explains why since Cabral's time (and the time of negritude) the idea of roots has developed a tarnish. As Gilroy notes with particular reference to diaspora intellectuals, "Whether their experience of exile is enforced or chosen, temporary or permanent, these intellectuals and activists, writers, speakers, poets, and artists repeatedly articulate a desire to escape restrictive bonds of ethnicity, national identification, and sometimes even 'race' itself" (19).

The phenomenon Gilroy describes is nothing new, of course. African American intellectuals involved in the pan-Africanism of the nineteenth century were decidedly ambivalent about the continent and its people; Africa to them was something of an embarrassment. For Alexander Crummell, for example, the African was a "man-child" who existed in a "half-animal condition" (Hickey and Wiley 247). Africa was a space in need of redemption through the agency of African diaspora descendants like themselves who had been redeemed, thanks to the middle passage. During the slavery period in North America the harshness of enslavement made the attraction of the idea of a return to the source most powerful, so much so that it gave rise to the phenomenon of metaphysical flying back to Africa. Now, after the end of slavery, and after independence has delivered to Africans what dispersed Jews always craved—that is, the opportunity to return to their ancestral lands and roots—we seem increasingly to be repelled by roots, and impelled to the competing notion of routes, to making tracks, in other words.

One must grant that the dismal performance of independent Africa provides enough reason for disappointment with the new African states, their institutions, and their bureaucrats; yet the current vogue of postmodernism and its challenges to supposedly settled verities, its space-clearing possibilities that permit alternative ways of seeing and of being, should have served to discourage any attribution of essential insufficiency to Africanity, and to mitigate the pathologization of Africa. But the continent continues to suffer in comparisons with the West, simply on account of its very difference from the presumed Western norm. It is ominous for Africa and Africanity that African and African diaspora intellectuals continue to be tempted, as a result, to distance themselves from Africanity and seek integration into westernity, and the hope that those Africans not directly involved in the middle passage would serve as a "faithful remnant" that would effect an African assertion dims as we mature in "independence."

Nor can one blithely assume, with regard to the lure of routes, that this too shall pass, for it is predicated on the conviction of the inevitability of our eventual westernization, on the certainty that, "as a matter of practical necessity, we have no choice but in the direction of Western culture and civilization" (Irele 215). The fact of being colonized thus proves as potent a refashioning force as the middle passage; the colonial condition was, for the colonized, passage in place.

The declaration must be taken as it was intended—as a fortunate revelation of our true calling, rather than as a lament. Among the practical ramifications of the conviction is the phenomenon that Tsenay Serequeberhan has ridiculed as the "tragicomic obscene duplication of Europe—in Africa and as Africa" (21). One instance of the phenomenon, and a manifestation of the nostalgia, occurred recently in the republic of Benin. In early February of 1996 (Sunday the 11th or Monday the 12th), the BBC broadcast news and commentary on the decision of President Nicephore Soglo's government to accord official recognition to Voudou as a state religion. The proposal immediately ran into determined and vocal opposition from officials of Christian denominations, who believed that the move was retrograde and inconsistent with African aspirations, or even with the African image. To them the progressive and preferred African image was decidedly Christian!

IDEOLOGICAL REVISIONISM

One effect of our acceptance and internalization of the colonialist valuation as regards the paradigmatic oppositions, of our pronouncements and actions asserting our preference for the boon of westernization, when

we compare them with our rhetoric and attitudes at the time of the decolonization campaign, is to suggest an ideological revision of our assessment of the colonialist adventure, and, therefore, to query our rhetorical
fault-finding with the Europeans who colonized us. Our exposure to westernity, even in the form of the middle passage, must be deemed fortunate.
Did not the Europeans, after all, bring us the possibilities of deliverance
from folklorism? Specifically, the revision calls assertions like the one in
Achebe's manifesto into question: if we prefer our refashioning to our pre-
European state, and, therefore, to the course of development that would
have obtained without European interruption, then we must, logically,
hold the process of our refashioning to be beneficial; we must then accept
slavery and colonialism as necessary evils; and, instead of asking for repa-
ration for these historical events, we should express gratitude to the slavers
and colonizers as deliverers.

The intellectual posture vis-á-vis colonialism and its aftermath unfortunately recalls Eldridge Cleaver's criticism of James Baldwin's attitude toward the white world as "lamblike submission—'You took the best,' sniv-
elled Rufus, 'so why not take the rest?' " (108). The reference is, of course,
to the homosexual hero of Baldwin's *Another Country* (1970: 77), who was
fatally seduced (in more than one sense) by whiteness. It also discounts
the experiences of large chunks of the African population that have existed
essentially beyond the reaches of European influence, that have not participated in any real sense in the trans-Atlantic crossings, recrossings, and
criss-crossings. (I grant that European adventures in Africa have affected
every African life to some degree, but one would be guilty of the easy error
of generalizing the experiences of the small fraction of the African population that has become truly and profoundly captured by the Western
way over the entire African population, even the dwellers in remote back-
woods, hamlets, and swamps.) This ideological revision, while rationaliz-
ing immediate apostasy, also guarantees a future in which there will be
no Africa to return to, even if alienation and apostasy were ever to go out
of fashion, for there is no doubt that the intellectuals are beacons that the
general populace follows. In any case, they largely determine the future of
the African world.

FROM FOLKLORE TO ORATURE:
ROOTS TO ROUTES

A variety of strategies have proved useful in the effort to historicize
Africa by distancing the continent, and ourselves, from conditions associated with "mytho-poeic imagination," and, in general and in effect, from
African specificity. Some of these seem insignificant, and are well meant,
but they suggest distancing nonetheless. For example, the recent adoption
by African literary scholars of the designation "orature" for what used to

be folklore reflects a desire to recognize the artistic properties of oral art forms, but it also indicates an assumption, mistaken I think, that *folk* products are inherently deficient in aesthetic qualities. The scholars concerned wish to habilitate folklore by investing it with assets appropriated from literature, to argue the artistic claims of folklore by adopting nomenclature that evokes literature. One wonders what an alternative tack could have been to insistence on "folklore," the term, and on the *difference* of what it designates as legitimate hallmarks of art. The jury is still out on the prospects of the new term as a respectable addition to the discipline.

Related to the foregoing is the sense of deprivation one sometimes detects in African discussions of literature, a defensiveness that expresses itself in claims, for example, that drama is native to Africa, not introduced by European settlers. V. Y. Mudimbe has recently cautioned us against assumptions that literature is a recent phenomenon in African life, citing several examples of African writers in antiquity. Many of them, he reports, exercised a great influence on important discourses, including religion. He wonders, therefore, if we could not "arrive at . . . explicative norms as to the real nature of African literature that will put it into some sort of relation with other literatures and not give us this uncomfortable feeling that it is somehow an indigenized imitation of something else, or an adapted reproduction of genres and their confusions imported from the West" (177). Why, one wonders, should the notion that the literature we describe today as African is actually derivative of Western genres give us any discomfort? Not so very long ago people in the West considered Russians as legitimate objects of fun for claiming the credit for every technological invention. Societies have always borrowed cultural practices from other societies; no stigma attaches to borrowing, or to not independently inventing *everything*.

The underlying dynamic in all of this, I am arguing, is the acceptance of the credentials for humanity as determined by Western (or Eurocentric) thought, and an effort to justify Africa on those terms by arguing that detractors who have placed African humanity in question have deliberately elided the evidence of our possession of the credentials. Accordingly, African scholars have gone to great lengths to prove that before the Europeans were human (according to the "arts and science" criterion), we already were. Thus, in *The African Origin of Greek Philosophy* Father Innocent Chilaka Onyewuenyi offers a most erudite discussion of the debt Western philosophy owes to early Egyptian thinkers. While the work is unquestionably worthwhile as an exercise in exploring the true history of philosophy and as a quest for enlightenment—a proper philosophical pursuit—its quest for knowledge, wisdom, or truth is not, I am afraid, for the sheer love of it. Its intent is to claim the glory that was Egypt for black Africa, because that glory has been validated by Western approval and adoption. The verification of Kemet's ethnicity is not significant in itself, but for its historicization of Africa, its restoration of Africa and Africans to history through the Egyptian, philosophical connection.

On close reflection, though, one cannot escape the basic contradiction in the objective and the means of achieving it. If Africa was excluded from history, it was because history was, as we have seen, endowed *by Europeans* with a Eurocentric complexion (essential to which, as Houn-tondji tells us, is writing), and qualification for inclusion made contingent on Europeanness. It is important to claim the origin of philosophy for Africa simply because we have accepted philosophy as, in Onyewuenyi's description, "that king of subjects" (65), so enthroned, of course, by Europeans. What his project and others like it do, then, is to accept a basic Eurocentrism and attempt a paradoxical (or ironic) Afrocentric coup through appropriating the Eurocentric instrument. Onyewuenyi is correct in his complaint:

> When Africans study anthropology in European and American universities and gain degrees under professors who extol the theory of early Caucasoid population of Egypt, there is every reason to believe that these "educated" Africans will return to Africa to teach false theories to young Africans right on African soil. What an intellectual and cultural suicide! (66)

But our Western education not only leaves us with "false" theories; it also leaves us with "false" values, such as would induce us to concede kingship of subjects to philosophy. It is, in any case, a "false" orientation to be so drawn to the achievements of peoples in far distant antiquity at the expense of what we have chosen to hold on to, for doing so implies a despair of ourselves and our present, an alienation from the here and now, and an inability to appreciate what of enduring Africanity is of value, or, perhaps, to conceive even that much of Africanity could be of value.

THE PERSISTENT QUESTION OF LANGUAGE

In the crucial and persistent matter of the choice of language for literary and official purposes in "post-colonial" Africa we have been most resourceful in ferreting out reasons for de-Africanization, so much so that Ngũgĩ (for one) wondered at our militant assertion of a claim to other people's languages and our correspondingly weak desire to claim our own (9). The ideological, cultural, and political resonations of the choice have usually been neutralized with appeals to pragmatism, political expediency, and the imperatives of development. In this discussion, though, I am primarily interested in some recent remarks by Alamin Mazrui. They invite a brief attention, because they represent an intriguingly unusual formulation of the argument against "linguistic or cultural nationalists," those who would like to see Africans do away with their dependence on colonial languages and re-embrace their own. The thrust of his argument seems to be that since Africa's current dependence on European languages did not result from a concerted European assault on African languages, that dependence should not be liable to tainting by colonialism. Colonial authorities, he writes,

> tend to be regarded as having pursued a monolithic language policy aimed at destroying African languages and establishing the supremacy of European languages. However, this monolithic view of the colonial experience obscures policy differences that ranged from the French goal of linguistic-cultural assimilation to the exclusivist German approach that denied the colonial subject any access to the language of the colonial master. The latter policy in fact contributed significantly to the consolidation of the Swahili language in what was then German East Africa. (1992: 68–69)

Mazrui nevertheless testifies to the perceived importance, among the colonizers themselves, of language as an instrument of power and control. This is true even among colonizers from the same colonizing country, in this instance francophone and Flemish Belgians in their Congo colony. He continues:

> For example, in the Belgian Congo Francophone Belgians controlled the administration from Brussels, but Flemish Belgians constituted the majority of the missionaries and educators who actually served in the colony. When Francophone Belgian authorities imposed French as the official language of the Congo and ensured the exclusion of Flemish, the Flemish-speaking missionaries and teachers subverted French assimilationist policy and strengthened their own position by promoting indigenous African languages. (69)

Mudimbe corroborates the point that the colonialists were by no means indifferent to the possibilities of language as means of controlling their colonial subjects. They promoted the use of French by Congolese *évolués*, and established a French-language journal as a forum in which the elite could sound off, and as a device to monitor the thinking of the colonized intellectuals. According to a contemporary policy statement,

> the administration has finally agreed to give the *évolués* a toy for expressing themselves: *La Voix du Congolais*. They can write to their heart's content; their texts—generally dealing with apparently inoffensive matters such as traditional life and customs, the politics of assimilation, or fiction—are, indeed, when accepted, carefully checked and edited by an editorial board, and then published. The journal has no ambition to call for the questioning of present rulers

in the country but, instead, is to be the sign of a Belgo-Congolese community yet to come. (123)

Mazrui himself cites instances from elsewhere (South Africa, Kenya, and Mozambique) where colonizers sometimes used European languages and sometimes African languages to further their aims. Referring to the two positions on the language issue—the relativist, which argues "a causal relationship among language, culture, and cognition," and the universalist, which claims that there is no real or necessary connection among them (68)—he writes, "This complex linguistic equation cannot be explained by either universalist or relativist theories of language precisely because both of them espouse an ahistoricity that predicates social progress on a pre-existing order of things, rather than on the open-ended, politico-economic dynamics of a constantly evolving society" (70–71).

But it is a historical fact that Europeans manipulated the propagation of languages in Africa to serve colonial purposes. It matters not whether they sometimes found it in their interest to promote African languages and sometimes European. Even in the case of the Portuguese in Mozambique, Mazrui points out that they called the shots, first promoting Portuguese, and later African languages, *to suit their own ends*. The same is true of the other areas he cites. The historical fact is that the linguistic picture in Africa today, especially the power relations between European and African languages, resulted from deliberate colonial policy, not from what could be described as "the open-ended, politico-economic dynamics of a constantly evolving society," as in the case of the relationship between Welsh and English, or Akamba and Swahili, for example. It is precisely because we must historicize the linguistic anomaly in Africa that we cannot simply ignore the present reality as though it arose from the normal dynamics of history, unless we intend to adduce normality to colonialism and imperialism, and refuse to redress their essential anomaly.

What Mazrui ultimately does, though, is to straddle the fence, concluding that "neither the psycholinguistic evidence nor the sociopolitical experience support[s] the deterministic positions that are characteristic of both relativism and universalism . . . any language can be a weapon of either colonization or liberation" (71). And so, one supposes, to bed! That conclusion, though, because of its noncommittal nature, does not help us toward a return to Africanity.

BEHAVIORAL AND ATTITUDINAL IMPLICATONS

The discussion of African refashioning, and of the move away from folklore, from roots, is not an idle exercise, for it carries important behavioral and attitudinal implications, which in turn have practical manifestations. We can look in fiction at the character of Toundi in Ferdinand Oyono's *Boy!*, especially his refusal to accept discipline from his father while opting for boyhood in the service of abusive and exploitative French masters on the eve of his becoming a man. Tsitsi Dangarembga offers us another instance in *Nervous Conditions;* I refer to Tambudzai's monstrous reaction to her brother Nhamo's death, with which Dangarembga opens the narrative. It is significant that the monstrosity results from the disaffection Tambu harbors toward her brother because he had been favored in their competition for the education the colonizers brought, and the Western appurtenances it promised. The refashioning of relationships, more than Nyasha's trauma, I believe, is the most important feature of the book.

I would like to cite another example, from real life, from my experiences with my friends in the years just after Nigeria's independence. One of them, Abiodun, lived in Lagos, and we admiringly called him *"Omo Wéè"* (meaning "Expert on Way," as in "ways and means"). The epithet celebrated his incurable and irrepressible addiction to irresponsible behavior, to irreverent and disrespectful attitudes toward others, especially venerable elders, and also his resourcefulness at getting away with his deviance. For us (who did not live in Lagos but only visited on holidays), he was the epitome of modernity and enlightenment; he was the wave of the future. In hindsight now I recognize in him the character that would have exemplified Peter Enahoro's quintessential Nigerian, according to his book *How to Be a Nigerian.* Abiodun was thoroughly emancipated from traditional sanctions, and in him was the genesis of the so-called indiscipline that has earned Nigerians a dubious reputation all over the world today. Obviously, one does not have to be a displaced African, removed from the old Africa and transplanted to the new world, in order to become refashioned. One can be nurtured in Africa and still become alienated from African values.

IMPLICATIONS FOR THE FUTURE

The overriding concern in all our discourses is undoubtedly what is best for Africa, and it is also what is at issue in our conflict of ideas. Those who favor westernization are convinced that only through that route can Africans thrive in the future; those who insist on reasserting the African difference are convinced, on the contrary, that westernization by definition means the death of Africanity, in which event any thought of *Africans* thriving would be a logical impossibility. The advocates of westernization, one might argue, choose either to forget the implications of the established reality that the African (more than any other non-European person) is the necessary manichaean Other against which the Western person is defined, or to believe that the age of manichaean otherization has passed. A recent incident serves both to jolt the forgetful back into full awareness of the still-contested humanity of the African, and to demonstrate the persistence of Afrophobia. I refer to the scandal that came to light toward the end of January 1996 about the Israeli Health Ministry's handling of blood donated by Ethiopian (Falasha) Jews. They were not told that the blood they donated in response to humanitarian impulses was unwanted, but the Ministry secretly discarded it, because, the explanation went, it was not considered safe for transfusion into other Jews. The incident compels a re-evaluation of the apparent concern that prompted Israel a few years earlier to mount a mass airlift of the Falashas from Ethiopia into Israel, where they now exist in what amounts to a quarantined space whose perimeters are patrolled and monitored for the safety of the remainder of Israel, or of Israel proper.

Nor is the Israeli demonstration of its reluctance to absorb and assimilate Blacks, even black Jews, into its corporate citizenry an isolated case. The Western media continue to purvey the notion of Africa as a corrupting influence that must be kept at bay. One result is the formidable obstacle in the path of would-be African immigrants into (or even visitors to) Western countries; another, certainly, is the gradual termination of Western involvement in (but not exploitation of) the continent. An observer blames the development on Robert D. Kaplan, saying that the reaction of the West to his "doomsday scenario," expressed in the February 1994 issue of *The Atlantic Monthly* and later elaborated in *The Ends of the Earth: A Journey at the Dawn of the Twenty-First Century*, "was to shrink from the source of the plague" (Sparks 6).

Unfortunately, professed Afrophobes are not alone in pathologizing Africa and Africans. The following apologia by a supposedly sympathetic Africanist says much about the regard of the continent in the second half of the twentieth century. Harold Collins, in a bid to encourage a sympathetic assessment of the African condition, calls attention to the numerous debilitating diseases he says the African must contend with:

> malaria, sleeping sickness, bilharziasis, leprosy, tuberculosis, hookworm, filariasis (including elephantiasis), pellagra, kwashiorkor, ascariasis, yaws, amoebic and bacillary dysentery, pneumonia, ulcers, pneumonic, bubonic, and septicemic plague, typhus, yellow fever, relapsing fevers, smallpox, and meningitis. (92)

"Considering the seriousness of these diseases," he observes, "we may wonder how Africans have been able to achieve anything at all." Or, he might have added, why anyone would not wish to distance himself/herself from Africa.

THE (UN)AFRICAN INTELLECTUAL OF THE FUTURE

Given the developing rout of roots by routes, one is prompted to wonder what the "African" intellectual of the future would be like? Recently, I listened to an American colleague trace the history of education in the West from the earliest times (among the Greeks) to the present. He began with the Ionians and moved to the Eleatics, the Socratics, on to Rome, the Renaissance, until he arrived at the present with the likes of Piaget, Chomsky, and Derrida. I listened in admiration, knowing that I could not rattle off all those schools and individuals in their proper order, even if I knew them in the first place. But then, I thought, the man was recounting *his* own cultural history. I knew more about the African world than he did, so, why should I envy him, especially when he does not envy me? What should interest me is whether we have Africans as erudite in African traditions as he is in Western ones. That was when the disturbing thought hit home.

The well-educated Western person can trace the history of ideas from Thales to Derrida, and the well-educated African person wants to prove his/her ability, nay, his/her *right*, to do the same, and thereby his/her worth. The Afrocentricist also wants to do the same, but, in addition, wants to assert that he/she is in fact tracing the history of *African* ideas. He/she would rather trace what has come to be identified as Western ideas and claim them for Africa, than claim (and trace) what is commonly identified and accepted as African.

I recall how impressed I was listening to my earlier colleague Wande Abimbola chant Ifa verses before the University of Ibadan Conference Hall in the late 1960s. He represents what one wishes was the model for the educated African of the future.

REFERENCES

Achebe, Chinua. "The Novelist as Teacher." *Morning Yet on Creation Day.* Garden City, NY: Anchor, 1976, pp. 55–60.
———. *Anthills of the Savannah.* New York: Anchor, 1988.
Baldwin, James. *Another Country.* New York: Dell, 1962.
Cleaver, Eldridge. *Soul on Ice.* New York: Ramparts, 1968.
Collins, Harold R. *Amos Tutuola.* Twayne's World Authors Series, 62. New York: Twayne, 1969.
Dangarembga, Tsitsi. *Nervous Conditions.* London: The Women's Press, 1988.
Enahoro, Peter. *How to Be a Nigerian.* Drawings by Chuks Anyanwu. Ibadan: Caxton Press, 1966.

Gates, Henry Louis, Jr. *Loose Canons: Notes on the Culture Wars*. New York: Oxford University Press, 1992.

Gilroy, Paul. *The Black Atlantic: Modernity and Double Consciousness*. Cambridge: Harvard University Press, 1993.

Hickey, Dennis, and Kenneth C. Wylie. *An Enchanting Darkness: The American Vision of Africa in the Twentieth Century*. East Lansing: Michigan State University Press, 1993.

Hountondji, Paulin J. *African Philosophy: Myth and Reality*. Bloomington: Indiana University Press, 1983.

Irele, F. Abiola. "In Praise of Alienation." *The Surreptitious Speech: Présence Africain and the Politics of Otherness, 1947–1987*. Ed. V. Y. Mudimbe. Chicago and London: The University of Chicago Press, 1992, 201–24.

Kaplan, Robert D. "The Coming Anarchy: How Scarcity, Crime, Overpopulation, Tribalism, and Disease Are Rapidly Destroying the Social Fabric of Our Planet." *The Atlantic Monthly* Vol. 273 No. 2 (February 1994), pp. 44–46, 48–49, 52, 54, 58–60, 62–63, 66, 68–70, 72–76.

———. *The Ends of the Earth: A Journey at the Dawn of the Twenty-First Century*. New York: Random House, 1996.

Mazrui, Alamin M. "Relativism, Universalism, and the Language of African Literature." *Research in African Literatures* 23,1 (Spring 1992), 65–72.

Mazrui, Ali. "From Sun-Worship to Time-Worship: Toward a Solar Theory of History." *Philosophy, Humanity and Ecology: Philosophy of Nature and Environmental Ethics*. H. Odera Oruka, Ed. Nairobi, Kenya: African Centre for Technology Studies, 1994, pp. 165–76.

Morrison, Toni. *Song of Solomon*. New York: Penguin USA, 1977.

Mudimbe, V. Y. *The Idea of Africa*. London: James Currey, 1994.

Naipaul, V. S. "The Crocodiles of Yamoussoukro." *Finding the Centre*. London: Andre Deutsch, 1984, pp. 89–189.

Ngũgĩ wa Thiong'o. *Decolonising the Mind: The Politics of Language in African Literature*. London: James Currey, 1981.

———. *Devil on the Cross*. London: Heinemann, 1982.

Onyewuenyi, Innocent Chilaka. *The African Origins of Greek Philosophy: An Exercise in Afrocentrism*. Nsukka: University of Nigeria Press, 1993.

Oyono, Ferdinand. *Boy!* New York: Collier, 1970.

Serequeberhan, Tsenay. *The Hermeneutics of African Philosophy: Horizon and Discourse*. New York and London: Routledge, 1994.

Sparks, Allister. "Help a Fragile Bright Spot in West Africa to Remain Alight." *Herald Tribune International*. March 29, 1996, p. 6.

18 BLACKNESS AS A PROCESS OF CREOLIZATION: THE AFRO-ESMERALDIAN *DÉCIMAS* (ECUADOR)[1]

Jean Rahier

Yo soy de aquí,
de esta tierra de mar,
de esta tierra de sol.

Negro soy,
negros, papá y mamá.

Yo soy de aquí,
y el hombro de alquitrán sabe del peso de una banana.
Yo soy de aquí,
y amo a la camisa verde de la tierra.
Yo soy de aquí,
y sé que el oro del guayacán es perfumado.
Yo soy de aquí,
y he temido a la tunda.
Yo soy de aquí,
y sé que la cáscara del coco mancha.
Yo soy de aquí,
y mís oídos se nutren de ¡BOM!
y la sangre enloquece.

Soy de carbón,
y mis pies zapatean por librarse de la candela de una rumba.
Soy de carbón,
y el fósforo del bombo enciende mi cintura.
Antonio Preciado, Afro-Esmeraldian poet (Preciado 1961:21–22)[2]

BLACKNESS AS PROCESSES OF CREOLIZATION

In an ethnohistorical perspective, blackness in the Americas is here understood as "processes of creolization." These processes brought cultural fragments from various origins, as well as original creations, to mingle in particular ways, to be reshaped within various time-space contexts, and to become singular cultural traditions associated with blackness. These traditions are still undergoing change and transformation. In this essay, I illustrate the value of such a conception with the study of the Afro-

Esmeraldian *Décimas* (Province of Esmeraldas, Ecuador). While establishing their Spanish origin, I also underline the fundamental differences between these and the Spanish glosses. These differences explain their classifications as two distinct poetic genres. The Décima, a traditional oral poetry recited by Afro-Esmeraldian men, has as its formal origin a written poetry that was quite popular during the Renaissance in Spain and in Europe in general: the gloss (*la glosa*).

To understand the Afro-Esmeraldian Décimas it is absolutely necessary to consider some details of the history of Spanish society, literature, and colonies which led to the transformation of the European (Spanish) gloss into the Décimas, one of the most characteristic elements of "Afro-Esmeraldian culture" and oral tradition. Thus, this essay does not participate in the "Afrocentric" or "Africentric" project. Exclusive references to Africa and African cultures would not serve to explicate this transformation. By their very nature, the Afro-Esmeraldian Décimas contradict the "ethnic absolutism" of Africentric writers such as Asante, for instance, who choose to understand blackness as an "entity" frozen in time and space, which implies the adoption of a concept of self as racialized, essentialized, and fundamentally monolithic, or "African" (Gilroy 1993; Gilroy 1995):

> One cannot study Africans in the United States or Brazil or
> Jamaica without some appreciation for the historical and cultural
> significance of Africa as source and origin. A reactionary posture
> which claims Africology as "African Slave Studies" is rejected
> outright because it disconnects the African in America from thou-
> sands of years of history and tradition. Thus, if one concentrates on
> studying Africans in the inner cities of the Northeast United States,
> which is reasonable, it must be done with the idea in the back
> of the mind that one is studying African people, not "made-in-
> America Negroes" without historical depth. (Asante 1990: 15)

My disagreement with Asante's Africentric view comes with a deep awareness of the complexity of Afro-Esmeraldian history; thus I prefer to approach blackness in terms of "processes of creolization." The expressions "creole," "creolized," and "creolization" have been used numerous times, in different places, by different people, to refer to very diverse populations and cultural institutions. A recurrent connotation of these terms, which justifies the application of the concept of "creolization" to the Afro-Esmeraldian Décimas, is that of *born in the Americas*, following the contact between different cultural traditions and populations in a colonial or neocolonial context. The transplanted Africans had no choice but to experience such processes of creolization. Hence Mintz and Price's statement that "the capacity to innovate, to elaborate, and to create" is one of the major characteristics of African-American cultures (i.e., self-fashioning of the African Diaspora) (Mintz 1992: 51). I follow Edouard Glissant when he defines "creolization" as a cultural process, a mode of entanglement, a *métissage sans limite*, a dialectic of mutations which is independent from specific cultural contents (Glissant 1990).

THE AFRO-ESMERALDIAN COMMUNITY

Black immigration in the province of Esmeraldas began in the sixteenth century, along with commerce between the Spanish colonies of Central America and the Caribbean on one hand, and the vice-kingdom of Peru on the other. This commerce moved through Panama. Cartagena de Indias was the main port of the slave trade for all the colonies of the region (Bowser 1977; Curtin 1969; Palacios Preciado 1973). In the sixteenth century, the number of slaves transported was considerably reduced. The merchants who traveled between Panama and Callao were dealing mostly with merchandise. Sometimes they completed their loading with one or two slaves, rarely more (Bowser 1977).

In the context of these commercial activities, and as a result of a shipwreck, the first black immigration originated in the province (1553). The facts were immortalized in the chronicle of Miguel Cabello Balboa (Cabello Balboa 1965), who obtained the information in 1577 from one of the shipwrecked former slaves, Sebastian Alonso de Illescas, who had become the leader of what historians have called the "Republic of *Zambos*."[3] The ship in question belonged to the Spaniard Sebastian Alonso de Illescas, from whom the slave had borrowed the name after his confirmation in Seville, Spain. The ship was en route to Callao and had merchandise on board, as well as 23 *ladino* slaves,[4] an important quantity for the time (17 men and 6 women). After 30 days at sea, the ship anchored off the Esmeraldian coast. The Spanish crew debarked with the slaves to hunt game and refill the reserve with drinking water. Before they could return to the ship, a powerful thunderstorm wrecked the ship against the reefs. The slaves took the opportunity and escaped into the forest (the central area of the Province), after having probably killed the Spanish crew.

In 1957, Robert West identified a vast region—including the southern province of Darién in Panama, the Colombian Pacific coast, and most of the Ecuadorian province of Esmeraldas—as a cultural area called the Pacific Lowlands (West 1957). This area is about 970 kilometers long and from 80 to 160 kilometers wide, mostly covered by a dense rain forest. The population of the Pacific Lowlands is principally composed of black communities whose way of life is still mostly based, particularly in rural areas, on subsistence agriculture, hunting, fishing, and exploitation of alluvial mines. Their forebears were imported into the region in the eighteenth century as slaves to work in the mines of Western Colombia, then called New Granada (Friedemann 1966–69, 1974, 1978; Sharp 1976; Wade 1993;

West 1952). At the end of the nineteenth century, an important number of blacks began to migrate from the Colombian region of Barbacoas into the Ecuadorian province of Esmeraldas to the south (West 1957). Migration took place in two waves. The first one, from 1850 to 1920, followed the abolition of slavery in Colombia and the province's development of a gathering-exportation economy based on forest products such as, most importantly, tagua nuts or vegetal ivory (*Phytelephas aequadorialiis*), rubber, tobacco, and some precious metals. The second wave, between 1930 and 1955, was the result of a decrease in the productivity of the mines of Barbacoas combined with the Esmeraldian banana boom of the late 1940s (West 1957; Jácome B. 1978, 1979; Rivera 1986).

The present population of the province (around 250,000) is mainly black. It is estimated that the blacks, mulattos and *zambos* represent around 70 percent. The rest of the population is composed of white-*mestizos* (the Esmeraldian elite) and mestizos who came principally from the northern Ecuadorian highlands, from the province of Manabí,[5] and from Colombia; a few of whom I call the Esmeraldian white-mestizos (born in the Province of Esmeraldas), who usually have some degree of black ancestry; and also of Amerindians (the Cayapas or Chachis).[6] These various ethnic groups migrated into the province at different times. The Chachis were the first to do so (Barret 1925; Carrasco 1983).

The northern sector of the province is often considered a place of "pure" blackness and backwardness by the multi-"racial" inhabitants, especially by the youth, of the city of Esmeraldas. They often call it *el Norte*, and its inhabitants *los norteños*. The northerners are also referred to by the expression *los negros azules*, "the blue blacks," to evoke the darkness of their skin color as well as, indirectly, its opposite, the *métissage*, "racial" mixture, and *blanqueamiento* ("whitening" of the way of life) that characterize the city's population. It is in the villages of the North, principally in the ones more distant in the forest, that the Afro-Esmeraldian traditions, such as the Décimas, survived, despite the decades-old process of progressive modernization and integration of the frontier areas of the country into the national and international economies.

No creole language has emerged among the black populations of the Pacific Lowlands, with the sole exception of the community of San Basilio in Colombia (Escalante 1954). Spanish is the language spoken by black Lowlanders. In the Province of Esmeraldas, as is the case elsewhere in the Pacific Lowlands, the Spanish spoken includes provincialisms which sometimes seem to be derived from African words.[7]

THE AFRO-ESMERALDIAN DÉCIMAS

The Spanish word *décima* signifies a stanza of ten verses. The Afro-Esmeraldians use the term *Décima* to refer to an oral poetry composed of forty-four verses.[8] These verses are mostly octosyllabic; however, verses sometimes have seven, ten, or even eleven syllables. There is no conscious, rigid rule which regulates the verses' meter. When asked about the existence of such a rule, the *decimeros*—the male poets who recite the Décimas—are quite surprised by the content of the question, as if the structure they had to respect to compose and recite Décimas was not demanding enough. They are very proud of the complexity of the formal structure of the poems. The forty-four verses are divided into five stanzas, in this order: one of four verses (a quartet), then four of ten (actual décimas).[9] Each verse of the initial quartet is repeated at the end of each ten-line stanza, in succession. In other words, the first verse of the quartet is the last line of the first ten-line stanza, the second verse of the quartet finishes the second ten-line stanza, the third verse finishes the third ten-line stanza, and so on (line 1 = line 14, 2 = 24, 3 = 34, 4 = 44). Sometimes, the verse from the quartet is slightly transformed when repeated at the end of a ten-line stanza, but maintains the same meaning. This variation is due to the particularity of the Afro-Esmeraldian oral tradition, which permits one to finish a ten-line stanza with some liberty. On rare occasions, the verse completely changes when repeated at the end of the ten-line stanza. Here is an example:

¿Quién es esta que está aquí?	Who Is This One Who Is Here?
1. *Quién es esta que está aquí?*	1. Who is this one who is here?
2. *Quién es esta hermosa rosa?*	2. Who is this beautiful rose?
3. *Pregunto: quién es tu madre?*	3. I ask: "Who is your mother
4. *Que te parió tan hermosa?*	4. Who gave birth to you so fair?"
5. *Quién es esta que está aquí?*	5. Who is this one who is here?
6. *Quién es esta bella rosa?*	6. Who is this beautiful rose?
7. *Pregunto: cuál es tu madre?*	7. I ask: "Which one is your mother
8. *Que te ha parido tan hermosa?*	8. Who gave birth to you so pretty?"
9. *Quién es esta tan bonita?*	9. Who is this good-looking woman
10. *que ha venido a dar aquí,*	10. Who came to establish herself here?
11. *que a penas la distinguí,*	11. Who as soon as I saw her,
12. *para contar su atención?*	12. I wanted to draw her attention?
13. *Y pregunto con atención:*	13. And I ask with great attention:
14. *quién es esta que está aquí?*	14. Who is this one who is here?
15. *Tu risa me ha cautivado,* a	15. Your laughter captivated me,

16.	*tu mirar mucho mejor,*	b	16. Your glance even more,
17.	*y tu talle con primor,*	b	17. And your incredible silhouette
18.	*sin sentido me ha dejao'.*	a	18. Left me numb.
19.	*Me hallo tan apensionado*	a	19. Passion overwhelms me
20.	*de verte tan buena moza,*	c	20. To see you as attractive as you are,
21.	*tan afable y cariñosa*	c	21. So affable and loving,
22.	*para ser tan bella dama.*	d	22. Such a beautiful woman.
23.	*Y se puede correr tu fama,*	d	23. May your fame travel,
24.	*quién es esta bella rosa?*	c	24. Who is this beautiful rose?
25.	*Cómo te llamas no sé,*	a	25. I don't know your name,
26.	*ni tampoco te conozco,*	b	26. Nor do I know you,
27.	*pero te diré que estoy loco*	b	27. But I'll tell you that I'm crazy
28.	*al tiempo que te miré.*	a	28. Since the first time I saw you.
29.	*Y a todos preguntaré*	a	29. And I will ask everybody
30.	*si tienes marido o padre,*	c	30. If you have a husband or a father,
31.	*o si está aquí tu madre:*	c	31. Or if your mother is around:
32.	*tengo que hacerle un secreto.*	d	32. I have to tell her a secret.
33.	*Y así con mucho respeto*	d	33. And that's with great respect
34.	*pregunto: quién es tu madre?*	c	34. That I ask who is your mother?
35.	*Tu madre debe de ser*		35. Your mother must be
36.	*una estrella reluciente.*		36. A shining star.
37.	*Tu padre por consiguiente,*		37. Your father consequently
38.	*es un hermoso clavel!*		38. Is a handsome carnation!
39.	*Que naciste de ella y d'el*		39. You were born from her and him
40.	*blanca, amable y buena moza,*		40. White, lovable and good looking,
41.	*alumbras más que una estrella.*		41. You shine more than a star.
42.	*Ay, dime a'ónde estará*		42. Ay, tell me where will
43.	*esta madre tuya, m'hijita*		43. Your mother be, my dear
44.	*que te parió tan hermosa?*		44. Who gave birth to you so fair?

An anonymous couplet known by all the decimeros summarizes some of these aspects of the Décimas' formal structure using "popular terminology," i.e., formal or technical terms with a new and very different meaning:

1.	*Cuarenta y cuatro palabras*		1. Forty-four verses
2.	*tiene la décima entera;*		2. Make the entire Décima:

| 3. *diez palabras cada pie,* | 3. Ten verses each ten-line stanza, |
| 4. *cuatro la glosa primera.* | 4. Four the first quartet. |

The decimeros use *palabras*, which literally means "word" in Spanish, for "verse"; *décima entera* for "the entire poem" (the Décima); *pie*, which means "foot" (rhythmic unit), for a ten-line stanza; and *glosa primera*, "the first gloss," for "the first quartet." This illustrates how the decimeros have transformed even the formal vocabulary of poetry. These structural rules of the Décimas make the initial quartet the synthesis of the central ideas of the poem, which are more fully developed in the four ten-line stanzas.

The declamation of the Décimas is similar with each poet, and emphasizes rhythm. The poems are delivered in nine parts separated by short pauses. First comes the initial quartet, and then the four first verses of the first ten-line stanza, then the six following verses of the same ten-line stanza, etc. (4-4/6-4/6-4/6-4/6). The decimeros' pitch usually rises in the last two syllables of the next-to-last verse of each ten-line stanza, and then falls in the last two syllables of the last verse. The goal is to emphasize the last verse, the conclusion of the stanza, which is the repetition of one of the lines of the initial quartet, thereby marking the rhythm of the declamation. Sometimes, older decimeros make pauses that the others do not make. Instead of saying the forty-four verses according to the model previously indicated, their declamation follows this pattern: (4-4/4/2-4/4/2-4/4/2-4/4/2), the pauses which separate the stanzas being slightly longer than the pauses which separate the verses of a same stanza. Logically, the described declamation is intimately related to the organization of the content, the story of the Décima, into groups of verses that correspond to grammatical sentences. When transcribing the oral texts, one can always finish the fourth verse of each ten-line stanza with a period or a semicolon. There is no overlapping between the fourth and the fifth verse. They are always clearly separated.

The decimeros distinguish between two categories of Décimas: the *Décimas a lo humano* (about human matters or profane) and the *Décimas a lo divino* (about divine matters). As I will explain later, these two categories of Décimas are not recited in the same contexts. The previously cited Décima is a poem *a lo humano.*

We can see in the Décima "*¿Quién es esta?*" ("Who Is This One?") that the majority of verses are octosyllabic, that there are forty-four verses divided into an initial quartet and four ten-line stanzas, that the verses of the quartet are repeated at the end of their respective ten-line stanza (with the exception of verse 2, *Quién es esta hermosa rosa?*, which becomes in verse 24 *Quién es esta bella rosa?*), and that each ten-line stanza constitutes the explanation, the gloss, of a verse of the quartet. This poem is also representative of the kind of rhymes one can find in the Décimas: They seem to be arbitrary rather than subject to strict rules.

THE AFRO-ESMERALDIAN *DECIMEROS*

In the small villages in the northern sector of the province of Esmeraldas, the tradition of reciting Décimas is reserved for men who are for the most part older and who are illiterate. They are respected for their knowledge and memory. Usually, Décimas have unknown composers, despite the fact that most of the decimeros will claim to have composed the Décimas they recite. It is quite common to find decimeros who live a hundred kilometers apart claiming to have written the same poem. However, even if authorship is sometimes manipulated by the poets as a source of prestige, nobody really argues against the identification of the (rural) Afro-Esmeraldian community at large as being the real author of the poems. The "author is a modern figure whose emergence is linked to the development of the modern culture industry and the capitalist valorization of the individual" (Lewis 1996). During my various journeys in the province of Esmeraldas, I met only one decimero (he was then in his mid-forties) who actually wrote his Décimas. He was living in the small town of Limones and was very proud that one of his compositions had been published by an organization that has as its objective the preservation of Afro-Ecuadorian cultures.

Like the decimeros, the Afro-Esmeraldian population in general divide the Décimas into the *Décimas a lo divino* and the *Décimas a lo humano*, each of which is context-specific.

THE *DÉCIMAS A LO DIVINO*

The Décimas about divine matters are recited in four different contexts: funerals for adults (*alabados*), funerals for children (*chigualos*), saints' day celebrations (*arrullos*), and as protection against forest spirits.

The alabados

According to Afro-Esmeraldian traditions, when young men or young women have had sexual intercourse, and it becomes known because of the resulting pregnancy, they begin their lives as adults and are independent from their families. Upon their death, after a series of rituals (called *la novena*), their souls will go to one of the "worlds" reserved for the souls of deceased adults: either purgatory or hell. The souls of adults do not go on to *Gloria*, or Paradise (Whitten 1974).

These funerals are accompanied by sad songs called alabados, which are sung without any musical background. Some Décimas about divine matters are also recited. They are usually sad poems that underline the inevitability of death, traditionally represented as a mysterious woman who acts upon the direct orders of God. The Décimas recited during the alabado ceremonies are part of the wider ambiance of sadness and fatality which characterizes such rituals (Whitten 1974; Barrero 1979b, 1979a; Quiroga 1994).

The separation between after-life worlds for adults and children is explained by an ideology which overemphasizes the Catholic doctrine of original sin. The past sexual activity of adults closes the door of Gloria for them. Purgatory is not conceived of as a place of transit before a final heavenly destination, but as a closed world that no soul can leave (Whitten 1974).

The chigualos

In the case of children, Afro-Esmeraldian traditions indicate that if they were young enough to not have been involved in sexual intercourse, and if they have been baptized, their souls (the *angelitos*) will leave for Paradise by the end of the funeral. There they stay in the company of God, the saints, and the Virgin. Funerals, called chigualos, are enlivened by songs (*arrullos*) accompanied by musical instruments, and short games performed around the corpse (called chigualos as well). In contrast with the alabado, the ambiance of the chigualo ritual is marked by a sort of happiness for everybody involved but the parents of the deceased child, who are physically present but who usually stay aside (Whitten 1974).

Roger Bastide wrote about funerals for children that can be found in various Afro–Latin-American communities:

> In the *velorio de angelito* (wake for a dead child) of Colombia
> and Venezuela we find a central idea which is strictly European.
> Faced with the extremely high rate of infant mortality which social
> contacts provoked in America [the Americas], the clergy thought
> up a new ideology according to which all little children who died
> became angels in heaven; thus one should not weep for them, but
> rather rejoice. All that Negroes added here was what they regarded
> as the characteristic manifestation of joy: a dance round the coffin
> (Venezuela), or dances, singing and games in Colombia. (Bastide
> 1971: 162)

The Décimas about divine matters recited during the chigualos are never sad poems dealing with mortality and the sadness of death or the wandering of the souls, as are the poems of the novena, nor do they emphasize the sins committed during one's lifetime, as is the case for the alabados. On the contrary, they participate in the joyous tone of the ceremony and sometimes establish an analogy between the angelito and Jesus Christ as a child (el Niño Dios). They talk in a positive way about the inhabitants of Gloria: God, the Saints, and the Virgin. The Décimas recited during the chigualos can also be addressed directly to a particular Saint or Virgin, or even to Jesus Christ.

The arrullos or Saints' Days

The term arrullo refers to both the ceremonies organized in honor of various saints and incarnations of Mary the night preceding the saint day, and the songs sung during the arrullo-ceremonies and the chigualos. In the traditional Afro-Esmeraldian context, women are in charge of the preparation of rituals in general. There are numerous saints and virgins who are popular in the province of Esmeraldas: San Antonio, San José, la Virgin de Fátima, la Virgin del Carmen, etc. To prepare an arrullo—which is always dedicated to a particular saint—the women ask some men to construct a shrine in which an image of the saint is placed. The women will sing arrullos around the shrine while shaking maracas to mark the rhythm. They are also accompanied by two percussion instruments played by men, the cununo and the bombo.

During the arrullo, which lasts from sunset to dawn, the woman of the house where the arrullo is held asks a decimero to recite Décimas a lo divino. These will usually be addressed to the saint or virgin being celebrated. However, since the ceremony provides an opening into Gloria, the Décimas can also be addressed to any other inhabitant of Paradise (saint or virgin). Here is an example of Décima a lo divino which is recited during the arrullo al Niño Dios, the arrullo performed on Christmas eve.

Yo vide a mi Dios chiquito	I Saw My God as a Baby
1. Yo vide a mi Dios chiquito	1. I saw my God as a baby,
2. dándole el pecho su madre	2. His mother was breast-feeding him
3. y San José como padre	3. And his father Saint Joseph
4. le decía: "calla, Niñito."	4. Was telling him: "Be quiet my son."
5. En un dichoso portal	5. In a happy crèche
6. ví a San José y a María	6. I saw Saint Joseph and Mary
7. que en los brazos lo tenía	7. Who was holding him in her arms
8. dándole al Niño mamar.	8. While suckling him.
9. Con tanta amorosidad	9. With so much love
10. le da sus pechos bendito,	10. She gives him her sacred breasts,

11. *le dice: "Mama, Niñito,*

11. Telling him: "Suck, my little one,

12. *este manjar oloroso."*

12. This perfumed sustenance."

13. *Tomando el sustento hermoso,*

13. He was drinking,

14. *yo vide a mi Dios chiquito.*

14. I saw my God as a baby.

15. *Los tres Reyes del Oriente*

15. The three Kings of the Orient

16. *se pusieron en camino*

16. Began their journey

17. *en busca del Rey divino*

17. Looking for the divine King

18. *donde lo hallaron presente.*

18. Until they found him.

19. *Herodes bajó en persona*

19. Herod welcomed them himself

20. *tan solo por degollarle.*

20. Because he wanted to kill Him.

21. *El ángel les vino a hablar*

21. The angel came to speak to them

22. *y para Egipto salieron.*

22. And they left for Egypt.

23. *Estaba el Niño en sus brazos*

23. The Baby was in her arms,

24. *dándole el pecho su madre.*

24. His mother was breast-feeding him.

25. *Cuando fueron a adorarlo*

25. When they went to worship him

26. *bajaron por el Oriente,*

26. They left toward the Orient,

27. *sólo de guía pusieron*

27. And their only guides

28. *las estrellas al poniente.*

28. Were the stars in the sky.

29. *Era tan resplandeciente,*

29. It was shining so much,

30. *no había con quién compararlo.*

30. There was nothing to compare it with.

31. *Cuando fueron a adorarlo*

31. When they went to worship him

32. *sólo tres santos habían:*

32. Only three saints were already present:

33. *la Magdalena y María,*

33. Magdalena and Mary,

34. *y San José como padre.*

34. And his father Saint Joseph.

35. *Cuando nació el Sumo Bién*

35. When the Supreme Good was born

36. *dijo el gallo: "Nació Cristo!"*

36. The cock sung: "The Christ is born!"

37. *Respondió Diego Laurito:*

37. Diego Laurito responded:

38. *"'Onde nació jue en Belén."*

38. "He was born in Bethlehem."

39. *Iban los Reyes también*

39. The Kings were going too

40. *con sus rosarios benditos.*

40. With their blessed rosaries

41. *Pastores iban contritos*

41. Shepherds were going repentantly

42. *hincaditos de rodilla.*

42. Kneeling down.

| 43. *Y el Cordero sin mancilla* | 43. And the Lamb without stain |
| 44. *le decía: "Calla Niñito."* | 44. Was telling him: "Be quiet my son." |

The Décimas a lo divino *and a forest spirit*

The northern sector of the province of Esmeraldas is covered by tropical rain forest; there are no roads, and rivers provide the only means of communication. Every Afro-Esmeraldian family has at least one canoe. Decimeros say that an evil spirit haunts the forest and sometimes surprises solitary travelers by reciting a *Décima a lo humano*. Nobody ever sees him and the only thing that is known about the spirit is that he has a very deep and powerful voice. If the traveler cannot respond immediately with a *Décima a lo divino*, he will faint and his canoe will drift aimlessly, perhaps resulting in his death. Any *Décima a lo divino* will suffice as a response to the spirit-decimero.

THE *DÉCIMAS A LO HUMANO*

The "profane Décimas" are not recited in religious or magical contexts. The decimeros say them during the male gatherings, which usually take place in the evening (Whitten 1974). During these gatherings, after a day of labor, men get together to comment upon the events of the day, play guitar, sing, relate tales, and recite Décimas. During these conversations, men try to boost their own prestige as much as possible. Norman Whitten underlined the importance of the expression *andar y conocer* ("to go elsewhere and learn") and its link to masculine prestige. To be able to cite faraway cities and countries and relate sexual adventures undoubtedly increases one's reputation. Older men talk more than the younger ones: they know more tales or Décimas, they have visited more cities and villages, they are not shy about referring to their sexual experiences, etc.

Profane Décimas could be subdivided into various groups according to their themes. In effect, some are hyperbolic compositions that, for example, exaggerate the circumstances of a particular event or the physical characteristics of an insect (or the bite of a mosquito). Other Décimas relate historical events (World War II or the Ecuadorian liberal revolution) or comment upon important changes in daily life (the arrival of a radio or of a hydroplane in the forest). Still others comment on women or present social and political demands.

Today, with the progressive integration of the province of Esmeraldas into the national and world economy, the Décimas are disappearing. Migration of young Afro-Esmeraldians from the small villages located deep in the forest of the northern sector of the province to urban areas interrupts the transmission of oral tradition from one generation to the next. Furthermore, many young people look down upon Afro-Esmeraldian Décimas that they see as backward, as a vestige of the past.

THE SPANISH *GLOSA* (GLOSS)

The gloss or *glosa* is a poetic form very popular among European writers from the fifteenth through the eighteenth century. What historians of Spanish literature call "the normal type of the gloss" was a poem composed of forty-four verses, divided in two parts: the "text" and the actual "gloss" or glosa. The text—in Spanish *texto, cabeza,* or *retuécano*—was a short poem which had been composed by a previous poet. Its extension could vary from one to twelve verses, and sometimes more. Nevertheless, the "most common form of the gloss"[10] presented a text of four verses (Baehr 1970: 330; Janner 1943, 1946; Le Gentil 1952; Spitzer 1943–1944).

The second part of this form of Spanish poetry, the actual gloss written by the *glosador* (glosser), was a commentary of the "text." It was used—as its name indicates—to gloss an already existing poem in a certain number of stanzas, by means of interpretation, paraphrase, and extension in general, of each initial verse. The number of stanzas of the gloss (second part of the poem) was determined by the number of verses included in the "text." Each stanza of the gloss interpreted and paraphrased one verse of the "text." The glossed verse was then found sometimes at the middle, more often at the end of the stanza.

The "most common type" of the Spanish gloss (entire poem) had for "text" a *ronda*, a four-line stanza, with *rimas envueltas*, "enveloped rhymes" (abba), or *rimas cruzadas*, "crossed rhymes" (ababa), which was commented upon in four ten-line stanzas, with the verse from the "text" repeated at the end of each stanza. The disposition of the rhymes followed the formal characteristics of the type of ten-line stanza chosen by the poet who composed the glosa.

Here is an example of Spanish gloss, composed by Lope de Vega to celebrate the wedding of Philip III and Princess Marguerite of Austria[11] (cited in Baehr 1970: 333–334):

Nace en el Nácar la Perla	The Pearl Is Born in the Nacre
1. *Nace en el nácar la perla,*	1. The Pearl is born in the Nacre,
2. *En Austria una Margarita,*	2. In Austria a Marguerite
3. *Y un joyel hay de infinita*	3. And a very special jewel
4. *Estima donde ponerla.*	4. Ponders where to place her.
5. *Cuando el cielo que el sol dora,*	5. When the sky gilded by the sun,
6. *Para formar perlas llueve*	6. Forms pearls of rain

7. *Las que en el norte atesora*	7. Which are stored in the north
8. *Abrese el nácar y bebe*	8. The nacre opens and drinks
9. *Las lágrimas del aurora.*	9. The tears of dawn.
10. *Desta suerte, para hacerla*	10. In this way she is made
11. *A Margarita preciosa*	11. A precious Marguerite
12. *Quiso el cielo componerla*	12. The sky wanted to compose her
13. *De la manera que hermosa*	13. In such a way so lovely
14. *Nace en el nácar la pera.* (14 = 1)	14. Is the Pearl born in the nacre. (14 = 1)
15. *Para un joyel rico y solo*	15. For a rich and solitary jewel
16. *Buscaba perlas España,*	16. Spain was looking for pearls
17. *Y piedras de polo a polo*	17. And stones from pole to pole
18. *O en nácares que el mar baña*	18. Or in nacres bathed by the sea
19. *O en minas que engendra Apolo.*	19. Or in mines engendered by Apollo.
20. *La fama, que en todo habita,*	20. Fame, that lives inside everything,
21. *Le dijo, viendo el joyel,*	21. Told her as he examined the jewel,
22. *Que al sol en belleza unita,*	22. That the sun with beauty unites,
23. *Que hallaría para él*	23. So would find for him
24. *En Austria una Margarita.* (24 = 2)	24. In Austria a Marguerite. (24 = 2)
25. *Austria también pretendía,*	25. Austria was also courting,
26. *Dudosa, informarse della,*	26. Doubtful, obtaining information for her,
27. *Y certificóle un día*	27. And one day guaranteed her
28. *Que Margarita tan bella*	28. That such a beautiful Marguerite
29. *Sólo en Felipe cabía.*	29. Could not be but for Philip.
30. *Luego España solicita*	30. Later Spain requested
31. *Con tal tercero a tal dama.*	31. Such a man to such a lady,
32. *Y con su pecho la incita,*	32. Be invited with all her heart,
33. *Donde hay oro de gran fama,*	33. Where there is gold of great renown
34. *Y un joyel hay de infinita.* (34 = 3)	34. And a very special jewel. (34 = 3)
35. *Este joyel español*	35. This Spanish jewel
36. *Se hizo a todo distinto*	36. Was very unique
37. *Y tan sólo como el sol*	37. He was like the shining
38. *Del oro de Carlos Quinto,*	38. Gold of Charles V,
39. *Siendo Felipe el crisol.*	39. Philip being the crucible.

40. *Deste, para engrandecerla,*	40. With it, to exalt her,
41. *Se engosta, adorna y esmalta,*	41. He adorns and embellishes himself,
42. *Este pudo merecerla,*	42. He does merit her,
43. *Que ninguna hay de tan alta*	43. No women is as exalted
44. *Estima donde ponerla.* (44 = 4)	44. Ponders where to place her. (44 = 4)

The "normal type" of Spanish gloss had different components: octosyllabic verses and four- and ten-line stanzas. The octosyllabic verse, also called by philologists *verso de arte real, verso de ronda mayor,* or *verso de arte menor,* is the most commonly used verse form in Spanish literature. In Spain, it is considered the national verse form and can be found in both aristocratic and popular poetry from the eleventh century on. It has retained its vigor in the popular poetry of Spain as well as that of Latin America (Baehr 1970: 102; Hidalgo Alzamora 1982: 54).

There are two types of four-line stanzas utilized as "text" in the "normal" or "classic" Spanish gloss: the *ronda* or quartet with "enveloped rhymes" (abba), which prevailed almost exclusively since the *Siglo de Oro* (see Lope de Vega's gloss, previously cited); and the quartet with "crossed rhymes" (abab), the oldest type of four-line stanza in Spanish literature. In Afro-Esmeraldian Décimas, despite the repetition of certain syllables at the end of each line, marking the rhythm of declamation, the rhymes are more arbitrary than the glosses' rhymes. However, some Décimas can be found with either an "enveloped rhymes" quartet or a "crossed rhymes" quartet. Here are two examples from the *Décima "San Lorenzo"* and the *Décima "El Cangrejo"* ("The Crab"), respectively:

Con justiciera razón,	a	With a justified reason,
San Lorenzo está pidiendo,	b	[the town of] San Lorenzo is asking,
diré mejor isistiendo,	b	Better said insisting,
ser elevado a cantón.	a	To become a county.
Un cangrejo con su espada,	a	A crab with its sword
me quiso poner un cacho.	b	Wanted to stab me.
Yo le dí una patada	a	I kicked him
y le quebré el carapacho.	b	And I broke his shell.

The ten-line stanza has been popular in Spanish poetry since the end of the Middle Ages: "Among all the metric combinations used by the traditional Castillan school to cluster *arte menor* verses (verses of less than nine syllables), none reached the fame and diffusion of the ten-line stanza. We can find it in all corners of *hispanidad*" (Mille y Gimenez 1937: 40).

To comment upon the four-line text, the classic or normal type of the Spanish gloss used two different kinds of ten-line stanzas: the *copla real* (royal couplet), and the *Espinela*.

The royal couplet is comprised of "two stanzas of five verses, that can have identical rhymes, or the first one some rhymes, and the second one others (ababacdcdc), which is better" (Baehr 1970: 295). Because the royal couplet is the combination of two five-line stanzas, it is also called the *falsa décima* (the false ten-line stanza) or also the *doble quintil* (the double five-line stanza). This distribution of the royal couplet into two five-line stanzas is also marked by the punctuation, which always divides the ten-line stanza in two parts of five verses (see the previously cited gloss composed by Lope de Vega) (Baehr 1970: 295–306).

The *Espinela*, from the name of its promoter Vicente Espinel (1550–1624) is, in its classic form, a stanza of ten octosyllabic verses with four rhymes which are invariably (abbaa–ccddc). It is actually composed of two quartets of enveloped rhymes which have identical rhyme schemes (abba and cddc), plus two connecting verses at the middle: the first one repeats the last rhyme of the first quartet, while the second anticipates the first rhyme of the following quartet: (abba–ac–ccddc). The rhyme scheme is not the only peculiarity of the Espinela. A ten-line stanza is considered an Espinela if, in addition to the indicated rhyme scheme, it shows a clear break in the content and delivery of the poem after the fourth verse. This pause gives the fifth verse a special status: according to the rhyme scheme it belongs to the first part of the ten-line stanza, but the content pertains to the second part. Juan Mille y Giménez summarized the role of the Espinela's fifth verse:

> This fifth verse is the axis, the key of the entire *Espinela*. If by the sound we have to consider it as united to the first part of five verses, in terms of meaning it belongs to the second. In this way, the composition is left symmetrical as far as the sounds are concerned, but presents a kind of overlapping by the meaning that unites one five line stanza to the other, giving birth to a new unit of versification. (Mille y Gimenez 1937: 41–2)

Rudolf Baehr also wrote about this break in meaning:

> Until the break in the meaning after the fourth verse, the argument has to dispose itself into the progression of its development, and in this way present the theme. The following six verses may not introduce a new idea; they have to amplify what has already been presented in the first part of four verses. Because of its rigorous presentation, form and development, the *Espinela* can be placed with dignity beside the sonnet. (Baehr 1970: 300)

Here is an example of an Espinela (composed by Vicente Espinel in 1592) (Baehr 1970: 300):

1.	*Suele decirme la gente*	a	1.	The people used to tell me
2.	*que en parte sabe mi mal,*	b	2.	That in part they know my pain
3.	*que la causa principal*	b	3.	That its principal cause
4.	*se me ve inscrita en la frente;*	a	4.	Is written on my forehead;
5.	*y aún me hago valiente*	a	5.	And even if I pretend
6.	*luego mi lengua desliza*	c	6.	My tongue always reveals it
7.	*por lo que dora y matiza;*	c	7.	With embellishment and nuances;
8.	*que lo que el pecho no gosta*	d	8.	What one cannot swallow
9.	*ningún disímulo basta*	d	9.	No dissimulation suffices
10.	*a cubrirlo con ceniza.*	c	10.	Even covering it with ashes.

This description of the formal components of the "classic model" of the Spanish gloss demonstrates quite well that the Afro-Esmeraldian Décimas originated in the "normal type" of gloss using the Espinela. All of the more than sixty Afro-Esmeraldian Décimas I worked on show this grammatical pause, characteristic of the Espinela's fourth verse. The first four verses serve to present the theme, which is developed in the six following verses and reaches a conclusion in the tenth verse. The dots and semicolons which separate the fourth and the fifth verse of the Décima's ten-line stanzas are placed, in the written version of the Décimas, by the ethnographer who recorded them. The decimeros, who most of the time do not put them in writing and have a purely oral relationship with the poems, do not place them at the end of a verse. The ethnographer does. It is significant that when transcribing Décimas, one always has to separate the fourth verse of a ten-line stanza from the fifth with a dot or a semicolon. The content of the stanza as well as the recitation of the poem asks the transcriber to do so. The pauses made by the decimero between the fourth and the fifth verse of a ten-line stanza are in accordance with the characteristic specialization of the verses of the Espinela; they do not interrupt the presentation of the argument. Furthermore, despite the fact that no strict rule systematizes the rhymes, sometimes one can find in particular Décimas the same characteristic Espinela rhyme scheme—or vestiges of that scheme. That is the case of the Décima "*¿Quién es esta?*," for instance, which has its second and third ten-line stanzas (verses 15–24 and verses 25–34) reproducing the Espinela rhyme scheme, while the first and the fourth do not.

Obviously, the formal structure of the Afro-Esmeraldian Décima is derived from the Spanish gloss format. However, the Décimas are not simply copies or bad imitations of the latter. Décimas and glosses constitute very

distinct poetic genres (texts and contexts). At the formal level—meter and
rhyme—the gloss is much more strictly defined than the Décima.

BRIEF HISTORY OF THE SPANISH GLOSS

The fundamental idea of the gloss—the explication or paraphrase of
another text—is a phenomenon characteristic of the European Middle
Ages. The objective of the gloss proceeds from "the deductive methods
of scholastic theology and philosophy, jurisprudence and the liberal arts,
methods which are shaped by the norms of the exegesis which characterizes the medieval thought in the Christian West" (Baehr 1970: 335–336;
see also Janner 1943; Le Gentil 1952).

> This desire to explain, to comment, to reason or more simply to
> paraphrase, represents one of the deepest tendencies of medieval
> mentality: Did not the teaching of the Arts in the [medieval] univer-
> sities consist only in commenting on particular manuals? And does
> not the gloss come directly from the deductive tradition of the
> scholastic thought? (Le Gentil 1952 295–6)

For H. Janner, the Spanish gloss also has roots in Arabic and Jewish
poetry. Both developed forms of gloss (Janner 1946 221–30): the *musam-
mat* and the *zejel* of Arabic poetry are glosses on religious texts; and in
the liturgy of Spanish Jews, we find similar forms used to paraphrase passages of the Bible. Other historians question the hypothesis of Arabic and
Jewish origins, arguing that they preceded the emergence of the Spanish
gloss by too short a time span to allow the attribution of any influence
(Baehr 1970; Le Gentil 1952).

Thus, the Spanish gloss had for a departure point not a precise form
but an intention—to paraphrase and to comment on an already existing
text. Initially, the number of verses was unimportant. What the historians
called the "normal type" of gloss was the result of an evolution. It is only
in the second half of the sixteenth century that this normal type transformed progressively into an established format. In the fifteenth century,
the first glosses used short proverbs, letters, or songs as "texts." These
were poems with numerous stanzas (glossed songs and letters) or glosses
with only one or two stanzas (glossed proverbs) (Baehr 1969: 335–336; Janner 1943; Le Gentil 1952).

The nostalgic desire to return to the lyricism of the Middle Ages—
which was disappearing in the fifteenth century—marked the beginning
of the gloss as a distinct poetic genre. The first glosses were paraphrases
of medieval texts, and their success in Spain was the result of the Spanish
elite's lingering on the culture of the Middle Ages. Initially, "Love" was
the major topic (*las glosas amorosas*), and the glosses about love were very

much appreciated in the court throughout the fifteenth century. Courtiers commented upon their content and proposed new themes (Janner 1943: 191).

At the beginning of the sixteenth century, the gloss progressively lost its exclusive relationship with the declining cult of courtly love and was more influenced by Renaissance philosophical and religious thought. To an extent, the metric diversity of the previous period was abandoned and the short glosses disappeared because they did not allow any development of religious or philosophical dogmas (Janner 1943: 196). This more "serious" thematic orientation was accompanied by a change in the objective of the glosser:

> In the sixteenth century, glosses were presenting religious and philosophical meditations and—in final analysis—they wanted to edify the reader. The glosser is no longer a troubadour according to the Provencal tradition: he takes on the dignity of a moral, philosophical and even sacred orator who indoctrinates, advises, threatens, fulminates, or exalts. (Janner 1943: 196)

In the second part of the sixteenth century began a tradition of religious glosses, among the first examples of which can be found the "long gloss" (glosses of orations) as well as the "normal type." These glosses expanded on the division of the Bible into Old and New Testaments. The redemption of Jesus Christ, the dual nature of God, divinity made human, the mystery of the Holy Eucharist, and the Mother of Christ were recurrent themes. All of these themes excited commentary and explanations, which in turn reaffirmed the didactic objective of the gloss: to reinforce the reader's faith (Janner 1943: 199). The second half of the sixteenth century also saw the development of a tradition of glosses on historical medieval romances, which were commenting upon historical facts.

By the end of the sixteenth century, the "long type" of the gloss had definitively disappeared and had been replaced by the normal type. With the advent of the normal type as a standard form, the gloss became a genre of poetry entirely independent of any specialized theme (Janner 1943: 204).

ARRIVAL OF THE GLOSS TO SPANISH COLONIES OF THE NEW WORLD

Since the beginning of the Spanish colonization of the Americas, the Jesuits—inspired by their teaching experience in Europe—founded many schools. In these schools, they sometimes organized competitions in which the gloss was one of the chosen poetic formats (Pacheco 1959: 532–543). Jesuits were known for their mastery in the composition of glosses.

One of these renowned glossers was Father Antonio Bastidas, who was born in Guayaquil, Ecuador, in 1615 and who died in Santa Fe de Bogotá in 1681. He is considered one of the first Ecuadorian poets of the colonial period. The majority of his compositions were glosses that focused on particular circumstances of the life of the royal family, for example the death of Queen Isabel de Borbón or the birth of Prince Felipe Prospero (Pacheco 1959: 317–329).

The presence of Décimas in various black communities of Latin America (Colombia, Peru, Puerto Rico, and Brazil)[12] is the direct result of missionary work: The glosses were one of the tools used by the Church to educate slaves. It used glosses-Décimas as mnemonic devices for indoctrination about divine matters. Before the conquest, there was already in Spain a tradition of using religious glosses to explain passages of the Bible to illiterate Spanish peasants (Hidalgo Alzamora 1982: 172).

In addition to this use of the gloss as a technique of evangelization, certain slaves would have observed their Spanish owners during their religious and secular festivals. Spaniards enjoyed public gatherings and the poetic competitions that were organized for royal holidays, canonization of Saints, the installation of viceroys, etc. An account of one of these events was preserved thanks to a report sent by the mayor of the Colombian city of Tunja to the king of Spain. In 1662, the municipality of Tunja held a poetry competition on the occasion of the birth of the Prince Carlos José (future Charles II) and the death of another prince, Felipe Prospero. The competition was organized in the Santa Clara convent and was open to the public. A jury of ten people had devised a series of ten tests in which every contestant could participate freely. The first test consisted of composing a gloss of the following "text":

Como el cielo de España ve	As the Sky of Spain sees
Que su desemparo arguye,	That its sadness develops,
Dió un ángel que sustituye	It gave an angel who substitutes
Mientras que a Carlos José.	By giving Carlos José.

The glosses were written in advance by each competitor, who had to submit his composition to the jury on the day of the contest. The jury had each poem read publicly by a secretary before pronouncing its decision. The gloss that won the first prize had been written by the Jesuit Father Juan Onofre, who was also a member of the jury (Gomez Restrepo 1938: 83–99; Pacheco 1959: 322–323).

When assimilating the gloss to create the Décima, blacks emphasized some of the rules of gloss composition, while downplaying others. The Décimas became an oral tradition with its own set of structural rules, an oral poetry which has a variety of sources of inspiration and is expressed in a very distinct vernacular or provincial form of Spanish.[13] They are declaimed in socio-cultural contexts very different from those in which the Spaniards read their glosses.

The penetration of the gloss into particular black communities of Latin America took place in different ways. In Peru, for instance, there exists a tradition called *el socavón*, in which Décimas are sung and accompanied by guitar (Cuche 1981; Santa Cruz 1964, 1971, 1982). In Colombia and in the Ecuadorian province of Esmeraldas, Décimas are recited without any musical accompaniment (García 1979, 1984; Coba 1980; Hidalgo Alzamora 1982; Rahier 1987).

THE AFRO-ESMERALDIAN DÉCIMAS AND THE ECUADORIAN "RACIAL"/SPATIAL ORDER

Ecuadorian society is spatially constituted, organized in a particular "cultural topography" (Wade 1993: 50) within which different ethnic groups (indigenous people, blacks, mestizos, white-mestizos, and whites) traditionally reside in specific places or regions (with particular histories), enjoy different concentrations of economic and political power, and occupy different positions on the national social ladder and in the racial order. Blacks and indigenous people are found at the bottom of the latter, and the two "traditional" regions of blackness (the province of Esmeraldas and the Chota-Mira Valley) are looked down upon by the white and white-mestizo urban citizenry as places of indolence and violence, laziness, backwardness, and unconquered nature. It is perhaps in this context that we have to understand the debate about the origin of the Décimas between a white-mestizo professor of literature, Laura Hidalgo Alzamora, and an Afro-Esmeraldian writer and political activist, Juan García Salazar.

Hidalgo Alzamora, in her book *Décimas Esmeraldeñas*, acknowledges a European origin of the poems and states that they now constitute an "original poetic genre." However, she later presents the texts of Décimas recorded and transcribed by García Salazar with a series of comments. More than once, using the laws of metric of written Spanish poetry of the Renaissance, she *corrects* the texts of Décimas she did not record, sometimes dividing verses in two, and other times suppressing prepositions to fit them into the model of octosyllabic verse so characteristic of the Spanish glosses, as if the Décimas were imperfect copies of the glosses (Hidalgo Alzamora 1982). García Salazar, on the other hand, is convinced of the African origin of the Décimas. He thinks that the Hispanic influence is limited to the use of Spanish language. The Décimas evoke to him the songs of the griots in Africa (García Salazar 1984: 32). Obviously, what he wants to do is question the representation of Ecuadorian blacks as violent and noncultured people by relating them to the respectability of African cultures and history.

What I tried to do in this limited space is trace the formal origin of the Afro-Esmeraldian Décimas to Europe, and Spain in particular. In doing so, my goal was also to underscore the striking differences—formal structure, content, and contexts—existing between the Décimas (oral poetry) and the European glosses (written texts), and thus underline the relevance of the concept of creolization. My intention was not to suggest, in any way, that all Afro-Esmeraldian cultural traditions are of Spanish origin. African influences in Afro-Esmeraldian culture can be observed, for instance, in the survival of certain words as well as in the Afro-Esmeraldian traditional music called *la marimba*, which includes a xylophone (the marimba itself) accompanied by percussion instruments (bombo and cununo) and maracas or guazás.

My objective was to focus the analysis on the oral tradition of the Décimas while profiting from the opportunity provided by the very nature of the Décimas to criticize en passant the absolutism of Africentric dogmas. When dealing seriously with African Diaspora cultures, one cannot simply dismiss time/space contexts in order to celebrate the greatness and the strength of a mythical Africa, or suggest the "undeniable" superiority of Europe. African Diaspora cultures, like any other, cannot be essentialized.

I am aware that my argument, constructed around the concept of creolization, is intertwined with a political position. I fully identify with Paul Gilroy when he writes:

> Striving to be both European and black requires some specific forms of double consciousness. By saying this I do not mean to suggest that taking on either or both of these unfinished identities necessarily exhausts the subjective resources of any particular individual. However, where racist, nationalist, or ethnically absolutist discourses orchestrate political relationships so that these identities appear to be mutually exclusive, occupying the space between them or trying to demonstrate their continuity has been viewed as a provocative and even oppositional act of political insubordination. (Gilroy, 1993)

NOTES

1. My special thanks go to two of my colleagues at Louisiana State University, Michael Hawkins and Ann Whitmer, for reading previous versions of this essay and helping me correct the imperfections of my English.

2. Antonio Preciado does not compose Décimas. He is a "modern" poet. He has been the rector of the University Luis Vargas Torres in the city of Esmeraldas and is actually the director of the Cultural Center of the Esmeraldas branch of the Banco Central Ecuatoriano.

3. A *zambo(a)* is a mixed-race person from black and Amerindian parents.

4. A *ladino* slave was a slave who had spent some time in Spain (Andalucía), who had been baptized in the Catholic religion, and who could speak the Spanish language before arriving in the Americas.

5. Also from other provinces (Loja, Los Ríos, etc.).

6. They call themselves Chachis, but were called Cayapas by their indigenous neighbors. The latter is still in use today among non-Chachis.

7. *Catanga* and *marimba*, for example, are, respectively, a fish trap and a xylophone.

8. I differentiate *décima* (a ten-line stanza) from *Décima* (the Afro-Esmeraldian poem of forty-four lines).

9. Ten-line stanzas.

10. I mean here the entire poem.

11. In Spanish, "Margarita" is a synonym of "pearl." In verse 31, *Tercero* is a reference to Philip III.

12. The gloss was also popular in Portugal.

13. Provincialisms are quite abundant in Afro-Esmeraldian Décimas.

REFERENCES

Asante, Molefi K. 1990. *Kemet, Afrocentricity, and Knowledge*. Trenton, N.J.: Africa World Press.

Baehr, Rudolf. 1970. *Manual de Versificación Española*. Traducción y adaptación de Wagner y F. Lopez Estrada, transl. Madrid: Editorial Gredos.

Barrero, Jacinto. 1979a. Costumbres, Ritualismos y Creencias en Torno a los Muertos en el Campo de San Lorenzo. *Apertura* 2:25–49.

———. 1979b. Creencias y Costumbres. *Apertura* 3:26–41.

Barret, S. A. 1925. *The Cayapa Indians of Ecuador*. 2 vols. New York: Heye Foundation.

Bastide, Roger. 1971. *African Civilizations in the New World*. New York: Harper and Row.

Bowser, Frederick P. 1977. *El Esclavo Africano en el Perú Colonial, 1524–1650*. Mexico City: *Siglo Veintiuno, Colección América Nuestra*.

Cabello Balboa, Miguel. 1965. *Obras*. Volume I. Quito: Editora Ecuatoriana.

Carrasco, Eulalia. 1983. *El Pueblo Chachi*. Quito: Abya-Yala.

Coba, Carlos Alberto. 1980. *Literatura Popular Afroecuatoriana*. Otavalo: Instituto Otavaleño de Antropología, Colección Pendoneros.

Cuche, Denys. 1981. *Pérou Nègre*. Paris: L'Harmattan.

Curtin, P. 1969. *The Atlantic Slave Trade: A Census*. Madison: University of Wisconsin Press.

Escalante, Aquiles. 1954. Notas sobre el Palenque de San Basilio. *Divulgaciones Etnológicas* IV(1).

Friedemann, Nina S., and Jorge Morales Gómez. 1966–69. Contextos Religiosos en un Area Negra de Barbacoas (Nariño, Colombia). *Revista Colombiana de Folklor* 4(10):63–83.

———. 1974. *Minería Descendencia y Obrería Artesanal: Litoral Pacífico Colombia*. Bogotá: Univ. Nac. Facultad de Ciencia Humanas.

———. 1978. "Troncos Among Black Miners in Colombia." In *Miners and Mining in the Americas*. T. G. a. W. Culver, ed. Manchester University Press.

García Salazar, Juan. 1979. *Décimas. Una Manifestación de la Poesía Oral en los Grupos Negros del Ecuador*. Quito: Centro de Investigación y Cultura del Banco Central del Ecuador, Poligrafiados.

———. 1984. Poesía Negra en la Costa de Ecuador. *Desarrollo de Base. Revista de la Fundación Interamericana* 8(1).

———. 1984. Black Poetry of Coastal Ecuador. *Grassroots Development. Journal of the Inter-American Foundation* 8(1):30–37.

Gilroy, Paul. 1993. *The Black Atlantic: Modernity and Double Consciousness*. Cambridge, Massachusetts: Harvard University Press.

———. 1995. "Roots and Routes: Black Identity as an Outernational Project." In *Racial and Ethnic Identity: Psychological Development and Creative Expression*. H. W. Harris, Howard Blue, and Ezra Griffith, eds. New York: Routledge.

Glissant, Edouard. 1990. *Poétiques de la Relation*. Paris: Gallimard.

Gomez Restrepo, Antonio. 1938. *Historia de la Literatura Colombiana*. Bogotá: Imprenta Nacional.

Hidalgo Alzamora, Laura. 1982. *Décimas Esmeraldeñas*. Quito: Banco Central del Ecuador.

Jácome B., Nicanor. 1978. "Un Modelo Diferente de Vinculación al Mercado Mundial: El Caso de Esmeraldas." In *Segundo Encuentro de Historia y Realidad Económica y Social del Ecuador*, Vol. III. Cuenca: Universidad de Cuenca y Banco Central del Ecuador.

Jácome B., Nicanor, and José Vicente Zevallos. 1979. La Formación del Estrato Popular de Esmeraldas en el Contexto del Desarrollo Provincial. *Revista Ciencias Sociales (Quito)* III(10–11):89–144.

Janner, Hans. 1943. La Glosa Española. Estudio Histórico de su Métrica y de sus Temas. *Revista de Filología Española* XXVII:181–232.

———. 1946. *La Glosa en el Siglo de Oro: Una Antología*. Madrid.

Le Gentil, Pierre. 1952. La Poesie lyrique espagnole et portugaise á la fin du Moyen-Age. *Les Formes* (Deuxième Partie):291–304.

Lewis, Reina. 1996. *Gendering Orientalism: Race, Femininity and Representation*. London: Routledge.

Mille y Gimenez, Juan. 1937. Sobre la Fecha de la Invención de la Décima o Espinela. *Hispanic Review* V:40–51.

Mintz, Sidney W., and Richard Price. 1992. *The Birth of African-American Culture: An Anthropological Perspective*. Boston: Beacon Press.

Pacheco, Juan Manuel. 1959. *Los Jesuitas en Colombia*. Volume I (1567–1654). Bogotá.

Palacios Preciado, Jorge. 1973. *La Trata de Negros por Cartagena de Indias*. Tunja: Ediciones "La Rana y El Aguila."

Preciado, Antonio. 1961. *Jolgorio*. Quito: Editorial Casa de la Cultura Ecuatoriana.

Quiroga, Diego. 1994. Saints, Virgins, and the Devil: Witchcraft, Magic, and Healing in the Northern Coast of Ecuador. Ph.D. Dissertation, Dept. of Anthropology, University of Illinois.

Rahier, Jean. 1987. La Décima. Poesía Oral Negra del Ecuador. Quito: Ediciones Abya Yala and Centro Cultural Afro-Ecuatoriano.

Rivera, Freddy. 1986. "La Comuna de Negros del Río Santiago en Cien Años de Historia." In Campesinado y Organización en Esmeraldas. F. Rivera, ed. Cuaderno de discusión popular n°11. Quito: Centro Andino de Acción Popular (CAAP) y Organización Campesina Muisne-Esmeraldas (OCAME).

Santa Cruz, Nicomedes. 1964. Cumana, Décimas de Pie Forzado y Poemas. Lima: Editorial J. Mejía Baca.

———. 1971. Décimas y Poemas, Antología. Lima: Campadónico.

———. 1982. La Décima en el Perú. Lima: Instituto de Estudios Peruanos.

Sharp, William Frederick. 1976. Slavery on the Spanish Frontier: The Colombian Chocó, 1680–1810. Norman: University of Oklahoma Press.

Spitzer, L. 1943–1944. The Prologue to the "Lais" of Marie de France and Medieval Poetics. Modern Philology XLI:96–102.

Wade, Peter. 1993. Blackness and Race Mixture: The Dynamics of Racial Identity in Colombia. Baltimore: Johns Hopkins University Press.

West, Robert. 1957. The Pacific Lowlands of Colombia: A Negroid Area of the American Tropics. Baton Rouge: Louisiana State University Press.

———. 1952. Colonial Placer Mining in Colombia. Baton Rouge: Louisiana State University Press.

Whitten, Norman. 1974. Black Frontiersmen: A South American Case. Cambridge, Mass.: Schenkman Pub. Co.

19

THE (T)ERROR OF INVISIBILITY: ELLISON AND CRUZ E SOUZA

Niyi Afolabi

The rich complexity of African experience in the Americas with particular reference to the African-American and African-Brazilian has been separately explored by critics. While the thrust of African diaspora literary historiography as manifest in these works resides in the marginalization of African presence, no attempt has been made to explore the commonality of this unique experience, especially in the literary criticism of both nations. My title takes the position that while ambivalence pervades the art of Ellison and Cruz e Souza, these writers are not ambiguous in expressing the "error" and "terror" of being invisible, as their parodic titles aptly capture.

This essay takes John F. Danby's[1] premise that "Literature is what happens in a man certainly. What can happen 'in' him, however, will be partly conditioned by what has happened 'to' him." I thus propose that the theme of *invisibility* and subversive ambiguity are persuasive theoretical foundations upon which to formulate a possible aesthetic in African-American and African-Brazilian literatures. Ralph Ellison's *Invisible Man* and Cruz e Souza's "Emparedado" ("Walled In") will serve as my representative texts, given their textual and contextual parallels.

HISTORICIZING INVISIBILITY

Invisibility as a thematic concern is indebted to both the history and culture of the African Diaspora, hence the legacy of slavery, abolition, and subsequent "double consciousness" (à la Du Bois) which informs invisibility as a state of consciousness. The African Diaspora has been nothing less than a laboratory of dispossession, dehumanization, and alienation. While the optimist would have us believe that, as with the colonized African on the continent, there are more gains than losses, the fact is that we cannot understand the feelings of the slave or the colonized until we have spent one second in the galleys or been displaced from our roots and culture.

The racial consciousness thus becomes for both Ellison and Cruz e Souza a necessary muse in the appreciation of the African diasporic experience in the United States and Brazil, respectively. While the case of Brazil is often portrayed as peculiar given the fallacious Portuguese philosophy of miscegenation as portrayed by Gilberto Freyre's "lusotropicalismo" in *Casa-Grande e Senzala*[2] (*The Masters and the Slaves*, 1933), Franklin and Moss, Jr. argue to the contrary, while alluding to the *Palmares* insurrection, that "one of the most desperate bids for freedom in the New World occurred in Brazil" (*From Slavery to Freedom* 51). David T. Haberly's comparative analysis in *Three Sad Races* captures the commonality and possible contrast between the Brazilian and North American racial experience, especially as translated in literature:

> And, despite the essential similarity of the racial backgrounds of the United States and Brazil, Americans have illogically but decisively defined themselves and their nation in terms of the white majority alone. American literature, with pitifully few exceptions, has been written by whites, for whites, and about whites. Non-white characters have been marginal at best, serving only to highlight the white heroes or heroines, the only conceivable national symbols. (2)

The implied stereotypical image of blackness in the white mind is what Toni Morrison explores in what she disturbingly and deliberately terms "Romancing the Shadow" in her *Playing in the Dark*. In an attempt to characterize American literature, its "antithetical" (35) portrayal of the American Dream, Morrison suggests that slavery and blackness as engaged by white writers became a romantic ideal, an escape from history, an instrument in the exploration of the "terror of human freedom" (37), which indeed was an outlet for overcoming their own fears and insecurities:

> Black slavery enriched the country's creative possibilities. For in that construction of blackness *and* enslavement could be found not only the not-free but also, with the dramatic polarity created by skin color, the projection of the not-me. The result was a playground for the imagination. (38)

Invisibility is thus not far from a fabrication or a necessary creation to buttress the image of the white man as the ideal American while excluding the Africanist presence or at least minimizing its place in the construction of American literary imagination, which Morrison sums up as the "highly problematic construction of the American as a new white man" (39). Morrison's position is that invisibility and visibility are, like black and white racial experience, a dialogical relationship, not a dialectical one.

Morrison's position responds to those critics who tend to frown at any mention of race in critical discourse as divisive, ideological, and sentimental. Morrison puts it graphically by comparing invisibility to the metaphor of the black hand being left intact despite erasure of the handprints and fingerprints with a "rhetorical acid":

> The imaginative and historical terrain upon which early American writers journeyed is in large measure shaped by the presence of the racial other. Statements to the contrary, insisting on the meaninglessness of race to the American identity, are themselves full of meaning. The world does not become raceless or will not become unracialized by assertion. The act of enforcing racelessness in literary discourse is itself a racial act. Pouring rhetorical acid on the fingers of a black hand may indeed destroy the prints, but not the hand. Besides, what happens in that violent, self-serving act of erasure to the hands, the fingers, the fingerprints of the one who does the pouring? Do they remain acid-free? The literature itself suggests otherwise.
>
> Explicit or implicit, the Africanist informs in compelling and inescapable ways the texture of American literature. It is a dark and abiding presence, there for the literary imagination as both a visible and an invisible mediating force. (46)

Morrison goes on to say that "Race," indeed, has become a metaphor which cannot be divorced from the "construction of Americanness" (47). The Africanist presence is such an inalienable part of the definition of American literature that invisibility as a theme becomes an irony, as race is definitely one of the structuring tropes of Americanness, hence Morrison's call for a quadripartite investigation into the import of the Africanist presence in American letters. First is the need to examine the extent to which the encounter of white writers with Africanism has enabled them to "think about themselves" (51). Second is the use of Africanist idiom to defamiliarize or express tension between "speech and speechlessness" (52). Third is the need to explore the strategic use of an Africanist character in propagating whiteness and fourth is the need to analyze the "manipulation of the Africanist narrative" to represent one's own humanity (53). These "topics for investigation" present a forum for dialogue rather than discord in the approach of race consciousness via the theme of invisibility in American literature.

The Brazilian experience of invisibility reflects the national character of contrasts as equally translated into the racial question. While the North American invisibility is derived from a deliberate denial of the "invisible" person's humanity by the dominant structure, the Brazilian case presents more a crisis of identity and consciousness from the viewpoint of "whitening" as an officially sponsored policy intended to eliminate the "color problem" in Brazilian society. As Haberly rightly points out, "much of Brazil's literature has been preoccupied with an anguished search for a viable racial identity—a search that has been both personal and national in scope" (*Three Sad Races* 2). This brings about a constantly changing identity or its ultimate crisis in terms of the varying shades of black and white:

> The far more complex Brazilian system operates in a very different way, but a system of racial categories, equally founded upon prejudice toward nonwhite peoples, does exist. The racial identity of any individual—his or her position on the continuum—is not necessarily fixed and immutable, as is so often in the United States, but is constantly redefined by the perceptions that can vary greatly from region to region and within different social settings. (3)

From this comparative historical background, the question of invisibility as addressed by Ellison and Cruz e Souza in their respective texts and contexts presents a common problematic, that of representation. While the reception of both works will be discussed later, it is worth examining Todd Lieber's[3] seminal article, "Ralph Ellison and the Metaphor of Invisibility in Black Literary Tradition," which provides a recent (pre-eighties) evaluation of the theme of invisibility as a theoretical framework in African-American literature. Lieber observes that "Ellison has given the metaphor of invisibility its most complete articulation" (87) but then opines that the form of *Invisible Man* is not necessarily new for it has been used by Afro-American writers in the treatment of their cultural experiences in America.

For Lieber, Ellison's *Invisible Man* becomes a symbolic articulation of African-American cultural experience in America via the inalienable question of race and cultural identity in American literature. Lieber identifies two types of invisibility: the "involuntary" (innate) and the "mask-wearing." The former is imposed by the society that refuses to recognize the humanity of the hero while the latter is self-imposed by the "conscious adoption of a false identity" (87) by the invisible person. Lieber acknowledges Ellison's achievement as the ability to synthesize these two approaches in *Invisible Man*:

> Ellison's primary contribution lies in the recognition that mask wearing and inherent invisibility are related aspects of the same problem. With this insight he is able to fuse these two approaches, which have for the most part been treated separately, into a new imaginative synthesis and move beyond despair to an affirmative

resolution of the difficulties and paradoxes involved in being an "invisible man." (87)

CRITICAL RECEPTION: FROM MYTH TO REALITY

Although a century apart, Ralph Ellison (1914–1994) and João da Cruz e Souza (1861–1898) share a common symbolistic imagination through their use of both intrinsic ambiguity and rhetorical strategies. The affinity of these two writers goes beyond their form of writing to their personality and thematic concerns. Ellison is a contemporary Afro-American writer whom Robert O'Meally has considered an adaptor of symbolism to "enrich the texture and meaning of his work" (*African American Writers* 118), while Cruz e Souza is the Afro-Brazilian leader of Brazilian Symbolism.

In terms of influences, Ellison is truly eclectic in his search of his own "form" and, as O'Meally points out, *Invisible Man* defies one critical method for it "owes as much to the symbolist tradition of Melville and Hawthorne as it does to the vernacular tradition of Mark Twain and Hemingway" (118). In the same fashion, Cruz e Souza, primarily a poet, was compelled to prove he could write like the Parnassians while still being his symbolist self, despite his African heritage. While my concern here is to compare the theme of invisibility in both writers, it is interesting to see the commonality of critical reception, from the myth to reality, and how these writers responded to such criticism of their respective works.

The metaphor of being "emparedado" (walled in) adequately captures the critical ambience of Cruz e Souza's poetical output, which indeed led to his response as portrayed in his poetic prose, "Emparedado." Faced with social rejection, a victim of racism and prejudice due to his African race, Cruz e Souza constantly strove not only to overcome the image of "inferiority" and literary "impotence" given his birth into slavery (1861), poverty, and loss of his entire family, but also to reinvent his literary reputation and defend his African origin.

The critical hostility was such that his artistic merit was diminished by reviewers like F. Margarida[4] who repudiates Cruz e Souza's works for their audacity and novelty and for refusing to follow the precepts of the "masters": "Nothing is new or admirable about Mr. Cruz e Souza's sonnet except for cacophonies and errors of metrification as recommended by reasonable, respectable and outstanding critics" (Montenegro 37). Cruz e Souza responds to his critics in "Emparedado," posthumously published in a collection titled *Evocações* (1898), where he scornfully ridicules their pettiness, mediocrity, and corruption: "Era uma politicazinha engenhosa de mediocres, de tacanhos, de perfeitos imbecilizados ou cínicos, que fariam da Arte um jogo caprichoso, maneirosos, para arranjar relações"

(*Obra Completa* 654). ("It was an ingenious device of narrow-minded mediocres, perfect imbeciles or cynics who have turned Art into a capricious game for selfish interests.")

In sharp contrast to the unfavorable reviews, David Haberly suggests that Cruz e Souza's difficulty with recognition in his time does not lie with his unquestionable genius, but with his blackness: "His black vitality and intelligence had been encircled and suppressed by white erudition and aesthetics, his whitened intellect was trapped within a black body, that black body was surrounded by an alien and hostile western white world (*Three Sad Races* 107). David Haberly equally dismisses Roger Bastide's anthropological misconception as simplistic when he characterizes Cruz e Souza's works as an effort at self-whitening in his article "A nostalgia do branco"[5] ("White Nostalgia"). Carlos Dante de Moraes's critical position complements that of Haberly in that it sees a more utilitarian function in Cruz e Souza's poetry: "The first condition of Cruz e Souza's poetry is his African origin. The second, his mystical conception of art. The third, his immense and perhaps tragic share of pain" (Coutinho 271).

In respect to Ellison, the critical reception was somewhat diversified by the mere fact that while Cruz e Souza had to contend with principally white critics who had the monopoly of the critical enterprise, Ellison had to deal with both white and black, left and right critics, all expressing their approval and disapproval for Ellison's *Invisible Man* (1952). Unlike Cruz e Souza, whose challenge was racial in nature, the central issue for Ellison was that of representation.

The allegations of ambivalence and lack of social realism are some of the critical echoes which call into question Ellison's commitment. Ellison, like Cruz e Souza, responds to this prescriptive criticism by using the very art of ambiguity that he has been accused of to defend his position when he contends that "I wasn't, and I am not primarily concerned with injustice, but with art," only to add almost self-contradictorily, "I recognize no dichotomy between art and protest" (*Shadow and Act* 169).

Jacqueline Covo's two-period classification of Ellison's critical reception in *The Blinking Eye: Ralph Waldo Ellison* (1974), namely 1952–1964 and 1965–1971, provides a foundation for my overview, while I take the liberty of adding a third period, 1972–1979. The first period is defined by the publication of *Invisible Man* (1952) and *Shadow and Act* (1953), which coincided with white-dominated or "reductionist" criticism. The second was the aftermath of Black Power and nationalist movements, hence its political orientation. The third was marked by intense black scholarship of the "black aesthetic," especially the metaphorical conceptualization of invisibility as a recurrent thematic concern in African-American literary tradition.

Of the three reviews selected for the first period, namely *Book Review Digest* (1952), *The Negro History Bulletin* (1953), and *Saturday Review*

(1964), the first was particularly informative in that it combined twelve different reviews from other journals and newspapers into one review piece. Essentially, this is a positive review in terms of Ellison's artistic accomplishment and attempt at universality. The humanist character of *Invisible Man* is rightly evoked by Edith Fowke when she considers the work "a remarkably vivid and compelling story about characters who are confused, deceived and betrayed—but who remain indisputably human" (284).

In sharp contrast to Fowke, Irving Howe considers *Invisible Man* "an angry book filled with symbolism. . . . written in an unusual style dealing with events more than people, it is not a 'protest novel' " (284). This critical claim of Ellisonian lack of commitment is further accentuated by C. J. Rolos's charges of "occasional overwriting, stretches of fuzzy thinking, and tendency to waver confusingly between realism and surrealism" (284).

For the second phase, I have selected the special Ralph Ellison edition of the *CLA Journal*[6] with a focus on articles by Darwin Turner, Phillis R. Klotman, and Eleanor R. Wilner, respectively. These three articles sum up the underlining and interconnected metaphors that give texture and meaning to the Ellisonian text: Sight, Running, and Ritual. The metaphor of "Sight" as proposed by Turner[7] contends that "invisibility" is either a deliberate "refusal or inability of white Americans to see the black hero" (258). The metaphor of "Running" as interpreted by Klotman[8] is both a therapeutic "inward journey" to self-discovery and an escape from the pressure of invisibility. Klotman sums up *Invisible Man* as "the culmination of the Running Man metaphor, the electric 'umbilical cord' that connects running men past to those of present" (277). The metaphor of "Ritual" as used by Wilner[9] implies the physical and psychological process of writing oneself from invisibility into visibility. Given the topicality of the third phase to the exploration of ambiguity as form in the two writers, I will discuss this in the following section.

AMBIGUITY AS FORM IN ELLISON AND CRUZ E SOUZA

The paradoxes of invisibility constitute both an artistic challenge and an opportunity for the writer, as Ellison and Cruz e Souza exemplify. Ambiguity becomes an experimental form for arriving at a point of harmony and equilibrium in the depiction of these realities. In his "Hidden Name and Complex Fate," Ellison proposes a creative "forgiveness" of the past and present "outrages symbolized by the denial and the division" (*Shadow and Act* 149) which ultimately creates a state of invisibility. For Ellison, the Afro-American experience of "ambiguities and hypocrisies of human history as they have been played out in the United States" (149) must be transformed into art through the use of imagination.

Invisibility thus poses a tripartite problem—the physical, the psycho-

logical, and the therapeutical. The last complexity puts an aesthetic burden on the African-American writer, which Ellison rightly calls the
"struggle with form" (145). Drawing from his personal experience as an
African-American writer, Ellison engages the challenges faced by the black
writer in white America, which Du Bois captures vividly, as follows: "One
ever feels this twoness—an American, a Negro; two souls, two thoughts,
two unreconciled strivings; two warring ideals in one dark body, whose
dogged strength alone keeps it from being torn asunder" (*The Souls of
Black Folks* 14).

The challenge, Ellison argues, is how the African-American writer
deals with the "implicit pluralism" (165) of Americanness and the elusive-
ness of the "American promise." In this regard, the search for identity becomes both an aesthetic goal and a creative process where the resort to
folk tradition is not only an artistic experimentation but a compulsion for
a faithful depiction of the African-American social reality:

> And with all of this there still remained the specific concerns of
> literature. Among these is the need of exploring new possibilities of
> language which would allow it to retain that flexibility and fidelity
> to the common speech which has been its glory since Mark Twain.
> For me this meant learning to add to it the wonderful resources of
> Negro American speech and idiom and to bring into range as fully
> and eloquently as possible the complex reality of the American
> experience as it is shaped and was shaped by the lives of my own
> people. (165)

Ellisonian ambiguity is thus better defined as "flexibility" to explore a
wider range of possibilities in his artistic resolution of invisibility.

Cruz e Souza's ambiguity stems more from his audience and identity
than his chosen form. As much as the symbolist would have loved to use
the African-Brazilian idiom to communicate his ideas and emotions, he
was faced with the challenge of nonacceptance and hostility from the Par-
nassian establishment, who refused to acknowledge his leadership in the
Brazilian Symbolist movement; all he represented was blackness, which
the Brazilian elite could not reconcile with his artistic refinement and
achievement. As Haberly observed: "He was justifiably proud of his ability
and accomplishments, but the white world was shocked and angered by
his display of pride, which seemed aggressive and insolent. Cruz e Souza
moreover, refused to make any gesture of compromise" (*Three Sad Races*
101). It was the challenge to prove himself as a competent Afro-Brazilian
writer that led to his "alienation" and ambiguity in relation to his audience. The question was, if he wrote in a sophisticated European tongue
alien to the majority of African-Brazilians who were mostly illiterates,
who was he writing for?

Given this background, Cruz e Souza opened himself to ambiguity on both sides of the racial spectrum. There were, on the one hand, those Brazilian elites who accused him of being deliberately sophisticated because he aspired to be white (Roger Bastide) in order to move up in the social stratum, and on the other hand there were those who claimed that by his use and repeated references to white colors and symbols in his works, he rejected his African origin. None of these allegations is verifiable, for a cursory look at Cruz e Souza's works reveals a deliberate juxtaposition of the black-white metaphors or codes for contrastive effects, in the Morrisonian style of *Playing in the Dark*.

An example of this deliberate ambiguity is found in his first volume of poetry, *Broqüeis* (1893) (*Shields*), whose thematic concern is conflict. There is an internal struggle for perfection and the ideal as faced by the despised and humiliated black race:

> Several longer poems present the ambiguous ideal of physical and moral purity (in the white symbolic code) and of whiteness (the black symbolic code); the sonnet sequences that fall between these longer poems explore the consequences of that double ideal, spiraling down to the level of human impurity before rising again to the sphere of perfection. (Haberly, 113)

"Antífona" ("Antiphony"), *Broqüeis*'s opening poem, sums up this conflict between the "imperfect" reality of blackness and the unconscious obsession with "perfection," symbolized in whiteness. A juxtaposition of opposites—light and darkness, whiteness and blackness—pervades the entire literary output of Cruz e Souza. For both writers, the missing link in ambiguity as form lies in the reconciliation of the Du Boisian "double consciousness" or "double presence" which, indeed, justifies my title. Invisibility is an error in perception on the part of those who choose not to see others but themselves; the terror lies in how such deliberate invisibility is reflective of the potentially dehumanizing effect of this attitude on the entire human condition, whether acknowledged or not.

SYMBOLS AND METAPHORS OF INVISIBILITY: *INVISIBLE MAN* AND "EMPAREDADO"

Ellison and Cruz e Souza exemplify Kenneth Burke's definition of humans as symbol-using animals in his "Language as Symbolic Action," not only in terms of identity but also in relation to symbols of authority. Given the preoccupation of both writers with the issue of identity, items 4 and 8 of Burke's "Twelve Propositions" in *Philosophy of Literary Form* become quite relevant. Burke's item 4 states that "the concept for treating relations to symbols of authority is *Identity*," while item 8 expands on this proposition with regard to symbol, language, artist, and audience as a complex interrelationship: "Identity and our study of it is a mystification. We can only attempt to resolve the conflicts caused by the complexity of identity through symbolic action, linguistic action, and the implicit commands of the artist to audience and self" (308).

Ellison complements Burke's position by emphasizing the "complex formulation" of language in his article "Twentieth-Century Fiction and the Black Mask of Humanity," where he insists that every word, as translated into a proverb, play, or novel, has an inherent power of ambivalence which is manipulated or slanted by the writer, as the stereotypical representation of African-Americans in American literature attests:

> The essence of the word is its ambivalence, and in fiction it is never so effective and revealing as when both potentials are operating simultaneously, as when it mirrors both good and bad, as when it blows both hot and cold in the same breath. Thus it is unfortunate for the Negro that the most powerful formulations of modern American fictional words have been so slanted against him that when he approaches for a glimpse of himself he discovers an image drained of humanity. (*Shadow and Act* 25)

From the foregoing, it is interesting to examine how Ellison and Cruz e Souza have used language symbolically or metaphorically to represent their respective concerns with invisibility. Ellison's contention that the "slanting" or stereotypical representation of the African-American image was more to console the white man than to strip the invisible person of all humanity, becomes a point of departure in the discovery of the writer's intentionality in *Invisible Man*: "A people must define itself, and minorities have the responsibility of having their ideals and images recognized as part of the composite image which is that of the still forming American people" (*Shadow and Act* 44).

Invisibility as a thematic concern is thus, for Ellison, an attempt at self-definition and possible escape from entrapment within the contradictions and ambiguity of symbols and images of invisibility. These metaphors, originally used to define the invisible person, are in turn subverted by the invisible protagonist's conscious assumption of the role of invisibility as a means of survival. Through symbolizing, the invisible person searches for visibility by embarking on a conscious rite of passage to reconstruct the fragmented self. Ellison addresses his use of symbols as intentionality in the construction of invisibility when he confesses in "The Art of Fiction,"

> The symbols and their connections were known to me. I began it with a chart of three-part division. It was a conceptual frame with

most of the ideas and some incidents indicated. The three parts represent the narrator's movement from, using Kenneth Burke's terms, purpose to passion to perception. These three major sections are built up of smaller units of three which mark the course of the action and which depend for their development upon what I hoped was a consistent and developing motivation. However, you'll note that the maximum insight on the hero's part isn't reached until the final section. After all, it's a novel about innocence and human error, a struggle through illusion to reality. (177)

The "illusion" and "reality" metaphors provide the reader with insight into the odyssey of the invisible protagonist as he moves from unconscious invisibility to conscious or voluntary invisibility. Each event or encounter further prevents the protagonist from discovering his true identity. The characters he comes into contact with either mislead him or serve as confirming agents of his invisibility. *Invisible Man* begins with the invisible protagonist affirming his humanity through an objective exposé of vivid circumstances which deliberately distort his visibility:

I am an invisible man. No, I am not a spook like those who haunted Edgar Allan Poe; nor am I one of your Hollywood-movie ectoplasms. I am a man of substance, of flesh and bone, fiber and liquids—and I might even be said to possess a mind. I am invisible, understand, simply because people refuse to see me. Like the bodiless heads you see sometimes in circus sideshows, it is as though I have been surrounded by mirrors of hard, distorting glass. When they approach me they see only my surroundings, themselves, or figments of their imagination—indeed, everything and anything except me.
    Nor is my invisibility exactly a matter of a biochemical accident to my epidermis. That invisibility to which I refer occurs because of a particular disposition of the eyes of those with whom I come in contact. A matter of the construction of the *inner* eyes, those eyes with which they look through their physical eyes upon reality. (3)

In this opening passage of the text, the protagonist juxtaposes both his undistorted image of self by affirming his humanity when he says he is "a man of substance, of flesh and bone," and the distorted self as depicted in the statement "I am an invisible man." This last symbolic image and identity that have been imposed on him by others often blind him to his own true identity. The coming to terms with this imposed invisibility suggests that the protagonist has not always been aware of his invisibility but only assumes the role following the contradiction of his world in order to resolve this conflict; hence his conscious choice of the "underground" as home.

The protagonist's home, a coal cellar located on the outskirts of Harlem, also depicts a dichotomy between the individual consciousness and social reality. His marginality becomes a conscious and symbolic action in the creative resolution of contradictions. It is in this conscious marginal state that he is able to reflect on his past and confusing symbolic illusion to arrive at a moment of self-discovery and acceptance of reality. Ellison's *Invisible Man*, as William Schafer points out in "Ralph Ellison and the Birth of the Anti-Hero," does not intend to blame the protagonist's experiences on society but to show "*how* he is affected, what the view is from inside the prison of blackness and invisibility" (118).

By the time he is writing, the invisible hero is no longer naive or blind, for he is able to reflect on his trajectory of invisibility and the erroneous and contradictory vision he hitherto had about social reality:

> It goes a long way back, some twenty years. All my life I had been looking for something, and everywhere I turned someone tried to tell me what it was. I accepted their answers too, though they were often in contradiction and even self-contradictory. I was naive. I was looking for myself and asking everyone except myself questions which I, and only I, could answer. It took me a long time and much painful boomeranging of my expectations to achieve a realization everyone else appears to have been born with: That I am nobody but myself. But I had to first discover that I am an invisible man! (*Invisible Man* 15)

Like Ellison's "invisible" protagonist, who chooses to accept his presumed invisibility by going underground to subvert social reality and discover his own humanity, Cruz e Souza's "walled in" narrator recognizes his existential drama as a member of a society which imposes limitations on his humanity by virtue of color. The "four walls" metaphor in "Emparedado" betrays the plot structure of the narrative, as the narrator identifies four main walls or obstacles which keep him from "running" (as in the *Invisible Man*'s "Keep this Nigger-Boy running"), physically and spiritually restless within the four walls of the society. This creates a feeling of stagnation and immobility, an enraging state of being captive, turning from one wall to the other:

> If you move towards the right, you are bound to be afflicted by the horrendous and vast wall of *Egoism and Prejudice*! If you move to the left, another wall, that of *Science and Criticism*, even higher than the former. . . . If you move forward, still another wall, made of *Resentment and Impotence*. . . . If finally, you move backwards, oh! yet another wall, closing everything, that horrible wall of *Narrow-mindedness and Ignorance*, you will live in the cold of absolute terror. (*Emparedado* 664)

This synoptic exposition of human bondage as expressed by Cruz e Souza satirizes social injustices which create such a state of being, while at the same time protesting the impact of such limitation on his artistic creation as an African-Brazilian writer. The blatant racism and prejudice typical of Brazilian and North American societies are further highlighted in a letter Cruz e Souza wrote to a friend confiding his pain and anguish. This time, instead of "walls" he refers to "portas" or doors:

> All the doors and passage-ways along the road of life are closed to me, a poor Aryan artist, yes Aryan, because I acquired, by systematic study, all the qualities of the great race. To what end? A sad black man, detested by those with culture, beaten down by society, always humiliated, cast out of every bed, spat upon in every household like some evil leper! But how? To be an artist with this color? (Magalhães Júnior, 130–131)

These rhetorical questions echo that of Ellison's invisible hero when he asks, alluding to Louis Armstrong, "What have I done to be so black and blue?" The answer, Ellison would argue, does not necessarily lie outside of but within the invisible person, for upon resolving the contradictions of his invisibility, Ellison's protagonist confesses: "I carried my sickness and though for a long time I tried to place it in the outside world, the attempt to write it down shows me that at least half of it lay within me" (*Invisible Man* 575).

This is probably where Ellison and Cruz e Souza agree—and yet differ significantly. For while the invisible hero in *Invisible Man* moves from unconscious to conscious invisibility, the invisible narrator in "Emparedado" does not believe in such a development. Rather, he contends that his invisibility makes him only a dreamer despite his white erudition, for he is still considered a poor black man. Writing about it only makes him more angry. It does not cure him of his "sickness." By placing his invisibility in the outside world, he is equally naive to think he could overcome this sickness by simply becoming "literate" or "immersed," to use Stepto's terms (*From Behind the Veil* 163). Where both agree, however, is in the recognition that invisibility is a sickness, and writing helps one alleviate and accept the state. It does not deny or negate it.

THE (T)ERROR OF INVISIBILITY: UNITY OF AFRICAN-AMERICAN AND AFRICAN-BRAZILIAN AESTHETIC

From unconscious to conscious invisibility, from conscious invisibility to conscious protest, the two protagonists of *Invisible Man* and "Emparedado" share one commonality, among others: the underground meta-

phor. Although *Invisible Man* offers more possibilities for the exploration
of invisibility, "Emparedado" provides the Brazilian perspective from the
viewpoint of a symbolist writer. While Ellison's invisible hero confronts
his invisibility through introspection, hibernation, and self-discovery,
Cruz e Souza rebels evocatively through a catalog of protests of which I
cite but a few: "A fundamentally unpleasant world is nothing but a geometric formula" (662); "I do not belong to the old genealogical lineage
of standard intellectualization" (662); "Against official ignominy of the
World, against perverse and hypocritical vice, against artificial universal
sentiment disguised in Liberty and Justice" (659). The evocative tone of
"Emparedado" reveals the symbolic appeal of Cruz e Souza in that it allows a dialogue between the writer and the society he accuses of dehumanization and his invisibility. Cruz e Souza's revolt goes beyond his immediate invisibility: indeed, he becomes a universal spokesperson against
all physical and psychological limitations, especially in the creative process which serves as the outlet for his anguish.

The theme of invisibility, coupled with subversive ambiguity as explored by Ellison and Cruz e Souza, provides the reader with some basic
assumptions about the African-American and African-Brazilian aesthetic.
John F. Danby's original premise (as alluded to in my introduction) that
there is a direct relationship between psychological and physical experiences of blackness and by extension, invisibility, becomes evident in both
texts. Richard Jackson, in *Black Literature and Humanism*, proposes Latin
American humanism as a model for "true American voices": "The black
presence has been a positive presence, and to read black literature is to
understand what it means to survive the inhumanities of the earth. . . .
Black voices in Latin America, by affirming black humanity, become models of what true American voices should be" (128). This complex calling
into question of the inhumanity of invisibility as defined in the historical
context of black experience in both Brazil and the United States explains
my position that from the perspectives of both Ellison and Cruz e Souza,
invisibility is erroneous and terrible.

The *error* derives from the primordial experience of subjugation and
dehumanization, where human beings are reduced to chattel and objects
of labor and thereby denied of their humanity. I am here referring to slavery and the stereotypical image of the African or African-American which,
indeed, is what Danby refers to as "what has happened 'to' him." This
error perpetuates a myth of inferiority-superiority that eventually translates into a master-servant relationship, as both texts under discussion testify. In fact, the humiliating experience brings about a divided self, a crisis
of consciousness and of identity which only finds meaning in an imposed
invisible personality. As J. J. Healy aptly observes in "Literature, Removal
and the Theme of Invisibility in America": "The curse of invisibility has

forced all Americans to do time on the cross of invisibility. That is part of the complexity and ambiguity of the fate" (135).

Cruz e Souza equally contemplates this "error of invisibility" in "Psicologia do feio" ("Psychology of the Ugly"), when he comes to terms with the contradictions of his erudition, intelligence, and sensibility in relation to his race. Although he has mastered European culture and language, he is still not accepted as an equal partner; his African heritage continues to be his permanent cross: "You come straight out of Darwin, I can clearly see your overhung brow, the heritage of the Orangutan; your lustful leer; the animalistic and rapacious air of the ape" (*Obra Completa* 411). That blackness becomes a "complex fate" to be borne by African-Americans and African-Brazilians, as the above allusions attest, can be better appreciated by analyzing how this error graduates into the terror of invisibility.

The *terror* of invisibility is what Danby refers to as "what can happen 'in' him," which becomes the psychological legacy of slavery, dispossession, and depersonalization. This is succinctly dramatized in the Golden Day episode when the Vet engages the invisible protagonist in a process of revelation, consciousness, and "literacy" vis-à-vis his image of Norton, which continues to blind him to his own individuality and humanity. While the Vet stresses that the fact that Norton is "only a man" and should not be treated as if he were some god, the invisible protagonist remains skeptical given the psychological damage already instilled in him by the former in relation to his being. As a result, the invisible man plays in the frontiers of ambiguity by not clearly accepting the Vet's attempt at raising his consciousness but reflecting on the error of invisibility, as his monologue reveals: "I wanted to tell him that Mr. Norton was much more than that, that he was a rich man and in my charge; but the very idea that I was responsible for him was too much for me to put into words" (*Invisible Man* 86). The role the Vet plays illuminates the protagonist's invisibility for our appreciation. Ironically the Vet, a supposedly insane inmate, makes several sane efforts to describe the invisible man as he sees him, and in the process provides not just Mr. Norton but the reader with a succinct profile of the invisible mind and personality, and its potential terror.

Ellison's epilogue, like Cruz e Souza's ending note in "Emparedado," provides the essential harmony with social reality: creative acceptance of invisibility and an end to hibernation. For both writers, it is not enough to have been "hurt to the point of invisibility" (580); indeed, invisibility provides the opportunity to give meaning to meaninglessness, to make sense of nonsense and, as Ellison suggests, approach invisibility with profound humanism: "I sell you no phony forgiveness, I'm a desperate man— but too much of your life will be lost, its meaning lost, unless you approach it through division. So I denounce and defend and I hate and I love" (580). This emphasis on humanism gives both texts their essential commonality. The very act of writing has "negated some of the anger and some of the bitterness" (579), providing the invisible protagonists a constructive understanding of their social plight.

NOTES

1. Richard L. Jackson, *Black Writers in Latin America* (Albuquerque: University of Mexico Press, 1979), 1.
2. Gilberto Freyre has been taken to task on this simplistic and cosmetic philosophy, which tends to justify Portuguese colonialism by the myth that of all colonizers, Portugal was the most tolerant in the sense that it encouraged racial mixing (miscegenation) and indeed brought about racial harmony and ideological diversity, especially as further argued in his *New World in the Tropics* (1959).
3. Todd M. Lieber, "Ralph Ellison and the Metaphor of Invisibility in Black Literary Tradition," *American Quarterly* 24.1 (1972):87–100.
4. Cited in Abelardo F. Montenegro, *Cruz e Souza e o Movimento Simbolista no Brasil* (Florianopolis: Fundação Catarinense de Cultura, 1988), 37. Unless otherwise stated, this and subsequent translations are mine.
5. Roger Bastide, "A nostalgia do branco," *Cruz e Souza*, Afrânio Coutinho, ed. (Rio de Janeiro: Civilização Brasileira, 1979), 157–163.
6. See *CLA Journal* 13.3 (1970).
7. Darwin Turner, "Sight in *Invisible Man*," *CLA Journal* 13.3 (1970):258.
8. Phyllis R. Klotman, "The Running Man as Metaphor in Ellison's *Invisible Man*," *CLA Journal* 13.3 (1970):277.
9. Eleanor R. Wilner, "The Invisible Black Thread: Identity and Nonentity in *Invisible Man*," *CLA Journal* 13.3 (1970):242–257.

REFERENCES

Burke, Kenneth. *Philosophy of Literary Form*. Chicago: University of Chicago Press, 1985.
Coutinho, Afranio (ed.). *Cruz e Souza*. Rio de Janeiro: Civilizaçao Brasileira, 1979.
Cruz e Souza, João da. *Cruz e Souza: Obra Completa*. Ed. Andrade Muricy, Rio de Janeiro: Aguilar, 1961.
Ellison, Ralph. *Invisible Man*. New York: Vintage, 1990.
———. *Shadow and Act*. New York: Vintage, 1972.
Fowke, Edith. Review of *Invisible Man*, by Ralph Ellison. *Book Review Digest* (Mar. 1952—Feb. 1953):284.
Franklin, John H. and Alfred A. Moss, Jr. *From Slavery to Freedom*. New York: McGraw Hill, 1988.
Haberly, David T. *Three Sad Races: Racial Identity and National Consciousness in Brazilian Literature*. Cambridge: Cambridge University Press, 1983.

Healy, J. J. "Literature, Removal and the Theme of Invisibility in America: A Complex Fate Revisited." *Dalhousie Review* 61.1 (1981):127–141.

Howe, Irving. Review of *Invisible Man* by Ralph Ellison. *Book Review Digest* (March 1952–February 1953):284.

Jackson, Richard L. *Black Writers in Latin America*. Albuquerque: University of New Mexico Press, 1979.

——. *Black Literature and Humanism in Latin America*. Athens: University of Georgia Press, 1988.

Klotman, P. R. "The Running Man as Metaphor in Ellison's *Invisible Man*." *CLA Journal*, 13.3 (1970):277–288.

Lieber, Todd M. "Ralph Ellison and the Metaphor of Invisibility in Black Literary Tradition." *American Quarterly*, 24.1 (1972):87–100.

Magalhães Júnior, R. *Poesia e Vida de Cruz e Souza*. Rio de Janeiro: Civilização Brasileira, 1975.

Morrison, Toni. *Playing in the Dark: Whiteness and the Literary Imagination*. New York: Vintage, 1992.

Muricy, Andrade. "Atualidade de Cruz e Souza." *Cruz e Souza: Obra Completa*. Rio de Janeiro: Editora Aguilar, 1961. 17–58.

Rolos, C. J. Review of *Invisible Man* by Ralph Ellison. *Book Review Digest* (March 1952–February 1953):284.

Schafer, William J. "Ralph Ellison and the Birth of the Anti-Hero." *Ralph Ellison: A Collection of Critical Essays*. Ed. John Hersey, New Jersey: Prentice Hall, 1974. 115–126.

Stepto, Robert. *From Behind the Veil*. Chicago: University of Illinois Press, 1979. 163–194.

Wilner, Eleanor R. "The Invisible Black Thread: Identity and Nonentity in *Invisible Man*." *CLA Journal*, 13.3 (1970):242–257.

20 RECOVER, NOT DISCOVER: AFRICA IN WALCOTT'S *DREAM ON MONKEY MOUNTAIN* AND PHILIP'S *LOOKING FOR LIVINGSTONE*[1]

Adetayo Alabi

> That return journey, with all its horror of rediscovery, means the annihilation of what is known.
>
> Derek Walcott, "What the Twilight Says: An Overture" (26)

> ... Dr. David Livingstone, 1813–73—Scottish, not English, and one of the first Europeans to cross the Kalahari—with the help of bushmen; was shown the Zambezi by the indigenous African and "discovered" it; was shown the falls of Mosioatunya—the smoke that thunders—by the indigenous African, "discovered" it and renamed it. Victoria Falls. Then he set out to "discover" the source of the Nile and was himself "discovered" by Stanley—"Dr. Livingstone, I presume?" And History. Stanley and Livingstone—white fathers of the continent. Of silence.
>
> Marlene Nourbese Philip, Looking for Livingstone: An Odyssey of Silence (7)

A substantial part of the history of the West Indies is a story of annihilation and exploitation. The destruction of the indigenous population of the area—the Taino, Siboney, Carib, and Arawak—by the invading European forces in the 1500s and the centuries that followed marked a significant change in the demography of the region. After the extermination of most of the original inhabitants of the area, enslaved people and indentured laborers were brought from Africa and Asia, respectively, and this further heightened the social, political, economic, and military tension in the region. Despite the fact that the West Indies was largely populated at this time by remaining indigenous peoples and people of African and Asian descent, political and economic power was wielded by the colonizing European forces.

The idea of "discovery" functioned as a prominent colonial trope used by the invading colonial powers to justify their seizure of land, torture, and genocide in the West Indies. The point, from their perspective, was that the area, despite the fact that it had its own organized and working structures before them, was empty, savage, and unorganized wasteland without a history. Just as they did in other parts of the world, like Africa, the colonial powers argued that they were just "discovering" the region. Since they were just "discovering" the place, they could justly ignore all other forms of law and order and organized structures and impose theirs. The result was that the customs and religions of the indigenous people were destroyed with the people, and the cultures of the enslaved and indentured people were not respected. The cultures, traditions, languages, and other structures of the old and new inhabitants of the area were either destroyed or debased and relegated to the background, where traces of them were still available. The end result was that colonized people were expected to accept only the cultures and traditions of the colonizers as the sole possible route to civilization and survival.

The post-emancipation era in the West Indies foregrounded again the carnage of the pre-emancipation period as residents of the area addressed the earlier destruction. Two options have since been available to both the writers and the residents of the area, namely to accept the concept of European "discovery," or to reject it and attempt to recover what was lost to slavery and colonization. To accept the European idea of discovery is for people of African ancestry to accept an inferior position to the colonizing power; it is to accept the debasement of the cultures of the colonized; it is to accept that colonialism was necessary. To reject the European concept of discovery, on the other hand, is to highlight the debased cultures and practices of the colonized and enslaved people, and orchestrate a process of recovering what has been lost in terms of the organized structures of the various inhabitants of the West Indies, including their languages, or whatever remained of them, after the era of slavery.

Many West Indian writers of African descent have addressed the notions of "colonial discovery" and "West Indian recovery" in their works. Principal among them are Tobagonian-born Marlene Nourbese Philip in *Looking for Livingstone: An Odyssey of Silence* and St. Lucian–born Derek Walcott in *Dream on Monkey Mountain*, among their other works. For many of these writers, particularly Walcott and Philip in the above texts, looking up to Africa is one way of recovering from colonial historiography. To them, establishing this African connection is one way of encouraging black West Indians to believe in themselves, remember their past, and use the knowledge gained for reconstructive purposes.

Central to *Looking for Livingstone* is the journey motif common in many world literatures. Philip's refreshing approach to this motif combines history, mystery, timelessness, reality, illusion, and dream as the unnamed Traveller journeys from an unidentified location—most likely somewhere in the "new world"—to Africa to meet David Livingstone, a European visitor to Africa, whom some have referred to as an explorer, who was supposed to have both "discovered" and named, in line with Eurocentric discourse, many parts of and things in Africa. The Traveller's journey is a physical trip that takes her through many places, all anagrams of silence (like ECNELIS, SINCEEL, LENSECI, AND SCENILE), and finally to somewhere in Africa where she confronts Livingstone. Though the Traveller's trip is a physical trip from the "new world" to her ancestral home in Africa, it is her movement from being an object that was "discovered" by colonialism to becoming a subject that recovers and locates herself in a resistant subject position in collision with ideas of colonial discovery and the experience of exploitation.

Unlike the movement in *Looking for Livingstone*, which is the Traveller's physical journey from the new to the old world, *Dream on Monkey Mountain*'s movement to the old world and the uplifting of the Afro-Caribbean is a mental trip. In other words, unlike Philip's Traveller, who leaves her physical space in the new world for the old, Walcott's characters Makak, Tigre, Souris, and Lestrade encounter the old world in the new world through a dream, which is the organizing framework of the play. The dream, according to Walcott in his "A Note to the Production" of the play, is

> one that exists as much in the given minds of its principal characters as in that of its writer, and as such, it is illogical, derivative, contradictory. Its source is metaphor and it is best treated as a physical poem with all the subconscious and deliberate borrowings of poetry. (208)

The fact that the dream exists not just in the minds of the characters in the play, but within the playwright's, shows how important it is. There is, however, logic in the illogicality and contradictions of the play. The dream pattern allows the playwright to dispense with a chronological progression of events in favor of those that are cinematic and immediate. This is why the principal characters can move very swiftly from Monkey Mountain to the police cell, the forest, and Africa.

Livingstone's journey foregrounds the workings of colonialism. He visits many places through indigenous guides, and after the visits, he claims to have discovered these places. One very symbolic place he visits is the falls locally named Mosioatunya, meaning "the smoke that thunders." Although this landmark had existed all along and had its own name, Livingstone renames it Victoria Falls (7). This renaming process shows the colonial ideology of rejecting everything before the advent of colonization as insignificant, and, as a matter of fact, not part of history.

The Traveller's task in *Looking* does not follow Livingstone's path of "discovery," but operates within a counter-discursive framework of recovery of the destroyed aspects of pre-colonial Africa and people of African descent. The communal nature of the Traveller's quest is underscored by the various places—such as ECNELIS, SINCEEL, and LENSECI—that she visits. Her visits to these places, which symbolize various African ethnic groups, educate her not just about the different cultures and traditions of her people that colonialism attempted to wipe out, but about the task ahead of her. She also learns to fend for herself. From the LENSECI, for example, she learns an important lesson in economic liberation, as she is expected to work for her upkeep.

The Traveller's final confrontation with Livingstone shows her attempt to educate him about the hypocrisy of his "discoveries." To her, he is a "cheat and a liar" (62) because he couldn't have discovered anything without the Africans who guided him everywhere. She reverses the colonial concept of discovery by suggesting to Livingstone that while he was under the illusion that he was discovering Africa, it was Africa that was discovering him (62). She also questions the colonial and racist inscription of Africa as the dark continent by reminding Livingstone that he and other imperialists "carried their own dark continents within them" (66). The Traveller also foregrounds the importance of "silence" by informing Livingstone that that was what she has discovered in her journey to Africa (67). In other words, the Traveller equates her discovered, or better still recovered, silence to all that Livingstone "discovered."

The issue of power relations between the colonizers and the colonized also features in the confrontation between Livingstone and the Traveller. Just as the colonizers overpower the silence of the colonized, they determine what the "facts" of a situation are, since the colonizers are in control of the means of production. This is why, according to the Traveller, "a fact is whatever anyone, having the power to enforce it, says is a fact. Power—that is the distinguishing mark of a fact. Fact—Livingstone discovered Victoria Falls. *That* is a fact" (67). Since the colonialists have the power of enforcement, they can change lies into facts; hence it is written in their history books, their books of so-called facts, that Livingstone discovered Victoria Falls, despite the indigenous African fact that the falls predated Livingstone and had their own name long before any European came to Africa. The more interesting issue about "facts" in this regard, however, is the ability of the dispossessed to question received "facts" from colonial discourse and posit their own facts from their own experiences, as the Traveller does in *Looking*.

Sartre's prologue to Fanon's *The Wretched of the Earth*, which functions as the epigraph to part one of *Dream*, provides a good way of understanding the play and its logic. Since the hallucinated person that Sartre talks about in the epigraph does not have any control over his or her many demeaning experiences, two options are available to the individual. The first is to accept the pressures of his or her experiences and succumb to the depth of his psychosis; the second is to imagine other possibilities that may not necessarily lead to the dissociation of the self. In *Dream*, Makak subscribes to the latter alternative as he reconstructs his heroic African heritage in his fight against his life of deprivation.

At the beginning of the play, Makak is presented as the lowest of the low in a number of ways. His job—charbonnier or charcoal-burner—fits with Monkey Mountain, his ugly and desolate residence. He is a recluse. Perhaps Moustique's description of him best sums up Makak's initial image in the play. According to Moustique, Makak is

> nothing. You [Makak] black, ugly, poor, so you worse than nothing. You like me. Small, ugly, with a foot like a "S." Man together two of us is minus one. (236)

Things start changing for the better from the moment Makak starts dreaming about and identifying with Africa, his ancestral home. It is at this stage that he starts the process of reconstructing his psyche. As the apparition that he encounters reminds him, he is of royal ancestry, a member of the family of lions and kings (236). His encounter with the apparition fits into the stage of "congratulations" that Sartre discusses in the epigraph to the first part of the play (211). Unlike the process described in the rest of the epigraph, Makak does not run amok. Instead, he starts believing in himself and improving his self-esteem, and he is able to assert later that he had "left death, failure, disappointment, despair in the wake of . . . [his] dreams" (305).

Makak is also able to educate his audience, at the healing scene, on their relationship to their new world. In a trancelike state, he recalls his sojourn on Monkey Mountain and the suffering of his people. Alluding to the histories of slavery, transplantation, and enslavement, Makak describes his people as trees "without names, a forest with no roots!" (248). The solution to the problem, from Makak's perspective, one that is supported by Moustique, his friend turned disciple, is for the people to recover their roots—a reference to their African heritage—by believing in themselves (249). Souris, one of the felons in the cell with Makak, questions him on how they can encounter Africa and what they will do there. Makak's response shows clearly that his recommendation is a mental and intellectual meeting with Africa. As Walcott puts it in "What the Twilight Says," "The voice must grovel in search of itself, until gesture and sound fuse and the blaze of their flesh astonishes them. The children of slaves must sear their memory with a torch" (5).

What happens after Makak is released from jail is a reiteration of his newly found hope and his regenerated self. The irony of his journey is that at the end of the play, he is more knowledgeable about his heritage, but economically he is still dependent on the institution that he is trying to use his ancestral heritage to undermine. For a total regeneration to take place, Felix Hobain has to do more than reject the derogatory identity of Makak and ally himself with his origins. He has to be economically independent, since the economy is the foundational structure on which others are based, as Karl Marx argues. Hobain's dream of survival has to move from the level of fantasy to the reality of the West Indies that he wakes up to. Like the Traveller in *Looking*, he has to be able to use the facilities available in his society to improve himself economically so that his political and ideological freedom will be meaningful.

One problematic aspect of the forward movement to Africa is the fact that the reconstruction of Makak's psyche starts with his encounter with the white goddess whom he kills later in the play. One may ask why the person to educate Makak about his self-esteem is white, what can symbolize his exploitation, and why the white goddess is beheaded in the apotheosis scene. The apparition is white because that is the color that the colonized has been taught to imitate and long for. As Corporal puts it, "She is the mirror of the moon that this ape look into and find himself unbearable" (319). She represents what the colonized is taught to desire, the other culture that has negated theirs in many ways. She, therefore, also represents all other concepts used by colonialism to exploit the colonized. Beheading her is symbolic of the resistance of the colonized to the tenets of colonialism.

Unlike *Looking*, which depicts Africa from a painstakingly affirmative perspective, *Dream* is critical of the continent, especially in the apotheosis scene. Unlike other scenes that depict Africa positively, this scene evaluates the autocratic tendencies of many African rulers. The reflection on the dictatorial tendencies of many African rulers is discussed through Makak, who is an African leader in the scene. Despite his hitherto revolutionary ideas and lofty ambitions about Africa, he becomes a tyrant as soon as he becomes a leader. Like some African rulers, he executes several people even when the reason for their execution is not clear. Even Moustique, his friend, does not escape the carnage that he unleashes.

Gender issues in *Dream* are more problematic than in *Looking*. *Dream* reconstructs the position of people of African descent in the new world through the male characters, who are also the principal characters. Even the white apparition that educates Makak about his heritage does not have a voice in the text. All we know of her is reported through Makak in his cell and Lestrade at the apotheosis scene. Women also feature as participants in the market scene and as Makak's wives in the apotheosis scene. Makak's several wives in the scene suggest the polygamous family structures that exist in many parts of Africa. The women still do not have a voice; they are not treated as individuals, but as a collective under the categories of "wives of Makak" and "chorus." This depiction is in contrast to *Looking*, which can then be read as Philip's reaction to the inability of male writers like Walcott to address gender exploitation and create a positive female role model for others to emulate. Women, therefore, play very significant roles in *Looking*.

The Traveller, the protagonist in *Looking*, is a woman; hence the text is the journey into recovery from a woman's perspective, a perspective that has been colonized hitherto by a collusion between patriarchy and colonialism. On her journey, most of her teachers are women, very successful role models who teach her that her journey is one of recovery and not discovery (10). These women, like Mama Ohnce of the CESLIENS (36), Marphan of the CLEENIS (41), and Arwhal of the NEECLIS (48) educate her about the rituals and traditions of their various societies, and they tell her stories about their societies, their art, and communal structures. In all these places, the Traveller forges a union with the women, a union that suggests their bond and collective resistance not only to colonialism but to patriarchy.

The women the Traveller meets are very independent and work very hard for their upkeep, just like anybody else. For example, when visiting the LENSECI, she has to join them in farming to earn her upkeep (14). From her encounter with the NEECLIS (48), she learns about weaving and needlework, spending long hours discussing aesthetics. From the EC-NELIS, she learns about the role of women in warfare. Women of the EC-NELIS, she learns, "had been going to war regularly ... ever since they could date their first memory, which was a long, long time in the past" (11).[2] Her encounter with the ECNELIS shows how their language, like many African languages, does not discriminate along gender lines. This is why in Bellume's story (11), God is female and in Chareem's (12), God is male. The fact that God is both male and female in this context shows that God is not of a particular gender. Furthermore, the three skill-testing questions she has to answer before she can continue her search when visiting the SCENILE foreground her need for a profound intellectual capacity for her ultimate confrontation with Livingstone, the symbol of colonialism. All these positive images of the female symbolize the gender rapport that existed in pre-colonial Africa,[3] and they inspire contemporary women of African descent to learn from their history of resistance.

The use of language in both *Looking* and *Dream* challenges the received form of the English language; hence language use is an integral part of the resistance tradition and recovery process developed in both texts. Philip's questioning of the received form of the English language and style of novel writing is appropriate to *Looking*. Since her subject matter, which is the recovery of what was lost to slavery and colonialism, is revolutionary, the form of her text is innovative: her style combines both prose and poetry. A poem follows her prose narrative of the Traveller's visit to a particular place. These poems reinforce the thematic preoccupation of the Traveller in the place just described. They also alert the reader to the combination of prose, poetry, drama, and autobiographies in many traditional African narratives.[4]

Philip questions the received form of the English language largely in her diction. Some of her word choices are unusual, a feature that works well with her innovative subject matter. For example, her use of the calendar is unconventional in a Western sense; she relies to a large extent on the calendar of many traditional African societies. There are various references to "the month of the moons" (7, 60), and instead of locating many events in terms of specific years, she locates them in terms of "the year of our word" (10, 35, 48), thus punning on "the year of our Lord." She also refers to hours in unconventional terms. Instead of the conventional twenty-four hours in a day, there are references to 1000 hours (19), 0100 hours (35), and 5001 hours (41).

Another important feature of language use in *Looking* is the contrast between silence and word which is used to educate the Traveller about power relations between the powerful colonizers and the overpowered colonized people. Throughout the text, the symbolic power of silence is stressed in relation to word. In other words, while indigenous Africans were silenced by the power of the word, the power of colonialism, they are not powerless; there is still power in their silence. Silence is, therefore, foregrounded as desirable by many ethnic groups she visits. While visiting the ECNELIS, she learns about how silence was overtaken by word:

> And so their ancestors, so their stories tell, mounted armies of words to colonise the many and various silences of the peoples round about, spreading and infecting with word where before there was silence. God rewarded them with an even greater hunger for words to drown out the silence they still sensed in unguarded moments. (12)

Although this parable is narrated as the story of the ECNELIS, it is symptomatic of the relationship between colonizers and colonized. She concludes, following her education by the CESLIENS, that

> Nothing in nature is silent . . . naturally silent, that is. Everything has its own sound, speech, or language, even if it is only the language of silence (there I go again—"even if"), and if you were willing to learn the sound of what appeared to be silence, you understood then that the word was but another sound—of silence. (35)

The symbolism of the Museum of Silence (57) is vital to understanding how colonialism tried to destroy the cultures of Africans and people of African descent. Silence in the museum represents the artifacts and inventions of various African peoples pillaged during slavery and colonialism. Even when the silences (the artifacts) are now imprisoned in the museum, the Traveller still acknowledges their power and requests that the proprietors of the museum return them to their various owners (57) because, according to her, when you "[r]emove a thing—a person—from its source . . . from where it belongs naturally . . . it will lose meaning—our silence has lost all meaning. . . . At the very least . . . we should own our silence" (58). Her lament over the meaninglessness of silence in the above passage is due to the destruction of various African cultures and artifacts and the transplantation of people of African descent to the new world. She not only laments the destruction, but saves an otherwise critical situation through her journey into herself.

Since Walcott's vision in *Dream on Monkey Mountain* is his attempt at uplifting the Afro-Caribbean, his ideology is coded in the language of the Afro-Caribbean (what Edward Kamau Brathwaite calls Nation-language). As it is presented in *Dream*, Nation-language is in a counter-discursive relationship to the received form of the English language. It is Walcott's way of asking Afro-Caribbeans not just to have pride in themselves but to have pride in the language they created. The importance of reconstructing the psyche of the Afro-Caribbeans through a language that they relate to is emphasised by Walcott in "What the Twilight Says," where he argues that what can save the Caribbean from servitude is

the forging of a language that went beyond mimicry, a dialect which had the force of revelation as it invented names for things, one which finally settled on its own mode of inflection, and which began to create an oral culture of chants, jokes, folk-songs and fables; this, not merely the debt of history [is] his [or her] proper claim to the new world. (17)

This language, Nation-language, or Caribbean talk, according to Edward Kamau Brathwaite in *The History of the Voice*, is:

the language which is influenced very strongly by the African model, the African aspect of our New World/Caribbean heritage. English it may be in terms of some lexical features. But in its contours, its rhythm and timbre, its sound explosions, it is not English, even though the words, as you hear them, might be English to a greater or lesser degree. . . . [It] is the *submerged* area of that dialect which is most closely allied to the African aspect of experience in the Caribbean. It may be in English: but often it is in an English which is like a howl, or a shout or a machine-gun or the wind or a wave. (13)

Nation-language is used in *Dream* by almost all the characters. Its use in the chorus sections of the prologue functions as a unifying factor for the exploited people who chart resistance to their enslavement and the received form of English in the language. The play starts in Nation-language with a song in the famous African call-and-response tradition. The conversation between Tigre, Souris, and Corporal Lestrade that follows the opening song takes place in Nation-language. To try Makak, Corporal Lestrade as a law enforcement agent switches from the Nation-language he was using to English. Lestrade questions Makak in British English because according to him, he is "observing the principles and precepts of Roman law, and Roman law is English law" (219). Makak's switch from Nation-language to British English in the trial scene shows that he is a man of two worlds—the worlds of the exploiter and the exploited—though he functions in the world of the exploiter as an exploited.

Nation-language is often musical, incantatory, panegyric, and poetic. Its musicality is shown in the rhythm of the songs in the prologue and other sections of *Dream*. The songs in both the prologue and the apotheosis scenes, as noted earlier, are based on the call-and-response feature of African poetry, which forms an integral part of the works of some African poets, like Nigeria's Christopher Okigbo and Niyi Osundare. The chants in the apotheosis scene also show the rhythm of African music, and are based on the panegyric and heroic forms of African oral poetry.[5]

Both Marlene Nourbese Philip's and Derek Walcott's works analyzed here portray Africa, to West Indians, with considerable nostalgia. The positive image of the continent in the texts functions as a source of inspiration to see Africa affirmatively. This affirmation of their heritage, as the texts suggest, is one way of combating the debilitating effects of slavery, transplantation, colonialism, and racism. While Philip's *Looking for Livingstone* suggests a physical encounter with Africa, Walcott's *Dream on Monkey Mountain* favors a discursive recovery of the continent. The choices made by both writers are valid responses to their circumstances and the patterns of their texts. Since *Looking* is patterned by the search for Livingstone, it is appropriate for the Traveller to confront him—or better still, discover him—in Africa, where he is supposed to be discovering places and things. *Dream on Monkey Mountain*'s dream framework, on the other hand, provides the characters with cinematic possibilities; hence they can move swiftly and mentally from their police cells to Africa for regenerative prospects. Perhaps what is more important is not the method of understanding Africa by people of African descent around the globe, but that the understanding takes place, and Africans and people of African descent are able to forge a union to fight their exploitation.

NOTES

1. This essay was presented at the "African Diaspora: African Origins and New World Self-Fashioning" Conference, State University of New York, Binghamton, April 11–13, 1996. I am grateful for comments on the paper at the conference and to Prof. Susan Gingell for hers.

2. The role of the women of ECNELIS in warfare recalls that of the women of Dahomey Empire, the Amazons.

3. See Ifi Amadiume's *Male Daughters, Female Husbands: Gender and Sex in an African Society* and Wole Soyinka's *Death and the King's Horseman*.

4. See Ruth Finnegan, *Oral Literature in Africa*, particularly her introduction, and Isidore Okpewho's *African Oral Literature*, particularly chapter 3—"The Oral Performance."

5. For a fuller discussion of the language of *Dream on Monkey Mountain*, see Susan Beckmann, "The Mulatto of Style."

REFERENCES

Amadiume, Ifi. *Male Daughters, Female Husbands: Gender and Sex in an African Society*. Atlantic Highlands, New Jersey: Zed Books, 1987.
Asein, Samuel Omo. "Derek Walcott: The Man and His Ideas." *The Literary Half-Yearly* 17 (July 1976):59–79.
Ashcroft, Bill, et al. *The Empire Writes Back: Theory and Practice in Post-Colonial Literatures*. New York: Routledge, 1989.
Ashcroft, W. D. "Constitutive Graphonomy: A Post-Colonial Theory of Literary Writing." *Kunapipi* 11.1 (1989):58–73.
Baugh Edward, ed. *Critics on Caribbean Literature: Readings in Literary Criticism*. New York: St. Martin's Press, 1978, 58–62.
Beckmann, Susan. "The Mulatto of Style: Language in Derek Walcott's Drama." *Canadian Drama (Special Issue: Commonwealth Drama)* 6.1 (Spring 1980):71–89.
Berghahn, Marion. *Images of Africa in Black American Literature*. Totowa, New Jersey: Rowman and Littlefield, 1977.
Brathwaite, Edward Kamau. *History of the Voice: The Development of Nation Language in Anglophone Caribbean Poetry*. London, Port of Spain: New Beacon Books, 1984.
Breiner, Laurence A. "Walcott's Early Drama." *The Art of Derek Walcott*. Dufour: Seren Books, 1991, 69–85.
Brown, Lloyd. "The Revolutionary Dream of Walcott's Makak." *Critics on Caribbean Literature: Readings in Literary Criticism*. Ed. Edward Baugh. New York: St. Martin's Press, 1978, 58–62.
Colson, Theodore. "Derek Walcott's Plays: Outrage and Compassion." *World Literature Written in English* 12.1 (April 1973):80–96.
Finnegan, Ruth. *Oral Literature in Africa*. Oxford: Clarendon Press, 1970.
Fox, Robert Elliot. "Big Night Music: Derek Walcott's *Dream on Monkey*

Mountain and the 'Splendours of Imagination.'" *The Journal of Commonwealth Literature* XVM.1 (1982):16–27.

Hamner, Robert D. *Derek Walcott.* Boston: Twayne Publishers, 1993.

——. "Mythological Aspects of Derek Walcott's Drama." *A Review of International English Literature (ARIEL)* 8.3 (July 1977):35–58.

Jeyifo, Biodun. "On Eurocentric Critical Theory: Some Paradigms from the Texts and Sub-Texts of Post-Colonial Writing." *Kunapipi* XI.1 (1989):107–118.

Morrell, Carol, ed. *Grammar of Dissent: Poetry and Prose by Claire Harris, M. Nourbese Philip, and Dionne Brand.* Fredericton, Goose Lane Editions, 1994.

Mukherjee, Arun. *Towards an Aesthetic of Opposition: Essays on Literature, Criticism and Cultural Imperialism.* Stratford: Williams-Wallace Publishers, 1988.

Okpewho, Isidore. *African Oral Literature: Backgrounds, Character, and Continuity.* Bloomington and Indianapolis: Indiana University Press, 1992.

Olaniyan, Tejumola. "Dramatizing Postcoloniality: Wole Soyinka and Derek Walcott." *Theatre Journal* 44.4 (December 1992):485–499.

Philip, Marlene Nourbese. *Looking for Livingstone: An Odyssey of Silence.* Stratford, Ontario: The Mercury Press, 1991.

Slemon, Stephen. "Monuments of Empire: Allegory/Counter-Discourse/Post-Colonial Writing." *Kunapipi* 9.3 (1987):1–16.

Soyinka, Wole. *Death and the King's Horseman* (1975). *Six Plays.* London: Methuen, 1984.

Terdiman, Richard. *Discourse/Counter-Discourse: The Theory and Practice of Symbolic Resistance in Nineteenth Century France.* Ithaca and London: Cornell University Press, 1985.

Trudgill, P. *Sociolinguistics: An Introduction.* England: Penguin Books Ltd., 1974.

Walcott, Derek. *Collected Poems 1948–1984.* New York: Farrar, Straus and Giroux, 1986.

——. *Dream on Monkey Mountain and Other Plays.* New York: Farrar, Straus and Giroux, 1970.

——. "Man of the Theatre." *The New Yorker,* June 26, 1971.

——. "The Muse of History: An Essay." In *Is Massa Dead? Black Moods in the Caribbean.* Ed. Orde Coombs. New York: Anchor Press/Doubleday, 1974, 1–27.

——. "What the Twilight Says: An Overture." In *Dream on Monkey Mountain and Other Plays.* New York: Farrar, Straus and Giroux, 1970, 3–40.

21 ISLAM AND THE BLACK DIASPORA: THE IMPACT OF ISLAMIGRATION

Ali A. Mazrui

Hinduism is partly predicated on the doctrine of the transmigration of the *soul* after death. Islam is partly predicated on the migration and physical motion of the *body* in life *before* death. Hinduism is sometimes a salute to absolute motionless and stillness. Islam is sometimes a salute to purposeful movement.

The Muslim formal prayer is one of the most physical forms of prayer among world religions. Five times every day hundreds of millions of Muslims bend, kneel, and prostrate themselves in physical worship. The Muslim rituals during the pilgrimage in Mecca go to the extent of symbolically *stoning* the evil spirit. Most other world religions believe that God is best approached by motionless postures, sometimes even by solemn silence and stillness. While Islam does allow for moments of silence and stillness, the five compulsory prayers are still *physically active* forms of worship.

When were these prayers commanded by God? Muslims believe that they were commanded when the Prophet Muhammad was physically transported first from Mecca to Jerusalem, and then physically transported from Jerusalem to the Heavens, where he met all the preceding great prophets, and where he came into the presence of the Almighty Himself. All this took place in a single miraculous night—the night of the Mi'raj.

Originally God demanded fifty rather than five physical prayers a day. It was Moses who convinced Muhammad to go back to the Almighty and beg for a reduction of the number of physical prayers for Muhammad's followers. Islam was indeed intended to be a religion in *motion* rather than stillness. It was intended to be a religion not of the transmigration of the soul but of the movement of the body and the migration of the person. The concept of Islamigration captures this paradox. The word "Islam" itself means submission (to the will of God), and submission implies *passivity*. "Migration," on the other hand, is an active principle of *movement*. This essay hopes to demonstrate that it is precisely this quality of Islam as movement and migration which gives it a special relationship with Global Africa. We define Global Africa as Africa plus, firstly, the *diaspora of enslavement* (such as African Americans) and, secondly, the *diaspora of colonialism* (such as twentieth-century African migrants to Europe and the Americas). Both diasporas involve migration and movement.

As the twentieth century comes to a close the world has over one billion Muslims. About a quarter of those are in Africa (including north Africa) and the African diaspora. There are more Muslims in Nigeria than in any Arab country, including Egypt. The Muslims of Nigeria, Egypt, and Ethiopia alone probably account for a quarter of the population of the African continent (over 130 million Muslims in the three countries).

The United States in 1996 has approximately as many Muslims as Jews. Forty-two percent of the U.S. Muslims are African Americans. It is expected that if present trends continue African American *Muslims* will outnumber American Jews by 2020 C.E. or soon thereafter. (At the moment the whole population of African Americans outnumber the population of the Jews of the whole world added together, including the Jews of Israel).

But what is the link between Islam as motion and Africa as migration? Let us look more closely at both the dynamics and the dialectic. To further understand the dynamics of *Islamigration,* let us take a closer look at the two great Hs in Islam—the *Hijrah* and the *Hajj.* The Hijrah was the migration of the Prophet Muhammad himself from Mecca to Medina to escape persecution. The Hajj is the annual movement of hundreds of thousands of Muslims from all the four corners of the world to make the pilgrimage to Mecca. Both the Hijrah and the Hajj involved people on the move. The original Hijrah was a displacement of people for reasons of their new religion. The Hajj is an annual reunification of people on the basis of their shared religion.

The theme of migration is at the heart of this entire dialectic. When did the Islamic Era begin? Once again *migration* rears its fascinating head.

The Hijrah is the beginning of the Islamic Calendar. The era *begins* not when the Prophet Muhammad was born in 570 C.E. Nor does it begin when he became a prophet in 610 C.E. The Islamic calendar does not begin when Muhammad died in 632 C.E. The whole *Islamic era is deemed* to begin when Muhammad was forced to migrate from Mecca to Medina in 622 C.E.—*beginning July 16, 622.* Migration inaugurates the Islamic era. The prophet moved under persecution from Mecca to go to a freer exile. *In the beginning was migration.*

Mecca and migration have entered some of the mythologies and histories of Black people, both Muslim and non-Muslim. The Yoruba possess more than one myth of ancestry. One of those ancestral legends traces Yoruba origins to Arabia. The Yoruba are thus seen as the remnant of the children of Canaan, who were of "the tribe of Nimrod."

In a book by the distinguished Yoruba historian and sociologist N. A. Fadipe, published by Ibadan University Press in 1970, a case is made that the Yoruba arrived in West Africa from Arabia via the Nile Valley:

The cause of their establishment in West Africa was . . . in consequence of their being driven by Yarrooba, son of Kahtan, out of Arabia, to the Western coast between Egypt and Abyssinia. From that
spot they advanced into the interior of Africa till they reached
Yarba, where they fixed their residence.[1]

According to a related Oyo mythological tradition, the Yoruba migrated from Mecca to their present abode, having been forced out of *Mecca*
following a civil war involving Oduduwa, son of King Lamurudu of Mecca.
Oduduwa became the common ancestor of the Yoruba as an African people, and Ile-Ife became the *Yoruba equivalent of Medina*—the place from
which the African phase of Yoruba culture flowered. Parts of what is today the Sultanate of Oman had a dynasty hundreds of years ago named
the *Yaaruba* dynasty. There is speculation as to whether the name of
this dynasty contributed to the Arabized version of the Oyo myth of ancestry.

During the Prophet Muhammad's own lifetime there was also movement of persecuted *Muslims* from Arabia to Africa. Especially noteworthy
historically was the migration of persecuted Muslims to Ethiopia in the
early seventh century C.E. seeking religious asylum. This event is celebrated in Ethiopia to the present day as a kind of pre-Hijrah.

Then there is the case of Farrad Muhammad, the founder of the Nation
of Islam, the black Muslim movement in the United States. According to
known history Farrad was born in Mecca in 1877. He arrived in the United
States in 1930 and established the Detroit Temple of Islam. This was a
nationalist version of Islamigration. Farrad told his followers that Christianity had been kidnapped by slave owners, that a racial war was coming
and Blacks should prepare for it, that their own moral superiority would
ultimately prevail—and they must begin by ceasing to call themselves
"Negroes." Farrad had undertaken a lifelong migration from Mecca (where
he was born) to Detroit (where he gave birth to a new religious movement).
Then Farrad performed the ultimate case of physical migration. He totally
disappeared without a trace in 1934, almost like the Hidden Imam of
Shiite Islam.

Theories about pre-Columbian Black crossings of the Atlantic also include Muslims on the move. In 1962 the official organ of the NAACP published an article by Harold G. Lawrence entitled "African Explorers of the
New World." In the article Lawrence referred to Abubakari II of Mali as
having employed Arab navigators and equipped them with a whole armada
of ships and African sailors to venture westward:

We can now positively state that the Mandingoes of the Mali and
Songay Empires, and possibly other Africans, crossed the Atlantic

to carry on trade with the western hemisphere Indians and further
succeeded in establishing colonies throughout the Americas . . .
Abubakari II (1305–1307) did not believe that it was impossible to
conquer the limits of the neighbouring ocean.[2]

Twenty years after Lawrence's article, Pathe Diagne, a Senegalese
scholar, initiated a project about Mansa Bakary II (another version of the
name Abubakari II) and whether his armada crossed the Atlantic before
1312 C.E. Columbus's trans-Atlantic crossing was in 1492. Pathe Diagne
argued,

> Both Bakary II and Christopher Columbus learned from the
> African navigators of Senegambia and the Gulf of Guinea about (1)
> trans-oceanic traffic and trade (2) the existence of a corridor fed by
> North Equatorial winds and (3) the existence of a current that was
> easy to navigate during the summer and fall and that led to the
> rich Maya, Olmeque, Aztec and Inca Kingdoms and civilizations.
> Neither Bakary II nor Christopher Columbus were ready to share
> this geopolitical secret with [rivals].[3]

According to this theory, Islam therefore arrived in the Americas at least
a century-and-a-half before Christianity. Mansa Bakary II was himself
a Muslim, and his sailors and navigators were either Muslim or followers
of indigenous African religions. But Islam does not seem to have either
spread or taken root in the Americas of pre-Columbian times. This seems
to have been a case of Islamigration which was still-born.

Islam's second coming to the Americas was also linked to Black
people—but this time through the enforced migration of slavery rather
than the Islamic concept of *hijrah*. Alex Haley made his grandfather,
Kunta Kinte, a Muslim. Haley made Islam part and parcel of Kunta Kinte's
roots.

The history of Islam in Trinidad is traced to enslaved Mandingos, who
began to be imported into the sugar plantations of Trinidad in the 1770s.
According to a study by Omar Hasan Kasule:

> In the 1830s, a community of Mandingo Muslims who had been
> captured from Senegal lived in Port of Spain. They were literate
> in Arabic and organized themselves under a forceful leader named
> Muhammad Beth, who had purchased his freedom from slavery.
> They kept their Islamic identity and always yearned to go back to
> Africa.[4]

In the twentieth century the majority of Muslims in Trinidad were East
Indians who had originally been imported as indentured laborers, but

there were also some Afro-Trinidadian Muslims. On July 27, 1990, members of a radical Afro-Muslim group known as Jamaat al-Muslimeen invaded the parliament building and held hostage Prime Minister A. N. R. Robinson and most of the cabinet for nearly a week. Next to the Million Man March in the U.S. in 1995, the 1990 capture of Trinidad's government was the most spectacular piece of Black diaspora action in the 1990s.

We said that the Senegalese adventurer who undertook the pre-Columbian trans-Atlantic crossing before 1312 was called Abu Bakari II. Who led the Muslimeen in Port of Spain, Trinidad, in 1990? One is tempted to call him Abu Bakari III. His name was indeed Abu Bakr (another version of the same name). His fist name was Yasin. Abu Bakr demanded a government in Trinidad more sensitive to the needs of the poor and more tolerant of religious pluralism. Prime Minister Robinson agreed to some of the demands of the Muslimeen, and also agreed to grant them amnesty. The policy demands were never really implemented, but the courts decided that the amnesty to the hostage-takers was legally binding. So the Muslimeen were never punished. The amnesty was even confirmed by the Privy Council.

But the first of all Muslim Abu Bakars was the first caliph of Islam after the death of Muhammad—Abu Bakar As-Siddiq. Among his advisors was a Black man who had also been an advisor to the Prophet Muhammad before him. The Black man's name was *Bilal*, and he had won his freedom as a result of Islam. In history Bilal was Islam's first link with Africa's diaspora. He was an Ethiopian at the birth of Islam—a migrant in Arabia, originally enslaved by non-Muslims, freed by a Muslim. In the twentieth century Bilal's name has been used by African Americans for their children, sometimes for their publications, at other times for their restaurants. Bilal is a Black Muslim name in history.

Bilal's voice is also part of the history of Black vocal power in human affairs—from Bilal to Paul Robeson and beyond. Robeson's voice made history in song and on the stage. Bilal's voice made history from the minaret—calling believers to prayer. He was the first great muezzin in the history of Islam—calling believers to those five physical forms of submission. Bilal (son of Rabah) used his Black vocal chords to call Muslims to their physical worship. Physicality and motion were once again intertwined in the history of Islam.

Is Louis Farrakhan a latter-day Bilal? As the author of the Million Man March of October 1995 in the United States, Farrakhan once again linked Islam to *movement*. I and other colleagues spent five hours with him at his home in Chicago in January 1996. He discussed a triad of tours—to Africa, to the Muslim world, and to different parts of the United States. Tours are also within an Islamic paradigm of movement.

Inseparable from the history of Islam is this link with the passions of the African diaspora. This is the dialectic of *Islamigration* as it has unfolded across space and time.

NOTES

1. N. A. Fadipe, *The Sociology of the Yoruba* edited by Francis Olu Okedji and Oladeji Okedji (Ibadan, Nigeria: Ibadan University Press, 1970) p. 31.

2. Harold G. Lawrence, "African Explorers of the New World," *The Crisis* (Organ of NAACP, USA) June–July 1962, pp. 2–4. Lawrence was Chair of the Research and Education Committee of the Detroit branch of the Association for the Study of Negro Life and History.

3. Project Outline, Africana Studies and Research Center, Cornell University, 1990.

4. Omar Hasan Kasule, *Muslims in Trinidad and Tobago* (Port of Spain, Trinidad: Pamphlet, 1978).

22 FROM LEGBA TO PAPA LABAS: NEW WORLD METAPHYSICAL SELF/RE-FASHIONING IN ISHMAEL REED'S *MUMBO JUMBO*

Pierre-Damien Mvuyekure

In his seminal work *Myth, Literature, and the African World*, Wole Soyinka discusses the "socio-religious reality" in the "African world of the Americas," and cogently argues that the "symbols of Yemaja (Yemoja), Oxosi (Ososi), Exu (Esu) and Xango (Sango) not only lead a promiscuous existence with Roman Catholic saints but are fused with the twentieth-century technological and revolutionary expressionism of the mural arts of Cuba, Brazil and much of the Caribbean" (1). Wole Soyinka's statement certainly points to both the African metaphysical presence in the New World and how Africans of the Diaspora have adapted the African-derived religions to the New World realities. My aim in this essay is to study the African origins of expressive traditions and metaphysical orientations in African Diaspora as illustrated in Ishmael Reed's novel *Mumbo Jumbo* (1972). Not only does *Mumbo Jumbo* theorize about how Africans in the Diaspora have succeeded in retaining and re-creating African religious beliefs, but it also shows how Reed has created an African-based multicultural aesthetic to negotiate the historical, social, political, and cultural conditions of Africans in the New World. Not only do Reed's novels like *Mumbo Jumbo*, *Yellow Back Radio Broke-Down* (1969), *The Last Days of Louisiana Red* (1974), and *Japanese by Spring* (1993) use gods and goddesses from or based on the African pantheon (such as Agwe, Damballah, Guede, Ifa, Legba, Obatala, Ogun, Olodumare, Orunmila, Shango, and Yemanjá), but they also condemn the conspiracy of Judeo-Christian religions to destroy African (based) religions. I argue that Reed's aim is not simply to assert "the blackness of blackness" or an Afrocentric aesthetic in the manner of Amiri Baraka, Molefi Asante, and others, but that his writing goes beyond the reconnection to African spirituality in order to create a space for cultural and spiritual pluralism. Actually, Reed has fashioned his own literary theory/aesthetic of syncretism and synchronicity called Neo-Hoodooism or the Neo-HooDoo Aesthetic.[1]

I argue as well that Neo-HooDooism adumbrates how Reed has adapted African cultural elements to the New World as suggested by three poems in his *New and Collected Poems*. In the poem "Neo-HooDoo Manifesto," Reed defines Neo-HooDooism as an aesthetic that borrows from several cultures from the world over, including Africa (Nigeria, Benin, Congo) and South America (Haiti, Jamaica, Cuba, Brazil).[2] More importantly, the poem reveals that "Africa is the home of the loa (Spirits) of Neo-HooDoo although we are building our own 'pantheon'" (23). This statement is very important insofar as it summarizes what Reed and his Voodoo characters do: Out of African deities, they create and invent new ones capable of surviving in the new environment. In another poem, "The Neo-HooDoo Aesthetic," Neo-HooDooism is described as an aesthetic of freedom with "Gombo Filé" or "Gombo Févi" as its metaphor. The idea is that just as "the proportion of ingredients depends upon the cook," so does writing style depend upon each individual writer. Reed further explores the food metaphor in *The Last Days of Louisiana Red*, a novel that opens with a gumbo recipe from *The Picayune Creole Cook Book*. The artistic freedom thus expressed is elaborated in "Catechism of d Neoamerican Hoodoo Church," in which the poet proclaims that writers' "pens are free" and "do not move by decree" (36). As the analysis of *Mumbo Jumbo* will suggest, the ideas embedded in the three poems underlie Reed's fiction.

Clearly, Reed takes up where Chinua Achebe has left off in *Things Fall Apart* and *Arrow of God*. Also, there is an interesting parallel between Reed and Ngugi wa Thiong'O in the sense that both writers address the European imperialism and conspiracy to destroy African cultures. But although both writers are tricksters, Reed is more of a Guede insofar as he demystifies European traditions by pointing their origins back to Africa. More importantly, in stark contrast to the fate of African gods and goddesses in Achebe's *Things Fall Apart* and *Arrow of God*, and Ngugi's *The River Between* and *Weep Not Child*,[3] Reed's gods and goddesses have survived Christianity by re-fashioning themselves, especially by becoming syncretic/creolized and improvisational. This has been done to such an extent that Christian saints coexist with African gods and loas in Voodoo (Jamaica, Haiti, Brazil, Cuba) and Hoodoo (New Orleans, North Carolina, Chicago, New York). It is noteworthy that in these New World metaphysical reconfigurations Reed shares the credit with other writers, such as Derek Walcott, Kamau Brathwaite, René Depestre, Maryse Condé, Zora Neale Hurston, John E. Wideman, David Henderson, Rudolph Fisher, and most recently Gloria Naylor and Jewell Parker Rhodes. But Reed is unique in the sense that for almost thirty years he has devoted his entire literary career to writing from the perspective of Voodoo and Hoodoo aesthetics.

Although *The Free-Lance Pallbearers* (1967), Reed's first novel, which contains a mambo who "hoodooes" her granddaughter's husband, represents Hoodoo as a negative force, it is in *Yellow Back Radio Broke-Down* (1969) that Reed begins to trace the origins of Voodoo and Hoodoo from Africa to demonstrate what happened to Africans and their deities when they crossed the Middle Passage into the New World. *Yellow Back Radio Broke-Down* is a Western novel with Loop Garoo Kid as an African Voodoo cowboy who threatens the American Wild West and Catholicism with his Voodoo and Hoodoo forces, forms of African spirituality. The novel exemplifies a case of self/re-fashioning through the reappropriation of the Western. This reappropriation is predicated on Reed's premise that the Western is traceable in both African Voodoo and African-American Hoodoo. When, in Voodoo and Hoodoo, spirits ride/possess human beings, the latter are called horsemen and horsewomen. Therefore, Reed "would naturally write a western, here again using the traditional styles of Afro-American folklore but enmeshing such styles with popular forms with which readers could identify."[4] As mentioned above, this is another indication of self-fashioning that translates itself into a creative writing aesthetic.

Through Loop Garoo Kid we see how African Americans have negotiated the political and cultural ideologies of the Western, from which they have been so long excluded. Whereas cowboys have traditionally negotiated with guns and ropes, Loop Garoo Kid does so with an African-derived metaphysics. Initially, the conflict between Loop Garoo Kid and Drag Gibson, who controls the town of Yellow Back Radio, seems to be political. But as Drag Gibson loses ground, the conflict shifts from personal to religious and cultural conflicts, with Loop Garoo Kid conjuring against guns from his headquarters in the cave. He achieves a metaphysical self/re-fashioning through an improvised "micro-Hoo-Doo" mass in which he conjures Drag Gibson and Yellow Back Radio by using pieces of cloth from Drag Gibson. In a prayer designed to end two thousand years of Christian monotheism, Loop Garoo Kid becomes the Father who commands Legba, an African loa of crossroads and interpretation, to connect his circuit to Guinea, Africa. Moreover, the Father (Loop Garoo Kid) summons forth different loas to help the black cowboy: cousin Zaka, Mack Hopson, Red-Eyed Ezili (Erzulie), Judas Iscariot, Jack Johnson, Baron-La-Croix, Doc Yah Yah, and ZoZo Labrique Marie Laveau. Clearly, Loop Garoo Kid's "micro-Hoo-Doo" mass is a parody of the Christian mass in which biblical figures are mixed with figures related to Voodoo and Hoodoo.

Analyzed closely, Loop Garoo Kid's "micro-Hoo-Doo" mass displays many elements that suggest how black people in the New World have had to improvise for the African gods and goddesses to survive. Also, one discovers that the aim of Loop Garoo Kid's credo is more than a desire to kill

Drag Gibson. For underneath the prayer lurks Loop Garoo Kid's syncretism and determination to bring back the respect that other people's religions and cultures deserve. In a very syncretic move, Loop Garoo Kid im-
plores a Black Hawk American Indian houngan of HooDoo to tell white
Americans to respect African American culture and cultural figures. This
syncretism is to be read as a means by which African-based religions have
prevailed through a coexistence with other cultures found in the New
World.

But as *Yellow Back Radio Broke-Down* suggests, the survival of New
World metaphysical reconfigurations in the African Diaspora does not
come very easily. As Loop Garoo Kid becomes more and more a real threat
to Christianity, Drag Gibson decides to invite the Pope, Innocent VIII,
whose mission would be to chase the Voodoo cowboy from the American
Wild West. Of course, calling upon the Pope to neutralize a Hoodoo cowboy bespeaks the tendency of the Catholic Church in the Middle Ages,
times of slavery, and colonial/postcolonial periods to suppress other cultures and religions.

One can argue that Reed has endowed the Pope with the powers of a
diviner and medicine man. John Mbiti has pointed out that the role of a
medicine man is to find out "why something has gone wrong" and to "tell
who may have worked evil, magic, sorcery or witchcraft against the sick
or the barren."[5] Indeed, it is through the Pope's lecture that we learn that
Loop Garoo Kid is practicing HooDoo, a North American version of Ju-Ju
religion, of Dahomean and Angolan origins. Also, the Pope's lecture
clearly explains why Africans in the New World had to reconfigure and
transform African deities. The Pope, for example, acknowledges that despite the Catholics' attempts to change and destroy the African pantheon
in the New World, African slaves simply placed their Damballah, Legba,
and other African deities alongside Christian saints. It is mentioned that
to avoid suspicion, women name their loas after their boyfriends.

Like a true diviner, the Pope sends his "spirits" (two black Judases) to
strip Loop Garoo Kid of his amulets, and decides to spare the HooDoo cowboy's life. The fact that the Pope refuses to kill Loop Garoo Kid, despite
Drag Gibson's insistence, is reminiscent of what Reed has said about Pope
Paul VI's book *Africae Terrarum*. According to Reed, Pope Paul VI's intentions suggested that the Church could benefit from "other traditions and
rites. It is a tenuous truce the Catholic Church has made with non-Western African deities and rites in the Americas. Even the most sophisticated
Creole Catholic has a Houngan tucked away somewhere in the background."[6]

The African ancestry and the New World self-fashioning are further
developed in *Mumbo Jumbo*, a novel in which Loop Garoo Kid becomes
the Voodoo detective and medicine man PaPa LaBas. To understand the
importance and significance of *Mumbo Jumbo* and PaPa LaBas, it is nec-

essary to briefly talk about Henry Louis Gates, Jr.'s theory of the Signifying Monkey, a theory partially inspired by Reed's *Mumbo Jumbo*. To elaborate his theory, Gates traces the origin of PaPa LaBas in Esu-Elegbara, the divine trickster figure of Yoruba mythology, also known as Legba among the Fon people in Benin. Additionally, Gates cogently argues that the New World figurations of Legba (Esu-Elegbara) "include Exú in Brazil, Echu-Elegua in Cuba, PaPa Legba (pronounced La-Bas) in the pantheon of the loa of Vaudu of Haiti, and PaPa LaBas in the loa of Hoodoo in the United States."[7] Furthermore, he concludes that the variations on Esu-Elegbara bespeak "an unbroken arc of metaphysical" relations shared by people in "certain black cultures in West Africa, South America, the Caribbean, and the United States."[8] Given the shift from Legba (Esu-Elegbara) to PaPa LaBas via the Haitian PaPa Legba, I argue that what Gates calls figuration is actually a reconfiguration and transformation of African gods and that in some cases the arc has been broken, refashioned, and then welded.

In her translation of René Depestre's book on Voodoo, Joan Dayan remarks that "unlike the original Dahomean version of Legba, who once loomed as the procreative and primal energy of all things, he appears in Haiti as suffering and aged."[9] Edward Brathwaite tells us that a "celebrant possessed by Legba [or Attibon Legba] assumes an aged, limping form and uses a crutch."[10] Reed concurs with this characterization of Legba when he states that in "Africa, Legba was a young man. In the New World, he is a wise old man."[11] In addition, while Legba is the god of the crossroads who mediates between the living and the spiritual world, PaPa LaBas of *Mumbo Jumbo* and *The Last Days of Louisiana Red*,[12] including trickster versions in Reed's other seven novels, is a Hoodoo detective and houngan who is still endowed with spirituality but who does not function as a loa.

Also from Gates's theory of the Signifying Monkey, one could argue that tracing the origins of Voodoo and Hoodoo is Reed's Afrocentrism, or the blackness of blackness.[13] This could not be further from the truth, for Reed is more interested in humbling Christianity by creating a multicultural space where African cultures coexist with other cultures from the world over.

The first indication of New World self/re-fashioning in *Mumbo Jumbo* starts with the title, which suggests many possible meanings, including "the received and ethnocentric Western designation for the rituals of black religions as well as for black languages themselves."[14] At the end of the prologue, Reed provides a dictionary definition of "Mumbo Jumbo" and suggests that it is an English corruption of "mā-mā-gyo-mbō," a Mandingo phrase that designates a magician who exorcises ancestors' troubled spirits. This is a clear example of how some African cultural elements were transformed in the New World to such an extent that they acquired new meanings and required new definitions.

Another indication that *Mumbo Jumbo* is about the origins of Voodoo and Hoodoo in the New World is that Jes Grew, a disguised form of Hoo-Doo, erupts first in New Orleans, the capital of Voodoo, before spreading to New York, Indiana, Minnesota, and Nebraska. Although its opponents describe it as a psychic epidemic that makes people do sensual things, a closer analysis reveals that Jes Grew is a popular and cultural manifestation of Voodoo, especially the phenomenon of being possessed by gods and goddesses. Not only is Jes Grew called "the delight of the gods," but one patient claims to have seen Unkulunkulu, the Zulu sky god, and a black python. Furthermore, Jes Grew is believed to resemble another phenomenon (Voodoo) that erupted in the 1890s in Place Congo. According to Jesse Gaston Mulira, Place Congo or Congo Square was "the site designated by New Orleans authorities for slaves and voodoos to gather on Sunday afternoons and dance." Mulira also points out that in 1920 nurses at Charity Hospital in New Orleans reported cases of voodoo and hoodoo and of patients who claimed to have been hoodooed.[15]

It should be made clear that in *Mumbo Jumbo* the Mayor of New Orleans is worried because Jes Grew, being a multiethnic and multicultural phenomenon, threatens his election and the hegemony of Western civilization. His efforts to eradicate Jes Grew translate into a cultural conflict between the Wallflower Order people, their Atonists and art curators, and PaPa LaBas and the Mu'tafikah. Despite the Wallflower Order and the Atonists' attempts to suppress Jes Grew by all means, the latter resists by appealing to people across race, class, and gender lines.

In a more direct way, *Mumbo Jumbo* is Reed's dissertation about the manifold aspects of Voodoo and Hoodoo, the role of Africa and Haiti in the origin of African-American culture, the Harlem Renaissance, Egyptology, the origin of monoculturalism, and the coming of multiculturalism. One of its theses is that African-American culture indirectly originates in Africa and is transmitted via Haiti. The novel involves a considerable amount of research on Haitian history, Voodoo, and Hoodoo (a North American version of Voodoo). It is noteworthy that Reed wrote *Mumbo Jumbo* after a research trip to Haiti in 1969. Throughout *Mumbo Jumbo*, the interest in Haiti stems from the idea that since Haitians are culturally closer to Africa than are African-Americans, it is normal that they provide a cultural base for North America. Reed has mentioned elsewhere that the *National Geographic* has described Haiti as the "West Africa of the Caribbean."[16] The same statement is made in *Mumbo Jumbo* when Benoit Battraville, a Haitian houngan, tells PaPa LaBas that Haitians can only provide North America blacks with a base, after which they have to figure out the rest on their own.

That Haiti provides the base for African-American culture is demonstrated by PaPa LaBas and his Hoodoo. A radio report in *Mumbo Jumbo* states that "IN HAITI IT WAS PAPA LOA, IN NEW ORLEANS IT WAS

PAPA LABAS, IN CHICAGO IT WAS PAPA JOE. THE LOCATIONS MAY SHIFT BUT THE FUNCTION REMAINS THE SAME" (77). Of course, in Africa, it was Legba in Benin or Esu-Elegbara in Nigeria—the god of crossroads and interpretations, who mediates between gods and human beings. As alluded to at the beginning of this essay, in *Mumbo Jumbo* PaPa LaBas's lineage is not as clear as it appears in Gates's study. While one version suggests that PaPa LaBas's ancestor might be "the long Ju Ju of Arno [Aro][17] in eastern Nigeria, the man who would oracle, sitting in the mouth of a cave," another version alleges that PaPa LaBas is "the reincarnation of the famed Moor of Summerland himself, the Black gypsy who according to Sufi Lit. sicked the witches on Europe" (23).

Things get even more complex when later in the novel PaPa LaBas suggests that Jes Grew and Voodoo are all traceable to the Egyptian Osiris and Isis. When PaPa Labas charges that Hinckle Von Vampton is related to Set and the Atonists, a Guianese art critic challenges him to provide evidence, because the whole theory would mean that Hinckle Von Vampton is one thousand years old. In a move that is only rivaled by Cheik Anta Diop, PaPa LaBas digs deep into Egyptology to explain how Set's legislators mutilated Osiris and how Isis later tried to gather the limbs of Osiris. PaPa LaBas adds that when Set tried to arrest Osirian guides who had learned the Work, some "of them [went] to Down Home where they matched their knowledge with the necromancers in Ifé, Nigeria. Dionysus traveled to Greece where the Dance 'spread like wildfire' although Homer doesn't mention it"[18] (168). If Set introduced and fostered monotheism through Atonism—the basis for Set's religion was Aton, the Sun's flaming disc; the latter is also the symbol of the Wallflower Order—Tutankhamen allowed people "to do their stuff, working out this way on the hall every which-a-way" (174). It is here that Moses comes into the story and tries to learn the Osirian dance and Work from Jethro.

In a reading that sharply contrasts that of the Bible, PaPa LaBas argues that according to the Voodoo tradition, Moses "learned the secrets of Voodoo from Jethro and taught them to his followers," including the Israelites, Jesus Christ, the Apostles, and the Knights Templar. What is important here is that Moses is believed to have been the first Voodoo man. Zora Neale Hurston has confirmed the fact that Moses learned from Jethro, "a great hoodoo man," and that "Moses was the first man who ever learned God's power-compelling words."[19] Also, in a letter to his cousin Zepho, Jethro brags about his son Moses being "the finest hoodoo man" who can send snakes and lice.[20] Given that Zora Neale Hurston describes Moses as "two beings,"[21] which makes him resemble Legba, one can argue that PaPa LaBas is also a version of Moses in *Mumbo Jumbo*.

Despite all these speculations about his origins, the novel insists that tracing PaPa LaBas's exact lineage is not as important as knowing that his grandfather was brought to America on a slave ship and was one of the people who brought African religion to the New World. Equally important is the legend behind his grandfather, because the latter was reputed to have hoodooed and killed white planters and slave masters. One could then misread these speculations about PaPa LaBas's lineage and argue that Reed is not as interested in being more accurate about PaPa LaBas's lineage as he is in emphasizing that PaPa LaBas and his Hoodoo are Haitian versions.

This reading would be erroneous, because despite the confused ancestry, what is more important is PaPa LaBas's connection to the survival of African religion in the New World. For his father had to adapt the Work to new conditions by selling roots through mail orders, which should be interpreted as a trait of religious self/re-fashioning. In Africa, medicine women and men or herbalists do not mail roots medicine, herbs, or charms; people who are interested must travel to the herbalists' compounds. But a New World requires new ways of operating, especially when the Work or Business is being threatened by the monoculturalists of Judeo-Christianity—in Reed's terminology Work and Business (used throughout *The Last Days of Louisiana Red*) are coded names for Voodoo and Hoodoo, and "Workers" designate Voodooists, Hoodooists, and healers.

As an heir to his ancestor's Voodoo traditions, PaPa LaBas practices Hoodoo in Mumbo Jumbo Kathedral, a derisive name that critics have given his headquarters. Like his ancestor, he has turned his Hoodoo practice into a lucrative industry, and Mumbo Jumbo Kathedral is referred to as a "factory which deals in jewelry, Black astrology charts, herbs, potions, candles, talismans" (24). Equally significant is how PaPa LaBas seems to have gone beyond what medicine men and women in Africa prescribe to their patients. To Mother Brown, a woman who suffers from "nightly visitations," PaPa LaBas gives "garlic, sage, thyme, geranium water, dry basil, parsley, saltpeter, bay rum, verbena essence and jack honeysuckle" (24). Mother Brown is to bathe in the potion, which "will place the vaporous evil Ka hovering above her sleep under arrest and cause it to disperse" (25). Despite the fact that this potion looks more like a cooking recipe than a therapeutic potion, we are told that people trust PaPa LaBas's powers.

What is more important, however, is the fact that PaPa LaBas has carried African metaphysics to a new level, Neo-HooDoo therapy. Whereas his enemies refer to him as an "Astrodetective," Papa LaBas describes himself as "a private eye" and a self-licensed Neo-HooDoo Therapist who in 1920 gave himself an Asson as a symbol of his power.[22] Abdul Sufi Hamid, a black Muslim who would rather believe in Islam than Voodoo and HooDoo, describes what PaPa Labas has developed as "HooDoo psychiatry" (37). In a lecture to students in the Epilogue of *Mumbo Jumbo*, PaPa LaBas calls himself "a jacklegged detective of the metaphysical who was on the case" when in 1920 "Jes Grew swept through this country" (212). In other words, not only is he a houngan and a Neo-HooDoo therapist, but he also is a lecturer and a scholar. In effect, PaPa LaBas has written two books, *Blue Back: A Speller*—everyone must read this book at Mumbo Jumbo Kathedral—and *The Forest Within*, which Benoit Battraville uses to capture those who wanted to disrupt PaPa LaBas's work and dismantle Jes Grew. Early in the novel, these manifold functions are epitomized in a description of PaPa Labas, in which he is said to be a "noonday HooDoo, fugitive hermit, obeah-man, botanist, animal impersonator, 2-headed man, You-Name-It" (45).

Whereas PaPa LaBas remains a HooDoo detective in *The Last Days of Louisiana Red*, it is Ed Yellings who practices Neo-HooDoo therapy, although he tells people that he is into Gumbo Business. With his Solid Gumbo Works (industry), Ed Yellings develops a gumbo that cures certain cancers. He is so successful that gumbo is seen "as a cure-all dish" that threatens to bankrupt other health-food stores (20). When Ed Yellings is killed, PaPa LaBas alleges that his opponents murdered him because he was close to developing a cure for heroin addiction.

Another aspect of New World metaphysical self/re-fashioning in *Mumbo Jumbo* is suggested in the ways South American, North American, and African rites resemble and differ from one another in terms of techniques and therapies associated with Voodoo and Hoodoo. The difference in attitude translates into the fact that "the Haitian elite pays homage to Catholicism but keeps a houngan tucked away in the background" (47). In other words, unlike North American blacks, Haitians practiced "Catholicism up front and Voodoo underground," a technique similar to the practice referred to by the "New Orleans expression 'doing the Calinda against the Dude'" (134). As the Haitian Benoit Battraville tells PaPa LaBas, people joked about how Haitians practiced Catholicism at 95 percent and Voodoo at 100 percent.[23] Furthermore, Haitians do not do the Work or practice Voodoo the way PaPa LaBas and other North American blacks do, because not only do Haitians believe in old mysteries, but they also improvise a great deal. In addition, Haitians occasionally practice the Petro loa, a family of loas who are bad but bring good luck when well fed.

In response to PaPa LaBas, Black Herman, an occultist, argues that because they were dumped in the New World "without the Book" to teach them about the loas, they had to refashion and make their own loas, including Blues, Ragtime, and the theories of Julia Jackson. For Black Herman, stretching out and opening up through improvisation is the key to metaphysical retention in the New World. Also, he predicts that soon some new artists will teach Africa and South America "some new twists." Black Herman's attitude clearly adumbrates the relation between Africa and its African Diaspora. Blacks in the New World have had to improvise and create new arts out of the African roots. Blues, jazz, ragtime, and the Work[24] are just a few examples of these improvisations and self/re-fashioning. When Nathan Brown asks him how to catch Jes Grew, Benoit Battraville criticizes him and his peers for not knowing the long list of deities and

rites because they have amalgamated "the HooDoo of VooDoo." Nevertheless, he advises Brown to ask Louis Armstrong, Bessie Smith, poets, painters, and other musicians how to get possessed (152).

That Benoit Battraville advises African Americans to ask Louis Armstrong, Bessie Smith, and other musicians how to catch Jes Grew is significant, given the close association between Voodoo (Hoodoo), music, and
dance. In *Mumbo Jumbo*, not only is Jes Grew associated with jazz and
dance, but also Reed makes several statements about dance, including
the fact that dance is the tune of life. At the end of his lecture in the Epilogue, PaPa LaBas emphatically declares, "The Blues is a Jes Grew, as
James Weldon Johnson surmised. Jazz was a Jes Grew which followed the
Jes Grew of Ragtime. Slang is Jes Grew too" (214). In "The Old Music,"
an essay in *Shrovetide in Old New Orleans*, Reed argues that for African
Americans to realize their tradition, they must recognize "Jelly Roll Morton, a HooDoo believer, as the guardian of spirit rhythms and Louis Armstrong as the King Zulu, the New Orleans Houngan" (64). Additionally,
he states that in the "old music the instruments sound like 'voices'" and
"substitute for the spirits who possess the human hosts in a ceremony,"
and that in early New Orleans "music even bore HooDoo titles such as
'Up Jumped LaBas,' most likely Creoles trying to say Legba" (65). Furthermore, Reed adds that the "'Blues' is often treated as a loa: 'Good Morning,
blues/blues, how do you do,' from 'Jailhouse,' the Houngan greeting a loa"
(65). Interestingly, *Mumbo Jumbo* contains a passage (repeated in "The
Old Music" essay) where Louis Armstrong describes people who are attracted by a funeral procession through music and dance. Thereafter, these
people are possessed by Baron Samedi, the spirit of cemetery—another
New-World-created deity—who forces them to follow the mourners.

The point that *Mumbo Jumbo* makes about the interconnectedness
between HooDoo/Jes Grew and Jazz/Blues is that, after being forced underground in the New World, African-derived religions had to appear in
the forms of music and dance to avoid suspicion. According to a radio report in *Mumbo Jumbo*, "CREOLE BANDS CONCEAL JES GREW FROM
CHICAGO'S PSYCHIC DEPARTMENT OF PUBLIC HEALTH. ERZULIE
WITH HER FAST SELF IS SHELTERED IN A 'VOCALIZING TRUMPET
WHICH SINGS FROM MUTE TO GROWL.' LEGBA TAKES REQUESTS
FROM BEHIND THE DERBY-COVERED BELL OF A 'TALKING' SLIDE-
TROMBONE" (77). Edward Brathwaite reminds us that "until the
drum/speaks" God is silent and that it is the drum that guides us where
God speaks.[25] The passage from *Mumbo Jumbo* demonstrates that Reed
has tapped into the African aesthetic regarding religions; for as Mbiti has
cogently argued, African religions are found in music and dance, in addition to places, religious objects, proverbs and riddles, or people's names.[26]

From Benoit Battraville's advice we can also deduce that for Reed, the
difference in attitude is of paramount importance, because the difference

in attitude is a difference in aesthetic freedom. Reed complains about the fact that, except for Oba Oseijeman in North Carolina, one does not see blacks up and down southern highways selling statues of African gods. He notes that the "'objective correlatives' of the Haitian African psychology are visible in everyday life, while here, where suppression of Afro-American cultures has been mean, they are invisible and abstract: jazz."[27]

It is then clear that for Reed and his characters in Mumbo Jumbo, Haiti is the symbol of political freedom from foreign oppressors, of awareness of cultural identity, and of aesthetic freedom—the freedom to write or create art from a syncretic or multicultural point of view. Throughout his report on Haiti, indeed, Reed demonstrates how Haitian art has influenced his writing: Haitian art "'distorts'" reality and is based on Voodoo principles; artists bring their own aesthetic sense to universal forms.[28] It is stated in Mumbo Jumbo that when artists discover new forms they proclaim that they have reached their Haiti. The text of Mumbo Jumbo accounts for the symbolic meaning of Haiti by recounting Haitian resistance against France in 1791, and then against the American occupation from 1915 to 1934, the very period in which Mumbo Jumbo takes place. In a sense, the novel celebrates Haitian heroes who fought for Haiti's independence. In PaPa LaBas's Mumbo Jumbo Kathedral there hang pictures of Toussaint L'Ouverture, Jean Jacques Dessalines, Henri Christophe, Boukman, the PaPa Loi, and André Rigaud.

Thus, PaPa LaBas and other North American characters also are interested in Haitian Voodoo because of its power to subvert threatening powers, as was exemplified during the U.S. occupation of Haiti. The text of Mumbo Jumbo contains several headlines (as in newspapers) that suggest that the Haitian warriors who surrounded the Marines at Port-au-Prince were Voodoo generals who were possessed by Ogun, the Voodoo loa of martial force and war. The repetition of these headlines in the text underscores the role that Voodoo has played in every political crisis in Haiti. The liberational aspect of Voodoo in Haiti is glorified throughout Mumbo Jumbo whose text maintains that the American occupation of Haiti forced writers and intellectuals to reembrace Voodoo and to rally to the banner of "Ogoun War Loa."[29] Rather than driving the U.S. Marines by force, Haitians returned to their ancient religion, Voodoo, "just as [their] ancestors the Egyptians the Nubians the Ethiopians did in times of trouble. The Marines became nervous. They didn't expect this" (135). In a sense, it is a cultural force against modern armed forces.

But despite these new coded forms of Voodoo and HooDoo, Jes Grew seems to wane at the end of Mumbo Jumbo, thus demonstrating the difficulty for Africans of the Diaspora to publicly practice their African ancestral beliefs and to successfully have them coexist with those of the Europeans, which slavery has forced them to live with. We are told that several people have sent congratulatory telegrams to the White House for having forced Jes Grew underground again. This is a transient victory, however, for we are told that Jes Grew cannot end as long as people live. As PaPa LaBas tells Earline, his assistant in the Work, they will "try to depress Jes Grew but it will only spring back and prosper. We will make our own future Text" (204). Encouraged by this optimism Earline vows to go to New Orleans, Haiti, Brazil, and other South American countries to learn more and study "our ancient cultures, our HooDoo cultures. Maybe by and by some future artists 30 to 40 years from now will benefit from my research" (206).

The urgency to learn more about HooDoo cultures, and therefore African-derived cultures, is also one of the themes in *Japanese By Spring* (1993). In this novel a Yoruba priest of Olódùmarè indicts African Americans for having forgotten their African deities, especially the Yoruba pantheon. Although the Yoruba language is used in the novel, besides English and Japanese, what attracts Reed (the author) to Yoruba culture—Ishmael Reed appears as a character in the novel to challenge his main character Benjamin Chappie Puttbutt—goes beyond the linguistic aspect: Yoruba exemplifies what has happened to the Africans in the New World. The greater fascination is about the epic of Yoruba Ifa in which Esu, Death, and Disease pay a visit to Orúnmìlà, who sells everything he owns to provide them with food and drink.

Reed achieves the highest point in his theory about what happened to African religions and the necessity for self/re-fashioning in the African Diaspora in "epilogue—Olódùmarè regained?", which can be regarded as the crowning moment of *Japanese By Spring*. "Though the descendants of Africans who survived the Atlantic crossing—the Olósun—still worship Yèyesun, or Òṣun (Olódùmarè's daughter)," Ògún Sànyà criticizes people of the African Diaspora for having forgotten Olódùmarè, "the omniscient, omnipresent, omnipotent." To restore the contact to Olódùmarè, Sànyà has invited people to attend the consecration of a temple to Olódùmarè on June 7, 1992. During the ceremony Ògún is to resurrect Olódùmarè, a god who is inactive in the African American experiences and "with whom African Americans lost contact after the breakup of Yoruba empire and the slave trade which the people at Whittle Books blame on what they refer to as 'African chieftains'" (217). For Sànyà, losing contact with Olódùmarè was tantamount to losing a phone contact with the deity, and resurrecting him would be like repairing the phone and restoring the Diaspora's direct line.

Besides the historicization of Africans' cultural and religious experiences in the Diaspora, the novel suggests a kind of improvisation as far as the temple is concerned, for Sànyà has chosen a community center in a shopping plaza as Olódùmarè's place of resurrection. This is probably a way of letting Olódùmarè go public. In this light, the novel makes a connection between Yoruba religion and A. M. E. Zion Church. At his stepfather's funeral, Ishmael Reed (the character) noticed that the Olósun wore nurses' uniforms, because in "a puritan country, Africans had to use camouflage in order to preserve their faith. Had to behave like chameleons" (219). In other words, self/re-fashioning came about not necessarily because Africans in the New World had forgotten the right African ways of worshipping, but because they wanted to survive and maintain their faith. One such instance is when the Olósun had to lie to the overseer that they were going to the river to get baptized, while they were actually in a procession to the Tennessee River to greet the goddess Ọ̀ṣun; that is, in order to survive, blacks had to hide African deities under the garb of Christian saints.

To be sure, this is a way for Reed not only to historicize the resistance of African-based religions, but also to showcase his knowledge of Yoruba language and culture—Reed has received two scholarships to study Yoruba language and culture. It is an opportunity to retell the Yoruba legend of creation—the novel tells us that it is a version recorded by G. J. Afolabi—according to which Olódùmarè created the earth with the chameleon, Obàtálá, and Orúnmìlà as messengers. The fowl and the pigeon had to spread sand on earth. Eventually, Olódùmarè gave the earth to Obàtálá to rule, with Orúnmìlà as counselor.

Just as the altar has been improvised, so the audience is as diverse as it can be: Ògún Sànyà has included professor Crabtree, a former Miltonian and Eurocentrist, who is dressed in a traditional Nigerian outfit. The adaptation to the new environment is so elastic that Ògún Sànyà has decided to use Native American and Eastern texts for future ceremonies just to illustrate the universalism of Yoruba. Interestingly enough, it is the European American Crabtree who leads "Awá Dé O, Olórun," a song of praise for Olódùmarè. The fact that a former Miltonian leads a prayer to Olódùmarè suggests to what extent African American culture can coexist with other American cultures and how even white Americans can learn about other cultures.

Although Ògún Sànyà's success is counteracted by the character Ishmael Reed's refusal to worship Olódùmarè, which deconstructs the very self/re-fashioning of the Yoruba deity, it is clear that Reed has used Yoruba as a metaphor of retention and self/re-fashioning in the African Diaspora. He has alleged that Africans of the Diaspora speak English with a Yoruba syntax and that it is by studying the literature of Yoruba civilization that "one can see some of the retention that has happened."[30] From my point of view, Yoruba should be seen as a metaphor for African cultures that crossed and survived the Middle Passage and as a synecdoche for Africa. Also, as seen in *Yellow Back Radio Broke-Down*, *Mumbo Jumbo*, *The Last Days of Louisiana Red*, *Flight to Canada*, *The Terrible Twos*, *The Terrible Threes*, and three collections of poetry, the use of Yoruba falls into Reed's Neo-HooDooism; it is a way to humble the monologue of English language, and the result is a multilingual voice. As the analysis of *Mumbo Jumbo* has demonstrated, Reed uses an African-derived aesthetic to endow his "(re)visions and (re)interpretations" with a discourse that transforms a discourse of monologue into a discourse of "polylogue."[31]

NOTES

1. For a full explanation of Neo-HooDooism or Neo-HooDoo Aesthetics see Ishmael Reed's poems "Neo-HooDoo Manifesto," "The Neo-Hoo-Doo Aesthetic," and "Catechism of d Neoamerican Hoodoo Church" in *Collected Poems* (New York: Atheneum, 1988), 20–25; 26; 36–41; Neil Schmitz, "Neo-HooDoo: The Experimental Fiction of Ishmael Reed," *Twentieth Century Fiction* 20.2 (1974):126–40; Reginald Martin, *Ishmael Reed and the New Black Aesthetic Critics* (New York: St. Martin Press, 1988), 63–108; Robert Elliot Fox, *Masters of the Drum: Black Lit/oratures Across the Continuum* (Westport, Connecticut: Greenwood Press, 1995), 49–62; James Lindroth, "Images of Subversion: Ishmael Reed and the Hoodoo Trickster," *African American Review* 30.2 (Summer 1996):185–196; Sämi Ludwig, "Dialogic Possession in Ishmael Reed's *Mumbo Jumbo*: Bakhtin, Voodoo, and the Materiality of Multicultural Discourse"; *The Black Columbiad: Defining Moments in African American Literature and Culture* (1994):325–336. For a full discussion of Reed's neo-HooDooism and food, see my article "Ishmael Reed's Neo-HooDoo Aesthetic, or the Proportions of Ingredients in Art and Food," *Poetic Briefs* 11 (April 1993): 2–3.
2. In his foreword to *Conjure: Selected Poems 1963–1970* (1972), Reed describes this poem as his "first attempt to define ancient Afro-American HooDoo as a contemporary art form" (ix).
3. Chinua Achebe, *Things Fall Apart* (1959; reprint, New York: Fawcett Crest, 1991); *Arrow of God* (1964; reprint, New York: Anchor Books, Doubleday, 1989). Ngugi wa Thiong'O, *Weep Not Child* (New Hampshire: Heinemann, 1964); *The River Between* (New Hampshire: Heinemann, 1965).
4. Ishmael Reed, *Writin' Is Fightin': Thirty-Seven Years of Boxing on Paper* (1988; reprint, New York: Atheneum, 1990), 137.
5. John Mbiti, *Introduction to African Religion* (1975; reprint, New Hampshire: Heinemann, 1991), 157.
6. Ishmael Reed, *Shrovetide in Old New Orleans* (1978; reprint, New York: Atheneum, 1989), 267.
7. Henry Louis Gates, Jr., *The Signifying Monkey: A Theory of African-American Literary Criticism* (New York: Oxford University Press, 1988), 5.
8. Gates, 6.
9. René Depestre, *A Rainbow for the Christian West*, trans. Joan Dayan (Amherst: University of Massachusetts Press, 1977), 59.
10. Edward Brathwaite, *Islands* (London: Oxford University Press, 1969), ix.
11. Ishmael Reed, *Shrovetide in Old New Orleans*, 271.
12. Ishmael Reed, *Mumbo Jumbo* (1972; reprint, New York: Atheneum,

1988); *The Last Days of Louisiana Red*, (1974; reprint, New York: Atheneum, 1989).

13. Gates, *The Signifying Monkey*, 217–238; see also Henry Louis Gates, Jr., *Figures in Black: Words, Signs, and the "Racial" Self* (New York: Oxford University Press, 1989), 235–276.

14. Gates, *The Signifying Monkey*, 220.

15. Jesse Gaston Mulira, "The Case of Voodoo in New Orleans," *Africanisms in American Culture*, ed. Joseph E. Holloway (Bloomington: Indiana University Press, 1990), 53; 58.

16. Ishmael Reed, *Shrovetide in Old New Orleans*. Reed justifies this concept by arguing that "having expelled Europeans very early, Haiti is more genuinely African than the actual place, invaded and occupied to this day, by Europeans" (266).

17. I am indebted to Professor Robert Elliot Fox for suggesting that "Arno" is probably a misspelling of "Aro"; the latter makes more sense in the sentence.

18. In his book *Myth, Literature, and the African World*, Wole Soyinka discusses the resemblance between the Greek pantheon and the Yoruba deities: "That Greek religion shows persuasive parallels with, to stick to our example, the Yoruba is by no means denied; the Delphic oracle and the Ifa Corpus of the Yoruba are a fascinating instance of one such structural parallel" (14).

19. Zora Neale Hurston, *Mules and Men* (1935; reprint, New York: Harper Perennial Library, 1990), 184.

20. Zora Neale Hurston, *Moses, Man of the Mountain* (1939; reprint, New York: Harper Perennial, 1990), 114.

21. Zora Neale Hurston, *Moses*, 60.

22. In *Shrovetide in Old New Orleans*, Reed defines Assons as "the symbols of the Houngan's power" that "resemble abstract human figures with arms but no legs" (273).

23. In *Shrovetide in Old New Orleans*, Reed gives the same number and adds, "I didn't know the truth of this until I discovered that Vodoun material was not only hidden in the murals of Christian themes but was being hustled right out of the church's gift shop! Not only were there vé-vés and other Vodoun paraphernalia for sale, but stationery with Vodoun symbols on it, Grand Bois, Agew [Agwe?] (Erzulie's husband, a sea loa), and Ghedes [sic], the cemetery loas" (281).

24. Work is a coded name for conjure, gris-gris, and possession, used to avoid detection. In *The Last Days of Louisiana Red* the term Business is also used; so a houngan would be referred to as a Worker/Businessman and HooDoo as the Work/Business.

25. Edward Brathwaite, *Masks* (London: Oxford University Press, 1968), 10.

26. John Mbiti, *Introduction to African Religion*. According to Mbiti, "music gives outlet to the emotional expression of the religious life, and it is a powerful means of communication in African traditional life" (27).

27. Reed, *Shrovetide in Old New Orleans*, 260–61.

28. Reed, 270.

29. It is noteworthy that Reed is not consistent in his spelling of Ogun; nor is he with Vodun.

30. Steve Cannon, et al., "A Gathering of the Tribes: Conversation with Ishmael Reed," *Conversations with Ishmael Reed*, ed. Bruce Dick and Amritjit Singh (Jackson: University of Mississippi Press, 1995), 371.

31. I borrow these concepts from Robert Elliot Fox's book *Masters of the Drum: Black Lit/oratures Across the Continuum* (Connecticut: Greenwood Press, 1995), 52.

REFERENCES

Achebe, Chinua. *Things Fall Apart.* 1959. Reprint, New York: Fawcett Crest, 1991.
———. *Arrow of God.* 1964. Reprint, New York: Doubleday, 1989.
Brathwaite, Edward. *Masks.* London: Oxford University Press, 1968.
———. *Islands.* London: Oxford University Press, 1969.
Byerman, Keith E. *Fingering the Jagged Grain: Tradition and Form in Recent Black Fiction.* Georgia: The University Press of Georgia, 1985.
Cannon, Steve. "A Gathering of the Tribes: Conversation with Ishmael Reed." In *Conversations with Ishmael Reed*, edited by Bruce Dick and Amritjit Singh. Jackson: University of Mississippi Press, 1995: 361–81.
Depestre, René. *A Rainbow for the Christian West.* Translated by Joan Dayan. Amherst: University of Massachusetts Press, 1977.
Fox, Robert E. *Conscientious Sorcerers: The Black Postmodernist Fiction of LeRoi Jones/Amiri Baraka, Ishmael Reed, and Samuel R. Delany.* New York: Greenwood Press, 1988.
———. *Masters of the Drum: Black Lit/oratures Across the Continuum.* Connecticut: Greenwood, 1995.
Gaston, Mulira. "The Case of Voodoo in New Orleans." In *Africanisms in American Culture*, edited by Joseph Holloway. Bloomington: Indiana University Press, 1990: 34–68.
Gates, Henry Louis, Jr. *Figures in Black: Words, Signs, and the "Racial" Self.* New York: Oxford University Press, 1989.
———. *The Signifying Monkey: A Theory of African-American Literary Criticism.* New York: Oxford University Press, 1988.
Gover, Robert. "Interview with Ishmael Reed." *Black Literature Forum.* 12.1. (Spring 1978):12–19.
Hardack, Richard. "Swing to the White, Back to the Black: Writing and "Sourcery" in Ishmael Reed's *Mumbo Jumbo*." In *Literary Influence and African American Writers*, edited by Tracy Mishkin. New York: Garland Publishing, 1996: 271–300.
Hurston, Zora Neale. *Moses, Man of the Mountain.* 1939. Reprint, New York: Harper Perennial, 1990.
———. *Mules and Men.* 1935. Reprint, New York: Harper Perennial, 1990.
———. *Tell My Horse: Voodoo and Life in Haiti and Jamaica.* 1938. Reprint, New York: Harper Perennial, 1990.

Lindrof, James. "Images of Subversion: Ishmael Reed and the Hoodoo Trickster." *African American Review* 30.2 (Summer 1996):185–196.

Ludwig, Sämi. "Dialogic Possession in Ishmael Reed's *Mumbo Jumbo*: Bakhtin, Voodoo, and the Materiality of Multicultural Discourse." In *The Black Columbiad: Defining Moments in African American Literature and Culture*. Eds. Werner Sollors and Maria Diedrich. Massachusetts: Harvard University Press, 1994: 325–336.

Martin, Reginald. *Ishmael Reed and the New Black Aesthetic Critics*. New York: St. Martin's Press, 1988.

Mason, Theodore, Jr. "Performance, History, and Myth: The Problem of Ishmael Reed in *Mumbo Jumbo*." *Modern Fiction Studies* 34.1 (Spring 1988):97–109.

Mbiti, John. *Introduction to African Religion*. 1975. Reprint, New Hampshire: Heinemann, 1991.

Mvuyekure, Pierre-Damien. "Signifyin(g) Revisions, Pretexts, Subtexts, and Posttexts: Elements of Multiculturalism in Ishmael Reed's Writing." Ph.D. diss., State University of New York at Buffalo, 1993.

Ngugi, wa Thiong'O. *The River Between*. New Hampshire: Heinemann, 1965.

———. *Weep Not Child*. New Hampshire: Heinemann, 1964.

O'Brien, John, ed. *Interviews with Black Writers*. New York: Liveright, 1973.

Reed, Ishmael. *Chattanooga: Poems by Ishmael Reed*. New York: Random House, 1973.

———. *Flight to Canada*. 1976. Reprint, New York: Atheneum, 1989.

———. *The Free-Lance Pallbearers*. 1967. Reprint, New York: Atheneum, 1988.

———. *Japanese By Spring*. New York: Atheneum, 1993.

———. *The Last Days of Louisiana Red*. 1974. Reprint, New York: Atheneum, 1989.

———. *Mumbo Jumbo*. 1972. Reprint, New York: Atheneum, 1988.

———. *New and Collected Poetry*. New York: Atheneum, 1989.

———. *Shrovetide in Old New Orleans*. 1978. Reprint, New York: Atheneum, 1989.

———. *The Terrible Threes*. 1989. Reprint, New York: Atheneum, 1991.

———. *The Terrible Twos*. 1982. Reprint, New York: Atheneum, 1988.

———. *Writin' Is Fightin': Thirty Seven Years of Boxing on Paper*. 1988. Reprint, New York: Atheneum, 1990.

———. *Yellow Back Radio Broke-Down*. 1969. Reprint, New York: Atheneum, 1988.

Schmidtz, Neil. "Neo-HooDoo: The Experimental Fiction of Ishmael Reed." *Twentieth Century Fiction* 20.2 (1974):126–140.

Shadle, Mark. "A Bird's Eye View: Ishmael Reed's Unsettling of the Score by Munching and Mooching on the Mumbo Jumbo Work of History." *North Dakota Quarterly* 54.1 (1986):18–29.

Soyinka, Wole. *Myth, Literature, and the African World*. 1976. Reprint, New York: Cambridge University Press, 1995.

23 DIASPORACENTRISM AND BLACK AURAL TEXTS

Robert Elliot Fox

[I]f history is a "web," it is one with many gaps and holes which
allow it to be constantly rewoven. . . . Thus one can see minority not
as a given, monolithic, traditional identity, but rather as a multiple,
unpredictable force which comes out from the *intervals* of official
memory to problematize and recompose traditions.
Rajchman "The Question of Identity" (ix)

In opposition to essentialist notions of race and the linear construction of history as progress, the term *diaspora* embraces a plurality of
different cultures and discontinuous histories. Not removed or separated from each other . . . these cultures and histories are interrelated
and are interwoven together in the tapestry of a wider history.
Tawadros "Beyond the Boundary" (257)

[A] construction of identity is not an imaginary process but a *processing of the imaginary. . . .*
Balibar "Culture and Identity (Working Notes)" (187)

This essay is premised in part on the notion that when dealing with
black cultures, we are not only performing *readings*, we are also holding *hearings*, for lit/orature[1] involves both the visual and the verbal, the
written/danced/mimed and the spoken/sung/played.

The ideas I am developing here were spun off, as it were, from an ongoing project dealing with the origins and influences of the Black Arts
Movement. Much of the critical writing focussing on this movement—
which isn't very extensive, given the crucial importance of this particular
period of cultural upheaval—explores its literary aspects, but it is increasingly clear that a good deal of the genesis of the Black Arts Movement and
much of its sustaining imagination and energy are to be found in black
music. Thus I sought out and began listening to an abundance of music—
much of it from the 1970s—that (then being preoccupied by other sounds)

I had neglected or missed out on when it first appeared: for example, George Clinton's "Supergroovalistic-prosifunkification" (to use the title of one of the tracks from the 1975 Parliament album *Mothership Connection*), the "theatre of sound" of saxophonist Julius Hemphill (probably best known for his work with the World Saxophone Quartet), the "improvisational acid-funk" of Miles Davis's *Pangaea* period, and the spirit-reach of Pharoah Sanders.

Many of the black aural texts I shall be referring to are instrumental jazz pieces which, I argue, tell stories, even though they are wordless, and these stories, while they may invoke or rehearse Africa, principally concern themselves with the experience of people of African descent in America; in short, they are diaspora tales. But to take a non-jazz example, and one that is word-laden rather than wordless, George Clinton's work with Parliament[2] and Funkadelic[3] in the seventies has, like all black music in America, an African inheritance, but it is most blatantly a product of, and a response to, a specifically *American* experience. In a manner very similar to that of poet/novelist Ishmael Reed, Clinton's work parodies—signifies upon—American experience, including *black* experience. Clinton's concept of nationalism, furthermore, is "one nation under a groove," and this nation—a "democracy of the dancefloor"—isn't exclusively black. The Funkadelic "freedom principle" is a pan-human one; so, too, is the blues phenomenology which preceded and nurtured it.

Listening to all this music—black art par excellence—I also was struck by the frequent embrace of what is now called "world music" and the implications of this for an operative multiculturalism "before the fact," or rather, before its political/academic vogue.[4] I am more of a diasporacentrist than an Afrocentrist because I am—bottomline—a multiculturalist (an allegiance I began to acquire in earnest while living in Africa). Most Afrocentrists seem to me to be monoculturalists. Diasporacentrism can't be "mono-" anything; it's a mixology, a morphing mindscape. In retrospect, this shouldn't have been surprising, given the schismatic and rhizomatic character of diaspora. As the painter R. B. Kitaj puts it, "Diasporist art is contradictory at its heart, being both internationalist and particularist" (35). (In contemplating the word "contradictory" in the foregoing, keep in mind Walt Whitman's avowal in "Song of Myself": "I contradict myself; / I am large . . . I contain multitudes.")

The term "diasporacentrism" may be an instigation, even a provocation, but it is not an oxymoron. Diasporacentrism is the articulation of a "centerless center" aimed at troubling the inward whirl of centrisms that tend to be unnatural focuses, retroactive and overdetermined. Diasporacentrism, on the other hand, is mobile, fluid, indeterminate. The diaspora may be envisioned as the dispersed site of an ongoing "middle passage"—not, now, the uprooting and dispossession caused by the slave trade, but a permanent intervention, marked by complex paths of possibilities. (We are dealing with *routes* as well as roots.) Keep in mind that a "passage" can mean transition, negotiation, interchange of communication. "Middle," of course, is something in a central position; similarly, "centrism" is a middle position between more divergent views. Diasporacentrism is situated between the excess of Eurocentrism on the one hand and the excess of Afrocentrism on the other.

The word *diaspora*, of course, is Greek and means "dispersion," from the verb "to disperse": *dia* (through) + *speirein* (to sow, scatter). A scattering which is also a sowing. This engenders the "aesthetics of reworlding" that Emmanuel Nelson has spoken of in connection with the Indian diaspora, but I believe it is characteristic of the cultural work of all deep diasporic experiences (xv–xvi). Diasporacentrism therefore is not a focus on loss or dilution; its emphasis is on struggle, survival, rebirth, the creation of new (albeit floating) "centers."

Edouard Glissant, in his book *Caribbean Discourse*, refers to "the universe of the Americas" (4). Apart from its native inhabitants, this so-called New World is a whole hemisphere of diasporists or diasporites; diasporacentrism, therefore, is not marginalism or peripheralism, which is one reason why I use the term, despite my suspicion of *all* centrisms.

In *Noises in the Blood*, an examination of Jamaican popular culture, Carolyn Cooper refers derogatorily to "the new decentering orthodoxies," part of the theoretical enterprise engaged in "post"-ing those portions of the world that have experienced colonialism (15). Endorsements of fragmentation and instability emanating from Babylon quite understandably will give the victims of empire pause; to use a term apparently coined by Rajagopalan Radhakrishnan, these theoretical pronouncements could be viewed as "'pre-post'-erous" (62). Nevertheless, I am partial to notions of decentering because the elaboration and promulgation of centers has tended too much toward inwardness in a negative sense: navel-gazing and all the ills and errors of nationalism/tribalism. Why, then, conceive of a term like *diasporacentrism*, which appears to reinscribe the very notion (of a locatable hub of identity) that it seeks to dissolve?

Admittedly, I have not put "centricity" under erasure. What I have done, I hope, is put it into a state of anxiety and irresolvable tension, in which the tendency of identity to congeal through a kind of centrifugal movement is constantly thwarted by the centripetal forces of diasporation, of recirculation. These cultural flows do re/turn to Africa, but they carry influences with them to the mother continent; it isn't only a matter of seeking "sources."

History has made it so: for people of African descent on *this* side of the black Atlantic continuum, the worlds of the diaspora *are* the central experience. For instance, when Alain Locke, in his classic essay "The New Negro," declared that Harlem "is the home of the Negro's 'Zionism,'" he was making a profoundly diasporacentric statement (14). So is Brazilian novelist Jorge Amado when he refers to Bahia as the "capital of all Africa" in his novel *The War of the Saints* (5). Of course, the original center of the black world was Africa—but for a long time, the region from which blackness has emanated globally as an influence has been the Americas (consider jazz, R&B, reggae, Black Power, etc.). Moreover, once the slave trade ended, the Caribbean arguably had a more powerful influence on the Africanization of the United States than did Africa. Furthermore, while a respectful glance always is cast back toward Africa by those of African descent in the diaspora, the real emphasis in the diasporan context is on the black future, not the black past (which is not to say that the black past should remain unknown or misunderstood). The diaspora broadened the African continuum, and from the diaspora, that continuum is still expanding—at least in the imaginations of the African Americans. Consider, for example, the emphasis on the extraterrestrial to be found in a good deal of black American music: for instance, Sun Ra's "Space is the Place" and many other works; John Coltrane's "Interstellar Space" and "Stellar Regions," etc. There also is an interplanetary mythos woven into George Clinton's work (cf. *Mothership Connection*, with titles like "Unfunky UFO" and references to "extraterrestrial brothers" and "citizens of the universe").

There are, in fact, diasporas within the diaspora—for example, the immigration of West Indian blacks to England and the exodus of Haitians and Cubans to the United States. As a result, London and New York "have become important Caribbean cities," while other migrations in the postcolonial period have made Paris, for example, into an African city as well as a European one (Lipsitz 122). "History," as Glissant has stated, "is fissured by histories" (231). Eurocentrism, which has arrogated History unto itself, has overlooked or "paged over" this fact. But Afrocentrism, too, tends to deal with History, not histories, whereas it is precisely these histories—complex, multiple, trackable but always in flight—to which, and out of which, diasporacentrism speaks.

The diaspora is a series—indeed, a tangle—of crossroads. The crossroads is a tricky, even dangerous, place, but it has the advantage of being a site from which one can look in many directions at once (Lipsitz 7–8). Meaning is both made and unmasked here (in short, there is signifying on all levels), and it is here that "hybridity happens" (Gates).

Antonio Benítez-Rojo, in his important book *The Repeating Island*, quotes Janheinz Jahn's comment that "the principle of *crossed rhythms*" is a common feature of African cultures. (Crossed roads/crossed rhythms. Intersecting worlds/intersecting modes of expression.) Benítez-Rojo believes that this concept of crossed rhythm is peculiarly apt for describing Caribbean culture, and asks, "Does this mean that the Caribbean rhythm is African?" His answer is, not entirely. I would say that the crossed rhythm that shows up in Caribbean cultural forms can be seen as the expression of countless performers who tried to represent what was already here, or there, at times drawing closer and at times farther away from Africa. (81)

In other words, "*History is a weaving labyrinth*" (Forrest 468) in which histories and their creators constantly work b(l)ack and forth. And (to repeat) hybridity happens; which is why we are required to seek "'xplanations" (Forrest 329): crisscrossed subjects, palimpsestic surfaces, knotted chords, the always-to-be-sought rather than the already found.

A mind- and ear-opening sense of what results when hybridity happens may be had by reading George Lipsitz's fascinating book *Dangerous Crossroads* and checking out some of the music he discusses there. Lipsitz writes about groups like the French rap group I.A.M. (Imperial Asiatic Men), whose members are of North African descent and who titled their first album *From the Planet Mars*, and about Bhangra musicians in England who blend folk music from their native India with "disco, pop, hip hop, and house music" (123, 129). Less spectacular but nonetheless revealing is Nelson George's chronicle of "Post-Soul Culture," an account of African-American culture, 1971–1991 (9–40). It's a fractal portrait no Afrocentric reading could do justice to, although Afrocentricity is an element in the mix.

Adventures in Afropea I (1992), the first album by the European-African female vocal group Zap Mama, perfectly illustrates the diasporacentric positionality arising from the shifts, syncretisms, and sedimentations noted above. *Afropea* is an amalgam of Africa and Europe. Black people in the diaspora may be said to be Afropean—but, given the extent of the influences of African culture and its derivatives, people of European descent in the Americas are (even if unwittingly) Afropeans to a degree as well. (Another Afropean example is the French band Les Négresses Vertes ["green black women"], a group that is both male and female, European and African [Lipsitz 124].) Indeed, despite stated intentions, but perhaps in keeping with repressed desires, America and other parts of the world have been Africanized. Thus the diaspora has done its work, transforming what was viewed as subservient into what is subversive, undermining and underdogging the so-called dominant paradigm.

In one of his poems, Clarence Major refers to "my middle / passage blues" (266). The "middle passage blues," as a form of sorrow, of alienation, is what Afrocentrism wants to assuage; but as a mode of performance, a creative matrix, it is what redeems the diaspora.

Black music—which cultural nationalists rightly celebrate—is not only a product of New World experience, it also responds to it, articulates it, critiques it. This follows from the fact that black cultural practice has always been both *against* and *on behalf of*. At the same time that it resisted the enslavement of the body, it also resisted enslavement of the spirit and the imagination. It sought freedom *to*, as well as freedom *from*. Moreover, the black music of the Americas has influenced contemporary African music, along with that of the rest of the world.

Whatever other constructions have since come into play regarding its identity, jazz, in its origins, is *creole*. This should not be surprising, for, as Michael Eric Dyson notes, "Creolization, syncretism, and hybridization are black culture's hallmarks. It is precisely in stitching together various fabrics of human and artistic experience that black musical artists have expressed their genius" (146). In a similar vein, on *The News Hour with Jim Lehrer* (March 25, 1996), Wynton Marsalis referred to "the consciousness, the will to integrate with other things" that is essential to jazz, the making of gumbo, and other aspects of African American culture. It's all in the mix, in other words.

This is the way a character in Leon Forrest's novel *Divine Days* puts it:

"[O]ur human rage [as black people in America] was always to make a way out of noway. And to create a synthesis out of all nightmares that our experiences kept throwing up at us. That will to synthesize . . . to absorb and reinvent; to take it all in and to masticate it, and process it, and spew it back out, as lyrical and soaring as a riff by Father Louie. . . ." (1062)[5]

Julius Hemphill's 1977 "audiodrama" *Roi Boyé and the Gotham Minstrels* originated as a mixed-media production, one of several Hemphill has done, but I believe it's the only one to be documented on record. (What I really wish we had is a recording of Hemphill's 1979 work exemplifying the black lit/oratorical tradition, *Ralph Ellison's Long Tongue*, inspired by the novel *Invisible Man*.) Most of the four sides of *Roi Boyé* consists of the "voices" of various instruments (alto and soprano saxophones, flute); only toward the end of the last side is there any substantial spoken text. (Interestingly, Bruce Thomas's transcription of Ornette Coleman's trumpet solo on the tune "The Golden Number," included among the liner notes on the 1977 Charlie Haden album of the same name, refers to individual instrumental passages as "sentences." I also recall what the Yoruba master drummer who made my *dùndún* drum said when he presented it to me: "This drum will talk good poetry." There are *aural* texts as well as oral and written ones. This is one reason why the musician can "preach" or "teach" on his instrument in a manner analogous to that of the singer or actual preacher/orator.)

The narrator of *Roi Boyé* talks of experimenting and being experimented on—references, one assumes, to black cultural practice in the laboratory of invention and racist practice in the laboratory of oppression (creation versus deformation). (It is worth noting here that Lester Bowie, trumpeter with Brass Fantasy and the Chicago Art Ensemble, frequently wears a laboratory coat on stage. In an interview on National Public Radio's program "Fresh Air" [November 3, 1989], Bowie said, "The lab coat suggests research. The musical stage is my laboratory.") What is being researched, explored, is what Richard Wright called "the forms of things unknown." Wright was referring to the blues and other forms of black folk expression as an inheritance denoting both African survival and African loss. But there is another sense in which "the forms of things unknown" refers to the very things that black culture, through a medium like jazz, pursues and strives to bring into being. As George Lipsitz notes in *Dangerous Crossroads*, "diasporic expressions constantly come back to what Franz Fanon called 'the seething pot out of which the learning of the future will emerge'" (44).

One of the questions that got me started on this topic of inquiry was, Is Julius Hemphill's album *Dogon A.D.* (recorded in 1972) Afrocentric or diasporacentric? The title can be read as "the year (or the time) of the Dogon," thus, in a sense, centralizing the Dogon of Mali. The Dogon are one of the African peoples who have especially captured the attention of writers and others in the diaspora.[6] The importance of an African culture usually depends upon its demonstrated influence on black diasporan cultures; this certainly is the case with, for example, the Yoruba, Ibo, and Kongo. In the case of the Dogon, however, their prominence would seem to depend less upon traceable Dogonisms on our side of the Atlantic and more on the imaginative power and complexity of their indigenous systems and the particular attention of European anthropologists who made the Dogon world available to the rest of us. Nevertheless, in his fascinating discussion of the *son*—the Spanish-Caribbean cousin of the blues—José Piedra states that it "has remained loyal to its remote, nonliterate source: the Dogon *sò*. Son and *sò* are core principles of Cuban and Dogon ontologies respectively. The evolution from the latter to the former likely involved the mediation of Afro-Haitian culture and language. . . . Moreover, *sò* is likely to be the source for the Anglo-African 'soul,' a Guillén-like 'unknown voice.'" Piedra further claims that "The African background of the *son* enriches and subverts the traditional logic of its own 'Spanish' lyrics," a process he calls "the neo-African logic of performance" (115, 109). The expression "neo-African" clearly specifies a diasporan context. A.D., then, also can be read as "After Diaspora," referring to that post-African experience which provides the matrix for jazz, Afrocentrism, and a great deal else. There is a looking back to Africa through the "lens" of the diaspora. Afrocentrism, after all, is an *interpretation* of Africanness, an interpretation colored, if you will, by the difficulties encountered in the diaspora and a longing for an imprisoned past that must be recalled, reclaimed.

In an essay on Caryl Phillips's novel *Crossing the River*, Anthony Ilona refers to "a neglected if not forgotten voice" emanating from this side of the Atlantic, a voice "with its rhythm in 'drum', 'skin', 'whip' and 'lash'; its 'song', its 'shout', its 'groan' and its 'dreams'..." which black writers of the New World still need to make us hear (3). But this voice can easily and perhaps more effectively be heard in black music. I became convinced through intensive listening that if you can grasp all the complexities of a piece like "Skin 1" from Julius Hemphill's album *'Coon 'Bidness* (recorded in 1972 and 1975), you will understand the black experience— which this music powerfully articulates, from the African past (in)to the future. I only wish I had the tools to analyze this music more technically and the vocabulary to express my findings in a more precise manner.

But consider: "Skin" is slang for a drum or drumset. It is also an expression of cultural solidarity, as in, "Give me some skin." Too much of our American history has been played out on "skin" (color/race). There also is the concept of the body as drum (hambone; patting juba). Compare Zora Neale Hurston's statement in her first novel, *Jonah's Gourd Vine* (1934), that Africans who made the Middle Passage brought the drum to the Americas "in their skin" (29).

The track entitled "Upper Egypt and Lower Egypt," which constitutes Side A of Pharaoh Sanders's album *Tauhid* (1971), is a piece of music with a development that is comparable to the shift from hieratic to demotic in Egyptian language, or from the "classical" to the "popular." It suggests, too, a movement from Africa to the Americas, but this movement is not from one self-contained experience/idiom to another, separate experience/idiom; it occurs within a matrix that embraces both. There is a shared context.

America is another Egypt, the realm of slavery, and slavery's aftermaths. Upper Egypt and lower Egypt are, in the American context, Upsouth and Downsouth. The first side of *Tauhid*, then, both connects and overlays Africa and Africa-in-America.

Side B of the album contains four titles: "Japan," "Aum," "Venus," and "Capricorn Rising." This is the global, multicultural side—not a "white" side, but another side to the black side. Taken as a whole, the two sides bespeak jazz as both a particular and a universal artform.

Pharaoh Sanders's album *Africa* (1987) contains three tracks that are relevant to our present discussion. "You've Got to Have Freedom" could be heard as an African-American resistance call, a pan-African political statement, and an assertion of the free play of the jazz innovator. The sax solos are lyrical and raw, ecstatic and agonized, in a testimony to both the promise and the betrayal of freedom. "Origin," which one might assume to have mythic connotations, is pure *American* music—although the drums at the end make a clearcut African connection, as a kind of coda. It's a working backward *to* Africa; the end here was/is the beginning.

The title cut "Africa" is the briefest piece on the disc, a bluesy instrumental featuring a chant of "Africa!" with an intonation that suggests loss as well as acknowledgment and celebration. One can also make out specific mention of several West African nations, including Nigeria and Togo. However, despite its title, the album as a whole doesn't deal mainly or centrally with the African continent. Most of the other tracks are ballads, standards. Africa, here, is Africa plus *all that follows* (i.e., the Diaspora).

Pharoah Sanders's latest album, *Message From Home* (1996), begins with a track entitled "Our Roots (Began in Africa)." The title is a chanted refrain, the music of which is distinctly African-American, with a soul feel and discernible hiphop rhythms. To say that black people's roots *began* in Africa is not the same thing as saying that their roots *are* in Africa, which, however, is true, but incomplete, since it also is necessary to say that black people's roots are *here*, in the diaspora. "Our roots began in Africa" isn't the end of the story, it's just the beginning. It is also important to point out that "Our roots began in Africa" is not an exclusively black statement; it is a pan-human one. Mankind originated in Africa and became global through *diaspora*.

Message from *home*. Where is "home"? The Afrocentric response would be, *Africa*. The diasporic reply would be, *here*. However, in this instance we are dealing with a double consciousness, since the message actually seems to be, "We are African *and* we are American." This is underscored by the album's final track, "Country Mile," whose title suggests the U.S. rural black experience but whose music has the style of South African township jive (a style strongly influenced by black American musics)—so that what we have here, beyond the political statement of an equivalency of antiracist struggle, is the intertextuality of black aesthetics, result of the black Atlantic tradition of intercontinental call-and-response.

The album *Old and New Dreams* (1979), by the quartet of Don Cherry (trumpet), Dewey Redman (sax), Ed Blackwell (drums), and Charlies Haden (bass), is another set that stitches together Africa and the diaspora. "Old and New Dreams" are expressions of there and here; then and now; tradition and innovation; past and future; repeating dreams of liberation and renewal. There is a piece entitled "Togo" (which actually is based on a traditional piece from Ghana) and another piece entitled "Guinea." "Guinea" is a generic term for Africa—especially the Slave Coast. But in Haitian voodoo belief, Guinea (*Guinée*) is an island beneath the sea where the *loa* dwell (Africa displaced).

The third piece I want to mention is called "Orbit of La-Ba." This "orbit" inscribes both Africa (Legba) and the diaspora (LaBas). It is a spiritual realm encoding cultural expressions that include the music we are talking about here, Ishmael Reed's concept of Jes Grew and his character Papa LaBas, and Henry Louis Gates, Jr.'s exposition of the signifying monkey.

Benítez-Rojo writes that "in the Caribbean orbit one historical stage does not cancel the earlier one as happens in the Western world" (203). It is a synchronic history—one of depths, layers, intersections, in which what is "originary" is both retained and reconfigured. The "orbit of La-Ba," then, like the orbit or trajectory of many African-derived "samples," is spiraling, dizzying, with a certain "spin" that could be said to correspond to that "certain way" in which, according to Benítez-Rojo, cultural style fashions and expresses itself in the Caribbean (Introduction).

The architextual soundings of black music draw, perhaps more intensely than any other mode, on the deep song of African-derived, diasporically reworlded cultures. Especially in their most unrestrained moments, jazz performers in particular weave incredibly rich tapestries (story-quilts?) of ancestry and community, commentary and desire. I'm not saying, therefore, that the heartbeat of Africa isn't to be discerned in the body of black diasporan cultures. What I am saying is that the contours of that body were shaped by the diaspora, and in this essay I'm examining some of the nuances of this body-building process, its sound/tracks.

NOTES

1. As I acknowledge in my book *Masters of the Drum* (Greenwood, 1995), I borrowed the term "lit/orature" from the Nigerian dramatist Femi Oṣofisan. Attempting a similar definition, the Caribbean poet Kamau Brathwaite, in his important essay "History of the Voice," uses the term "auriture" to describe that broader expressive continuum of which oral literature is a part (267). The musical (aural) "texts" that I am discussing in this essay clearly come under the category of "auriture."

2. Despite the fact that a parliament would be recognized by most of us as a British institution, there is nothing Eurocentric about this name choice, let alone the group's music. A parliament (according to the *OED*) is a council for the discussion of important matters; thus Clinton invokes a certain dignity for a popular/populist cultural enterprise that (among other things!) embodies "parley," "palaver." But there is also an obsolete meaning of parliament—that is, a "spell" or "bout" of speaking, which is suggestive of the "trance mission" of the rhetorics of song/dance/drum.

3. The name Funkadelic foregrounds a fusion of the visceral and the visionary, of "feets" and "heads." It's not precisely counter-countercultural; rather, it reminds us that the counterculture wasn't a predominantly white phenomenon but a mixed bag, a coalition of colors.

4. In his book *Jazz in the Sixties*, Michael J. Budds speaks of various "turns"—to Africa, to Asia, to Brazil, even to Europe—which jazz musicians made in an effort to expand their resources (15–26).

5. Father Louie is, of course, trumpeter Louis Armstrong.

6. Note, for instance, the Dogon materials in the poetry of Jay Wright. There also are Mexican and other cultural materials to be found in the work of Wright, who is far more of a diasporacentrist than an Afrocentrist.

REFERENCES

Amado, Jorge. *The War of the Saints*. Trans. Gregory Rabassa. New York: Bantam, 1993.
Balibar, Etienne. "Culture and Identity (Working Notes)." *The Identity in Question*, ed. John Rajchman. New York: Routledge, 1995. 173–196.
Benítez-Rojo, Antonio. *The Repeating Island: The Caribbean and the Postmodern Perspective*. Trans. James E. Maraniss. Durham: Duke University Press, 1992.
Brathwaite, Kamau. "History of the Voice." *Roots*. Ann Arbor: University of Michigan, 1993. 259–304.
Budds, Michael J. *Jazz of the Sixties*. Iowa City: University of Iowa, 1978.
Cooper, Carolyn. *Noises in the Blood: Orality, Gender, and the "Vulgar" Body of Jamaican Popular Culture*. Durham: Duke University Press, 1995.
Dyson, Michael Eric. *Between God and Gangsta Rap: Bearing Witness to Black Culture*. New York: Oxford, 1996.
Forrest, Leon. *Divine Days*. New York: Norton, 1993.
Gates, Henry Louis, Jr. "Hybridity Happens: Black Brit Bricolage Brings the Noise." *Voice Literary Supplement* (October 1992): 26–27.
George, Nelson. *Buppies, B-Boys, Baps and Bohos: Notes on Post-Soul Black Culture*. New York: HarperCollins, 1992.
Glissant, Edouard. *Caribbean Discourse: Selected Essays*. Trans. Michael Dash. Charlottesville: University Press of Virginia, 1989.
Hurston, Zora Neale. *Jonah's Gourd Vine*. New York: HarperPerennial, 1990.
Ilona, Anthony. "Crossing the River: A Chronicle of the Black Diaspora." *Wasafiri* 22 (Autumn 1995). 3–9.
Kitaj, R. B. *First Diasporist Manifesto*. New York: Thames and Hudson, 1989.
Lipsitz, George. *Dangerous Crossroads: Popular Music, Postmodernism and the Poetics of Place*. New York: Verso, 1994.
Locke, Alain. *The New Negro: An Interpretation*. New York: Boni, 1925.
Major, Clarence. "Swallow the Lake." *From the Other Side of the Century: A New American Poetry 1960–1990*, ed. Douglas Messerli. Los Angeles: Sun and Moon, 1994. 266–267.
Nelson, Emmanuel S., ed. Introduction. *Reworlding: The Literature of the Indian Diaspora*. Westport, Connecticut: Greenwood, 1992. ix–xvi.

Piedra, José. "Through Blues." *Do the Americas Have a Common Litera-ture?* Ed. Gustavo Perez Firmat. Durham: Duke University Press, 1990. 107–129.

Radhakrishnan, R. *Diasporic Meditations: Between Home and Location.* Minneapolis: University of Minnesota Press, 1996.

Rajchman, John. "Introduction: The Question of Identity." *The Identity in Question*, ed. John Rajchman. New York: Routledge, 1995. vii–xiii.

Tawadros, Gilane. "Beyond the Boundary: The Work of Three Black Women Artists in Britain." *Black British Cultural Studies: A Reader*, ed. Houston A. Baker, Jr., Manthia Diawara, and Ruth H. Lindeborg. University of Chicago Press, 1996. 240–277.

24 THE REINTERPRETATION OF AFRICAN MUSICAL INSTRUMENTS IN THE UNITED STATES

David Evans

Many folk musical instruments in the United States have been identified as being derived from African prototypes. This essay is a brief survey of these instruments, concentrating on examples that persisted to the twentieth century. Its purpose is to identify common processes in the reinterpretation of these originally African instruments in the North American cultural and historical context. Past studies have generally examined only a single instrument or presented a less complete inventory.[1]

First, however, let me say a few words about terminology. Even after the lapse of about half a century and the inevitable progress of scholarship in that period, I must say that I still prefer much of the old terminology of the American anthropologist Melville Herskovits for discussing the processes of acculturation between peoples of African and European descent in the New World. I especially find useful his terms *retention, syncretism,* and *reinterpretation.*[2] To these we could also add the term *revival* to describe recent processes that were not anticipated by Herskovits in his day, but which ironically his own research served to promote. I like these terms because they describe mental and/or behavioral *processes.* They are not based on analogies or derived from population groups or geographical locations. They are, in fact, applicable to situations of acculturation anywhere in the world and are not confined to the situation of African-European contact.

Retention should be used to describe the process whereby an African cultural trait and its associated meaning have been perpetuated without significant modification in a New World setting. In most cases those who retain an African cultural trait should be aware of its African derivation. The term should not be used loosely for traits and behavior that have some African quality but also have significant qualities that were acquired or developed in the New World.

Syncretism is the term most prone to be used loosely and inaccurately.

Used only in intellectual discourse, often it serves as a fancy-sounding descriptive term for the overall process of cultural blending or hybridization. Syncretism for Herskovits originally meant a process whereby an African cultural trait is equated with or likened to a European or Euro-American trait encountered in the New World on the basis of some perceived similarity between the two traits. Those who engage in this process of syncretism are aware of the bicultural derivation of the trait. This largely mental process of equating or likening is an important one in the history of encounters of musical instrument traditions, and it is often embodied in naming practices. Our recognition of this process should not be lost through loose usage of the term that specifically describes it.

Reinterpretation is the process whereby an African cultural trait is given a new meaning in terms of European or Euro-American culture, or conversely a European or Euro-American trait is given a new meaning in terms of the African culture. As a result of this process, the knowledge of the bicultural derivation of the trait is lost or greatly obscured. Frequently reinterpretation takes place in both directions (African to European and vice versa) and continues back and forth over time, resulting in a new trait that is perceived by everybody to be simply "American" or "African-American" or not even associated with any particular ethnic group.

Revival is a self-conscious reintroduction of an African cultural trait that has died out in the past or possibly never existed in the New World. It usually occurs for ideological, political, or social reasons and is seen most clearly in the United States in the adoption of African clothing and hair styles, religious practices, personal names, etc. Certain African musical instruments, such as lamellophones and various drums, have been adopted in recent years, especially by jazz musicians, where they have a symbolic as well as musical function. This adoption has not resulted in any new musical form or style that has gained currency in the United States at the folk or popular level, although it is possible that this could happen in the future.

I prefer these terms to others, such as "Africanism," "African survival," "creolization," and "Americanization," even though Herskovits himself also used some of these terms.[3] *Africanism*, although it is used to describe a cultural trait, sounds too much like a self-conscious ideology. It places the emphasis entirely on the African component of the cultural trait and fails to describe processes. Its only usefulness as a term is in pointing out that something has an African quality. *African survival* has the same limitations, with the added disadvantage of suggesting that the African quality is something left over from the historical past that really ought not to exist but has somehow avoided extinction. Without denying the importance of "survival" in African-American culture and history, this is ultimately a limited way of looking at the creative dynamics of the situation. *Creolization* is a term that is often heard in the United States today, and it has been used for a longer time in the Caribbean and Latin America. It has the positive quality of referring to a cultural process, but it is ultimately derived from a descriptive term for a population group, i.e., Creoles. Since people calling themselves "Creole" in the United States can be of purely European, purely African, or mixed descent, having in common only their status of being born in the New World, the term is inherently confusing and not descriptive of a single process. In the United States it represents an *ideal* more than a *reality*. While I recognize that this term can be very useful in Caribbean and Latin American studies and in some geographical regions of the United States (e.g., Louisiana), it is confusing in most situations in the United States, and I fear that it often functions as another fancy-sounding intellectual term with a vague meaning. The term *Americanization* has similar problems and is even vaguer in its meaning, although it may have some usefulness at a very general level.

Retention, syncretism, and reinterpretation can be viewed as sequential stages in a process of acculturation, although they cannot be assigned to specific historical periods because of ongoing cultural contact with Africa and other outside areas. In other words, Africans did not all arrive in the United States at one time and collectively launch a process of acculturation that began with retention and ended with reinterpretation or even revival. Instead, this movement toward reinterpretation (sometimes continuing to revival) can be viewed as a complex and ongoing process that continues to affect and modify cultural traits and behavior. Of all of these processes, reinterpretation has been the most important one in the history of African-American folk musical instruments in the United States, especially in the twentieth century, although it is sometimes possible to identify earlier stages of syncretism and retention.[4]

In surveying African-derived musical instruments we can detect several patterns of reinterpretation that they have typically undergone. These include:

1. The use of found, discarded, or commercially made objects, either singly or in combination, in creating musical instruments. A consequence of this is a minimum of special fashioning of these folk instruments, such as carving, casting, or decoration. The United States has always been a society of abundance, materialism, and waste, and these qualities have affected even the poorest citizens. Many objects have long been available for use in creating musical instruments, such as metal cans; glass and ceramic jugs; washboards; cheese and cigar boxes; and metal wire from screens, brooms, and cotton bales.

2. The instruments are often accommodated in some degree to European instruments in their forms, names, or materials of con-

struction. If not, they take on a novelty and/or humorous function that serves to mediate and reinterpret their non-European
character. In other words, their overt African characteristics become obscured in the eyes of non-Africans so that they become
less exotic and less culturally "threatening."

3. The instruments have generally been used in the performance
of distinct African-American types of music rather than purely
African music, and new playing techniques or musical roles have
been created for them.

We can see these processes at work as we survey a variety of African-
derived folk musical instruments:

Kazoo. This instrument, which exists in both homemade and commercially manufactured forms, is derived from African membrane instruments that serve as voice disguisers or "vocal masks," often in ritual contexts. Usually the membrane is made from the egg sac of a spider. In the
United States the instrument is said to have been "invented" in the 1840s
in Macon, Georgia, by a black man named Alabama Vest and a German
clockmaker named Thaddeus von Clegg, who made it to Vest's specifica-
tions. The instrument was later manufactured commercially under the
name of "Down South Submarine."[5] The names *kazoo* and *bazooka*, by
which it is often known, may be African in origin, possibly exhibiting
Bantu prefixes. Most black players in the United States call it a "jazz horn"
or "jazzbo," and they play it in ensembles as a cheap and novel equivalent
of a real jazz horn, such as a muted trumpet or saxophone. I have encountered the kazoo as a voice disguiser to obscure the sound of risqué blues
lyrics,[6] and in general it seems to be especially used with risqué and other
humorous songs. It is almost always heard in combination with one or
more other instruments, such as guitar or piano, harmonica, jug, etc. Thus,
its original African meaning, which was usually "serious," has been reinterpreted to something humorous in the United States, and it has gone
through a sort of fictive syncretism with wind instruments of a jazz ensemble. In the United States it is played in new types of instrumental ensembles not known in African music, and it has become a melodic instrument more than a voice disguiser.

Jug. This instrument is also derived from African prototypes of hollow
vessels that serve as voice disguisers or spirit voices. In one example from
the BaBembe near the mouth of the Congo River four hollow wooden effigy
figures with holes in the back serve this purpose, symbolically representing spirits of father, mother, son, and daughter.[7] The instrument is played
by making a buzzing and flapping sound with the lips facing the opening
of the vessel. In the United States this instrument usually is simply a

ceramic, metal, or glass jug, at one time a common household object, used as a novelty bass instrument in combination with other instruments. It is thus a counterpart to the kazoo in the bass register. There exists, however, a report from 1888 of a band of four boys in Palatka, Florida, all of them with jugs and possibly a harmonica and kazoo.[8] Reports of similar ensembles of four instruments of this type come from Haiti and the Dominican Republic.[9] But around this same time the jug was becoming a bass instrument in string ensembles, as can be seen in a photograph taken in 1898 in Atlanta.[10] By the 1920s, jug bands of this sort, with a single jug as a bass instrument, recorded as urban novelty ensembles from the cities of Louisville, Memphis, Birmingham, Dallas, Cincinnati, and Chicago.[11] The jug had thus undergone a process of reinterpretation from its African prototypes similar to that of the kazoo.

Panpipes. This is a set of tuned bamboo pipes of varying length and pitch, bound together in a row. Versions of this instrument are found in Central Africa as well as other parts of the world, including southeastern Europe, Melanesia, and among South American Indians. In North America the instrument is found only in black musical tradition, and it is quite clearly derived from an African prototype. It varies in size from four to ten pipes. Often the player employs the characteristically African technique of alternating blown notes with vocal "whooping."[12] Another clue to the instrument's African origin is the name which players give to it: the "quills." Although the North American versions are always made of bamboo, there are reports of some African versions made from the large tail quills of the African porcupine.[13] It would appear that this African practice has survived in the name of the instrument in North America but not in the technique of manufacture, since the quills of the North American porcupine are too small for this purpose. (Possibly large bird feather quills were once used.) The instrument is usually played solo, in panpipe ensembles, or with percussion instruments in Africa. In North America it was usually played solo, but in the twentieth century there are some reports and recordings of it being played with the guitar.[14] The instrument is probably extinct today, as it has not been encountered since the 1960s. Possibly it exists in the form of a small glass bottle of the type used to contain artificial flavorings, played by children. The technique of alternating blowing and whooping has been transferred to the harmonica in the twentieth century.[15] An alternative form of the "quills," a set of tuned whistles, has been reported several times but never recorded. This version of the instrument was used for playing religious songs, and its form is possibly modeled on that of a church organ.[16]

Banjo. This instrument is based on West African prototypes found in the Savannah region from Senegambia to Chad. African forms of this instrument have a sound box covered with skin, one or more strings that run only part way up the neck, and a playing technique featuring a downward stroke with the backs of the fingernails while the thumb plucks a short string, giving the instrument its characteristic high-pitched "ringing" sound.[17] These same characteristics are found in forms of the banjo in the United States, but the materials of construction are new. Most U.S. instruments have been commercially manufactured since the late nineteenth century. They have frets on the neck, like a guitar, and the skin head is stretched over a metal ring instead of a wooden box. Older players performed solo, but by the early nineteenth century the banjo began to be played together with the fiddle, and it has continued to be played with other instruments in the twentieth century.[18] Its role in such ensembles has thus been reinterpreted, as in Africa it is primarily a solo instrument or played with another instrument of the same type or with percussion instruments. The five-string banjo, with its one short string, is the closest U.S. variety to the African prototypes, but there also exist four-string, six-string, and eight-string varieties with all the strings of the same length. These are strictly a development within the United States, and the latter two represent banjo versions of the guitar and mandolin. This is obviously a further reinterpretation. The name "banjo" is not African. Instead it is derived from a family of European lute-like instruments called variously bandora, bandoura, bandola, etc. These instruments were popular in western Europe in the sixteenth and seventeenth centuries and still exist in South America. Some of the earliest North American banjos lack the short string. This fact, along with the similarity of the names (early reports often use the spelling "banjar"), suggests that the African prototypes were syncretized with the European bandora with reinterpretation taking place in the nineteenth century as the banjo became a distinctly North American instrument.

One-string Fiddle. The European four-string fiddle (violin) was the most prominent of all instruments in North American black folk music during the nineteenth century. But there are also several reports of one-string fiddles. Most descriptions are very imprecise, but it is clear that some of these were rather similar to West African one-string fiddles.[19] It is not certain that we have any recordings of this instrument from the United States. The guitarist and singer in a 1935 blues session, Big Joe Williams from Mississippi, claimed that the fiddler on this session played a one-stringed instrument, but Williams is well known for many exaggerations.[20] Its use in blues, if true, would be a reinterpretation.

One-string bass. The African prototype of this instrument is the "earth bow," also known as a "ground harp."[21] It consists of a membrane stretched over a hole in the earth. One end of a string is attached to the membrane and the other end to a flexible stick inserted in the ground. A similar instrument exists in Haiti, called the "mosquito drum." This instrument is known widely in the New World, made from new materials.

In the United States an inverted tub or bucket is normally used. It functions as a bass instrument in ensembles, whereas in Africa it is a solo instrument. It tended to replace the jug in the 1930s. Its U.S. role as an ensemble instrument represents a reinterpretation, with possibly an earlier stage of syncretism with the western four-string bass.

One-string glissed zither. African forms of this instrument are idiochordic and usually made from the leaf stalk of the raffia palm. Sometimes a bow is substituted. There are two players. One strikes the string with two sticks, and the other slides an object along the string, usually a cup or bowl of some sort. A similar instrument found is in Jamaica as the *benta* and in Venezuela and Colombia as the *carángano*, with other versions in Brazil and elsewhere. In the United States it is played by a single person, usually a child. Most African players are also children. The U.S. instrument is constructed on a board or the side of a house. The string is made from wire, usually from a broom, and the slider is usually a glass bottle. It is not reported until the twentieth century and is found mostly in northwest Mississippi and adjacent regions. It has several different names, including diddley bow, bo diddley, jitterbug, banjo, drum, unitar, one-string guitar, and guitar-board. The first of these names possibly represents a retention of the idea of using a bow, which is found in African tradition. But there clearly has been a reinterpretation in terms of the guitar. This is seen in some of the names, its use by a single player, and its association especially with blues music. The instrument often functions for children as a step toward learning the guitar, and it has contributed the "slide" technique to blues guitar style.[22]

Mouth bow. There are many African varieties of the mouth bow, but they all utilize two fundamental notes, each with a harmonic series of notes which can be enhanced by using the mouth as a resonator. The second fundamental is created by shortening the string by pressing a hard object against it. The mouth bow exists in the United States with reports in the nineteenth and twentieth centuries, but it always has only a single fundamental. It is used to play fiddle tunes and spiritual songs. It is sometimes called a "home-made Jew's harp," suggesting a syncretism with the Jew's harp, which uses the same technique of sound production with the mouth. Its role in playing fiddle tunes and spirituals represents a reinterpretation.[23]

Washboard. This is a common household object, which African-American musicians in the United States evidently considered to be an adequate substitute for African scraping instruments, which were normally fashioned from hard wood or metal. An older version of this instrument in the United States was simply the jawbone of a horse, donkey, or mule. In Louisiana, since the 1960s, a special type of corrugated aluminum vest has been manufactured. It is called a "frottoir" and is used with a type of rhythm and blues music called *zydeco*, often sung in French.[24]

Drums. African types of drums have been reported in the United States, but they have never been documented by recording and only rarely by photography or drawings. Most accounts are from the eighteenth or early nineteenth centuries, but there are a few from the twentieth century.[25] It is difficult to tell whether these drums underwent any process of acculturation beyond retention. I did, however, record a recollection from southern Mississippi early in this century of three drums made from barrels of different sizes and played together by a single player with tambourines, guitar, and harmonica played by other musicians.[26] It would appear that these drums had undergone a process of reinterpretation in their manufacture and in their use by one player, as in a jazz drum set. I have acquired a hand-made bass drum from northern Mississippi, made around 1900, but it is entirely in the style of a European rope-tightened instrument.

Other instruments, such as the *fife*, have no clear African prototypes or may be simply home-made versions of European instruments, although their manner of playing or context may display African qualities.[27]

Some African instruments, such as xylophones and lamellophones, were reported in the United States in the eighteenth and early nineteenth centuries, even with African names. The *barrafoo* of Virginia is clearly the Senegambian *balafon* xylophone, and the *marimba brett* of New Orleans is clearly a lamellophone of the African *mbira* type.[28] But these are isolated cases, and they seem to have disappeared after an initial period of retention. In other words, they did not undergo syncretism and reinterpretation, and this may explain why they died out in the United States. These instruments had no obvious European equivalents, either in form or in name, either as a musical instrument or a common utilitarian object. They also required extensive fashioning. (Drums also require much fashioning in most cases, which may explain why European military drums were so readily adopted or barrels were used.) Some other complex African instruments, such as the pluriarc, the harp, lyre, iron bell, and hourglass drum, never made a known appearance in the United States.

Finally it is interesting to note a further process of acculturation: the adoption of many of these instruments by Americans of non-African ancestry and often their abandonment by African-Americans. This had been the case with the banjo, mouth bow, kazoo, jug, one-string bass, and to some extent the washboard and frottoir. The banjo has even become emblematic of white southern music, while there are now hardly any black players of this originally African instrument. On the other hand, African-American musicians have continued to adopt and adapt European instruments, such as the guitar, piano, violin, brass and woodwind instruments, drums, etc., injecting their performances with stylistic traits derived from the African musical tradition. This exchange of musical instruments between white and black Americans is perhaps the most important process of reinterpretation.

NOTES

1. See, for example, Harold Courlander, *Negro Folk Music U.S.A.* (New York: Columbia University Press, 1963); Bruce A. MacLeod, "The Musical Instruments of North American Slaves," *Mississippi Folklore Register* 11 (1977): 34–49; Dena Epstein, *Sinful Tunes and Spirituals* (Urbana: University of Illinois Press, 1977); David Evans, "African Elements in Twentieth-Century United States Black Folk Music," *Jazzforschung* 10 (1978): 85–110; and David Evans, "African Contributions to America's Musical Heritage," *The World & I* 5, no. 1 (January 1990): 628–639.

2. Melville J. Herskovits, *The Myth of the Negro Past* (Boston: Beacon, 1958; originally published in 1941).

3. For recent uses of some of these terms see, for example, the essays in Joseph E. Holloway, ed., *Africanisms in American Culture* (Bloomington: Indiana University Press, 1990).

4. For an example of the complexity of the ongoing process of acculturation within one African-American musical family see David Evans, "The Music of Eli Owens: African Music in Transition in Southern Mississippi," in *For Gerhard Kubik: Festschrift on the Occasion of His 60th Birthday*, August Schmidhofer and Dietrich Schuller, eds. (Frankfurt: Peter Lang, 1994), pp. 329–359.

5. Barbara Stewart, *How to Kazoo* (New York: Workman, 1983), pp. 14–17.

6. David Evans, *Big Road Blues: Tradition and Creativity in the Folk Blues* (Berkeley: University of California Press, 1982), pp. 229–230.

7. *Musique Kongo*, Ocora OCR 35, 12" LP, side B, tracks 4 and 5.

8. Bruce Bastin, *Red River Blues: The Blues Tradition in the Southeast* (Urbana: University of Illinois Press, 1986), p. 35, photograph following p. 160.

9. *Rara in Haiti: Gaga in the Dominican Republic*, Ethnic Folkways FE 4531, 12" double LP (1978).

10. Bastin, *Red River Blues*, pp. 34–35, photograph following p. 160.

11. Samuel B. Charters, *The Country Blues* (New York: Rinehart, 1959), pp. 107–130; Paul Oliver, *The Story of the Blues* (London: Barrie and Rockliff, 1969), pp. 47–57; Bengt Olsson, *Memphis Blues and Jug Bands* (London: Studio Vista, 1970), pp. 22–62.

12. Bruce A. MacLeod, "Quills, Fifes, and Flutes before the Civil War," *Southern Folklore Quarterly* 42 (1978): 201–208; David Evans, notes to *Afro-American Folk Music from Tate and Panola Counties, Mississippi*, Archive of Folk Song AFS L67, 12" LP, side A, track 4.

13. Percival R. Kirby, *The Musical Instruments of the Native Races of South Africa* (Oxford: Oxford University Press, 1934), pp. 88–89, 101–102.

14. Henry Thomas, *Ragtime Texas*, Herwin 209, 12" double LP (1974); John Lee, "Baby Please Don't Go," Federal unissued (1951), issued on *Rural Blues, Vol. 1 (1934–1956)*, Document DOCD-5223, track 15 (compact disc).

15. See, for example, *Sonny Terry, Complete Recorded Works, 1938–1945, in Chronological Order*, Document DOCD-5230 (compact disc).

16. Evans, "The Music of Eli Owens," pp. 340–344.

17. Dena J. Epstein, "The Folk Banjo: A Documentary History," *Ethnomusicology* 19 (1975): 347–371; Michael T. Coolen, "Senegambian Archetypes for the American Folk Banjo," *Western Folklore* 43 (1984): 117–132; Cecilia Conway, *African Banjo Echoes in Appalachia: A Study of Folk Traditions* (Knoxville: University of Tennessee Press, 1995).

18. Karen Linn, *That Half-Barbaric Twang: The Banjo in American Popular Culture* (Urbana: University of Illinois Press, 1991).

19. John Minton, "West African Fiddles in Deep East Texas," in *Juneteenth Texas: Essays in African-American Folklore*, Publications of the Texas Folklore Society No. 54, Francis E. Abernethy, Patrick B. Mullen, and Alan Govenar, eds. (Denton: University of North Texas Press, 1996), pp. 290–313.

20. *Big Joe Williams, Complete Recorded Works in Chronological Order, Vols. 1 and 2*, Blues Document BDCD 6003–6004 (compact discs).

21. Courlander, *Negro Folk Music U.S.A.*, pp. 206–207.

22. David Evans, "Afro-American One-Stringed Instruments," *Western Folklore* 29 (1970): 229–245; Evans, notes to *Afro-American Folk Music from Tate and Panola Counties, Mississippi*, side B, tracks 2 and 3; Richard Graham, "The Diddley Bow in a Global Context," *Experimental Musical Instruments* 6, no. 5 (February 1991): 1, 10–11.

23. Evans, "The Music of Eli Owens," pp. 345–352; Richard Graham, "Ethnicity, Kinship and Transculturation: African-Derived Mouth Bows in European-American Mountain Communities," in *For Gerhard Kubik*, Schmidhofer and Schuller, eds., pp. 361–380.

24. Courlander, *Negro Folk Music U.S.A.*, pp. 207–208; Kip Lornell, notes to *Virginia Traditions: Non-Blues Secular Black Music*, BRI 001 (12" LP), pp. 2, 5; Ann Allen Savoy, *Cajun Music: A Reflection of the People*, Vol. 1 (Eunice, LA: Bluebird, 1984), pp. 305–306.

25. Epstein, *Sinful Tunes and Spirituals*, pp. 46–54; Georgia Federal Writers' Project, *Drums and Shadows: Survival Studies among the Georgia Coastal Negroes* (Athens: University of Georgia Press, 1940), passim.

26. Evans, "The Music of Eli Owens," pp. 337–339.

27. David Evans, "Black Fife and Drum Music in Mississippi," *Mississippi Folklore Register* 6 (1972): 94–107; Evans, notes to *Afro-American Folk Music from Tate and Panola Counties, Mississippi*, side A, tracks 1, 2, and 3.

28. Epstein, *Sinful Tunes and Spirituals*, pp. 55–58; George Washington Cable, "The Dance in the Place Congo," in *The Negro and His Folklore in Nineteenth-Century Periodicals*, Bruce Jackson, ed. (Austin: University of Texas Press, 1967), p. 192.

REFERENCES

Bastin, Bruce. *Red River Blues: The Blues Tradition in the Southeast.* Urbana: University of Illinois Press, 1986.

Cable, George Washington. "The Dance in the Place Congo," in *The Negro and His Folklore in Nineteenth-Century Periodicals.* Bruce Jackson, ed. Austin: University of Texas Press, 1967, pp. 189–210. (Originally published in 1886).

Charters, Samuel B. *The Country Blues.* New York: Rinehart, 1959.

Conway, Cecilia. *African Banjo Echos in Appalachia: A Study of Folk Traditions.* Knoxville: University of Tennessee Press, 1995.

Coolen, Michael T. "Senegambian Archetypes for the American Folk Banjo," *Western Folklore* 43 (1984): pp. 117–132.

Courlander, Harold. *Negro Folk Music U.S.A.* New York: Columbia University Press, 1963.

Epstein, Dena J. "The Folk Banjo: A Documentary History." *Ethnomusicology* 19 (1975): pp. 347–371.

———. *Sinful Tunes and Spirituals.* Urbana: University of Illinois Press, 1977.

Evans, David. "African Contributions to America's Musical Heritage." *The World & I* 5, no. 1 (January 1990): pp. 682–689.

———. "African Elements in Twentieth-Century United States Black Folk Music." *Jazzforschung* 10 (1978): pp. 85–110.

———. Notes to *Afro-American Folk Music from Tate and Panola Counties, Mississippi.* Archive of Folk Song AFS L67, 12" LP.

———. "Afro-American One-Stringed Instruments." *Western Folklore* 29 (1970): pp. 229–245.

———. *Big Road Blues: Tradition and Creativity in the Folk Blues.* Berkeley: University of California Press, 1982.

———. "Black Fife and Drum Music in Mississippi." *Mississippi Folklore Register* 6 (1972): pp. 94–107.

———. "The Music of Eli Owens: African Music in Transition in Southern Mississippi," in *For Gerhard Kubik: Festschrift on the Occasion of His 60th Birthday*, August Schmidhofer and Dietrich Schuller, eds. Frankfurt: Peter Lang, 1994, pp. 329–359.

Georgia Federal Writers' Project. *Drums and Shadows: Survival Studies among the Georgia Coastal Negroes.* Athens: University of Georgia Press, 1940.

Graham, Richard. "The Diddley Bow in a Global Context." *Experimental Musical Instruments* 6, no. 5 (February 1991): pp. 1, 10–11.

———. "Ethnicity, Kinship and Transculturation: African-Derived Mouth Bows in European-American Mountain Communities," in *For Gerhard Kubik: Festschrift on the Occasion of His 60th Birthday*, August Schmidhofer and Dietrich Schuller, eds. (Frankfurt: Peter Lang, 1994), pp. 361–380.

Herskovits, Melville J. *The Myth of the Negro Past.* Boston: Beacon, 1958; originally published in 1941.

Holloway, Joseph E., ed. *Africanisms in American Culture*. Bloomington: Indiana University Press, 1990.

Kirby, Percival R. *The Musical Instruments of the Native Races of South Africa*. Oxford: Oxford University Press, 1934.

Linn, Karen. *That Half-Barbaric Twang: The Banjo in American Popular Culture*. Urbana: University of Illinois Press, 1991.

Lornell, Kip. Notes to *Virginia Traditions: Non-Blues Secular Black Music*, BRI 001 (12" LP).

MacLeod, Bruce A. "The Musical Instruments of North American Slaves." *Mississippi Folklore Register* 11 (1977): pp. 34–49.

———. "Quills, Fifes, and Flutes before the Civil War." *Southern Folklore Quarterly* 42 (1978): pp. 201–208.

Minton, John. "West African Fiddles in Deep East Texas." in *Juneteenth Texas: Essays in African-American Folklore*. Publications of the Texas Folklore Society No. 54, Francis E. Abernethy, Patrick B. Mullen, and Alan Govenar, eds. Denton: University of North Texas Press, 1996, pp. 290–313.

Oliver, Paul. *The Story of the Blues*. London: Barie & Rockliff, 1969.

Olsson, Bengt. *Memphis Blues and Jug Bands*. London: Studio Vista, 1970.

Savoy, Ann Allen. *Cajun Music: A Reflection of a People, Vol. 1*. Eunice, LA: Bluebird, 1984.

Stewart, Barbara. *How to Kazoo*. New York: Workman, 1983.

25 THE CONCEPT OF MODERNITY IN CONTEMPORARY AFRICAN ART

Nkiru Nzegwu

For 425 years the world has lived with a distorted image of itself. In 1569, the German cartographer Mercator visually skewed the world to the advantage of countries in the northern hemisphere. He presented Europe as larger than South America, which is double its size. The old Soviet Union became double the size of Africa, a much larger continent. India, which is three times the size of the Scandinavian countries, became smaller. Greenland dwarfed China, even though China is four times larger. Alaska ballooned to three times the size of Mexico, although in reality Mexico is larger. By the end of Europe's three Ages of Discovery, Enlightenment, and Colonialism, this cartographic distortion had carried over into all facets of human life, so that today the world gazes at itself through badly fractured lens.[1]

Throughout this century, in the visual arts, Modernism has been the cartographic lens through which global visual creative expression is framed. Its distorting Mercator-type assumptions about visual creative production ignore the fact that Modernism's privileging of art and visuality obscures the multiple trajectories of cultural development, and mystifies the deep political, moral, and social considerations that are powerful catalysts to creativity and to new ways of seeing. Shaped within a particular cultural location, though denying its cultural specificity, Modernism's authoritative insistence that art be created just for art's sake prescribes a limiting ideal that justifies the denial of moral responsibility in the art. Thus, this separation of artistic production from the larger questions of morality and political vision provided the requisite basis for preserving the centrality of a Eurocentric vision of art and artistic practice in the Age of Colonialism and its aftermath, and for curtailing the transformational force of competing creative visions.

In a historical period of reexaminations of traditional assumptions about forms of knowledge, visual representation, and artistic practice, a critical reevaluation of old terminologies, interpretive frames, and justifications of Africa's twentieth-century contemporary art are very much in order, and sorely needed. The question that institutes this process is: Is the "modern" in modern Nigerian art the same as the "modern" in modern European art? Rephrased: Is modernity, as conceptualized in European artistic practice in the first quarter of the twentieth century, fundamentally the same as Africans' deployment of this term in the description of its twentieth-century representational practice? The tendency has been to assume that it is, especially since a radical rupture occurred in the 1900s in both the European and the African representational traditions, and the rise and influence of modernism in Europe temporally overlapped with the spread of European social values in colonial Africa.

Using the early history of Nigeria's contemporary art as an example, I undertake a historicized examination of the history of the concept of modernity in contemporary African art. Attending closely to the formative influences of this art in Nigeria, I consider the eliding processes that facilitate the construal of contemporary Nigerian art as direct derivations of European Academy art and Modernism; next I examine the extent to which "modern" in modern Nigerian art shares ideological or stylistic roots with Euromodernism; and lastly, I shall expose the teleological conception of history that seduces proponents of Euromodernism into thinking that there is only one path and one homogenous view of modernity.

THE SHIFTING MEANINGS OF "MODERN" AND "CONTEMPORARY"

The words "contemporary" and "modern" have interchangeably been used to characterize much of Africa's twentieth-century art distinct from the forms which some historians have claimed are directly tied to traditional rites and rituals. Over the years, the enduring nature and limits of this set of works have been debated, and subsequently linked to Modernism. In one of the older publications in the area of study, *Art in Nigeria 1960*, the Swiss-Austrian art scholar Ulli Beier (1960) drew a boundary between traditional African art on the one hand, and "modern" and "contemporary" art on the other. Without explicitly defining the meaning of the terms, he deployed "modern" in ways that suggest a current, up-to-date historical process, so that the expression "modern art" consequently referenced the entire range of artistic expression produced since the beginning of colonial encounters in Nigeria.[2]

As stipulatively deployed, the expression "contemporary Nigerian art" lacks temporal specificity; it does not refer to the here-and-now or to works of art created a few years ago as may be supposed. Like the term "modern European art," and as Salah Hassan notes about contemporary African art, the classificatory expression "contemporary Nigerian art" "denotes a wide range of artistic forms and traditions without a real concern for theoretical or methodological questions of definition" (Hassan 1993, 6). This definitional imprecision, however, is more apparent than real. At the genre level, Beier explicates the denotative contours of the expression by juxtaposing it to the following categories of creative production—"the cement sculpture art of the new middle class," "Christian workshop art of Oye-Ekiti," and "commercial or signage art." A consequence of the juxtaposition is that the term "contemporary art" refers narrowly to the creative works of two artists whom he describes as "pioneers in the truest sense of the word" (1960, 9). These are Ben Enwonwu (1921–94) and Felix Idubor (1928–91).

Adhering to Beier's account, Nigeria's modern art history is coextensive with the history of the political formation of Nigeria, hence beginning either on or slightly before 1900. On this account, all works are modern if they have been created in the twentieth century. By contrast, the history of the genre of contemporary art commenced in the 1940s, presumably when the two "pioneers," Enwonwu and Idubor, became professional artists. Although membership in this latter category was broadened by Beier in 1968, it is significant that his selection of the two artists as markers of contemporary art is based on teleological grounds that tacitly link these artists' creative output to European art in general, and to Euromodernism in particular.

Several assumptions underlie Beier's approach to the construction of contemporary African art. Central among these is his preferred German expressionist conception of art that deploys the principles of a European artistic practice: lack of inhibitions, absence of preconceived ideas, and free, colorful, and imaginative art. This enables him to conceptualize African artists as contemporary, not because he sees their works as reflecting any vital social and cultural influences that are Nigerian, or because they have appropriately contemporized and extended their indigenous artistic tradition, but because he considers them as instantiating the three critical features that on Western European reference frames define both artistic production and artistic progress. These are artistic individualism, the receipt of Western European artistic education, and international (i.e., in the West) exhibitions. Though the blurring of "contemporary [Nigerian] art" and Euromodernism occurs because the non-naturalistic works of these Nigerian artists stylistically *appear* to be modernist in form and character, Euromodernism enters into, and mediates Beier's conception of contemporary Nigerian art by representing it as systematically developing along the preordained track laid out by European artists. Most pertinently, it enters through Beier's cultivation and promotion of the expressionist-type works of "illiterate" individuals who have received no formal training whatsoever in any artistic practice.

Beier contextualizes contemporary Nigerian art by assigning a marginal position in his writings to Nigeria's cultural traditions and stylistics, to the artists' social expectations, and to their cultural experiences in the production of their art. His representation makes it seem that contemporary Nigerian art is modernist, while the artists' training in European-style art schools and their exposure to European art through participation in international exhibitions are proof that the artists are following the path "discovered" by European artists at the turn of the twentieth century. At this stage of analysis, the historical meaning of "modern art" is clearly being replaced by the ideological meaning of the term and is being made equivalent in meaning to works in the Euromodernist style. Since "contemporary Nigerian art" is understood as "modern Nigerian art," and since "modern" does double duty for European worldviews, it is generally assumed that the "modern" in the "modern art" of a European colony is conceptually identical to the "modern" in Europe's "modern art."

To firmly secure this idea Beier forces familiar European expectations about stylistics and the practice of art to bear disciplinary responsibility for the popular understanding of contemporary Nigerian art. He contends that "[t]he modern African artist has little real connection with tradition" (1960, 9) because Christianity and the British educational system had taught them to reject their culture "as superstitious or even as evil" (1960, 9). This thesis of culture rejection is used to insinuate that contemporary art is alien and inauthentic, and that only the artistic production of "illiterates" is acceptable, as they are uncontaminated by the new cultural values of Europe. Beier, an adherent of artistic expressionism, carefully conceals the ideological basis of his evaluative criteria and hides the fact that his preference in art is for "primitivist" works that are unencumbered by received ideas and in which emotion and imagination are unrestrained. An immediate consequence of this carefully concealed prejudice is that contemporary Nigerian art (produced by educated individuals) is represented as one in which the style, choice, and modes of visual representation are informed by European artistic vision and practice.

Elaborating further in 1968, as if to deflect charges of misrepresentation, Beier reinforces his 1960 reading by assigning indigenous artistic principles and practices a location of marginality in contemporary art. He states unequivocally that "the traditional arts of Africa died away quickly . . . [and that] the artists were already abandoning the tradition (1968, 12)."[3] The implication he expects us to draw is that there is a legitimate way in which cultural rootedness is established, that no indigenous artistic tradition remained to sustain, nourish, and provide an appropriate grounding for contemporary Nigerian art, and to make matters worse, that the contemporary artists have embraced a European tradition. This radical elimination of the indigenous artistic traditions permeates his evaluation of the *Africa Dances* series of Enwonwu, in which he closes the door to the possibility of selective imaginative reinterpretations or conceptual linkages to local artistic universes. Instead of addressing Enwonwu's social aspirations and aiming to understand what the artist sought to achieve with *Africa Dances*, and to understand the complex ways the images were reinvigorating the artist's cultural tradition, Beier's Mercator-style evaluation entrenches the idea that this educated contemporary artist and his works are, indeed, alienated from his culture. By this means he summarily disqualifies any images that exemplify philosophical, social, and political ideas that he sees as sophisticated, and that do not meet with his expectations of what Africans should be doing.

Drawing heavily from a German expressionist framework that is animated by stereotypical views of Africans' primitive nature, Beier foists his aesthetic views on Nigeria's modern art in the process of reconstructing the history of that art. This maneuver enables him to state disparagingly of Enwonwu's disciplined style, "The approach is intellectual rather than emotional. The artist is not experiencing but observing the traditional ceremonies. He is excited by them, but is not part of them" (1968, 10). This underestimation of the relevance, cultural importance, and implications of Nigeria's creative, social, and political histories for its contemporary art occurs because Beier assigns normative value to the idea of European expressionism and artistic practices in global art. The possibility that there are different traditions of modernity and different understandings of what counts as modernity in art is tightly regulated. Through hegemonic manipulation of disciplinary assumptions, terminologies, values, and ideas, modernity unfolds along an inexorable path as one unitary process. This illegitimate move ties the concept of modernity to European modes of visual representation so that the expression "modern Nigerian art" is interpreted on a model that inevitably treats the Euromodernist formulation of expressionism as the archetypal ideal. The idea that different histories and creative visions may inform and shape people's understanding of what modernity is and what modern art means is never seriously considered. What is missed by scholars upholding this Eurocentric frame of interpretation is that Africa's idea of contemporary art need not overlap with that of Europe's, and that the history of its own process of modernism need not preserve the creative and intellectual dominance of Europe.

Writing in the prevailing intellectual climate of the period, Beier insulates his reading from critique by discursively drawing from the prevailing fretwork of assumptions of the widely influential modernization theories of economic development of the period. These assumptions of a clearly defined path to economic progress legitimized the utilization of Euromodernism and the views of Europeans as the model of artistic progress. In the economic development climate of the 1960s in which he was writing, the conventional wisdom of the fashionable modernization theories were that Africa needed to be modernized and constructively placed on the path of progress, if it was ever to develop. The Rostowian idea was that the "backward" underdeveloped peoples of Africa and the Third World would arrive at a modern condition of life provided they employed Europe as a model for development. Given this framework, the term "modern" increasingly came to stand for Westernization and progress, the propaedeutic process for development. As a result, Beier's deployment of European creative practices and experiences as a panacea for artistic development in Nigeria was then seen, not as the hegemonic move that it was, but as both beneficent and progressive. Thus, in contemporary African art history constructed by Beier, "modern" became ideologically coincident with progress and modernization, and functioned as a hegemonic tool that instituted the suzerainty of European artistic assumptions.

Though it is generally assumed that the influence of modernization theories is limited only to economics and the economic development sector, a careful study reveals its far-reaching impact on other disciplines too. That the normative principles of Eurocentrism implicit in economic modernization theories are also presupposed in statements about representational practices is evident in Beier's attempts to saddle Nigeria with polemical aesthetics that laud expressive emotionalism typified by Oshogbo. The central problem of his position is that in *speaking for* contemporary Nigerian artists, and in constructing the history of that tradition, Beier never factored into analyses the artistic philosophies of pioneer artists like Aina Onabolu (1882–1963, who predates Enwonwu and Idubor but whom Beier never acknowledged), Enwonwu, Idubor, and Akinola Lasekan (1916–74). Curiously enough, although a scholar of Beier's caliber should be aware of the vital relationship between the principles of creative production and artistic output, he chooses not to illumine the creative rationale of early contemporary artists who addressed the social issues, political problems, and historical concerns of their time. Consequently, the construction of contemporary Nigerian art ends up abrogating the rights of Nigerian artists to articulate their artistic objective, denies them agency, and makes them appear as pathetic beings.

Indeed, Beier's failure to adequately contextualize the early stages of Nigerian art, as is routinely done for European and American artists, results in a worrisome distortion. This occurs because his authoritative narrative, his teleological view of history, including his tacit selection of expressionism as the artistic ideal, methodically occurs within the assumptions of Europe's representational structures and practices, in which Euromodernism is the authorizing artistic ideal of twentieth-century art.

RUNNING LOOSE: OTHER DEFINITIONS OF "CONTEMPORARY"

Other definitions of "modern" and "contemporary" art by Nigerian art historians and writers abound, though none seriously challenges the Eurocentric tenets of Beier's view. While some, like Lawal, have rejected the modernist thesis of "art for art's sake," and have replaced it with the expression "art for life's sake," they remain essentially in agreement with the view that Nigeria's contemporary art is an extension of Western Europe's representational practice. In unwittingly carrying on the crude Westernization agenda of Beier, these scholars have not only given legitimacy to, but also have more deeply entrenched Nigeria's twentieth-century art into, a conceptual scheme that preserves the centrality of European assumptions of artistic progress while eliding the creative ethos of Nigeria's art.

Agreeing substantially with Beier's account of art forms in the "modern art" category, Pat Oyelola differs slightly by working with two senses of "modern" in *Everyman's Guide to Nigerian Art*. The first sense operates at a broad historical level, in which she collapses "modern" into "contemporary" so that the two words are interchangeable. In this broad sense, "modern" simply marks a historical distinction between nineteenth-century, precolonial art, and the artistic production of the twentieth century. This means that works which were created during and after colonization are modern. In the second sense "modern" functions as a stylistic marker that separates certain styles and types of artworks (such as paintings and sculptures) from works with different stylistic roots. In this narrower sense, "modern" loses its historicity and acquires analytic overtones. The result is that the expression "modern art," in this second sense, refers to a cluster of works (paintings and sculptures which include the work of Onabolu, never referred to by Beier) that correspond roughly to Beier's category of "contemporary art."

Under this reinterpreted meaning, the historicity of "modern" is replaced by the evaluative sense of the word, making it difficult to sort out the exact meaning of the term. Because of this blurring of boundaries, the neotraditionalist style of a Lamidi Fakeye is not viewed as contemporary even though the work may have been created recently. Since Oyelola's use of "modern" and "contemporary" holds out the promise of historicity and change, it needs to be underscored that once the words are deployed in practice they lose their descriptive essence and acquire a prescriptive force. Not only do the words end up stipulating that artistic individualism, an "art for art's sake" philosophy, and a Western-style education are prerequisites for this art; most importantly, they function as organizational tools of difference, enthroning the normative superiority of European artistic vision. Under this guise, the expression "modern Nigerian art" implies development, or progression toward the Western, while "traditional art" implies the unchanging and the African.

Again like Beier, Oyelola justifies her definition by epistemically grounding it on the traditional/modern dichotomy that treats the artistic values and the social and political aspects of the two disjuncts as fundamentally distinct and separate. The evidence that the dichotomy is chimerical given that it is continually being breached by artists is ignored.

The implication is that Oyelola's claim that new, colonial, and postindependence art is created in accordance with the Euromodernist concept of "art for art's sake" (which differs fundamentally from the community-oriented artistic values of precolonial Africa), is advanced without determining whether the envisioned overlap is accurate. Yet the overlap is secured by insisting that the rise of contemporary Nigerian art facilitated the decline of the traditional art and displaced its life-oriented values. The consequence of this insistence is that the emergent modern-contemporary art forms are seen as Nigeria's variation of European modernist art; any differences are assumed to be technical.

Oyelola's formal linkage of modern Nigerian art to European modernism is coincident with Babatunde Lawal's characterization of a particular strand of contemporary Nigerian art as "avant-garde." A close examination of his views in an essay on identity in contemporary Nigerian art reveals that like Oyelola,[4] he too reads "contemporary" and "modern" as indicators of a historical period. The expression "contemporary art" is interchangeably used with "modern art" to reference the country's twentieth-century art. However, unlike Oyelola, Lawal bypasses the problem of equivocation by using the French expression "avant-garde" rather than "modern" to distinguish the works of artists who were trained in art schools. The move automatically relocates Idubor (one of Beier's markers of contemporary art) to the category of "neo-traditionalist," airport art manufacturers, and Lamidi Fakeye, who sculpts in Yoruba abstract style, is characterized as unimaginative for producing "'neo-traditional' works . . . that are severed from [their] umbilical sustenance [of] traditional culture and religion" (1977, 146). Interestingly, while Lawal's category of "avant-garde" captures the individualistic and Euromodernist emphasis of Beier's notion of contemporary art, it differs in his insistence on the importance of art school training as a prerequisite for membership in the "avant-garde" club.

The problem in Lawal's position begins with his employment of terminologies with a longstanding history and tradition. His choice of the Euromodernist expression "avant-garde" as a classificatory term for new stylistic-cum-technical changes frames the artistic objectives of a segment of contemporary Nigerian art as a variant of Euromodernist art. The issue here is not that the expression "avant-garde" is French but, given that the expression is steeped in the tradition and ideology of Euromodernism, its usage for Nigerian art automatically projects Euromodernist artistic values on Nigerian art, whether or not this is intended. Insofar as Lawal's reliance on "avant-garde" (at the cutting edge) denotes a specific artistic practice, we need to understand how its usage devalues the culturally rooted rationale of that segment of contemporary art.

As Barry Hallen demonstrates in his essay "The Art Historian as a Conceptual Analyst" (1979), the ascriptive aspect of language is hardly ever considered by art historians as they cross conceptual boundaries of vastly different cultures. The example of Robert Farris Thompson, the notable Africanist art historian, is a case in point. Seduced by the compelling imagery of the heart in an informant's (Mashudi) expression "We take our measurements from our heart" (1973, 45), Thompson postulates an artistic criterion of emotional proportion for Yorubas in which the psychological importance of things is stressed over strict measurement (1973, 43). This postulation effectively portrays Yorubas as sharing the belief that emotions are rigidly distinct from reason. As Hallen makes clear, Thompson's unwitting imposition of the European dualistic framework on Yorubas ignores the Yoruba conceptual framework in which *okon* (heart) is the repository of mind or consciousness (1979, 305). Unbeknownst to Thompson, whose knowledge of the Yoruba conceptual scheme is limited, *okon*, as used by the informant, refers to what most closely approximates the European conception of reason, deliberation, and measurement, not the emotional and the psychological, as Thompson's representation erroneously supposes.

The reverse is the case in Lawal's use of "avant-garde." Concerned as he is with presenting contemporary Nigerian artists as a legitimate part of a modern art movement, his use of the expression maps Euromodernist assumptions and visual expectations about art onto this category of Nigerian art. Similar to *okon*, the expression "avant-garde" describes a list of ideas and images that in the Euromodernist framework refer to radical, provocative, cutting-edge works that are essentially abstract in depiction and divergent from the naturalistic style of their tradition. By relying on "avant-garde" as the classificatory term for the category, Lawal lays emphasis on innovative experimentation and movement away from tradition, not on conformity to traditionally validated norms. As such, Lawal's usage of "avant-garde" incorrectly describes a category of works by Nigerian artists whose objective, he claims, is to synthesize the new and the old, and to contemporize the traditional. As he describes it, the objective of Nigerian "avant-garde" artists is not to avoid tradition but to extend it (1977, 148). Their primary goal is not an obsessive search for the novel, the different, or a new language of stylistics, as Lawal puts it; it is to indigenize the forms through "an *analytic* study of traditional forms and symbols to be followed by a synthetic adaptation to contemporary painting, sculpture, architecture, etc." (1977, 148). Because these artists are striving for the culturally familiar, and not for cultural difference, by using "avant-garde" as the defining expression, Lawal summarily subsumes their creative vision under the European modernist ideal.

A consequence of Lawal's reliance on terminologies from Europe's representational practice is his insistence on Western education as a criterion for inclusion into the "avant-garde" category, that being the only way an artist is appropriately trained. Yet his deployment of this educational requirement promotes cultural alienation by suggesting that the artists are searching for identity. Representing the educated pioneer artists as alienated from their indigenous identities and cultures enables him to describe their works as "a provincial extension of European modes" (1977, 145). If indeed the artists are alienated, Lawal needs to determine the circumstances of their alienation rather than simply positing it. It may very well be that in the process of examination it would be revealed that what he thought was alienation is actually a cogent affirmation of cultural identity and an unapologetic resistance to subjugation. Given that Onabolu's brief sojourn in Europe occurred long after he was a proficient artist, Lawal ought to have examined how Onabolu became an artist, who taught him, and who influenced him; as well, he should have interrogated the idea that the European-type art school is crucial to the development of Nigeria's contemporary art. Rather, in a circuitous move, he drew from Onabolu's utilization of the naturalistic style and represented this as indicative of his colonized status and cultural alienation. The failure to probe the politics underlying Onabolu's naturalistic representation allows Lawal to assert erroneously that, in its early phases, modern art was a provincial extension of European modes of creativity.

Though, as Lawal admits, a cross-cultural exchange occurred between Europe and Africa in which "contemporary Western art is trying to 'Africanize' [and] Nigerian avant-garde art is trying to 'Westernize'" (1977, 148), he fails to examine the full theoretical implications of this seemingly innocuous exchange. If indeed the exchange is as equitable as he represents it, why is it that the abstract style of artists like Picasso, Matisse, Derain, and Braque are treated as modern when the abstract style of Africa that facilitated them is dismissed as premodern and primitive? Why is Europeans' twentieth-century use of the abstract mode of representation characterized as modern and "avant-garde" while Africans' historic usage of the technique is represented as premodern and primitive? Further, why does Lawal portray the African side of the exchange as a "provincial extension of European modes" without representing the European *avant-garde* side of the equation as a provincial extension of African modes? If cross-cultural exchange is mutual and equitable as Lawal wants to suggests, why does he assume that Europe's employment of Africa's "premodern" abstract mode of representation is not alienating and does not contaminate its concept of modernism, while Africa's use of naturalism is presented as alienating and as subverting the independent status of its modern art?

It is noteworthy that Lawal readily accommodates Euromodernism and its hegemonic construction of history as well as the corollary idea that the artistic Africanization of Europe did not imply an alienation from European culture. It is also instructive that he readily accepts the idea that the works of the pioneers of contemporary Nigerian art are derivative and

passé, and represents the Westernization of Nigeria as signifying alienation from African culture. The crucial problem is not simply that the hy-
brid culture of Europe remains essentially European and uncontaminated
despite the African cultural mix, while Nigerian cultures are represented
as contaminated at the mere hint of Western influence. It is more that, in
accepting the validity of European stylistic experimentations and shifting to a different standard when evaluating Nigerian stylistic experimentations, Lawal unwittingly endorses a teleological view of modernity in
which the European model of exchange constitutes a better, more acceptable model of a secular understanding of modernism. By implicitly treating
the latter as normative, and by shifting to a different standard of evaluation and suggesting that pioneer artists are compromised by their education, Lawal throws his weight behind a hegemonic agenda that denies
agency and self-determination to Nigerian artists and represents contemporary Nigerian art as inauthentic.[5]

MODERNIST HUBRIS: THE CONTEMPORARY AS INAUTHENTIC

Two other definitional features of modernism emerge strongly in Uche
Okeke's and Dele Jegede's writings: elitism and the urban-centered nature
of modern art. In "A History of Modern Nigerian Art," Okeke gives a
fairly detailed profile of Onabolu, Akinola Lasekan, Enwonwu, and Demas
Nwoko, playing up what he takes to be their privileged status as well as
the elitist character of their art (1979). In "African Art Today: A Historical
Overview," Dele Jegede extends this viewpoint, stating unequivocally that
"contemporary African art, like modern art elsewhere, is individualistic,
and elitist . . . fiercely independent . . . uninterested in illustrating or remaining subservient to a socioreligious consensus" (1990, 34), and also
urban-centered (1990, 37). Although Jegede's views seem laudatory and
positive, he cuts the ground from under contemporary Nigerian art when,
interrogating its cultural relevance, he rhetorically asks: "[O]f what use
is a landscape painting to a farmer in whose thatched homestead it
would be rendered redundant by soot, masks, and other cultic objects?"
(1990, 37).[6]

A close reflection on the tone and content of the question reveals that
Jegede treats elitism and urbanity as definitive of modern art, and as establishing a divide between it and rural, proletarian Nigerians. This dichotomy casts contemporary art as alien and culturally irrelevant. By
drawing the line of authenticity on the basis that it is "like modern art
elsewhere," he hitches Africa's contemporary art onto Euromodernism,
making it subject to those rules. While Jegede's point is that contemporary
art lacks functional value and that it is not reflective of, or subservient to,
the traditional "socioreligious consensus," his choice of a farmer as the

arbiter for artistic authenticity is problematic. Even if, as he implies, a landscape painting is of no use to a farmer in a thatched homestead, it does not follow that such paintings lack cultural validity or authenticity. The relevant question is not "How useful are these works to Africa's farmers (the image of the average African)?" but "How legitimate is it to set up indigent farmers as artistic arbiters?"[7]

The subtle introduction of the issue of relevance and authenticity for contemporary African art derives from the idea that urbanity, and the artistic forms created in such spaces, is somewhat at variance with the ethos of traditional living, the ascriptor of cultural legitimacy. But even if we concede Jegede's contentious point that there is a sharp rupture between traditional art and modern art, it does not follow that urbanity defines a "foreign," nontraditional space that seemly developed with colonialism. Urban living has historically been a part of African indigenous life given that Yorubas, Hausas, or Binis have traditionally lived in the urban environments of Oyo, Eko, Abeokuta, Ibadan, Ijebu Ode, Kano, Zaria, and Benin. So even if contemporary art is urban-based, to what degree is it any more urban-centered than traditional Yoruba arts in Oyo or Ijebu Ode, Hausa arts in Kano or Zaria, and Edo arts in Benin and Warri? Indeed, to what degree were traditional arts in Yorubaland, Hausaland, and Benin a rural or farmland phenomena?

There is an absence of sociohistorical contextualization in Jegede's construction of the urban/rural distinction that derives from his ready acceptance of white Africanists' construction of contemporary African art, and from his construal of the history of that art as "in part, the story of expatriates who saw in Africa a transitional territory in need of creative husbandry" (1990, 36). This unremitting focus on the histories and narratives of European and white American expatriates prevents Jegede from recognizing that Africans had cities, that not all farmers in Africa fit his picture of the indigent farmer, and that there are many ways in which art works have come to be in farmers' homes—all of which undermine the plausibility of his assertions. The widely popular cement sculptural forms (e.g. elephants, roosters, lions, seated or kneeling male or female figures, and male figures in the act of writing) of the 1940s to 1970s were found in the countryside of southern Nigeria. Influenced more by traditional themes and values than by modern (colonial and post/neocolonial) cultural values, these forms were commissioned by fairly affluent farmers and produce merchants to decorate the frontage and courtyards of their homes. From the 1980s, as retired army generals, ambassadors, industrialists, bank CEOs, and managers went into farming, they filled their opulent country homes with treasure-troves of paintings and sculptures that volubly spoke to the sociopolitical and cultural issues of relevance to Nigerians. Other ways in which art has come to be in rural areas is through some not-so-wealthy individuals who have houses in their hometowns and home-villages. Sometimes these individuals have either purchased or commissioned artworks for these country estates, or have the paintings of their children or relatives displayed in their homes.

Furthermore, as Beier (1960) and Lawal (1977) have recognized, acquisition of contemporary art was affected by income, but that does not mean that average Nigerians are uninterested in the artistic products of their times. Even in the 1950s to 1970s, low-, lower-middle- and middle-income Nigerians, in urban areas, typically beautified their homes with slick enamel-on-board paintings of mangrove swamps, river/lagoon scenes, mermaids, and fishermen in canoes they purchased from signwriters. Even today, works of art are increasingly to be found in the homes and offices of Nigerians. Granted these classes of Nigerians are not the farmer in Jegede's example, they nevertheless fit the bill of the average Nigerian, whose artistic taste must be factored into analysis. The implicit problem in Jegede's analysis is that his image of the farmer as the average African is too restrictive given the reality of African social life. Secondly, he fails to grapple with the complexity of Africa's social reality today, and accepts too easily the simplistic model of Africa as inherently rural. Thirdly, he ignores that the primary consumers of artworks in any society, including the indigenous societies, are typically the elite. Since it is not a necessary condition for cultural legitimacy that every citizen own an art work, it is unjustified to arbitrarily set up questionable standards of validation for contemporary societies in Africa.

In characterizing contemporary African art as individualistic, elitist, and urban, Jegede implies that these properties are not associated with traditional art. But how accurate is this assertion in light of the well-documented fact that the patrons of the high end of the traditional arts and crafts (carving, beadwork, and textiles) have historically been the affluent members of the society?[8] So, what does it really mean, for Jegede, to say that contemporary art is elitist, individualistic, and fiercely independent? Again, to what degree is it any more elitist and individualistic than are the Yoruba traditional arts of Abeokuta or Oyo? What evidence is there to show that individuality is not a cherished ideal in traditional art forms given that each carving style constitutes a signature, and given what we know of Bandele Areogun of Osi Ilorin, Alani Adigbologe of Abeokuta, Bamgboye of Odo Owa, and Olowe of Ise? And lastly, how "fiercely independent" are contemporary artists who have to depend on a patron's largesse for their livelihood and who have switched styles to keep pace with the vagaries of the marketplace?

Explanations are crucial since Jegede intends to portray the artistic universes of the older traditional art as radically different from those of contemporary art. His reference to "masks and cultic objects" suggests that the older reference frames were religious-oriented while the new reference scheme of art is secular. Apart from the fact that being religious does not give a work greater authenticity than secular works, there is no way to rank the legitimacy of the two states in a society. But even if "masks and cultic objects" have a socioreligious basis, it does not follow that art in the indigenous context is necessarily religious. This portrayal is misleading given that a vast amount of traditional art works are secular in orientation and do not have any religious connotations. There is a vast amount of secular objects like the elaborately carved veranda house-posts (or caryatids), ornately carved doors, textiles, pottery, and mural paintings, even as there are cultic objects. Similarly, this same blurring of the secular-religious boundary occurs in contemporary art. While it is true that contemporary Nigerian artists like Grillo, Onabrakpeya, Enwonwu, Onabolu, Emokpae have created a large cache of works that are secular, some of their major works have been religious, and are to be found in the following places of worship: Cathedral Church of Christ, Lagos; All Saints' (Anglican) Cathedral, Onitsha; Chapel of the Resurrection, Ibadan; Chapel of the Apostolic Delegate, Lagos; St. Paul's Church, Ebute Metta; St. John the Evangelist Church, Lagos; Holy Trinity Anglican Church, Lagos; All Saints Church, Lagos; and Chapel of the Healing Cross, Lagos.

An answer to these issues at the very least would radically revise the simplistic model of African societies underlying Jegede's position. One way to quickly uncover the complexities in the society is for Jegede to re-think his rhetorical question. Since "masks" and "other cultic objects" are not the regular run-of-the-mill farming tools, Jegede needs to elaborate on the social stature of the farmer in the community so that readers could understand why the thatched homestead is a storage place for communally owned cultic objects. Could it be that the farmer is not as socially incon-sequential as Jegede suggests? The issue here is not simply that the farmer is not socially inconsequential, but that in the traditional universe of vis-ual representation (as in the contemporary universe) there is a one-to-one correlation between an audience and the type of artworks produced. Jegede should realize that he mismatched contemporary art and its audience. He incorrectly presents "farmers in thatched homesteads" as the primary audience of paintings, rather than the segment of the population that is the conventional audience of this art. Had Jegede correctly correlated the varieties of contemporary art to their rightful audience, a different history would emerge that would not be the story of expatriates. Since the art of any society is essentially integrated into some aspect of the political and social culture of the community and has a local audience of salience, its cultural rootedness and legitimacy are given.

Because for some theorists the historical state of modernity shares terminological roots with the artistic position of modernism, the distinc-tive attributes of the latter constantly work in art historiography to mask, elide, and supplant the historicity of the word "modern." Though intended as functional terms, the essentially European formulations of twentieth-century art have often served to set the ideological tone and boundary for what is and is not contemporary Nigerian art. In doing so, these terms reveal that they are theoretical constructs with prescriptive connotations of what art works must possess to be described as "contemporary art." Since "modern" and "contemporary" never really functioned as ordinary everyday terms, they bypass Salah Hassan's complaint that a paradoxical situation is created when that which is created half a century ago is still labeled "contemporary" (1993, 31–2). The paradox dissolves once it is clear that the word "contemporary" is a technical term, and logically behaves in the same fashion as "modern" does in the expression "European modern art."

AN ARCHAEOLOGY OF THE "CONTEMPORARY" AND THE "MODERN"

In Nigerian parlance, contemporary art refers to a body of works, created from the 1890s with internationalized materials, and that are the products of people's artistic and political interests in defining their own reality. These representations are executed with European-manufactured materials and techniques to meet the aesthetic tastes and artistic ideals of the new social classes.[9] Those who enter the discourse on contemporary African art as defined by Africans know that the expression "contemporary art" is no different from Europe's choice of the expression "modern art" to label its African-inspired works that were produced by a group of artists in the first half of the twentieth century. While the choice of terms is each culture's prerogative, what is really important is that the preference for "contemporary art," as the denotative term, makes it clear that Africans do not necessarily attribute modernist values to their art.

Once the special semantics of the expression are acknowledged, a different sort of epistemological problem arises, which is that in current art historiography, it is assumed that what occurred before 1900 (in "precolonial times") was traditional, and that what has occurred since that date is modern and contemporary. The problem with taking colonialism as the defining historical moment for the genesis of contemporary art is that a sharp divide is introduced that fails to recognize the historic links and cultural exchanges between various ethnic groups in West Africa.[10] Furthermore, it misses the diverse ways the traditional and the contemporary are interlinked, and ignores the precolonial emergence of necessary social formations needed for the development of the latter art. By suggesting that the philosophy and creative production of indigenous works were brought to a closure by colonization, it is not clear to many that traditional art works continued in different sections of the country, and that contemporary art draws substantially from Africa's social reality, and from the iconography of diverse indigenous artistic traditions. Moreover, the tacit suggestion that the requisite social processes of modernity did not begin prior to colonization prevents many from seeing the extant local conditions that gave rise to an Onabolu and made his art possible.

When the historical phenomenon of colonialism is taken as the single most defining moment, colonialism takes credit for structures, events, and processes that predate it, or that occurred in resistance to it, and whose logic derive from sources other than subjugation. Also, a colonized reading occurs when colonialism is taken as a marker for Europe and the "story of expatriates in art" occupies a larger-than-life space in art historical imagination, the result of which is the trivialization of Nigerians' role in creating their art. As may be seen in Jegede's essay, the centering of Europe through colonialism compels a near obsessive attention on Europeans' artistic policies, intuitions, and interventions rather than on the resistance/interactional/appropriational forces at play in Nigeria between 1880 and 1920. This sidelining of Nigeria's sociopolitical activities and interventions not only makes Europe the model, but indeed suggests that no complex of social and political structures and processes existed in Nigeria, prior to British domination, that could have facilitated the emergence of a distinctive creative phenomenon.

The reason local influences are absent in scholarly narratives of the emergence of Nigeria's contemporary art is that inadequate attention is paid to the sociopolitical resistance culture of Lagos. Because of this inattentiveness the resultant analyses remain trapped within a narrow explanatory framework that misses the links between the sociopolitical climate of 1890 to 1945 and the emergence of works produced with European-manufactured materials and techniques. This elision persists because in the pursuit of international scholarly recognition and prestige, scholars are pressured through prepublication reviews to ignore Africans' agency and to uphold conventional Eurocentric narratives. Inevitably, they are compelled to utilize, rather than transcend, a distorting framework that subordinates contemporary Nigerian art and Nigerians of a certain period to a colonial ideal. Caught in this Euro-privileging trap, scholars who are anxious to publish may ignore the pertinent fact that the temporal overlap of the emergence of contemporary art and the establishment of colonialism does not establish a causal relationship between the two. The existence of a temporal overlap does not imply that contemporary Nigerian art is "rooted" in colonialism since there were other initiating factors—such as photographs and people's desire for self-representation—that account for its development. Hence, it is false to assume that contemporary Nigerian art is an art of subjugation.

In fact, a review of the roots of Nigeria's contemporary art and the social and political history of Lagos from the 1890s (the time of Onabolu's residence in Lagos), reveals a convergence in resistance objectives, which indicates that despite the overlap in time-frames, contemporary art was not materially dependent on colonialism but flourished in spite of it. Probing Onabolu's (the recognized father of modern Nigerian art) history, we find that his artistic sensibilities were, in fact, shaped by the arts and artistic tradition of Ijebu Ode long before the introduction of European artistic values. His subsequent preference for the naturalistic style derives both from photographic illustrations in publications and a visceral resistance to the racism of the colonial system.

Born in September 1882 in Ijebu Ode,[11] Onabolu's attempt to draw realistically began while he was a student at St. Saviour's Primary School, Ijebu Ode, after the British punitive expedition of May 1892. Prior to the expedition, Onabolu had little contact with European values, as Rev. Samuel Johnson's history of the Yorubas (1976) and E. A. Ayandele's history of the Ijebus (1983) indicate. Between 1800 and 1891, Ayandele asserts, the Ijebus pursued a policy of "splendid isolation" in which they treated British agents, missionaries, and non-Ijebu Yorubas as "strangers" (1983, 90). So complete was their distaste of Europeans and their way of life that in 1852, the Awujale (ruler of Ijebu nation) promulgated a new immigration policy instructing the Remo, on the borders of Ijebu proper, not to allow any missionary into their part of Ijebuland (1983, 94). This hostility to European cultural influence was so unrelenting that the Ijebus would not even allow Ijebu Saro[12] as members of their community. In their eyes, the latter "had betrayed their fatherland by adopting European religion, manners and clothing" (1983, 91).

Though the policy of isolationism helped the Ijebus to "retain intact their religious ideas, cosmology and religious system" (1983, 93), Ayandele notes that it did not debar them from pursuing their economic activities and trading, even with the Europeans they despised. They traded with other Yoruba "strangers" in markets (in Ilugun, Ketu, Apomu, Ode-Ondo, Ibadan, Oyo, and Ilorin), as well as with the Portuguese and the British, whom Obanta (their guardian force) had decreed to be evil. Exceedingly prosperous when the rest of Yorubaland was caught up in debilitating civil wars, Ijebus became dominant economic players, controlling major markets and importing a variety of goods into Yorubaland. Attributing their peace and prosperity to the efficacy of their religion, "which pervaded society in all spheres of life" (1983, 93), their arts flourished and resulted in the production of skillfully carved religious reliquaries in wood, such as the Gbedu drums, ornate house posts and doors of Osugbo lodges, and metal *edan* and *ipawo ase* that sometimes reflected the neighboring styles of Benin and their Yoruba neighbors. Their economic wealth led to elaborate observances and performances of rituals, and to the production of secular and religious arts in bronze, wood, textile, pottery, and beadmaking.

An exclusive focus on colonialism, Christianity, and Western education hinders an understanding of the ways in which Onabolu's art derived from and is anchored on Ijebu art. Western education was finally introduced into Ijebuland after May 1892. By this time, Onabolu was ten years old and was already familiar with both the secular and religious arts of his culture. It is obvious that he had acquired some technical knowledge in art since he was able to freelance as an artist by 1894, less than two years after commencing primary education in which art was not part of the curricula. He taught himself to draw by copying illustrations in textbooks and newspapers since art books were not available then. By 1894, when he was twelve and a student in St. Saviour's Primary School in Ijebu Ode, he was designing charts and teaching aids for teachers who were his first local audience. That he was able to attain significant proficiency in art in a short amount of time shows that he must have been engaged (probably as an apprentice) in some form of artistic production, such as sculpting and modeling human forms and faces, prior to the 1892 expedition. As Ayandele points out, childhood education among the Ijebu starts very early, with every boy or girl "expected to be shrewd and was made independent at an early age" (1983, 92).

Though a complete detail of his early life is not available, however, knowledge of Ijebu history in 1885 to 1895 reveals that, at its inception, Onabolu's art was not developmentally dependent on the forces of colonialism. His adoption of the naturalistic style that evokes the naturalism of Ife art really began from the partially abstract figurative forms of Ijebu secular and religious art of the time. The shift from an abstract naturalistic style of the human forms on the caryatids and temple statuary to the illusionistic naturalistic style of the Academy is a short one, which Onabolu managed easily by adhering to the illustrations contained in publication materials that were circulated by missionaries.[13] Since his artistic genius was kindled primarily by photographic illustrations rather than by Western education per se, it is misguided to restrict the genesis of his art and the history of modern Nigerian art to colonialism.

Other equally important factors need to be considered, not least of which is the emergence of a third new powerful force in the political equation that existed between the British and indigenous rulers of Lagos. Constituents of this force were the group of educated Africans (Saro, Egba, Oyo, Ijesha, Ibadan, and Ijebus) whose aims and objectives were not necessarily coincident with the interests of the two established groups,[14] and who saw themselves as creators of a new society that was to be the equal of other nations in the world.

THE POLITICS OF FASHIONING MODERNITY

After the 1852 restoration of Oba Akitoye to the throne of Lagos, and before the British annexation of the area in 1861, a burgeoning cultural center had begun to develop with the influx into Lagos of numerous Christian missionary groups, Sierra Leonean immigrants (or Saro), self-emancipated Africans from Brazil (Agudas or Assimilados, as they were known), Egbas from Abeokuta, Oyos, Ijesha, and Ijebus from the Yoruba heartland, Akans from the Gold Coast, and European (English, German, Austrian, and Italian) merchants of different trading missions. Yorubas traveled back and forth between home in the hinterland (Ake, Ibadan, Oyo, Ilorin, Ilesha, Ondo, and Ekiti), and the coast. Families like the Assumpcaos, who were originally from Ikija, returned from Brazil and settled in Ake, and changed their name to Alakija (Folarin Coker 1972, 21). Shortly after 1861, more ethnic groups—Efiks, Ibibios, Igbos, Nupe, and Hausa—arrived from eastern and northern Nigeria, bringing with them diverse social, cultural, and artistic values. The presence of this diverse multiethnic, multicultural population gave cosmopolitan Lagos a vibrancy and independence at odds with the picture of passive subjugation we regularly encounter in colonial literature. Ayandele reveals that Governor Freeman complained in a report to the Colonial Office in 1863 about the hostility of the Lagosian elite, whose motto was "Africa for the Africans," and who wanted the British "either swept from the coast or subjected to the dominion of the blacks" (1979, 206).[15]

In this polyglot mix of Yoruba, Hausa, Igbo, Portuguese, and English speakers, predominantly Orisha-worshipers, Christians, and Muslims, the political interests of the educated group with whom Onabolu was later to associate was sometimes antithetical to the interests of the British colonial government. Led by Dadi Imaro and Ojo Martins, this group monitored, critiqued, harangued, and legally challenged the repressive ordinances of the colonial administration. Saburi Biobaku reports that in 1864 the missionaries of the Church Missionary Society (CMS) and the Saro routinely attacked the policy of the Lagos government for seizing people's properties without adequate compensation and for excluding "educated natives" from the Colonial Council (1991, 75). In return, Commander John Glover, the Lieutenant-Governor and Acting Colonial Secretary, termed the activities of the Saro "evil," and "passed an ordinance in Lagos obliging them to take the oath of allegiance" in order to break their organized resistance to his policies (1991, 80).[16]

Against this political backdrop, Lawal's description of the works of early artists as a provincial extension of European modes of representation raises profound questions about his reading of the political climate and the sociopolitical consciousness and identity of Lagosians of this early period. By suggesting that pioneer artists were engaged in alienated forms of representation because they employed the naturalistic style, he ignores the history of the period and represents naturalism as European, rather than as a technique of representation that could be utilized by any cultural group, as was done in ancient Ife by the forebears of Ijebus (Ayandele 1983, 89) and other Yorubas. The critical issue here is not that Nigerian art

should not take its cue from Britain if it really drew from that artistic practice, but that a Europeanized lens, artistic prejudices, and biases are being
used to frame our idea of the modern. Given that each society constructs
its own tradition of modernity, Lawal's focus of investigation should be on
Nigerian society, its artists, and prevailing social issues, rather than on the
art tradition of Britain.

Conceptually, modernism or modernity in art is defined by three formal elements, namely experimentation, a radical shift to a new stylistic
form, and a movement away from conventional modes of representation.
In the same formal way that Picasso, Matisse, Derain, and Braque experimented with abstract style in making a radical shift from the conventional
naturalistic mode of representation, Onabolu experimented with naturalism in facilitating a radical shift form the conventional abstract mode of
representation. Though the trajectory of the two artistic forms of representation and the socially specific pattern of action is radically different,
the formal properties of the concept of modernity remain essentially the
same. Since modernity is not inherently teleological, it is wrong to devalue
Onabolu's genius because he charted a different path from Europe, and to
celebrate Picasso's genius, especially since Onabolu did not borrow from
European art, and Picasso copied from African art.

Even if Nigeria's contemporary art was called into existence by the
intellectual and cultural forces unleashed by the historical forces of colonialism, that art cannot be circumscribed by colonialism since the latter
does not exhaustively explain it. The same is the case with Euromodernist
art which was called into existence by the artistic values of Africa, yet
is not explained by the latter given that there are other compelling factors. A review of historical evidence and editorial opinions in the following leading newspapers reveals that the establishment of contemporary art
was not part of the British colonial agenda. Between 1862 to 1900, Lagos
was a hotbed of activities.[17] The five newspapers dominated the intellectual climate of Lagos and nurtured a critically informed citizenry, with a
sharply defined sense of their image and identity. These were the bilingual
(English and Yoruba) Iwe Irohin (1859–67, published in Abeokuta), African
Times (1862–82), The Lagos Observer (1886–89, founded by J. B. Benjamin), The Lagos Times (1880–91, founded by Richard B. Blaize), The
Lagos Weekly Times, which began in 1889, and The Lagos Standard (1889–
1920, established by G. A. Williams).

Resisting domination, yet astute enough to recognize that the colonizers had the advantage of military might, Lagosians lobbied intensely for
the creation of the Lagos Legislative Council. Under the sponsorship of
Rev. James Johnson,[18] John Augustus Otunba-Payne, Sheriff of Lagos in
the 1870s, sought representation on the Council. The objective of Otunba-
Payne's candidacy was to participate in the governance of the colony and,
where necessary, intervene to check the unwelcome and racist policies of

the British colonial administrator. By 1885, thirteen years after the creation of the Legislative Council in 1872, Lagosians sought greater autonomy and petitioned the Secretary of State for the Colonies for the separation of Lagos from the Gold Coast colony. The granting of the petition on January 3, 1886, gave Lagos residents greater room for intervention. This was the sociopolitical climate of Lagos in which contemporary art developed and flourished, and in which the sociopolitical significance of the new art was framed.

Following his move to Lagos in the early 1900s to attend CMS Grammar School (the oldest secondary school in Nigeria), Onabolu lived in the home of his guardian and mentor J. K. Randle, a medical practitioner and a family friend. At the time of his arrival in Lagos, the racist policies of Governor MacCallam (1897–1904) were gradually eroding the progressive integrationist policies of the previous governors of Lagos. Prior to 1897, Governors Glover (locally known as Goloba, 1864–72), Moloney (1886–90) and Carter (1891–97) had undertaken major rezoning and replanning of the spatial environment of Lagos, further complicating and obscuring the assumed spatial and architectural distinction between traditional life and modern life. Construction had commenced on the Railways, Five Cowries Creek, Carter, and Denton bridges, and Lagos had been connected to the United Kingdom by telegraph (1886). Soon after, the introduction of telephones and electricity in 1898 increased Lagosians' sense of participation in the larger world.

Yet even as all these changes were occurring, the indigenous family life, habits, Orisha worship, and rites continued unabated for the 42,000 noneducated and non-English-speaking African residents of Lagos, and even among the 4,000 educated African elites. Use of Yoruba language, marriage ceremonies, burials, Ogboni freemasonry, and the annual celebrations of the Adamu Orisha festivities in which the white-clad *Eyo* "spirits" performed continued, and left no doubts about the uniquely distinct character of Lagos society in the 1920s.

Though some identification with England was being fostered by telephonic and telegraphic connections, the public impact of these technological devices was limited. In contrast to the metropole, there was greater identification with other West Africans in the other British colonies, given their historic ties and trade activities, geographical proximity, patterns of migration, kinship, and shared colonial experience. In the first two decades of the twentieth century, Lagosians possessed a well-defined Pan–West African outlook, which was further reinforced by the setting up of regional financial, educational, and judicial institutions in British West Africa. Led by the antiracist politics of Holy Johnson (Rev. James Johnson, born in Sierra Leone of an Ijesha father and Ijebu mother), this regionalism brought with it an expansive sense of political and social unity that explains the 1890 visit to Lagos of Edward Wilmot Blyden, a man then rec-

ognized as "the Greatest Defender of the Negro Race." Blyden returned four
years later, in 1894, for the formal opening of the imposing Shitta Mosque,
named after the wealthy Sierra Leonean–born merchant, Mohammed
Shitta Bey.

By the 1920s, when Onabolu successfully organized his first solo exhibition, a corps of distinguished Nigerian lawyers, doctors, engineers,
clergy, and businessmen had emerged as an influential intellectual class
and as the prospective audience for Onabolu's art. In the legal profession
these included such luminaries as Adeyemo Alakija, Sir Akitoye Ajasa,
Sapara-Williams (who had an unmatched reputation in advocacy and an
intimate knowledge of unwritten customary law), Montague Thompson,
Egerton Shyngle, and Eric Oladipo Moore (who filed leading cases against
the Colonial Secretary of Southern Nigeria related to land tenure and customary law), Sanni Adewale, and E. J. Alex Taylor, leader of the Nigerian
Bar and popularly referred to as "the Cock of the Bar" (Folarin Coker 1972,
28–9). In the medical profession were J. K. Randle, Akinwande Savage,
Oguntola Sapara, Magnus Macaulay, and Adeniyi Jones; and in the mer-
chant class these distinguished personages included P. J. C. Thomas,
Samuel H. Pearse, Daddy Vaughan from Alabama, J. H. Doherty, C. O.
Blaize (known as "Merchant Prince"), A. W. U. Thomas, and W. A. Da-
wodu. Politically active in associations formed to protest the abuses of the
British administration and to agitate for self-representation were Mojola
Agbebi (formerly D. B. Vincent), Herbert Macaulay, Randle, Savage, Ernest
Ikoli, W. B. Euba, Rev. S. M. Abiodun, Babington Adebayo, Shyngle, Ajasa,
Rev. J. G. Campbell, and Adebayo Deniga.

ART AND STYLE: IDENTITY DISCOURSES THROUGH ART

In an essay on theorizing in historical writing, Rifaat Ali Abou-El-Haj
argues against historiographical strategies and assumptions that construe
events (such as nation-states or a nation's history of art) "as the inevitable
issue of modern history" rather than seeing modernity as the outcome of
a possible set of choices (1994, 1).[19] Such immutability of logic in history,
he contends, excludes alternative paradigms that are part of the transitory,
open-ended nature of historical process, and makes it difficult to see the
constantly transforming, variegated character of what are assumed to be
traditional norms and events. Once a nation-state, or art as in this case, is
stripped of its historicity (that is, its transitory, changing nature), it takes
on a fixed, ahistorical character. This shift not only eliminates other competing paradigms that reveal the interrelationship of social interests, histories, and influences, but treats tradition as a stable, unchanging, fixed
body of ideas, beliefs, norms, and images.

Abou-El-Haj convincingly argues that a critical perspective must view
events (such as nation-states or Nigerian art, as in this case) as "simulta-

neously representing a transitional object" that is created from diverse, shifting, socially situated interests and forces. If not, a literalist interpretation occurs because historical meaning is tied unreflexively to unchanging contexts. Thus, a multicausal, historicized analysis must necessarily shift from unsubstantiated theoretical speculations about state, or the nature of art, to the actual environment of the society in which the convergent, interactive forces of change have their base.

Applied to art-historical analysis, Abou-El-Haj's insight facilitates a radical reframing of the contexts within which the history of contemporary Nigerian art has been articulated. In the first instance, it represents Lagos society as a continually vibrant multicultural environment in which Yoruba norms and Christian and Muslim values were continually being transformed; second, it investigates the symbiotic and synergetic interaction between traditional and modern artistic values and philosophy; and third, it recoups into analysis the occurrent social and cultural influences that shaped the art. Framed in this critical manner, a theoretical reconstruction of Nigeria's contemporary art subverts the traditional/modern schism and shifts the focus of interpretation to the socially situated concerns, issues, and objectives of the time. The shift enables us to recognize the specific concerns of the citizenry, and to see the transitory sites of engagement within which the formative issues of the chosen style in modern art were raised and settled.

Given Abou-El-Haj's emphasis, contemporary art and the preferred style of representation begins to appear not as the inevitable product of Nigerians' experience of colonialism, but as the outcome of a possible set of choices in which a new cultural identity was articulated, and in which Onabolu emerged as an artist. Read critically, then, Onabolu's art and his preference for realism (i.e., the naturalistic style) direct our attention to the rationale and multipronged process of the formation of modernity in Nigerian art, his rejection of the abstract style that was the rave in Europe, and to the diverse, shifting, socially situated interests and forces that influenced his path.

During the early days of the development of contemporary art, and after completing his secondary school, Onabolu worked as a marine clerk in the Customs Department. On the side, he continued practicing his art, studying and copying nature in still-lifes and landscapes, using photographs and the pictures and illustrations he came across in magazines to perfect his skill. He decided to go into portrait painting because of the challenges it offered (Agoro 1980, 37). Proximity to Randle, a well-connected political activist and art patron, fortunately validated and reinforced Onabolu's art as well as placing him in the hub of the upper echelon of Lagosian society. This facilitated the establishment of ties with prospective clients and the families of future clients whose interest in portraiture converged with his preference for realism.

With Randle as a mentor, Onabolu's artistic development converged with his political development; he learned about the nationalist issues championed by his mentor in such political associations as the People's Union (formed 1908), the Anti-Slavery and Aborigines Protection Society (organized 1912), and the Nigerian branch of the National Congress of British West Africa. Randle had formed the People's Union with Dr. Obasa to provide a secular arena where Lagosians could express anticolonial political sentiments and strategize against the increasingly racist policies of the administration of Governor Walter Egerton (1904–12).

While association with Randle ensured that Onabolu learned about the deleterious features of colonialism and how these must be combated, it also suggested to him the best stylistic tool for exposing the falsity of the colonial maxim that Africans were biologically inferior to the white man. Strategic professional and political interests led to realism's becoming his artistic technique of choice. In the face of Egerton's segregationist programs, a naturalistic representation of Lagos, its peoples, and the differing aspects of their lives was a most effective and powerful weapon for countering stereotypical images of Africa's cannibalism and primitivity replete in the narratives of colonial officials. A consummate artist, Onabolu's professionalism and artistic excellence attracted a clientele of Nigerian luminaries (businessmen, lawyers, doctors, and clergy), whose portraits he executed. At his first salon in 1901, at the home of Randle, the drawings, still-lifes, landscapes, and portraits he produced while in Lagos were exhibited and favorably received. The most memorable of his early works were the portraits *Mrs. Spencer Savage* (1906), a photographic likeness of Augusta, Spencer's wife, and *Dr. Randle* (1910) a posed image of his mentor.

A formalist reading of Onabolu's portraits, especially the later ones, reveal individuals that are distinguished by the dignified countenance of their age or posture, the intimidating garb of their respective professions, and the rich, subtly contrasting coloration of the overall work. This is evident in the portraits of *Rt. Rev. I. Oluwole* commissioned by CMS Old Boys Association, *The Barrister*, and *Bishop James Johnson* (45″ × 32″), presently at the main entrance of the rebuilt Glover Memorial Hall, Lagos. Bishop Oluwole's portrait presents him in a seated pose, dressed in episcopal robes, and gazing with equanimity at the viewer, with a benevolent smile playing on his lips. Like Oluwole's portrait, Johnson's portrait was framed in oak with a brass inset. It was commissioned in 1917 shortly after Johnson's death by the women's branch of the Committee of the West African Bishoprics Fund. The commission cost twenty-four pounds sterling while an additional eight pounds sterling was paid to obtain twenty-four smaller copies for friends and admirers. According to Ayandele, forty-eight pounds was raised from every woman in Lagos, most of whom contributed a maximum of one shilling (1970, 372). At its dedication ceremony in November 26, 1918, in which Henry Carr (a Nigerian) gave the address with Governor General Frederick Lugard in attendance, the portrait was placed in a prominent position at the entrance of the old Glover Memorial Hall (1970, 372).

In ·the portrait, Johnson was represented "in the closing years of his life . . . standing upright, a tall gaunt figure in episcopal robes, ascetic in appearance, with the light of battle in his eyes and his aged face worn deep with the lines of thought, struggle, and sorrow" (Ayandele 1970, 372). Another preferred pose was that of the *Barrister*, in which the restrained demeanor of the formally garbed lawyer, seated among his law books, filled the central space of the canvas. The slightly angled face of the man is illuminated with soft, diffused light with shadows cast to the back of the head, creating depth of field. Onabolu sometimes sought skillfully structured moods, as in *Man with a Beret*, creating an evocative romantic atmosphere with a fascinating tale that is strongly suggestive of Rembrandt. As with photography, Onabolu's pictorial style allowed the educated Lagosians of the 1920s to capture their likenesses and their achieved status. Other than the cost, the significant difference between Onabolu's portraits and the photo-portraits of the renowned Lagos photographer George S. A. Da Costa was that Onabolu rendered his clients' images in color. His expertise notwithstanding, Da Costa could only produce black-and-white images of his clients given the level of photographic technology at the time. Onabolu's critical edge and popular appeal lay in the lifelike hues and tones of his color palette.

Most scholarly analyses of the early history of contemporary Nigerian art are basically reductive, and oblivious to the complex dynamics of appropriation, resistance, and retranslation of human experiences taking place in an existential context of colonial domination. By 1924, Onabolu's reputation as an artist and politically informed being was already well established in Lagos. Thus, it is instructive that Beier contended forty years later in the 1960s that contemporary art had not begun in Nigeria at this time, and that Lawal dismissed as British provincialism the artistic products of the period. It is these sorts of historiographical misrepresentations that reinforce the need for painstaking reexaminations of the tradition of contemporary art production in Nigeria. In revisiting this period, and given the cursory treatment it has received, there is need to ascertain whether indeed the social and political climate of colonial Lagos in the first quarter of the twentieth century constricted artistic imagination and independence, a factor that would explain scholarly disinterest. Given that Onabolu's entrée into art came by means of photographic images and illustrations in magazines, the question is: To what extent is his art an extension of British provincialism? Was there thematic coherence or other aesthetic cues? How dominant was the impact of his two-year art program?

As indicated earlier, Onabolu's role in creating Nigeria's modern art began in Ijebu Ode and was influenced by the photographs and illustrations he saw in the newspapers, periodicals, and textbooks. Between 1915 and 1920, after completion of his secondary school education, he had mastered a full range of drawing techniques and was perfecting his skill in portraiture while teaching part-time at numerous primary schools. Onabolu was fascinated with portraiture and viewed portrait painting as "the highest and the most difficult of pictorial art[s]." His services were keenly sought after as evidenced by the 1917 commission of the portrait of Holy Johnson. In 1920, he held a solo exhibition of 200 works to show the public "some of the pictures he had been able to paint without the aid of an Art master, and thereby . . . prove that God is impartial in his endowment of various talents to mankind" (Agoro 1980, 9).

The incessant demands and politics of certificates forced him to travel abroad to obtain a certificate from an art school. In those days of colonial rule, obtaining a certificate was imperative if one was to secure permanent employment as a teacher in any secondary school. Weeks after the end of his solo exhibition, he departed for a two-year art course at St. John's Wood School, London, and Julien Academie, Paris. The time in both places was spent brushing up and perfecting technical skills that would enhance his work in portraiture and paintings from real life.[20] Although the Euromodernist art movement was in full swing, Onabolu found the images uninspiring and weakly imitative of traditional African works. Besides, the implicitly racist language used by the European artists to characterize their movement did not endear the Euromodernist ideal and stylistic experimentations to him. He found the whole exercise disrespectful and offensive. On completion of this program in 1922, Onabolu returned and opened a studio in Lagos that same year, where he established a reputation for artistic excellence and innovation. He was hired as an art teacher at King's College and CMS Grammar School, Lagos. Some of his early pupils were Geoffrey Okolo, Albert Odunsi, Eyo Ita, Nkure, Festus Idowu, Holloway, Osula, Odubanjo, Solanke, Orisadipe, and Ajidasile.

Onabolu was particularly drawn to portraiture and the naturalististic style of representation for a variety of reasons, not least of which is the political one. The illusionistic effect of naturalism could conveniently be deployed to expose the fallacious narratives of colonial histories. Its selling point was that it fulfilled his clients' aspirations and preference for self-representation and family portraits, while at the same time satisfying his political objective of visually subverting the racist argument of Africans' inability. As the demand for his services increased owing to the communicative effectiveness of his style, in 1923 Onabolu was commissioned by the Lagos Town Council to design a poster advertisement for the sale of new buildings that were under construction. The public's response was overwhelming. Mr. Rumen, then secretary to the Town Council, and other members were suitably impressed since they wanted to quickly recoup the money invested in the houses. Taken in by the illusion of the painting, some people came to pay for a unit, believing the houses to have been completed, and the following employees of the Town Council enrolled for art classes with him: Messrs S. I. George, Bankole Williams, and Balogun.

The vast amount of Onabolu's portraits and compositions reveal them to be less concerned with the polemics of colonialism and more concerned with people's personal, family, and professional interests. For instance, in 1924, Onabolu's gouache painting *Nigerian Weaver*, depicting a Yoruba female weaver seated on a low stool at her loom, was submitted by the Colonial government to London, and was selected in a world-wide competition as a poster for the British Empire Art exhibition in Wembley, London. In the same year, *The Trumpeters* (1924), an imaginative painting, was commissioned by the Colonial government for presentation to the Prince of Wales. Another well-known oil painting, *The Village Belle* (1924), a portrait of his wife, Mabel, in *aso oke* (a richly woven cloth), also dates to this period.

A correct approach to contemporary Nigerian art is critical both for understanding the artists of the period and for presenting the influences, rationale, and formative impulses of contemporary art. The importance of naturalism as a style of representation could be better understood against the politics of the sociopolitical life in Lagos between 1900 and 1935. This period of Onabolu's maturation was a contestation ground of opposing interests and objectives, not all of which were responses to the political issues and intellectual and cultural forces of colonialism. A perusal of the leading papers and the events chronicled reveals a very articulate citizenry, affirming British social norms and cultural values yet virulently contesting their subject status. Paradoxical as this may seem, Ayandele correctly contends that Lagosians of the period manifested "a spirit of self-identity" and were the "purveyors of the concept of Nigeria for the Nigerians" (1979, 205). The power and success of colonialism, however, was that it provided spaces for people to aspire toward what has been defined as European ideals even as they publicly resisted and opposed their subjugation. In this prevailing push-pull dynamic, the colonial administrators tried desperately and unsuccessfully to control and rechannel the unrelenting political expression; however, after independence, the residual effects of colonization accomplished the psychic subjugation that the colonizers themselves had failed to achieve.

In the identified historical period, the Lagos press, namely *The Lagos Weekly Record* (1910–30), owned by the Lagosian-born Thomas H. Jackson, *The Nigerian Times* (1910–), *Nigerian Pioneer* (1914–36), owned by Akitoye Ajasa, *The Times of Nigeria* (1915–23), *Lagos Daily News* (1925–37), *The Lagos Daily Records* (1930), and Ernest Ikoli's *African Messenger* provided the fora for, and played a large role in determining the issues for these public debates. Seeking the implementation of the principle of equality, the press spiritedly assailed the racially discriminatory policies of the colonial administration that placed Nigerians in a subordinate position. The Lagos Town Council was a particular target since it had successively tried through differing policies and decisions to marginalize the educated elite. In 1906, after Lagos became the seat of Southern Nigeria, Lagosians responded sharply to the colonial government's residential segregation of European Government officials from the African population under the pretext of health and sanitation measures.

Sometimes the anticolonial challenges were more radical as people fathomed the implications of colonization. In 1913, there was intense agitation over the payments of water rates, and there was protracted litigation filed by the Idejo "White Cap" Chiefs over acres of land which had been expropriated by the colonial administration. For a small fee, Nigerian letter-writers systematically inundated the Colonial Office in London with reports of the mismanagement of colonial officials in Lagos, and repeatedly called for inquiries to be instituted. Under the auspices of the Anti-Slavery and Aborigines Protection Society, S. H. Pearse led a delegation of the Nigerian Land Deputation to Downing Street, London (MacMillan 1920, 98).

The "spirit of self-identity" manifested itself with the introduction of each new program and policy, and in each decade of colonial rule. In 1919, Lagos became the capital of Nigeria following the amalgamation of the Southern and Northern Protectorates and the Colony of Lagos. Even as the country battled the after-effects of the 1918 influenza epidemic, the amalgamation of the country was a focal point of volatile debates. The Lagos press fearlessly galvanized public opposition to Lord Lugard's imposition of the reactionary Northern Nigeria model of administration on the more moderate Southern administration. This repressive system, in operation in Northern Nigeria, was roundly denounced by the *Lagos Weekly Record* (February 22, and June 14, 1919) as "the most infernal system that has ever been devised since the days of the Spanish Inquisition" (1919). The refusal of Lagosians to acquiesce to pernicious colonial policies did not endear them to the Lagos administration, yet it was a clear indicator of the people's heightened awareness, and evidence of their ideological resistance to political subordination.

THE ESSENCE OF LAGOSIAN MODERNITY: 1850–1950

In *Formations of Modernity*, Stuart Hall offers a number of interesting features and defining strategies that free the concept of modernity from a Eurocentered framework, in which it has long been held hostage. The thrust of his argument is that the formation process of modernity occurs "across several centuries in a slow uneven way" with no precise cut-off point (1996, 10). With no single time-frame or universal date of emergence, it is easier to appreciate that modernity began at different times in different societies. As Hall states, "Modern societies certainly display no singular logic of development" (1996, 12). The implication of this idea of multiple histories is that modernity did not assume the same form or characteristics in all societies, but rather was conditioned by the peculiarities of each cultural context. This conceptual emancipation of modernity from the clutches of Europe allows us to undercut teleological propulsion and to more vigorously interrogate and debate the constitutive features of modernism in different societies without necessarily treating Europe as *the* model. The recognition that modernity relates to a possible set of choices enables us to see that some of its identified features, such as dominance of secular forms of political power and authority, a clear separation of powers between the executive, judiciary, and the legislature, a monetarized exchange economy, and interethnic migrations were already taking place in parts of Nigeria long before 1900. Some of these features were exploited by the colonial powers.

Hall's enumeration of the formal traits of modernity offers a way to understand complex historical events without racializing the distinctive features of the period. By directing attention to the character of social processes, he brings to attention the specific spirit of modernity—dynamism, change, optimism, transformation, and forward movement to displace older paradigms. He makes it clear that modernity is a social process of change and is not equivalent or reducible to a European phenomenon, as Hassan misguidedly claimed. Modernity or modernism is not coincident with Eurocentrism but with social processes. Hassan had claimed that " 'modernity' itself is a European construct that was articulated initially and most forcefully at the same time 'traditional' Africa was being colonized" (1995, 32).[21] While Hassan makes an important point about the way modernity has been construed, his notion of "traditional" Africa needs to be radically interrogated since its implicit representation of modernity is a concession to Europe's hegemonic construction of history and art. It is this concession that prevents him from recognizing that the formal elements of modernism or modernity in art are basically the processes of experimentation, a radical shift to a new stylistic form, and a movement away from conventional modes of representation.

Modernity, as David Held most succinctly puts it, "is a deeply structured process of change taking place over long" (1996, 73) historical timescales and is marked by the emergence of certain social features, such as the birth of a new intellectual and cognitive world. Because the process of modernity is a societal phenomenon, not a racialized one, it occurs everywhere at differing times, and understandably differs in character from nation to nation. If anything, Held's construal of the formal elements of the modern state—territoriality, control of the means of violence, impersonal structure of power, legitimacy—allows us to acknowledge that the emergence of modernity in the global arena predates the onset of Europe's colonization of Africa. Once the Eurocentric model of historical explanation is laid aside, modernity (within the context of modern states) emerges in different ways in different countries. Interestingly enough, what is revealed in the tumultuous nineteenth century in Yorubaland is that certain nation-states,[22] namely Ibadan, Egba, Ijebu, Ijesha, and Ekiti, had emerged into modern states and were experiencing the growth of "new intellectual and cognitive worlds." The thoroughgoing military republicanism of Ibadan, utterly independent of European political discourses, highlights a form of modern state that is completely homegrown.

In analyzing the historical development of contemporary art through Lagosian modernity and of the character of Lagos through art, we find both to be the variegated expressions of dynamic individuals in the nexus of sociopolitical transformation. In a very important sense, Onabolu's philosophy of modern art was shaped in a complicated, interactional context of resistance that rejects the artistic authority of Europe, the primitivizing ideal of Euromodernism, and the overbearing universalism of that conceptual scheme. Like most professionals of his time (lawyers, doctors, teachers, engineers), Onabolu appropriated the technical tools and style of representation most suited for visually confronting the racist rhetoric of colonialism, just as legal practitioners strategically deployed Britain's legal principles of liberty and equality against its philosophy of racial difference. The value of portraiture and verisimilitude in representation is that it effectively countered the racist musings of such distinguished personalities as Governor Hugh Clifford, who believed that "Africans have to be treated very much as one would treat children . . . [since] . . . the organizing ability is the particular trait and characteristic of the white man" (West Africa, 26 July 1924, quoted in Crowder 1962, 264).

Contesting subjugation as they fashioned their own brand of modernity, Lagosians of the period reserved the right to take whatever they wanted from England's cultural and intellectual arsenal to advance their cause, rejecting what they believed complicated their lives. They dismissed as naive the separatist idea that utilization of technological devices or the borrowing of certain values for their own ends represented a colonized status. In their view, it was wise to appropriate intellectual and technological resources to expand their world-sense. After all, their studies in classics, history, philosophy, and law had revealed to them that Britain's strength derived from its constant borrowings and appropriation of ideas from diverse cultures to fashion its own unique culture.

Nevertheless, as with all processes of appropriation and voyages of discovery, feelings of ambivalence occasionally surfaced in Lagos residents as a resentment of their political subjugation and subject status, and in their social and cultural appropriation of certain English mores. This African audience of Onabolu resented their subject status and demanded equal treatment from Britain, insisting on political representation at the legislative, judicial, and administrative levels of government. At the social level, they protested and lobbied against racial discrimination, insisted on merit in the workplace, pay equity, being appointed to posts to which they were qualified, and on becoming members of taxpayer-funded clubs like the Lagos Dining Clubs, frequently patronized by top government officials. In particular, Onabolu fought for fully developed educational curricula for Nigerian youth, asserting their right to receive instruction in the creative arts. Yet, while championing the principle of social and political equality, Onabolu and other Nigerians systematically communicated to the British colonial officials their intruder status by closing them out of their own cultural affairs. Many Lagosians in the 1930s and 1940s routinely conducted their social ceremonies and affairs in ways that expressed respect for their cultural norms and beliefs. Onabolu, for example, was a member of Egbe Omo Ijebu Ode, a Society of Ijebu Ode citizens, a situation that enabled him to retain his Ijebu-Yoruba identity and participate in its political and cultural activities, even as he lived the cosmopolitan life of Lagos.

Engaged in the dialectical discourse of identity formation and modernity construction, affluent Lagosians, both the educated and uneducated, inscribed their presence in the physical spatial environment of Lagos. Their influences were evident in the imposing architectural edifices they constructed in a mixture of styles that uniquely transformed the city's physical landscape. Noticeable among these palatial homes were Ebun House, the opulent late-Brazilian-style home of Oyo-born A. W. U. Thomas, auctioneer and produce merchant; the magnificent Elephant House of Pearce; Sir Akitoye Ajasa's elegant Godstone House; and the Branco House, the Vaughan House, and the Da Rocha's Waterhouse, all on Kakawa Street. Other noteworthy edifices were the stately Caxton House of the Merchant Prince, Richard Beale Blaize, a major landmark at 53 Marina; the grand Ijeun House at the corner of Wesley and Joseph Streets; Prospect House, the home of W. A. Dawodu, at the corner of Bishop and Breadfruit Streets; and Orange House, the home of the pioneer law-maker and former Sheriff of Lagos, Otunba-Payne, at the junction of Tinubu and Customs streets.

Though clearly recognized as a portrait painter and teacher, Onabolu did not limit himself to portraiture and the teaching profession. He participated in the aesthetic edification of the spatial environment of Lagos, exploring new media and different techniques when the opportunity presented itself. In 1932, for example, he designed the pews of the Cathedral Church of Christ, Lagos which was dedicated on July 6 of the same year. Between 1940 and 1950, he produced a number of oil portraits, pastel compositions, and studies which found their way to people's homes; and in 1954, he completed the construction of his home at Osolake Street, Ebute Metta, with its own permanent gallery, open to the public.

Despite these accomplishments, a general reluctance remains at the theoretical level to claim Onabolu's work as Nigerian, especially by those who find it difficult to accept the legitimacy of the burgeoning culture of Lagosian elites as Nigerian. This hesitance evidently derives from misguided fears that both the artist and audience are alienated, and that Nigeria's contemporary art is authentic only if, thematically and conceptually, it is linked to and demonstrates a clear extension of the artistic traditions of any of its 250 ethnic cultures. This restrictive reading draws its logic from a separatist ideology, and rests on the mistaken idea that discontinuities or ruptures are not a constitutive and legitimate part of the creative tradition. An additional error is that it fails to appreciate that traditions are created, stabilized, and/or modified in a dynamic context of social interaction and change.

A theoretical problem, however, arises when the older Yoruba tradition intersects with Onabolu's contemporary tradition in an unpredictable, nonlinear time-frame. Without a full historical view of Yoruba artistic tradition Onabolu's preference for naturalism may be seen to interrogate the conventional Yoruba sanction against this mode of representation. Yet, this reading runs into difficulties when we realize that naturalism is an implicit part of Yoruba artistic convention. Once seen as alien, Onabolu's preference for naturalism takes on new significance when interpreted in the light of Ife's artistic legacy. Not only does the recovery of ancient Ife's bronze and terracotta works provide cultural legitimation for Onabolu's naturalistic art, in temporally suturing the split in Yoruba artistic consciousness, his art contemporizes the Yoruba stylistic corpus and analytically extends the forms in novel ways. This expansion of the corpus is in no way different from the creative expression of the "Nigerian avant-garde" artists that Lawal held in high esteem, or from the modernist expansion of European art by its artists. Equally, Onabolu's disenchantment with the abstract style of his artistic tradition parallels the disenchantment of European modernist artists with realism, so that realism became the "avant-garde" for him in Nigeria, just as abstraction became the "avant-garde" for Picasso in France.

Thus, a close reading of the multiethnic, multicultural, politically active, intellectual climate of Lagos in the 1930s makes it abundantly clear that the social, political, and ethical concerns and objectives of contemporary Nigerian art spoke to the modern social and political aspirations of Nigerians. These messages were audible and comprehensible to the local audience in a way that was closed to the Eurocentric evaluators who believed modern art should be apolitical and profoundly formalistic. According to the purist art critic/theoretician Clement Greenberg, the best in

Euro-American modern art is abstract (1990), a credo that is based on the idea that the only way painting and sculpture could become fully independent is to be freed from imitating nature. By contrast, contemporary Nigerian art consciously sought verisimilitude through the illusionistic portrayal of its transforming social life, ushering in a new way of seeing as a means of making painting and sculpture culturally meaningful to people in the newly emergent state of Nigeria. In effect, the very nature of the difference between contemporary Nigerian art and Euro-American modernism exposes the error in presenting the two as tracking the same evolutionary path.

NOTES

1. Arno Peter's map publicly revealed the gross distortions of the Mercator map, which remains the most familiar map of the world. It is still being used in classrooms across America and in television newscasts. I first learned of this distortion and the existence of Peter's map only in 1992 at a teacher's seminar organized by the Education Department of the New Museum of Contemporary Art, New York. *Arno Peter's Map* (Oxford, Oxford Cartographer's Ltd).

2. With colonialism as the marker, anything that occurs before 1900 is traditional and precolonial, and any works (including those that may conventionally be described as traditional works) that occur after that date are modern.

3. Only among the "illiterate" locals who never left to "seek wisdom or skill" and "who had grown up with the festival of Oshun and Shango and Ogun" is he able to find the right artistic and aesthetic mode (Beier 1968, 107). As Susan Wenger, a former collaborator of his, succinctly puts it, they were looking for art from the authentic primitive African uncontaminated by Western values. Personal communication (1989) during the preliminary research for the film of *Nigerian Arts: Kindred Spirits.*

4. Babatunde Lawal's "The Search for Identity in Contemporary Nigerian Art," *Studio International*, vol. 193, no. 986, (March/April 1977), 145–150.

5. Lawal's assumption divorces most of the preindependence works of artists who derived their character from their cultural roots. Also, he might argue that this portrayal is a realistic recognition of the dominant power of Europe in the cross-cultural exchange equation. But what he seems to have ignored is that at this stage in history, the effect of Europe's social and cultural values were not as pervasive as is being suggested.

6. Jegede must be aware that during the early years of the evolution of contemporary art not all rural farmers were as destitute as he made them out to be, that there were rural elites too who were farmers. However, even if we grant the arguable point that farmers do not live in opulence, it does not follow that their thatched homesteads and all items, including their *odun* clothes, are soot-coated. His characterization does not take cogni-

zance of the architectural structure of most homes. Apart from the fact that kitchens in the rural areas do not necessarily adjoin the living part of homes, those that do have the smoke vented outside. Hence, it is false to suggest that people's homes were soot-coated.

7. Nothing about the constitutive nature of the world suggests that art patrons and enthusiasts must necessarily be poor, or that they must be farmers, or that they must reside in the rural areas. Indeed as products of someone else's labor, works of art cannot be productively thought of as free gifts of exchange.

8. This is still the case today.

9. By contrast, "traditional art," the term of popular usage in Nigeria, refers both to pre-nineteenth- and twentieth-century works that closely reflect the stylistics of any ethnic groups.

10. Olabiyi Yai (1994) discusses the fact that by the seventeenth century, Yoruba linguistic influence extended to the Fon region of Dahomey. According to his research, early traveler accounts of Alonso de Sandoval and Frei Colombina de Nantes, a Jesuit missionary, reveal that Oyo Yourba was the lingua franca of trade and intellectual discourse (109).

11. Aina Onabolu's parents were Jacob and Oshunjente Onabolu. His father was a successful merchant while his mother was also a trader.

12. "Saro" is the term for Sierra Leonean immigrants.

13. We should remember that the turbulence of the Yoruba wars in the late nineteenth century meant that not all of Yorubaland (including Ijebu) had been militarily pacified and colonized. Besides, as Onabolu's confrontation with the colonial administrations in the 1930s showed, his educational policy was hostile to art. British colonial administration viewed art as irrelevant to the principal objective of colonial education, which was to produce clerks for the colonial machinery.

14. To his credit, Uche Okeke began to make this point in the essay "History of Modern Nigerian Art" (1979).

15. So as not to create the impression that the spirit of self-identity and the desire for political independence was peculiar only to the educated Lagosians, Leo Frobenius unwittingly provided, in 1910, an interesting picture of the assertive spirit of ordinary, uneducated Lagosians:

> I saw one of the higher grade officials driving along in his gig close to the near side of the road according to regulations; a crowd of Yoruba "boys" in trousers plants itself in his way to the left of him; when the gentleman comes up to them the crowd does not budge an inch, and the official of rank is obliged to drive round them in a wide sweep to the off; not a single one of the "boys" so much as thinks of recognizing the familiar uniform and its wearer's personality by the slightest salute.

Now for the companion picture:

> A white man is walking on his right side of the road and meets a grotesquely bedizened company of negroes, some of whom are already in liquor. There is a policeman in the road. The black crowd

is a christening party on its way home from the breakfast. The black policeman steps up the the white man and none too politely requests him to get out of the way of the blacks. (1968, 38–39)

16. Again, the so-called "natives" (uneducated Africans) did not present a passive, acquiescing front to British imperial objectives. The mental and physical health, material resources, and imagination of the handful of colonial officials were tasked to the limit as the Egbas in the northern hinterland, Dahomey to the west, Ikorodu to the immediate north, and Ijebu to the northeast squabbled for control of trade routes. The religious sector too was not immune to African resistance and agitations as the CMS and the American Baptist Mission splintered into an African arm and a foreign arm, with Bishop Ajayi Crowther in charge of the African arm of the CMS.

Colonialism succeeded as it did in West Africa because Africans had no clue as to the ultimate objective of the Europeans, hence they did not devise any contingency plans. However, as they increasingly perceived the long-term objectives of White colonial rule, they created an extraordinary amount of attritional events which led to the modification of imperial policies in the region. It is a testimony to the power of these events and the people's anticolonial organizational skills that within eighty years of colonial rule states were gaining their independence even though British technological superiority did not diminish. Unfortunately, the new states failed to foresee the impact of the residual effects and surviving structures of colonialism long after the physical departure of the Europeans.

17. These include but are not limited to the 1861 annexation of Lagos, the abrogation of some of the land-tenure rights of the Idejo "White-Cap" Chiefs of Lagos, the Egba-Dahomey war, the Lagos-Abeokuta power tussle, and the deterioration of relations following the banishment of the powerful Iyalode (Madam) Tinubu from Lagos to Abeokuta, and the creation of a settlement at Ebute-Metta suburb of Lagos for Egba refugees fleeing the Egba-Dahomey war.

18. James Johnson's parents were Yoruba. Born in Sierra Leone, his father was Ijesha, from Akure and his mother was Ijebu.

19. The methodological importance of Abou-El-Haj's work is that he is methodically raising relevant and similar questions regarding the life and living conditions of people in the Ottoman Empire.

20. He took courses in human anatomy, chemistry of painting, comparative anatomy, landscape drawing and painting, simple designs, lettering, drawing for reproduction, and art history. He won the second-best award in drawing details from the classical figures of Greece and Rome. Onabolu also attended two years of lectures offered to advanced students at the Royal Academy of Arts in London. He exhibited his works twice in Europe before returning to Nigeria in 1922 (Agoro 1980, 10–12).

21. If, as Hassan fully recognized, "African art forms must be perceived as expressions of a more complex African reality" (10), then his attempt to treat the "development of a modern idiom in African art [as] closely linked to modern Africa's search for identity" (4) or as indicative of the artist's residency in "the Western centers of artistic production" is mis-

guided. Artists like Onabolu or Oshinowo, who work in a realist style, undoubtedly see themselves as modern, do not live in Western centers of artistic production, and are not searching for a new identity given that they have already determined for themselves what their identity is. Given the dearth of literature on the matter, one wishes that art historians would increasingly examine the complex interfaces of colonial rule and nationalist debates, and of the artists' conceptualizations of their role. Terms and categories need to be interrogated and rethought. It is usually the case that when information is presented about African artists' search for identity, much of that talk derived from white theorists' postulations (initially Ulli Beier and Frank McEwen but with Africans now following their lead) about what they take Africans to be doing. A rethinking of Africa's contemporary art warrants that these earlier postulations must be separated from the crucial question of whether or not artists share this endeavor and what the history of the period reveals. Unfortunately, much of the legitimacy of theorists' identity-talk has been taken for granted or treated as correct, precisely because there has been no systematic examination of the complex processes of social interaction and change in the period between 1860 and 1960.

22. By any definition of the term these Yoruba kingdoms satisfy the formal requisite conditions of statehood, notwithstanding any treaty they may have signed with the British government. In fact, the very existence of a formal treaty with England is a recognition of their statehood.

BIBLIOGRAPHY

Agoro, Oladeninde O. "Aina Onabolu: Pioneer of Modern Nigerian Art Tradition." B.A. thesis, University of Nigeria, Nsukka, June 1980.

Ali Abou-El-Haj, Rifa'at. "Theorizing in Historical Writing Beyond the Nation-State: Ottoman Society in the Middle Period." *Armagan: Festschrift Andrets Tietze,* ed. Faroque Sureyya (Prague: 1994), 1–18.

Ayandele, E. A. "Ijebuland 1800–1891: Era of Splendid Isolation." In *Studies In Yoruba History and Culture.* Ed. G. O. Olusanya (Ibadan: University Press Ltd., 1983), 88–107.

———. "The Phenomenon of Visionary Nationalities in Pre-Colonial Nigeria." In *Nigerian Historical Studies* (London: Frank Cass, 1979), 204–225.

———. *Holy Johnson: Pioneer of African Nationalism* (London: Frank Cass and Co. Ltd., 1970).

Beier, Ulli. *Contemporary Art in Africa* (London: Pall Mall, 1968).

———. *Art in Nigeria 1960* (London: Cambridge University Press, 1960).

Biobaku, Saburi O. *Egba and Their Neighbours 1842–1872* (Ibadan: University Press, PLC, 1991).

Coker, Folarin. *Sir Adetokunbo Ademola: A Biography* (Lagos: Times Press, 1972).

Crowder, Michael. *The Story of Nigeria* (London: Faber, 1962).

Frobenius, Leo. *The Voice of Africa*, vol. 1 (New York: Benhamin Blom, Inc., reissued 1968, 1913).

Greenberg, Clement. "Towards a Newer Laocoon." In *Abstract Expressionism: A Critical Anthology*. Ed. David Shapiro and Cecile Shapiro (Cambridge: Cambridge University Press, 1990), 61–74.

Hall, Stuart. "Introduction," *Modernity: An Introduction to Modern Societies*. Ed. Stuart Hall, David Held, Don Hubert, and Kenneth Thompson (Cambridge, Mass: Blackwell Publishers, 1996), 1–18.

Hallen, Barry. "The Art Historian as a Conceptual Analyst." *Journal of Aesthetics and Art Criticism* 37, 3 (Spring 1979), 303–313.

Hassan, Salah. *Creative Impulses/Modern Expression* (Ithaca: Africana Studies and Research Center and the Institute for African Development, Cornell University, 1993).

Held, David. "The Development of the Modern State." In *Modernity: An Introduction to Modern Societies*. Ed. Stuart Hall, David Held, Don Hubert, and Kenneth Thompson (Cambridge, Mass: Blackwell Publishers, 1996), 55–89.

Jegede, Dele. *Contemporary African Artists: Changing Traditions* (New York: Studio Museum of Harlem, 1990), 29–43.

Johnson, Rev. Samuel. *The History of the Yorubas* (Norfolk: Lowe and Brydone Printers Ltd., 1976).

MacMillan, Allister, ed. *The Red Book of West Africa* (Ibadan: Spectrum Books Limited, rpt. 1993, 1920).

Okeke, Uche. "History of Modern Nigerian Art," *Nigeria Magazine*, 128–29, (1979), 100–118.

Oyelola, Pat. *Everyman's Guide to Nigerian Art* (Lagos: Nigeria Magazine, 1976).

Thompson, Robert Farris. "Yoruba Artistic Criticism," In Warren L. d'Azevedo (ed.), *The Traditional Artist in African Societies* (Bloomington: Indiana University Press, 1973), 19–61.

Yai, Olabiyi. "In Praise of Metonymy: The Concepts of 'Tradition' and 'Creativity' in the Transmission of Yoruba Artistry Over Time and Space." *The Yoruba Artist*. Ed. Rowland Abiodun, Henry J. Drewal, and John Pemberton III (Washington D.C.: Smithsonian Press, 1994), 107–115.

26 HABITS OF ATTENTION: PERSISTENCE OF LAN GINÉE IN HAITI

LeGrace Benson

"Grandmother told mother, mother told me, and I tell you now. And your brother knows where to look, because his father told him what Grandfather and the uncles told him. We know where to look for what we need and what we like; what is dangerous, and what saves. We are always looking and looking, and so will you." Jean Price-Mars told how this happens among Haitians in *Ainsi Parla l'Oncle*.[1] Many scholars have pointed out and discussed survival of artifacts, notably drums and *asseins*; of retained spiritual presences such as Legba or Ogun; and of numerous other African objects and ideas continued in the New World religion *Vaudou*.[2] Others have discussed theories of how African grammar supports the European, primarily French, lexicon of Haitian Kreyol. Receiving less notice is how these evidences also indicate persisting modes of attending to the world—habits of attention; that these habits of attention, preserved from Lan Ginée, are also manifest in much of the painting and sculpture of Kreyol-speaking Haitians. Although the content and even styles of such masters as Obin, Duffaut and Bigaud, Liautaud, Nacius Joseph, Pointjour, and Bien-Aimé are markedly individual, they all share a common, Kreyol, visual and philosophical stance. Like the grammar of their speech, these include African continuities. Their distinctive regard (the orientation of their attention) is directly apparent in the works: their compositional structures strikingly contrast with those of European artists, and they transpose the "vocabulary" of European-derived iconography into quite other symbolic meanings. The result is newly fashioned material expressions distinctive to diasporic life in the New World.

Africans from many homelands, enslaved in the Americas, preserved important features of their original cultures by sustaining attention. Those for whom ritual recollection and veneration of ancestors was deeply felt directed attention to the most cherished beliefs and practices by means of stories, songs, dances, dramatized rituals, and the creation of objects,

Nacius Joseph, untitled work depicting agricultural spirits. Tree-bole carving, ca. 1960. Musée de l'Art Haïtien, Port-au-Prince, Haiti.

inculcating the necessary habits of attention in themselves and into the next generations. Stories, music, objects, coming into being as a result of this focus, served further to *draw* attention. The cultural objects are thus direct evidence of the continuance of habits of attention formed first among Malinke or Ashante, Yoruba or Kongo, Angolan or Mozambiqan. At the latter-day moment of this continuity that is sometimes material, sometimes spiritual and most often both, let us observe how the works manifest the habits of attention.

FOUR SCULPTORS

"Sculptor" is a Western art historian's word for a person—an "artist"—who produces three-dimensional works intended primarily to be viewed and only secondarily, if at all, for some useful function. In contrast, the pieces under discussion here came into being in one case at the hands of a person who called himself a woodworker (*ébenist*), or *bos pié-bwa* and in the second case by a man who called himself a forger or ironworker (*ferronier* in French, *bos fé* in Kreyol). The terms they use show a difference of attention. "Sculptor" points attention to the artistic functioning of a certain person, while "woodworker" or "ironworker" calls attention to *both* material to be worked *and* the person who will accomplish the tasks. Such conjunctive attention is characteristic of most African traditions of making.

First then the woodworker, Nacius Joseph.[3] There is an old tradition in Haiti, continuing into the present, of carving from the trunk-base and roots of trees—*travay rasin*, root work. Joseph did a piece, now in the Museé d'Art in Port-au-Prince, circa 1960, using an entire small tree bole, the identity of which is fully retained despite the complexity of figures and objects carved into and from it. It is at once tree bole and Papa Loko, the *lwa* or spiritual energy of agricultural work, accompanied by his implements and by the great West African lwa Danballah, the beneficent serpent who will insure rain and harvest. The piece is subtle as well as complex, for it is not a literal "finding in the wood" of the figures, but results from the artist's using the physical nature of the wood in such a way as to reveal its immanent spiritual content. Thus Joseph paid attention both to the material as a workable substance and as holding a spiritual presence.[4] Joseph's attitude—his habit of attention—is like that reported from the West Africa of antiquity, and into the recent present, where woodworkers often attended to their material as having this double affordance: practically useful, yes, and also the carrier of recognized sacred presences that inhabited the tree. This contrasts sharply with the utilitarian attitude toward wood as substance to be used for some purpose, even including artistic expression.

The ironworker George Liautaud, active until his death in 1989 at age

90, directed his attention to the remarkable characteristics of the malleable, weldable oil drum sheet steel (*dwom*) and to the tools devised to work on it, including the mystery of fire. He exercised skill and imagination to bring into being a new creation that as a result of the smith's imposing action, *embodies* a spiritual presence.[5] It is not necessary to describe to scholars of African cultures the pan-African valuation of the work of the blacksmith and the quasi-mystical efficacy of the tools, even to the point of effecting healings. Nor would there be any need to explain to anyone who has farmed how essential such skills are to life. On the plantations of St.-Domingue the skills of the blacksmith spirit, Ogun, would have provided certain slaves a locality where the utilitarian needs of the plantation could shelter the continuation of a transcendently crafty craft, the smiths carrying forward the spiritual content even as they shod the mules.

As a *bos fé*, Liautaud ably fashioned the many metal parts needed for the peasants' two-wheeled carts and harness and shoes of draft animals. Around 1950, he created a remarkable work just less than a meter in length and one-fourth as wide, some 30 centimeters high. At first look, it seems simply to depict a peasant on his cart, encouraging a straining four-ox team forward.[6] Working with a thin sheet of dwom and some pliers, Liautaud bent each ox once at the haunch to inscribe into the void a massive horned creature. Cart, peasant, and animals are materially all of a piece; where there is no-iron breathes the spirit, all of a piece too. This is the manner of using material and no-material to present the earth's hard stuff and transcendent stuff at once, which Pablo Picasso saw in the African works in Paris, and which caused him to change his ways.

Liautaud was a prolific worker: even now, small pieces come to light out of the crannies of his atelier. Even the least works manifest the simultaneous attention to iron and spirit. How? By subtleties of unique edges and surfaces; voids, like those of the oxen, "filled"; cuts that track the energetic purposefulness of the hand and tools that made them; and always an object never-before-visible, adumbrating an elusive spirit. This can be seen, but defies description. The objects out of old oil drums call attention to the numinous as Liautaud learned from his father and uncles, and they from the grandfathers, the directed line and lien of gaze.

Recent pieces from younger ironworkers show a conscious reach for African style or motif in addition to, or perhaps instead of, the continuities of tradition that marked earlier works. For example, Paul Damien, in his 1970 "Temptation of Eve,"[7] uses a story foreign to non-Christianized African lands as a starting point, but his dramatization has more in common with West African mask and costume reversals of solid and void, observable surface and spiritual presence, than with the Italian Renaissance paintings with their solid bodies and receding spaces that served as a partial model. In a sense this is African restoration work, rather than continuity. This artist, trained partly in Western methods by Western artists, sought out African habits, finding them in the works of Liautaud, but in those of Picasso as well.

The even more recent (1995) "Antelope Mother,"[8] by Haitian ex-patriate Fontanel Pointjour, recalls "Spirit Antelopes" of the Bamana peoples of Mali. These are a part of the attention of this Haitian artist because he went looking for them in the museums of Boston. Here again is restoration of attention at work: but something called out that attention. Was it the talk of a parent, an uncle of the artist?

Gerald Bien-Aimé takes up the same oil drum material that Liautaud had incorporated into the traditional blacksmith stuffs; takes up, too, the Renaissance Eden themes added by U.S. artists to Haitian awareness in the 1940s. An excellent example of his efforts stands in the reception area of the office of Institut Français in Port-au-Prince.[9] In this 1994 work, he maintains the oldest traditions by incorporating signs of spiritual mysteries, substantive and insubstantial, palpable and ineffable, as did Liautaud. He acknowledges the debt, and there is probably here a continuity of habit of attention, as well as a will to preserve and a desire to restore.

Haitian artists selecting the Eden theme (a heavily favored iconography) devote as much or more technical attention to the tree with its associated animals and flowers as to the two human figures. In the Bien-Aimé work cited, one must seek out the figures in the complexities of flora and fauna. Where European artists make the figures prominent by placement, size, dramatization, or color, Bien-Aimé and other Haitians strongly relocate the center of attention away from the moral fable and toward the tree and its environment. This strategy directly renders visible an important habit of attention consistent with practices and beliefs of a number of different West African religious faiths, including Islam.

The woodworker makes visible the spirit present in the wood, while the ironworker calls the spirit down into the construction—two ways of working, both attending to spirit presence, both habits of attention brought to the Americas from Lan Ginée. As one visits Africa, reads reports as recent as this year or as old as the traveler Ibn Battuta, as one views surviving or recent works done in or as continuation of traditions, this habit of attending to both material affordances and the resident spiritual energies is evident. For Nacius Joseph and Liautaud it was central. For Damien, Pointjour, and Bien-Aimé attention may be drifting; they call themselves "artists" or "sculptors," not "ironworkers."

Certain twentieth-century artists from Italy or Spain or France recognized the results of the habit of simultaneous attention to the material and spiritual. Notably Picasso saw it, reported on it, and changed his own attitudes, materials, and even tools in response. In Haiti and the Haitian Diaspora workers/artists did not have to rediscover spirit immanence: for them it was a result of generations of Haitian bos fé ironworkers or bos pié-bwa woodworkers drawing attention in a process of conversation and demonstration of skill and tools and arcana from master to apprentice, father to son, calling attention to the specifics of the craft and what its meaning is in and for the people with whom one lives. In the recent generations attention has shifted, and we shall return to that theme after considering two painters of the older traditions.

THE PAINTERS

Easel painting appears in Egypt and, if one stretches the definition, in Coptic lands in the east of Africa. It seems to be absent or at least unattended in the south and west, whereas floor or ground designs and those on walls are fairly common. The portable easel work is surely a European form in Haiti, one introduced in the earliest days of colonization and slavery, and continued with vigor in the art schools chartered by King Christophe in the North and General Pétion in the south. Yet for all the dominance of the French tradition, Haitian artists of this century have clearly brought different habits of attention to easel works.

Philomé Obin's work renders into visibility another set of African habits of attention—those of telling or dramatizing in a reserved space the stories and histories of family and community and nation. It is appropriate to call it "griot staging" as a way of marking its echo of Lan Ginée. Obin mastered Western perspective drawing in the art academy in Cap Haitian, but set the lessons aside in favor of designing a system better suited to his purpose. Wishing to make the history of Haiti known to his family and neighbors and fellow citizens, he took on the role of griot, telling his sacred, patriotic, or everyday story by means of images whose compositions were put to the service of dramatization. Perspective rendering of the world on a canvas or wall comes about as a result of certain ways of paying attention to the world. These paths into what lies ahead have been followed notably by the Italians of the Renaissance, and later by other Europeans. In contrast, Obin staged the action and characters in a layout that brings the viewer face to face with the essentials of the story and of the actors in it—the *zanzet*, or ancestors.

In both versions of his "Martyrdom of Peralte,"[10] Obin places the dead hero of the Haitian national movement (Cacos)—who had been strapped to a common door by the U.S. Marines and dragged through the city streets—upright, center, backed in sky blue. In one version, Peralte's mother, in black, stands weeping at the side. Comparison with European crucifixions is hard to miss, but Obin much more intimately confronts his viewers with the martyr, leaving no exit from the stark blue pressed against the figure. In the 1965 "Caco Heros Murdered by the Marines,"[11] he tilts his stage to provide maximum visibility and encloses it so there is no route away from the dead weight of Cacos piled down on the lower left margin. They strongly unbalance the composition, impelling an unavoidable after-shock of the terrible event.

Obin composed nearly every one of his works in this fashion. There is a sort of apron stage, tilted, hemmed in by people, interior or exterior architecture, fences, or vegetation. Sometimes he places himself, the griot, upstage center, the focus of converging diagonals—but not of "perspective." The visible griot's purpose and strategy is not accidental. Obin grew up in a time and place where such story-telling or pageantry or reenactment would take place in at least three localities: any of the several lakou-courtyards of the village he lived in as a small child; the Voudou peristyles which he knew well, though he was not a believer; and the formal squares and ronds of Cap Haitian. The first two are Kreyol manifestations of living and social arrangements carried into the New World Diaspora from Lan Ginée. The third is French, of course, the layouts of every city in Haiti being the result of French city and military planning principles.

But Obin does not depict the French layouts in a French manner, characterized by vistas and parade routes into and out of the area; rather, as can be seen in such a work as 1947's "On the Way to the Market" (now in the Milwaukee Museum of Art) he reorganizes them as theater stages to confront his viewers with events directly, not in the future and not in the distance. His attention is on the story and its emotive qualities—the people and their events. This clever griot requires viewers to direct and confine their attention within the demarcation of his lakou, that is, his familial, story-telling space.

The importance of the role of griot was much discussed in patriotic circles while Obin was growing up and especially during the years when he began to paint. One influential group of intellectuals and scholars used the term as their sobriquet. Painted in an era of Dr. Price-Mars's greatly influential book, *Ainsi Parla l'Oncle (Thus Spoke the Uncle)*,[12] that is, the griot, it is appropriate to say of this body of work, *"Ansi pent l'Onk,"* "Thus Painted the Uncle." Obin used the European technique of easel painting to accomplish purposes brought generations before from Africa, just as Liautaud used oil company drums to incarnate the old spirits. Content, costume, and props are all vernacular and the history is local and recent. The heroes are the zanzet—the ancestors, still in lively communication with the visible members of the extended family, and remaining present to advise and protect. Peralte was martyred in the presence of many who would see Obin's work. Some of the Caco guerrillas were alive when the painting of their fallen companions came into sight. The paintings are at once the story of the zanzet and the necessary commemoration and homage, the firm establishment in diaspora of a necessary habit of attention from Africa.

Obin attended school at a time when students still read a standard text imported from France, which began with a now infamous phrase: *"Nos ancêtres, les Gauls. . . ."* Those ancestors were not the zanzet of Obin and his compatriots. He then took upon himself the mantle of griot, to keep the good efficacies of the true zanzet present by calling attention to them. Also in the tradition of griots, Obin reported on the doings of the still-visible members of the community. His 1970 "Obin Academy," portraying himself and members of his family of painters, interestingly features the artist in the position and posture of Piero della Francesca's "Christ Rising from the Tomb." To the side of the artist's head is a small square window framing a view into infinity, probably a "quotation" from the sky of Piero's work. He quotes from Piero, but uses his own Ginée story-space instead of the Italian artist's perspective. Attaching value to passing on his work via family and apprentices in an academy shows that he was engaged in the process of preserving the habits of attention, in making sure there would be griots able to continue to tell all the stories.

A Haitian of quite different sensibilities from those of the insistently Christian Obin, Préfèt Duffaut brings Lan Ginée into twentieth-century Haiti as though on one of those filaments that float around the world on trade winds and jet streams, dropping their arachnid passengers thousands of miles from birthground: Anansi's children. In numerous versions of "Reine Araigne" ("Spider Queen"), he couples the visual imagery of the Akan Ginée lwa Anansi with that of the Virgin Mary. Often he brings notice to the spider web itself, to the connectors that join this edge to that. Thus Anansi and the Virgin Mary are more powerful than either would have been alone. The displayed sense of conjunctions is perhaps even more distinctively a continuity of Lan Ginée than the repetition of symbols: an assumption that wisdom consists of and is efficacious by means of a conjoining web of human relationships. Duffaut gives *Sedes Sapentiae* (*Virgin Mary as the Seat of the Wisdom of Solomon*) the binding outreach of Anansi, the clever trickster of West Africa. From his earliest painting, he combines these themes. The works directly manifest that, although it was the Virgin who appeared to him in a dream and told him to paint an aureole around her head in the local church, and although he clearly had an array of attentional habits formed in his primary school directed by Breton teaching friars, old Akan habits had persisted in the stories and songs, and probably Vaudou wall images, of his family and neighbors.

Atelier, land, water, village, ordinary people, and mystical personages come together as one in the prolific work of this artist and his family, with a sensibility concerning the interconnectedness of all things that was a deep persistence from his living and deceased family. Queen Anansi, in the 1986 "Rêve Mystique," presides over good and evil, sun and moon, the sky and the earth floor of a Voudou peristyle. The visions are Duffaut's; the habit of attention is the ancestral legacy from Lan Ginée.

THE SHIFT OF ATTENTION

Until mid-century this calling attention very much focussed on skill and on finding and/or bringing or manifesting spirit presence in the material object. The work of bos fé, bos pié-bwa, or bos tablo involved in part the same kind of action and attitude of the *houngan* calling down the spirits into the community through the *vèvè* and *poto mitan* of the *vaudou temnp*, even in the case of Obin. The shift of attention around 1950 is clearly discernable and quite radical: the art market strongly comes into view. French and United States teachers and critics drew the Haitians' attention to possibilities of personal, artistic, creative expression which then could go to the art market. This shift effected a radical relocation of the focal center away from the search for immanent creative spirits and the relating of the memory stories of the fathers and mothers. At the new center is the individual and the market.

The paintings of Wilson Bigaud exemplify the emergence of new habits of attention, visible in his work as a display of contending forces. Bigaud was scarcely eighteen when his ability, demonstrated in the school art classes and at the Centre d'Art, resulted in a commission to paint one of the murals for the Episcopal cathedral. His "Marriage at Cana" (1946)[13] unmistakably reveals attention divided between the Christian Gospel story of Jesus turning water into wine at the wedding of a friend, and the Kreyol story of the spiritual marriage of the lwa Ezulie to her servitors.

The compositional focus is the booth where the nuptials are celebrated, and where in Voudou practice the mystical joining of the spirit Ezulie to that of the servitor takes place. Other marks of the Kreyol religion, with its African habits of attention, include the depiction of drums, connoting the essential inclusion of rhythmic procedures, contrasting with Christian service music in which the melodic line or polyphonic structures are under attention; the tree with its branches cut to allow free passage of spirits, contrasting with Christian notions of the Tree of the Knowledge of Good and Evil, and the Tree of the Cross of Crucifixion of Jesus Christ. Bigaud's trees have more in common with those of Liautaud, or Bien-Aimé. The affordances of trees, including their spiritual affordances, are approached over a different path than that followed by the Episcopalians of Ste.-Trinité, and looked at for different possibilities. The cigar-smoking visitor to the nuptials is Baron Samedi, a Vaudou lwa of the important *gedé* family, associated with death and sexuality. Such an

Eros/Thanatos presence is familiar in West African religions, but virtually absent in Christian teachings.

It was apparently the U.S. director of the Centre d'Art in Port-au-Prince who called young Wilson's attention next to the theme of Earthly Paradise—Adam and Eve in the Garden of Eden just before the Fall. This seems to have been the moment when the theme first came to Haitian awareness. Dewitt Peters made available to the talented teen-ager the plates in art books in the Centre library, including works from the Italian Renaissance.[14] Note that at the same time, Wilson's attention went to the possibility of easel painting, itself a shift away from Afro-Kreyol traditions of wall and fabric pieces. Furthermore, the possibility of his doing a work to express his own personal spirit and the possibility of gaining a prize in the art market also shifted his focus. He indeed won a prize and became favored in the international art market.[15]

To win prizes and favor is, of course, a factor in Africa or in Haiti, as anywhere; the point is that the scope of attention widens to include not just friends, neighbors, and the usual nearby trading partners, but the world; the focus is no longer communal communication and spiritual efficacy, but personal exploration and expression of the immediately present sensibility yoked to a distant buyer. Wilson Bigaud went global, so to speak, several years in advance of the suggestions from the World Bank and International Monetary Fund that Haiti would thrive under market globalization. His painting took first prize in an international art show in Washington. The ironic companion to "Earthly Paradise," "Murder in the Jungle" (1950) went into the permanent collection of the Museum of Modern Art in New York City.

The shift of focus was effected from outside. Traditional habits of attention apprenticed from one African generation to another appeared before eyes that could not see. The Americans and French who saw the works had their own habits of attention and did not comprehend, and thus did not experience, the efficacy of the ancient ways. They *did* see that the works incarnated some mysterious, lively spirit. However, the works and their creators were relocated into a different mode of attending to the world. The new focus powerfully enabled bringing down food, medicine, education, and money for choices—but not spirit presences. Two modes of attention, two sets of compelling interests. Two still-contending forces.

Recent generations of Haitian artists, both in the Diaspora from Africa which is modern Haiti, and in the several countries of what might be called the "Double Diaspora," sometimes continue the attentional focus taught them by the grandmothers and grandfathers, and sometimes the focus learned from the international art market. In any case, they fashion out of available materials a Kreyol expression that more often than not pulls the eyebeams in line with the old, still valid, still efficacious attention points of the zanzet, still able to show them where to look for the dangers and the goods.

NOTES

1. Jean Price-Mars, *Ainsi Parla l'Oncle.* Québec: Editions Leméac, 1973 (1928).

2. See, for example: Lilas Desquirons, *Racines du Vodou*, Port-au-Prince: Editions Henri Deschamps, 1990; Louis Maximilien, *Le Vodou Haïtien*, Port-au-Prince: Imprimerie H. Deschamps, 1982 (1945); Alfred Métraux, *Le vaudou Haïtien*, Paris: Gallimard, 1958; or Robert Farris Thompson, *Flash of the Spirit*, New York: Vintage Books, 1984.

3. The work discussed, as well as other pieces by Nacius Joseph, are held at the Musée d'Art Haïtien in Port-au-Prince, and are on view from time to time. His works can be seen also at the Centre d'Art in Port-au-Prince. The work of George Liautaud likewise may be seen in these two locales. The works of the other sculptors are in private collections in Haiti and elsewhere, including collections in galleries dealing with Haitian and Latin American art.

4. The piece is illustrated in the author's "A Report from Haiti," *Art International*, vol. XXV/5–6. May–June, 1982, p. 128.

5. An exceptional collection of Liautaud's work is in the Milwaukee Museum of Art, Milwaukee, Wisconsin. Illustrations of his works appear inter alia in Ute Stebich, *Haitian Art*, New York: Abrams/Brooklyn Museum, 1978.

6. This work is currently in a private collection. It is illustrated in Stebich, op. cit.

7. The work is in the Flagg Collection of the Milwaukee Museum of Art.

8. The work is in the collection of the artist, Somerville, Massachusetts. An image is filed with Arts of Haiti Research Project, Ithaca, New York.

9. An image of the work, currently in the reception office of Institut Français, Port-au-Prince is on file in the Arts of Haiti Research Project, Ithaca, NY.

10. One version of this work is in the Flagg Collection of Haitian Art at the Milwaukee Museum of Art. An image is in on file at the museum.

11. This work is currently in the National Museum of Haiti, Port-au-Prince.

12. Price-Mars, *Ainsi Parla l'Oncle*, Port-au-Prince: Editions Henri Deschamps, 1928.

13. The mural is on the left apse wall of Ste.-Trinité in Port-au-Prince. It is illustrated in several books on Haitian art.

14. Several people who were associated with the Centre d'Art in those years have remarked about this to the author. The books Bigaud would have seen are still in the library of the Centre.

15. The "Earthly Paradise" is currently in restoration at the Museé d'Art, Port-au-Prince.

27 REPRESENTING JEAN-MICHEL BASQUIAT

Andrea Frohne

The diverse cultural and spiritual identities Jean-Michel Basquiat expressed in his powerful paintings are informed by his Brooklyn upbringing as well as his Puerto Rican and Haitian descent from his mother and father, respectively. In this essay, I explore social, cultural, and spiritual elements in Basquiat's representations of himself that derive from his African, American, and Diasporic backgrounds. For instance, I suggest that Basquiat represented himself as Oshoosi, the Yoruba deity of hunting, as well as the trickster deity, Exu, of the African Diaspora. While I do not deny his interaction with European traditions, I choose to focus on African influences, as they are often erased or redefined as European.

Thus, I also discuss how Basquiat was represented by others in the United States to define the archetypal black. His African American identity was cultivated by art critics and buyers as primitive, wild, an Other unknowable to buyers in the white art world. We may consider the positioning of pop singer Grace Jones or Chicago Bulls basketball player Dennis Rodman in our society. How much control do they possess in representing themselves and how much is dictated by white societal stereotypes? We may conjure images of these stars as wild, primitive, sexualized blacks. While Basquiat was manipulated by constructed identities, he himself also perpetuated them at times. Thus ambiguities arise in the multifarious representations of his identity. In drawing upon Africa and its Diaspora, Basquiat rendered himself as a celebration and embodiment of power, as a participant and rebel against an oppressive colonial and postcolonial world, and as a victim of subjugation. Basquiat also played a primitive, victimized black who infiltrated and dominated an art market controlled by white men as well as an empowered artist who deconstructed histories of marginalized, oppressed Africans and Africans of the Diaspora.

I suggest that in the art painted around 1981 and 1982, Basquiat rendered himself as Oshoosi, the Yoruba *orisha*, or deity, of hunters. Oshoosi is the hunter who shoots his arrows with the utmost skill, confidence, and purpose. He ensnares his animals through concentrated, cunning tactics, approaching his kill stealthily and imperceptibly. The bold, hieroglyphic-like image of Oshoosi's metal bow and arrow is rendered in full size on two separate pages in the book *Flash of the Spirit*, which Basquiat read. The author, Robert Farris Thompson, later visited Basquiat. As Basquiat held a penchant for such simplistic symbols, the bow and arrow must have captured his attention. Basquiat certainly knew of *orisha*—he painted the trickster Exu and he painted the word "ASE," the lifeforce or spiritual energy of the Yoruba, in an untitled 1981 painting.

Oshoosi served as a fitting persona for Basquiat. Having just begun his advance in the art market, Basquiat was determined to be rich and famous. He declared, "I wanted to build a name for myself,"[1] and he told his housemate Fab 5 Freddy (Fred Braithwaite), "I know I'm going to make it."[2] Like Oshoosi, the "Hunter who shoots and does not miss,"[3] Basquiat hunted his goal methodically and purposefully. Oshoosi is the best and most respected in his art of hunting and Basquiat sought this position ardently in the white art world. Just as Oshoosi cleared the way and blazed a path for others to follow, Basquiat strove for a heroic breakthrough into the art world.

Basquiat's struggles with heroism emulate aspects of Oshoosi's identity. Lines of an Oshoosi song tell us,

> Crowned one that slashes, be careful . . .
> Pick the leaves of the hunter,
> The powerful child [Oshoosi] becomes famous, power becomes fame
> The child wants the head of a king
> The one known to the dead relatives will come to give himself the head of a king
> Power becomes fame. The child is known to the dead relatives and takes pleasure in being known to the dead relatives[4]

Like the young artist who yearned for heroism, the song describes Oshoosi as a crowned orisha who possesses fame and power. Indeed, Ajuwon notes that "Heroism improves the social status of Yoruba hunters."[5] Thus, it is in the funeral dirges, or *iremoji*, chanted for deceased Yoruba hunters that grief, praise, and heroism are expressed for the dead hunters.[6] Furthermore, Mande people in Mali understand that hunters aspire to be heroes.[7] Hunters strive to acquire heroic status and fame by surpassing the reputation of their ancestors in order to secure their immortality.[8] To achieve this position, hunters may threaten society and disrupt its stability. They break its constraints by aggrandizing and promoting themselves to establish reputations as individuals, although it is ultimately up to society to perpetuate their fame. It is not necessarily important to know how familiar Basquiat was with Yoruba and Mande concepts of heroism; rather, I consider Basquiat in terms of African concepts of heroism instead of locating him in European or Euro-American traditions.

Basquiat's *Untitled* paper collage from 1982 exemplifies a powerful rendering of Basquiat as Oshoosi. The repeated images of a mutilated and empowered Oshoosi are drawn on squares of paper. The edges of the squares are cut or overlap each other to reveal partial identities. Nonetheless, the quintessential components that energize and vivify Oshoosi remain intact and are repeated across the canvas. The triumphantly held arrows and the prominent biceps on the simulated hunter visually describe a verse from Oshoosi's praise song printed in *Flash of the Spirit*: ". . . stronger than most men."[9] Also, the red and black crowns hovering in space over the Oshoosi figures visualize words cited earlier in the praise song to the crowned Oshoosi. Crowns that pervade Basquiat's works convey his ardent desire for heroism and his declaration of royalty. Basquiat explained that his subject matter was comprised of "Royalty, heroism, and the streets"[10] and according to the graffiti culture in which he engaged, "a King is the best with the most."[11]

Basquiat was the apparent ruler and hero of the contemporary art scene.[12] The young black artist broke into a white-dominated art market, introducing empowerment, resistance, and oppression of black histories. At the height of Basquiat's career, works sold for thousands of dollars and were reserved by buyers before he had completed them. In early 1983, a painting by Basquiat in a show at the Tony Shafrazi Gallery sold for $12,000. Basquiat was shown on the cover of *The New York Times Magazine* in 1985, when his paintings sold for $25,000 in the galleries and higher yet at auctions. Indeed, Basquiat ensured legendary fame and recognition. Larson recognizes that Basquiat knew "the ultimate career move for a hip artist is death."[13] His overdose on heroin at age 27 in 1988 revitalized his name, granting him further fame. Paintings fetched the highest prices ever and the Whitney Museum organized a retrospective of his works in 1992. In late 1988, a painting sold for $110,000 and a record-breaking $228,000 was paid for *Everything Must Go* at Christie's in 1992.

Basquiat recognized, according to Tate, that "making it to him meant going down in history, ranked beside the Great White Fathers of Western painting in the eyes of the major critics, museum curators, and art historians who ultimately determine such things."[14] Yet Basquiat also satirized this scene. In order to gain attention early on, he mocked "high" art by strategically painting graffiti in the Soho area and outside of galleries before opening nights. His signature was SAMO—Same Old Shit. Basquiat's actions emulated those of an African hero who deconstructed social values in order to break convention and establish a reputation:

The unfortunate thing was, once one did figure out how to get into
the art world, it was like, Well, shit, where am I? You've pulled off
this amazing feat, you've waltzed your way right into the thick of
it, and probably faster than anybody in history, but once you *got*
in you were standing around wondering where you were. And then,
Who's here with me? In Jean's case I think all this had a lot to do
with his drug problem. . . .[15]

What is the price a hero pays? Basquiat rendered himself not only with
royal crowns, but also with crowns of thorns. Like Jesus, Basquiat was a
victim who sacrificed himself as well as his identity. bell hooks views
Basquiat's crowns as a mockery of the obsession for being at the top and
the inevitable dehumanization that accompanies such status.[16] In the
painting *Crowns (Peso Neto)* of 1981, several ghostly, hollow black faces
(one white) are donned with crowns. The one just off-center wears a crown
of thorns. Basquiat's alignment with Jesus is confirmed by the date of
Christ's birth and signature at the bottom of the canvas: "DEC 25 81 JEAN
MICHEL." An arrow belonging to Oshoosi shoots toward the thorned
head, and other upward-pointing arrows are placed sporadically throughout the canvas. Heroic crowns transformed into crowns of thorns illustrate that with fame comes sacrifice. Basquiat's commodified and weighted
value was now inextricably proportionate to his reputation as a success
and hero. Thus, Basquiat's identity was not price-less, but carried a particular value or a net weight (*peso neto*). Like the salt represented by boxed
rows of the letter "S," Basquiat became a commodity attained through exploitation. Hebdige aptly notes that the "painterly heroics is the singularity of Basquiat's position as American modernism's first (and last?) officially appointed black savior."[17]

Basquiat's identity remains an unresolved paradox teetering precari-
ously between victim and ruler. In the 1982 painting *Obnoxious Liberals*,
three distinct figures are presented in triptych form (Fig. 1). The assertive
central figure stares straight back at the viewer. The crown identifies this
figure as Basquiat, and his five arrows define him as Oshoosi. Labeled by
others, he claims the phrase OBNOXIOUS LIBERALS as his own by means
of a copyright symbol. His chest proclaims, "NOT FOR SALE." He and
his art works are not commodities; his power and identity cannot be purchased.

Basquiat is blocked in a fiery red color that is like the hotness and
aggressiveness of Ogun. Oshoosi's brother is Ogun, orisha of iron, hunting,
and warfare. He enjoys spicy foods, becomes a warrior in battle, smelts and
forges iron, and has a strong temper. The funeral dirges or iremoje are performed to honor Ogun. Aggressive painting and colors in Basquiat's works
can be likened to Ogun as well as to spaces hunters occupy. Both Yoruba
and Mande hunters dwell outside of society and beyond the West African

FIGURE I.
Jean-Michel Basquiat. *Obnoxious Liberals*, 1982. Acrylic and oil stick on canvas. 68 × 102 inches. The Eli and Edythe L. Broad Collection, Los Angeles. © 1999 Artists Rights Society (ARS), New York/ADAGP, Paris.

village for periods of time. The hunter journeys deep into the forest that is inhabited by lifeforce or energy. These energies are unknown and dangerous to those who do not possess knowledge to manage and control the power. A chanter of iremoje explains, "Forest is the heart of town for hunters."[18] Mande hunters in general are recognized as hot, aggressive people.[19] A popular line in West African epic poems that relays the death of a hunter is, "The world has cooled off."[20]

As hunter and hero, this central figure designates a space of opposition and assertion. Oshoosi raises disproportionately large arrows threateningly above his prey, the dwarfed American cowboy on the right. Three leaves above the cowboy define Oshoosi's domain and mark the victim who occupies his territory. They are in the bush or forest, a space where power is known and controlled only by hunters such as Oshoosi who possess the necessary knowledge. Basquiat strives to obfuscate the legacy of the cowboy, the legendary hero who pacified Native Americans, the mythological figure children perpetuate by playing Cowboys and Indians. Here, two dollar signs identify the white cowboy as perpetrator of economic exploitation. He is devoid of arms, his eyes are crossed out by an X, and he is clad in a wimpy pink shirt and humiliating blue-spotted underwear to reveal a humorously small phallus. Saliva drools from exaggerated fangs.

The notion of sacrifice pervades the left segment of the painting. The black monster labeled Samson is stripped of his hair, eyesight, and clothes. The body is disfigured, deformed, fractured down the middle, and poisoned by asbestos. Samson straddles a rectangle labeled "GOLD," a commodity associated with exploitation of blacks. The adversary has gained possession of Samson's secret; his long hair, now absent, was what empowered him. Yet Samson's palms are splayed on the pillars flanking him. The debilitated, subjugated figure who appears devoid of power actually possesses enough to bring the entire structure confining him crashing down. While on the one hand exploited and commodified, Basquiat/Samson also possessed the secret to superhuman power on the other. Basquiat realized that oppressed and oppressor are symbiotic and only destruction of both could abolish the system.

Basquiat's identities manifest an apparent disparity between a victimized Other and strong, heroic characters such as Samson and Oshoosi. In order to attain heroism through fame, Basquiat became caught between enforcing his own identity and playing on other people's perceptions of him as an African American. He propagated myths that portrayed him as an exotic Other who exhibited wild, unpredictable behavior. For instance, it was rumored that he spent large sums of money—at times $1,000 to $2,000 per week—for his drug addiction. In the photograph on *The New York Times Magazine* cover, Basquiat played as both colonizer and colonized, as cultured and primitive. He wears a Giorgio Armani suit in an artist's studio, but sits barefoot. A painted cowboy grabs at him and a primitive, tooth-baring monster grins savagely. Yet his raised paintbrush tells us he creates and controls his work and himself.[21] Thus, Basquiat occupied an exotic space as Other on the front cover of a mainstream, reputable magazine. Collectors in the white art market were drawn to this participant who had entered and disrupted their system. Yet in attaining a ruling stature overnight, Basquiat inadvertently sacrificed his humanity, and ultimately his life. Basquiat gave away the freedom he desperately sought from (post)colonial oppression, exploitation, and objectification. He became enmeshed in Oshoosi's own traps by overdosing. Hunters must be able to absorb large amounts of life force or energy that is emitted from each animal who is killed.[22] In turn, this release of energy protects and empowers the hunter. Basquiat did not take into account the amount of power he would accumulate, and the sudden rise to stardom ultimately overpowered him.

Basquiat did not assume self-control when he achieved fame and fortune, but relinquished it. His addiction to drugs raises questions about his ability to think or paint rationally as well as the amount of awareness he possessed while painting. His lack of control was apparent not only in reconstructions of his identity by others, but also in the drugs that controlled him.

Basquiat acknowledges his ambiguous identities by performing and honoring the African-based orisha named Exu. Exu is the trickster who resides at the crossroads; it is said that beggars who stand at street intersections are Exu. Once, Basquiat recognized Exu by offering $50 to a window washer working at a crossroads.[23] In keeping with his excessive behavior, Basquiat was also known to supply street people with expensive bottles of liquor. As trickster, Basquiat played with constructions of his identity, presenting himself in multiple ways to the public. He saw himself as victimized and exploited, as victorious and heroic, as part of oppression in African histories and as empowerer of oppressed peoples. Also, Basquiat deconstructed his marginalized identity and reconstructed himself as his oppressors viewed him.

In Basquiat's 1988 painting *Exu*, a plethora of eyes floating around the diabolic donkey translate into the letter "I" to refer to himself and to the letters that spell "TO BACEQUIT" (Fig. 2). The artist becomes an avatar of Exu and he designates his painting as an offering to the orisha. Exu is often accompanied by Oshoosi (as well as Ogun) and we see here the powerful arrows belonging to Oshoosi. In the painting, Exu declares histories of subjugation and exploitation. The X in Exu, highlighted with a square, marks African slavery and the Middle Passage because the (anglicized) Yoruba spelling of Esu with an "s" in Nigeria became Exu with an "x" in Portuguese in Brazil when Africans carried their spiritual practices with them. While cigarettes at the donkey's feet are a standard offering to Exu, the tobacco also symbolizes European exploitation of enslaved Africans on the triangular trade route. Finally, the boxed X visually defines the trickster's place at the crossroads.

While Basquiat manipulated his image for the public, others also constructed representations of him. For some, his "primitive" style of painting defined the Euro-American mythological concept of primitivism. In the article "Royal Slumming: Jean-Michel Basquiat Here Below," McEvilley writes that while Basquiat himself was not primitive, he chose to "practice a form of primitivism."[24] For McEvilley, this means an artist consciously decides to paint from "pre-Modern or traditional societies," and he adds that a person who originates from such physical spaces possesses limited exposure to global culture. Thus, the author has effectively eradicated any links between Basquiat and those "traditional societies"; his ancestry to Africa and the Diaspora is cleanly and clearly severed. Furthermore, such a definition, which McEvilley acknowledges derives from the 1984 exhibition "'Primitivism' in Twentieth Century Art: Affinity of the Tribal and the Modern," presupposes that modern art can only be Western, that only the West can have modern art, and that traditional spaces are not civilized,

FIGURE 2.
Jean-Michel Basquiat. *Exu*, 1988. Oil on canvas. 78 × 100 inches. Galerie Enrico Navarra, Paris. © 1999 Artists Rights Society (ARS), New York/ADAGP, Paris.

but primitive. As an opposition to "the white art tradition," primitivism is separate and Other. McEvilley isolates white art from the rest of the world to preserve its supposed pristine state. He supplies us with a comparison between Basquiat's art and Picasso's desire to mimic nonwhite culture: "This black artist was doing exactly what classical-Modernist white artists such as Picasso and Georges Braque had done: deliberately echoing a primitive style."[25] Such a statement simultaneously erases the existence of African, Asian, and Oceanic elements in modern European art and pejoratively redefines them as primitive. It also removes Basquiat's blackness and recreates him as white ("He was behaving like white men who think they are behaving like black men"). McEvilley considers this mimicry akin to "royal slumming," "like the visits of downtown white esthetes to upper Manhattan during the Harlem Renaissance."[26] The royal Picasso travels to the undesirable, low-class slums of primitivism; the crowned Basquiat debases himself to express his black roots.

In Julian Schnabel's recent film *Basquiat*, Schnabel firmly planted Basquiat in European art history in the opening scenes. A young Basquiat and his mother are deeply moved by Picasso's *Guernica*. As the mother sobs, Basquiat is divinely crowned with a glowing, golden crown. To magnify the point, critic Rene Ricard sits in a park and reads aloud about a genius named Van Gogh while a noble savage emerges from a cardboard box behind him. As a successful artist himself, Schnabel enjoyed parodying the New York art scene with its greedy gallery owners and jealous critics. The dealer Annina Nosei presents "The true voice of the gutter" to potential clients. In confirmation, Basquiat (played by Jeffrey Wright) peels and eats a banana in front of his freshly finished paintings.

The scenario I have outlined concerning Jean-Michel Basquiat in the '80s only repeats itself with Dennis Rodman in the '90s. Rodman has cultivated an in(famous) reputation by superseding the norms of society. The Chicago Bulls basketball player is heroic for his basketball skills, his disruptions on the court, and his creation of himself as a spectacle. Like Basquiat, Rodman has formed a powerful, popular identity by also performing stereotypical white conceptions of Africans and African Americans. Rodman's recent autobiography, *Walk on the Wild Side*, presents a sexualized and savage black. On the eye-catching front cover of the book, Rodman faces us naked, on his hands and knees with teeth bared. His bare body is painted with thick, black stripes; his face, chest, and hair are colored white; and his lips and eyes are outlined in black. Two more naked Rodmans from different angles illustrate the back cover. We are confronted with a self-assured Rodman who brazenly returns our gaze. On the one hand, he possesses the power of a confident hero who controls his identity through the words of the book. On the other, his identity is manipulated by American society's historically repeated conception of African Americans. He wears the typical body paint and he enacts the supposed sexualness of an African and African American. Rodman represents the stereotypical black who is wild, dangerous, and primitive. He is more animal-like and sensual than human and modern.

Despite victimization, I contend Basquiat at times transcended histories of subjugation and exploitation to assert his multidimensional identity. He used his white clients, who perpetuated colonial attitudes (including the Western myth of primitivism), to buy and view his art. They possess re-visualized histories that offer mutilated, angry, oppressed blacks and empowered, heroic blacks. Basquiat could force and challenge viewers to look at themselves, their histories, and their identities. I conclude with Basquiat's 1983 painting *Untitled (History of Black People)*, in which he reclaims Egyptians as African and subverts the concept of an-

FIGURE 3.
Jean-Michel Basquiat. *Untitled (History of Black People)*, 1983. Acrylic
and oil paintstick on canvas with exposed wood supports, three panels,
68 × 141 inches. Galerie Enrico Navarra, Paris. © 1999 Artists Rights
Society (ARS), New York/ADAGP, Paris.

cient Egypt as the cradle of Western civilization, while all along reminding
us of histories of slavery (Fig. 3). Any suggestion that Basquiat was uneducated or primitive dissipates when one considers this reclamation of
historical identity. Labeled the "Grand Spectacle," we see an Egyptian boat
in the center guided down the Nile by a yellow, mummified Osiris, god of
the dead. To the left, two letters in the word "Nile" are crossed out. To the
right, a coded "Osiris" is spelled with some Greek letters. The boat that
Osiris guides to the next world may also refer to slave ships. Indeed, in
the right panel a figure is labeled "Esclave, Slave, Esclave," and an arrow
points to it. The letters that are wiped out and scribbled over perhaps reflect the acts of historians who have conveniently forgotten that Egyptians
were black and blacks were enslaved. Words on the guard dog reveal another identity of the armless, legless, and therefore immobile and powerless slave: "A DOG GUARDING THE PHAROH." It is no longer the
monumental, intimidating sphinx who guards the pharaoh's tomb, but a
vicious, savage dog, watching a dehumanized slave. In the lower right, poi-
sonous hemlock emanates from the wild. Once a place of power and energy, the woods are now deadly and dangerous. The tip of Oshoosi's white
arrow is blotted over and powerless.

   Other images of subjugation and oppression fill the painting. A clearly labeled sickle in the lower center refers to tools that slaves used on plantations. Again, we see salt of the triangular trade route. On the far left, two Nubian masks stare straight at the viewer. Historically, the darker Nubians were considered slaves to Egyptians and it is only recently that their rich culture is being recognized and explored by Western scholars.

Just as ancient Egypt has been extracted from Africa and adopted by the West, Basquiat's African and African Diasporic identities have been ignored, altered, or erased. These connections were reconceived to signify primitive or European-influenced art. Mirzoeff suggests that for Basquiat personally, "It was a tripartite process, involving a consideration of what it meant to be in America but not of America; what it meant to be of Haitian and Puerto Rican extraction while growing up in Brooklyn; and finally what it meant to be an artist who was not white."[27]

Was Basquiat victim or victor? He displayed virtues belonging to Yoruba and Mande heroic hunters by superseding the reputation of his family ancestors and acquiring fame that remains secure to this day. Yet part of his fame was based upon other people's conceptions and representations of his identity. Also, his drug addiction usurped his power and control. Basquiat recognized he was caught, commodified, and manipulated by others; Oshoosi couldn't free him from entrapment. Upon his death, Basquiat physically transgressed the pervasive system that bound him. While representations of Basquiat continue after his death, he himself asserts his voice and identities visually, through his art.

NOTES

1. Andrew Decker, "The Price of Fame," Art News (January 1989): 98.

2. Ingrid Sischy, "What Made Jean-Michel Basquiat So Great as an Artist?" Interview 22 (October 1992): 120.

3. From a song to Oshoosi. John Mason, Orin Orisa (New York: Yoruba Theological Archministry, 1992), 108.

4. Mason, 104.

5. Bade Ajuwon, Funeral Dirges of Yoruba Hunters (New York and Nigeria: Nok Publishers International, 1982), 30.

6. Ajuwon, 28.

7. Patrick McNaughton, "The Shirts That Mande Hunters Wear," African Arts (May 1982): 54.

8. Charles S. Bird and Martha B. Kendall, "The Mande Hero," Explorations in African Systems of Thought, eds. Ivan Karp and Charles S. Bird (Bloomington: Indiana University Press, 1980), 24.

9. Robert Farris Thompson, Flash of the Spirit (New York: Vintage Books, 1983), fn. 111.

10. Henry Geldzahler, "Art from the Subways to Soho, Jean-Michel Basquiat," Interview 13 (1983): 46.

11. Dick Hebdige, "Welcome to the Terrordome: Jean-Michel Basquiat and the 'Dark' Side of Hybridity," *Jean-Michel Basquiat*, ed. Richard Marshall (New York Whitney Museum of American Art, 1992), fn. 5.

12. Basquiat's fame was not solely self-propelled. For instance, he established a friendship with Andy Warhol and relations with gallery owners.

13. Kay Larson, "Wild Child," *New York* (November 9, 1992): 76.

14. Greg Tate, "Jean-Michel Basquiat, Lonesome Flyboy in the '80s Art Boom Buttermilk," *Village Voice* (November 14, 1989): 33.

15. Interview with Fred Braithwaite. Sischy, 123.

16. bell hooks, "Altars of Sacrifice: Re-Membering Basquiat," *Art in America* 81 (1993): 73.

17. Hebdige, 62.

18. Ajuwon, 29.

19. Patrick McNaughton, *Mande Blacksmiths: Knowledge, Power, and Art in West Africa* (Bloomington: Indiana University Press, 1988), 71.

20. Ibid.

21. I do not know whether the photograph was set up by Basquiat, the photographer, or both of them. Such information would help to illuminate who controls the presentation of Basquiat to the public.

22. McNaughton, 16.

23. Robert Farris Thompson, "Royalty, Heroism, and the Streets: The Art of Jean-Michel Basquiat," *Jean-Michel Basquiat*, ed. Richard Marshall (New York: Whitney Museum of American Art, 1992).

24. Thomas McEvilley, "Royal Slumming: Jean-Michel Basquiat Here Below," *Artforum* (November 1992): 95. hooks's own critique of McEvilley led me to further probe his piece.

25. Ibid.

26. Ibid.

27. Nicholas Mirzoeff, *Bodyscape: Art, Modernity and the Ideal Figure* (London and New York: Routledge, 1995), 189.

REFERENCES

Ajuwon, Bade. *Funeral Dirges of Yoruba Hunters*. New York and Nigeria: NOK Publishers, 1982.

Basquiat. Dir. Julian Schnabel. Miramax, 1996.

Bird, Charles S. and Martha B. Kendall. "The Mande Hero." *Explorations in African Systems of Thought*. Ed. Ivan Karp and Charles S. Bird. Bloomington: Indiana University Press, 1980. 13–26.

Decker, Andrew. "The Price of Fame." *Art News*. January 1989: 96–101.

Geldzahler, Henry. "Art from the Subways to Soho, Jean-Michel Basquiat." *Interview* 13 (1983): 44–66.

Hebdige, Dick. "Welcome to the Terrordome: Jean-Michel Basquiat and the 'Dark' Side of Hybridity." *Jean-Michel Basquiat*. Ed. Richard Marshall. New York: Whitney Museum of American Art, 1992. 60–70.

hooks, bell. "Altars of Sacrifice: Re-Membering Basquiat." *Art in America* 81 (1993): 68–75, 117ff.

Larson, Kay. "Wild Child." *New York*. November 9, 1992: 74–76.

Marshall, Richard, ed. *Jean-Michel Basquiat*. New York: Whitney Museum of American Art, 1992.

Mason, John. *Orin Orisha*. New York: Yoruba Theological Seminary, 1992.

McEvilley, Thomas. "Royal Slumming: Jean-Michel Basquiat Here Below." *Artforum*. November 1992: 92–97.

McNaughton, Patrick. "The Shirts That Mande Hunters Wear." *African Arts*. May 1982: 54–58.

———. *Mande Blacksmiths: Knowledge, Power, and Art in West Africa*. Bloomington: Indiana University Press, 1988.

Mirzoeff, Nicholas. *Bodyscape: Art, Modernity and the Ideal Figure*. London and New York: Routledge, 1995.

Rodman, Dennis. *Walk on the Wild Side*. New York: Delacorte Press, 1997.

Sischy, Ingrid. "What Made Jean-Michel Basquiat So Great as an Artist?" *Interview* 22 (October 1992): 119–123.

Tate, Greg. "Jean-Michel Basquiat, Lonesome Flyboy in the '80s Art Boom Buttermilk." *Village Voice*. November 14, 1989.

Thompson, Robert Farris. *Flash of the Spirit*. New York: Vintage Books, 1983.

———. "Royalty, Heroism, and the Streets: The Art of Jean-Michel Basquiat." *Jean-Michel Basquiat*. Ed. Richard Marshall. New York: Whitney Museum of American Art, 1992. 28–43.

Tully, Judd. "A Boost for Basquiat." *Art News*. March 1993: 27.

28 OPTIC BLACK: IMPLIED TEXTS AND THE COLORS OF PHOTOGRAPHY

Charles Martin

In essence, this essay asks, "What is black photography?" By extension, it also ponders some of the implied, but usually unwritten, textual comments attached to photography. Do we call photographs black, or afrocentric, according to their subject matter? Does the race of the photographer play a part in our calling a photo "black"? What is expected of a "black" photograph, how can it be recognized, how categorized?

The discussion to follow draws upon a wide variety of photographers, photographic subjects, approaches, and types of photos to comment about photography, the visual arts in general, and the cultural contexts which give rise to such attempts at color-coding art and its practices. We will see some of the *implied* texts that accompany photographs, and it will be clear how often the viewer, scanning and thinking through a print on a page or on a wall, holds as important the use of the photograph and the supposed intention of the photographer.

Such concerns underline how closely intertwined the creation and consideration of art can be with issues of perception, but also with imaginative license and social constraints. In relation to the diaspora notable questions are also raised regarding forms of visual representation. The diaspora has been historically linked, on the one hand, with questions of legalized mistreatment by antagonistic "host" societies and, on the other, to aspirations of establishing identity through positioning and repositioning with respect both to a homeland and a new land. Social questions have played so large a part that it is to be expected that there are significant spillovers into the visual arts. The spillovers, we shall see, can be both enabling and restricting.

In Ralph Ellison's *Invisible Man* (1952) we learn of "Optic white" paint, bright and "purest" white, made so through the addition of drops of black pigment. In this famous formulation, *Invisible Man* questions what constitutes whiteness and, in pointing to the blend of colors, implicates the cultural practices that make use of and benefit from, but omit, African American and African-derived components—from, say, the wealth of a slave-holding society to, simply, the nonmention that an innovator was of an ancestry of color. Such leavings-out can suggest the overlooking of contributions of black people to United States culture and can be extended without much difficulty to official/authorized overlookings in other parts of the New World, and around the world, for that matter. Correctives to those slights often are expected to be found in black artistry and expression—from the slave narrative, to black autobiographies such as that of Richard Wright, to the politicized novel and poetry (even in extremely open forms such as that of *Invisible Man* or Césaire's *Cahier d'un Retour au Pays Natal* [1947]), to films reaffirming sexual orientation, such as those of Marlon Riggs.

Such arts have at times been assessed, to borrow a phrase from Houston Baker, in search of a "peculiar subjectivity."[1] The hope that black arts will identify and attempt to rectify social ills has led, at times, to the anticipation that they be immediately comprehensible, utilitarian and efficient tools of impeachment. Such utility is juxtaposed by some to Western art's tenet that art not be a practical tool. Black art, according to this argument, would celebrate community and problem-solving, while Western traditions praise and fall prey to the ravines of self-obsession. But we should not overlook that the idea of art for the sake of art is not, in fact, use-free, but rather is meant—not altogether in clandestine fashion—to imply the superiority of the Western mind, one that, supposedly, rises above use and contemplates the abstract, the un-obvious. Such a formulation holds art to be metonymically associated with a superior culture of superior minds. To accept the idea that art is for art's sake alone, that any art is without use, is to be misled by art into a tarpit. All art has use, be it for statements about the culture from which it has sprung, for disinterested contemplation, or to rally troops, sects, populations, or initiates. Understanding this places into context not only the "useless" aspect of some traditional Western art, but also the call for committed art, which, for example, was certainly the slogan of French writers such as Camus and Sartre equally as it has been for later Black Nationalists.

Given such polemical usage of the arts in general, and taking into account the place photography has held and continues to hold, especially in the history of photojournalism, as a medium apt at attesting to wrong and denouncing it, we here turn our attention to photography and through it consider aspects of New World self-fashioning of African origins. It will be evident that photographers and photographs regularly have been made use of in regard to the above-mentioned "peculiar subjectivity." In short, we find that in looking at photographs, viewers sometimes want to feel that a photograph shows some affection or at least empathy for the things it pictures within its borders. And, in the spirit of a simplifying identity politics, speculations—even pronouncements—occasionally are made about the very backgrounds of photographers, based on the pictures they make.

Aside from expecting to find promoted in black art a "peculiar subjectivity," some have thought of it (as some have thought of much photography in general) as best and most authentic when seemingly a transparent wrapper that shows "real life," or a thing "like it is." For some viewers black art is best when *journalistic*, conveying information simply and downplaying the form itself, virtually claiming to situate mechanically the reader or viewer as a fly on a wall, who would report the same events in the same manner and attitude if given a chance.

In theater, this expectation for "realism" in black art is found in the predominance of the family drama and other traditional forms, and the avoidance of more experimental structures and controversial subject matter. It should be noted, though, that all black arts have not been so conservative. In jazz there have been significant times of freedom where innovation was encouraged and respected, where the medium has resisted calcifying along rigid structures, perhaps precisely because it has been a relatively new and unstabilized form and because music, itself, is in some ways abstract, or at least nonrepresentational. In the visual arts figuration and representation have generally had the upper hand, but there are significant abstract artists, such as those featured by the Studio Museum in Harlem's 1996 show *Exploration in the City of Light: African-American Artists in Paris, 1945–1965*. (Of course, as the site of the creation of these paintings was Paris, it is inevitable that some will categorize this work as European.)

Returning to photography, let us consider some subject matters and stances whose illustration, in photographs of mine, reflects the questions under discussion. What are some of the ways that black photography might be defined? First of all, it will be identified with black cultures and race. It may be photography that is about black people—that is, photographs of black people. Another possibility for black photography would be photography by black people. And, putting the two together, black photography might be about black people and made by black photographers. Such photography could also underline or document black cultures, traditions, and histories in the New World, in Africa, and wherever else black peoples have traveled—willingly or not.

But in speaking of black traditions, one must recognize that part of that tradition has been survival, adaptation, and change. Thus, we find that innovation and refashioning are as integral as is continuity. Such refashioning and adjustment to changes of time, locale, and so forth emphasize that art—indeed much of life itself—ultimately is bricolage: the use of things in previously unintended ways, making for new usages of already existing items. Bricolage automatically challenges and raises questions of

FIGURE I.
Paule Marshall. Paris,
France. © Charles Martin.

authenticity, as new uses often run counter to earlier sanctioned or accepted uses and practices. Bricolage thus encounters obstacles offered by
traditional restrictions of use and prior, approved intentions.

Thinking further of what might be black photography, one answer
would be work that is flattering to black people. An obvious place to begin
is with the portrait of black people (Fig. 1). In the language of portraiture—
be it photographed or painted—the frontal, direct view of a person generally is held to be made with respect and of a respectable act, a respectable
moment. Such, for example, are wedding, anniversary, graduation photos
and the like. There are, of course, exceptions: the mug shot generally is
frontal, and it carries with it no societal compliments, unless the status of
outlaw is thought of as special.

The frontal portrait often features its subject dressed well and, looking
fully out at the viewer, composed—either smiling or neutral in expression.
The subject usually gives the impression of being relaxed, complicit, or
commanding, but, in any case, does not appear to be threatened or afraid.
Not far in spirit from such generally static portraits are more animated

ones of a person in an acceptable or bourgeois occupation: the business executive at the office, a school teacher, a friendly cop. Related to these photos of people in positions of esteem, respect, or acknowledged importance are images of people respected for their effort, especially the effort of hard work. Thus respectability can be conferred upon laborers on the job, satisfied at the end of the work day, or relaxing after it. Another group of people who merit respect, not for their position or work but for their status as innocents, are children, presumably uncorrupted.

Images of these sorts are, for example, the stuff of Roy DeCarava and Langston Hughes's effort, *The Sweet Flypaper of Life* (1984), which opens with a portrait of a black girl (9), follows with a child asleep in bed (10), a girl dressed for cold weather (10), and Rodney (11).[2] The girl of the first photo looks directly, close-up, at the viewer. Her expression is neutral, featuring her attentive, relaxed eyes. Her hair is neatly combed. She is seated on a chair at a table, but the support of the chair, and the room's background, are blurred so the viewer's attention can focus only on her. With the next picture, a caption says that the sleeping child is a grandchild— suggesting the warmth and continuity of generations—and the room is clearly orderly and decorated with care for the child: in view is a cartoon-like drawing of a dog, affixed to the dresser. The girl, dressed for cold weather, clutches books; a caption tells the viewer that she is on her way to school: i.e., to higher learning and social graces. Her clothing is nice and her look to the viewer is direct and relaxed.

Rodney does not look at the camera. The view is a candid moment and he is relaxed, evidently in a restaurant or diner. Rodney is conventionally well dressed in white shirt, bow tie, sport jacket, trench coat, and dapper felt hat. Following, are images of women with substantial jewelry and elegant clothes, and the cityscape includes its share of nice cars. Other figures throughout, more humble, are couples, parents, hard workers, and children at play.

The book closes with a photo of an elderly woman (112), the narrator who has guided this tour of Harlem. She is hatted and wears earrings, a black skirt, and a blouse clasped with a brooch or pin and accented by a handkerchief in the breast pocket. The woman looks directly to the viewer and has one hand on a wrought-iron fence while the other, adorned with a ring, rests at her side. The narrative, written by Hughes, generally describes upbeat activity and employs an equally upbeat tone that counters the occasional brushes with difficulty, such as the narrator's mentioning sadness, a shortage of front stoops in Harlem, or that Rodney was kicked out of his father's home but was readily taken in by the narrator of whom, the reader is told, Rodney is the favorite grandchild.

It it worth noting that DeCarava's photos were, he has explained in conversation, regularly rejected for publication until Hughes took it upon himself to organize the photos according to a narrative, a show-and-tell of good folk, with the by then well-known signature of Langston Hughes.

The Sweet Flypaper of Life carries out a tour of the kind of acceptable characters written of during the earlier Harlem Renaissance by many black writers, such as Hughes, Jessie Fauset, Nella Larsen, James Weldon Johnson, and others. These types of photos are a sort of "uplift": positive statements about positive people with positive attitudes, whether or not their dreams and hopes have been recognized or acknowledged by much of society. An earlier example, or precursor, of this visual approach—in attitude, though not exactly in camera style—is the work of James Van-DerZee. VanDerZee's imagery, unlike that of DeCarava, usually looks posed and static. Deborah Willis-Braithwaite, in her introduction, "They Knew Their Names," to the book of photographs *James VanDerZee: Photographer, 1886–1983* (1993), observes that VanDerZee was extremely directorial, contrary to, she says, his reputation as a "neutral observer of his times" (8) whose work was presented by the Metropolitan Museum of Art as essentially "historical documents."[3] She remarks, as well, what she calls the "professed astonishment" of white American critic A. D. Coleman at VanDerZee's aesthetic sophistication, and Willis-Braithwaite observes that "viewers are often challenged, engaged, and overwhelmed by VanDerZee's celebration of black middle-class life, for his photographs are an overt celebration of black middle-class life, and particularly family life" (10). Willis-Braithwaite goes on to characterize his work as "transformative[,] visionary and optimistic" (11).

Willis-Braithwaite contrasts the photos of VanDerZee with those of Aaron Siskind, who emphasized social difficulties and disadvantages when he photographed Harlem in the 1930s–40s. As Willis-Braithwaite points out, Siskind became known as a "concerned" photographer and awakener of social consciousness[4] (Fig. 2.) In her words, "to VanDerZee Harlem was home; to Siskind it was a ghetto" (24). She admits that Siskind produced beautiful photos of Harlem, and also that VanDerZee may have had in mind the tastes of his future portrait and documentary clients in producing such work, but Willis-Braithwaite asserts that the photographs by Van-DerZee "reveal more about the Nature of Harlem[,] and its capacity for renewal[,] its growth" (25).

Ultimately, despite her beckoning to issues of form, aesthetics, and sociopolitical orientation, Willis-Braithwaite declares VanDerZee's work to be superior to that of Siskind. She justifies her decision in deference to VanDerZee's fictitious uplift look and clearly explains his superior rating via recourse to his identity: he is a black man at home, and thus, photographing his home, his work comes across better than that of the outsider looking at an *other*. Willis-Braithwaite acknowledges that, since VanDerZee was dressing up and covering over his sets and portrait sitters, her

FIGURE 2.
Child in Street. Bahia, Brazil. © Charles Martin.

opinion ultimately is not based on reality or method, but upon final photographic stance which, again, is clearly one that flatters.

Willis-Braithwaite writes of Max Yavno, too, who worked with
Siskind.[5] However, it should be noted that although Siskind later moved
to abstraction, and thus moved away from black people as icons of social
necessity, an acquaintance with Yavno's work shows that its social realism
is not limited to subjects of color.

Returning to VanDerZee, let me point out that French critic Roland
Barthes in *Camera Lucida* (1984) writes that he saw in a photo by VanDer-
Zee those decorative anthems to the bourgeoisie and Barthes goes on to
say that "[the image] utters respectability, family life, conformism, Sunday best, an effort at social advancement in order to assume the White
Man's attributes (an effort touching by reason of its naiveté)."[6] It is significant that Barthes falls into the racial quicksand that imagines comfort and family life to be "White Man's attributes." But, despite his flawed
expression of it, Barthes speaks to the same quality in VanDerZee that
Willis-Braithwaite does. He finds it naive while she finds it laudable, but
they both find it touching.

The list of photographers, past and present, whose photos speak this uplift (or uplifted) language goes on and on and includes—noted by Deborah Willis in *Early Black Photographers: 1840–1940* (1992)—early portrait photographers James Presley Ball and Alexander Thomas (working at least since 1865 in Cincinnati) and James Conway Farley, whose work dates from the 1870s in Richmond, Virginia. Ball and Thomas, aside from their "Panorama of Negro Life in the Ohio, Susquehanna and Mississippi Rivers," photographed white society of Cincinnati.[7]

Other photography, current, stressing the dignity if not the uplift of black folk, includes work of Dawoud Bey, Coreen Simpson, and Marilyn Nance. In the popular press, photography of VanDerZee's flattering sort can be seen in every issue of magazines such as *Jet*, *Ebony*, and *Essence*. Flattering work is not in any way limited to photographers who are black, as is shown by the book and exhibit *I Dream a World* (1989) by Brian Lanker (photographs of well-known African American women), and by the book *The Eyes of Harlem* (1985), by Nobuo Nakamura.[8] *The Eyes of Harlem* is a beautifully photographed, evidently lovingly made tribute—largely portraits—by a Japanese photographer who writes in his foreword that he began this photo project when "at dusk one day as I was walking through Harlem, I was suddenly struck by how beautiful the people living there looked in the setting sun. I heard parents, children, as well as grand-mothers and grandfathers laughing. . . . [T]hese people appeared to be living everyday to the fullest" (10). His story of empathy ends, he tells us, with the Schomburg Center purchasing 47 of his Harlem photos. His photography is not exactly black photography, if we want work by black photographers, but it certainly is flattering and, we have seen, endorsed and bought by a black institution.

Another area regularly plumbed by flattering photography is the black church, particularly evangelical congregations. Such pictures have recently been exhibited in the Museum of Modern Art's (New York) *Come Sunday* (1996), by Thomas Roma—an Italian American photographer who depicts congregations and services in black churches in Brooklyn. Along with the photos Roma states that, at the age of 40, he became interested in spirituality and began to photograph churches. A minister who saw him invited him to photograph not the exteriors, but the people inside. This led Roma on a church-to-church pilgrimage through Brooklyn.

Sulaiman Ellison has photographed the churches of Ethiopia. His photos attest to a positive journey to Africa, and a journey that ends affirming Christianity, or at least its churches and its faithful. Not restricted to churches, Marilyn Nance has for some time photographed what she calls black spirituality: Christian churches, but also New World derivations of the Yoruba religion of West Africa. A predecessor of hers, working from Brazil, would be Pierre Verger, whose photos of *candomblé* society, for

FIGURE 3.
Spiritual Guidance. São Paulo, Brazil. © Charles Martin.

example in *Orixás* (1981), are extensive and were carried out over many years[9] (Fig. 3). All of these photographs, regardless of the race of the photographer, speak well of black peoples. Are they black photography because of their subject matter and the attitudes conveyed? The question of subject matter has a special place within considerations of photography since photography, more than is the case with other of the arts, is at times identified more with its subject matter than with its presentation of that subject matter. The publication, during the course of the criminal case against O. J. Simpson, of an intentionally darkened photograph was a rare instance where attention was given to the alteration of a photograph—and even that attention came about more because national newsmagazines coincidentally published at the same time mugshots of Simpson and thus the difference between the manipulated and unmanipulated images was manifest. This is not the place for a discussion of manipulation but, to greater and lesser degrees, such manipulation is common but usually less dramatically clear, and so is usually overlooked; the viewer takes most of these images to be accurate.

Another area often explored in "black" photography is the world of jazz (Fig. 4). Roy DeCarava, again, has contributed greatly to this branch

FIGURE 4.
Flash. New York, NY. © Charles Martin.

of photography as have, to name but a few others, Hugh Bell, Anthony Bar-
boza, and Frank Stewart. Jazz's central status in culture as an embodiment
of black creativity, originality, and authorship—a form genuinely new and
different from earlier art forms—made the music's history, atmosphere,
and style a deep source from which to dip, as did, for example, numerous
writers of the Harlem Renaissance in search of a black creative art to inspire and shape their fiction and poetry. It is not surprising that some
black photographers have returned to this same well to establish artisti-
cally an explicit link with black culture. This photography might be called
flattering in the sense that it prizes the culture of which it is part.

    In discussing what I have called "flattering photography," I have intro-
duced, as well, photography that is not so much flattering but rather is
instructive in its focus upon social crises of special pertinence to black
communities. Siskind and Yavno—neither of them black—have already
been mentioned. Some of the work of Gordon Parks can be seen in this
light, pointing to social issues and stereotypes. These photographs, often
of difficult or unpleasant subject matter, direct themselves toward exposing social evil, bringing it to view for an airing out before, presumably,

an eventual eradication. Such work, of course, is not exclusively aimed at black people: the famous exposé photos of Jacob Riis, *How the Other Half Lives* (1971), showed New York poor in general.[10] A modern exponent of the exposé might be, say, Eugene Richards—a white photographer—whose work on crack smokers in New York showed the horror of a particular slice of life in order to call more attention to it.

It is an error to reject social realism for more flattering work, imagining that the steely, icy stance is due to the attitude of the photographer toward the subject just as, in the reverse, it is equally mistaken to look at flattering photos and think that the photographer must be black. To take the example of a white photographer detachedly showing white people, we have only to look at much of the work of Nan Goldin, whose photos in *The Ballad of Sexual Dependency* (1986) are largely of her friends, though they feature battered women, debauched partygoers, and a host of others of a new "lost generation."[11] She shows their difficulty, but that hardly means that she shows them positively or exuberantly.

The place of social commitment, or lack of it, in black photography repeats a desire for many that black art be obviously "useful." In a variant of the "useful" expectation placed upon the black arts, playwright Philip Hayes Dean has remarked in conversation that the black playwright is often expected to produce work that, in journalistic style, relays generalist information to a largely uninformed audience.

Following these examples of work that might be flattering and other work that might be a call to conscience, let us here think of some photography that, unlike the above, seems to call for, exclusively, contemplation of the imagery itself. Such imagery is nonspecific and sometimes abstract, and some might want to label it "irrelevant" or "frivolous" (Fig. 5).

Shawn Walker, in an issue of the photography journal *Nueva Luz*, presented a group of photographs, a "cloud series."[12] These black-and-white photos feature cloud-filled skies; the white clouds range in texture from fluffy cumulous to streaky cirrus, and they stand out against dark sky. Most of the images have, in a lower, foreground area, a building or rooftop that appears in silhouette as a large dark or black area. The light in the photos comes only from the sky and from the opposite, blocked sides of the buildings. Occasionally, also in silhouette, there are treetops, lampposts, or railings. There are no people in the photographs.

The photos are serene and formally beautiful in compositional arrangement and shape, and in selection of lighting effects. Sometime after the photos were published I met Walker and he explained that much of the response to the publication had been negative, that many people felt that he should show photos of black faces and of identifiably black places—Africa, Harlem, etc.—things that he had done for a long time and has continued to do. But this series of photos, a departure from that subject area,

FIGURE 5.
Reflections. Pinacoteca Museum. São Paulo, Brazil. © Charles Martin.

was, for many, intolerable and seen neither as an addition to his work nor as a breather for himself and his viewers, but simply without value.

Some of the work of Hugh Bell, whose jazz photos have been mentioned already, could be subjected to questions similar to those directed to Walker's photos, not because the work is absent of people, but rather because the people are not black: his many photos of Ibiza detail town life that is almost exclusively Iberian. Is there anything to be gained by comparing the jazz photos to those of Ibiza and finding one group more black, more appropriate for their maker or for certain viewers?

Frank Stewart, whose photos have recently been published in a book with Wynton Marsalis about the jazz scene, *Swing Street: Blues on the Road* (1994), and in another book on barbecue, *Smokestack Lightning* (1996), has also produced photograms, images made without film by directly exposing photographic paper to light cast over objects so the shadows of the objects and the light itself form unpredictable shapes and imagery.[13] The resultant images are abstract, and those in question produce a series of light and dark patterns not unlike small pieces of paper cut and arranged on a table top. An appreciation of such work requires an affinity for form, for light and dark, but no more. Other work that I mention only in passing, and also published in various issues of *Nueva Luz*, would be the fern and plant landscapes of Hilton L. Braithwaite, the industrial structure cityscapes of Accra Shepp, the abstractions of Conrad Barclay, and the mysticism-tinged, often blurry and hazed, images of Albert Chong.[14]

Some of the work of Roy DeCarava, such as that of the monograph *Photographs* (1981), though not completely abstract, is free of a recognizable locale.[15] Would it be reasonable to say that these photographers, when photographing pieces of pork or musicians on the bandstand, are doing something that is "blacker" or more African American than when they are making abstract light-and-dark images or photographing flowers—such as the recent work of Gordon Parks?

For an exhibit that I was asked to do at a college, the black woman who made the request asked in afterthought if the photos were going to be "black" photographs, which she went on to explain as photos of black people, or at least of recognizable cultural items: bushy hair, dreadlocks, African sculpture, etc. Presumably she would not have been happy with watermelons—though the contemporary rage for collecting mammies and jockeys might mean that watermelons would do just fine (and such imagery does figure prominently in some of the work—for example of photographers such as Carrie Mae Weems, Lorna Simpson, and others—of those who direct attention to stereotypes). In another instance, at another college, the curator, a white woman, went through a portfolio of mine, commented pleasantly about the work, then rejected all photos of whites and Asians to exclusively select images of black people. She would not accept any images of other people, but did eventually agree to add some still lifes and scenics.

Interestingly, at the gallery talk about the show, a white male student asked why all the photos were of black people. At the reply that all the photos were not of black people—there were photos, too, of objects and so forth—he conceded the point, but said that he meant why were there no pictures of white people. I told him that I could not answer that, as the person who did the selection was not myself. I do not know if he pursued the question with the curator, to whom he was directed. But here we see the same attitude toward "black" photography: the two curators in these examples—one black and one white—feel comfortable with a black artist mainly when that person presents images of black people. Further examples are not necessary, as the point, I hope, is made.

I offer it here as only a fleeting reference, but another topic that one might think about is the presentation of African people in a journal such as *National Geographic*, where imagery of Africa and the Pacific was, aside from travelogs, an opportunity for a clothed society to look at unclothed ones, and also to imagine that Africa, for example, was almost entirely unclothed. At play in the *Geographic* is the assumption that there is no manipulation in the weighting of the images toward animals, natural landscape, and naked societies to the exclusion of city or other imagery. The diminished sense of urban usages in favor of the picturesque is seen to be "natural," and so influences the idea of Africa as "natural," as valued primarily for its flora and fauna but not its people who knowingly face contemporary global issues.

A last area of discussion, somewhat ushered in by the comments about the *Geographic*, has to do with photography that is considered disrespectful, shocking, or even blasphemous. Take, for example, the work of the late Nigerian photographer Rotimi Fani-Kayode. In images from a 1991 *Revue Noire* that pay homage to the sensual male figure and, more particularly, to homoeroticism, Fani-Koyode confronted the idea that homosexuality is alien to Africans.[16] (Granted, he did live in England and the United States, before settling in the former.) Among his images are some that show African masks as sex toys, certainly not representing them merely as cultural icons or as guides to an African past. Rather, he adapted traditional items, at least in the photographs, to flagrantly untraditional ways. One photo (37) presents the rear end and legs—down to above the knees—of a black man. The man is straddling an African bronze head on a pedestal.

Another image (36) presents an athletic male body hunched forward. The man's hands grasp two large leaves on long stems. The leaves block his eyes and he would seem to be in some way recalling the stance of a warrior. Around his waist, though, is a studded black belt, likely indicative of sado-masochism. Clearly this work challenges African traditions or transforms them into very different circumstances. It does, in fact, ask how these traditions get transplanted or what traces they carry for some who have come to live far from the source. However, it would be shortsighted to say that the questions raised by this work apply only to those who live far from home. Traditions are not impervious to change, not even when they stay at home, and they do find themselves attached to unexpected and unintended carriers. An affront to sensibility may be an investigation of change, even if not widely spread or endorsed.

Ultimately, we must recognize that the artist responds to everything that he or she knows or meets in the world. It is unreasonable to assume that artists will arbitrarily reject certain avenues of investigation, of expression, of attempted mastery simply because traditionalists have not gone that way before. And it is illegitimate to argue that, say, the appropriation of new forms and instruments, in the case of jazz, was fruitful only because the artists had no choice, because they were cut off from Africa and Africa's particular instruments and musical contact. Art—and photography is no exception—grows from tradition but also expands, challenges, and sometimes breaks it. Even when an artist chooses to work with traditional materials or with traditional imagery, the final artistic product can break drastically with accepted convention and fly in the face of it.

Art truly does challenge essentialism, in this case the notion that a certain take is black while another is not. This question has been asked by generations of black writers, both implicitly and explicitly. In the wake of the *Narrative of the Life of Frederick Douglass* (1845) questions arose about Douglass's language, which some abolitionists argued was spoken too well for one who had been a slave. In essence, they wanted him to fit a paradigm. Years later, Hurston's emphasis on dialect in works such as *Their Eyes Were Watching God* (1937) and *Moses, Man of the Mountain* (1939) led some to what amounted to a charge that she was "too black," so black that it was a disgrace to be black. She was not properly middle class, in line with the aspirations of rising African Americans. Langston Hughes was referred to as the "poet low-rate" because, in his choice of simple black characters, setting, and language he, too, was "too black," or at least "improperly" black. Facing the question of allegiance or interest in a country, Martin Delany argued that black people should live wherever it was comfortable: in Africa, Brazil, the U.S. There was, he argued, no one black place.

Photography, like so many other aspects of the production of black peoples, demonstrates that New World black cultures develop a variety of relationships to the plural societies among which they function, and that, curious, responsive, and critical of traditions both black and other than black, the artist, indeed the human being, responds in a way that makes it clear that the claim of Africa in Western cultural discourse is not limited to an orthodox recitation of past values, past origins, past methods, or past boundaries. In essence, to be black is to be informed, aware, and open. Janie, in Hurston's *Their Eyes Were Watching God*, found out something about herself through the outside viewpoint of an itinerant photographer whose interest was neither in her nor the others in the photograph, but in selling his picture product. Janie, a black child, had never differentiated herself from the white children around her; she had not yet come to an awareness of race and color. Seeing herself in a picture, Janie began to understand that she had an identity and that it was evident to others just as it, now, was evident to her. She learned at that moment that having a specific identity could be a clarification and not a setback, an understanding that valuably replaced ignorance. None of these insights had anything to do with *why* the photographer took the photo. This brief moment in Hurston's novel portrays the power and reward of contemplating a photograph for its content rather than surmising and supposing its intent.

NOTES

1. Houston Baker. *Blues, Ideology and Afro-American Literature: A Vernacular Theory*, p. 1. See also Baker's *Afro-American Poetics: Revisions*

of Harlem and the Black Aesthetic and Reginald Martin's *Ishmael Reed and the New Black Aesthetic Critics.*

2. Roy DeCarava and Langston Hughes. *The Sweet Flypaper of Life.*

3. Deborah Willis-Braithwaite. *James VanDerZee: Photographer, 1886–1983.*

4. See, for examples of Siskind's work, Deborah Martin Kao and Charles A. Meyer, eds., *Aaron Siskind: Towards a Personal Vision, 1935–55.*

5. For examples of Yavno's work, see Max Yavno and Ben Maddow (text), *The Photography of Max Yavno.*

6. Roland Barthes. *Camera Lucida.*

7. Deborah Willis. *Early Black Photographers: 1840–1940.*

8. See Brian Lanker, *I Dream a World: Portraits of Black Women who Have Changed the World*, and Nobuo Nakamura, *The Eyes of Harlem.*

9. Pierre Verger. *Orixás.*

10. Jacob Riis, *How the Other Half Lives*, and see Alexander Allard, Sr., *Jacob A. Riis: Photographer and Citizen.*

11. Nan Goldin. *The Ballad of Sexual Dependency.*

12. Shawn Walker in *Nueva Luz.*

13. Frank Stewart in *Nueva Luz;* in his *Smokestack Lightning;* and in Wynton Marsalis, *Swing Street: Blues on the Road.*

14. Conrad Barclay, Albert Chong, and Accra Shepp, each in *Nueva Luz.*

15. Roy DeCarava. *Photographs.*

16. Rotimi Fani-Kayode in *Revue Noire.*

REFERENCES

Allard, Alexander, Sr. *Jacob A. Riis: Photographer and Citizen.* New York, Aperture, 1973, 1993.

Baker, Houston. *Afro-American Poetics: Revisions of Harlem and the Black Aesthetic.* Madison, U of Wisconsin P, 1988.

———. *Blues, Ideology and Afro-American Literature: A Vernacular Theory.* Chicago, U of Chicago P, 1984.

Barclay, Conrad. "Photographs." *Nueva Luz* 3.3 (1991):2–11.

Barthes, Roland. *Camera Lucida.* Trans. Richard Howard. London, Flamingo, 1984.

Braithwaite, Hilton. "Photographs." *Nueva Luz* 3.3 (1991):12–21.

Césaire, Aimé. *Cahier d'un Retour au Pays Natal*, bilingual edition, trans. Emile Snyder (Paris: Présence Africaine, 1971). First definitive edition Paris, Présence Africaine, 1956. Originally Paris, Bordas, 1947.

Chong, Albert. "Photographs." *Nueva Luz* 2.2 (Spring 1988):2–11.

DeCarava, Roy. *Photographs.* Introduction: Sherry Turner DeCarava. San Francisco, The Friends of Photography. 1981.

———, and Langston Hughes. *The Sweet Flypaper of Life.* Washington, D.C., Howard UP, 1984. First published New York, Hill and Wang, 1955.

Douglass, Frederick. *Narrative of the Life of Frederick Douglass, An American Slave.* New York, Penguin Classics, 1982.

Ellison, Ralph. *Invisible Man*. New York, Vintage Books, 1989.

Fani-Kayode, Rotimi. "Photos." *Revue Noire* 3 (Dec. 1991):30–50.

Goldin, Nan. *The Ballad of Sexual Dependency*. New York, Aperture, 1986.

Hurston, Zora Neale. *Moses, Man of the Mountain*. Urbana, Illini Books, 1984.

———. *Their Eyes Were Watching God*. New York, Perennial Library, 1990.

Kao, Deborah Martin and Charles A. Meyer, eds. *Aaron Siskind: Towards a Personal Vision, 1935–55*. Chestnut Hill, MA, Boston College Museum of Art, 1994.

Lanker, Brian. *I Dream a World: Portraits of Black Women Who Have Changed the World*. New York, Stewart, Tabori and Chang, 1989.

Marsalis, Wynton. *Swing Street: Blues on the Road*. New York, Norton, 1994.

Martin, Reginald. *Ishmael Reed and the New Black Aesthetic Critics*. New York, St. Martin's Press, 1988.

Nakamura, Nobuo. *The Eyes of Harlem*. Tokyo, Chikuma Shobo, 1985.

Riis, Jacob. *How the Other Half Lives*. New York, Dover Publications, 1971. First published New York, Charles Scribner's Sons, 1890.

Shepp, Accra. "Photographs." *Nueva Luz* 3.3 (1991):22–31.

Stewart, Frank. "Photographs." *Nueva Luz* 3.1 (1989):12–21.

———. *Smokestack Lightning*. New York, Farrar, Straus and Giroux, 1996.

Verger, Pierre Fatumbi. *Orixás*. Salvador, Bahia, Editora Corrupio, Comércio Ltda., 1981.

Walker, Shawn. "Photographs." *Nueva Luz* 1.4 (1987):22–31.

Willis, Deborah. *Early Black Photographers: 1840–1940*. New York, The New Press, 1992.

Willis-Braithwaite, Deborah. *James VanDerZee: Photographer, 1886–1983*. New York, Harry N. Abrams, 1993.

Yavno, Max and Ben Maddow (text). *The Photography of Max Yavno*. Berkeley, U of California P, 1981.

29 CARIBBEAN CINEMA, OR CINEMA IN THE CARIBBEAN?

Keith Q. Warner

When Ivan, hero of the widely acclaimed Jamaican film *The Harder They Come*, first comes to town, one of the places he is most anxious to visit, to the surprise of his new-found and streetwise friends, is a cinema. He had, he claimed, read about the Rialto while he was still in the country, and could not wait to experience the cinema firsthand. We subsequently witness several instances of Ivan living out his cinematic fantasy, complete with posed photographs in cowboy garb. Finally, we see him felled by a hail of bullets that, for him, could easily have been fired as part of the gunfight at the O. K. Corral. It is significant that one of the more popular and authentic films to emerge from the Anglophone Caribbean—the focus of this study—would have as a subtext this tribute to the pervading presence and importance of the cinema. Similarly, another widely acclaimed film, *Sugar Cane Alley*, this time from French-speaking Martinique, also highlights the importance of the cinema, for we see one of its characters, Carmen, striving to improve his reading skills so that he can eventually go to Hollywood. Why was there this fascination with the cinema, especially among lower classes? And how did this preoccupation with the cinema manifest itself?

Given our tendency as colonial subjects in the Caribbean to give special value to whatever came from abroad, it was not at all surprising that audiences would take so readily to this new and totally non-Caribbean medium. If we look at the period following the Second World War, and at the emerging popularity of cinema attendance, we find that the majority of the films shown were American in origin. This fact brought the following observation from keen but acerbic observer V. S. Naipaul in *The Middle Passage*, after he had noted that the influence of the cinema in Trinidad is incalculable:

> Favourites are shown again and again: *Casablanca*, with Humphrey Bogart; *Till the Clouds Roll By*; the Errol Flynn, John Wayne, James Cagney, Edward G. Robinson and Richard Widmark films; vintage

Westerns like *Dodge City* and *Jesse James*; and every film Bogart made. Films are reputed for their fights. *The Spoilers* is advertised as having the longest fight ever (Randolph Scott and John Wayne, I believe). (p. 63)

Incidentally, in one of his first pieces of sustained writing, later published as *Miguel Street*, Naipaul would name one of his characters Bogart, and give his narrator the following possible explanation for the origin of the name: "It was something of a mystery why he was called Bogart; but I suspect that it was Hat who gave him the name. I don't know if you remember the year the film *Casablanca* was made. That was the year when Bogart's fame spread like fire through Port of Spain and hundreds of young men began adopting the hard-boiled Bogartian attitude" (p. 9). Michael Thelwell, in his novel *The Harder They Come*, based on the film of the same name, also notes the popularity of some of the very actors mentioned by Naipaul, leading one to surmise that this was a pan-Caribbean phenomenon. Of Ivan, alias Rhygin, the author writes that

> It wasn't long before his judgment matured and his taste became more selective. Gangster movies didn't appeal to him much, they seemed to lack the clean-cut heroism of the westerns. Of course there were certain names: Humphrey Bogart, Edward G. Robinson, Richard Widmark, Sidney Greenstreet, or George Raft, which evolved a certain style, a cynical tight-lipped toughness which he liked. But in his innermost heart Rhygin was a cowboy. To miss a western, almost any western, brought sadness and deprivation to his spirit. (195)

It mattered not that these were white actors on whom the predominantly Afro-Caribbean youth in these pre-independence years were modeling themselves. Sidney Poitier, Harry Belafonte, and the other black actors who desegregated Hollywood's film industry came much later, and did not really affect the bond the masses had by then developed with their favorite characters. There was a reason for this. To quote from *The Middle Passage* again: "In its stars the Trinidad audience looks for a special quality of style. . . . For the Trinidadian an actor has style when he is seen to fulfil certain aspirations of the audience: the virility of Bogart, the man-on-the-run romanticism of Garfield, the pimpishness and menace of Duryea, the ice-cold sadism of Widmark" (p. 64). Clearly, style transcended race, a notion to which some of Trinidad's calypsonians and Jamaica's D.J.s with their non-Caribbean sobriquets can relate. Clearly, too, screen image transcended local reality, or at least created another one, as Thelwell notes: "The movie was a flowing reality, unfolding like time made visible before one's eyes. With the parting of the curtain a wall had collapsed and Ivan was looking into a different world, where *pale people* [my emphasis] of giant dimensions walked, talked, fought, and conducted their lives in a marvelous and quite convincing reality" (p. 148). What mattered most, then, was the new world that the cinema opened up for this devoted crop of film viewers. Michael Thelwell writes of the post-film occurrence in *The Harder They Come*: "Afterward the show moved into the street. The boys reenacted the good scenes. With amazing facility of memory and mimicry they drawled the best lines through their noses, walked the walks with hands hanging like claws above imaginary holsters, and made the moves" (p. 194). This scenario finds a longer and more poignant development in Earl Lovelace's *The Dragon Can't Dance*, where we read of the hero Fisheye:

> He began to go to the cinema. Every night almost, he went to Royal or Empire, whichever was showing a western double; and after the show, walking home up the Hill, the picture fresh in his mind, walking kinda slow, he would feel for a few moments his strength, his youth, his promise fill him, and he would walk, the fastest gun alive, his long hands stiff at his sides, his fingers ready to go for the guns he imagined holstered low on his hips. . . . He began to develop a crawl, a way of walking that was kinda dragging and slow, in which his knees barely bent, his feet were kept close and his legs spread apart to give the appearance of being bow-legged from riding a horse. (pp. 50–51)

In the colonial and pre-independence setting, this yearning, extreme as it is, to adopt everything served on the foreign platter was understandable, given the overwhelming diet of extra-Caribbean culture forced upon the region's inhabitants. However, Carolyn Cooper, in her excellent study of Jamaican popular culture, sees this utter fascination and total identification with film heroes on the part of both Ivan and Fisheye as "clearly pathological," a far cry from "the discriminating responses of habitual moviegoers in the Caribbean . . . who are ultimately able to maintain a sane critical distance from the text" (p. 98). But, one could argue, those who would maintain this distance are precisely the ones on whom any influence would appear to manifest itself the least, for such gut reactions to mere images on a screen could only be seen as the result of an uncultured and unlettered mind.

Going to the cinema—or "theater," as it was called in many instances—was obviously a favorite activity among the poorer masses. They flocked to an activity that was relatively inexpensive, that provided them a look at another world, and that allowed them to believe make-believe. The cinema also provided a wonderful communal opportunity for certain sections of the population to indulge in open grandstanding, and there are countless stories of the goings-on among patrons inside the cinema. In particular, those who sat in the cheaper pit or stalls sections nearest the screen were renowned for their interaction with what was taking place on the screen, for, as Michael Thelwell reminded us in his novel, "there was no such thing as watching in silence; the identification was high and a contagious excitement spilled down from the screen and rolled in waves through the theater" (p. 194). In this regard, Carolyn Cooper's observation is instructive:

> As anyone who has attended the cinema in predominantly oral societies like Jamaica will attest, film is an art-form in which an open-ended dialogue with the narrative/visual text is transacted. Loud comments on the action, not simply non-verbal laughter or tears, articulate the viewer's responses to this intimate medium. Characters are addressed directly and are often warned of impending danger; the viewer, after all, is more knowing than they and can "read" the meaning of events the character merely experiences. (p. 96)

In *The Middle Passage*, Naipaul also gives a glimpse of what transpired in a similar setting at the other end of the Caribbean chain of islands:

> The Trinidad audience actively participates in the action on the screen. "Where do you come from?" Lauren Bacall is asked in *To Have and Have Not*. "Port of Spain, Trinidad," she replies, and the audience shouts delightedly, "You lie! You lie!" So the audience continually shouts advice and comments; it grunts at every blow in a fight; it roars with delight when the once-spurned hero returns wealthy and impeccably dressed (this is important) to revenge himself on his past tormentor; it grows derisive when the hero finally rejects and perhaps slaps the Hollywood "bad" woman (of the *Leave Her to Heaven* type). It responds, in short, to every stock situation of the American cinema. (p. 63)

The sections of the audience which responded so viscerally to what was happening on the screen were, as we have seen, mostly from the lower rungs of the economic ladder, the very people who would not have all of the competing pastimes enjoyed by the upper classes. This fact was most noticeable in the case of one such section of the Trinidad public, namely the first wave of players—young, poor, and black for the most part—of the new instrument forged from discarded oil drums. "Their background," writes Stephen Stuempfle in *The Steelband Movement*, "was one of poverty; some lived in the crowded barrack yards in the downtown area, while others resided in the depressed neighborhoods on the east side of the city"

(p. 47). The attraction of the cinema for this group, as well as for their counterparts in the world of carnival revelry, was extraordinary:

> Though the panmen enjoyed liming on the streets, they also spent a great amount of time at the cinemas. Movies, most of which were American, were very popular in Trinidad, and panmen were among the most devoted patrons. Sometimes they attended several shows a day. They particularly liked war movies but also enjoyed other types of films such as gangster dramas, Westerns, and musicals.
>
> Through these movies the panmen experienced a foreign world of grandeur, battles, and romance that had a major influence on the cultural style that they were developing. They appropriated ways of dressing, walking, and talking from the movies and creatively combined these with parallel practices from the local street culture. Sometimes they even adopted the names of movie stars such as Humphrey Bogart and Cesar Romero, but they used many locally-created nicknames as well. Similarly, during the war and the immediate postwar years, panmen often named their bands after movies: Casablanca . . . Destination Tokyo . . . Cross of Lorraine . . . Night Invaders . . . Desperadoes . . . Sun Valley . . . and Bataan. . . . Once the war was over and Carnival was again permitted, the movies had a tremendous impact on military masquerades played by steelbands. Uniforms, equipment, and maneuvers observed in the cinema were replicated with great precision on the streets. (pp. 49–50)

The carnival connection would achieve its climax in the 1950s and 1960s with the parading of masqueraders in bands whose themes and costumes came almost directly from Hollywood, and one prominent bandleader, Harold Saldhena, was dubbed the local Cecil B. De Mille.

Further, Trinidad's other folk artists, the calypsonians, also showed a love for the cinema, and either sprinkled their songs with references to exploits of their favorite film stars, or commented on the attitudes of parts of the cinema-going public. The Mighty Sparrow even associated a spate of hooliganism that swept Port of Spain in the 1960s with idle youth who spent a lot of their time going to the cinema, in particular to the early afternoon shows notorious as the refuge of the lowly employed or unemployed. This same calypsonian, who had glorified young ruffians and their love of the cinema in "Gunslingers," comparing them to Audie Murphy in *To Hell and Back* as they gave their victims "a one way ticket to Boot Hill," now turned on them in "Renegades":

> Every day they going theatre twelve thirty
> And believe me they going in free
> One will call the gate man here
> Talk in he ears, ten gone through there

The gate man rush to put a stop
They push him down and the whole theater full up.

Sparrow is also aware that the cinema is where you took a young lady on an important date. "I have a nice señorita / last night I took her to theatre," he sang in "Nice Señorita." No question here of going to the 12:30 show, since the calypsonian wants to make the best impression possible in the relative seclusion of the highest-priced seats "in balcony."

Even without the technological sophistication of the modern cinema, the early silver screen still held vast sections of the Caribbean public enthralled. There was hardly any criticism, say in the popular Trinidad calypsoes, of the fare that Hollywood served, though, curiously enough, the portrayal of black characters in the cinema was criticized by one writer, Joseph Zobel, of Martinique, French West Indies. In his novel *Black Shack Alley*, itself adapted for the screen (and retitled *Sugar Cane Alley* for United States cinema audiences), the narrator asks:

Who was it who created for the cinema and the theater that type of black man, houseboy, driver, footman, truant, a pretext for words from simple minds, always rolling their white eyes in amazement, always with a silly irrepressible smile plastered on their faces, provoker of mockery? That black man with his grotesque behavior under the kick in his backside proudly administered by the white man, or when the latter had him hoodwinked with an ease that is explained by the theory of the "black man being a big child?"

Who was it who invented for the blacks portrayed in the cinema and in the theater that language the blacks never could speak and in which, I am sure, no black man will manage to express himself? Who was it who, for the black man, agreed, once and for all, on those plaid suits that no black man ever made or wore of his own choice? And those disguises in shoes worn down at the heels, old clothes, bowler hats and umbrellas with holes in them, weren't they above all the sordid apanage of a section of the society that, in the civilized countries, misery and poverty made the sad beneficiary of the offscourings of the upper classes? (pp. 168–169)

First published in 1950, this novel seems slightly ahead of its time with regard to the criticism of the portrayal of black characters in the cinema. Similar criticism was slow to filter through to the rest of the Caribbean public as a whole, whether French- or English-speaking, though the 1957 film *Island in the Sun*, shot on location in Barbados, Grenada, and Jamaica, aroused a great deal of controversy. According to film librarian Valerie Bloomfield, "the Caribbean press was particularly critical of its treatment of race." Ironically, though, the Caribbean scenes were "still greeted by local audiences with delighted recognition" (p. 286).

Meanwhile, films kept coming to the region, kept finding fans for whatever was shown. For example, Tarzan movies were openly enjoyed without the cringe of embarrassment that would come with the awareness that Hollywood's vision of Africa was unflattering at best. Indeed, calypsonian The Mighty Spoiler sang uncritically about his preference for the older, stereotypical Tarzan over the modern one. In his calypso "Tarzan," he sang:

> Ah rather see Mickey Mouse drive a train
> Than to go and see a Tarzan picture again
> Now he riding bike; Tarzan going to dance
> Tarzan eating hot dog; he wearing pants
> Now he talking fluent more than you or me
> Like he eat up a Webster's dictionary
> . . . .
> If they want to get meh money out of meh hand
> Bring back pictures like *Tarzan the Apeman*
> Two pictures again which were very great
> *Tarzan Finds a Son; Tarzan and His Mate.*

Clearly, sophistication was not what guided the average film spectator as represented here by the calypsonian. Such critical appreciation of what a film was "saying," or what it "meant," would come much later, as audiences learned to place the fascination with things foreign into proper perspective.

Fascination with the cinema was everywhere in the Anglophone Caribbean long before there was any attempt to develop what could remotely be termed a cinema industry. As we have seen, it was in the nicknames that young men took as they searched to give meaning to their lives; it was in the early calypso in Trinidad as the bards celebrated the exploits of matinee idols like Rudy Vallee and Bing Crosby; it was ever present in the birth of the steelband. In other words, it was in the consciousness of the masses, conditioned as they were to turn their gaze to the exterior. It would seem only natural to expect that the people of the Caribbean would have parlayed their love of viewing films and their ready assimilation of the on-screen characters and situations into an equally ardent love of producing their own films. Unfortunately, for the most part, this has not been the case.

The early identification with the world of film did not immediately create an urge for, or an insistence on, a similar insertion of the Caribbean landscape into this celluloid world. Many years would elapse before the Caribbean saw films that showed, however briefly, meaningful scenes set in the islands, and, in any case, where such films did exist, the perspective was not one set by us in the Caribbean. The region started off as backdrop, and remained so for some time.

The concept of the Caribbean as backdrop has meant that crews from the larger film-producing capitals would occasionally ship themselves to the islands for certain scenes, and eventually for entire location shoots. News of film crews shooting on the various islands would be enough to start a mini-rush to the selected locations not only to see how films are made, a reasonable pursuit even to this day, but also to see if any islanders would be fortunate enough to be in front of the camera. With the film crew's departure, there would be an anxious wait for the release of the finished product, and hope that, first, the film came to the Caribbean; second, that the censors allowed the public to see it; and third, that the particular scene survived editing. Finally, audiences would view the film with the sole purpose of identifying certain people and locales, as if they had now found a new purpose, and certainly notoriety, with their inclusion in a feature film.

Of course, this development would not have been possible with the earliest scenes that purported to depict the Caribbean on film. They were not shot on location, but were rather done on back lots in Hollywood, the usual source of the vilest of stereotype, or in other parts of the United States that closely resembled the Caribbean's tropical landscape. For example, *Captain Blood* (1935), a story of piracy in the Caribbean, was filmed in part at Corona, Laguna Beach, and in Palm Canyon near Palm Springs, as producers no doubt argued that the authenticity of the backdrop was less important than the intrigue of the plot. And what did these films, ostensibly set in the Caribbean, offer? According to Kennedy Wilson, "Since Hollywood's early days, filmmakers have depicted the region as an illusory paradise peopled by dubious natives, ravishing temptresses, and swashbuckling heroes. Themes of black magic and voodoo, gangsters and spies, and pirates and villains have recurred in nightmarish proportions over the years" (p. 93). Interestingly, one notes that few of the types that fascinated the early Caribbean movie lovers are listed here, just as none of their favorite films were set in the region.

While it would be unfair to maintain that all of the films set in the Caribbean concentrated on the now familiar stereotypical themes, it is nonetheless true that the vast majority of them paid scant attention to life in the region as such. The stories were, for the most part, centered on the foreigner's adventure in the islands, rather than on the islanders' lives. "Very often," writes Kennedy Wilson, "in pictures like these the Caribbean and its islands are the real stars of the films, lending hackneyed plots a touch of sunny glamour or a beach-party atmosphere" (p. 95). The James Bond series of films, the first of which, *Dr. No*, was shot in Jamaica in 1962, with seven others also featuring Caribbean settings, is a good example of this use of the exotic lushness of the Caribbean as backdrop. The audience sees the Caribbean flora and fauna, and a few local actors in bit parts, but cannot really claim to learn very much about the region. The situation has improved somewhat, to the point where a film like *The Mighty Quinn* (1989), an American production, actually has Denzel Washington and Robert Townsend playing Caribbean (Jamaican to all appearances) characters, complete with island accents, alongside a number of Jamaica's better-known actors. The foreignness of the past is thus attenuated, though not totally eliminated, and one suspects that this does not necessarily work against a film of this nature, given the Caribbean audiences' historical propensity to see themselves from the outside.

The feature films shot, in whole or in part, on location in the Caribbean—Kennedy Wilson lists some sixty—have used scenes from throughout the region, from Cuba to Puerto Rico down to Tobago, with an obvious edge going to Jamaica (one third of the films on Wilson's list). Advancing technology has made location filming easier, though not necessarily less expensive, so one would expect that the beauty of the Caribbean, and its proximity to the United States, source of so many of today's feature films, would attract more works highlighting the region. The problem, however, is that in a world that counts a film's success in terms of receipts in the millions of dollars worldwide, the returns from the Caribbean, or lack thereof, do not warrant too much concern from the corporate side of the film industry. In other words, there really is no great market incentive driving non-Caribbean film producers to make a product more geared to a Caribbean audience. From all appearances, Caribbean cinema aficionados are assumed to be happy once a few scenes in films produced outside of the region are shot on location in the islands, for that would give the necessary tourist-oriented exposure, and once a reasonable number of local extras and artists are employed.

And if the films featuring the Caribbean in some meaningful way do not come from the usual source, namely abroad, then where will they come from? Should they not naturally come from the Caribbean itself? It is in this light that we must view the outstanding success of Jamaica's *The Harder They Come* (1972), though it should be pointed out that this success did not come without its detractors. Critics were uneasy with the film's portrayal of crime and violence. Harry Milner, writing in the *Sunday Gleaner* of June 18, 1972, said: "I still think it is a pity that the first fictional movie made here for international circulation, and which, through its quality, its sensationalism and its novelty, is bound to resound abroad, should have been this film of murder, violence and crime" (p. 5). Clearly, the concern was with image. After many years of being seen by the other, of being described by the other, Caribbean people were at last turning the table. It was the other that would now be the outsider, that would need help in understanding everything from language to music.

Although generally credited as the first full-length all-Caribbean feature film, Perry Henzell's *The Harder They Come* was preceded by at least two others, *The Right and the Wrong* and *The Caribbean Fox*, both directed in Trinidad in 1970 by Harbance Kumar. Valerie Bloomfield provides the following snapshot of these films and their reception:

> *The Right and the Wrong*, set in Trinidad at the time of slavery, was a tale of a sadistic plantation owner, escaping slaves and sudden death. The film won a gold medal for photography at the Atlanta Film Festival. *The Caribbean Fox*, a mixture of crime story, romance and musical comedy, portrayed the exploits of rival gangs, prostitutes and drug smugglers in the Trinidad underworld. Against a background of steel band, calypso and sitar music. Both films did well at box offices in the Caribbean, although subject to Black power demonstrations in Guyana. In Britain they were shown as a double bill, receiving their European premiere at the Classic Cinemas in Kilburn in September 1971. *The reviewers welcomed the development of a West Indian film industry* [my emphasis], but could find little good to say of its first offerings, apart from praising the beauty of the scenery. They were particularly critical of the lack of authenticity in the scripts and the sensationalism of the treatment. One writer, after commenting on the thematic banality, the embarrassed love scenes and the historical inaccuracies (such as the director's introduction of East Indian slaves), argued that such criticism was necessary if Trinidad were to produce worthwhile films in the future. (p. 288)

One notes that this fledgling attempt was not all bad (gold medal for photography, for example), and that, all things considered, the subject matter was not unlike what the Caribbean public had been gobbling up over the years. Still, this was not to be the longed-for start of a "West Indian film industry."

The film that really raised hopes that such an industry had been born was, as mentioned earlier, *The Harder They Come*. The plot is simplicity itself: poor country boy comes to town with no skills bar his good voice and a burning desire to make a record; unable to find a job, he eventually seeks help from a preacher, but that lead turns sour when he courts the preacher's protégée; he ends up making a record (an eventual hit), but is ruthlessly exploited, and suffers the same fate when he turns to selling ganja; he ends up killing a policeman, becomes a folk hero of sorts, and is hunted and gunned down trying to escape to Cuba. The soundtrack features Jimmy Cliff, who plays the role of Ivan, and a variety of songs that are considered the forerunners of the reggae craze. Gordon Rohlehr, one of the Anglophone Caribbean's most perceptive literary critics, called this film "the first West Indian movie which attempts to look at the West Indian reality, with sensitivity and frankness" (p. 106). Director Perry Henzell, in several interviews following the film's enthusiastic reception, explained what he had set out to do. "I had a choice," he told the *Daily Gleaner* of June 22, 1972, "when I set out to make this film—to make a film for Jamaica, or to make a film for the rest of the world. I chose to make a film for Jamaica" (See Rohlehr, p. 95). He went on to claim that, in view of the reaction to the film by its first non-Jamaican audience (in Ireland), he had apparently achieved both things; while in another interview with Martin Hayman, published in *Cinema Rising*, he expressed the hope that this film marked the beginning of an indigenous film industry.

The film clearly struck a nerve, with its down-to-earth social realism, its unapologetic use of Jamaican creole (with subtitles in standard English), and with its very effective use of its soundtrack. It is not surprising that it became an instant hit throughout the Caribbean and beyond, achieving cult and classic status, and that despite the reservations mentioned earlier. One would have thought, then, that with a film of this nature having garnered international success—a surefire way of legitimizing anything we do in the Caribbean—film producers throughout the region would have rushed to capitalize on the renewed interest in local production. Unfortunately, it is the nature of filmmaking that it is expensive, and not many financial backers were found for subsequent scripts, for, as Victoria Marshall has confirmed: "potential sponsors and investors are reluctant to risk their money, particularly the large sums needed to produce even a modest film" (p. 99).

In 1974, Trinidad and Tobago, on the brink of an oil bonanza, made *Bim*, a story of pre-independence political and interracial intrigue, that pulled together, as was the case with Jamaica's film, the best of local talent. Jamaica produced a second feature film in 1975, *Smile Orange*, directed by Trevor Rhone, who had co-written *The Harder They Come*. But the anticipated boom in Caribbean filmmaking supposedly spawned by such efforts did not materialize, though by the end of the 1970s and through the 1980s Jamaica's independent (read "relatively small and underfinanced") filmmakers would produce most of the significant Caribbean feature films in English: e.g., *Rockers* (1978), *Children of Babylon* (1980), *Countryman* (1982). None of these, however, has achieved the success, or the wide distribution, of *The Harder They Come*, or of Martinique's *Sugar Cane Alley* (1983), which has become the virtual quintessential Caribbean film as far as non-Caribbean audiences are concerned.

Competition for scarce private-sector dollars is one factor that has worked against the development of a thriving cinema industry. Kennedy Wilson quotes Lennie Little-White on the reason for this state of affairs: "It's difficult to get financing to make films in the Caribbean because there's not that tradition. Investors are happy to put money into sugar or bananas or something they can see. They don't appreciate the possibility of the enormous market for films" (p. 96). Nonetheless, in its attempt to attract financing Jamaica has set up an agency, Jampro, that actively seeks to have foreign film companies use the island for location shooting. The result of this effort has been an increase in the number of films set on the island, but not necessarily in the number of films that could be called Caribbean. But, as I have already asked in my article "Film, Literature, and Identity in the Caribbean," "[W]hat *is* a Caribbean film? If a film is shot in the Caribbean, but its entire conception, and its entire production team are non-Caribbean, save for a few minor local characters, is it a Caribbean film?" (p. 51). This question can be posed from another perspective in the case of Caribbean filmmakers who have worked extensively outside of the region, the case, for instance, with Trinidad's Horace Ove and Frances-Anne Solomon. If you are from the Caribbean, but work almost exclusively in Europe, are you producing Caribbean cinema?

Films, like books, need audiences, and without major distribution networks, the ones produced by the independent filmmakers have not always been seen by the wider cinema-going public. Meanwhile, any other feature production from the companies that surface from time to time must still compete with the ever-present American movies (or with Indian ones in Trinidad and Guyana, given the racial breakdown of these two countries). Unfortunately, there is no way around this situation, for the sheer volume of films readily available from abroad makes it impractical for the Caribbean public to wait patiently for a local production, and to hope that it likes what it sees. It is conceivable, however, that more work will be done in video production for television, as was the case with Derek Walcott's direction of *The Rig* in Trinidad in 1983, for example. Similarly, extremely popular television dramas like *Turn of the Tide* in Trinidad or *Royal Palm Estate* in Jamaica showcase the wealth of talent available for possible film production, but also serve to highlight the problems inherent in the budding industry as a whole. The large following for the televised episodes proves that there is interest in the dramas per se. Still, when *Turn of the Tide*, developed from the serial into a regular film for cinema audiences, was distributed locally, it did not recapture the popularity of the original television production. This is a probable indication of a shift from cinema attendance to in-home television viewing, a shift occasioned more by changing economic fortunes than by the dominance of video versions of first-run films. There is literally no competition between Caribbean films shown in the cinema and their ensuing video versions, for the volume and frequency of production are far too low to make this an issue.

Finally, several pan-Caribbean film festivals have resulted in the establishment of loose federations of professionals, whose aim would obviously be to work toward the establishment of some semblance of a film industry. According to Kennedy Wilson, "initiatives like Images Caraïbes and the Caribbean Film and Video Federation have encouraged Caribbean-set films to move away from stereotypical tourist fantasies. They also have helped promote other themes while encouraging cinema to become a vital, indigenous art form" (p. 96).

The full-length Caribbean film made for cinema screens, the one destined to bring together the audience in the same way that the non-Caribbean film does in the communal act of cinema-going, is indeed rare, though attempts are still made to correct this situation. As late as 1996, cinema viewers saw *Men of Grey II: The Flight of the Ibis*, a sequel of sorts since the original *Men of Grey* had been a television serial. Heavily touted as produced and filmed entirely in Trinidad and Tobago, this movie attempted to translate the fast-action-type drama, the current craze after the karate and kung fu days, to a Caribbean setting, with the hope, no doubt, of capturing some of the same cinema audiences that patronized the American action pictures. In the same vein, Jamaica made *Klash*, with well-known American star Jasmine Guy to help improve its attractiveness, and the now usual dose of popular reggae music. But, once again, a Caribbean production ran into trouble. It bombed in Jamaica, prompting the *Jamaica Herald* to make a plea for a delay in its "swift departure," and, when shown in Trinidad, was criticized for being too violent. This double standard shown in the rejection of the local film by some of the very audiences that feast on similar foreign films is a source of constant concern and annoyance, and a situation that calypsonians know only too well. For years, these artists have complained that the same public that criticizes its calypsoes for being "smutty" openly and avidly enjoy equally suggestive songs from the American hit parade.

One cannot help but wonder, then, if cinema in the Anglophone Caribbean is not destined to live forever in the shadow of comparison with other well-established ones. One remedy constantly proposed is to have filmmakers turn inward, to forget about North America and Europe, and to follow the examples set by Cuba, by India, or by many of the African countries. But this solution will remain more theoretical than practical unless there is a commitment to a change of mentality among those who will inevitably have to facilitate the arrangements necessary for a successful production. The providers of financing, and the granters of the myriad approvals filmmakers need, will have to come together with a view to making any eventual film industry a viable undertaking.

Further, one also wonders if the economic situation of most of the Anglophone Caribbean countries will not preclude full development of such an indigenous industry. The region is caught between the progress and modernization that it constantly hankers after, or has foisted upon it, and the retention of traditional practices that made for a certain cohesiveness in the society. Cinema audiences in the 1990s are naturally quite different from those of the postwar and pre-independence years. Increased educational opportunity has begun to produce more sophisticated cinema patrons, who can appreciate a Caribbean production for something else beside the fact that it was filmed in a location they recognize. However, reduced economic opportunity has also begun to take its toll among the very class of patrons who so enjoyed the cinema in the past, making it more practical for them to resort to in-home viewing of rented videos.

Film uses images, and images are powerful. The people of the Caribbean, like people throughout the African diaspora, relate and respond to this power. Indeed, it is often through these powerful images that one area of the diaspora learns about another, making it imperative that the perspective be the one a particular people or region wants to project. It will be unfortunate if the Anglophone Caribbean cannot harness the power of images to its own benefit; if it is perpetually forced to enjoy cinema and film from someone else's perspective; and if it cannot reasonably expect to produce and appreciate its own Caribbean cinema.

REFERENCES

Bloomfield, Valerie. "Caribbean Films." *Journal of Librarianship* 9 (October 1977).

Cham, Mbye (ed.). *Ex-Iles: Essays on Caribbean Cinema*. Trenton: African World Press, 1992.

Cooper, Carolyn. *Noises in the Blood: Orality, Gender and the "Vulgar" Body of Jamaican Popular Culture*. London: Macmillan Caribbean, 1993.

Lovelace, Earl. *The Dragon Can't Dance*. Burnt Mill: Longman Drumbeat, 1979.

Marshall, Victoria. "Filmmaking in Jamaica: 'Likkle But Tallawah.'" In Cham, Mbye (ed.). *Ex-Iles: Essays on Caribbean Cinema*. Trenton: African World Press, 1992.

Naipaul, V. S. *Miguel Street*. Middlesex: Penguin Books, 1959.

———. *The Middle Passage*. Middlesex: Penguin Books, 1962.

Rohlehr, Gordon. *My Strangled City and Other Essays*. Port of Spain: Longman, 1992.

Stuempfle, Stephen. *The Steelband Movement: The Forging of a National Art in Trinidad and Tobago*. Philadelphia: University of Pennsylvania Press, 1995.

Thelwell, Michael. *The Harder They Come*. New York: Grove Weidenfeld, 1980.

Warner, Keith. "Film, Literature, and Identity in the Caribbean." In Cham, Mbye (ed.). *Ex-Iles: Essays on Caribbean Cinema*. Trenton: African World Press, 1992.

Wilson, Kennedy. "On Location." *Caribbean Travel and Life* (May–June 1996).

Zobel, Joseph. *Black Shack Alley*. Washington, D.C.: Three Continents Press, 1980.

RECONNECTING WITH AFRICA

30 THE EMERGENCE OF BILATERAL DIASPORA ETHNICITY AMONG CAPE VERDEAN–AMERICANS

Laura J. Pires-Hester

This essay discusses the emergence of bilateral diaspora ethnicity among a little-studied diaspora population, Cape Verdean–Americans. It suggests that this more recent stage in Cape Verdean–American ethnic development represents the maturation of a relatively small ethnic population as it begins to use its acquired skills in its current homeland, the United States, to benefit its overseas original homeland, Cape Verde.

Studies of diaspora populations have usually focussed on either the sending or receiving side of the migration cycle. Diaspora relations with the ancestral homeland have been of relatively recent concern. Among the first to cross this boundary was Elliott P. Skinner (1982), who compared the diaspora–homeland relations of diaspora Africans, Chinese, Indians, Jews, and Irish. His exciting 1992 volume *African-Americans and U.S. Policy toward Africa 1850–1924: In Defense of Black Nationality* chronicled the mid-nineteenth- to early-twentieth-century efforts of African-American leaders to influence United States policies toward Africa. His rich analysis spotlighted a little-known segment of United States history, all the more noteworthy because it occurred at the height of European expansion when many believed, despite Franz Boas, that Africa and African peoples were less than ready for full participation in modern society.

More attention is now being paid to both sides of the migration chain. Examples include George Gmelch's (1992) oral histories of Barbadian emigrants to London or North America and their *return* migration decision and experience, and José Llanes's (1982) presentation of Cuban-Americans' own "legends of migration." On another level of bilateral relationships are Eugenia Georges's (1990) wonderful analysis of a "transnational community" created by "Los Pineros" migrating to New York City from the Dominican Republic and Gisèle L. Bousquet's (1979) look "behind the bamboo hedge" at the homeland politics of the Parisian-Vietnamese community and their international network of politically involved Vietnamese refugees and immigrants.[1] The development and emergence of bilateral diaspora ethnicity among Cape Verdean–Americans, a little-studied population and a population little-recognized outside New England,[2] is another example.

THE EMERGENCE OF CAPE VERDEAN–AMERICAN BILATERAL DIASPORA ETHNICITY

"Bilateral diaspora ethnicity" is defined as the strategic use of ethnic identification with an *original* overseas homeland to benefit that homeland, through relations with systems and institutions of the current *actual* homeland. The original homeland is the Republic of Cape Verde, an archipelago off the western coast of Africa and former Portuguese colony/"overseas possession."[3] The current actual homeland is the United States. The term and its definition borrow from a distinction made by Amilcar Cabral (1973), the brilliant leader of the Cape Verdean and Guinea-Bissau independence struggle and theoretician of liberation and culture: "The identity of a being is always a relative quality. . . . It shows the need not to confuse the *original* identity, of which the biological element is the main determinant, and the *actual* identity, of which the main determinant is the sociological element [italics added]" (p. 65). Bilateral diaspora ethnicity represents a maturing of relations between diaspora populations and their old and new homelands (Skinner, 1982). In the late 1970s to early 1980s Cape Verdean–Americans started to use their acquired skills and networks to influence policies in their current actual homeland (i.e., lobbying) to benefit their original homeland.

Historical Context

The Cape Verdean–American ethnic experience has several uniquenesses and illustrates the broad diversity within the African diaspora. It combines both immigrant origin *and* color, powerful factors within the dichotomous United States "Black-White calculus," and thus brings together issues of ethnicity, race, and national origin. Its immigration dates back at least two and most likely three centuries[4] and was also *voluntary*—although impelled also by conditions of drought, poverty, and famine—thus demonstrating that the story of Africans in America is not only the story of the slave ship. In fact, starting in 1892 passenger and cargo schooners were owned and crewed by Cape Verdeans themselves (Michael Cohn and Michael K. H. Platzer, 1978; Laura Pires Houston and Michael K. H. Platzer, 1982). The population has maintained continuous and active ties with the original homeland since the outset, thus creating very early an "imagined community" (Benedict Anderson, 1983) with enduring and

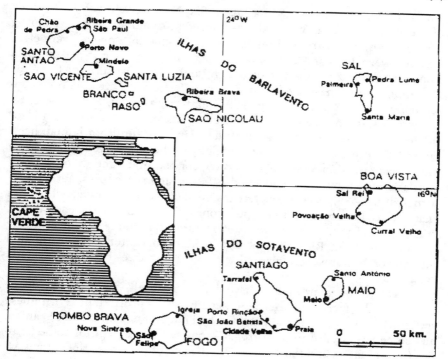

FIGURE I.

Cape Verde and Its Region
Source: Colm Foy, *Cape Verde: Politics, Economics and Society*
(London and New York: Pinter, 1988, page xx)

material substance. Because the Islands were *uninhabited* at the time of
being claimed by the Portuguese in the mid-fifteenth century (Elisa Andrade, 1974; Carreira, 1982; Walter Rodney, 1974),[5] the new country was
in fact created in Portugal's image, leading to a clearly mixed indigenous
population and also to inevitable contradictions and tensions in definition.
Finally, the United States diaspora population is roughly equivalent to that
in the original homeland (approximately 300,000).

Cape Verde itself is a paradox. Part of Portugal's wide-ranging "estate"—nearly three times its own size (P. Calvoressi, 1968)—the volcani-
cally formed islands were claimed by Portugal between 1455 and 1462.
The ten major islands (see Figure 1) are usually divided into two groups:
the southern Brava, Fogo, Maio, and Santiago, and the northern Boa Vista,

Santo Antão, São Vicente, Santa Luzia, São Nicolau, and Sal. Only three of the rugged Sahelian-band islands have year-round streams of running water, leading to recurrent drought cycles. For example, one of every eight years between 1748 and 1947 saw famine, and almost 96,000 persons died from drought and famine between 1774 and 1922 (Institute for Overseas Research, 1970). The 1947 famine is remembered with great pain by contemporary Cape Verdeans (Jorge Pedro Barbosa, 3/18/77; Helder Ferreira, 4/7/77). A sixteenth-century letter back to Lisbon from a no-longer-identifiable Portuguese settler described the islands as "unfit for human habitation." Centuries later, Sidney Greenfield (in the 1980s) would agree with the characterization, and when I visited for the first time in 1981 I was similarly struck by the islands' aridity, scale, and ruggedness. Yet on a return visit in 1987, I saw a concrete example of the perseverance which has characterized the history and population: hillsides outside the capital city, Praia, covered with growth from reforestation programs heralded during the previous visit. Richard Lobban and Marilyn Halter (1988) estimated that 20,000 hectares were planted with 9 million trees between 1975 and 1984 (p. 9).

People throughout history have defied "natural" odds, and the development and survival of this new people were no different. Portuguese settlement was sparse but augmented by French, English, Dutch, Spanish, and some Jews exiled from Portugal—mostly male except for some families from Madeira and the Algarve. By the end of the fifteenth century Africans were being brought by the Portuguese from the Upper Guinea Coast for the growing of cotton and sugar, which grew almost spontaneously in Santiago and Fogo. Carreira (1982) remains the best source for the still-incomplete population data and has analyzed the patterns leading to an indigenous population widely regarded as 70 percent "mixed," with greater Africanization on the largest island, Santiago. Carreira and T. Bentley Duncan (1972) agree that the largest number of Africans—an estimated 28,000 in the seventeenth century—were actually further transported, either to the Spanish Indies or to Europe.

The islands' location at the Atlantic intersection of trade winds, currents, and shipping routes to and from Europe, Africa, the Caribbean islands, and Brazil made them key ship-servicing points between the sixteenth and eighteenth centuries, with periodic declines followed by major decline in the nineteenth century. By 1816 there was a United States consular office in Brava (island of earliest emigration to New England) and 27 representatives from 11 countries (including Brazil, Britain, and the United States) among 7 islands (Duncan, 1972). The 1850s saw a short-lived peak commercial period for the northern port of Mindelo as a major coaling and supply station. Colonial tariff policies added to competition with other ports and finally the substitution of oil for coal led to major economic decline, while Portugal consistently ignored the need for assistance to cope with the physical disasters of drought and famine. Merchant ships often carried messages of the disastrous conditions in the isolated islands and these sometimes led to "people-to-people" assistance, but rarely was the assistance officially accepted. In 1936 such isolation led poet Jorge Barbosa (Norman Araujo 1975) to pen words such as: "nimguém dá, nimguém dá por isso" (no one cares, no one cares about this).[6]

The islands had a "special status" within the Portuguese orbit. They were granted exclusive trading privileges on the Upper Guinea Coast, the "assimilado" codes were not applied there, and at the beginning of the nineteenth century Cape Verdeans were trained abroad and assigned as functionaries in other Portuguese colonies—contradictions which contributed to the inevitable separation from Portugal. Cape Verdeans' ultimate resistance was of course the successful struggle for political independence in 1975, but prior to that they bypassed colonial trade restrictions, they developed a surprisingly[7] prodigious literature—and they emigrated.

The precise contours of Cape Verdean emigration to the United States are still not available. Immigration and census records are woefully inadequate because of the broad-banding of Cape Verdeans with "Portuguese," "other Africa," "Atlantic Islands," etc. Scattered New England records suggest recognized Cape Verdeans in Massachusetts or Connecticut in the eighteenth century, and the presence of foreign whalers in Cape Verdean waters going back to the early eighteenth century suggests strongly that crewmen joined these voyages starting at least that early. At the height of the whaling industry in New Bedford, Massachusetts, whalers were largely Cape Verdean. Emigration was often clandestine but also seen by Portuguese officials and Cape Verdeans alike as a necessary outlet.[8] With the decline of whaling and the nineteenth-century advent of steamship travel, wooden schooners were given up or sold by many New England merchants and Cape Verdean entrepreneurs bought several old vessels. In 1892 an important transatlantic packet trade began by which passengers and goods were transported back and forth in Cape Verdean–owned and crewed schooners until well into the second half of this century. Carreira's seminal work was recently augmented by Lobban and Halter's (1988) estimate of 35,000 to 45,000 emigrating between 1820 and 1976 to New England. Halter (1993) added an important dimension to this emigration story by documenting the arrival of *women* as far back as 1863—in fact, "a higher proportion of women and children were arriving in the late 19th century (28.6% for 1860–99) than in the years of mass migration that followed (1900–19, 15.4%)" (p. 46). Carreira (1977) had also posited a significant *retornado* phenomenon, and Halter (1993) suggests that one of three New Bedford–bound passengers between 1900 and 1920 had been to the United States before.

The islands became the independent Republic of Cape Verde as part of the liberation struggle led by Amilcar Cabral. The independence process itself was complicated, involving armed struggle only in Portuguese Guiné but not in the Atlantic islands; an Independence Party (PAIGC, Partido Africano da Independência da Guiné e Cabo Verde) platform that advocated unification between the two new countries of Cape Verde and Guinea-Bissau (pre-independence contradictions forecast its improbability [Pires Houston 1978a]); intense and controversial support-building activites in diaspora communities worldwide; the brilliant and charismatic (in the specifically Weberian sense)[9] leadership of Cabral and his untimely assassination only two years before the formal independence in 1975. The political independence would have a dynamic impact on Cape Verdean–American ethnic development.

Roots of Bilateral Diaspora Ethnicity: Remittances, Associations, and Attitudes

The roots of bilateral diaspora ethnicity can be found in long-standing remittance patterns, gradual politicization of voluntary associations, and transformed attitudes of Cape Verde toward its diaspora population. Its earliest base can be found in the diaspora population's bilateral ties with its original homeland that were never really broken, and the resulting transatlantic community that was always real as well as "imaged/imagined." Regular "cartas" (letters), "mantenhas" (warm greetings), and "bidons" (barrels of food, clothing, supplies) joined transatlantic households in cycles of family sickness, births, deaths, celebrations, and good or bad harvests. Drought and famine pressures propelled Cape Verdeans to seek any available outlet, and the merchant ships in their harbors offered the opportunity for earnings to help support families, delivered either personally or by returning colleagues. In the mid-nineteenth century Cape Verdeans and other concerned Americans had privately sent supplies of corn and other foodstuffs in response to messages of devastation communicated by U.S. officials and returning merchants.

Thus diaspora Cape Verdean remittances—a "person-to-person" strategy documented in anthropological studies of African migration to the cities and of worldwide importance to the economies of developing countries (Aderanti Adepoju, 1974; Georges, 1990; Gmelch, 1992; J. N. Kerry, 1976; Skinner, 1982a; Myron Weiner, 1983)—have a long and continuing heritage. A 1912 German visitor (Immanuel Friedlander, 1975) reported a postman's estimate of approximately $100,000 arriving in the 10,000-person island of Brava. The Agency for International Development (1982) estimated that "official transfers" had gone from 10.2 percent to 18.4 percent from 1972 to 1978, as compared to 8.7 percent to 18.7 percent for "private transfers" during the same period (p. 2). The World Bank (2/10/83) estimated in 1983 that "large emigrant remittances" raised Cape Verde's GNP per capita income from $200 to $300 (p. 1). Remittances often spelled survival but they also spawned visible differentiations such as painting, tiled roofs, shingles on housing—very evident in my 1981 visit, as also seen by Georges in Los Pinos. Remittances had also enabled nineteenth-century Cape Verdeans to buy properties of struggling Portuguese landlords and to become retail traders (Andrade, 1974).

The gradual politicization of voluntary associations also supported the emergence of bilateral diaspora ethnicity. With the earliest recorded in 1916, the New England associations represent the gradual collectivization of individual effort (in New Bedford, Cape Verdean Beneficent Association 1916, Cape Verdean Ultramarine Band Club 1917, Cape Verdean–American Veterans' Association 1946, and Cape Verdean Band Club Auxiliary 1962; Cape Verdean Women's Social Club 1937 [Bridgeport, CT]; Cape Verdean–American Scholarship Committee 1972; Wareham [MA] Cape Verdean Relief Association [for Cape Verde] 1973). The earliest ones were dedicated to survival and flourishing in the new environment and for exchanging original homeland news.

The early associations were organized mostly by persons with leadership abilities, commitment, the ability to galvanize kin, friendship, and local networks, and usually limited formal education. The intervening years between the earliest associations and the 1970s saw the growth in skills, capabilities, and networks galvanized through formal education, professionalization, and deepened experience in and access to political networks. The early leaders were predominantly male and ancestrally connected to the islands of Brava and Fogo. Women, nonetheless, played an important role in organizing and resistance, as exemplified by the remarkable Belmira Nunes Lopes, born here in 1899.[10]

The second- and third-generation cadre of leaders was active in a wider array of fields (including law, secondary and higher education, community development, social work, business, travel, communications, government, and politics) and in locations beyond New England. Especially in the tumultuous pre-independence period, their attitudes forecast a broader politicization. In the spectrum of ideological positions vis-à-vis the Independence Party platform and strategies, many of these younger representatives generally supported or communicated the perspectives of the PAIGC, while those first-generation representatives who did engage in independence-period activities tended to support positions opposing the party, often under the banner of the newly formed Congress (O Congreso) in Support of Total Independence. On both "sides" the early 1970s was a period of gathering, selecting, disseminating, and interpreting/reinterpreting information about Cape Verde and its historical features. This sometimes contributed to divisions and tensions within family and kinship networks, a process cited also by Bousquet (1979).

Two new initiatives signaled diasporic change, as the developing skills and networks were used to obtain official recognition as a *named* ethnic population. The Boston-based Cape Verdean Educators Collaborative, comprised of a core group of Cape Verdean and Cape Verdean–American teachers, guidance counselors, and supporters from Massachusetts and Rhode Island, organized successfully to have "the Cape Verdean *Crioulo* language . . . recognized as a separate classification, thereby adding it to the list of official 'living foreign languages' cited in the Transitional Bilingual Education Act" (Commonwealth of Massachusetts, 7/2/76:1–2), and created Cape Verdean language transitional classes. During the same period, the Cape Verdean Recognition Committee, a subcommittee of the New Bedford Verdean Veterans Association, succeeded in establishing "Cape Verdean" as a recognized ancestry classification in the 1980 Federal Census (U.S. Department of Commerce 3/21/79). Both of these efforts represented *outward* movement, of engaging and lobbying political systems for benefits in the *current* homeland. It was also during this pre-independence period that the younger generation developed the estimated "numbers" (about 250,000) for the Cape Verdean and Cape Verdean–descent United States population.

The *Ernestina* repatriation movement represented a further "bridge" phase toward bilateral diaspora ethnicity. This movement began in the late 1960s and tenuously united two different ethnic and maritime traditions. Both the New England Cape Verdean and Yankee shipbuilding/yacht club/sailing traditions had legitimate interests in the 120-foot historic schooner. Launched in Gloucester in 1894 as the *Effie M. Morrissey*, with an illustrious career that included Grand Banks fishing, Arctic exploration, and World War II reconnaissance missions, and renamed *Ernestina* after being bought by Cape Verdean Henrique Mendes in 1947, the ship made twelve transatlantic voyages carrying passengers and goods to and from Cape Verde and New Bedford or Providence. While struggles between the two groups were taking place, the government of the newly independent Cape Verde agreed that the vessel could participate in the 1976 Tall Ships Parade, the only African ship to do so. Dismasting of the hastily repaired schooner only thirteen miles into the voyage stimulated formation of a National Friends Committee under the auspices of the New York–based National Maritime Historical Society. The six-year repatriation campaign was co-led by the Austrian-descent UN Program Officer for Cape Verde (himself a sailor and member of the New York Yacht Club) and a New York–based/New England–born Cape Verdean–American woman. Aided by local support committees in Wareham and New Bedford, Bridgeport, and Providence, the successful campaign garnered multilevel support: the Cape Verdean government for repairs and restoration of the vessel; Cape Verdean–American and other ethnic organizing, financial support, and volunteer assistance; political support for legislation for an official Massachusetts Commission that would take official title to the vessel; and local municipalities for future berthing and support. In 1982 the schooner returned under sail to the United States. It was an official "gift to the people of the United States" acknowledging the long-standing relations between the two countries and people.[11]

A most compelling force driving the emergence of bilateral diaspora ethnicity was the post-independence transformation within Cape Verde itself, its changing international role and its changing attitude toward its United States diaspora. In earlier diaspora studies, there was little attention paid to the impact of political independence on overseas populations, except for a passing reference by Morton Klass (1960) to the impact of Indian independence on East Indians in Guyana. In the pre-independence early 1970s, a few younger-generation Cape Verdean–Americans and supporters had started to visit the Islands—not only to visit kin but also for more "political" purposes, e.g., to see and/or record the conditions of their ancestral homeland and to communicate these conditions to potential supporters in the New England area. This was perhaps the first public action to influence directly the course of affairs within the islands (there was considerable clandestine diaspora involvement in the independence struggle from exiled Cape Verdeans in European capitals where they were being or had been educated), and of course their purposes had to be seen by the colonial government as nonsubversive. Still the general responses they received from many Cape Verdeans were not unlike the original homeland responses to visiting diaspora representatives cited by Skinner (1982)—from ambivalence to suspicion, although usually mediated by intense cross-cutting kinship ties. It should be noted that Amilcar Cabral was unusual among the independence leaders in the breadth of his travels, which included not only the socialist countries—the backbone of support for the liberation struggle—and Europe but also the United States. Therefore the sometimes reactionary views of the PAIGC carried from 1973 to 1975 in a Cape Verdean–American newspaper became a major source of information about the "americanos."

After the 1975 independence the new republic established its United Nations Mission, embassy in Washington D.C., and consular office in Boston. Between 1975 and 1980, Cape Verdeans and Cape Verdean–Americans in and around these cities reached out to the new representatives. That five-year "acquaintanceship" period was marked by stops and starts and more than one rebuff, but these were met by persistence, regrouping, and organizing, including an American Committee for Cape Verde (TCHUBA,[12] for "rain") and the *Ernestina* campaign.

A turning point in this bilateral relationship was the 1980 coup in Guinea-Bissau, widely believed to have been motivated by the desire to oust Cape Verdean leaders. Although this explanation was more simplistic than a total explanation, the event did galvanize an explicit change in Cape Verde's attitude toward its United States diaspora. The newly appointed and energetic English-speaking ambassador to the United States and the

UN ambassador now reached out to key Cape Verdean–Americans in New England and New York. They conceded the need to reach a "broader spectrum/'bridge-types' . . . in this critical period for Cape Verde" and admitted the inadequacies of their own past overtures. In informal sessions with ideologically mixed groups they acknowledged that some arguments used in the pre-independence phase to support the PAIGC platform (for example, exclusive historical connections with Portuguese Guiné to reinforce the unification goal) were pursued dogmatically but were strategically necessary.

In the immediate post-independence years Cape Verde itself was also broadening its positive public image, cited, for example, for its prudent management of foreign aid and for its trustworthy international role. In 1979 it hosted the first secret meeting between Angola and South Africa (Colm Foy, 11/29/82). In early 1981 the new government organized its first Invitational Conference and Tour, inviting forty Cape Verdean–Americans and Cape Verdeans away since before the independence. The purposes of the tour were to introduce "key communicators" to the new Cape Verde, to show the impact of bilateral aid, and to spread the word about development efforts. The three-week tour included meetings with officials and cultural figures, visits to development projects, and time in ancestral villages. This set the stage for the explicit bilateral diasporic ethnicity phase.

BILATERAL DIASPORA ETHNICITY AT WORK

This new phase was first marked by the formation of a different kind of association, the National Coordinating Council for the Development of Cape Verde (NCCDCV). It was organized in 1981 by the Conference and Tour group at its first conference in New Bedford. Its primary goal was to "plan specific strategies to involve Cape Verdean–Americans as a *group* in a process which can generate economic assistance to the Republic and people of Cape Verde" (Manuel Pires Monteiro, 9/21/81:1). It would not replace but build explicitly upon the population's long tradition of "people-to-people assistance," using educational, political, intellectual, and expanded network assets of the ethnic population matured within the new homeland environment. It would exploit the members' ethnic identification and knowledge now deepened by the trip to the original homeland. It would also exploit their identification as *U.S. citizens*, with the rights and responsibilities of monitoring and influencing policies and workings of their own government.

NCCDCV's resolve was soon put to the test. While preparing for fall 1981 sessions with AID, State Department, and elected officials to advocate for Cape Verde, Council members learned that AID's annual appropriation to the Sahelian countries was in jeopardy. A recent General Accounting Office (GAO) report citing poor management and accountability procedures was being used to justify the proposed cut, projected from 50 to 100 percent. Cape Verde was specifically excepted from this negative assessment; in fact, the newly independent country's procedures were praised and some of its distribution innovations were especially singled out. NCCDCV members made the case for continued assistance to the Sahelian region as a whole, while using their specific knowledge and commitment to Cape Verde as a centerpiece for the argument. By tapping local association networks now augmented by the multistate networks represented by the Conference and Tour group, the Council launched an aggressive mail and telephone advocacy campaign. The final allocation was in fact higher than that of the previous year, attributable partly to the advocacy efforts. The Council's next major campaign involved its role in helping to release administration emergency assistance for repair of homes, inter-island transport ships, and telecommunications facilities destroyed by Hurricane Beryl in August 1982, only days after the *Ernestina* arrived in Newport after a sometimes harrowing 41-day return voyage under sail. In 1983 the Council network helped organize parts of President Aristides Pereira's first visit to the United States, including visits with local and regional political leaders.

In 1985 Congressman Mervyn Dymally observed that "foreign ethnics don't understand the importance of lobbying" (Paul Findley, 1985:77). Dymally's was not an unusual observation in the halls of Washington. Elected officials and their staffs often expressed surprise at the Council delegation, not only that *African* development was being advocated by African-Americans but also that the focus was other than the "more sexy" South African situation. They cited also the value of the specific and named (village, project, etc.) information and issues connected to specific homeland conditions.[13]

Through the NCCDCV and its activities, Cape Verdean–Americans were therefore making a different kind of statement about their possibilities as an ethnic population in the United States: "We have been here a long time, this 'current actual homeland' is where we live, move and have our being; we also believe that our 'original homeland' deserves access to the resources shared around the world by [the U.S.] and we want to exercise our rights and responsibilities as citizens to ensure that this happens." This maturation and enhanced political sophistication were being mirrored in the 1975 to early 1980s post-independence years by similar transformations in Cape Verde itself. The new government's decision to host the Cape Verdean–Americans on the official Conference and Tour and to structure not only official and cultural meetings but also "family/kin" time in homeland villages represented its growing understanding of the political and economic importance of its diaspora. Ambivalences about the "americanos" still persisted,[14] but in the 1981 encounter visitors heard the explicit beginnings of a reconceptualization of a definition of Cabo

Verde: "*Nos tudos é Caboverdeanos*—We're all Cape Verdeans". The transformation was most eloquently reflected in the changing commentary by
the first president of the new republic, Aristides Pereira, who had been
Cabral's most trusted lieutenant. As secretary-general of the PAIGC
Pereira had distanced himself and his about-to-become-independent country from the New England diaspora: "It has been claimed that there are as
many Cape Verdeans in the United States . . . as . . . in Cape Verde. [He]
pointed out to the Mission, however, that the figure includes large numbers of people with a Cape Verdean background who were not born in Cape
Verde" (UNGA 1975:10). His message was different on his first visit in
1983 (*Voz Di Povo*):

> I was immensely impressed . . . to see a community that is
> not only large but also very old. . . . We must pay attention to
> this phenomenon. . . . There actually exists already a number of
> Cape Verdean–Americans who are integrated into American politi-
> cal-administrative life and who will have some influence . . . a com-
> munity which is . . . well-regarded, because our fellow countrymen
> have always shown themselves to be serious workers and citizens.
> (pp. 2–3)

Six years later, the government would also invite visitors to inaugurate the
Boston–Cape Verde flights following the imposition of the South African
sanctions. This time the invitees would include non–Cape Verdean as well
as Cape Verdean–descent "key communicators"—especially travel, media,
and business representatives—and the broader goal would be to encourage
diaspora *and* other private investment and business involvement.

In 1992 the newly elected prime minister of Jamaica would proclaim
a similar reconceptualization (and new investment incentives) at his first
meeting with New York Jamaicans: "Jamaica is a 'country without borders.' We have 5 million citizens, 2.5 million inside our borders and the
rest in this country and abroad. If Jews can build a Jerusalem in the des-
ert, then Jamaicans can build rock at home." Nehru had apparently undergone a similar transformation: after India's independence he had urged diaspora loyalties to the new homelands, but economic pressures led him to
urge remittances and incentives for original homeland investment (Arthur
W. Helweg, 1983).

The emergence of the bilateral diaspora ethnicity phase in Cape
Verdean–American ethnic development represents, then, a political maturation of the Cape Verdean–American population. Could a similar use
and impact of ethnicity be seen at the local, domestic level? Other research (Laura Pires-Hester, 1994) on the comparative use of ethnicity
within a southeastern New England locality showed a mixed picture. Electoral campaigns did not use explicitly ethnic themes, campaigns that

might be called "social action" were limited or nonexistent, and there was a consistent impression (both internal and external to the Cape Verdean–descent population) that the population's potential political power was unfulfilled. However, contrary to a widely held perception, historical analysis also showed significant Cape Verdean–American participation in the locality's electoral races. From 1960 to 1981 their candidates were elected in ten of eighteen races in which they had run and in these eighteen races they were among the top four vote-getters for the Board of Selectmen, Assessors, and School Committee. Precinct data also showed support across ethnic boundaries. Members had traditionally participated in voluntary association activities, some of which had engaged non–Cape Verdean support: for scholarship, Cape Verdean relief, or *Ernestina* berthing or financial support purposes. The population's use of ethnicity was more latent—even while the *locality's* use of ethnic "counting" of the population grew more explicit as it sought to position itself for first-time community development funding. The ethnic population's "maturity" was thus represented in different ways at the locality and bilateral levels.

LOOKING AHEAD

In the 1980s the role of modern diasporas in international politics was so untouched that it was declared "a new field of study" by political scientist Gabriel Sheffer (1983), and Cynthia Enloe (1981) stressed that it defied traditional thinking by challenging the primacy of the nation-state as the only vehicle for international action and development. Increasingly complex communications and transportation networks have made even more possible not only the *imaging* but also the *actualizing* of communities that cross physical, psychological, and intellectual boundaries. The created "global ethnoscapes" (Arjun Appadurai, 1991) reach well beyond territorial units. Within this changing world context, resource competition sharpens. Indeed what gets defined as assets or resources in the international arena may also shift. Strategic use of the ethnicity resource may be a way of leveling the playing field for those populations which were previously absent from the field. The emergence of bilateral diaspora ethnicity among Cape Verdean–Americans suggests the possibility of utilizing this asset to improve positions where people are *actually* and where they are *ancestrally*. Occurring within a population with features ordinarily regarded as disadvantageous in the United States context (color, immigration status, small size), the example also demonstrates how ethnic populations strive to maintain multiple identities around a central core, develop new and different forms of "community" in increasingly fragmented and complex societies, and live simultaneously in different kinds of communities. It does not offer easy solutions to issues of access, whether domestically or in the overseas homeland. What it does do is suggest the existential *reality* of ethnicity, its human meaning and significance, and the diverse ways this reality manifests itself in different contexts.

On New Year's Eve 1973, just before his assassination by the Portuguese, Amilcar Cabral offered a prophetic message to his compatriots, who would soon be faced by challenges even greater than the winning of political independence itself: "I draw the attention of comrades to the diversity of new questions we have to study and solve in the appropriate way" (1979:293). On the eve of a new century, our own "new questions" challenge us as well.

NOTES

1. These accounts show a "selection" of features that become part of the "legends" (Robert Dentler, 1982:ix) or definitional stances. Also noted by Cabral, this selection process was quite evident in the Cape Verdean pre-independence debates (Laura Pires Houston, 1978, 1978a).

2. This history of silence is not confined to academics or to the U.S. António Salazar had never visited the islands, as António de Barros observed in 1961: "de todas as partes de nosso Ultramar, Cabo Verde é a menos conhecida e a menos visitada [of all the parts of our overseas possessions, Cabo Verde is the least known and the least visited]" (source unknown). A most insightful Cape Verdean *participant*-observer, Basil Davidson, also cited this gap: "On journeys up and down the world I have heard it said that these islands . . . came up out of the sea in the famous year of 1975 (Independence). . . . If such islands really existed . . . (they) say, then people would have heard of them" (1989:39). On the other hand, Charles Darwin identified the island of Santiago as a place where he had first examined rocks (Marston Bates and Philip S. Humphrey, 1956); historian T. Bentley Duncan observed that from 1830 to 1920 much literature had described the islands (1972:237); and Boasian Elsie Clews Parsons (1923) had collected Cape Verdean folk tales in New England.

3. In 1952 Portugal renamed its colonies "overseas possessions" (David M. Abshire and Michael A. Samuels, 1969) to forestall decolonization. Although ultimately unsuccessful the strategy was a very good example of Benedict Anderson's "imagined communities" (1983).

4. António Carreira (1977, 1982), Cape Verdean historian whose immigration research is widely used (sometimes unattributed), asserted that Cape Verdean crewmen probably started joining American whalers at least by the late seventeenth to early eighteenth centuries. I am also indebted to the late Robert Packard of Wareham, MA for the reference to a Cape Verdean crewman on a Wareham whaler in 1788 (Frederick W. Hower, 1941).

5. In 1977 Cape Verde's new Foreign Minister reportedly responded to a Portuguese diplomat's account of the islands' "discovery" with: "I didn't know we were ever lost."

6. Basil Davidson (1989) found recently accessible 1940 archival rec-

ords of pleas from Juvenal Cabral (Amilcar's father) for "water conservation, intensive planting of trees, reforms of land tenure and taxation, and the immediate funding of agrarian credit" (p. 59). Poet Jorge Barbosa's poignant words signaled the literary outpouring that strove to communicate the colonial conditions to an unknowing world (Norman Araujo, 1966; Manuel Ferreira, 1975).

7. Norman Araujo expressed his surprise at the literary richness in the "poor and rain-forsaken land" (1966:x)—a common reaction of Cape Verdean–Americans, who have grown up with the orally transmitted tales of "miséria" and struggle and knowing objectively the smallness of the islands. Although many of the key figures in this tradition were regarded as "pro-European" by the independence leaders, their contribution as a "cultural precursor" to independence was finally acknowledged ten years after the independence (Instituto Caboverdiano Do Livro, 1986).

8. The best-known Cape Verdean composer, Eugénio Tavares, reportedly stated in official debate in 1918 that "stopping Cape Verdean emigration to the United States . . . would be like a law obliging us to fold our arms while our wives and children were dying of famine" (Carreira, 1982:63).

9. Max Weber (1947) reserved "charisma" for those "set apart from ordinary men and women and treated as endowed with supernatural, superhuman qualities. . . . what is alone important is how the individual is actually regarded by those subject to charismatic authority, by his 'followers' or 'disciples'" (p. 359). Cabral was called by his most trusted disciple, Aristides Pereira, "the architect of our building, the strategist of our military successes, the diplomatist of our initiatives in the international field, and finally the leader who by his intelligence and by his generosity had shaped the singular character of the war in Guinea-Bissau" (Mário de Andrade, 1979:xxxv). Others remember Cabral as a man who "could see into the future," "had revolution in his heart," and was a "brilliant poet and student" (Gil Fernandes [4/2/77], first UN Ambassador from Guinea-Bissau, and boyhood friends Helder Ferreira [3/18/77] and Jorge Pedro Barbosa [4/7/77]).

10. Linguist Maria Louise Nunes (1982) collaborated with her aunt on Lopes's extraordinary autobiography, as well as recording other family accomplishments such as that of Judge George Leighton of Chicago.

11. Pires Houston and Platzer, 1982; The Courier (9/3/82); The Providence Sunday Journal (9/12/82); The Standard Times (8/31/82); Voz Di Povo (7/23/82).

12. TCHUBA was organized by Raymond Almeida, who had begun his visits before 1975 and has made over fifty trips since that time. The committee was comprised of Cape Verdeans and others, focussed on education and support-building for the new country, and published a monthly newsletter with news of both homelands. Almeida was also named the embassy's first public relations officer in 1980 and organized the 1981 tour.

13. Tour members also shared this information with others, with one person making over thirty-two slide presentations to mixed audiences in the northeast. Older Cape Verdeans were moved by views of their home-

land villages. Those removed generationally from the oral transmission of stories by grandparents and from the regular letters or new arrivals linking transatlantic households were not surprised at the poverty but were surprised at the absence of starving children in the streets—even to see streets. Across ethnic lines, there was general surprise at seeing avenues and housing in the main cities, the uniformed schoolchildren, and the wide phenotypic range.

14. On the 1981 tour some members had often distressing conversations with host officials about their continuing attitudes about the "American crazies," whom leaders judged as misunderstanding the "socialist/communist" leanings of the PAIGCV, or as "wanting to be European," or not supporting independence at all. Some privately insisted to their hosts that a new bilateral relationship required more Cape Verdean openness and had to be a two-way street.

REFERENCES

"A Day to Celebrate." *The Courier* (9/3/82):1.

Abshire, David M. and Michael A. Samuels. *Portuguese Africa: A Handbook.* London: Pall Mall Press, 1969.

Adepoju, Aderanti. "Migration and Socio-Economic Links Between Urban Migrants and Their Home Communities in Nigeria." *Africa* 44 (1974):383–396.

Agency for International Development. *Annual Report on Cape Verde* (1983):30–39.

Anderson, Benedict. *Imagined Communities: Reflections on the Origin and Spread of Nationalism.* London and New York: Verso, 1983.

Andrade, Elisa. *The Cape Verde Islands: From Slavery to Modern Times.* Dakar: United Nations African Institute for Economic Development and Planning, 1974.

Appadurai, Arjun. "Global Ethnoscapes: Notes and Queries for a Transnational Anthropology." In *Recapturing Anthropology: Working in the Present.* Edited by Richard G. Fox. Santa Fe, NM: School of American Research Press, 1991, pp. 191–210.

Araujo, Norman. *A Study of Cape Verdean Literature.* Boston: Boston College, 1966.

Barbosa, Jorge Pedro. Interview, 3/18/77.

Barker, Harold E. "It took much more than a crew to bring Ernestina to America." *The Providence Sunday Journal* (9/12/82):C10.

Bates, Marston and Philip S. Humphrey, eds. *The Darwin Reader.* New York: Charles Scribner's Sons, 1956.

Bousquet, Gisèle L. *Behind the Bamboo Hedge: The Impact of Homeland Politics in the Parisian Vietnamese Community.* Ann Arbor: The University of Michigan Press, 1979.

Cabral, Amilcar. *Return to the Source: Selected Speeches of Amilcar Cabral.* New York and London: Monthly Review Press with Africa Information Service, 1973.

Calvoressi, P. *International Politics since 1945*. New York: F. A. Praeger Publishers, 1968.

Carreira, António. *Migrações nas Ilhas de Cabo Verde*. Lisboa: Universida de Nova de Lisboa, 1977.

——. *The People of the Cape Verde Islands: Exploitation and Emigration*. Translated from the Portuguese and edited by Christopher Fyfe. London: C. Hurst and Company and Hamden, CT: Archon Books, 1982.

Cohn, Michael and Michael K. H. Platzer. *Black Men of the Sea*. New York: Dodd, Mead and Company, 1978.

Commonwealth of Massachusetts. "Memo from Gregory R. Anrig to Superintendent of Schools and Program Directors" (7/2/76):1–2.

Davidson, Basil. *The Fortunate Isles: A Study in African Transformation*. London: Hutchinson, 1989.

De Andrade, Mário. "Biographical Notes." *Unity and Struggle: Speeches and Writings of Amilcar Cabral*. New York and London: Monthly Review Press, 1979, pp. xviii–xxxv.

Dentler, Robert. "Foreword." In *Cuban Americans: Masters of Survival*, by José Llanes. Cambridge, MA: ABT Books, 1982, pp. ix–xii.

Department of Commerce. "Letter from Meyer Zitter, Chief Population Division/Bureau of the Census to Manuel Lopes, Chairman, Cape Verdean Recognition Committee" (3/21/79):1–2.

Duncan, T. Bentley. *Atlantic Islands: Madeira, the Azores, and the Cape Verde Islands in Seventeenth-Century Commerce and Navigation*. Chicago: University of Chicago Press, 1972.

Enloe, Cynthia. "Foreword." In *Ethnic Identities in a Transnational World*. Edited by John F. Stack. Westport, CT: Greenwood Press, 1981.

"Ernestina regressa aos Estados-Unidos: President Reagan envia mensagem á Aristides Pereira." *Voz Di Povo* (7/23/82):1,8.

Fernandes, Gil. Interview, 4/7/77.

Ferreira, Helder. Interview, 4/7/77.

Ferreira, Manuel. *No Reino De Caliban: Antologia Panorâmica de Poesia Africana de Expressão Portuguesa*. Lisbon: Seara Nova, 1975.

Findley, Paul. *They Dare to Speak Out*. Westport, CT: Lawrence Hill and Company, 1985.

Foy, Colm. "Cape Verde in the Role of Honest Broker." *West Africa* (11/29/82):324–325.

Friedlander, Immanuel. "Observations on the Cape Verde Islands: The Results of an Educational Trip in the Summer of 1912." Translated by Birgit Herbert and Michael K. H. Platzer, 1975, pp. 1–10.

Georges, Eugenia. *The Making of a Transnational Community: Migration, Development, and Cultural Change in the Dominican Republic*. New York: Columbia Unviersity Press, 1990.

Gmelch, George. *Double Passage: The Lives of Caribbean Migrants Abroad and Back Home*. Ann Arbor: The University of Michigan Press, 1992.

Greenfield, Sidney. "The Cape Verde Islands: Their Settlement, the Emergence of Their Creole Culture, and the Subsequent Migrations of Their People." Unpublished manuscript, 1980s.

Halter, Marilyn. *Between Race and Ethnicity: Cape Verdean American Immigrants, 1860–1965*. Urbana and Chicago: University of Illinois Press, 1993.

Helweg, Arthur W. "The Indian Diaspora: Influence on International Relations." In *Modern Diasporas in International Politics*. Edited by Gabriel Sheffer. London: Croom Helm, 1983, pp. 47–74.

Hower, Frederick W., ed. *Voyages of the Columbia*. Boston: The Wareham Historical Society, 1941.

"In Our View: Ernestina has returned as a monument to perseverance." *The Standard Times* (8/31/82):6.

Institute for Overseas Research. *Seroantropologia das Ilhas de Cabo Verde*. Lisbon, 1970.

Instituto Caboverdiano De. Livro. *Claridade: Revista de Arte e Letras*. 1986.

Kerry, J. N. "Studying Voluntary Associations as Adaptive Mechanisms: A Review of Anthropological Perspectives." *Cultural Anthropology* 17 (1976):23–47.

Klass, Morton. "East and West Indians: Cultural Complexity in Trinidad." *Annals of New York Academy of Sciences* 83 (1960):855–861.

Llanes, José. *Cuban Americans: Masters of Survival*. Cambridge, MA: ABT Books, 1982.

Lobban, Richard and Marilyn B. Halter. *Historical Dictionary of the Republic of Cape Verde*. Metuchen, NJ and London: The Scarecrow Press, 1988.

Monteiro, Manuel Pires. "Opening Remarks." National Coordinating Committee Conference for Development of Cape Verde, New Bedford, MA (9/12/81):1–6.

Nunes, Maria Louise. *A Portuguese Colonial in America: Belmira Nunes Lopes, The Autobiography of a Cape Verdean–American*. Pittsburgh, PA: Latin American Literary Review Press, 1982.

Parsons, Elsie Clews. *Folklore from the Cape Verde Islands*. Cambridge and New York: The American Folk-Lore Society, 1923.

Pires-Hester, Laura. "A Study of Cape Verdean–American Ethnic Development: The Emergence of Bilateral Diaspora Ethnicity and Its Impact in a Southeastern New England Locality." Unpublished dissertation, 1994.

Pires Houston, Laura. "Cape Verdeans in the United States: Continuing a Story of Struggle, Creativity, and Persistence." Cape Verdean–American Scholarship Committee, 1978, pp. 1–28.

———. "Unification of Cape Verde and Guinea-Bissau." Unpublished manuscript, 1978a, pp. 1–40.

Pires Houston, Laura and Michael K. H. Platzer. *Ernestina/Effie M. Morrissey Commemorative Journal*. National Friends of the Ernestina/Morrissey, 1982.

Rodney, Walter. *How Europe Underdeveloped Africa*. Washington, D.C.: Howard University Press, 1974.

Sheffer, Gabriel. *Modern Diasporas in International Politics*. London: Croom Helm, 1983.

Skinner, Elliott P. "The Dialectic between Diasporas and Homelands." In *Global Dimensions of the African Diaspora.* Edited by Joseph E. Harris. Washington, D.C.: Howard University Press, 1982, pp. 17–45.

———. "Voluntary Associations and Ethnic Competition in Oagadougou." *Ethnicity in Modern Africa.* Edited by Brian du Toit. Boulder, CO: Westview Press, 1982a.

———. *African Americans and U.S. Policy Toward Africa 1850–1924: In Defense of Black Nationality* (Washington, D.C.: Howard University Press, 1992).

United Nations General Assembly. "Report of Visiting Mission to Cape Verde Islands." UNGA Document A/AC.109/PV995. Reprinted in *Objective: Justice* (April–June 1975):3–10.

Weber, Max. *The Theory of Social and Economic Organization.* New York and London: The Free Press and Collier MacMillan Publishers, 1947.

Weiner, Myron. "Labor Migrations as Incipient Diasporas." *Modern Diasporas in International Politics.* Edited by Gabriel Sheffer. London: Croom Helm, 1983, pp. 47–74.

World Bank News. "IDA approves first credit to Cape Verde" (2/10/83):1.

31 BLACK AMERICANS AND THE CREATION OF AMERICA'S AFRICA POLICIES: THE DE-RACIALIZATION OF PAN-AFRICAN POLITICS

Alvin B. Tillery, Jr.

S cholars have traditionally taken for granted that instances of cooperation between Africans and their descendants in the diaspora are based on similar views of race and racial obligation. This essay takes issue with this view. It argues that in the post-independence, post–civil rights, post–Cold War era, the potential for transnational interactions to arise from a multitude of circumstances other than race consciousness is great. And the potential for these interactions to be confounded by the pursuit of interests derived from other factors is just as great. These other factors include: (1) political economy—meaning that actors may not always view Pan-Africanism as the most efficient way to obtain political and economic ends; and (2) the rise of cultural nationalism—the tendency of actors to stress political and cultural differences. Implicit in this argument is that, even when actors cite racial ideology as the driving force in establishing a transnational interaction, the above two factors impact the way in which these ideologies are formed and acted upon. This essay examines transnational interactions in the creation of America's Africa policies.

HISTORICAL OVERVIEW OF TRANSNATIONAL RELATIONS

There is a rich tradition of cooperation between black groups in the development of America's foreign policies toward Africa.[1] Even before attaining full franchise rights in their own nation, African-American leaders stressed the importance of building an active lobby for African interests.[2] The Council on African Affairs and the National Association for the Advancement of Colored People were the first groups to develop strategies to impact America's foreign policies.

The CAA, founded in 1937, "was the first organization established for the express purpose of influencing American foreign policies toward Africa, and as such is considered the first African-American foreign policy lobby."[3] The organization spent the majority of its time directing letter-writing campaigns and contacting government officials. The group also had strong ties to the only African-American in Congress, Adam Clayton Powell, and tried to use him for access to governmental authority.[4] Given its founder Max Yergan's experiences as a missionary in South Africa, the major thrust of CAA activities was lobbying the federal government to take action against that racist regime.[5] The NAACP joined in many of these efforts during the late 1930s and 1940s. The organization was instrumental in targeting multilateral policy initiatives adopted by the government. The high point of NAACP involvement in African affairs was their campaign for African independence and the alleviation of worldwide racism among American representatives to the 1945 San Francisco Conference tasked with drafting the United Nations Charter.[6]

Although important milestones, the efforts of these groups were largely unsuccessful. One scholar describes their tepid impact, writing that "[d]espite the fact that [officials like Assistant Secretary of State for African Affairs] Stettinius responded to the activities of the CAA on occasion, neither the CAA nor the NAACP exerted influence on the decisions of US Foreign policy-makers" (Leanne 1994, 170). Early black American attempts to lobby for Africa fell largely on deaf ears for several reasons. First is the general weakness of the African-American leadership class in this period. Although members of government, from the lowest level bureaucrat to President Truman, often corresponded with and allowed these lobbyists to present their views, the CAA and NAACP were in no position to broker the kinds of political trade-offs that generally impact the creation of foreign policy. Thus, government officials offered mere lip-service to these groups without the threat of paying political costs for inactivity around their causes.

Around 1947, the rise of the Cold War and the perceived close association that the leaders of these organizations maintained with communist sympathizers began to significantly weaken the little access these groups had to governmental authority.[7] The government took it upon itself to silence these organizations because of their supposed communist threat.[8] These efforts crushed the CAA, and forced the NAACP to shift gears to maintain domestic credibility with its constituents.

The "black power" decades of the 1950s and 1960s witnessed the growth of African-American political clout on two important levels. First and foremost, scores of black voters entered the voter registration rolls in this period. Secondly, as a result of increased black voting strength, the ranks of black elected officials swelled on all levels.[9] These developments placed diaspora activists in a wholly new position; for the first time they had the political capital to exercise real influence over policy decisions.

Recognizing the dawn of this new era, they sought ways to return to the task of representing Africa's interests. The founding of the Congressional Black Caucus and TransAfrica in the 1970s represent the culmination of these efforts.

The primary goal of the Congressional Black Caucus is to ensure that black interests are well represented on the domestic level. However, just like the NAACP before it, the CBC actively engages in foreign policy issues that impact African and other majority black states. Raymond Copson, a specialist in international relations at the Congressional Research Service of the Library of Congress, writes:

> The Congressional Black Caucus (CBC), widely known for its domestic policy impact, has also been active on foreign policy issues since its founding in 1971. Electoral politics did not force this active role on the CBC, since for Caucus members—as for most other members of Congress—foreign policy has typically not been a critical issue in the elections they have faced. Yet, Caucus members have repeatedly taken firm positions on foreign policy issues, led discussions and debates on foreign policy topics in Congress and sought to inform and engage the wider black American community, and others as well, on a variety of foreign affairs subjects. During the 1970s, these subjects mostly related to Africa, particularly southern Africa.[10]

For years after the founding of the CBC, many members, particularly Congressman Charles Diggs, felt that the organization's foreign policy activities should be supplemented by a full time African-American lobby representing the interests of blacks in other parts of the world (Copson 1996, 11). This desire was formalized at the CBC's African-American Leadership Conference in 1976 with the founding of TransAfrica.[11] TransAfrica emerged as one of the leading advocacy groups for African and Caribbean interests in the world; the organization has joined the CBC in a number of policy initiatives, and has served as a constant source of informational and technical support (Copson, 11).

Although CBC and TransAfrica campaigns focus on issues similar to those pursued by their predecessors, their tactics are significantly different. The primary difference is that, unlike CAA and NAACP lobbying, their efforts are led mostly from within government. In 1971, the CBC was comprised of twelve members; the membership stood at forty in 1996. Both are a far cry from the one African-American member of Congress at the disposal of the CAA and NAACP in the 1940s and 1950s. As the numbers of African-American members increased they continued to pool their resources in order to have the greatest impact on policy. The enhanced position of these leaders in domestic politics has had a profound impact on their ability to represent Africa's interests inside the Beltway.

They are not easily dismissed by other members of Congress, executive agencies, or the president. Again, African-American agitation against the racist regime in South Africa stands as the most instructive case when seeking to gauge their effectiveness.

Members of the CBC began to hold hearings, introducing anti-Apartheid legislation as early as 1971. These early measures had little impact on the actual course of American policy toward South Africa for several reasons. Leanne points out in her work the fact that the majority of CBC members were not seasoned veterans, and that this inexperience yielded poor results as the CBC continually endorsed too broad a range of approaches (292). For example, the CBC endorsed seventy-two distinct actions from a 1972 conference on Africa (Leanne, 291). This frenzy of activity in the early years distracted members and left the CBC unprepared for the political wrangling of more seasoned legislators, like Senator Robert F. Byrd of West Virginia, who forced through legislation counter to their interests.[12]

Racism also played a role in their early lack of effectiveness. It is no secret that President Nixon was openly hostile to many interests of the African-American community, and his political agenda sought to dismantle most of Johnson's "Great Society" programs.[13] These attitudes manifested themselves in the way that he dealt politically with the CBC; Nixon continually refused to meet with them to hear their concerns about his agenda.[14] Racism was not limited to the executive branch of government. Members of the CBC also faced subtle and sometimes overt racism on Capitol Hill. Nadine Cohodas describes early CBC reception on the hill as follows: "They came to Congress as the ultimate outsiders, a sprinkling of black faces in a sea of white."[15] Other legislators often doubted the credentials of African-American congresspersons and placed challenges to their authority on substantive issues. A black political analyst characterizes this early period: "Blacks regularly ha[d] to establish fundamental credentials that would for the most part never be required of white members. . . . The first line of inquiry that any black member encounters is whether he can cut it on the issues of substance" (Cohadas, 677).

It is ironic that what separates the level of influence enjoyed by the latter groups—namely, government access or institutional clout—was achieved prima facie through extra-institutional means. The Caucus gained greater access to the Nixon administration by manipulating public opinion through the news media (Leanne, 287). The most conspicuous example of this strategy was the CBC boycott of Nixon's 1971 State of the Union address, forcing him to finally meet with the group to hear their concerns (Poinsett 289). Although Nixon continued his short-sighted and implicitly racist policies in South Africa, this major coup shaped the way future American presidents would deal with the CBC. For example, President Ford convened the group at the White House three days after assuming office.[16] This gesture had a moderating effect on politics on the Hill, and during the remainder of his term, "tensions eased between the Republican leadership and Caucus" (Leanne, 287).

As members reached political maturity as legislators, the CBC narrowed its objectives and focused on pragmatic legislative strategies for influencing policy (Copson, 10–11). The introduction of bills, resolutions, and alternative budget proposals advocating for Africa were the centerpieces of this strategy. This strategy, coupled with more experience and seniority, gave members increased credibility and coalition-building potential in the Congress (Cohodas, 675). The need to build and maintain coalitions was stressed in Copson's work. He describes Caucus activities as follows:

> Congressional Black Caucus activities in the foreign affairs
> field have generally been marked by considerable pragmatism and
> moderation, as well as persistence in pursuit of some issues over
> many years. This style of operation reflects the Caucus' need to
> build and maintain coalitions if it is to have any hope of achieving
> its objectives. Extreme language, inflexibility and an unwillingness
> to compromise, and hasty or ill-prepared legislative proposals would
> only have driven away potential allies, dooming progress for success. (Copson, 12)

By the mid-1970s, the CBC was successfully articulating its position on Southern Africa to other legislators and executive agencies by bringing a barrage of alternative measures to the House floor. Although the vast majority of these measures died, they succeeded in educating other members about the plight of black Southern Africans and the complicity of our government in allowing these racist systems to flourish unchecked.[17]

In the 1980s, the CBC and TransAfrica began to combine an intensified legislative agenda with protest politics.[18] By the middle of the decade, TransAfrica had earned the respect of the public and members of government and was viewed as the "principal organization spearheading the drive for comprehensive, mandatory sanctions against South Africa."[19] Together, they continued to win support for the sanctions movement from notables within and outside of government. This became increasingly apparent, in the period of activism between 1986 and Mandela's release, when votes on anti-Apartheid legislation neared passage in both chambers (Pressman, 1384–5) and prominent white members joined Robinson and CBC members in popular protests at the South African embassy in DC.[20]

In late 1985 and 1986, the CBC and TransAfrica began to reap the benefits of more than fifteen years of hard work to make sanctions a reality. Against the hostile backdrop of the Reagan administration and a Republican-controlled Senate, House Democrats began passing measures barring U.S. bank loans to the South African government, prohibiting new U.S. investments, and ending the importation of South African gold coins.[21] The tide had completely turned by June of 1985, when the Republican-controlled Senate Foreign Relations Committee imposed immediate economic sanctions against South Africa, putting the Reagan administration under extreme pressure to redirect policy. Although the Reagan administration vetoed the sanctions legislation, the movement was not to be denied, as the Congress voted overwhelmingly to override.[22]

The culmination of this ten-year effort placed considerable pressure on South Africa to move toward multiracial democracy. The CBC and TransAfrica continued to agitate on behalf of black South Africans, pressing the United States to support democratic reforms right up to the ascension of Nelson Mandela to the presidency. Their success in influencing government policies far exceeded that of their predecessors. As insiders they possessed the skills and resources to reshape policies. They proved that they could not be dismissed or diverted from the goal of representing Africa's interests. Although the sanctions movement is the most visible effort on behalf of Africans by the two organizations, it should be noted that these groups have been the major advocates influencing Africa policy on all levels (Copson, 17–30).

DEFINING PAN-AFRICANISM

Following Ali Mazrui, this work holds that many types of Pan-Africanism have existed throughout history. He claims that there are five dimensions of Pan-Africanism: trans-Atlantic, continental, trans-Saharan, sub-Saharan, and global.[23] This study is obviously about "trans-Atlantic Pan-Africanism," as transnational interactions between black American and African leaders are the focus of inquiry.

Although this diversity of Pan-African movements exists, there are shared elements between these forms. Exploring these commonalties will contribute to our understanding of the interactions we are interested in and lead to greater precision in providing a definition for the concept. P. O. Esedebe argues that there are "major component ideas" present in almost every variation of Pan-African ideology.[24] Describing these common elements, he states that "with some simplification we can say that Pan-Africanism is a political and cultural phenomenon which regards Africa, Africans and African descendants abroad as a unit" (Esedebe 1982, 3). He continues: "[Pan-Africanism] seeks to regenerate and unify Africa and promote a feeling of oneness among the people of the African world" (Esedebe, 3). Thus, from Esedebe, we get the point that Pan-African movements typically use African heritage to relay political and cultural symbols aimed at building bonds between disparate groups.

According to scholars like Colin Legum and Adekunle Ajala, Pan-

African ideologies and movements grew out of the need for a systematic response to European racist movements in world history. Says Legum:

> The emotional impetus for its [Pan-Africanism's] concepts flowered from the experiences of a widely dispersed people—those of African stock—who felt themselves either physically through dispossession or slavery, or socially, economically, politically and mentally through colonialism, to have lost their homeland; with this loss of independence, freedom and dignity. Dignity: that majestic magical word in the vocabulary of Pan-Africanists; to regain dignity is the mainspring of all their actions.[25]

Ajala extends this:

> The common experience of discrimination based on skin colour, and flagrant injustices and degradation, combined to make people of African descent . . . realize that they faced the same problems and must therefore unite in order to find a solution. This realization led to an awareness of their common heritage and to a desire for some link with their African origins. Out of this grew the ideals of Pan-Africanism.[26]

Thus, Legum and Ajala suggest that Pan-African movements arose in response to white racism. This fact gave race a central role in the production of Pan-African ideologies, as intellectuals and political leaders in the black world countered white racism, using notions of racial pride and unity centered on Africa and its development. Drawing these strains together, we may define Pan-Africanism as: *a trans-Atlantic movement seeking to promote the development and well-being of peoples of African heritage in the diaspora and on the continent through transnational political cooperation.* Furthermore, this movement often seeks to use race to bridge the disparate linguistic, religious, and cultural traditions of these black groups.

MOTIVATIONS

This section seeks to: (1) begin modeling the behavior of African-Americans when acting in the interest of Africa; and (2) explain the intersection between shifts in Pan-Africanism's intellectual and ideological trajectories and the factors impacting the decisions of black Americans to serve as advocates for Africa. The efforts of the CAA and NAACP were largely a response to white racism and oppression. The CAA and NAACP activists viewed the African-American and African freedom struggles as inextricably linked.[27] Leanne describes the tendency of these organizations to link the domestic civil rights and anti-colonial movements: "The CAA drew occasional parallels between the situation of African-Americans and the situation of black Africans, for instance, referring to both groups as 'Negroes,' and calling racial discrimination in each country 'Jim Crow' practices" (117). The rationale behind this belief was the hope that black freedom attained on one side of the Atlantic would accelerate the freedom movement on the other. Thus, the view that African-Americans and Africans were united in struggle against white supremacy and racism on an international scale best characterizes the nature of Pan-Africanism as practiced by the CAA, NAACP, and their African contacts. It was this sentiment that made the racist regime of South Africa the most likely point of attack.

The lobbying efforts of the Congressional Black Caucus and Trans-Africa are also motivated, at least in part, by the idea that black people around the world are somehow connected by race: "Many Caucus Members have also felt that their experiences as African-Americans created a bond with—and a responsibility toward—Africans in Africa itself and the Caribbean. Representative William Gray argued in 1981 that 'as blacks, we share many common heritages, struggles, and concerns [with Africans]'" (Copson, 5). Representative Walter Fauntroy, the District of Columbia's delegate, made similar statements while he was CBC Chairman. Although he was addressing a group of lobbyists from Caribbean nations, the racial rhetoric of his speech is easily extended to the African context: "Black Americans and people from the island nations of the Caribbean are brothers and sisters caught in an involuntary African Diaspora. . . . We are cousins in the African family. . . . [W]e here in North America are a valuable constituency for Black people wherever they may be" (Copson, 5).

At first glance it would seem that the motivations of African-American lobbyists run parallel in both eras. However, a very subtle difference in the rhetoric of the two periods indicates that the motivations of the contemporary groups has shifted, ushering in a new era in the history of Pan-Africanism. This study has stressed that the enhanced success of contemporary lobbying efforts results from the fact that these groups are now working from positions of institutional clout with enhanced access to governmental authority. Therefore, unlike the CAA and the NAACP, these groups do not readily equate their objective material and political condition as African-Americans to that of Africans. Contemporary black advocates for Africa have tended to narrow their focus and differentiate between the sources of domestic misery for blacks and the problems plaguing their African cousins.

Their tendency to differentiate between African and black American political problems results from a series of factors, including (1) shifts in Pan-African ideology; (2) the closeness of black American leaders to centers of government power; and (3) the demise of colonialism in Africa. Although these factors are listed separately, it should be noted that they are closely related and often intertwined.

This essay's definition of Pan-Africanism suggests that race is often used to bridge gaps in the objective realities among disparate groups. More specifically, race has often had a dual meaning in Pan-African theory. The first connotation is interchangeable with the wealth of phenotypic or "gross descriptions" associated with African heritage (i.e., skin color, hair texture, etc.). This meaning allowed Pan-Africanists in the movement's formative years to scan the globe and seek allies in struggle against the common enemies who made these same phenotypic characteristics a source of oppression and exploitation in the modern world.

The second meaning closely approximates a worldview or a life philosophy. Race in this sense was viewed as a tool for alleviating the burdens of racism placed on Africa's descendants. The implications of this second meaning are best explained in two ways. First and foremost, recalling Legum and Ajala, we know that Pan-Africanism is a response to white racism and oppression. Given the fact that no ideology or political movement develops in a societal vacuum, it is safe to reason that the intellectual founders of Pan-Africanism were influenced by trends in the international society they sought to respond to. Taking this organic view, it is easy to see how these activists responded to a scientology of race with a scientology of race. International society told them that whites were superior because of whiteness, which imbued them with special characteristics and qualities for world leadership. They responded by telling the world that blackness or Africanity endowed them with the same qualifications, if not more.[28] This strategy was completely rational and absolutely necessary if they were to ever regain, promote, and preserve the dignity that Legum describes.

Both of these meanings have vacillated in the course of Pan-Africanism's ideological development; however, the latter meaning (or race as a worldview) has typically been more difficult to pin down. Even using Mazrui's "five dimensions" distinction, one sees that although phenotypic classifications vary, descent from African heritage is closely associated with the first meaning of race in all five dimensions. Thus, race may be equated with some sort of Africanity (whether Negroid, Arab, or both). Turning to race as a philosophy of action or system of thought, several subtle distinctions emerge: Garveyism, Negritude, Afro-Centricity, etc. The common point of departure for all is the belief that the key to black world development was recognition that its phenotypic race was not inferior. The methods for achieving this international confidence boost are the source of the subtle distinctions mentioned above. For Garvey, the physical return of diasporan blacks to Africa was the best way to achieve dignity. For Du Bois, a multitude of liberal tactics, stressing political agitation and intellectual development, exists within the philosophy of race. With the demise of Henry Sylvester Williams and Garvey, Du Bois emerged as the major luminary of twentieth-century trans-Atlantic Pan-Africanism. Therefore, it is no great surprise that the tactics adopted by the CAA and NAACP and the spirit in which they pursued their aims reflected many of the notions central to his thinking. The point is that ideas matter in politics. The close contact that these organizations had with the black intellectual community had a tremendous impact on the ideological content of their messages and the ways they sought to influence policy.

The simultaneous ascension of African independence leaders to governmental authority in Africa and the attainment of political rights for blacks in America challenged the traditional way both meanings of race have been employed in Pan-African theory. Elites on both sides of the Atlantic have been forced to open their hearts and minds to the possibility that underdevelopment results from a multiplicity of complex factors, and white racism and political domination are just pieces of a larger puzzle.

In the 1960s, race confidence as a philosophy of development gave way to the practical concerns of nation-building in Africa. This occurred primarily for two reasons. First and foremost was the recognition by African leaders that colonialism had left similar patterns of underdevelopment all over the continent. Second was the rise of cultural and political nationalism in Africa. African leaders found the development of economic and political unions far more pressing and relevant challenges than uplifting the black race on an international level. If the project of continental unity was ever to work, black African leaders realized that all of Africa, not just black or "Negro" Africa, must be included, and that the nationless African-American's role in forging this union would be marginal at best. Ronald Walters describes this turbulent time in Pan-Africanism's history: "In 1963, it appeared that simultaneously an era had passed and another was being born as the Organization of African Unity came into existence and W. E. B. Du Bois died and was buried in Africa on September 29."[29]

The joys associated with self-government created a new sense of introspection in Africa. James Coleman says that with independence "there emerged a new pride in being African."[30] African intellectuals, often at the behest of political leaders, delved into detailed explorations of Africa's past. Says Coleman:

A particularly striking feature of African nationalism has been the literary and cultural revival which has attended it. A renewed appreciation of and interest in "African" culture has been manifested. . . . In some cases this cultural renaissance has had a purely tribal emphasis; in others it has taken a neo-African form, such as the African dress of Dr. Nnamdi Azikiwe, nationalist leader in Nigeria. (1954, 25)

The point is that these were new nations, and the experience of modernization brought a tremendous amount of uncertainty. Africans responded to this uncertainty with nationalism. Nation-building, particularly in Africa, is what scholars of nationalism call a process of "imagining political community."[31] When "imagining" their national communities, Africans used culture as the fictive glue between citizens. They sought to invent senses of Nigerian-ness or Ghanaian-ness out of smaller communal identities by stressing the commonalties of cultural traditions. Ernest Gellner has argued that "Nationalism is not the awakening of nations to self-consciousness: it invents nations where they do not exist."[32] In their quest to build one fictive tie, African elites seemed to quickly turn away from another, the "imagined" Pan-African community based on race.

Shifting patterns in American politics also contributed to the decline of international race thinking. At the time of Du Bois's death, African-Americans were beginning to make significant strides in the civil rights movement (Walters 1993, 54). By 1965, major legislative packages promoting minority rights in America had been secured. Just like the Africans, when their primary political goals were attained black Americans began to reexamine their role in the world. Although they never forgot about Africa, their interest was put on the back burner as they found themselves, for the first time, in a position to successfully deliver the goods to their domestic constituents. Furthermore, these were times of high optimism because it seemed that Pan-Africanism had accomplished its central goals; Africa was independent and African-Americans were approaching full citizenship status. This situation left black elites on both sides of the Atlantic "groping for new fixed patterns of relationships with one another."[33]

A generational split in the black American civil rights movement kept the racial component of transatlantic Pan-Africanism alive. Attaining full franchise rights and ending Jim Crow were the major goals of older civil rights leaders. For younger activists, these achievements were a mere beginning and enhanced freedom gave them opportunities to push the limits of being both full citizens and black in American society. The result of this exploration was the formation of a "Black Power" movement centered on race and the African-American's connection to his/her African past (Walters, 55).

Thus, the leaders of the Black Power movement became the stewards of transatlantic Pan-Africanism as well. During the short life of the movement, the young civil rights activists tried to establish strong ties linking continental and transatlantic Pan-Africanism. Communism became the common language upon which this new fictive Pan-African community would be based. This attempt to undergird traditional racial Pan-Africanism with Marxism was a failure. Marxism's message was less and less palatable to the African-American masses in light of the increased political power of more conservative black leaders (Plummer, 218). Furthermore, the Marxist approach pointed to the significant differences in objective material realities that the two groups faced. The second reason was the general failure of continental Pan-Africanism (Ajala, 181). Together, these two factors contributed to the demise of the Black Power movement's attempts to link the two. However, before its decline, the Black Power movement momentarily revitalized the racial component of trans-Atlantic Pan-Africanism.

By the early 1970s, the old-guard black leaders completely gave way to the younger group. These men and women had participated in the civil rights movement on many levels. Some were involved with the Black Power movement, while others sought to bring some aspects of that militant spirit to mainstream civil rights groups. These leaders would eventually earn seats in Congress, and be in the vanguard of the movement to form the Congressional Black Caucus and TransAfrica. The way that these leaders behave when seeking to influence policy indicates that they were significantly influenced by the shifts in Pan-African ideology reported above. In recent decades, a new type of trans-Atlantic Pan-Africanism has emerged, one in which transnational cooperation is based on more than a response to international racism. This new variant allows for the possibility that a series of complex factors may work in conjunction with or in lieu of race thinking to motivate African-American leaders to act on behalf of Africa.

This is increasingly clear when one questions black American leaders involved with lobbying for Africa on the factors motivating their involvement. All of the Congressional Black Caucus members interviewed for this essay cited a reason grounded in racial ideology as the force motivating their initial interest in African affairs. Congresswoman Eva Clayton says that her interest in Africa was initially sparked from "a sense of pride, and a sense that Africa was part of [her] history as a black American."[34] Representative Floyd Flake, from New York's Sixth Congressional District, cites his connection to the African Methodist Episcopal church (a denomination with very strong Pan-African ties) as the primary impetus motivating his interest in African affairs.[35] Congressman William Jefferson, second District, New Orleans, characterized his initial interest in Africa as "Remote, romantic, [and] the same type of interest that most African-Americans exposed to some information about Africa would have."[36]

The interesting thing is that these same members recognize that although their initial interest in Africa may have been based on notions of racial connections, they do not see their work on behalf of Africa as part of a linked struggle for worldwide racial justice. Instead, they recognize the complexities of the newly emerging transnational relationships. Clayton views her participation in influencing African affairs as an added bonus to her domestic legislative activities. She clearly differentiates her belief in helping Africa from the work she has to do on behalf of her black

American constituents in North Carolina's first Congressional District: "I am not on the International Relations Committee. So although I have this interest [in Africa] I do not feel that it is strong enough to motivate me to serve on that committee. I feel like my first interest should be closer to home . . . to people in my district. So, although I was offered a spot on International Relations by the leadership, I decided not to take it" (5 March 1996). Furthermore, she sees her fight for Africa's interests, particularly her involvement with the Nigeria campaign, as part of a larger fight to promote worldwide democracy and freedom. She seeks to ensure racial parity in government practice when advancing global freedom. She told me, "I am interested in Nigeria for the same reasons we [the United States] are interested in Bosnia; to promote democracy" (5 March 1996).

Congressman Jefferson notes that, although his sense of racial allegiance motivated him to become interested in Africa, it was business that first took him to the continent (6 March 1996). Furthermore, he feels that his substantial involvement in the push for Nigerian democratization is based more on the fact that he has traveled extensively in the country than any special credentials his race bestows upon him (Jefferson 1996). It is also telling that during our interview Mr. Jefferson assumed the tone of a member of Congress, a government leader, not exclusively a black leader: "I am warmly welcomed and received as a member of Congress because they see me as a sympathetic ear who they can tell what is missing in the relationship between our government and their countries" (Jefferson 1996). He continues:

> Africa has in almost every occasion that I have been there had very warm impressions about the United States. Perhaps it is because all of Africa's oppression has come from Europe, not the United States. In most instances, their contact with *our* government has been through programs providing educational support, medical and technical support, what have you. So the attitudes [toward Americans] starting out are not bad. (Jefferson 1996)

Congressman Floyd Flake strikes a similar chord, stating, "I would suggest that movement [in Africa] as a member of Congress is obviously much freer than when I was a private citizen" (Flake, 11 March 1996). He continues:

> I serve on the Banking Committee and the Sub-Committee for International Monetary policy. And in that role, I am responsible for some oversight of the IMF and World Bank. So that generally if I go abroad, the response of leadership and government is very strong, because the majority of the African countries have a major albatross around their necks with regard to their debt structure to these organizations. . . . So every [African] country I have been in, I have

met with the president and other leaders and this issue is always
their primary concern. So I have always had great entree on that
issue. I am singled out as a member of Congress who places great
emphasis on economics. (Flake 1996)

Furthermore, it seems that financial relationships will play an increasingly important role in the emergent Pan-Africanism of development. Continuing with the comments of Congressman Flake:

My primary goal has been to figure out how you merge social
and economic strategies with this whole political model that I try
to work within. I have always felt that if you can strengthen Africa
as a continent, African-Americans would be better off. . . . My contention is that if you can ever train young African-Americans to the
reality of trying to learn the necessary skills and marry that with
what [Africans] have naturally [in terms of resources], you will have
blacks all over the world in a stronger position. (Flake 1996)

Flake's Pan-Africanism is not completely devoid of racial motivations. He
clearly believes that there are some commonalties in black world underdevelopment. However, unlike his predecessors, he does not see the alleviation of international racism as the major strategy for resolving this underdevelopment. Instead of building ties stressing race pride, Flake wants
to build Pan-African connections by marketing African-American skills
to Africans. Flake readily draws parallels between his proposals and the
American Jewish Diaspora's financial support of Israel when he says, "Jews
give to make Israel strong, blacks who may not have the resources to provide that same type of financial support may be able to provide a similar
contribution in technical skills" (Flake 1996). Jefferson also stresses financial relationships and compares the black American situation to Zionism
when characterizing the emergent Pan-Africanism of development:

Jews seem to live with thoughts of Israel. Our persecution took
place on these shores and that type of connection was erased by
the culture of slavery. Our memory is very short, because there has
been a supreme effort to erase these historical connections. So it is
not any wonder that we don't feel like Jews. They still have their
historical memory, religion and cultural customs. We are just now
rebuilding this same type of connection with Africa for solid reasons having to do with trade, diplomacy, and international justice.
(Jefferson 1996)

These statements indicate that a hybridized Pan-Africanism is emerging, one that combines the "romantic notions" of building an "imagined
community" of African descendants with pragmatic realizations that a

philosophy of race is not necessarily the best way to build such a community. Their roles as government insiders have given them expertise and access to authority that make the traditional rhetoric of the "Pan-Africanism
of liberation" obsolete. With African leaders, they are attempting to forge
new relationships more reflective of their changed political and material
circumstances. A wealth of political and economic motivations seemingly
lie behind these new relationships, all of which have the potential to lead
to continued de-racialization of transnational interactions between diaspora and continental blacks. Under this view, there is a greater potential
for the pursuit of group interest to complicate the manner in which transnational cooperation occurs.

PAN-AFRICANISM OF DEVELOPMENT AND THE RISE OF INTEREST-GROUP POLITICS

The recent controversies over African states' refusing to hire African-
American lobbying firms are one example of the complicated group interactions that result as black groups struggle to bring the embryonic Pan-
Africanism of development to life. In early 1995, Congressman William L.
Clay (D-Mo.) began investigating this ironic lack of racial parity. The language used by Kenneth Cooper in an article reporting on Clay's investigation is telling. He writes, "Clay has done some checking on whom Africans hire to look out for their interests in Washington and found that
few African and Caribbean countries have contracted with African-Americans."[37] Cooper continues, writing that Clay's study discloses that "[o]f
the 53 African nations recognized by the United Nations, six are represented by Black-owned firms: Gabon, Nigeria, Sao Tome and Principe, the
republics of Benin, Mauritania and Cameroon" (1995, 18).

The responses of Clay, other members of Congress, and African-
American lobbyists to this record clearly demonstrates how specific group
interests have the potential to supplant traditional views of racial obligation and transnational cooperation in the emergent Pan-Africanism of development. Clay argues that the problem "extends far beyond the limited
number of African-American lobbyists in Washington, their possible lack
of international contacts or even the plausible assumption that White lobbyists can get more from a white-run government" (18). He sees this record
as a blatant betrayal of racial solidarity steeped in African notions of black
American inferiority. He is quoted in the Emerge article as follows: "Africans have never wanted to be identified with Black Americans. They feel
superior to Black Americans" (Clay quoted in Cooper, 18). Clay finds this
attitude a particularly tough pill to swallow given the African-American
political elite's strong tradition of championing African interests inside
the Beltway. He states, "They [Africans] are expecting the Black commu-

nity to do the work. When they get resources, they turn around and use them to enhance the economic status of whites" (18).

Congresswoman Clayton agrees that it is unacceptable for African nations to rely on the Black Caucus and TransAfrica to build a black constituency for African affairs but fail to hire black Americans in the private sector. She states:

> I am aware that Africans do not hire in any appreciable amount African-American lobbyists and lawyers to represent their interests. It has not been a natural assumption on the part of Africans to think of us as the ones to turn to in this country with regard to these matters. It is unacceptable, that time in and time out we go to the floor begging for them and when they have the opportunity to engage our professionals they do not do it. (Clayton 1996)

Unlike Clay, however, she believes an African assumption that whites have more influence with a white-run government is a plausible explanation for their hiring practices, describing African leaders as "stuck in that mentality that they need to have a white lobbyist or attorney to gain access to government power" (Clayton 1996).

Congressman Jefferson believes that the fact that foreign policy is driven by the president contributes to this perception:

> Africans not hiring black American lobbyists is a problem. Since the president drives foreign policy he should be responsible for African affairs. The Congress presides over trade, but we have no real trade policy with Africa. We have no real treaties with Africa. So African heads of states have basically been dealing with presidents from one to another. So, the decisions that the Africans are making with regard to who they employ to represent their interests in Washington are based more on which firms have access to the presidency than anything else. If George Bush is the president, then you will see Africans hiring a lot of large, white, Republican-oriented law firms and lobbying outfits. (Jefferson 1996)

He also believes that these practices will change as the Caucus gets more and more involved with African affairs: "There was very little talk in the Congress about Africa until very recently. Now, since the Congress is getting more involved in African affairs through human rights issues and what have you, the Caucus will get more and more involved and will be in a position to get more black firms hired" (Jefferson 1996). Jefferson believes that African nations will have to increase the number of black lobbyists they employ or potentially lose access to America's sympathetic black power brokers:

I think that Bill Clay is right though, now that things are changing and the Congress is showing more interest and there are black
firms capable of doing the work, Africans have to be more sensitive
to searching out and hiring black professionals to carry their messages up here. They may still decide that to get to Newt Gingrich
they need to hire Republican firms. But to deal with the Democrats
they need to hire Democratic firms and to deal with us [African-
American members] they need to hire black or multicultural firms.
(Jefferson 1996)

Flake turns again to the nature of the African economic crisis as an
explanation for black American exclusion in this field. He believes that
African perceptions about black lobbyists are founded on the way that Africans perceive black Americans handle their own political and economic
affairs: "I don't quite think that Africa, like a lot of other regions of the
world, sees at the moment the overall product of what the African-American community is capable of producing" (Flake 1996). He thinks that this
situation will continue "until the African-American begins to understand
that people abroad are not looking for our [racial] rhetoric, they are looking for solutions built on solid economic theories and foundations" (Flake
1996). The congressman continues:

If you look at our [black] leadership both politically and otherwise,
we almost give a glorification to poverty as opposed to an acceptance of the reality that banks and financial investment institutions
determine the direction of this country and to a large extent the
world. We exclude ourselves from this reality. So that if Africa sees
itself as trying to become liberated, once you get beyond the issues
of Apartheid in South Africa, their primary concerns are building
their economies and the problem is that they do not see enough
African-Americans with enough capabilities and skills to make
enough of a difference. (Flake 1996)

CONCLUSIONS

It is interesting that in one instance members of the Congressional
Black Caucus readily admit that race is declining as a solid basis for transnational cooperation, then go on to describe the failure of African nations
to hire black American lobbyists as an insult to their racial sensibilities.
It is also interesting that cultural nationalism and political economy are
two prominent explanations African-Americans offer when trying to interpret the hiring practices of these nations. One thing is for certain: the
domestic race-thinking of African-Americans has made the goal of getting
more black American lobbyists hired by African nations a top priority. To
the extent that this group interest runs counter to the concerns Africans

have demonstrated about cultural nationalism and political economy, there is increased potential for conflict or the breakdown of traditional patterns of transnational interaction between the two groups.

NOTES

1. Brenda Gayle Plummer provides one of the most comprehensive examinations of this tradition in her book *Rising Wind: Black Americans and U.S. Foreign Affairs, 1935–1960*; a particularly clear synopsis is provided on pp. 12–35.

2. Elliot P. Skinner, *African-Americans and U.S. Policy Toward Africa: 1850–1924*, p. 1.

3. Shelly Leanne, *African-American Initiatives Against Minority Rule in South Africa: A Politicized Diaspora in World Politics*, p. 113.

4. Henry F. Jackson notes Congressman Adam Clayton Powell's membership in the Council on African Affairs on page 142 of his book *From Congo to Soweto: U.S. Foreign Policy Toward Africa Since 1960*. Although the literature makes clear that the scope of his daily involvement in the group was limited, largely because of the central control over the organization exhibited by William Alphaeus Hunton, given his pattern of behavior in the foreign affairs arena, it is reasonable to assume that his membership gave the group symbolic legitimacy and access to governmental authority. This assertion is bolstered by Brenda Gayle Plummer's vivid descriptions of Powell's foreign affairs activism and of his withdrawal from the CAA because of his fear that it was a communist front; see particularly pp. 117 and 191.

5. David Anthony, "Max Yergan and South Africa: A Transatlantic Interaction," pp. 191–92.

6. W. E. B. Du Bois, Department of Special Research, Report, 9 April–May 1945, NAACP Papers, Reel #7. See also, Plummer, *Rising Wind*, pp. 132–152.

7. James Roark, "Black American Leaders: The Response to Colonialism and the Cold War," p. 253.

8. See Gerald Horne, *Black and Red: W. E. B. DuBois and the Afro-American Response to the Cold War*, pp. 62–65; David Caute, *The Great Fear: The Anti-Communist Purge Under Truman and Eisenhower*, pp. 330–331; and also Shelly Leanne, *African-American Initiatives Against Minority Rule in South Africa*, pp. 160–163.

9. One of the better treatments of this expansion of black political capital is Lucius J. Barker and Mack H. Jones, *African-Americans and the American Political System*.

10. Raymond Copson, *The Congressional Black Caucus and Foreign Policy: 1971–1995*, p. 1.

11. Frank McCoy, "TransAfrica Explores New Challenges," p. 58.

12. The Byrd Amendment of 1971 permitted the U.S. to import over seventy strategic minerals from Rhodesia in direct contravention of UN sanctions against that nation. For a detailed description of this action, see

Wellington Nyangoni, *United States Foreign Policy and South Africa,* p. 60.

13. Poinsett, "The Black Caucus," p. 289.

14. William L. Clay, *Just Permanent Interests: Black Americans in Congress, 1870–1991,* p. 139.

15. Nadine Cohadas, "Black House Members Striving for Influence," p. 675.

16. Lucius Barker and Jesse McCorry, *Black Americans and the U.S. Political System,* p. 270.

17. Pressman, "Stunner in House: Tough Anti-Apartheid Bill," p. 1385.

18. TransAfrica, "Congress Overrides Veto: Sanctions as a First Step," p. 80.

19. Pauline Baker, *The United States and South Africa: The Reagan Years,* p. 31.

20. *Congressional Quarterly,* December 1, 1984, p. 3047.

21. *Congressional Quarterly Weekly,* 9 March 1985.

22. TransAfrica, *TransAfrica News,* p. 1.

23. Ali Mazrui, *Africa's International Relations,* pp. 68–69.

24. P. O. Esedebe, *Pan-Africanism: The Idea and Movement,* p. 3.

25. Colin Legum, *Pan-Africanism,* p. 15.

26. Adekule Ajala, *Pan-Africanism: Evolution, Progress and Projects,* p. 4.

27. This sentiment is made vividly clear in Committee on African Affairs, *New Africa,* February 1946 and the NAACP's *Crisis,* December 1951, pp. 647–51; January 1954, pp. 19–22.

28. Okon Edet Uya describes this response in his powerful essay "Conceptualizing Afro-American/African Relations: Implications for African Diaspora Studies," pp. 70–73.

29. Ronald Walters, *Pan-Africanism in the African Diaspora,* p. 55.

30. James Coleman, "Nationalism in Tropical Africa," p. 25.

31. Benedict Anderson, *Imagined Communities,* p. 6.

32. Ernest Gellner, *Thought and Change,* p. 169.

33. St. Clair Drake made this statement and it was quoted by Walters in the text of *Pan-Africanism in the African Diaspora.*

34. The Honorable Eva Clayton, personal interview, 5 March 1996.

35. The Honorable Floyd Flake, personal interview, 11 March 1996.

36. The Honorable William J. Jefferson, personal interview, 6 March 1996.

37. Kenneth Cooper, *Building the Ranks of Black Lobbyists,* p. 18

REFERENCES

Books

Ajala, A. 1973. *Pan-Africanism: Evolution, Progress and Prospects.* London: Deutsch.

Anderson, B. 1983. *Imagined Communities.* New York: Verso.

Anthony, D. 1994. Max Yergan and South Africa: A Trans-Atlantic Interaction. In *Imagining Home: Class, Culture and Nationalism in the African Diaspora*, ed. Sidney Lemelle and Robin Kelley. London: Verso Press.

Baker, P. 1989. *The United States and South Africa: The Reagan Years.* New York: Ford Foundation Foreign Policy Association.

Barker, Lucius J. and Mack H. Jones. 1978. *African-Americans and the American Political System.* Boston: Little Brown.

Caute, D. 1978. *The Great Fear: The Anti-Communist Purge Under Truman and Eisenhower.* New York: Simon and Schuster.

Clay, W. 1992. *Just Permanent Interests: Black Americans in Congress, 1870–1991.* New York: Amistad Press.

Coleman, J. 1994 (1954). Nationalism in Tropical Africa. In *Nationalism and Development in Africa: Selected Essays of James Smoot Coleman*, ed. Richard Sklar. Berkeley: University of California Press.

Esedebe, P. O. 1982. *Pan-Africanism: The Idea and Movement.* Washington, DC: Howard University Press.

Gellner, E. 1965. *Thought and Change.* Chicago: University of Chicago Press.

Horne, G. 1986. *Black and Red: W. E. B. Du Bois and the Afro-American Response to the Cold War.* Albany: State University of New York Press.

Jackson, H. 1983. *From Congo to Soweto: U.S. Foreign Policy Toward Africa Since 1960.* New York: Morrow.

Legum, C. 1976. *Pan-Africanism: A Short Political Guide.* Westport: Greenwood Press.

Mazrui, A. A. 1977. *Africa's International Relations.* London: Heinemann.

Nyangoni, W. 1981. *United States Foreign Policy and South Africa.* New York: World Research Committee of the Society for Common Insights, African Institute for the Study of Human Values.

Plummer, B. G. 1996. *Rising Wind: Black Americans and U.S. Foreign Affairs, 1935–1960.* Chapel Hill: University of North Carolina Press.

Poinsett. 1982. The Black Caucus. In *Black Americans and the Political System*, ed. Lucius Barker and Jesse McCorry. Boston: Little Brown.

Skinner, E. 1992. *African-Americans and U.S. Policy Toward Africa: 1850–1924.* Washington, DC: Howard University Press.

Uya, O. E. 1982. Conceptualizing Afro-American/African Relations: Implications for African Diaspora Studies. In *Global Dimensions of the African Diaspora*, ed. Joseph Harris. Washington, DC: Howard University Press.

Walters, R. 1993. *Pan-Africanism in the African Diaspora.* Detroit: Wayne State University Press.

Articles

Cohodas, N. 1986. Black House Members Striving for Influence. *Congressional Quarterly Weekly Report*, v. 43.

Cooper, K. June, 1995. Building the Ranks of Black Lobbyists. *Emerge.*
McCoy, F. August, 1992. TransAfrica Explores New Challenges. *Black Enterprise*, v. 23.
Pressman. S. June 21, 1986. Stunner in House: Tough Anti-Apartheid Bill. *Congressional Quarterly Weekly Report*, v. 44.
Roark, J. 1971. Black American Leaders: The Response to Colonialism and the Cold War. *International Journal of African Historical Studies* 4(2).

Dissertations

Leanne, S. 1994. *African-American Initiatives Against Minority Rule in South Africa: A Politicized Diaspora in World Politics.* Ph.D. Dissertation, University of Oxford, England.

United States Government Documents

Copson, R. 1996. *The Congressional Black Caucus and Foreign Policy: 1971–1995.* Washington, DC: Congressional Research Service.

Newspapers, Clipping Files, and Serials

The Crisis.
New Africa.
TransAfrica News.

Interviews by Author

The Honorable Eva M. Clayton, Washington, DC, March 5, 1996.
The Honorable Floyd Flake, Washington, DC, March 11, 1996.
The Honorable William J. Jefferson, Washington, DC, March 6, 1996.

Archival Material

Howard University (Moorland-Spingarn Center, Washington, DC) NAACP Papers, Reel #7.

32 ALICE WALKER AND THE LEGACY OF AFRICAN AMERICAN DISCOURSE ON AFRICA

Joseph McLaren

Since their forced removal from the Continent during the Atlantic slave trade, Africans in North America have engaged Africa in a variety of ways. In the nineteenth century, emigration through African colonization and Christian missionary movements began to generate Pan-African concepts. In the first decades of the twentieth century, along with the growth of Pan-Africanism and black nationalism, creative writers depicted Africa as a distant homeland and a source of heritage. African American discourses have tended to view Africa as monolithic, a natural outcome of a Diasporic vision shaped by the scattering of discrete ethnic identities. Pan-Africanism and Afrocentricity are evidence of this global tendency that can conflict with the interest in ethnic specificity that perhaps underlies the critique of Alice Walker.

Walker's portrayal of African American missionaries and female circumcision represents a critical juncture in the legacy of African American interaction with Africa. This legacy is based on the contributions of such figures as Martin Delany, W. E. B. Du Bois, Langston Hughes, Richard Wright, Malcolm X, Maya Angelou, and Molefi Asante, a partial list of African Americans whose ideas form a discourse on Africa. These discourses have contributed to the formation of a Diasporic identity by focusing on cultural and political issues that have repeatedly emerged in the self-definitions of African Americans.

In general, the writings of these intellectuals have had a varied reception by their African counterparts, who have viewed African Americans sometimes as allies, sometimes as intruders. For the most part, African American discourses have been supported by Africans when the pronouncements have sought to overturn the hegemony of the West as part of the anticolonial or anti-imperialist struggle—interventions in a classic "political" sense. Alice Walker's dilemma suggests the problems of accepting the African American spokesperson who is critical of traditional practice, ritual, religion, or worldview—areas that represent "culture" as opposed to international power relationships. Controversies can also arise when African Americans present themselves as authorities on indigenous culture or propose African-based theories such as Asante's Afrocentricity.

THE DEVELOPMENT OF A LEGACY

In the nineteenth century, African American discourses on Africa were often the result of temporary sojourns or permanent relocations in Africa. Black American clergy, such as Alexander Crummel, who journeyed to Liberia (1821–22), were part of missionary activities that questioned indigenous African religion and cultural practices. The notion of bringing enlightenment to the "heathens" resembles the intentions of European missionaries. Few black missionaries valorized traditional African cultural systems. Black missionaries not only wanted to "make Africans over into Americans" but targeted traditional practices such as polygamy and sacrifice. In other words, "racial identity did not imply a cultural identity with contemporary African societies." William Sheppard, a Presbyterian missionary in the Congo in the 1890s, was an exception in his regard for the Bakuba traditions (Williams 1982, 104–06, 123).[1]

Martin Delany, a social historian and creative writer, described areas of West Africa in "The Official Report of the Niger Valley Exploring Party." The tone of his presentation is one of Western superiority, a valorizing of Christian morality, although Delany has been considered a Pan-African patriarch—the African American counterpart to Caribbean-born Edward Wilmot Blyden of Liberia. Delany's observations on Liberia, Yorubaland, and Igboland emphasize the topographical elements, and his notions of "civilization" are similar to those voiced by European missionaries. Since his mission was to find a site for emigration, in many respects he echoes the observations of Europeans in seeking colonial outposts, where the emphasis is on the suitability of the environment and proselytizing. Episcopalian, Baptist, and Methodist churches placed African American missionaries strategically in West and Central Africa because of the genetic factor, the adaptability of the African gene to the climatic conditions that created the so-called white man's graveyard (Williams 1982, 6).

Although Delany undoubtedly realized this, he saw the missionary effort as somewhat beneficial: "To deny or overlook the fact, the all-important fact, that the missionary influence had done much good in Africa would be simply to do injustice, a gross injustice to a good cause" (Delany and Campbell 1969, 102). However, Delany does critique Catholic missions and their association with the continuation of the slave trade. His sole challenge to the Protestant missionaries is their renaming of Africans, equating this erasure of the African name with a "loss of identity" (Delany and Campbell 1969, 106). Unlike Delany, Robert Campbell, who documented his own experience in West Africa in "A Pilgrimage to My Motherland: An Account of a Journey Among the Egbas and Yorubas of Central Africa, in 1859–60," seemed to have experienced cultural linkage. Furthermore, Campbell and Delany differ in the "gendering of their African homeland," Delany preferring the term "fatherland" (Gilroy 1993, 25).

Like Delany, Du Bois has been directly associated with Pan-Africanism. He was instrumental in its organizational development—the Pan-African congresses of 1900, 1919, 1923, and 1927—as well as its theoretical extension, posing a counter-historiography that reevaluated Africa's internal relationships and its contact with the West. Du Bois's *The World and Africa*, originally published in 1946, articulates the reasons for a Pan-African conception emerging from the Diaspora. Though he was perhaps the most politically conscious African American to develop a discourse on Africa, one of his statements contains the ironic "dark" imagery associated with European views of Africa: "The idea of one Africa to unite the thought and ideals of all native peoples of the dark continent belongs to the twentieth century and stems naturally from the West Indies and the United States" (Du Bois 1965, 7). Since quotation marks are not used in this passage, how must one read his inscription of "natives" and "dark continent"—as an echo or as mockery of the West's image? This minor lapse by Du Bois indicates the pervasive influence of Western concepts, even if we assume his intended irony.

By the 1960s, Du Bois had become a prominent ally and advisor of Kwame Nkrumah. Du Bois, who received Ghanaian citizenship in 1963, achieved one of the most successful associations between an African American intellectual and an African leader. When Du Bois addressed the economic challenges of newly independent Ghana, he was prophetic, anticipating a critique by contemporary African Americans, such as John Henrik Clarke, of Rawlings's policies. Du Bois referred to Nkrumah's economic policies: "He is not scaring private investment away; neither is he inviting it with promise of unlimited profit. If he can get capital on reasonable terms he will welcome and protect it" (Du Bois 1965, 303).

Du Bois's support of Nkrumah's vision of a unified Africa bolstered the political possibilities of Pan-Africanism, and his choice of Ghana foreshadowed the numerous returns of African Americans. (The return of Stokely Carmichael [Kwame Touré], a symbol of the black power movement, to Guinea in the 1970s is another example of African emigration and political association.) In the late twentieth century, Ghana has become the "default" African American site of reconnection at a time when certain observers have perceived Africa as an invention of the West.

In addition to the Pan-Africanism of Du Bois, more concerned with geopolitical issues and the African state, there has also been an African

American "literary Pan-Africanism" established by such figures as Langston Hughes, who was one of the first twentieth-century African American literary figures to not only support Pan-Africanism but to actually set foot on the Continent, journeying to West Africa—Ghana, Nigeria, and Angola—in 1923, the same year Du Bois had made his first visit to Africa. Like Du Bois, Hughes did not challenge specific traditional practices but he did observe the social predicament of mixed-blood Africans, a theme that was easily linked to race issues in the American context.

Hughes's "The Negro Speaks of Rivers" (1921), written prior to his journey to West Africa, suggests the literary seeds of Afrocentricity, especially in its allusions to black Egypt through references to the Nile and the pyramids. The recognition of black Egypt was later reinforced by *Fire!!* (1926), published by the younger writers of the Harlem Renaissance. On the cover of the magazine was a drawing of a Sphinx. In other poems, such as "Afro-American Fragment," "Danse Africaine," "Negro," and "Sun Song," Hughes uses Africa as a trope for black American identity and heritage. Hughes's "Johannesburg Mines" (1925), published in *Good Morning Revolution* (1973), is a plea for social justice for black South African laborers.

Hughes's African journey is retold in *The Big Sea* (1940). "Burutu Moon" recreates an evening walk when "the full moon hung low over Burutu and it was night on the Nigerian delta" (117). Hughes hears the drums of "Ju-Ju" and concludes the narrative with a recreation of commentary by Africans. This ending shows Hughes's support of the anticolonial struggle expressed in both economic and social terms. The dialogue identifies the white men as those who "'come to take our palm oil and ivory, our ebony and mahogany, to buy our women and bribe our chiefs'" (Hughes 1940, 120).

For the most part, Hughes did not fall out of favor with African intellectuals, primarily because he did not veer from his challenge to the colonial enterprise, unlike Richard Wright, who critiqued ritual and tradition. Wright's West African journey was the source for his critical statements in *Black Power: A Record of Reactions in the Land of Pathos* (1954). Wright was unable to analyze the social, cultural, and political situations he observed without the encumbrances of a consciousness shaped by Western thoughts and values, which are often in direct conflict with the cultural-value systems of Africans.

Wright's meeting with Nkrumah and his trip to James Town is one of the significant events of the journey. Nkrumah is described as having "moved in and filled the vacuum which the British and missionaries had left when they smashed the tribal culture of the people!" Wright witnesses the dancing of women bared to the waist; their "shuffling dance," as he describes it, brings home to him the links between his experiences with dance in America: "what I was now looking at in the powerful improvised dance of these women, I'd seen before in America." These remarks suggest a dilemma that Wright observed in his own character and cultural life: his inability to partake in the dance, to feel the emotion and to move with its intuitive rhythms. "I had wanted to, *but I had never been able to!*" (Wright 1954, 60–61, 57–58).

This dilemma is echoed in later comments concerning his trip to the interior regions and Kumasi. Wright's most forceful criticism of the traditional Ghanaian life is leveled at indigenous religion, which he believes prevented Ghanaians from achieving true independence and self rule. His criticisms of juju and "fetish worship" are numerous although he is occasionally sympathetic to the different worldview. Such comments as "mumbo jumbo" and other negative remarks are interspersed throughout the text. For Wright, the power of African religion is purely psychological and is not the result of actual spiritual or divine power. Wright's critique of traditional religion and chieftaincy were undoubtedly shaped by his radical politics.

An African journey was also a basis for Malcolm X's statements, which are more concerned with the anticolonial position than a challenge to ritual, though his Muslim perspective could have led to a discourse on Christian Africa. His commentaries are essentially Pan-Africanist. His visit to Ghana at the height of the Nkrumah era is reflected in a general utopian optimism resulting from his meeting with Nkrumah (Malcolm X 1973, 356). In Ghana, Malcolm, hosted by African American expatriates such as Maya Angelou, experienced his own reidentification when he began to use the term "Afro-American" instead of "Negro" and expressed a more definite sense of Africa's significance, especially in relation to his spiritual quest in the Middle East:

> I knew that after what I had experienced in the Holy Land, the second most indelible memory I would carry back to America would be the Africa seething with serious awareness of itself, and of Africa's wealth, and of her power, and of her destined role in the world. (Malcolm X 1973, 360)

Ironically, Malcolm challenged Maya Angelou's remarks about Shirley Du Bois, who Angelou thought to have isolated herself and to have been "sitting in the catbird seat in Ghana" (Angelou 1986, 144–45).

Angelou's Ghanaian experience occurred as well during the 1960s. However, unlike Hughes or Wright, she spent a considerable time in Africa and was able to articulate the difficulties of repatriation, suggesting an ironic linkage to nineteenth-century emigrationist narratives; Angelou is clearly a Pan-Africanist. *All God's Children Need Traveling Shoes* (1986) is more a personal odyssey than a political statement. Like Malcolm, she also expresses a euphoric idealism, an "adoration of Ghana," but her remarks are complicated by her recognizing the complexities of return for

African Americans to "a home which had shamefully little memory of them" (Angelou 1986, 20). Angelou faces Ghanaian traditional culture as a novice, rather than as a critic, but ultimately comes to a realization of the barriers between African American expatriates and Ghanaians. Gender politics is an element of her critical perspective, though she is more concerned with issues of communal interchange and the legacy of slavery as a ghost haunting the relationships of returning Africans. The question of African languages is also relevant, especially in the closing sections of the memoir, where Angelou's inability to communicate with an Ewe-speaking woman shows a disjuncture in sisterly understanding. This moment of miscommunication is purely linguistic.

The acceptance rather than the critique of traditional culture is at the core of Molefi Asante's discourse on Africa, clearly an outgrowth of Pan-Africanism; he has been the subject of critical attack by certain African intellectuals. In *The Afrocentric Idea* (1987), Asante challenges the types of metaphors, names, and contexts derived from the dual legacy of colonialism and racial oppression. He defines Afrocentricity as "placing African ideals at the center of any analysis that involves African culture and behavior" (Asante 1987, 6).

Asante's *Kemet, Afrocentricity and Knowledge* (1990), which poses alternate organizational structures for Africalogy, received a scathing attack from Uzo Esonwanne, who challenged Asante's fundamental definitions: "Who is 'the African,' what is the nature of his/her perspectivism . . . and what is the validity of a perspectivist theory of knowledge?" (Esonwanne 1992, 205). In *Malcolm X as Cultural Hero and Other Afrocentric Essays*, Asante responds to Esonwanne's remarks in equally combative terms, generally arguing that Esonwanne "does not understand the concepts" in his work. Asante challenges Esonwanne's claim that Afrocentricity developed as an alternative to Eurocentrism and concludes that Esonwanne did not thoroughly examine the text (Asante 1993, 62–63).

This scholarly conflict has parallels to the dispute between Alice Walker and her critics, although Walker does not initiate a theoretical approach to African culture but questions a specific element of certain cultures, namely, female circumcision. This issue is itself "political," but not necessarily in relation to international or state power. Gender politics is inherently critical of "culture" and the power discrepancies that exist between men and women.

WALKER'S DISCOURSE ON AFRICA

Walker's *Possessing the Secret of Joy* (1992) and *Warrior Marks: Female Genital Mutilation and the Sexual Blinding of Women* (1993), a collaborative work with Pratibha Parmar based on "field work" in Gambia and elsewhere, have generated significant controversy over the issue of female circumcision. Walker has been challenged by certain continental African women who view her approach as part of the legacy of Western intrusion in Africa. This controversy reveals the political implications of African American writing that uses the African woman's body as a text for contesting traditional ritual practice.

Walker's "intrusion" can be contextualized as part of a legacy of engaging Africa in a manner that blends nineteenth-century emigrationist-missionary perspectives with Pan-Africanist/anticolonial positions and gender politics. The critical firestorm following the publication of *Possessing the Secret of Joy* and *Warrior Marks* implicitly suggests that Walker had "intruded" into a culturally sensitive area involving ritual. In *Warrior Marks*, Walker refers to the "African mothers / forced to 'forget' / their pain," a broad reference to the general act of female circumcision (Walker and Parmar 1993, 57). In a commentary on *Warrior Marks* in the *New York Times*, 7 December 1993, entitled "The West Just Doesn't Get It," Seble Dawit and filmmaker Salem Mekuria explained the underlying reason for the strong opposition by certain African women to Walker's presentation of the issues in the novel and the film, citing a number of women who have themselves fought for the "eradication" of the practice.

> As is common in Western depictions of Africa, Ms. Walker and her collaborator, Pratibha Parmar, portray the continent as a monolith. African women and children are the props, and the village the background against which Alice Walker, heroine-savior, comes to articulate their pain and condemn those who inflict it. (Dawit and Mekuria 1993, 27)

The authors conclude that those in the West cannot "speak for" continental African women who are themselves waging a battle against the practice but instead can "forge partnerships" (Dawit and Mekuria 1993, 27). A related issue is whether East African or South Asian women can "speak for" West African Gambians.

Notions of sisterhood associated with Walker's articulation of womanism are sometimes lost in this phase of her connection to a segment of her African sisters. Walker's definition of "Womanist" joined black feminists in a bond that underscored a commitment to "survival and wholeness of entire people, male *and* female" (Walker 1983, xi). However, Walker is not alone in her critique of female circumcision. Certainly, numerous African women have also challenged the practice. What sometimes appears to be an overly defensive response from certain African women is based on the implications and mode of Walker's discourse, the suggestion that a practice that varies from "mild sunna" to infibulation, removal of the external labia as well as the inner layer of the labia majora, will be understood by the West as a universally practiced mutilation widespread throughout Africa. Other critics stress the importance of placing female circumcision within its correct cultural context.

It is more the context, tone, and implication of Walker's critique than the issue itself that apparently generated the controversy, although for Dorothy Randall-Tsuruta, "sometimes it is necessary for an artist with the gift of aesthetic rendering to bring the world up short with graphic depiction of abuses that must be stopped" (Randall-Tsuruta 1992, 87). The critical tension is also a reaction to the cultural perspectives of those African Americans who speak to or for Africa but who are seen as products of Western acculturation and the "fetishizing" of Africa.

Walker's treatment of African issues is not a recent theme in her work. Perspectives on Africa can be traced to her writings of the 1960s. Prior to her novels dealing with Africa, Walker articulated her connection to the Continent in poems that typify a broad and somewhat romanticized idealization of Africa as floral space, a mode of discourse found in other writers influenced by Pan-Africanism. In "African Images, *Glimpses from a Tiger's Back*," a section from *Once*, Walker's 1968 collection of poems— included in *Her Blue Body Everything We Know: Earthling Poems, 1965– 1990 Complete* (1991)—Walker fashions a version of African identity.[2] Like her Pan-Africanist antecedents, she too journeyed to Africa, spending the summer of 1965 in Kenya, where she helped in the building of a school and wrote a number of poems collected in *Once*. One of her poems cleverly plays with the notion of Africa as the wildlife locale, an idea that stems from her journey to East Africa, the region most often associated with the safari: "There are no tigers / in Africa!" (Walker 1991, 4).

Her sixties poems about Africa, sometimes tinged with ironic humor, are delicate and sensitively capture impressions of East Africa; some of the poems focus on young women, the central concern in her later critique of female circumcision. In one verse, she describes a young girl's dance movements: "I see a girl / Go limp." The persona of the poem questions the ability to recognize transcendence. Other images of young African girls include the child who is "holding three fingers" and another of one who flees from the persona and her "white friend" because "She thinks he wants her / For his dinner" (Walker 1991, 27, 31). Walker's treatment of Africa in these early poems is not demonstrably political in an anticolonial sense; generally, her collected poetry is not primarily devoted to African themes, although references to Africa emerge in a number of other, later poems.

Like many African Americans of the 1960s, she was influenced by primarily positive associations with the Continent, as seen in *Revolutionary Petunias and Other Poems* (1973), where she attributes her first associations of Africa to her sister Molly, who, in the fifties, "coached me

[Walker] in my songs of Africa / A continent I never knew / But learned to love" (Walker 1991, 176). Another African-related poem, alluding to East Africa, is "In Uganda an Early King," which appears in the collection *Good Night, Willie Lee, I'll See You in the Morning* (1979). This poem does not romanticize traditional culture but shows an ironic gender-oriented perception that mocks male dominance, signified by the king who fattens his wives, once "straight and lithe," "natural as birds of paradise" (Walker 1991, 281–82). Here Walker's womanism is revealed in a poem that articulates the seemingly powerless position of the "wives."

However, her verse also explores the ironies of the colonial experience and economic exploitation. "The Diamonds on Liz's Bosom," for example, from *Horses Make a Landscape Look More Beautiful* (1984), strikes a definite critical note concerning African mine laborers and the apparent indifference of the consumers of their product; the rubies and diamonds symbolize "despair" and the distance between the haves and the have-nots: "Oh, those Africans! / Everywhere you look / they're bleeding / and crying / Crying and bleeding / on some of the whitest necks / in your town" (Walker 1991, 328).

The development of Walker's poetic treatment of Africa is suggested in her "previously uncollected poems"; one of these pieces considers African heritage as an element in a mixture of "Triple Bloods," including black, white, and red. Another, more prose-like, makes a link to "ancient Egyptian Africa," the central symbol of Afrocentricity, experienced through the poet's imaginative response to the natural elements in Northern California (Walker 1991, 416, 411). There is also a poem about Ndebele pride, of their exploitation and the plight of the mother whose brothers and sons are "dying on the long / bus rides / to Pretoria's / mines" (Walker 1991, 434–35). Her poems of individual praise include pieces devoted to Ghanaian author Ayi Kwei Armah and Winnie Mandela.

Walker's novels dealing with Africa use the African American missionary as a way of entering the cultural life of West Africa. Walker's Olinka village, used in *The Color Purple* (1982), *The Temple of My Familiar* (1989), and *Possessing the Secret of Joy* (1992), is an example of literary improvisation that borrows from both the actual and the imagined. Walker considers the recreation of ethnicity her right as an author. The Olinka are used to explore the complex interrelationships of African Americans and West Africans engaged in the process of conversion.

The Color Purple presents the initial image of Africa as experienced by Nettie, the African American who, to a degree, signifies anticolonial and Pan-African consciousness when she recognizes that "Africans once had a better civilization than the European," an idea she gets from reading J. A. Rogers. Her missionary work with her husband, Samuel, is placed in the context of British missionary efforts in India, China, and Africa. Nettie, whose duties as a missionary are to work with children as a kindergarten teacher, first sees Africa in a way that resembles the initial impressions of Delany, Hughes, and Wright—observations of people and locales, as in Nettie's recollections of Senegal: "try to imagine a city full of these shining, blueblack people wearing brilliant blue robes with designs like fancy quilt patterns. Tall, thin, with long necks and straight backs." It is *The Color Purple* that introduces Tashi, the central figure of *Possessing the Secret of Joy*. In *The Color Purple*, Tashi signifies for Olivia, the daughter of Nettie and Samuel, the "Africa she [Olivia] came beaming across the ocean hoping to find" (Walker 1982, 129, 131, 145). Walker has been critiqued for certain "static" portrayals in *The Color Purple* of traditional culture during a period when both missionary and colonial structures were becoming entrenched in West Africa (Wilentz 1992, 74).

However, in *The Temple of My Familiar*, Walker more clearly addresses the contradictions inherent in African Americans returning as missionaries. Olivia ultimately recognizes, as does her father, that African religion is valid in its own right:

> We had all begun to see, in Africa—where people worshiped many things, including the roofleaf plant, which they used to cover their houses—that "God" was not a monolith, and not the property of Moses, as we'd been led to think, and not separate from us, or absent from whatever world one inhabited. (Walker 1989, 144)

Though Walker presents the ironies of conversion in *The Temple of My Familiar*, she is decidedly more absolute in the challenge to the practice of female circumcision in *Possessing the Secret of Joy*, which has parallels to Ngugi wa Thiong'o's *The River Between* (1965), in which female circumcision is treated as a desired rite of passage by Muthoni, who views it as the mark of a "real woman" (Ngugi 1965, 25–6). Like Tashi's sister in *Possessing the Secret of Joy*, Muthoni also dies from the operation, but Ngugi's work is not essentially a condemnation of the practice, but rather a statement of the conflicts between Christian missionary conversion and traditional practices. In some respects, *Possessing the Secret of Joy* seems to mimic the methodological paradigm of the Western anthropologist (Gourdine 1996, 240–41). Rather than being perceived as anti–black male, the label resulting from *The Color Purple* and reinforced in such counterattacks as Ishmael Reed's *Reckless Eyeballing* (1986), Walker has been viewed, on the basis of *Possessing the Secret of Joy*, as a critic of the African woman. Unlike in *The Color Purple*, where the African American male is the symbolic nemesis (especially in the portrayal of two abusive characters, Pa and Mr. Albert), in *Possessing the Secret of Joy* it is the African midwife, M'Lissa, the woman who performs the circumcision of both Tashi and her sister Dura, who is cast as the agent of woman's suffering. M'Lissa's characterization no doubt contributed to the hostile response of certain African women critics, for, in a sense, her portrayal is a criticism of African mother figures. Tashi's physical disabling and her revenge against M'Lissa are, respectively, the symbolic result of and the solution to the practice of female circumcision. Just as Tashi perceives her confrontation of M'Lissa as retribution for her sister's death from the operation, Walker assumes the role of defender of her African sisters and "daughters" who are subject to the practice. In a postscript to the novel, Walker reinscribes her mission, placing her in the role of teacher: "A portion of the royalties from this book will be used to educate women and girls, men and boys, about the hazardous effects of genital mutilation" (Walker 1992, 285).

Walker's position on female circumcision is a cultural issue related to gender politics rather than to the economic or political dominance of the West, an element of her writings that links her to those African American antecedents—such as Du Bois and Malcolm X—who were mostly concerned with challenging colonial rule or assessing its aftereffects. As a creative writer, she has more in common with Hughes and Angelou in fashioning "literary" representations of her cultural and political positions, although Hughes and Angelou tended to value traditional culture rather than challenge it, as did Richard Wright. In her movement to "vaginal politics," Walker has channeled the discourse to issues that resemble the nineteenth-century emigrationist-missionary interventions of Crummel and commentaries of Delany that sought to revise certain traditional practices and define notions of "civilization." However, Walker has been more focused in her challenges, in that her attack has been centered on a particular practice rather than broad issues concerning religion or ritual. Most importantly, it is evident that continental Africans themselves have revised traditional practices and that there exists a dynamic assertion by African women in the area of gender politics.

Overall, African intellectuals have more readily accepted Pan-Africanist ideology and anticolonial critiques, exemplified by the writings of Du Bois, Langston Hughes, and Malcolm X. Commentaries on state oppression have also had a favorable hearing. The interventions of TransAfrica in both the anti-apartheid struggle and the election process in Nigeria have been generally supported by African critics. However, the case has not been the same for Asante's Afrocentricity or challenges to African religion and ritual practice, as in the work of Wright and Walker.

The sensitivity to critiques of ritual results from the perception that African Americans may not have the "cultural credentials" to act as spokespersons, or, as implied by Dawit and Mekuria, that the mode of presentation, the heroic savior bringing enlightenment, endorses Western hegemony. Despite instances of "falling out," African Americans con-

cerned with furthering the discourse on Africa will continue to search for
modes that foster connections, expressing viewpoints from the Diaspora
that are sometimes dissonant but which are intended as useful contributions to the transatlantic dialogue.

NOTES

1. The issue of Christian views of traditional African belief systems
is complicated if one considers Christianity to have early African origins,
an argument expressed in Yosef ben-Jochannan's *Africa: Mother of Western
Civilization* (1988) and in Elizabeth Isichei's *A History of Christianity in
Africa* (1995). Although these texts discuss East African origins, there are
still interesting ironies to be uncovered in exploring West African conversion to European Christianity.

2. All references to poems are cited from *Her Blue Body Everything
We Know*, which contains the collected poems from 1965–1990.

REFERENCES

Angelou, Maya. 1986. *All God's Children Need Traveling Shoes*. New
    York: Random House.
Asante, Molefi. 1987. *The Afrocentric Idea*. Philadelphia: Temple Univ.
    Press.
———. 1990. *Kemet, Afrocentricity and Knowledge*. Trenton, N.J.: Africa
    World Press.
———. 1993. *Malcolm X as Cultural Hero and Other Afrocentric Essays*.
    Trenton, N.J.: Africa World Press.
Dawit, Seble, and Salem Mekuria. 1993. "The West Just Doesn't Get It."
    New York Times 7 Dec., sec. A, p. 27, col. 1.
Delany, M. R., and Robert Campbell. 1969. *Search for a Place: Black Sepa-
    ratism and Africa, 1860*. Ann Arbor: Univ. of Michigan Press.
Du Bois, W. E. B. [1946] 1965. *The World and Africa*. New York: Interna-
    tional, 1965.
Esonwanne, Uzo. 1992. Review of *Kemet, Afrocentricity and Knowledge*,
    by Molefi Asante. *Research in African Literatures* 23(1): 203–07.
Gilroy, Paul. 1993. *The Black Atlantic: Modernity and Double Conscious-
    ness*. Cambridge: Harvard Univ. Press.
Gourdine, Angeletta KM. 1996. Postmodern Ethnography and the Woman-
    ist Mission: Postcolonial Sensibilities in *Possessing the Secret of Joy*.
    African American Review 30(2): 237–44.
Hughes, Langston. 1940. *The Big Sea*. New York: Hill and Wang.
Malcolm X. [1965] 1973. *The Autobiography of Malcolm X*. New York: Bal-
    lantine.
Ngugi wa Thiong'o. 1965. *The River Between*. London: Heinemann.
Randall-Tsuruta, Dorothy. 1992. Review of *Possessing the Secret of Joy*, by
    Alice Walker. *Black Scholar* 22(3): 85–87.

Walker, Alice. 1982. *The Color Purple.* New York: Washington Square Press.

———. 1983. *In Search of our Mothers' Gardens: Womanist Prose.* New York: Harcourt Brace.

———. 1989. *The Temple of My Familiar.* New York: Pocket Books.

———. 1991. *Her Blue Body Everything We Know: Earthling Poems, 1965–1990 Complete.* New York: Harcourt Brace.

———. 1992. *Possessing the Secret of Joy.* New York: Pocket Books.

Walker, Alice, and Pratibha Parmar. 1993. *Warrior Marks: Female Genital Mutilation and the Sexual Blinding of Women.* New York: Harcourt Brace.

Wilentz, Gay. 1992. *Binding Cultures.* Bloomington: Indiana Univ. Press.

Williams, Walter. 1982. *Black Americans and the Evangelization of Africa, 1877–1900.* Madison: Univ. of Wisconsin Press.

33 AFRICAN-CENTERED WOMANISM: CONNECTING AFRICA TO THE DIASPORA

Joyce Ann Joyce

African
Don't keer where you come from
As long as you're a Black man
You're an African.

No mind your nationality
You have got the identity of an
African. . . .

Peter Tosh, transcribed from the cassette Equal Rights,
Columbia Records, 1977

The reggae singer Peter Tosh, in his song entitled "African," cited above, beautifully and comprehensively espouses the political perspective that charges all my work as an African-American woman literary critic. Reflective of its title, the song bestows an African identity upon all Blacks in the diaspora. Thus Blacks from all over England, other parts of Europe, the Americas, and Asia share an African origin. And regardless of the varying shades of the color of their skin or their diverse religious affiliations, Blacks, implicit in Tosh's song, share a history of oppression. And despite this history, it is ironically their African origin and a strong sense of identity with that origin that should instill Blacks with pride and solidarity.

Although it is true that African-American culture today is quite pluralistic and thus it is difficult to speak of a monolithic African-American experience, African Americans, Africans, West Indian Blacks, and other Blacks in the diaspora share a common history of oppression based on the color of their skin. And this common history has shaped Black psyches. After many years of on-site research in Africa, Chancellor Williams in his *Rebirth of African Civilization* rejects the stereotypical idea that the numerous tribes and languages in Africa make various African peoples sharply different from each other: "Too many students of Africa have stressed the differences in culture, language, religion, and even race as un-surmountable barriers to overall unity of purpose, thought and action. One of the unexpected developments [of Williams's research] . . . is an under-lying sense of unity among Africans throughout the continent" (14).

Chancellor Williams's observations have their roots in the network that binds traditional African life. In explaining the relationship of the in-dividual to the community, John S. Mbiti in his seminal study *African Religions and Philosophy* both gives the source of Williams's findings and thus affirms the interconnectedness of African societies. In the chapter en-titled "Ethnic Groups, Kinship & the Individual," Mbiti explains,

> In traditional life, the individual does not and cannot exist alone except corporately. He owes his existence to other people, including those of past generations and his contemporaries. He is simply part of the whole.
> . . . When he [the individual] suffers, he does not suffer alone but with the corporate group; when he rejoices, he rejoices not alone but with his kinsmen, his neighbors and his relations whether dead or living. (106)

The interrelationship between the individual and the community that de-scribes traditional African culture lies at the root of Peter Tosh's song and at what is referred to in contemporary intellectual circles as Afrocentricity or—the term I prefer—African-centeredness.

An African-centered ideology is an African-American intellectual concept that places all of Africa (not just ancient Egypt) and its history at the center of its research and pedagogical investigations. An African-centered approach is interdisciplinary, with practitioners who are historians, philosophers, sociologists, psychologists, cultural analysts, anthropologists, and literary critics. An African-centered ideology is comprehensive with its goal of influencing both the intellectual and the emotional components of Black lives. Although African-American literature has always focused on racial oppression, it was in the late 1960s and early 1970s that African-American literary critics and writers who were a part of the Black Aes-thetic movement began to emphasize the need for literary criticism to ground its exegesis in African culture and thus to address the intercon-nectedness of Black peoples' sociological, psychological, economical, politi-cal, educational, and spiritual needs. Viewed from this perspective, the Black Aesthetic emerges as the literary application of Afrocentricity, which includes the responsibility of the African-centered literary critic to bring about social change. Thus African and African-American scholars who define Afrocentric texts as those that are "vernacular or culturally grounded" (Ogunyemi 111) use the term/concept so loosely that they mis-appropriate it by failing to move beyond mere discussions of language/dialect and culture to address issues that underscore the racism that has shaped African lives on the continent and in the diaspora. The African-centered scholar's emphasis on Africa as the beginning of humankind and on the Black race as the first human beings attempts to destroy Black self-hatred and White superiority. African and African-American literary texts using deconstructive strategies that undermine racial issues "cannot" re-buke social problems that stifle Black intellectual and environmental de-velopment.

Understanding that self-hatred is often reflected in an individual's treatment of others in his or her family or racial group, African-centered scholars emphasize the African-American's African heritage and the need for a strong African-centered identity, rooted in the same sense of commu-nal connectedness in traditional African culture described by Mbiti. For the political climate in America has proven that the survival of African Americans is a communal struggle rather than an individual one. The de-piction of the interconnectedness of all members of the community emerges in African-American literature from the slave narrative to Ernest Gaines's A Gathering of Old Men (1983). However, no one has captured the essence of African-centered thought and the connection between Afri-cans and African Americans more beautifully and movingly than Ayi Kwei Armah in his novel Two Thousand Seasons.

This lyrical, philosophical novel provides a lesson in Black history by tracing the lives of several Africans in a single village before and during the Arab and European invasions that brought the devastating slave trade to Africa. At the same time that Armah depicts the movement of the novel's major characters from freedom to slavery to freedom, he interweaves into the story a philosophical and political ideology that illuminates both the physical and psychological ramifications of slavery, especially those psy-chological developments that destroy the strength of group thinking and unity. Armah's explanation of Sobo's loneliness as Sobo works to under-mine the slaveholders continues the description of what Armah refers to as the way, the holistic components of traditional African society.

The narrator's insight into Sobo's emotional isolation from the group also suggests how a deviation from group identification and solidarity weakens the survival of the African and analogously the African-American community. The narrator says,

> How infinitely stupefying the prison of the single, unconnected viewpoint, station of the cut-off vision. How deathly the separation of faculties, the separation of people. The single agent's action is waste motion; the single agent's freedom useless liberty. Such indi-vidual action can find no sense until there is again that higher con-nectedness that links each agent to the group. Then the single per-

son is no cut-off thing but an extension of the living group, the
single will but a piece of the group's active will, each mind a part
of a larger common mind. (134)

An extension of the earlier Black Aesthetic movement, African-centered
literary criticism embraces a communal doctrine that has its roots in the
interconnectedness and well-being of all Blacks in Africa and the diaspora.
It is essential to note here that many of the societal values indigenous to
traditional African culture have now been weakened seriously by corruption and disruption. Maryse Conde's *Segu* and *The Children of Segu* comprehensively trace the decline or dissolution of traditional African culture
with its communal structure. This communal emphasis, as demonstrated
by Armah's comments above, emerges as an essential aspect of traditional
African society.

Armah's disembodied narrator in *Two Thousand Seasons* also describes a time in traditional African society, before the introduction of
Christianity and Islam, when *reciprocity* defined the relationship between
men and women. This exploration of the connection between Black men
and women in Africa and the diaspora attempts to exemplify an African-
centered, balanced perspective through its use of diverse intellectual contributions of Black men and women in Africa and the diaspora. Given the
complex history that makes up the Black woman's experiences in Africa
and in the diaspora, the role of the African-centered female scholar born
in America is fraught with complexities. In order to accentuate the intellectual, cultural, and political connection of African women born in Africa
to Black women in the diaspora, it is useful to examine Black women's
voices in Africa and in the diaspora from both historical and literary perspectives. Four very different scholarly works—*Life Histories of African
Women*, edited by Patricia W. Romero; *The Black Woman Cross-Culturally*, edited by Filomina Chioma Steady; *In Their Own Voices: African
Women Writers Talk*, edited by Adeola James; and Mbiti's *African Religions and Philosophy*—provide a diverse view of the Black woman's historical heritage in Africa and the diaspora.

According to Mbiti, "traditional religions permeate all the depart-
ments of [African] life, there is no formal distinction between the sacred
and the secular, between the religious and non-religious, between the spiritual and the material areas of life" (2). This merger of the sacred and the
secular is perhaps nowhere as important in African life as it is in the African's traditional attitude toward marriage. "In some African societies,
marriage is not fully recognized or consummated until the wife has given
birth. . . . Unhappy is the woman who fails to get children for, whatever
other qualities she might possess, her failure to bear children is worse than
committing genocide: she has become the dead end of human life . . ."
(Mbiti 107). Both sexual activity outside of marriage and adultery are forbidden in traditional African culture. Thus childbearing must result from

marriage only. Children manifest the point of connection between the dead, the living, and those to come. Thus "without procreation marriage is incomplete. . . . It is a religious obligation by means of which the individual contributes the seeds of life towards man's struggle against the loss of original immortality" (Mbiti 130).

Not only were marriage and children expected components of the traditional African woman's life, but she also, in most cases, had no voice in choosing her husband. The ties that most frequently connect the women interviewed in *Life Histories of African Women* involve the issue of marriage, childbearing, and the women's feelings about not being able to choose their own husbands. For Nongenile Masithathu Zenani, a Xhosa woman of South Africa, explains how her father and relatives plotted to have her marry someone of her father's choosing and how she ran away to avoid being forced to marry against her wishes (19–22). Also Mercha, an Ethiopian potter, ran away (though she was found) from her intended forced marriage (171). And Mama Khadija of Lamu, an island in East Kenya, explains, "In Lamu today most daughters of the poor or the illiterate marry just past puberty. And most marriages are arranged, just as they were earlier in the century" (145).

Marriage and the Black woman's place in society also reflect interconnections between the African woman and her sister in the diaspora. In her essay "Women's Role in West Indian Society," Joyce Bennett Justus shows that marriage in the Caribbean also manifests a connection between the sacred and the secular. She writes, "Marriage . . . is an ideal shared by all, regardless of social class, and is a prerequisite for full church membership. Church membership *and* marriage are marks of respectability, a status to which all members of society aspire" (Steady 441). Thus the merger of marriage and religion has traditionally been the essential determining agent that has bound the African and Caribbean woman to the home.

An examination of the comments on the place of African women in society made by those African women writers collected in Adeola James's *In Their Own Voices* provides some insight into the African woman's perspective on her place in the home and the larger society. Writers Zaynab Alkali, Pamela Kola, Ellen Kuzwayo, Muthoni Likimani, Molara Ogundipe-Leslie, Penina Muhando, Rebeka Njau, Flora Nwapa, and Asenath Odaga all agree the need exists for improvement in the quality of life for the African woman. Flora Nwapa addresses the conditions that underlie the psychological differences that distinquish African men and women:

> The oppression of women starts in the home. In our homes today, we treat girls differently, and we treat boys as if they are kings. I remember the problem I have in my own home when I make my only son go to the kitchen to cook, wash the plates and so on. He

does it. But my mother-in-law comes in and says in a raised voice, "Why are you allowing this boy to do this, he is a man, he is not supposed to be in the kitchen." That is where the trouble stems from, the double standard we use in bringing up our children. . . . A woman who says she is oppressed and then has a son and treats him like a king, such a woman is perpetuating the problems we are complaining about. (113–14)

While Nwapa emphasizes how the differences in childraising influences the difference in the development of African children, Rebeka Njau and Asenath Odaga caution against oversimplifying the intricacies of African family life. Odaga says,

I come from a large family, we are seven sisters and two brothers. Our father brought us up on equal terms and gave us equal opportunities. All of us passed through high school and some of us have gone to univesity. Why I think I have succeeded is because I come from that firm background where it doesn't matter whether you are a boy or a girl, it is your ability that counts. . . . I am fortunate, too, that when I got married, my husband never tried to put me down, he always allowed me. I say "allowed" because in our society if a husband is against your progress you cannot get anywhere to to develop as a person. . . . (124)

Odaga points out that despite the equality she experienced growing up in her parents' home, had she not married an open-minded or supportive husband, her success would have been seriously stifled by marriage. Odaga's comments and Njau's suggest that despite the balanced role-modeling some African men receive as children in their homes, their attitude toward women follows the more conformist view Nwapa describes as the young men become adults. Njau says,

I remember my mother was very strong. I come from a big family. There are twelve of us, five sisters and seven brothers. There was no difference in the way my mother treated all of us. Going to fetch water, we all went including my brothers; cooking, we all did it. If there was a farm to cultivate, my mother would measure it out, a piece for me and a piece for you, whether you are a boy or a girl. That was the way we lived, there was no difference and there was respect. When I got married I never thought I would be made to feel that "You are a woman, you are inferior." That came to me as a kind of shock. (105–106)

Despite Odaga's and Njau's positive childhood experiences, they acknowledge the unequal ways in which African men and women are raised. Their observations corroborate the experiences of other African women.

For example, when the Europeans began to open schools in Africa, girls, especially pregnant girls, were not allowed to attend. Bitu, a Muganda woman, opened a school in the 1940s for girls because she "realized that women would continue to be educationally backward in her society as long as girls got pregnant and schools expelled them because of their condition" (Romero 99). Husiana, a northern Nigerian herbal medicine woman, explained that her husband forbade his daughters to go to school. While their brothers went to school, Husiana's daughters helped her with the housework and with cooking food to sell (Romero 87).

This sharp difference in preparing males and females for society also manifests in Caribbean culture. In "Women's Role in West Indian Society," Justus explains, "At the age of five male-female socialization patterns diverge sharply and females begin role training, while boys are permitted, and expected, to continue to be 'babies' and are allowed to play" (Justus 437). Because males are not trained to assume responsibility, those in the lowest strata of Caribbean society make up the highest percentage of the unemployed. Despite the fact that many of the grassroots females are either unemployed or underemployed, "there are more avenues open to them in the informal sector, and they are thus better able to support themselves and their offspring" (Justus 446). While African, Caribbean, and African-American men have viewed themselves as superior to Black women because of their dominant position in their respective societies, Black women, particularly in the homes of the underclass, are the stabilizing agents that provide for the family.

At the same time that the African male refuses to permit his daughter to attend school and the medicine women in some countries are paid fifty cents more for delivering male babies than girl babies, African women have traditionally been the economists who manage their marketplaces. The African legacy of male superiority and female inferiority connects Black men and women in the diaspora to their African heritage (despite the omnipresence of sexism on all the continents). And, of course, the brutal experiences of colonialism on the continent and slavery in the diaspora have seriously exacerbated how sexism affects Black men and women. Because slavery and racial oppression have socialized Black males and females quite differently, African-American and Caribbean males' trauma over their experiences affect their self-respect and self-confidence and thus their ability to function as emotionally healthy adults. The end result is that many of the males in the grassroots culture leave their families. Therefore, African-American and Caribbean women have had to become as economically productive as their African sisters.

Sociologist Delores Aldridge explains that the differences in the ways in which African-American men and women are raised set up problems for them when they attempt to relate to each other as adults. She explains that Black families encourage definitions of femininity in which the women experience conflicts between passivity and emotional and economic dependence, and expressiveness, warmth, and nurturance (54). Black men, she adds, experience a contradiction between the ways they are expected to present themselves in small and large groups and the reality of their true feelings (55). Black American males' masking of their true feelings and Black women's conflicting behavior contribute greatly to the disharmonious relationships between Black American men and women. Moreover, this dichotomy between passivity and strength in the African-American woman and between illusion and reality in the Black American male psyche echoes the contradictions in the interrelationships between African men and women as well.

Despite the fact that African, Caribbean, and African-American women have played a leading role in getting food to the table for their children, they clearly suffer from sexist oppression both in the home and in the professional arena. Interviews with African women writers such as Bessie Head, Flora Nwapa, Ama Ata Aidoo, and Buchi Emecheta verify that their personal and professional experiences are not very different from those of some of the characters they create in their fiction. And while the novels of the African woman fiction writer have only a marginal presence in American intellectual circles, the African woman scholar is even less well known than the creative writer. While my university has at least seven African male professors on its faculty, we have only one African woman. Ellen Kuzwayo suggests the historical background as to why African men in the American academy far outnumber African women:

> In the process of growing up we encounter it [the problem of being Black and a woman]. In school we were told that we couldn't do certain subjects, that certain subjects were good for certain people. I think this has given women a double exclusion from all sorts of sources. We've always been stereotyped and I think it is this stereotyping that has given the black woman an extra burden, as a black and as a woman. (55)

Yet, despite the history of sexist oppression suffered by the African woman, novelist and poet Ama Ata Aidoo, like her African-centered sisters born in America, affirms her need to empower her African nationalist consciousness. In response to Adeola James's question about the African female artist's commitment as a writer, as a woman, and as a Third World person, Aidoo explains, "I don't deny that we belong to a larger non-northern world and the dynamics that operate in a situation like that, but find my commitment as an African, the need for me to be an African nationalist, to be a little more pressing. It seems there are things relating to our world, as African people, which are of a more throbbing nature in an immediate sense" (15). Aidoo's commitment to African nationalism connects her directly to the African-centered womanist in the diaspora who affirms her familial and political bond with the Black man.

The heroines in Aidoo's *Changes* and in Buchi Emecheta's *Double Yoke* experience the same lack of fulfillment and problems associated with a male-dominated university structure as Black women in the diaspora. While Emecheta uses the metaphor of the double yoke to represent the conflict between modernity (the woman's freedom to choose the direction of her life) and tradition (the restricting of the African woman's life to marriage and children), I use it to suggest the African-centered Black woman's commitment to joining forces with the Black man to eradicate racism and her conflicting need to challenge Black male sexism. For the Black womanist scholar's position in the academy is indeed a double yoke. Like Aidoo, the African-centered womanist scholar in the diaspora finds herself in that very difficult position of focusing on racism first and then on its relationship to the sexist and economic oppression of Black women. In her book *Africana Womanism: Reclaiming Ourselves*, Clenora Hudson-Weems joins Afrocentric sociologists Delores Aldridge and the late Vivian Gordon in her desire to distinguish Africana womanism from feminism and to emphasize unabashedly the importance of the family to the Africana womanist. While most African-American womanists stress Black male sexism through discussions around differences, the Africana womanist focuses simultaneously on deconstructing Black male sexism, reconstructing the Black family, and paradoxically achieving female psychical and professional autonomy.

Though the African-centered womanist looks to traditional African culture for models of family structure and values and seeks identification with African women, the African-American womanist, at the same time, must consider that the African woman born in Africa possibly views the African-American scholar as an outsider. In her very impressive study *Africa Wo/man Palava: The Nigerian Novel by Women*, Chikwenye Okonjo Ogunyemi implicitly suggests that African-American women readers of African women's novels are voyeurs. In a very significant passage, she writes:

> For whom and to whom do African women then write or tell their stories? Ideologically, African womanism's inherent ambivalence toward feminism is related to questions of style and authority. Feminism's feisty spirit predisposes it to use the headlines, the expose, personal and public. This propensity for confrontationally "telling all," the African woman critic has no authority or inclination to adopt, since her target audience, with its numerical superiority and spending power, reads the foreign language in which she writes, creating a rupture in the competing audiences. The notion of an invasive addressee, who should be an eavesdropper/voyeur now turned primary audience, is part of the postcolonial dilemma Edward Said addressed in his *Orientalism* (1978). Therefore, the

African woman critic bites her tongue, distrusting her pen and
computer as she speaks and writes. (12)

With her African "propensity" against "telling all" or disclosing the nature of her culture, critic Ogunyemi hides beyond her own "palava/pa-
laver" (obfuscating language) here. It is neither our pens nor our computer
that we distrust, it is ourselves and the thoughts the pen and computer
transcribe.

The above passage suggests that African women creative writers distort their subject matter to satisfy the expectations or requirements of a
Western reading audience unfamiliar with the realities of African culture.
It would seem then that the African woman critic's responsibility is to
explain the nature of the "rupture" Ogunyemi says separates the target
audience from the primary audience. Moreover, Ogunyemi does not reveal
what the African woman creative writer or critic gains from avoiding the
"propensity for telling all." In other words, in its encounter with the West,
how does African culture grow or find stability or improve itself through
its tendency toward privatization? Ogunyemi's own reading of the fiction
of African women's novels demonstrates that these texts focus most consistently on the way in which marriage and children shape the African
woman's life. This emphasis on traditional family structure binds the
African woman to her husband in ways that differ from the contemporary
western White and Black *feminists* as well as Black *womanists*, whose
agendas do not include complementarity or reciprocity between Black men
and women.

In characterizing her target Western audience as voyeurs, Ogunyemi
does not exclude Black American women. Yet African-centered womanists, like Clenora Hudson-Weems and myself, recognize that the contemporary sexism that describes relationships between American Black men
and Black women in the diaspora finds its source in our African ancestry
and in the ways slavery impacted our lives and that the value system that
motivates contemporary African-American culture, though highly contaminated, has African origins. A metaphorical paraphrase of Ntozake
Shange's phrase "The slaves who are ourselves" appropriately describes the
relationship between the African-centered womanist and the African
woman: we are reflections of each other. Simply put, the African woman
would be psychologically and psychically the same as Black women in the
diaspora had the African woman been taken to the diaspora as a slave centuries ago. Again to paraphrase Shange, the African woman is a diasporan
Black woman and the Black woman in the diaspora is an African woman
changed by time and acculturation. Ogunyemi's mistrust of the Black
woman in the diaspora and her designation of the Black woman in the
diaspora as a Western "eavesdropper/voyeur" emerges as an actual manifestation of Maryse Conde's fictionalized account of the dissolution and

dispersion of the African family members estranged from each other. When African women intellectually reject embracing the critiques of their art by African-American women, they stifle communication among family members as well as intellectual growth that describes the complementarity of the outsider/insider relationship. For just as the African-centered womanist seeks to explore her connections with African women, the African woman can learn much from African-centered womanists who are comfortable with the inherent risk of embracing Black men and challenging their sexism simultaneously and openly.

The African-centered womanist's agenda, then, is triple-pronged because not only does she struggle against White racism and White male and Black male sexism, but she also must confront the African woman's rejection of her Americanness. In my African-centered approach to literary criticism, I attempt to place this triad at the center of my critical investigations. While it is true that since the early 1970s many African-American scholars have been deeply influenced by the pedagogy of the hegemony, at the same time the African-centered approach to literary criticism, through its connections with the Black Aesthetic movement, has increased in momentum since the 1970s. Influenced by this enhanced interest in the African American's African heritage, a number of Black women writers have now turned the focus of their fiction to those cultural and spiritual aspects of the African American community that have their roots in Africa. It is disturbing then that while the Black Arts movement has inspired Black writers to turn backward/forward to Africa for the source and framework of their creativity, Africa, according to Ogunyemi, looks toward the demands of a Western reading audience.

The African-centered womanist is a scholar who is alone with no secure niche. The African-centered womanist critic corroborates Vivian Gordon's call for cooperative relationships between Black men and women. According to Gordon, "Black liberation represents freedom from sexism and racism and embraces a Black female/male co-partnership in struggle and love. To the extent that the movement fails in this focus, Black women and men who are enlightened must actively work to teach and influence others; thereby, maintaining the Black struggle focus" (46). Not only is it necessary that the African-centered womanist critic work against the notion of isolation from males that describes the White feminist movement, but also the African-centered womanist must establish linkages between African and Black women in the diaspora that are sensitive to the cultural and historical issues that undergird these Black women's varying points of view. The African-American womanist, rather than falling into the trap of a Eurocentric view of Aidoo's, Emecheta's, and Nwapa's portrayals of their women, should instead highlight how colonialism and slavery totally disrupted the natural course of African history and thus the history of Africans in the diaspora.

If the African-centered intellectual community is going to be success-ful at establishing harmonious, equitable relationships between men and women, sensitive Black men willing to deconstruct their sexism will need to challenge the sexism of their male peers. For it is especially essential for the Black male sensitive to sexism and womanist issues to read the works of Black men from a womanist position. For men know men's ways better than women do; they know each other's psyches better and from a different perspective than women. And importantly, because slavery and racism have removed the African-American father from a position of authority and from the home, the son's relationship with his mother sug-gests that he has the experience necessary to seek the repressed female inside himself (Spillers 80). This psychical experience provides the Black man with the tools he needs to critique the destructive nature of male power and thus contribute greatly to the destruction of male power or dominance.

In addition to the need for Black male self-critique, we also need to be more inclusive in our reference to Black women intellectuals. The ideas of African-centered Black women sociologists Vivian Gordon and Delores Aldridge do not appear in any of the works that I have read by Black womanists or White women feminists. Given the political nature of Gor-don's and Aldridge's ideas, their absence from mainstream feminist criti-cism is not surprising. In discussing the weaknesses of the women's lib-eration movement, Aldridge, I believe, implicitly provides the answer as to why she and Gordon are usually excluded as references in the criticism of both Black and White women feminists. She writes, "The essence of this writer's disagreement with women's liberation is the basically conserva-tive mode of its beliefs and functions. Women's liberation operates within the capitalist tradition and accepts the end goals of sexist white males; simply stated, women's liberation strives to place women on an equal par with men without considering whether the male position—the white male position—is basically a humanizing position" (35). Vivian Gordon, to some extent, echoes Ogunyemi's rejection of a women's liberation move-ment that lacks focus on the unique, historical position of the Black woman: "Black women who identify with the women's liberation move-ment [run the risk of internalizing] the rhetoric and perspective of that movement and becom[ing] alienated from themselves (self-hate), and alien-ated from the race, as well as from a splendid record of activities against racism" (2–3). Gordon's comments here reflect Ama Ata Aidoo's emphasis on her African nationalism, which she finds to "be a little more pressing" than her commitment as a writer, woman, or Third World person.

Aidoo's novel *Changes* reflects the same contradiction as that found in the criticism of Black womanist scholars. Although she states in her interview with Adeola James that she sees nationalism as more important than feminism, the novel does not provide us with a positive characterization of an African male, nor does it present a relationship between a man and a woman in which they both find emotional fulfillment.

Analogously, a look at some of the more recent landmark Black womanist collections of essays reveals the same contradiction. Many of the essays by Black womanist writers in *Reading Black, Reading Feminists; Wild Women in the Whirlwind: Afra-American Culture and the Contemporary Literary Renaissance;* and *Changing Our Own Words: Essays on Criticism, Theory, and Writing by Black Women* assert that Black womanist scholars do not lose sight of the way in which slavery and racism have shaped the lives of Blacks in the diaspora. Yet, the criticism of Black womanist scholars follows the same one-sided perspective as the fiction of most Black women novelists. For Black womanist scholars must go further than making statements about how racism separates their views from those of White feminists. We must demonstrate the importance of this realization by providing balanced critiques of Black male and female characters.

Black womanist scholars, of course, take their lead from Black women fiction writers. Too many contemporary novels written by women that dramatize Black male-female relationships present only negative characterizations of Black males. The contemporary African-American literary arena is in dire need of African-centered womanist scholars to present a balanced analysis of the Black men in the fiction of both male and female Black writers. These scholars must also challenge the implied glorification of Black women in these same novels. For example, most of the criticism on Toni Morrison's *Sula* characterizes Sula as an eccentric, free-spirited, independent Black woman. While Sula is alluring on paper, few of us, I believe, would want to have someone as distrusting, selfish, and unethical as she for a friend. Black womanist criticism needs to explore those traits in Black women that are peculiarly feminine and independent of the woman's relationship to a man.

It is interesting that some intellectuals propose that some problems in contemporary Black culture have nothing to do with racial oppression or the economic, social, and political relationships between Blacks and Whites. Yet, in our critique of Black literature (both in Africa and the diaspora), we fail to make the similar observation when analyzing relationships between men and women. We fail to question if the three sisters in Tina McElroy Ansa's *Ugly Ways* are the type of women we would like to have as sisters.

The African-American men who were disturbed by Alice Walker's *The Color Purple* and who continue to be disconcerted over the characterization of Black men in the fiction of Black women writers should not be dismissed merely as guilty men wallowing in denial. African-American men reading the fiction of African-American women novelists have the same response to the male characters in this fiction as African and Caribbean men have to Maryse Condé's *Segu* and *The Children of Segu*. During a telephone conversation, well-known Nigerian scholar Oyekan Owomoyela said that all of Condé's male characters emerge as very weak, driven primarily by their overwhelming libido. While Owomoyela's observation is not ill founded, the breadth of the novel reveals men who are tormented by their inability to escape first the expectations of tradition and later the humiliation, shame, and anger of colonialism. The African-centered literary scholar, male or female, understands the importance of presenting a comprehensive critique of the negative characterizations of Black men in the fiction of Black women writers and of illuminating the political and social expectations and clichés that camouflage the richness, depth, and ingenious craftsmanship of some of the world's greatest literary artists.

In her historical novels, *Segu* and *The Children of Segu*, Maryse Condé provides a connection between the aesthetics of African, Caribbean, and African-American women writers, the connection we find addressed both in Karla Holloway's *Moorings and Metaphors: Figure of Culture and Gender in Black Women's Literature* and in Joanne V. Gabbin's "A Laying on of Hands: Black Women Writers Exploring the Roots of Their Folk and Cultural Tradition." In discussing Paule Marshall's treatment of Avey Johnson in *Praisesong for the Widow*, Gabbin writes, "The same way that Rosalie Parvay is the channel for Avey's spiritual rebirth, black women writers are transforming Afro-American literature. By exploring the roots of their folk and cultural tradition they have discovered an aesthetic foundation upon which to build art that is vital, original, and rich in emotional and spiritual depth" (248).

Margaret Walker's *Jubilee*, Toni Morrison's *Song of Solomon* and *Sula*, Gloria Naylor's *Mama Day*, Alice Walker's *The Temple of My Familiar*, and Paule Marshall's *Praisesong for the Widow* treat the interconnectedness (to varying degrees and in varying ways) of the spiritual and psychological lives of Africans in the diaspora. Condé's *Segu* and *The Children of Segu* provide the historical context, far more comprehensive than Armah's *Two Thousand Seasons*, for the African's and African American's severance from their cultural roots and thus begin the "journey of self-recognition and healing" (Busia 197) that we find in the works of other West Indian as well as African and African-American women writers. In *The Afrocentric Idea*, the African-American cultural analyst Molefi Asante provides a comprehensive but succinct definition of Afrocentricity that, for me, approximately defines African-centeredness as well. "Afrocentricity," he writes, "is the most complete philosophical totalization of the African being-at-the-center of his or her existence. It is not merely an artistic or literary movement. Not only is it an individual or collective quest for authenticity, but it is above all the total use of method to effect psychological, political, social, cultural, and economic change" (125). African-centeredness in literary criticism, then, is a matter of focus, of concentration. It is a matter of what the scholar chooses to emphasize.

The African-centered womanist position is to focus on how Africans on the continent and in the diaspora are carriers of cultural memory that demonstrates the connection of the African-centered womanist to her roots and her sisters in the diaspora. The works of African writers around the world provide the African-centered scholar with the historical tools she needs to "transcribe cultural meaning," to borrow Karla Holloway's phraseology, or transform cultural memory into action. By interpreting or "telling all" of the political, sociological, economical, historical, psychological, and spiritual codes of African and African-American literature and history, the African-centered scholar provides a means for Black people in the diaspora to reconnect with their African heritage. The purpose of this reconnection is to take one step toward giving Blacks in the diaspora a sense of pride in their history and destroying the self-hatred that is in part a result of people being totally disconnected from their roots.

This disconnection from the source has caused Blacks in the West and many of those Africans educated by the West to privilege individuality over collectivism. The African-centered scholar understands that the quest for individual freedom is inherently connected to the collective struggle for political, social, cultural, and economic freedom. In the pursuit of this collective struggle, the African-centered womanist scholar must maintain a balance when discussing issues that cause a schism between Black men and women. It is essential that Black women remain mindful of the ways in which colonialism and slavery have affected the Black male. Though it is important to give empathic attention to the sociological conditions that have shaped the Black male's psyche, it is also necessary that we be candid and thorough in describing sexist behavior.

Although African and African-American women writers understand the forces that have shaped the Black male psyche, they nonetheless still struggle to conquer the Black male sexism that oppresses them. For example, Flora Nwapa explains that Buchi Emecheta's husband dared Emecheta to write by burning her manuscript (116). A contemporary African-American woman writer revealed to me that her ex-husband, out of jealousy, destroyed one of her manuscripts. While I was teaching at the University of Maryland, I had an older student who after raising three children decided to return to college to complete her degree. Her husband, whose salary was (fifteen years ago) close to $100,000 a year, refused to help her with her tuition. And the sparsity of African women writers and the absence of Black women Egyptologists or historians with book-length manuscripts and thus with the stature of Molefi Asante, Ivan van Sertima, John Henrik Clarke, and others reflect the oppressed position of Black women in the academy. This undermining of women's accomplishments and of their needs is not, of course, limited to the academy. For example, though we know much about the inside of male prisons, the public is given very little information about the activities inside female prisons. "While much publicity is given to the disproportionate number of Black males in the nation's prisons, limited attention is given to the fact that 48% of the women's prison population is Black" (Gordon 30).

Despite their history of sexist oppression, Black women, from ancient Egypt to contemporary times, have historically taken risks in their roles as mothers, queens, warriors, farmers, cooks, weavers, potters, artists, priests, economists, doctors, judges, politicians, teachers, writers, etc. Because my goal is to effect social change and because I believe that this change must be brought about inside and outside of the academy, I am influenced by Black women across all cultures and class strata who have cared more about the efficacy of their work than they have for public opinion of them. These women—from Hatshepsut, Nefertari, and Nzinga to Ellen Kuzwayo, Ama Ata Aidoo, Flora Nwapa, Buchi Emecheta, Winnie Mandela, Margaret Walker, June Jordan, Rita Marley, and Sonia Sanchez—are the real motivating forces in the struggle for liberation from racism and sexism. All of these women, including Chikwenye Okonjo Ogunyemi, recognize that Black men and women are "mutually dependent" (Ogunyemi 126).

Black people have a choice about fulfilling White society's expectations and assumptions about what it means to be Black. Both Buchi Emecheta and African-centered historian Chancellor Williams believe that Black women have the power to effect overwhelming change not only in Black people's lives, but in the dominant culture as well. While Emecheta holds that the "tragic disruption of society" in Achebe's *Things Fall Apart* is due to the absence of the female principle needed to counter the male's "strong-headedness and inflexibility" (42), Williams in his *Rebirth of African Civilization* holds that the mothers of men must assume a more aggressive role in "bringing about a better world." He adds that because women are more spiritual than men, men need the woman's "civilizing influence" (244). And Marimba Ani, in her seminal study *Yurugu: An African-Centered Critique of European Cultural Thought and Behavior*, explains that in the African view a "harmonious interaction" describes the complementarity of the "Divine Feminine and Masculine" as opposed to their opposition in European culture (174–75).

Finally, understanding the need for this complementarity and thus working to minimize sexism and change the world, Black women scholars have a clear responsibility as African-centered scholars: they must be balanced and inclusive in their treatment of their former oppressors. The global, racial identification of which Peter Tosh sings must be transcribed into a recognition of our African social history and of how the impact of the West has estranged members of the African family and exacerbated the weaknesses in the familial chain that links Black men and women on the continent and in the diaspora.

REFERENCES

Aidoo, Ama Ata. Interview. *In Their Own Voices: African Women Writers Talk.* Ed. Adeola James. London: Heinemann, 1990. 9–27.

Aldridge, Delores P. *Focusing: Black Male-Female Relationships.* Chicago: Third World P, 1991.

Armah, Ayi Kwei. *Two Thousand Seasons.* 1973. London: Heinemann, 1979.

Asante, Molefi. *The Afrocentric Idea.* Philadelphia: Temple UP, 1987.

Busia, Abena P. A. "What Is Your Nation? Reconnecting Africa and Her Diaspora through Paule Marshall's *Praisesong for the Widow.*" In *Changing Our Own Words: Essays on Criticism, Theory, and Writing by Black Women.* Ed. Cheryl A. Wall. New Brunswick: Rutgers UP, 1989. 196–211.

Emecheta, Buchi. Interview. *In Their Own Voices: African Women Writers Talk.* Ed. Adeola James. London: Heinemann. 1990. 35–45.

Gabbin, Joanne V. "A Laying on of Hands: Black Women Writers Exploring the Roots of Their Folk and Cultural Tradition." In *Wild Women in the Whirlwind: Afra-American Culture and the Contemporary Renaissance.* Ed. Joanne M. Braxton and Andree Nicola McLaughlin. New Brunswick: Rutgers UP, 1990. 246–263.

Gordon, Vivian V. *Black Women, Feminism, and Black Liberation: Which Way?* Chicago: Third Third World P, 1987.

Justus, Joyce Bennett. "Women's Role in West Indian Society." In *The Black Woman Cross-Culturally.* Ed. Filomina Chioma Steady. Cambridge: Schenkman, 1981. 431–450.

Kuzwayo, Ellen. Interview. *In Their Own Voices: African Women Writers Talk.* Ed. Adeola James. London: Heinemann, 1990. 53–57.

Mbiti, John S. *African Religions and Philosophy.* 1969. London: Heinemann, 1990.

Njau, Rebeka. Interview. *In Their Own Voices: African Women Writers Talk.* Ed. Adeola James. London: Heinemann, 1990. 103–108.

Nwapa, Flora. Interview. *In Their Own Voices: African Women Writers Talk.* Ed. Adeola James. London: Heinemann, 1990. 111–117.

Odaga, Asenath. Interview. *In Their Own Voices: African Women Writers Talk.* Ed. Adeola James. London: Heinemann, 1990. 123–135.

Ogunyemi, Chikwenye Okonjo. *Africa Wo/Man Palava: The Nigerian Novel by Women.* Chicago: U of Chicago P, 1996.

Romero, Patricia. Ed. *Life Histories of African Women.* London: Ashfield P, 1988.

Spillers, Hortense. "Mama's Baby, Papa's Maybe: An American Grammar Book." *Diacritics* 17 (Summer 1987): 65–81.

Williams, Chancellor. *The Rebirth of African Civilization.* 1961. Chicago: Third World P, 1993.

CONTRIBUTORS

NIYI AFOLABI is Assistant Professor of Spanish and Portuguese at Tulane University in New Orleans, Louisiana.

ADETAYO ALABI is Assistant Professor of English at the University of Windsor, Ontario (Canada).

CELIA M. AZEVEDO is Professor of History at the Universidad Estadual de Campinas in São Paolo, Brazil.

ANTONIO BENÍTEZ-ROJO is Professor of Romance Languages at Amherst College in Amherst, Massachusetts.

ELIANA GUERREIRO RAMOS BENNETT teaches in the Department of Social Science at the University of Texas in Brownsville, Texas.

LEGRACE BENSON works with the Arts of Haiti Research Project in Ithaca, New York.

IRA KINCADE BLAKE is Assistant Professor of Psychology at Susquehanna University in Selinsgrove, Pennsylvania.

JACK S. BLOCKER, JR. is Professor of History at Huron College of the University of Western Ontario (Canada).

SHARON ANETA BRYANT is Assistant Professor in the Decker School of Nursing at the State University of New York in Binghamton.

CAROLE BOYCE DAVIES, formerly Professor of English and Africana Studies at the State University of New York, Binghamton, is currently Professor and Director of African–New World Studies at Florida International University.

MICHAEL J. C. ECHERUO is William Safire Professor of Modern Letters in the Department of English at Syracuse University in Syracuse, New York.

PETER P. EKEH is Professor and Chair of African American Studies at the State University of New York in Buffalo.

PATIENCE ELABOR-IDEMUDIA is Associate Professor in the Department of Sociology, University of Saskatchewan, Saskatoon (Canada).

DAVID EVANS is Professor of Music at the University of Memphis in Memphis, Tennessee.

ROBERT ELLIOT FOX is Professor of English at Southern Illinois University in Carbondale, Illinois.

ANDREA FROHNE is pursuing a doctorate in African Art History at the State University of New York, Binghamton.

JOSEPH E. INIKORI is Professor of History at the University of Rochester in Rochester, New York.

JOYCE ANN JOYCE is Chair of African American Studies at Temple University in Philadelphia, Pennsylvania.

CHARLES MARTIN is Professor of Comparative Literature at Queens College of the City University of New York.

ALI A. MAZRUI, Director of the Institute of Global Cultural Studies at the State University of New York, Binghamton, is also Senior Scholar in Africana Studies at Cornell University and Walter Rodney Distinguished Professor at the University of Guyana.

JOSEPH MCLAREN teaches in the English Department of Hofstra University, New York.

PIERRE-DAMIEN MVUYEKURE is Assistant Professor of English, American, and African American Literature at the University of Northern Iowa in Cedar Falls, Iowa.

NKIRU NZEGWU is Associate Professor of Africana Studies and Art History at the State University of New York in Binghamton.

ISIDORE OKPEWHO, Professor of Africana Studies, English, and Comparative Literature at the State University of New York in Binghamton, was Chair of Africana Studies and Convener of the conference from which this book arose.

OYEKAN OWOMOYELA is Professor of English at the University of Nebraska in Lincoln, Nebraska.

LAURA J. PIRES-HESTER received a Ph.D. in Anthropology from Columbia University and is currently Program Officer at the DeWitt Wallace Reader's Digest Fund, New York.

RICHARD PRICE divides his time between rural Martinique and the College of William and Mary in Williamsburg, Virginia, where he is Dittman Professor of American Studies, Anthropology, and History.

SALLY PRICE divides her time between rural Martinique and the College of William and Mary in Williamsburg, Virginia, where she is Dittman Professor of American Studies and Anthropology.

JEAN RAHIER is Associate Professor of Anthropology and African–New World Studies at Florida International University in Miami.

SANDRA L. RICHARDS is Professor of African American Studies and Theater at Northwestern University in Evanston, Illinois.

Contributors

557

ELLIOTT P. SKINNER is Franz Boas Professor of Anthropology at Columbia University, New York.

ALVIN B. TILLERY, JR. is a doctoral candidate in the Department of Government at Harvard University in Cambridge, Massachusetts.

KEITH Q. WARNER is Professor of French at George Mason University in Fairfax, Virginia.

MAUREEN WARNER-LEWIS is Reader in African-Caribbean Language and Orature at the University of the West Indies in Mona, Jamaica.

KIMBERLY WELCH is Assistant Professor of Latin American history at St John's University in Jamaica, New York.

INDEX OF NAMES

DEMCO